Contents

Adobe®

Premiere Pro® 1.5
STUDIO TECHNIQUES

Jacob Rosenberg

Adobe Premiere Pro 1.5 Studio Techniques

Jacob Rosenberg

This Adobe Press book is published by Peachpit Press. For information on Adobe Press books, contact:

Peachpit Press
1249 Eighth Street
Berkeley, CA 94710
(510) 524-2178
Fax: (510) 524-2221
http://www.peachpit.com

To report errors, please send a note to errata@peachpit.com
Peachpit Press is a division of Pearson Education

For the latest on Adobe Press books, go to to www.adobepress.com.

Acquisitions Editor: Elise Walter
Development and Copy Editor: Linda Laflamme
Project Editor: Kristy Hart
Technical Editors: Charles Liss, George Lamore, Bruce Bowman
Compositor: Amy Hassos
Indexer: Lisa Stumpf
Cover design: Aren Howell

Notice of Rights

Notice of Liability

Trademarks

ISBN 0-321-22052-8

9 8 7 6 5 4 3

Printed and bound in the United States of America

Part IV Advanced Editing Techniques

Part V Advanced Effect Techniques

DVD Contents

Part VI Before You Edit

Dedication

I would like to dedicate this book to my friend Michael Anthony Ternasky and to my father Joel Rosenberg.

My mentor Michael "MT" Ternasky was killed in an automobile accident shortly before I started film school. Mike was the impetus for my pursuing that dream and for naming my production company Formika Films. I dedicate the work I do to his memory.

Mike grew up as a rebel with a passion to be the best at whatever he did. When I first met him, he ran a skateboard company called H-Street, and he ran it to top capacity. When Mike died, he had formed his own "super" skateboard company, Plan B, which pooled together the best skateboarders in the world and produced some of the most groundbreaking and influential skateboard videos to date. I was fortunate enough to be a part of those videos and to have been educated in the "MT Filming and Editing School of Hard Knocks" under his direction.

In dealing with the grief that followed Mike's death, I became close friends with his older brother Joe who, at the time, worked at Adobe Systems. Knowing that my editing skills were strong, Joe suggested that I try my hand at testing Adobe editing software. After I was turned down as a tester for the Quality Assurance Team (no college education and no formal computer experience), Joe got me an interview with the engineering team that wrote the code for Adobe Premiere. Nick Schlott (then the engineering manager) took a gamble and hired me to test the program from an editor's perspective. I was to communicate directly with the engineers about what wasn't working and what needed changing. That was almost a decade ago, and my relationship with Adobe continues to this day.

I tell this story as a means of showing the amazing and positive twists and turns that can come from a tragic event. By acknowledging the impact of someone's life and death on my own life, I am able to keep pushing forward.

At age 65, my father sets a precedent for enthusiasm, energy, and passion. Riding a few hundred miles a week on his bicycle and challenging himself daily, he continually aspires to do more and learn more about the world. My father has contributed greatly to the person I am today by teaching me the power of communication and the overwhelming value of educating and inspiring the people around you.

I dedicate this book to my two friends and two fathers. Thank you for your knowledge, passion, and guidance.

About the Author

Jacob Rosenberg is a Los Angeles-based filmmaker and Adobe Premiere expert. Jacob has worked extensively with Premiere as part of the Adobe software development team for almost a decade. Most recently, he has been the sole featured instructor for Premiere Pro on the highly acclaimed Total Training instructional DVD series.

Jacob got his start in high school by filming and editing skateboard videos, as well as taking photographs for a variety of print publications. After graduating from Emerson College, Jacob moved to Los Angeles and began his film career. Today, he is an accomplished independent filmmaker having directed national commercials, music videos, and several short films. His most recent film, *Bleach,* starring Brian Austin Green and Adam Scott can be seen on the festival circuit. His most recent music video was for the multi-platinum-selling group The Baha Men.

From IBC in Amsterdam to NAB in Las Vegas, Jacob teaches classes around the world about editing with Premiere. Constantly striving to make each course practical as well as educational, Jacob supplements his technical instruction with the use of his own film footage to provide a real-world context for how Premiere helps to deliver a professional-quality end product.

About the Technical Editors

With more than ten years experience in the graphics and video industry, **Charles Liss** has worked for such companies as Adobe Systems and Canopus Corporation. Charles has made Premiere Pro the cornerstone of his work for the last four years, testing such areas of the product as the new Effect Controls window, project workflow, and the window docking behavior. Currently a test automation engineer, he continues to work with Adobe and the Premiere team, inventing new ways to make this product better. Away from Premiere and Adobe, Charles can be found climbing Castle Rock, snowboarding at Tahoe, or taking the occasional co-pilot seat in preparation of his flight training. He lives in Silicon Valley with his wife Kimberly and their two dogs.

George Lamore is a lead quality engineer on the Adobe Premiere Pro development team. Although he earned a BA in English from UC Davis, he found himself drawn to the revolution in desktop computer graphics and animation and crammed two years of study into one. Tired of the slow pace at school, he bought all the software and as many books as he could get his hands on and immersed himself in Photoshop, Premiere, After Effects, and Lightwave. He began freelancing as an After Effects artist shortly thereafter. When the opportunity to work for the Premiere team came, he jumped on it. For the past three and a half years, he has been responsible for testing effects, compositing, color correction, the titler, and product interoperability with After Effects, Photoshop, and Illustrator among other areas.

Bruce Bowman is the product manager for the Adobe Video Collections and is now going on his eleventh year as an Adobe employee. He spent more than eight years working on Premiere, holding positions on both the engineering and product management teams. Bruce and Jacob are longtime friends and have shared their passion for digital video while working together on many projects over the years.

Acknowledgments

I first need to acknowledge the people who first gave me the opportunity to work at Adobe Systems year after year:

Joe Ternasky, for getting my back, lobbying for me, and getting me the second interview.

Nick Schlott, for taking a chance and hiring me.

Greg Gilley, for continuing to have me back, again and again and again.

Marianne Deaton, for helping to ensure that everything was in order for me to keep coming back.

Steve Warner, for hiring me again and again and again.

Bruce Bowman, for the tradeshow work, friendship, opportunities that he helped create, and some last-minute tech editing duties.

Richard Townhill, for his trust and the opportunities he extended to me.

Dave Trescot, who not only extended me opportunities, but also encouraged me to take my training and education skills a bit further and build a relationship with Total Training. His guidance has been valuable.

It's a curious thought for me to ponder where I would be had John Warnock and Chuck Geschke not been rebels themselves and created such a sound company.

For this book, I would like to acknowledge Jeffrey Warnock, who first suggested the idea and put me in touch with Peachpit. A very special nod of appreciation goes to my technical editors: Charles Liss, who has been the backbone of the tech team, and George Lamore. During their own work at Adobe, Charles and George have been very generous with their time and feedback, ensuring that the details and jargon that I tossed around where very well grounded in fact. I feel very privileged to have such a tight group supporting me and being a part of the creation of this book. I would also like to thank John Warnock for his contribution of the Foreword and his continued support of my artistic work.

To my patient acquisitions editor Elise Walter, who has put up with my fluctuating artist lifestyle and taken my word on impending deadlines far too many times. I also wish to thank my editor Linda Laflamme, who has helped me hone in and focus on what's important. I am not one short on words, but I am a bit shorter and more concise thanks to Linda! We have all put a lot of time into the writing of this book and I thank all of those involved with its creation.

I would feel bad not identifying people that have supported me at Adobe and elsewhere during the writing of this book. In no particular order, I want to make sure these people know that I appreciate their support: Mike Berry, Jason Levine, Bob Currier, Addison Liu, Gerhard Koren, Jason Woliner, Kelly Ryer, Marjorie Baer, Brad Pillow, David Kuspa, Bob Moll, Trent Happel, Matt Davey, Liz McQueen, Zachary Lam, Tina Eckman, Kristan Chan, Paul Young (I), Paul Young (II), Daniel Brown, Andrew Huebscher, Wally Buch, Tracy Moon, Mitch Wood, Barbara Ross, Marc Johnson, Barbara Driscoll, MT, Ganoush, Robert F., Lorbs, Al Tse, Matthew Toledo, and everyone else I forgot.

On another Adobe note, I would like to extend a general nod of approval to the folks on the Premiere team who single-handedly brought an application out of the dark ages and into the new millennium with a vengeance. Adobe Premiere Pro 1.5 is an application to be proud of! I say this not only as a loyal user, but as someone who has been in the trenches of the past versions and understands what it takes to make the type of radical changes that were necessary in order to re-brand this product and raise its potential. To the ninth floor in San Jose, my kudos!

And finally, I would like to thank my family for their patience with such an enthusiastic and hyper-curious child who was allowed to explore all of the things that interested him. If not for their patience, I have no clue what my life would look like today. I have been blessed with a tight family that supported my growth and individuality even when it wasn't comfortable for them. Mom, Dad, and Jessica, thank you. Elisabetta, you are so patient, ti amo.

Foreword

I have known Jacob Rosenberg for most of his life, and I can truly say that he has a creative spark and passion for video and filmmaking.

Over the last ten years, he has tracked the development of Adobe Premiere as a tester, consultant, user, and critic. He has very extensive experience with Premiere, Premiere Pro, and other Adobe products from both inside and outside Adobe.

What most impresses me about Jacob is that he is a smart, sensitive, and artistic filmmaker who demands that the tools he uses live up to the vision he has for his projects. This combination of artistic drive and extreme technical competence makes Jacob the perfect person to guide you through the ins and outs of Adobe Premiere Pro 1.5.

In this book, you will find that Premiere Pro is a very different application than the previous versions. Many new features were added and a great deal of attention was paid to how these features integrate into the workflow. You will find many new editing features, new integrated sound facilities, new titling, and new color control features.

While reading this book you will see Premiere Pro through the eyes of someone who lives his life with the product. I am sure you will find the journey rewarding.

John Warnock

I

Introduction

A little over a year ago, I was approached to write a book on Adobe Premiere Pro. My gut reactions were fear and wonder. Having touched nearly every element of the program from testing to development to tradeshows to training, I felt that writing a book would truly test my passion for the product.

For the last ten years, I have dedicated a large portion of my life to solving problems and trying to create problems using Premiere, now Premiere Pro 1.5. This has left me with my hands full of lessons, tips, tricks, and techniques. I am pleased to be able to share what I have learned with you, so that you do not have to suffer the same setbacks and so that features can make sense right away.

I have always used Premiere for small work and professional jobs. Although there were plenty of other nonlinear editing choices out there, Premiere made sense to me when I first started editing, and it still does. I am a highly visual person, and I'm comfortable with Premiere's dragging and dropping, shifting and moving—it fits the right visual editing model. With Premiere Pro, the user interface had a major overhaul; many features changed, and some were left behind.

During the initial development of Premiere Pro, I was a little uncertain whether or not Premiere would shake its legacy issues and step up to bat with the big boys. Part of my motivation to write this book was to affirm that Premiere Pro *did* step up to the plate. It now has a ton of features that work better than ever. If you are intimidated by the UI changes or curious about the power of Premiere Pro, read on to see the many benefits of choosing it as your nonlinear editor.

With Premiere Pro, Adobe offers a very reasonably priced, compelling program that helps you get real-world work done. At the end of the day, it all comes down to money and to a budget. Sure you can pay high prices and get great integrated editing systems, but throughout its history Premiere and its diverse feature set have offered a high value for a relatively low price. Think about it: You can digitize video, add titles, effects, fine-tune audio, and export directly to a DVD without having to use any other software—that's fantastic. With the new advances in hardware, cameras, and processors, now is as good of a time as ever to invest in a simple editing solution. In this book, you will find lots of lessons and tons of tips that will help you make the most of your investment. At the end of the day, I consider myself an editor and filmmaker who wants a tool to get the job done. With Premiere Pro 1.5, Adobe provides a worthy tool.

Who Should Read This Book?

Adobe Premiere Pro Studio Techniques is for anyone who wants to get more out of using Adobe Premiere Pro—from new users to old hands.

If you are new to Premiere, the "Fundamentals of Premiere Pro" section and bonus appendices on the accompanying DVD will give you a good foundation to build on. This material serves as an alternate manual to the program and contains very specific and direct descriptions that cover the entire application. I am not a big fan of manuals, so I attempted to keep the book's format easy to read and reference.

If you're looking for step-by-step lessons to help you hone your skills, the "Advanced Techniques" sections will give you plenty of resources to mine. Jump to the subject you desire, and dig in. The straightforward step-by-step lessons cover real-world examples and techniques that I have used and developed during my own work, and many include some of my original video and audio files. It is not enough to learn how to edit with Premiere using below-adequate editing material. I believe that you learn how to edit by editing with real editing material, such as shots that make up a scene that must be tailored into a whole. Using this idea, each lesson helps you achieve a viable and practical goal.

Being a visual person, I sometimes need to *see* exactly what a feature does in order to understand it. On the accompanying DVD, you will find video tutorials to supplement the discussions of the more difficult concepts. Access the short video clips to learn more about difficult, technical, or purely visual concepts. Notes in the book's text will direct you to the clips at the time viewing them would be most helpful.

What's in This Book?

Adobe Premiere Pro Studio Techniques is composed of nine sections, each focusing on a different aspect of Premiere Pro. Here's a quick preview of what you'll find where.

- **I: Fundamentals of Premiere Pro.** Here you will find almost every Premiere Pro feature, window, and button explained in simple terms and clear illustrations. Not only will the section provide a solid overview of the application, but also a strong reference for your later questions.
- **II: Advanced Graphics and Titles.** Now it's time for the hands-on lessons. In this section, you will learn how to properly import layered Photoshop files, nest sequences to build more controllable effects, create custom image pan effects with presets, and get better results from the Adobe Title Designer.
- **III: Advanced Audio Techniques.** Imagery is only half of your project, and this section shines the spotlight on the other half: audio. After a complete overview from fine-tuning your system's audio settings, you will learn to record a voiceover, edit it, add effects, and mix it all down.
- **IV: Advanced Editing Techniques.** Working with professional footage from a short film and a couple music videos, you will refine your editing skills in this section, as well as be introduced to my down-home multi-cam editing

technique. In addition, you will use Premiere Pro 1.5's new Project Manager to consolidate and compact projects for storage, delivery, and backing up.

- **V: Advanced Effect Techniques.** Focusing on several of Premiere Pro's most important effects, this section provides plenty of real-world examples. You will practice properly white balancing your footage, creating a custom color look, and using the Color Match effect. You will also create moving track mattes, key green screen material, and create a good looking picture-in-picture effect.

What's on the DVD?

Accompanying this book is a DVD chock full of reference reading, lesson files, video tutorials, and add-on plug-ins. When you put the DVD in your drive, you will see a graphic launchpad with several options: Read Me, Get QuickTime, Install Training, Start Training, Book Lesson Files, Third-Party Plug-Ins, and Book Appendices. Clicking on one of these launches its associated task.

To use the training on the DVD, you must first install QuickTime (click the button), install the training (click the button), and start the training (click the button). You can then navigate through the video tutorials.

The video tutorials are arranged in sections that correspond to the book sections. For example, the DVD's Section I, "The Fundamentals" includes the video lessons referenced in the book's Section I (Chapters 1 through 9). Throughout the book, you will be directed to the DVD when a video tutorial exists to explain or illustrate something in the chapter. The video tutorials were recorded and created in conjunction with Total Training, a company that offers comprehensive, professional video-based training.

To follow along with the lessons in Chapters 10 through 27, be sure to click the Book Lesson Files button on the graphic launchpad to copy the lesson files onto your computer. Alternatively, you can copy the extras folder from the DVD to your hard drive. The Lessons folder contains all the media and project files you need to work through the lessons. Copy the Lessons folder to a secondary system drive; you'll need just over three gigabytes of free space. After you click the button, you will be prompted with a dialog in which you can specify where to copy the files.

The Third Party Plug-Ins folder is full of trial versions and demo copies of third-party plug-ins that add extra functionality to Premiere Pro. Documentation and installation instructions for using each of the plug-ins are also inclued. After you click the button, you will be prompted with a dialog in which you can specify where to copy the files. With the files on your system, you can run the installers.

The Book Appendices folder contains bonus material that supplements this book. If you have a question that isn't answered elsewhere, consult these sections, which are listed in a rollover menu on the DVD:

- **VI: Before You Edit.** These PDF appendices define the terms, technical presets, and system settings you need to review before and during your initial launch of Premiere Pro. You'll learn about all the nuts and bolts that go into creating a DV system from the ground up, as well as definitions of common digital video terms. Most importantly, you'll learn the proper settings for your system and Premiere Pro to keep them working together at their best.
- **VII: While You Edit.** Sometimes you need a little help while you work. This section provides it in two ways: Appedix E spotlights a variety of plug-ins and 24P solutions that you can purchase to add capabilities to your Premiere Pro system. Appendix F will help you troubleshoot your way out of that conundrum that is driving you crazy.
- **VIII: After You Edit.** If you need to export your production, consult this section's single appendix. You'll learn all about the features and functions of the Adobe Media Encoder. The Media Encoder was introduced in version 1.0 and has some valuable new pre- and post-processing features to help streamline the process of getting video out of Premiere Pro.

The appendices are formatted as PDF files. Copy them to your system, then you can open and read them using Acrobat Reader.

Where Do I Go Beyond This Book?

If you want to continue your quest for Premiere Pro knowledge and experience beyond this book, consider looking into the Premiere training series from Total Training. When you purchase a training series, you get several interactive DVDs containing video lessons and source lesson files. After you install the lesson files on your computer, you pop in the DVD and watch the video lessons. While the instructor guides you through the lesson and interface in the video, you can create the same project with the same files on your machine at home.

I have created three series on Premiere Pro for Total Training: "Total Training for Adobe Premiere Pro," "Total Training for Adobe Premiere Pro 1.5," and "Tips & Tricks for Adobe Premiere Pro 1.5," as well as a single update disk: "What's New in Adobe Premiere Pro 1.5." Although some lessons are similar to projects in this book, the DVDs contain more real-world lessons, examples, and additional footage to give you more exposure to the application. For more details about the curriculum, explore the Premiere Pro/Digital Video links on Total Training's website at **www.totaltraining.com**.

If you want to stay current with the films, music videos, and productions that keep me busy, check out my website at **www.formikafilms.com**. If you want to stay current with my Adobe Premiere Pro work, visit **www.premiereprotraining.com**. You can also contact me to share your thoughts about this book and your Premiere Pro experiences by e-mailing studiotech@premiereprotraining.com.

Fundamentals of Premiere Pro

CHAPTER

1

Capturing Video

Video capture is at the heart of Premiere Pro—you can't do much until you have some clips to work with. To get the clips you want at the best quality for your project, you'll need to understand the Capture window, as well as some capturing fundamentals, such as logging your tapes and striping them with timecode. This chapter will take you on a tour of what's new and what's necessary, examining, for example, how Premiere Pro's Capture window is now more tightly integrated with your open project. Along the way, you will learn a workflow that provides better media management and long-term project stability.

Scratch Disks and Device Control

Before you get to the Capture window, however, you need to make sure your Scratch Disk and Device Control preferences are set correctly. These help establish where your captured files are recorded and which method Premiere uses to communicate with the attached video device (a camera or deck).

I recommend that you do not use your root disk (C:) as the primary scratch disk for capturing. Instead, create a unique folder to which you target your captured files on your scratch or capture disk. To assign your scratch disks, choose Edit>Preferences>Scratch Disks and specify the disks you want (see Figure 1.1). If you want the captured media from separate projects to be captured into separate subfolders, you must create and target those subfolders separately for each project before you start capturing. You can always change your scratch disks before you capture a clip, and this can be done quite easily in the Capture window.

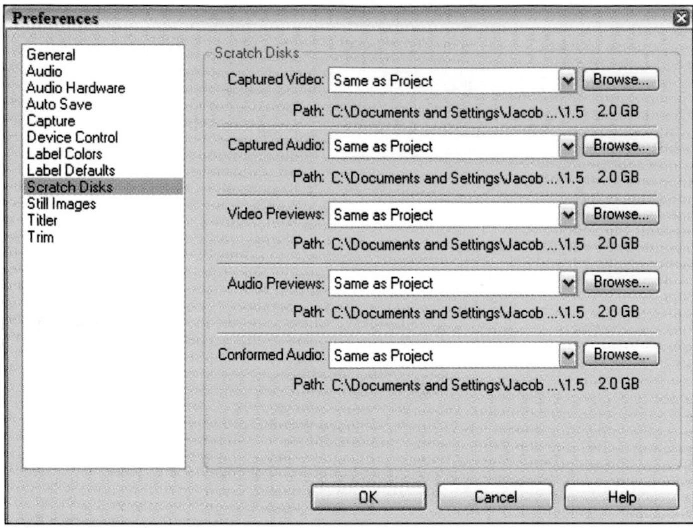

Figure 1.1 In the Preferences dialog, you assign your scratch disks.

For DV capturing, make sure that your drives have the proper spin rate (7200rpm), and if you are capturing to external FireWire drives, make sure they are not daisy chained together (see Figure 1.2).

Daisy chaining is the linking together multiple external drives. Typically, FireWire drives have two input/output ports. If your computer had only one available FireWire port, you would daisy chain both drives so both could be recognized by your computer. The first drive (E:) would connect to your computer via FireWire and the second drive (F:), using the extra FireWire port on the first, would connect to drive E: and be recognized as an additional drive on your system. Although it is fine to configure drives in this manner, the DV Specifications do not support this configuration for capturing DV footage from a DV device.

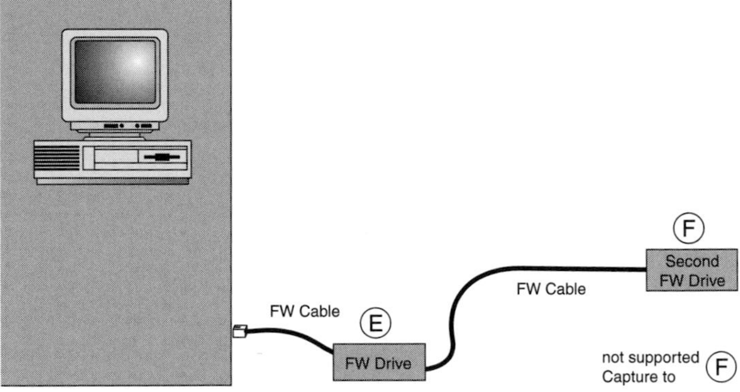

Figure 1.2 The FireWire drive E: is connected to the computer with a FireWire cable, then drive F: is then daisy-chained to E: with a FireWire cable. Drive F: is not supported for capture and playback with a DV device.

For DV device control, choose Edit>Preferences>Device Control. In the Device Control pane of the Preferences dialog (see Figure 1.3), select the device control method from the Devices drop down menu, then manually adjust those controls by clicking the Options button and entering the information that matches the device you are using. (See Figure 1.4.) Each camera or deck has its own unique protocol and method of communicating using device control, and it's important that you set the Options before you start capturing.

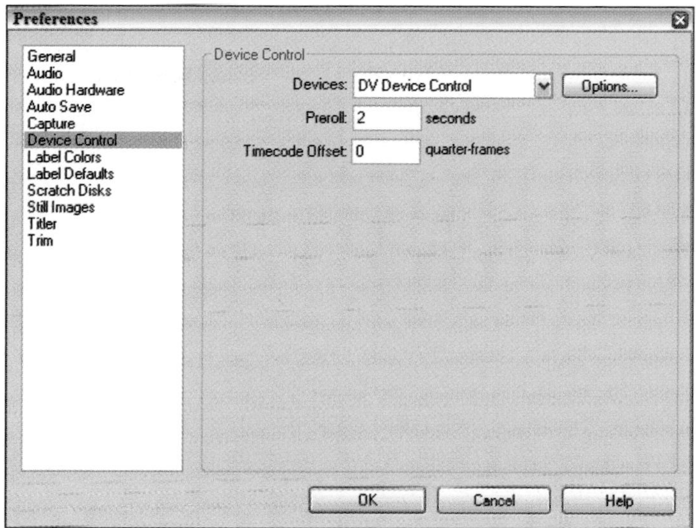

Figure 1.3 You can also assign your device control settings in the Preferences dialog.

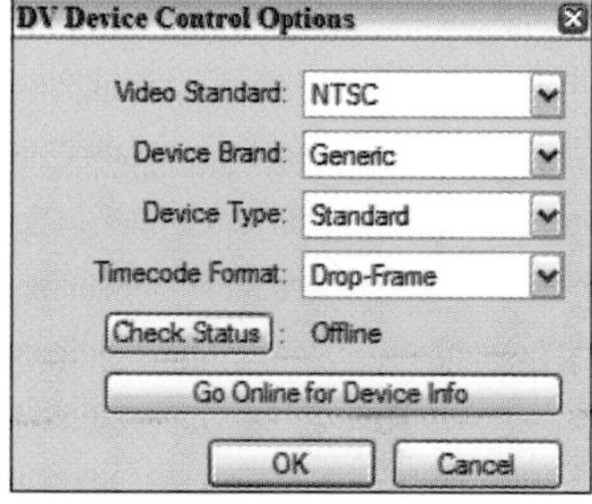

Figure 1.4 In the Device Controls Options dialog, you specify your device's video standard, brand, and type. Click the Check Status button to find out whether the device is communicating with Premiere Pro. Offline means there is no communication, Online means there is.

Out of habit from my earliest Premiere days, I always turn on my camera and connect the FireWire cable before I launch Premiere Pro. It is still correct to assume that you will have more immediate communication with your device once the application is open; however, it's not the only way to go. Because Windows XP supports hot plugging of external devices (it loads the drivers and activates the device without having to reboot), you can power on your camera at any time during your Premiere session. I don't recommend turning your camera on and off while you work, but if your battery dies or you want to turn your camera off, it's okay. The application will be all right and so will you. If you do power up your camera in the middle of a session, you may have to wait 10 to 20 seconds for the drivers to load and communication and transmission to be engaged.

If you have your DV camera turned on and connected, but you are unable to transmit and communicate with it, check the device status in your DV Device Control Options dialog box first. Go to Edit>Preferences>Device Control, then click Options. If the device is listed as online but you cannot transmit to it, power off the device then power it back on. When it powers off you should hear the Windows Device Management bell chime off, then when the device powers back on, the bell sound should chime on. I typically check all FireWire insertion points and re-insert the cable. Also, check your own internal brain error, and make sure you aren't turning on the camera in Camera mode as opposed to VCR or VTR.

What's New with Capture

With your device settings in place and your camera on, you are ready for a tour of the Capture window. To open it, choose File>Capture or press F5. (See Figure 1.5.) On the left side of the window is your viewing area for the signal that is being transmitted to your Capture window. The top bar always contains feedback as to what the Capture window is doing—rewinding, playing back, batch capturing clips, and so on. Below the viewing area is the timecode feedback area, which displays (from the left) the current timecode, marked In timecode, marked Out timecode, and duration of In/Out. Below the timecode are your transport controls, which are made up of three group boxes. (See Figure 1.6.)

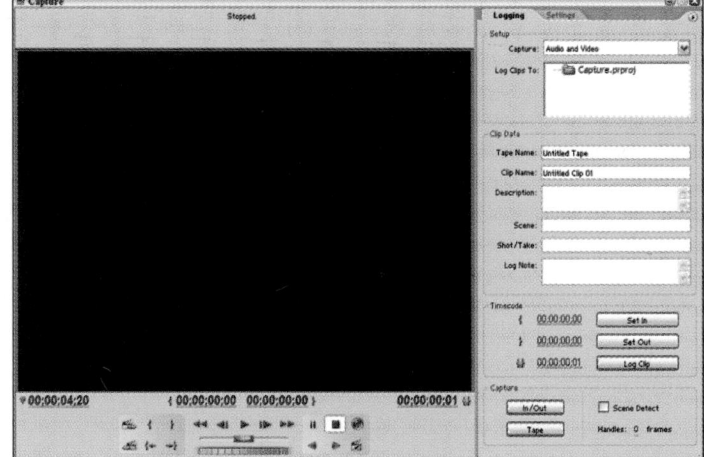

Figure 1.5 The new Capture window, which arrived with Premiere Pro, offers full shuttle and deck control, advanced logging functionality, and scene detection.

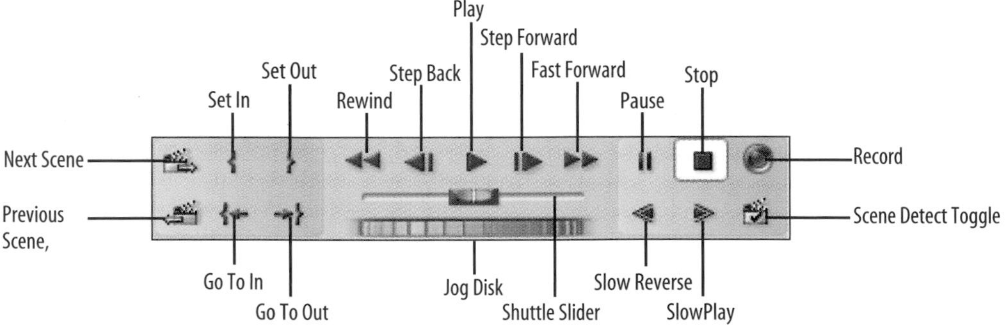

Figure 1.6 The Transport controls consist of three group boxes: left, center, and right.

Transport Controls

The left group box of transport controls begins with the Next Scene (top) and Previous Scene (bottom) buttons. The number of times you click these buttons, determines how many scenes you advance forward or backwards: Two clicks moves two scenes. The viewing area displays a message as it is rewinding back the number of scenes you specified. If you click Previous Scene twice, for example, it displays "Searching 2 Scenes Back." The next buttons are quite straightforward and common to most of the transport areas in the other Monitor windows. The top row holds Set In Point and Set Out Point, while the bottom row contains Go To In Point and Go To Out Point. If you have an In or Out point marked, clicking on the Go To buttons advances your tape to the specified point.

In the top row of the center group box, you'll find the familiar tape controls: Rewind, Step Back (one frame increment), Play, Step Forward (one frame increment), and Fast Forward. Below is the shuttle slider, which dynamically changes the forward or backward playback speed. Pull the shuttle right to change the forward speed, left to change backward playback speed. The farther away from the center you move the shuttle, the faster playback will be. Dragging the shuttle all the way to the right is the equivalent of fast forward, while dragging just a hair to the right increases the speed only slightly. At the bottom of the center box is the jog disk, which steps through frame by frame. You can just roll your mouse over the jog to keep it going. The nice thing about the jog is that once you start scrubbing it, your mouse doesn't get lost off screen left or right. It stays centered on the wheel so you can scrub, scrub, scrub to your heart's content.

The right group box has the Pause, Stop, and Record buttons in the top row. The Slow Reverse button, the Slow Play button, and the Scene Detect toggle are on the bottom.

Although all of these controls are here for your clicking, I capture more efficiently with the keyboard alone.

J, K, and L: More Than Three Letters

J, K, and L are critical keys whenever you are playing back in a Monitor window or the Capture window. Here's how these shortcuts can help you:

- **J** Plays in reverse at normal speed, press again for double speed, and again for quadruple speed
- **K** Stop
- **Spacebar** Toggles between pausing and playing
- **L** Plays forward at normal speed, press again for double speed, and again for quadruple speed
- **R** Rewind
- **F** Fast forward
- **G** Capture

Say you're stepping through your tape doing normal captures (or logging). Press L to start playing, if you want to fast forward at the highest speed while still seeing your video, press F to play very fast with the video still visible. If you see something you like, press the Spacebar to pause, then maybe press J twice to rewind, L to play, and finally G to capture. Once you're happy with the capture, press G again (or Esc or Spacebar) to end the capture. Name your file, and move on. If you want to fast forward at the camera's fastest speed, press K to stop, then press F to engage fast forward again while the camera is in Stop mode to have the fastest forward speed possible. The same is true for R (rewinding). So, navigate with J, K, L, F, and R. When you see the shot you want, press pause (Spacebar). If you want to step frame by frame, use the Left and Right Arrow keys to go forward or backwards (right and left respectively); one press moves one frame, two moves two frames, and so on. Shift+Arrow steps at five-frame increments. When you are finished with your tape, press K to stop, then E to eject the tape. Pop a new one in and continue.

When you are paused at a specific tape location, the instant you click the Capture button, the camera plays and starts recording at the same time.

Logging and the Logging Tab

If you have the time, always log your videotapes before you begin editing with them. You will spare yourself a lot of hassles this way.

Logging a tape consists of scanning through your tape, noting the timecode In and Out points of specific instances, then assigning these instances a unique name and various descriptions. Logging a tape is beneficial, because it provides a running description with exact timecode locations for every shot on the tape.

You will log your tapes using the Logging tab (see Figure 1.7), which is the default tab that is open on the right side of the Capture window. It is critical to managing your captured media that you become familiar with this tab's fields.

When you log your clips, you are defining parameters of the media. Because you can define a number of specific values, it is very easy for Premiere Pro to make an *offline file* that respects all of these parameters.

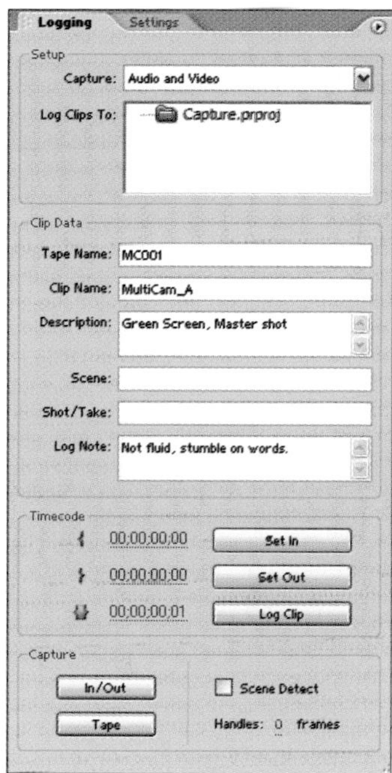

Figure 1.7 The wealth of information that you manually enter in the Capture window's Logging tab will be attached to the logged offline file or captured clip.

Offline file is a term used for media that is not detected on your system, while the parameters of the media still exist in your Project window. If a file is accidentally deleted from your system, the icon and information for the file will still exist in your project (see Figure 1.8), but be listed as offline. Additionally, if you were to log a clip to your Project window but did not yet capture it, the logged clip would be offline until you captured it and the media was added to your computer.

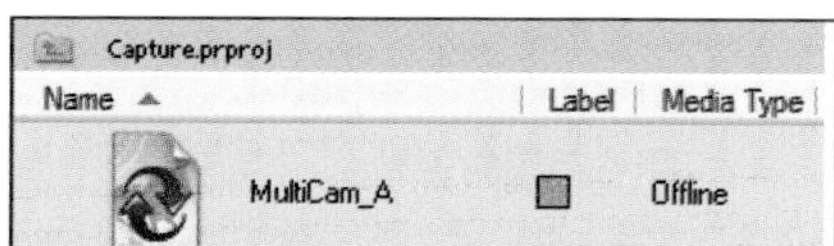

Figure 1.8 Once a clip is logged directly to the Project window it appears offline. An offline file simulates the physical clips with all its properties, but no video or audio.

For example, when you log an audio and video clip named Clip01 that has a duration of ten seconds between the In and Out points, Premiere Pro creates an offline file in your Project window with the same parameters and filename. In fact, there will be a tangible ten-second offline file that you can edit in your timeline.

If you are logging only, there will be no media linked to the logged clip. The filename, the tape name, the timecode In and Out points, descriptions, and so on are all attached to the file. To give the clip online status, simply choose File>Batch Capture. Because you have all the parameters logged, Premiere Pro knows exactly which tape the file comes from, where it is on that tape, and what you want to name it. If you choose not to batch capture the clip, you can still use the clip within your project, but Premiere Pro will display the message "Media Offline" instead of playing that clip back.

The power of this feature is that you can edit right away after logging, even if you have not captured any media. Even if you lose all of your media and retain only your project file, as long as you digitized and logged your footage properly, you will only have to batch capture the missing clips to get your project back into its former shape. Label your tapes clearly, and you can rescue your project from disaster.

Setup

The Setup area has two parameters:

- **Capture.** Defines the properties of the capture you want to log. From the drop-down list, choose Video, Audio, or Audio and Video.
- **Log Clips To.** Specifies the location to which you are logging your clips. Because you log directly to the Project window, you can target a specific bin in which to place the logged clips.

Your entire project bin structure will be revealed in the Log Clips To field (see Figure 1.9). I always make a unique folder called Logged Clips that I log into. Once I capture my files, I copy or move them to a new, more appropriate folder.

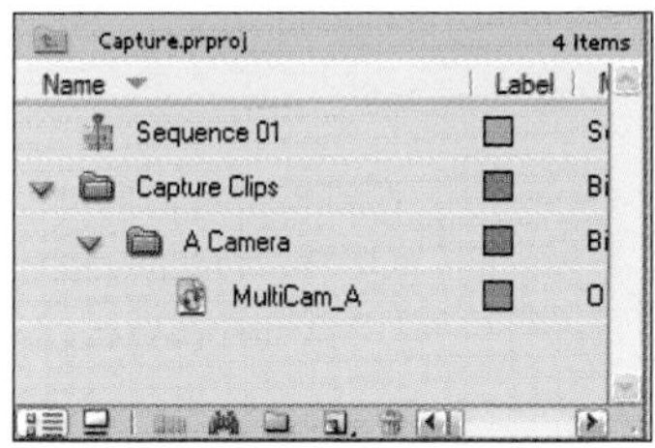

Figure 1.9 The bin structure of the Project window (left) is the same as in the Log Clips To field of the Setup group box (right). The bin you select in the Log Clips To field is the bin in which the logged or captured clips will be added to the project.

In the initial release of Premiere Pro, once you log a clip as Video, you cannot open that log file and change it to Audio and Video. You cannot reload the logged instance back into the Capture window. Certain parameters can be updated, but the capture properties (audio and video, only audio, or only video) are locked once you log the file.

Clip Data

Ahh, the most important fields are right here in the Clip Data section (see Figure 1.10). If your tapes are labeled clearly this should be simple. The parameters are:

- **Tape Name**. The name of the tape currently in your camera. You should change this only when you put a new tape in and begin logging from the new tape.
- **Clip Name.** The name you apply to the clip that you are logging. Premiere Pro auto-increments your names with a +01 numbering system. If you name your first clip Dad_Party and press Log Clip, for example, Premiere logs the clip and displays the name Dad_Party01 in the Capture window. This is helpful, but not always what you need. Fortunately, all your logged data gets verified before you physically create the logged clip in the Project window.
- **Description**. Details you want to remember about the file. I always name my files something plain and then save the specifics for the Description and Log Notes. For Dad_Party, the Description might be: "Jessica arrives with Joshua, early."
- **Scene** and **Shot/Take**. A scene number and a shot number, respectively. Use these only if they apply to your clip.
- **Log Note**. Details about the file that will actually be written into the captured file itself. A file's Description, Scene, and Shot/Take are associated with it in your project only. If you were to open the file in another

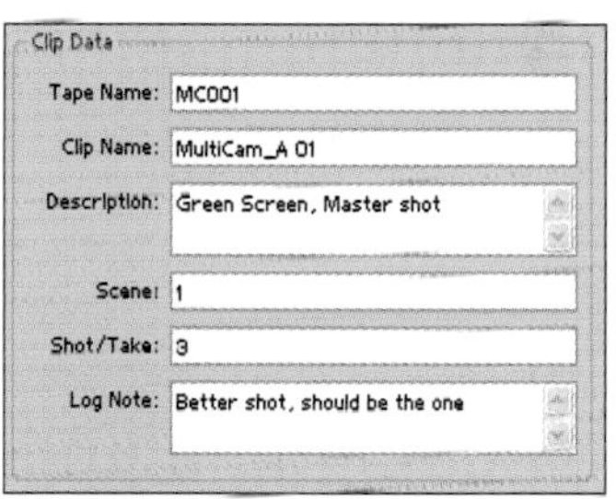

Figure 1.10 The Clip Data fields are where you can add all the details regarding your logged or to be capture clip.

I cannot emphasize enough the importance of properly logging a tape's name, at the very least.

editing application, you would not know it was scene 3, shot 2, you would just see the tape name, file name, and log note. If you think that your captured clips will be used in separate projects, then use the Log Notes field to duplicate your Description, Scene, and Shot/Take information. For the Dad_Party example shot, I would write, "Dark and out of focus when Jessica talks to Joshua, Use only at the end." This is a description and note about my thoughts during the log and a suggestion for the editor (myself or someone else).

All of these fields will be persistent, meaning once you enter information into the Description, for example, that information stays in the field for the next clip that you log. You can, of course, clear a field before you confirm the logging of any clip. Only the Clip Name auto-increments.

Timecode

The Timecode fields are pretty slick. Not only is this area another place to click a button to set your timecode In and Out points, but also the Timecode fields are displayed as hot text fields so modifying them is simple (see Figure 1.11). Instead of having to reset a misplaced In or Out point from scratch, you can very easily click and drag the timecode display left or right to reduce or add to the marked point. Click the Set In (or Set Out) button when you're satisfied. After defining the In and Out points, you can see the duration. To the right of the duration is the Log Clip button, which puts all of the data from the entire Log tab into a dialog box for you to verify. Click OK to add a new clip as an offline file to the destination log folder you specified.

Figure 1.11 You can easily modify the timecode values by clicking on them and dragging to the left or right.

Capture and Scene Detection

To capture a clip you just logged, go to the Capture window's Logging tab and click the In/Out button (see Figure 1.12). This button instructs the program to capture from the Capture window's current In point to its current Out point.

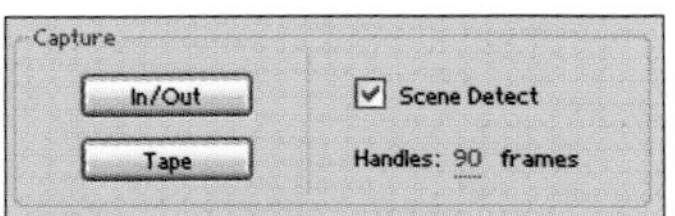

Figure 1.12 The Logging tab's Capture controls enable you to capture the current In/Out instance or to engage Scene Detect capture of the entire tape starting at the current position. Use Handles to define how many extra frames before and after your In/Out instance to record.

If you need to capture an entire tape, however, consider Premiere Pro's powerful new Scene Detect feature. Because your DV camera records data to the tape, it writes time and date stamps to the tape every time you stop and start recording. If you were to look through the data of the tape, you could find every unique shot based on the changes in the time and date stamps. Additionally, using scene detection, you can advance forward or backwards at specific increments. You use the Scene Detect feature in conjunction with the Tape button.

Clicking on the Scene Detect check box puts capturing into Scene Detect mode. This does not affect logging. When you click the Tape button with Scene Detect turned on, however, Premiere Pro starts capturing your tape from the current position and continues to the end of the tape using scene detection. Premiere Pro rolls through your tape in one pass, treating each time/date stamp instance as an individual clip. While it appears that Premiere Pro is recording one long file, every time/date stamp instance results in an individual captured clip. When I don't have the time to log a tape or I am not sure which portions I want to use, I capture the entire tape using Scene Detect and Tape, drop all the clips in the timeline, and just delete those I don't want.

In Scene Detect mode, Premiere Pro uses the Tape Name in the Clip Data area and then it uses the active Clip Name with auto incrementing for each individual capture. You cannot give each file a unique name as you record, you have to modify that later in the Project window.

The final setting in the Capture area is Handles. Handles are extra frames at the beginning and end of your capture. If you have an In point of 1;01;20 and an Out point of 1;05;10 and Handles is set to 20 frames, your captured clip will start at 1;01;00 and end at 1;06;00. When you open that clip in your project, the In and Out points will still be 1;01;20 and 1;05;10, but you will have 20 extra frames. I always set Handles at 15 to 30 frames so that I never have to recapture additional material to get my shots right. Handles are assigned to batch captures and Scene Detect captures only. If you do a *free record* capture, no handles will be assigned.

A free record capture does not rely on timecode In and Out instances, it just captures what is being played from the time you click Record until you stop playback or stop capture. Free recording uses the Tape Name, File Name, timecode values, Description, and other meta fields that are active when you first press Record. After you stop recording, you can then verify or adjust the fields before saving the captured file.

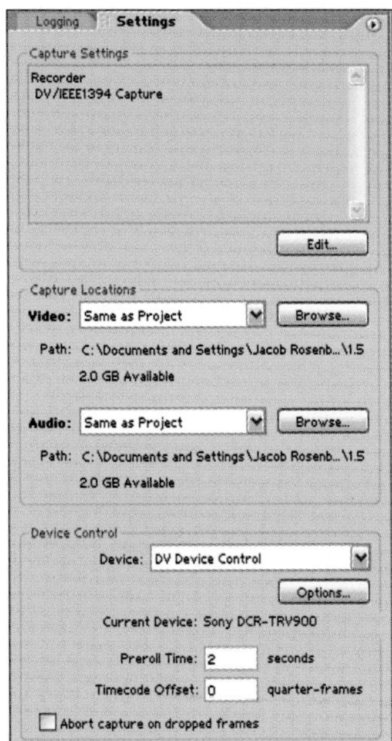

Figure 1.13 The Settings tab provides you quick access to Capture Settings, Capture Locations (scratch disks), and Device Control. There is no need to open your preferences, just activate the Settings tab.

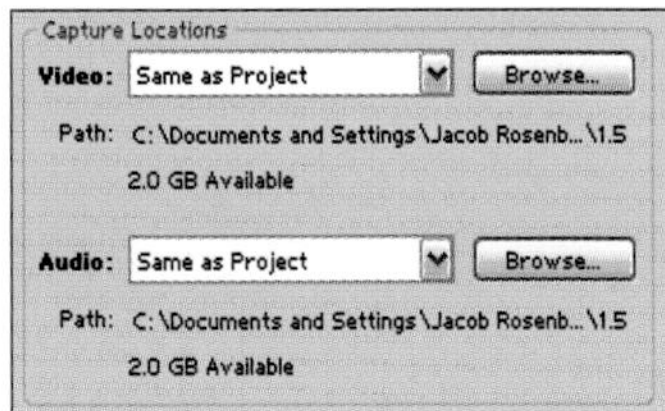

Figure 1.14 In the Capture Locations area, you can assign your Scratch Disks, which are the paths to which your captured video and audio media is automatically saved.

Settings Tab

The Capture window's Settings tab (see Figure 1.13) allows access to a number of typically buried presets and preferences related to your capture settings, the capture location, and device control.

Capture Settings

The Setting tab's Capture Settings area displays the Capture Format (here called the Recorder) you specified for your project. To change it, click Edit button. The Capture pane of the Project Settings dialog opens; click on the Capture Format drop-down list to select a capture module. For all of the DV presets, the capture module is DV/IEEE1394 Capture. If you have a third-party capture card installed, you will have other choices listed.

Capture Locations

The Capture Locations area (see Figure 1.14) displays the Scratch Disks Preferences you set for capturing video and audio. As you capture, it also updates the amount of disk space available on your assigned scratch disks. You can change them as you capture. Click the appropriate Browse button (Video or Audio) and navigate to the folder you need, then choose Custom from the drop-down menu. For a shortcut to Premiere Pro's default document folder, choose My Documents from the drop-down list, or choose Same as Project to capture to the folder you specified as a Scratch Disk Preference. If you have a project where you want different tapes captured to different folders, capture your first tape, make a change in Capture Locations, then capture your second tape, and so on.

Device Control

The Device Control field is a shortcut to your Device Control Preferences. You can change all these values as you would if you accessed them from Edit>Preferences>Device Control. Additionally, your device type (if you specified one) will be revealed in the Current Device field. If your camera is not responding, you can switch to the Settings tab, click Options in the Device Control section, and verify your settings in the DV Device Control Options. If your camera does go offline, a message to that effect appears in the Capture window above the display area.

Capture Wing Menu

Every window in Premiere Pro has a wing menu (see Figure 1.15). The wing menu is a shortcut area to certain features and modes. Because Premiere Pro has a fully customizable keyboard, putting functions in the wing menus allows these functions to be mapped to the keyboard. From the wing menu, you can access your capture settings, set your capture mode, turn scene detection on or off, and collapse the Capture window.

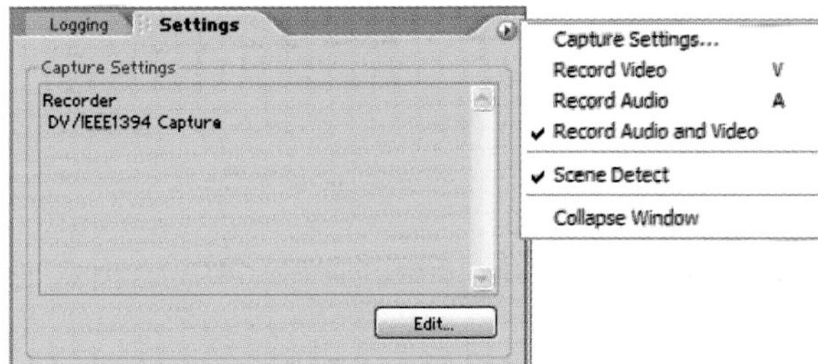

Figure 1.15 The wing menu provides access to a few shortcuts. Because the shortcuts populate the menu, they can be assigned as keyboard shortcuts.

The Right Workflow

Knowing what the capture parameters and controls are and what they do is only half the equation. Following an efficient workflow is vital. Striping and labeling your tapes should be your first task. (See Figure 1.16.)

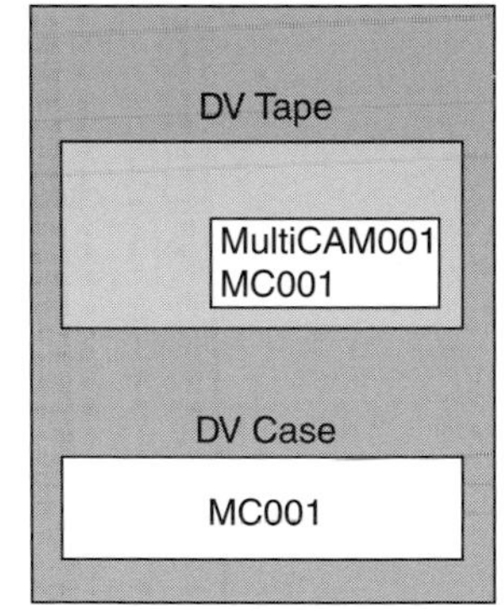

Figure 1.16 Make sure your tape and its case have the same name. This may feel like basic stuff, but it goes a long way towards better organizing your library of footage. Here the tape label has a descriptive name and a shortened name used for logging and capturing (MC001).

Timecode and Striping Your Tapes

When using Premiere in a DV environment, do not underestimate the benefit of *striping* your MiniDV Tapes. The timecode format for MiniDV is such that if the camera detects blank tape (static) and you begin recording, the timecode always begins at 00;00;00;00. This can cause trouble.

Say you record for ten minutes, then you watch your last shot. You try to press Stop exactly at the shot's end, but inadvertently stop in the blank space just after it. When you next press Record, the timecode starts all over again at

00;00;00;00. You then record for another 50 minutes and finish the tape. Technically, you now have two identical timecode values on different portions of your tape—which can make logging and batch capturing with this tape a nightmare.

Or, you may play through and mark In and Out points, passing the brief blank space not knowing that it is there. When batch capturing, Premiere Pro automatically captures all the clips you logged. Because the first recorded instance has ten minutes of content then blank space, as soon as the batch capture hits the stoppage, Premiere will seek for three seconds looking for new timecode. If Premiere does not find any new timecode in those three seconds, it assumes it has hit the end of the tape and it stops. Of course, with a MiniDV tape, you might not actually be at the end of your tape. (See Figure 1.17.)

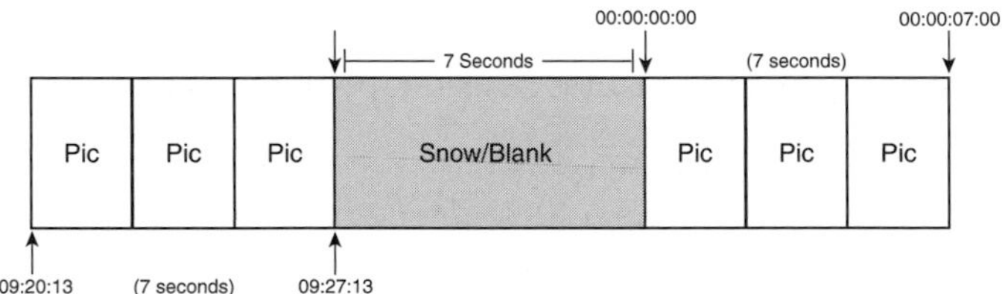

Figure 1.17 In this diagram, the strip represents 21 seconds of your DV tape and the timecode represents the timecode value for the associated frames of video. Because there is no recorded video in the snow/blank section, timecode starts all over again at 00;00;00;00 when recording re-engages.

To properly prepare and to work more efficiently with MiniDV, I recommend two steps before your shoot with your camera:

1. Stripe your tape with a full recording pass so that there is a continuous run of timecode and data on your tape from beginning to end. It will not damage the tape or affect future recordings on that tape.
2. Label your tape clearly and with an alpha+numeric value, such as Bleach001 (ProjectName+NumericValue). If you pre-label your tapes, you can find specific tapes more easily once you start logging. You can also add the description of the tape after you record.

Capturing Best Practices

With your video recorded, it's time to capture. Pop your tape in, set the camera to VTR mode, and press F5 to open your Capture window. Before I try my first capture, I like to press Play (L) to make sure my timecode numbers are being transmitted and I am seeing my video. The basic steps for a capture are:

1. Cue up your tape, and then specify the parameters of what you're logging. I usually create a new folder in my Project window and name it Logged Clips, then select it from the Log Clip To field.
2. Enter the name of your tape in the Tape Name field. If you have a good sense of what the filenames will be, enter that for the Clip Name. For example, I might use Bleach_BTS (Bleach is my short film, and BTS means behind the scenes).
3. Press L to start playing back.
4. When you find the first In point, press I to set it.
5. You can keep playing if your shot is long and enter the description as it plays back. If you do click within a text field while playback is engaged, you cannot access your keyboard shortcuts (because of text conflicts) until you click out of the field.
6. Enter any additional meta data, set your Out point, then click Log Clip. All of the data you entered will appear in a dialog box that you can modify.
7. Click OK, and Premiere adds a new offline file to your chosen bin. For me, that's the Logged Clips bin.

From there, you can continue logging one tape or switch to any others that you need to log. Because Premiere Pro supports offline files, you need not capture immediately after you have logged. At any time, you can select individual or groups of offline files to batch capture and get the media online.

Offline Files

Once you have successfully logged clips to your Project window, you do not have to capture them immediately to use them in your project. Clips with no media linked will be displayed as offline files. If you scroll through the columns of the Project window, you can see all the data associated with the file that you logged. Offline files can be edited and used in your project, as would any normal media file (see Figure 1.18). They do not, however, display any media that would be associated with them. You can edit, trim, and adjust offline files. Once you batch capture or link media to them, the media will show up exactly as you edited it.

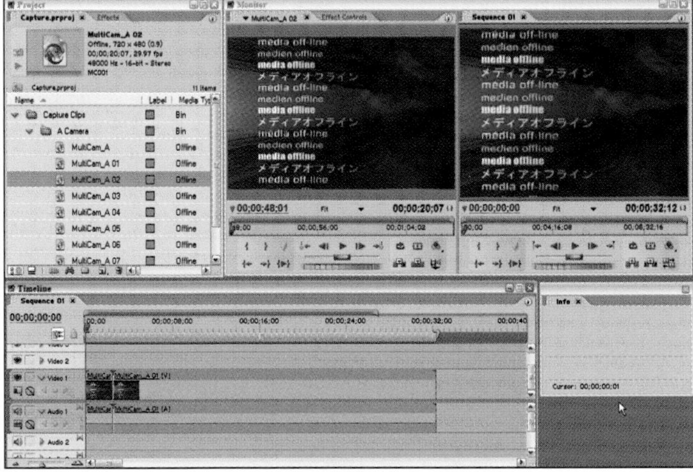

Figure 1.18 Offline files can be opened in the Source Monitor and edited in the timeline. In all these windows, the timecode properties and audio/video attributes are represented and a graphic placeholder is open to let you know that files are offline.

Batch Capturing

Premiere Pro builds on Premiere's earlier batch list capturing features. Now, not only can you create and import traditional text batch lists, but your project can also act as a master batch list enabling Premiere Pro to log your clips (captured or not) directly into the open project (into a bin you define). There is no batch list functionality lost with Pro: You can still import and export individual batch lists in a comma-delimited format. Instead, a highly intuitive method has been added that makes your project file more valuable and much deeper. Logging directly to the Project window saves the clip data into the project file (See Figure 1.19). As long as you don't delete the clip reference from your Project window, you will always be able to recapture, based on the original logged parameters.

Capture.prproj × Effects

A Camera
Bin

Capture.prproj — 11 Items

Name	Status	Tape Name	Log Note	Scene	Shot/Take	Media Start	Media End	Media Duration
Capture Clips								
A Camera								
MultiCam_A	Offline: User Requested	MC001	Not fluid, stumble on words.			00;00;04;20	00;00;07;05	00;00;02;16
MultiCam_A 01	Offline: User Requested	MC001	Good take, won't use	1	1	00;00;16;13	00;00;46;08	00;00;29;26
MultiCam_A 02	Offline: User Requested	MC001	Better shot, should be the one	1	2	00;00;48;01	00;01;08;09	00;00;20;07
MultiCam_A 03	Offline: User Requested	MC001	Best!	1	3	00;01;31;02	00;01;57;03	00;00;26;02
MultiCam_A 04	Offline: User Requested	MC001	Bad lighting	1	4	00;02;07;13	00;02;33;06	00;00;25;24
MultiCam_A 05	Offline: User Requested	MC001	Good shot, audio level too low	1	5	00;02;29;25	00;03;06;21	00;00;36;25
MultiCam_A 06	Offline: User Requested	MC001	Good Shot, cuts early.	1	6	00;03;00;27	00;03;37;27	00;00;37;01
MultiCam_A 07	Offline: User Requested	MC001	Unusable	1	7	00;03;33;00	00;03;55;19	00;00;22;20
Sequence 01								

Figure 1.19 Depending on which columns you choose to view and in which order, you have access to all the meta data that was logged to the clips. Additionally, you can see a number of other details and add comments into custom fields.

With all your clips logged and a bin of offline files, you can do a couple of different things to specify what you want to capture. If you select File>Batch Capture with the Log Clips bin selected from your Master Project view, all of the offline files in that folder that have proper tape, name, and timecode In/Out information will be captured. If you have one specific file selected, Premiere will batch capture only that file.

Not all DV devices automatically eject the tape when capture is complete. You can expect DV decks to always eject, but not all DV cameras support the automatic eject feature. Once capturing from a tape is complete, while the dialog is open telling you to insert another tape, you safely can manually press eject and then insert the new tape.

If you need several clips, Ctrl+click to select multiple files within a folder. Premiere Pro will batch captures only those selected files. The program first asks you to put into your camera the first tape associated with your media, then it engages playback and captures all the specified clips that are on that tape. When finished with a tape, it ejects the tape and prompts you to put in a new one. You insert the next tape, then click OK to continue batch capturing.

For error reporting, I recommend that you turn on Generate Batch Log File Only on Unsuccessful Completion so that if there are any errors with your batch captures, a file listing the errors will be waiting for you in the same bin location as the offline files.

Linking Your Media

Because your project file holds all the meta data associated with each captured clip, you can unlink and delete the media that is currently linked (associated) with your clips. When you unlink a file, you can break the link with files on the disk, or you can break the link and delete the media file on disk. In both cases, the clip reference in the Project window would still be preserved. If you are trying to free space on your system, for example, you can break the links and delete all the unused files in your project. These files would remain visible, but be offline. If you decide you need them after all, select them and choose Batch Capture to bring them back online. (See Figure 1.20.)

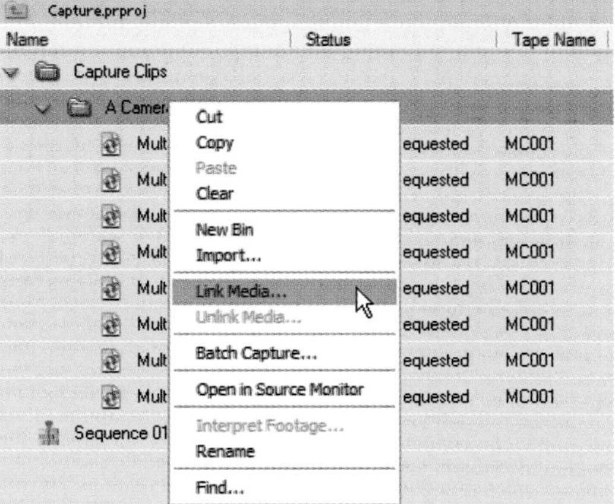

Figure 1.20 With a bin full of offline files, you can right-click on bin and choose Link Media from the context menu to relink every file in descending order. If you choose Batch Capture, Premiere will execute a batch capture of all the offline clips in the bin.

This reinforces the importance of using a consistent naming convention for your tapes and files: Doing so makes relinking and recapturing quite easy, which in turn makes your project more mobile and more flexible. If you want to give your project to someone else, send your tapes with the project file (which compresses down to a very small size). When the project is opened, all of the files will show up offline. All your friend needs to do is run Batch Capture and insert the proper tapes when instructed.

If you moved a file and Premiere Pro cannot find it, select the offline file and choose Clip>Link Audio and Video (assuming you need both media types). Whatever you link to then associates itself with the file in your project.

Exporting and Importing Batch Lists

To make sure the logged files from your tapes exist in a portable format, you have the ability to create and export batch lists or import existing batch lists. To export a text batch list, select the folder, clip, or clips that you want to make the batch list from and then choose Project>Export Batch List. Premiere Pro creates a comma-delimited text document that honors the data associated with the clips. (See Figure 1.21.)

	A	B	C	D	E	F	G	H
1	MC001	00;00;04;20	00;00;07;06	MultiCam_A	Not fluid stumble on words.	Green Screen Master shot		
2	MC001	00;00;16;13	00;00;46;09	MultiCam_A 01	Good take won't use	Green Screen Master shot	1	1
3	MC001	00;00;48;01	00;01;08;10	MultiCam_A 02	Better shot should be the one	Green Screen Master shot	1	2
4	MC001	00;01;31;02	00;01;57;04	MultiCam_A 03	Best!	Green Screen Master shot	1	3
5	MC001	00;02;07;13	00;02;33;07	MultiCam_A 04	Bad lighting	Green Screen Master shot	1	4
6	MC001	00;02;29;26	00;03;06;22	MultiCam_A 05	Good shot audio level too low	Green Screen Master shot	1	5
7	MC001	00;03;00;27	00;03;37;28	MultiCam_A 06	Good Shot cuts early	Green Screen Master shot	1	6
8	MC001	00;03;33;00	00;03;55;20	MultiCam_A 07	Unusable	Green Screen Master shot	1	7

Figure 1.21 In this batch list file, you can see how each of the fields correlate with fields from Premiere Pro: A is Tape Name, B is In Point, C is Out Point, D is Clip Name, E is Log Comment, F is Description, G is Scene, and H is Take.

Importing a batch list is pretty cool. You choose Project>Import Batch List, target the batch list that you want, then click OK. Premiere Pro creates a new folder in your project that has the same name as the batch list. Inside that folder are offline clip instances of all the items in the batch list. A text file that becomes physical clip instances—Premiere Pro has definitely entered the new millennium.

Manual Captures, No Device Control

If you have a camera connected that does not support device control or if you are using an RCA to DV converter box (called a bridge), which takes an analog signal and converts it to a DV stream of data on a FireWire cable, then you should turn off DV Device Control. In the Capture window's Settings tab, choose None from the Device drop-down list. You will still be using the DV Capture Recorder because you do have a signal into your FireWire port, but you will not have device control for that signal. (See Figure 1.22.)

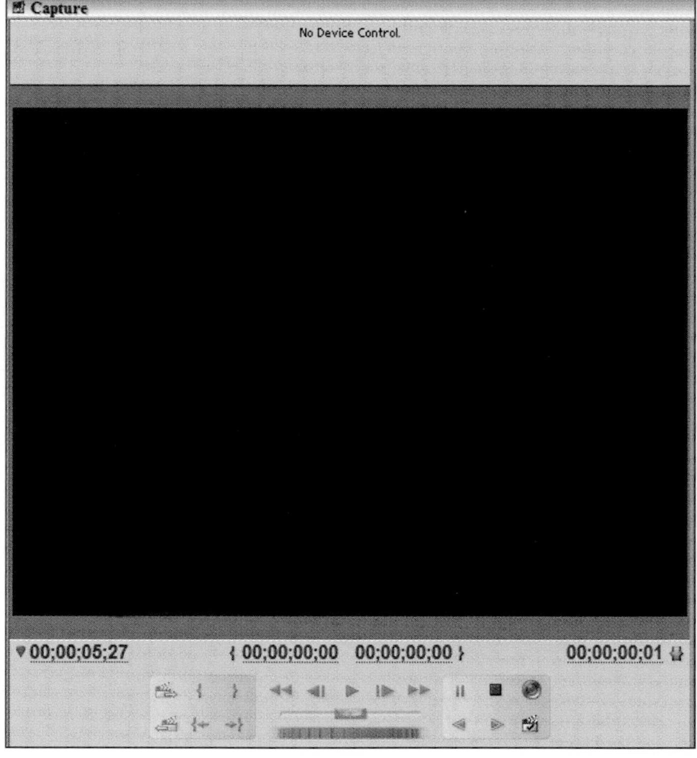

Figure 1.22 With no device control available, you are unable to access any of the transport controls.

If you have a VCR wired through a DV converter, for example, you just press the VCR's Play, Pause, Fast Forward, and Rewind buttons to find the segment that you want to capture. Press G on your keyboard (or click Record in the Capture window) to begin capturing, and then press G or Esc to stop (or click the Stop button). In the Capture window's Clip Data area, you can enter a tape name and filename, as well as the other meta details that you want associated with the captured file. After you click OK to confirm the data in these fields, Premiere adds the newly captured clip to your project.

Clips captured via FireWire using a converter box have a timecode value starting at 00;00;00;00 for frame 1. Because the FireWire port does not detect any timecode information on the cable, it starts timecode from zero.

If you have captured clips without device control and thus without timecode, think carefully before deleting the media and making those files offline. Because there is no absolute method of insuring that you can recapture these files with exactly the same In and Out points, your edit will change if you have to re-capture your media.

Background Capture

A new feature for Premiere Pro 1.5 is the capability to capture in the background. You begin capturing, then minimize Premiere. The program will continue capturing while you are doing other things on your computer. To see a video tutorial on this feature, watch the "Background Capture" in the Fundamentals section of the DVD.

Things to Remember

Striping and labeling your tapes is fundamentally the most important part of the capture process. It ensures that your media can be found with relative ease if any problems arise. Additionally, you can back up a text batch list of all the clips in your project. This list can be used as a reference or it can be imported into another separate project.

Traditional issues relating to capture usually entail problems with your tapes, such as discontinuous timecode or mislabeling. If you have good timecode and proper naming conventions, then all you need to observe is your camera habits and the temperament of DV device issues on your system. The lessons from this chapter provide the groundwork of where to go and what to do to capture and log properly into Premiere Pro.

The next chapter will help you work more efficiently with the clips once they are captured, introducing the display views and functionality of the Project window.

CHAPTER

2

Using the Project Window

The Project window is pretty much the center of the universe for Premiere Pro. Every element that is used in your edited sequence first must be imported and opened in your project. All video clips, audio files, still images, and sequences have icons and instances that you can access in your Project window. (See Figure 2.1.) Although your project size can get pretty large (four to ten megs) depending on how much content you have imported and saved, it will zip into an incredibly small file, because the project file format is XML based. Over the course of this chapter, I will give you an overview of the Project window's functions, features, and behaviors.

Because so many of these functions relate to clip handling, it's important to understand how Premiere Pro manages clips. When you first import a file into your project, that file is referred to as a *master clip*. It is the master file from which all edited and used instances will come. If clip01 is edited into a sequence using only half of its duration, the edited instance of clip01 is referred to as a *subclip* or *child* of the master clip. The subclip, if opened separately, can access all the information of the master clip, while honoring its assigned In/Out points and duration. Deleting an edited subclip does not delete the master clip. Deleting a master clip from your project will delete all of the subclips, because the subclips point to the master clip to get their information. Because Premiere Pro supports offline files in the timeline, if you accidentally delete a master clip from your hard drive, all project clip instances will remain intact with the media appearing offline.

You'll dig much deeper into working with clips later in the chapter. For now, though, start with importing and opening your media.

A cousin of the HTML format, XML is a self-describing file format that is used to transfer information from one place to the next. None of the XML file data is compressed, and it is not written in a binary language. Instead, XML files contain readable human language and data followed by descriptions of the data. XML files can be read and opened in word processing applications, making it easy to search for specific fields of information.

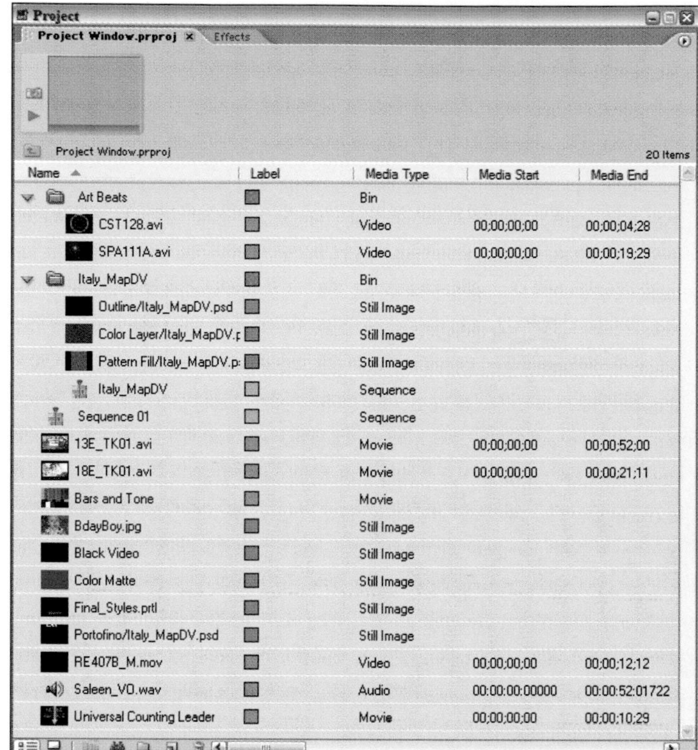

Figure 2.1 The Project window can display its contents in Icon view (left) or List view with icons turned on (right).

Importing Files

If you wanted to open and look at a clip in previous versions of Premiere, you would select File>Open and then target the video clip. The video clip would open in your Source Monitor, but would not be added to your project until you either dragged it into the Project window or dropped it in the edit of your timeline. With Premiere Pro, the only things you can *open* are other projects. You can, however, *import* files into the Project window to examine them before adding them to the timeline. To add or open any media files, you must import them. You can access the Import dialog (see Figure 2.2) by:

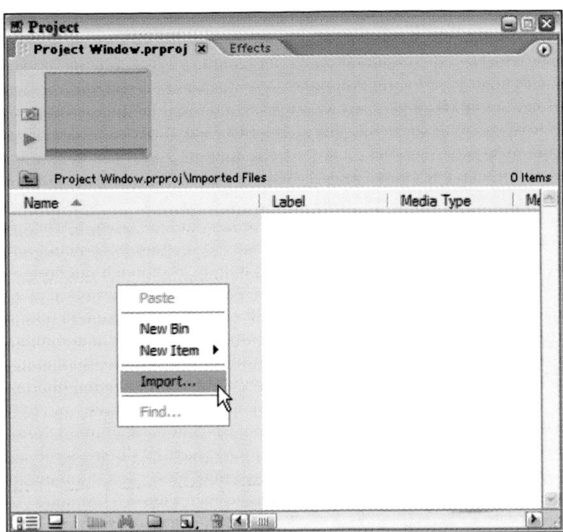

Figure 2.2 You can access the Import dialog in multiple ways. You can right-click in empty space of the Project window, then choose Import from the context menu, for example, or you can double-click in the empty space of the Project window to immediately open the Import dialog.

- Choosing File>Import
- Double-clicking in blank space of the Project window
- Right-clicking in the blank space of the Project window and selecting Import
- Pressing Ctrl+I

Then simply click and select the file you wish to import. You see there are still four ways to do one thing—Premiere hasn't really changed that much. To import multiple items, select them using the Shift or Ctrl modifier keys when targeting the files (see Figure 2.3). Each media type has some importing specifics, as well.

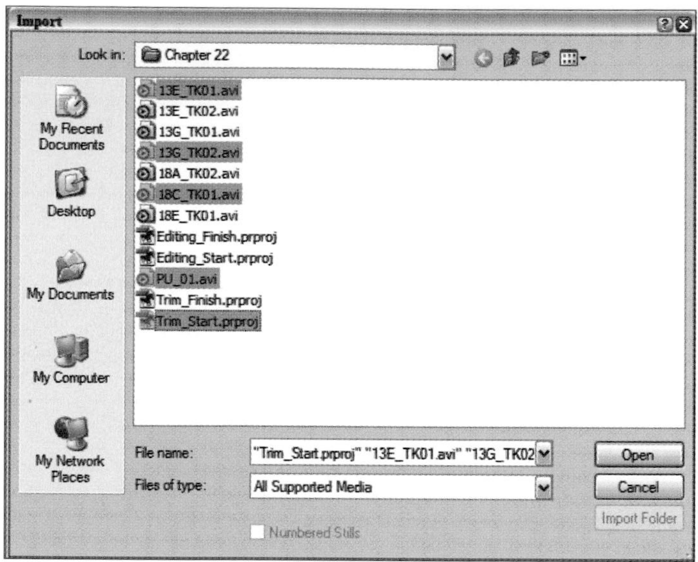

Figure 2.3 By holding down the Ctrl key, you can click and target the files you want to import. Here, multiple media files and a project file are selected for importing.

Video

When you import a video file, it will not conform to your project settings upon importing. Say that you have project settings of 320×240 with Video for Windows as your editing mode. If you import a DV clip, it will remain at 720×480 rather than be scaled down to 320×240. When you edit or add a new clip to a sequence, you choose whether of not you want it auto-scaled to conform to the project size. This means all of your imported elements preserve their original format and size when importing. To resize the file to your project's settings, choose Project>Project Settings>General then click the Scale Clips to Project Dimensions When Adding to Sequence check box in the Project Settings dialog box (see Figure 2.4). Remember, however, this setting affects resizing only when you add that file into a sequence.

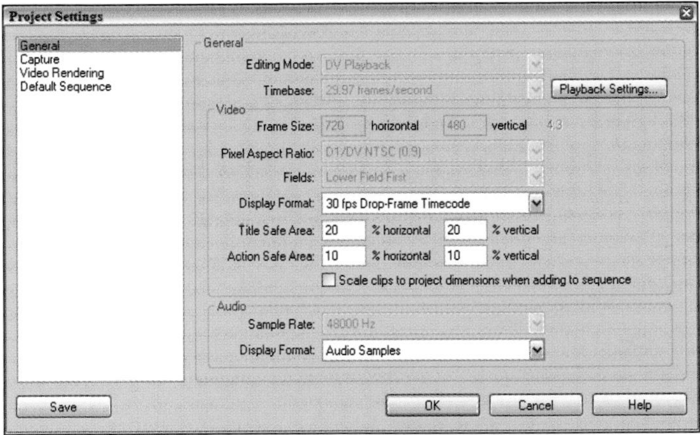

Figure 2.4 In the General area of the Project Settings dialog you can choose whether to scale clips to the project dimensions when adding them to a sequence. The media files import at their full size and are scaled only when they are added to a sequence.

Audio

Importing audio is slightly different. To reduce access time and increase the details to be extracted from your audio files, Premiere Pro converts your audio when it is imported into your project; this process is called *conforming*. (See Figure 2.5.)

Figure 2.5 In the bottom-right corner of the application window, a small conforming progress bar displays the name of the file being conformed and the file's progress.

You can import all sorts of audio files—WAVs, MP3s, AIFFs, and so on—but the most important setting to remember is your project's sample rate. If you import an audio file that is less than or greater than your project's sample rate, the conformed audio file will be up-sampled or down-sampled so that its sample rate matches that of your project.

Your audio project settings are commonly expressed as 16-bit 48kHz. The bit value (*bit depth*) reflects the resolution of your audio file. The more bits, the clearer the detail in the audio file. Premiere Pro supports up to 32 bits. The kHz value is your *sample rate*, also known as your Hertz rate (1kHz equals 1000 Hertz). The sample rate reflects the number of samples in your audio file. For example, 48kHz means your audio file has 48000 audio samples per second. Premiere Pro supports up to 96kHz or 96000 samples per second.

The higher the bit depth, the more dynamic the range of the audio file is. A *fixed-bit* format has a ceiling, or limit, to its range. A *floating-bit* format is a way of expanding the bit depth to provide a much more dynamic range for applying effects. The bit depth is called floating, because once the effect is applied at the floating bit depth, the file is reduced back to the preset bit depth for playback. Although 24 bits is the ceiling for audio files in Premiere Pro, all of your conformed audio files will be conformed at a floating 32-bit depth. The benefit is that effects and clip adjustments are assigned on the 32-bit floating file, which results in much more accurate and higher quality adjustments.

Conforming

A lot of high-end audio editing and video editing applications adjust their imported media, conforming it to a format that accurately matches their settings and can be accessed easily. Although Premiere Pro can extract plenty of information from a standard WAV, MP3, or AIFF audio file, it created a standard audio file format in which it optimized access time, waveform displaying, playback, and effect application.

If you set your project's audio sample rate to 48kHz, all of your audio will be conformed to 48kHz. Additionally, conformed audio files alter the bit depth to a floating bit rate of 32. When Premiere Pro conforms your audio, it creates two unique files that associate themselves with the original audio file in your project. One of the files has a .cfa extension, the other a .pek extension. These two files are created in whatever scratch disk path you chose for your conformed audio files and they are specific to the project that you have open (see Figure 2.6).

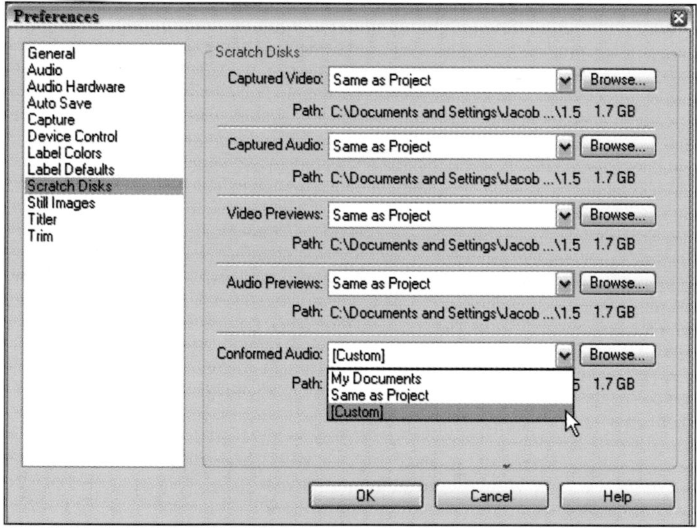

Figure 2.6 In the Scratch Disks Preferences dialog, you can assign the location your conformed audio file will populate. Choosing Same as Project ensures that the conformed audio files will be saved in their own subfolder of the folder in which you save your project.

Consider a typical conforming process: You start with a project with a sample rate of 48kHz, and you import a DV clip that has an audio setting of 16 bits, 32kHz. As Premiere Pro adds the clip to your project, the progress bar in the bottom-right corner of the application tells you the audio is being conformed. In the conformed audio folder associated with your project, Premiere creates two new files. The CFA file is the conformed version of the audio from the DV file, and a PEK file (Peak file) is associated with it (see Figure 2.7). When you play or reference this imported DV clip in your project, the audio that plays is not the original audio from the clip, it is the conformed audio file.

Peak files contain visual waveform information for their associated CFA files. Because the PEK file stores the waveform information, anytime you display or zoom into the waveform of an audio file, the results are almost instantaneous. If a PEK file is deleted, it will be created again the next time the waveform display is called upon for a selected audio file. It will take a moment to build the PEK, but once it's created, the visual feedback will be almost instantaneous.

Why? Conforming allows more efficient audio processing because real-time conversion is not needed. By conforming the file, the audio now exists in a format that Premiere Pro can access, display, and adjust much more quickly. Once you start to make tweaks and adjustments, you are referencing the conformed file that has the audio converted to match your project settings.

A few notes about conforming: When you import a large file it will take a while to conform, but once your audio is conformed you will not be prompted to do it again. Conformed audio files are *project sensitive*, so if you have the same clip in three separate projects, you will have three conformed files—one for each project. This is why one project with multiple folders to reflect different edits is a great way to work. Because Premiere Pro supports multiple timelines, you should structure your project accordingly to minimize disk usage.

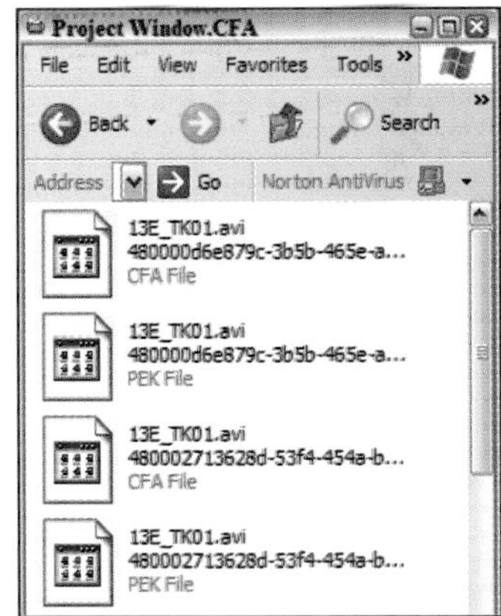

Figure 2.7 Within the conformed audio folder for my active project (called Project Window), the Project Window.CFA folder holds all the CFA and PEK files for the audio in this project. If I were to delete this folder, the project would automatically reconform the audio and create a new conformed audio folder.

Although conforming will pause if you do certain actions, you can safely work with an audio file in Premiere Pro 1.5 before its conforming is complete. When testing pre-release versions of Premiere Pro, I had a three-hour project that I had to reconform with every new test release of the program. It took about ten minutes to conform each time. That may sound like a lot of time, but the benefit in quality and speed is worth the wait. Just think of it as ten minutes you can spend with the life you have been neglecting.

Stills

A major new benefit with importing video and still files in Premiere Pro is that their original frame size and dimensions are respected when you import them. A still image that is 2000 × 1000 imports at that size, not scaled down to 720 × 480 upon arrival. In fact, the still's original size can be preserved when you edit with it in the timeline. This is a *huge* improvement, because it means that there is no quality degradation of your image when editing with it in Premiere Pro—no compromises or quality loss when you begin to zoom in and scale your still image. (See Figure 2.8.)

Figure 2.8 In the Source Monitor, the Still Rome01 is open, and you can view its full frame. When this file is added to the timeline and auto-scaling is turned off, you can see only a small portion of the image in the video frame. In the Program Monitor, the scale is set to 25%, and you can see the full size of the still image represented by the thin gray lined square in the Program Monitor.

A frame of video has 72 dots per inch, but a still image can have many, many more. When you are creating stills for use in Premiere Pro, I recommend modifying them to have a 72dpi. Make their frame size as big as you want, but reduce the dpi when you can. This speeds up the process in which Premiere Pro samples your image. Anytime you have a filter or effect on your still image, Premiere Pro looks at the entire image (sampling) then does the math and processing of the effect. A higher dpi setting creates more work for the sampling and processing. Having a large frame size with 72dpi will yield a faster response from the application.

Photoshop Documents

Premiere has always been able to import Photoshop documents (PSD files), but Premiere Pro drastically improved this function. Because you can have multiple sequences in your project, you now have the option to import a layered Photoshop file as a unique sequence with all its layers stacked one on top of the other, respecting the hierarchy of the original document. (See Figure 2.9.) This is a powerful feature, because it makes it quite easy to add motion to what was originally a static document.

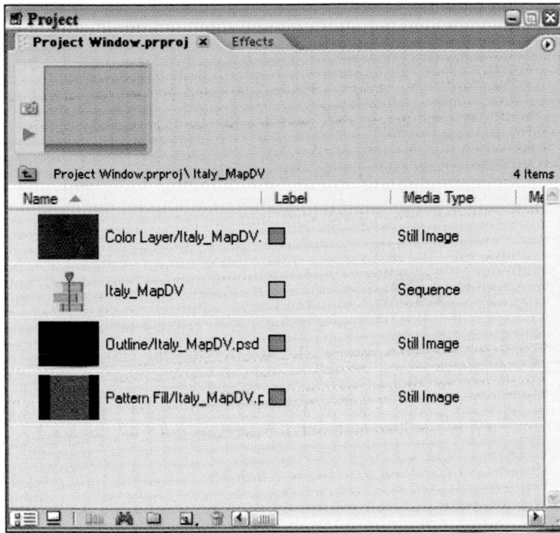

Figure 2.9 Once a bin is created with the same name as the imported PSD, in this case "Italy_MapDV," Premiere Pro creates a unique still for each layer of the Photoshop file. Because this PSD was imported as a sequence, Premiere Pro also creates a sequence that is named for the PSD and holds all the layers on separate tracks.

When the program imports layered PSDs, every layer of the Photoshop file can be imported as a separate still image, and all the stills are stacked directly on top of each other in separate video tracks to provide an accurate reflection of the original layered PSD. When you import a PSD with layers you get three choices:

- **Import as a single still image with all the layers merged.** This gives you a single still image that has the same name as the Photoshop file. (See Figure 2.10.)

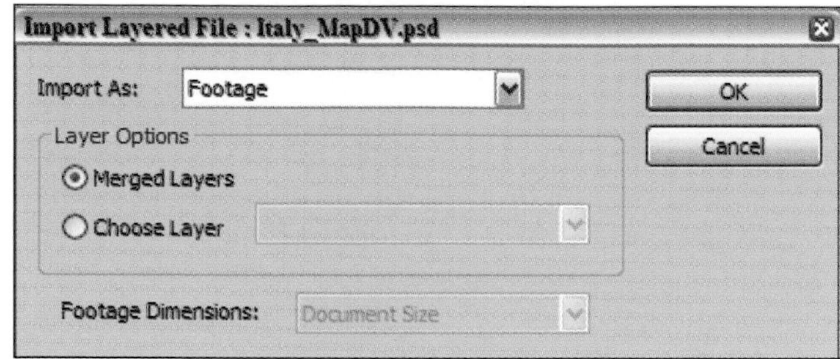

Figure 2.10 When you import a layered Photoshop file as a single merged file, Premiere Pro creates a single clip to represent the composite of all the layers. This appears as an option when you select to Import as Footage.

- **Import just one of the layers as a still image.** This imports the selected layer as a single still image with the name of the layer/name of the PSD as its filename. For example, with the PSD file named Italy_MapDV and a chosen layer named Portofino, the imported layer name would be Portofino/Italy_MapDV.psd. (See Figure 2.11.)

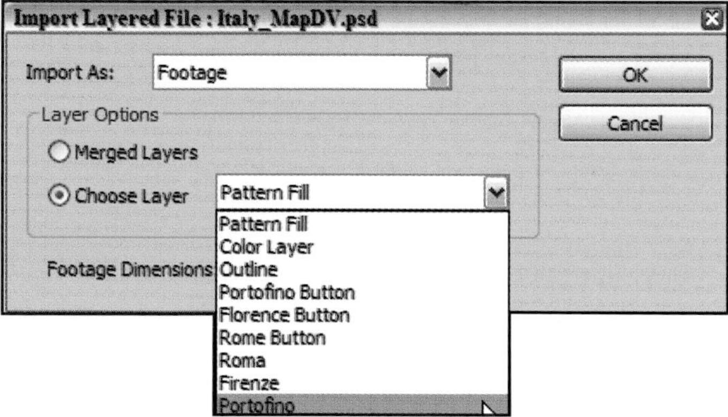

Figure 2.11 When you select Choose Layer, Premiere Pro imports only the chosen layer and adds it to your project file. Again, the option to import a single layer is only available when you choose to import the PSD as Footage.

- **Import as a sequence with all layers.** This option does a lot more: It creates a new folder in your project that is named with the exact name of the PSD file. In that folder are still images and a sequence. Each still represents a unique layer of the file, named in the form layer name/filename. Finally, the created sequence is named after the imported PSD. If you open it, it will contain all of the layers stacked on unique tracks, thus representing the original file. (See Figure 2.12.)

Figure 2.12 Importing a layered PSD as a sequence yields no additional options, because all layers will be imported to accurately represent the original PSD.

Because of the proper importation of Photoshop files, it is a breeze to animate and add motion to even the most simple logo. The only trick to remember when you are creating your Photoshop file is to use different layers for different image elements.

Old Projects

Premiere Pro may have advanced into its next incarnation, but it still supports the opening of legacy projects (from former versions Mac and PC). All you need to do is select your .ppj files from the Import dialog. When you import an old project, Premiere Pro creates a new bin in your current project. The bin is named for the project and inside of that bin is all the media associated with that project plus a new sequence that reflects the edited timeline of the old project. Virtual clips from legacy projects are created as unique sequences inside of this folder, and your older title files can be opened and saved anew in the new Adobe Title Designer. There are two methods of opening old projects.

If you double-click on the project file icon for a project created with a former version of Premiere, Premiere Pro will prompt you with a dialog box that tells you the project is from a former version and needs to be updated to

Premiere Pro project files have the extension .prppj; project files from former PC versions of Premiere have the extension .ppj.

Premiere Pro's file format (see Figure 2.13). To save a new version of the file and not overwrite the original, the dialog gives you the option to rename the updated project file. Once you have properly named the file, the project will open inside of Premiere Pro.

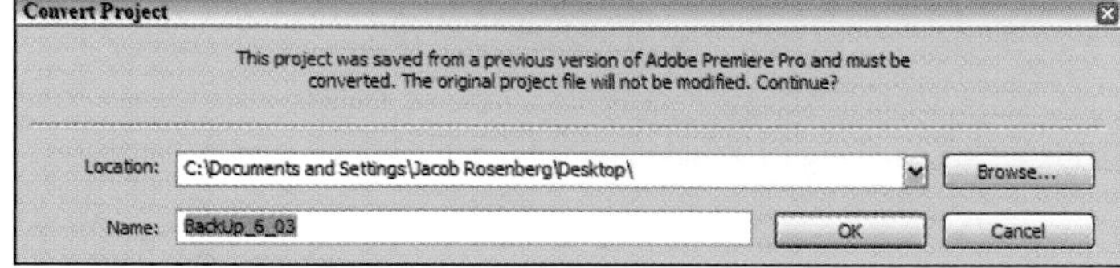

Figure 2.13 When opening an older project, you can automatically rename the file so that the Premiere Pro version does not overwrite the original.

The second method of opening a former Premiere project is by importing it into an open Premiere Pro project. When you import a legacy Premiere project into an open project, Premiere Pro creates a new bin using the name of the imported project file. Inside of the bin will be the entire bin structure of the legacy project with a sequence that reflects the edited timeline of the project. (See Figure 2.14.)

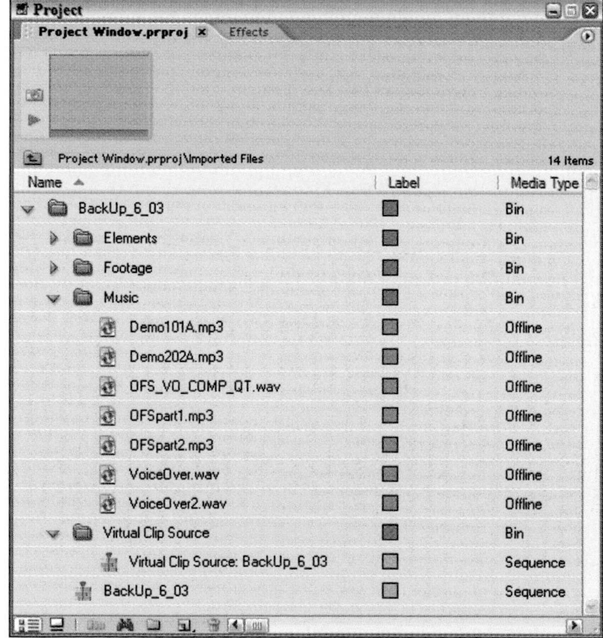

Figure 2.14 When I imported an old Premiere 6.5 project into Premiere Pro 1.5, Premiere Pro created a new bin named for the original project file. Inside that bin is the exact contents of the old project with a sequence file that reflects the timeline of the old project. Here you can see the BackUp_6_03 sequence at the bottom of the window matches the name of the imported project. Also notice that because my old project had a virtual clip instance, a separate sequence was created to reflect that.

Project Views

With your project full of media, you have a few choices in how to view the contents of your project. Former versions of Premiere offered three views: List, Icon, and Thumbnail. For Premiere Pro, List and Thumbnail were unified into the new List view and Icon was added storyboard view elements. The two icons in the lower left corner of the Project window toggle between List view (the left icon) and Icon view (the right icon).

List View

List view not only accommodates smaller icon sizes, it uses a number of columns from which you can organize and order your project. In List view, the project name is always on the left. To the right of the name column are the columns you can reorganize and customize. When displaying items and bins in List view, Premiere Pro follows the standard Windows Folder view functionality. Twirling down a bin to open it reveals its contents within the window, and double-clicking on a bin causes the bin's contents to fill the entire Project window view. To navigate back up one level, you must click on the Up Folder button. (See Figure 2.15.)

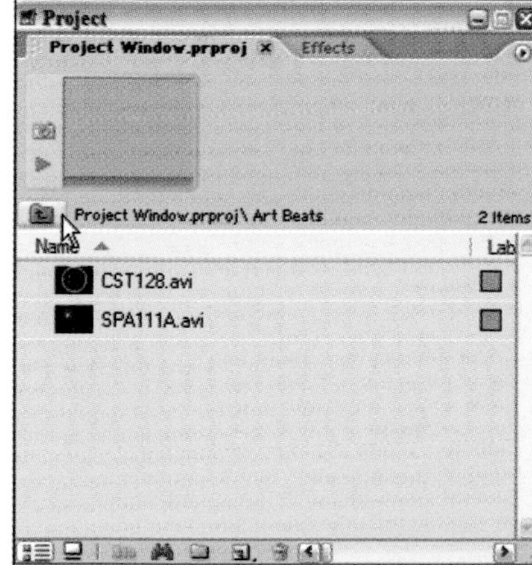

Figure 2.15 When you double-click on a bin, it assumes the full display of the Project window. When you are inside of a bin and want to go up one level of bins or back out to the root project bin view, click the Up Folder button. Here you can see that the Art Beats bin is currently active in the Project window. Pressing the Up Folder button you would be at the root level of the project and could see the other items in the project.

List View Columns

You can customize and sort the information columns in List view and use them for a number of different tasks. If you don't care for the default listing of columns, change their order by clicking and dragging on the column headings to move them around. You can also increase or decrease their size to a set amount by dragging from either of a heading's edges. (See Figure 2.16.)

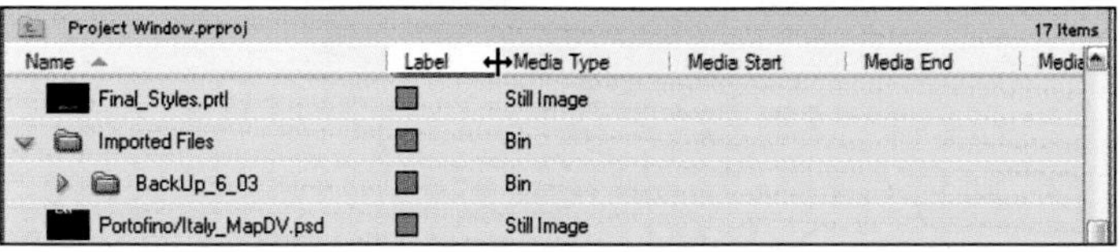

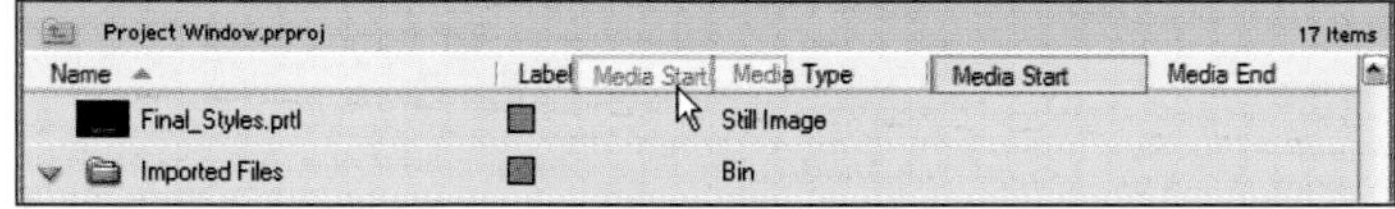

Figure 2.16 You can easily resize the width of a column (top) or drag and drop a column to change its horizontal position (bottom).

Certain columns can yield information that can be adjusted. By using the hot text interface, you can change the In point of clip within the Project window by scrubbing for the listed in the Video In Point column. You can do the same with the Video Out Point and Video Duration columns. (See Figure 2.17.)

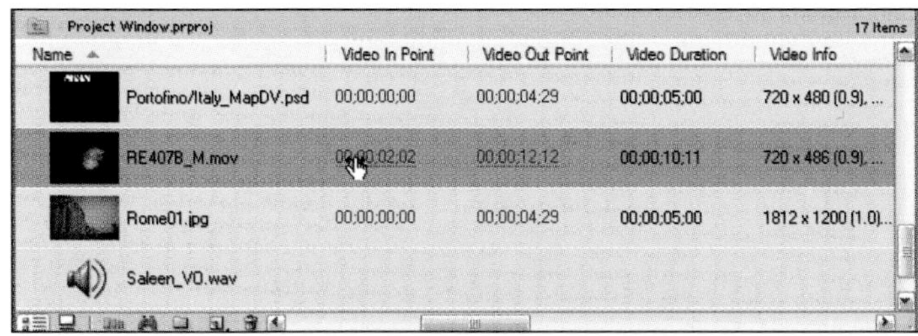

Figure 2.17 You can adjust any of the blue hot text fields by clicking and scrubbing on the numbers.

Custom Columns

You can create custom columns and turn on or off specific columns by choosing Edit Columns from the wing menu. In the Edit Columns dialog, choose the check boxes for the columns you want listed. You can change the order by selecting an item and moving it up or down within the dialog's list. (See Figure 2.18.)

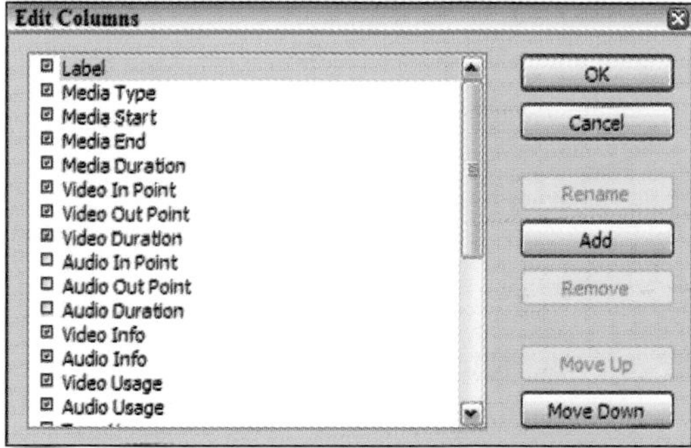

Figure 2.18 Accessed from the Project window wing menu, the Edit Columns dialog box enables you to adjust the order and display of any column in the Project window.

Most importantly, in this dialog you can create your own custom columns. Clicking the Add button creates a new column. You can create two types of columns:

- **Text columns.** These have fields to which text can be written. If you need additional space to make notes for your media in your Project window, you can create a custom column called My Notes. In that column, you will be able to click and write any text information. You can sort the information by highlighting (clicking on) the My Notes column heading and then clicking again to sort based on an ascending or descending order. This is helpful if you have an alternative order in which you want your files to be edited. I will make a custom column and then enter number values, such as 01, 05, 07, and a comment after. If I want to edit based on this order, I just select the column and chose my sort order.

- **Boolean columns.** These are check box columns. To create a custom column in which you can easily identify an attribute with a check, this is what you use. When I edit photo montages, I usually want to know whether the picture is a portrait (vertical orientation) or landscape (horizontal orientation). I create a new Boolean column and name it Portrait, then click in the check box for every image that is a portrait. If I want to list all my portraits together, I click on the Portrait column name to sort based on that criteria, either ascending or descending.

In addition to a flexible column structure, List view has multiple display modes.

List Display Modes

In List view you can decide how you want to view listed items by clicking on the wing menu. (See Figure 2.19.) Choose View>List or View>Icon to toggle the view from List to Icon, and choose the Thumbnails submenu to change the size of the icons in the Thumbnail Preview area or turn it off entirely. If you do not want to see an icon for your video clip, but instead want to see a thumbnail displaying the poster frame, you can uncheck the Off item and then select the size that you want the thumbnails to be. The bigger the size, the fewer items you will see within your viewing area of the Project window. (See Figure 2.20.) I always use the small size and toggle thumbnails on or off. The thumbnails settings are global, so there is no way to turn off thumbnails for one folder in your project leave them on for another.

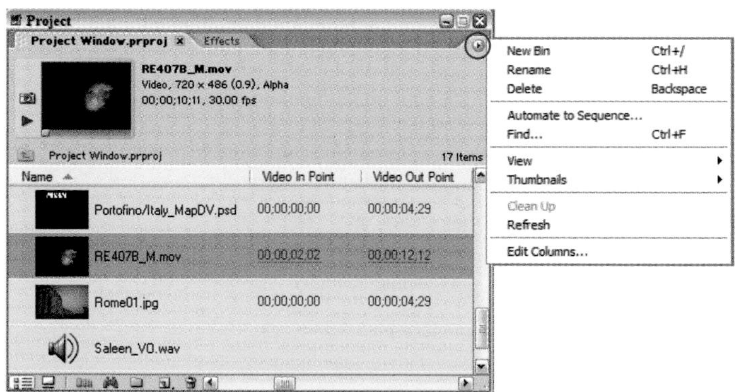

Figure 2.19 The Project window wing menu offers a bunch of quick access features. By having items in this menu, they can be assigned as unique keyboard shortcut items.

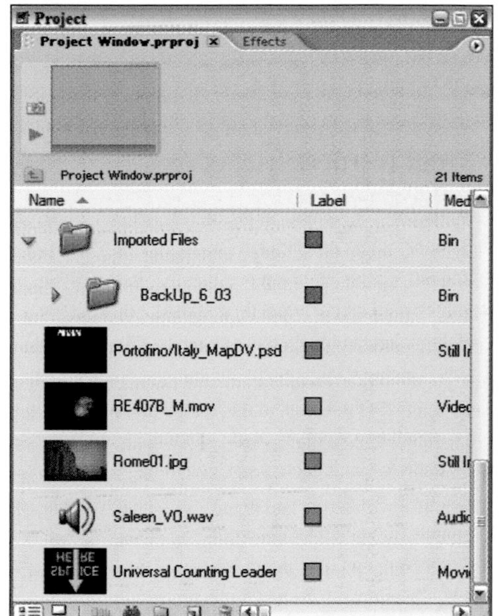

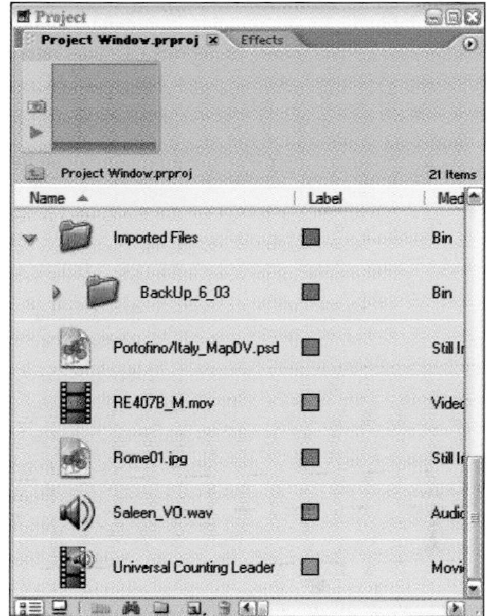

Figure 2.20 The image on the left shows thumbnails on for Medium List view. The image on the right shows thumbnails off; Premiere instead displays a default icon for the different media types.

Icon View

I am a bit critical of Icon view, because I don't think it is a very intuitive or completely developed view mode. The Storyboard window in older versions of Premiere, which does not exist in Premiere Pro, was a pretty straightforward window with a sequential grid that all of the items would snap to. The grid was only as wide as your window size, and if you made the window larger, the grid would fill the space and still keep the sequential order of the items in the window. The Icon view in Premiere Pro follows a similar grid format, but it does not have a defined size. Additionally, if you resize your window or move items, they do not snap to a set sequential order.

To see an overview of exactly how to organize and arrange your Project window in Icon view, watch the video tutorial, "Arranging Icons in the Project Window," in the Fundamentals section on the accompanying DVD.

I find the Icon view helpful when working with still images, because you can create an order of items that is not as easy to create in List view. Because List view presents your items based on an ascending or descending order, you can't just drag your items into a different order within List view.

With Icon view, you can drag them anywhere you want and the respected order will be left to right, top to bottom. Icon view is best used in conjunction with the Automate to Timeline function (bottom button bar) that allows you to automatically edit a sequence of clips using their listed or sorted order in a Project window.

Viewing and Adjusting

Once you have imported files into your project, you can extract a lot of information from them and make a number of adjustments to the files before you edit with them. You know the List view contains a ton of columns that reveal all the data associated with each file. Now I want to show you some additional functions and features that make working with the files a bit easier.

Thumbnail Preview Area

In the top left corner of the Project window, the Thumbnail Preview area provides a preview of and some information about the selected item in your Project window (see Figure 2.21). If you click once on an audio, video, or sequence file, you will get the associated thumbnail and a little transport control to play that file. If you are editing DV files in DV mode, they will play on your FireWire device as well as in the Thumbnail Preview area. I love the fact that you can playback a sequence in this area without having to open it in the Timeline window.

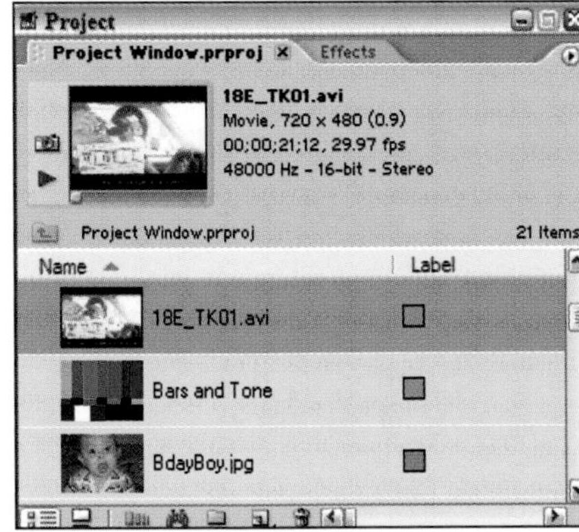

Figure 2.21 With any clip selected in the Project window, the Thumbnail Preview area (top left corner) displays a preview with some additional details about the file. Not only can you turn off this area, you can also playback and assign poster frames for any of the select media.

Properties

You can view properties for the selected file in two different places. Although you will get a brief bit of information in the Thumbnail Preview area, if you right-click on a file in the Project window and choose Properties, you will get a lot more. In addition, you can access this function by File>Get Properties for>File/Selection.

Viewing your properties is the way to verify certain settings and parameters associated with your file (see Figure 2.22). If you are unclear which compressor is used with an imported video clip, for example, the compressor will be revealed when you get properties for the clip.

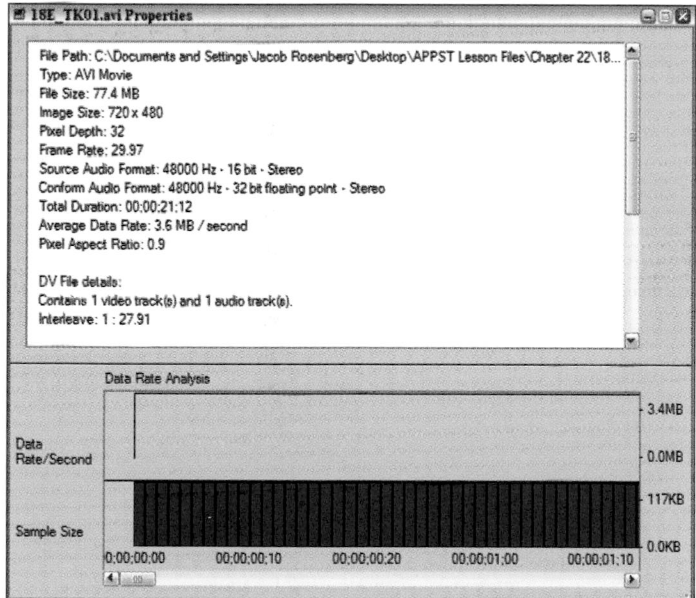

Figure 2.22 The Properties dialog not only gives you details of the selected file's audio, video, and timecode attributes, but also a graphic analysis of the data rate.

Project Settings

To access your Project Settings once your project is open, go to Project>Project Settings then choose the area you want to adjust or change. Because the project has already been created and is open, certain parameters will be locked.

Clip Settings

You can adjust and access a few settings for certain selected media in your Project window. For example, if you want to switch the incorrect field order of a video clip, you can access the field order from the Clip menu once you have your video clip selected.

Adjusting your clips within the Project window keeps you one step ahead of your edit. If you have a clip that you want to use in slow motion only, you don't have to always adjust its speed in the Timeline window, you can preset the speed to the master clip directly in the Project window (see Figure 2.23).

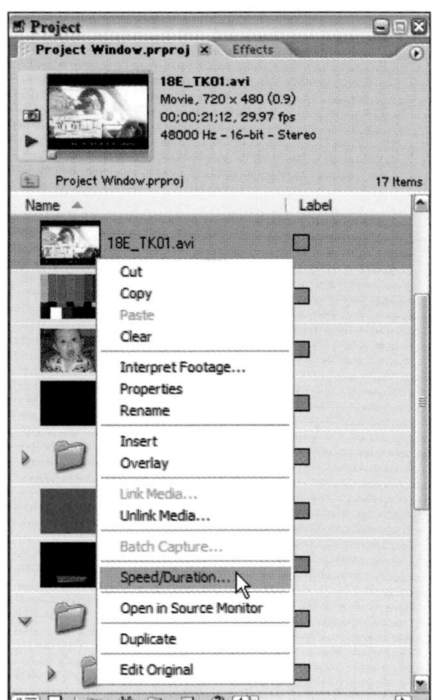

Figure 2.23 Right-clicking on any file in the Project window reveals a context menu of options for that file. For example, you can adjust the speed of a clip within the Project window before it is added to your sequence.

Video Clip Menu

With a video clip selected, the Clip menu reveals a handful of functions that you can apply to the clip (see Figure 2.24). Rename allows you to change the alias for the file in the Project window. It does not modify the linked file on disk, just the displayed file in the project. You can edit your clip directly to the Timeline window by using Insert and Overlay. Choose Clip>Video Options>Field Options. From the resulting Field Options dialog, you can change any of the field settings associated with your clip. The last Clip menu choice is to modify the speed or duration of the file.

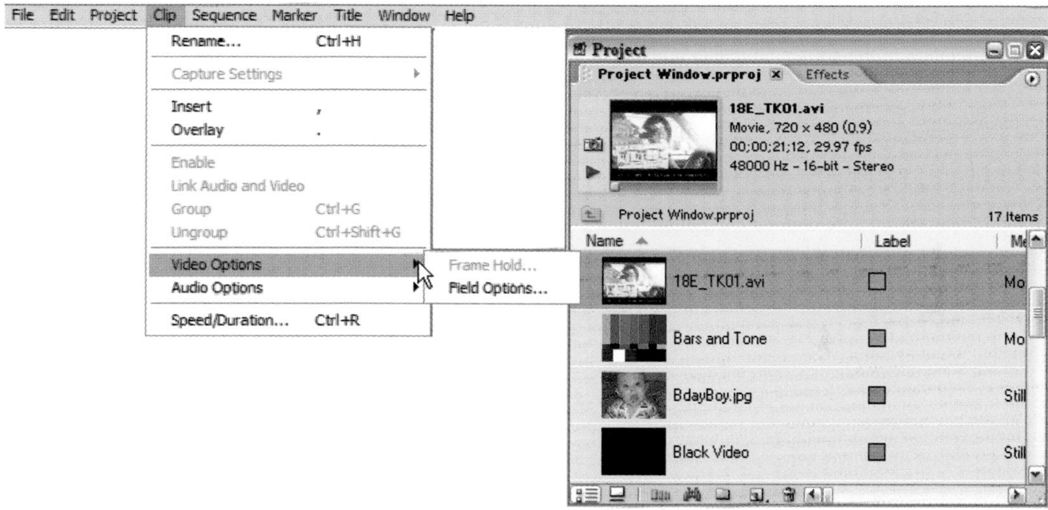

Figure 2.24 If a selected clip contains audio and video, you gain access to the Video Options and Audio Options submenus in the Clip menu.

If you modify a master clip in the Project window, it affects all edited instances from that point forward. If you previously edited five instances from one master clip then changed its speed to 50%, those five instances would not change to 50%.

Audio Clip Menu

With audio files selected, a number of the Clip menu items are the same, but two new ones—Clip>Audio Options>Audio Gain and Clip>Audio Options>Breakout to—are very special.

Audio Gain and Normalizing Your Audio When you Import an audio file, it has a set volume level associated with it. Once you edit the audio file into your timeline, its volume can be increased or decreased a number of ways. An incredibly powerful feature that is somewhat hidden,

Audio Gain allows you to perfect the audio level of your master clip so that you do not need to make constant adjustments of the edited subclips. Adjusting your Audio Gain setting allows you adjust your audio level based on an increase or decrease in decibels (dBs).

If you have an audio clip selected or a video clip with audio, go to Clip>Audio Options>Audio Gain. The Gain dialog allows you to either increase or decrease the dB of your selected clip. The Normalize button takes this one step further (see Figure 2.25).

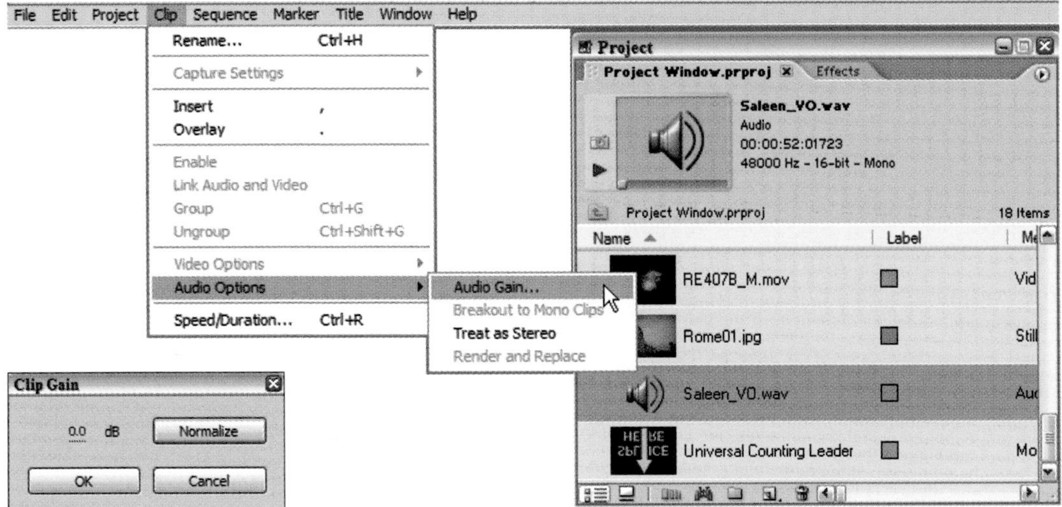

Figure 2.25 From the Clip menu (left), you can access the Clip Gain dialog (bottom left), which allows you to normalize your clip gain level.

Within the range of audio volume levels, there are some decibel ratings that don't register any sound at all (low) and others that register sounds too loud (high). If sound levels register too high you will usually get pops, crackles, or distortions. If your original recording has pops, crackles, and distortions, there is not too much you can do to remove those sounds as you cannot undo the audio that was recorded. If the volume for the audio file you import is too low or too high once it arrives in Premiere Pro, however, you can make a uniform adjustment to compensate for that.

Normalize is an intelligent, automated function that looks at your entire audio file, at the peaks and valleys (highs and lows), then recommends the gain setting that will give you the best volume adjustment value without exceeding the proper ceiling of 0dB during playback. Normalize gives you a positive or negative dB value that will bring your volume to a safe overall level where there is no distortion. Normalize saves a ton of your time tinkering to find the right level. Normalizing in the Project window on the master file ensures that all of the master clip's associated subclips will honor that level adjustment.

I recommend that when you import audio clips and audio/video clips you first normalize their levels to get them to the best dB setting. You can worry about specific instances where you want to make minor adjustments later.

Breakout To The second very special audio clip feature is the capability to break out each channel of a stereo or 5.1 surround file into its own separate file. A stereo file contains two channels, left and right. If you select a stereo file in your Project window then go to Clip>Audio Options>Breakout to Mono Clips, Premiere Pro creates two separate mono files (see Figure 2.26). One file has an L (left) at the end of the filename and the other an R (right). You can now use these files as single mono tracks in your sequences. Premiere Pro breaks 2.1 files into six separate mono tracks.

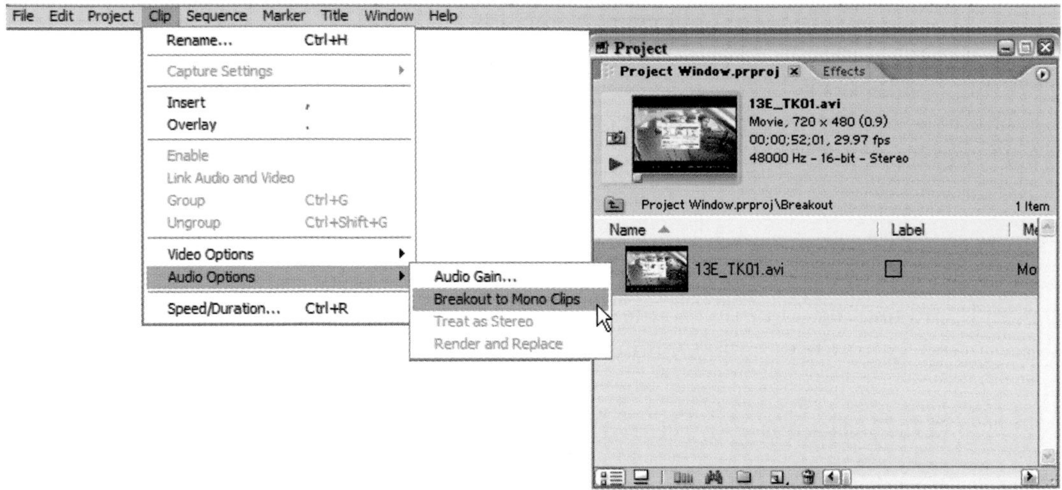

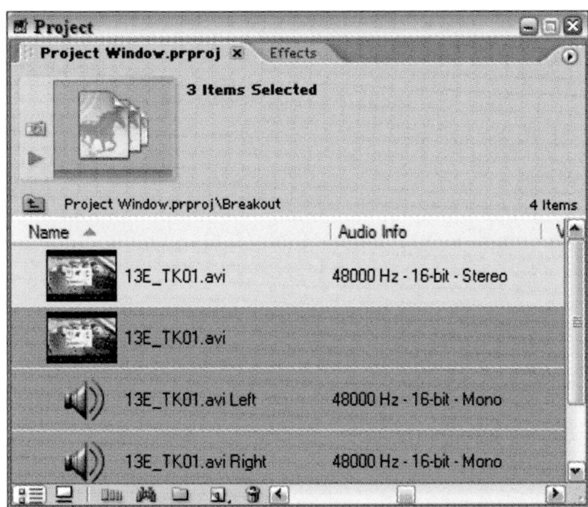

Figure 2.26 When you select Clip>Audio Options>Breakout to Mono Clips for a video clip with a stereo track (top), Premiere Pro duplicates the video clip as a video-only file with left and right mono audio clips that have the same timecode value as the master video clip (bottom).

Why is this so important? Consider a couple recording scenarios. Say you are recording a family dinner from the right end of the table. All of your sound is coming from the left side of your camera's stereo microphone. When you look at the waveform for the audio, you can see that the left channel is much louder and more robust than the right. Another example is recording an interview where one channel has the lavalier microphone and the other a directional microphone. In both cases, being able to break the channels out to separate tracks gives a substantial amount of value and control into the future work you will do with those files. While there are filters to fill both stereo channels with one of the channels, I want to emphasize the power of the Breakout To feature.

Just to make sure your single channel mono clips don't get too lonely, you can treat them as stereo, duplicating their channels and making a new stereo file. If you have a mono clip selected, go to Clip>Audio Options>Treat as Stereo.

Creating New Elements

The last territory I want to discuss is the bottom bar area of the Project window (see Figure 2.27). This is where you can perform a number of tasks and create numerous items for your project.

Figure 2.27 From the left, the icons in the bottom menu bar of the Project window are List View, Icon View, Automate to Timeline, Search, New Bin, New Item, and Trash.

From the left, the icons are:

- **List View and Icon View.** Click these icons toggle between the Project window's two views.
- **Automate to Timeline.** Click the third icon to automatically edit a selection of clips by having them placed back to back with the option of having transitions between them. This function is explored completely in Chapter 11, "Working with Still Images."
- **Search.** Click the binoculars to bring up a Search tool that allows you to search the Project window from any column based on a number of criteria: Column is which column you want to search in, Operator is the criterion, and Find What is the area where you type the characters you are looking to find. Case Sensitive ensures the search respects upper- and lowercase character values.

In the next chapter, you will move forward to playing media in the Monitor window, exploring the differences and similarities between the Source and Program Monitors.

CHAPTER

3

Playing and Watching Your Media

I like to think of the Project window as the container for all of your media. The Monitor window is where you can view that media in detail and decide which portions you want to work with. As you'll see in the next chapter, the Timeline window is your virtual videotape or canvas where you arrange and create your edit.

Within the Monitor window are two monitors: Source and Program (see Figure 3.1). In the Source Monitor, you open source material and pick the portions you want to incorporate into your sequence. In the Program Monitor, you open and view the sequences that you are editing. Although their buttons and transport controls are almost identical, the function of each window is quite different, as you'll see.

Figure 3.1 The Source Monitor is on the left of the Monitor window and the Program Monitor is on the right.

As you may remember from Appendix D, "Workspaces and Preferences," there is a third monitor: the Trim window. Because the Trim window is much easier to understand in the context of its own workflow, Chapter 19, "Advanced Timeline Editing Techniques," has a lesson that illustrates how you use the Trim window to visually trim precise cuts between edit points.

Figure 3.2 The Source Monitor features a drop-down menu and wing menu (right corner), as well as timecode fields, a time navigation area, transport controls, and editing group boxes.

The Source Monitor

In previous versions of Premiere, the Source Monitor was called the Clip window and it was not attached to the Program Monitor. You can still think of the Source Monitor as a clip window, because it is the only window where you can open and play individual clips. You use the Source Monitor to open and review media that you wish to edit and incorporate into your sequences. (See Figure 3.2.)

What You Can Open

In the Source Monitor you will be able to open and view:

- Video clips
- Audio clips
- Audio and Video clips
- Stills
- Sequences

Additionally, you can open synthetic media, such as:

- Color mattes
- Black video
- Offline files
- Bars and tone
- The Universal Counting Leader

When you drag media from your Project window into the Source Monitor window, the pointer changes to a hand, signifying that you can drop (open) the media in the window. Double-clicking on most files opens them, but sometimes you must Ctrl+double-click. For example, if you double-click on an offline file, it opens its parameters for you to edit. If you Ctrl+double-click on an offline file, it will load into the Source Monitor. The same is true for sequences: A standard double-click opens the sequence in the Timeline window, and a Ctrl+double-click opens the sequence in the Source Monitor.

Window Layout

As shown in Figure 3.2, the Source Monitor has a few distinct regions that display information and give you access to transport controls and features. Although the Source Monitor has a tab area, media does not open as separate tabs. Media opens and is listed within the Source Monitor tab. You use the other tabs in the tab area when the Effect Controls window or Reference Monitor is docked into the Source Monitor, as in the Effects or Color Correction Workspace.

To the right of the tab area is the wing menu (see Figure 3.3), which has physical links to some of the button options at the bottom of the window. These physical links can be assigned to unique keyboard shortcuts using the Keyboard Customization function.

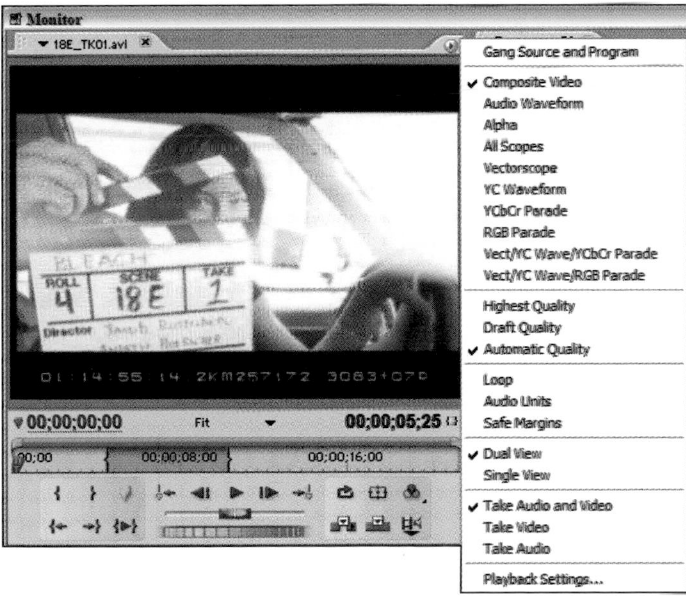

Figure 3.3 Like all windows, the Source Monitor has a wing menu that allows direct access to features that can be routed to customized keyboard shortcuts.

The center of the Source Monitor is the viewing area, where media plays back. You can load multiple items into the Source Monitor by dragging multiple selections or folders into its viewing area. Dragging a folder full of items loads all of the items into the Source Monitor. To open an individual item, select it from the drop-drown menu. You can close the open media from the window by selecting Close from the drop-down menu or by pressing Ctrl+Backspace. You can also close all the listed items by selecting Close All.

Below the viewing area, you have the timecode display, time ruler, viewing area bar, and the transport controls arranged in three separate groups, similar to the Capture window.

Timecode and the Time Navigation Controls

When you open media in the Source Monitor, the lower left text area reveals the timecode value of the current frame that is being played or scrubbed on in the monitor. The timecode value to the right is the total duration of the media in the window. Once you start modifying the In and Out points, the duration updates dynamically.

New for Premiere Pro, the *time ruler* is basically a visual counter for your open media that can scrubbed in and zoomed into and out from. (See Figure 3.4.) Time is delineated by tick marks that represent the Timebase specified in your Project Settings. Any markers, In points, and Out points assigned in your clip also are visually represented in the time ruler. Above the time ruler is the *viewing area bar*, which you stretch and drag to zoom into and navigate through portions of your open media. In the time ruler, the blue playback head that you click and drag around to scrub through your media is called the *Current Time Indicator (CTI)*. The CTI also exists in the timeline where it is referred to as the CTI or Edit Line.

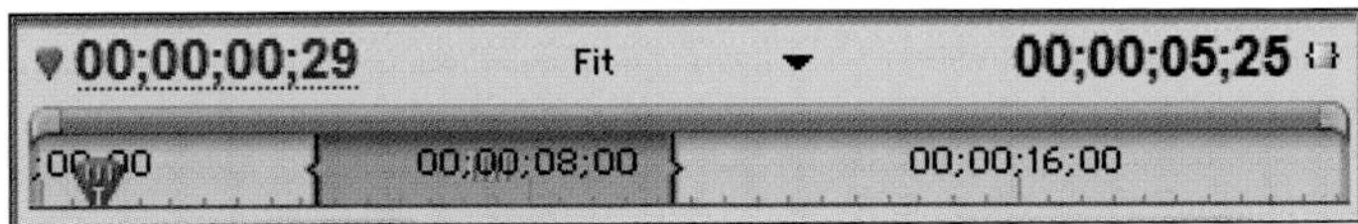

Figure 3.4 The blue timecode value reflects the current position of the CTI. The black timecode value reflects the duration of the In/Out instance visible in the time ruler. You can resize the gray viewing area bar to zoom in and out of the time ruler.

Scrubbing through a one-hour clip frame by frame would be difficult, for example, if there was not the capability to zoom into a specific area of the time ruler. By being able to zoom in (dragging inwards from the edges of bar), you can get down to whatever magnification you want. Once you are zoomed in, you can click and drag from the center of the bar to reveal different areas of the open clip. The viewing area bar does have an intelligent zoom: If the CTI is within view, the viewing area bar will zoom in and out around the CTI position.

To see a video tutorial on the time navigation area's behavior, watch the "Time Navigation" video tutorial in the Fundamentals section on the accompanying DVD.

Buttons and Transport Controls

Below the time ruler are your transport controls and various buttons associated with marking and navigating to In and Out points in the source media. These buttons and controls are broken up into three separate group boxes (see Figure 3.5). The left group assigns and navigates to In and Out points for your open media. The center group holds the transport controls for playing back your media. The right group contains buttons specific to the editing tasks of the Source Monitor window.

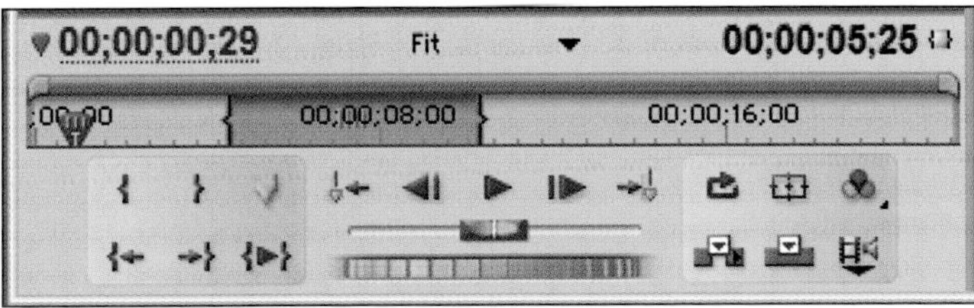

Figure 3.5 The Transport area of the Source Monitor contains three group boxes of controls. The left group manages In and Out points, the center group handles playing back your media, and the right group houses editing-related buttons.

TIP

If you hold down the Alt key, Play In to Out becomes the Play Edit button.

Although some buttons do not have keyboard shortcuts assigned to them, you can search the Edit>Keyboard Customization>Windows>Monitor and Trim Windows to see which keyboard shortcuts are available to be assigned.

Holding the Shift key when clicking Step Back steps back five frames at a time. Likewise, holding the Shift key when pressing Step Forward steps forward in five-frame increments.

In the left group are six buttons:

- **In Point** (shortcut key: I). Marks an In point at the current CTI position.
- **Out Point** (shortcut key: O). Marks an Out point at the current CTI position.
- **Set Unnumbered Marker** (shortcut key: * on the number pad). Assigns an unnumbered marker at the current CTI position.
- **Go to In** (shortcut key: Q). Automatically moves the CTI from its current position to the assigned In point.
- **Go to Out** (shortcut key: W). Automatically moves the CTI from its current position to the assigned Out point.
- **Play In to Out.** Automatically plays back your media from your assigned In point to your assigned Out point.
- **Play Edit.** Plays back from the current CTI position using the values you entered for Preroll and Postroll in your General Preferences dialog. For example, if the CTI was resting on 10 seconds and both Preroll and Postroll were set to 3, Play Edit would play from 7 seconds to 13 seconds only. This is great feature for quick previews, just remember to assign your preferred values for Preroll and Postroll in General Preferences.

The center group houses your primary transport controls, which are (from the left):

- **Go to Previous Marker.** Moves the CTI from its current position to the position of the nearest assigned marker prior to it.
- **Step Back** (shortcut key: Left Arrow). Moves the CTI back one frame at a time. You must click every time you want to step, holding down this button will not continuously step.
- **Play/Stop Toggle** (shortcut key: Spacebar). Plays or stops the media in the viewing area. This toggle has two states. When you are stopped, the Play icon displays. Click it to engage playback. When you are playing a clip, the Stop icon displays. When you press it, playback stops.

- **Step Forward** (shortcut key: Right Arrow). Moves the CTI one frame forward with each click. You cannot hold down this button to have the CTI continuously step.
- **Go to Next Marker.** Updates the CTI position to the next assigned marker nearest to the CTI's current position.
- **Shuttle slider.** Allows you to dynamically throw the Monitor into variable playback speeds. The farther from the center, left, or right the slider is, the faster playback will be. The closer to the center you drag, the slower playback will be. The shuttle is great for watching in slow motion as it will play beautifully without stuttering.
- **Jog disk.** Enables you to scrub through your media, either forwards or backwards, with greater detail. Jogging is like scrubbing through your clip in slow motion, you can control the scrubbing by dragging. While the shuttle controls variable playback speeds, the jog disk steps through your media at a constant frame-by-frame rate.

On the right, the third group has specific functions unique to the Source Monitor:

- **Loop.** Activates a state of playback. If you have Loop pressed, whenever you engage playback you will be in Loop mode, meaning when the CTI hits the end of the media or an Out point, it continues playing from the beginning or In point of the clip.
- **Safe Margins.** A display state for the Source Monitor. When you click Safe Margins, they will be visible in your Source Monitor (see Figure 3.6), adhering to the value you assigned for them in your General Project Settings. Safe Margins are best used when trying to make sure graphics, stills, and clips have action within the television safe area of the video frame. (See Appendix C, "Project Settings and Presets," for details.)

Figure 3.6 With Safe Margins turned on, the gray overlaid boxes reflect the Title Safe (inner box) and Action Safe (outer box) areas.

- **Output.** Refers to what is being output or displayed in your Source Monitor window. The first group of choices in the drop-down menu includes all your vectorscope and waveform monitors, and the second group includes the output display quality (see Figure 3.7). Briefly, if you were to select Waveform for your output display, your same media would playback in the Source Monitor, only it would be displayed as if it was being output to a waveform monitor. Using the different scope views allows you to gauge color and brightness values of your media. It is very helpful to use these scopes when performing such tasks as color correction.

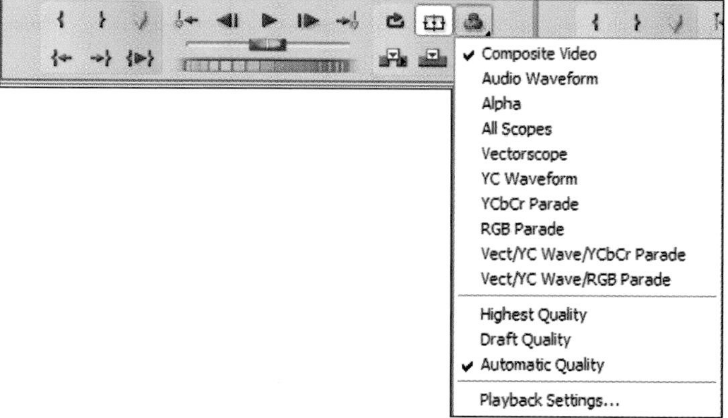

Figure 3.7 From the Output button's drop-down menu you can specify the Source Monitor's viewing mode. Additionally, you can toggle the display quality between Highest, Draft, and Automatic.

The quality settings are Highest, Draft, and Automatic. Highest displays the media in the Source Monitor at its full resolution. Draft displays media at quarter resolution. Automatic plays your media at full resolution when it does not detect instances with filtering or effects (which require rendering). If Automatic mode detects an instance that needs to be rendered, it switches to quarter resolution for that instance, then back to full resolution when finished with the instance. The changes in sizes will affect playback performance. If you have a sequence with a lot of effects open in your Source Monitor, you may not experience excellent real-time playback if you are set to Highest quality, because it will try to render the sequence in real-time at high quality, which requires a lot processing. Leave your Source Monitor in Automatic mode, instead.

- **Insert** (shortcut key: ,). Inserts selected media from the Source Monitor into the timeline at either an assigned In point or the CTI (if you don't have an assigned In point). An Insert edit does not overwrite media in the timeline. An Insert edit splits whatever media is in the timeline so that your shot can be placed without replacing or overwriting any other media.
- **Overlay** (shortcut key: .). Overlays the selected media from the Source Monitor into the timeline at an assigned In point or the CTI (if you don't have an assigned In point). An Overlay edit is the opposite of an Insert: It overwrites the material that it is being edited over. With an Insert edit, if you inserted a five-second clip in the middle of your timeline, the overall duration of the timeline would increase by five seconds. Using the same example with an Overlay edit, the duration would not change; you would have replaced five seconds of your edit with a different five seconds of material.
- **Take Audio and Video toggle.** Determines which elements of your media will be edited into your timeline. If you have a clip with both audio and video, you have the option of adding the video only, audio only, or audio and video together to your timeline. Clicking the toggle activates the different states of the button to give you the proper feedback for each state. If the toggle is in Audio mode, only the audio portion of your clip will be used for edits (see Figure 3.8). Video mode means only video will be used, and Audio and Video mode means audio and video both will be used.

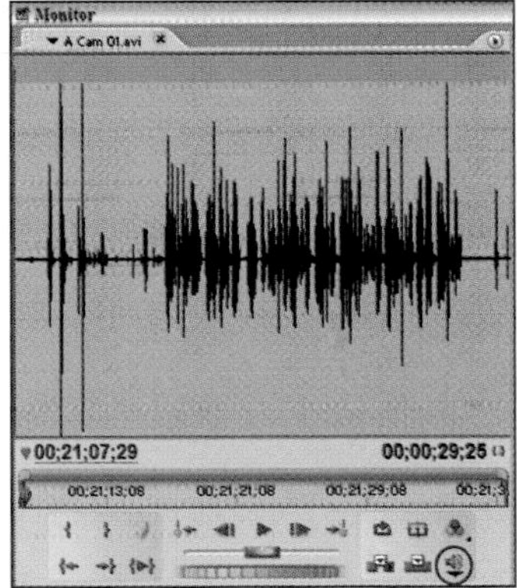

Figure 3.8 When the Take Audio and Video toggle is Audio mode, the Source Monitor displays the audio waveform for the active clip and will edit only the audio attributes into the timeline.

The Source Monitor group boxes contain all the tools necessary for navigating and defining which portions and attributes of the open media will be added to your sequence. Once media is added to your sequence, you can continue to use the Source Monitor to edit material from the active sequence.

Editing Functions

In the Source Monitor, you can perform edits using the Insert and Overlay buttons, or you can drag and drop from the Source Monitor into the Timeline window. The usual workflow is to open the media in the Source Monitor, to determine the In/Out instance of the media, then to add it into the Timeline window (see Figure 3.9).

Figure 3.9 You can designate a subclip within the source material by assigning In and Out points (notice the dark gray region in the time ruler). You then can drag that subclip from the Source Monitor and drop it in the timeline.

Additionally, a clip instance edited into the Timeline window can be opened in the Source Monitor by double-clicking on the clip in the timeline (see Figure 3.10). The clip opens as a subclip in the Source Monitor window, and any adjustments to its In point or Out point automatically update the clip instance in the timeline.

Figure 3.10 Double-clicking on the subclip instance from the timeline does not open the master clip from which the In/Out was assigned. Instead, it opens the subclip as its own clip instance in the Source Monitor. Any modifications made to this subclip's In or Out points in the Source Monitor immediately effects the clip instance in the timeline. Notice that the clip name in the top of the Source Monitor reflects that of the subclip in Figure 3.10, as opposed to the master clip in Figure 3.9.

Wing Menu Options

The Source Monitor's wing menu is where you can choose features or viewing modes specific to the window. Most of the choices are self-explanatory, but two important functions aren't that obvious:

- **Gang Source and Program.** Gang Source and Program means that you are locking certain transport controls together. If you gang the two monitors, all scrubbing in the Source Monitor will be mimicked in the Program Monitor. If you step one frame forward in the Program, you will step one frame forward in the Source. Although this does not seem like an obvious and useful function, it proves very powerful for certain workflows. For a video tutorial that explores this function, see Chapter 25, "Effects: Track Mattes."

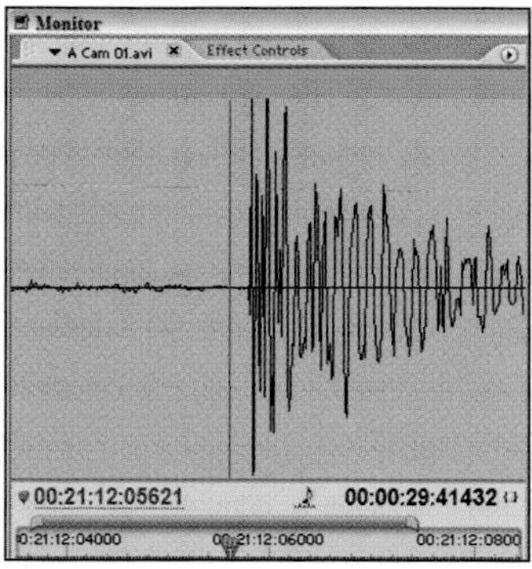

Figure 3.11 With the Source Monitor set to display audio units, you zoom closer into audio files. In addition, the timecode reflects time in 1/100000ths units so that you can isolate, identify, and edit an exact sample of audio.

- **Audio Units.** Because you now have conformed audio files of greater bit depth and detail, you may want to zoom in, scrub, and assign In or Out points at the subframe level (see Figure 3.11). To switch your counter display from Video Frames to Audio Units, simply select Audio Units from the wing menu. Remember, once you switch to Audio Units, the Step Forward button will step one sample at a time and that will barely register any sound. Although there is an increase in detail, you may have to do a bit more physical scrubbing and clicking within the scrub area to navigate to your desired locations.

The wing menu's Dual View and Single View options are also very useful. To conserve real estate, choose Single View to have just the Program Monitor open in your workspace. The standard view of the Source and Program Monitors is referred to as Dual view. If you are in Single view and you double-click a video clip, the Monitor updates to Dual view to display the clip in the Source Monitor. If you close the clip, it will not revert the view back to Single.

Magnification

Finally, you can magnify the viewable area of your open media, by choosing the Source Monitor's drop-down Magnification menu, between the timecode displays. Clicking it reveals a list of zoom states. The default choice, Fit, considers the current size of the window then resizes the media so that the entire frame fits inside the window. You will notice that if you set your magnification to Fit, any resizing of the window results in dynamic automatic resizing of the media. If you choose 25% from the Magnification menu, the media takes up a quarter of its normal full-sized space. If your Source Monitor window is larger than the 25% size, there will be gray space surrounding edge of the media. If you select a size that is greater than the size of the Source Monitor window, the edges of the clip exceed the edges of the Source Monitor window. (See Figure 3.12.)

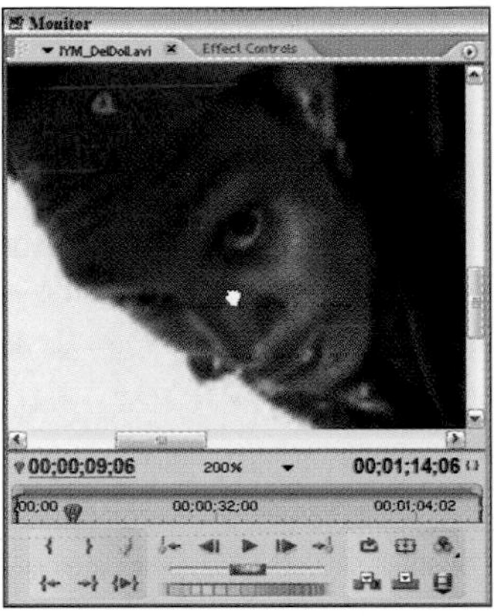

Figure 3.12 Two zoom states for the Source Monitor: Fit (left) always fits the image as large as possible into the current window size. If you are zoomed in close (right), you can use the Hand tool to drag the frame inside the view area to look at a different region of the image.

The Program Monitor

The Program Monitor is your television screen for the timeline's edited sequences. From the Program Monitor, you can make edits and adjustments to the open sequences, as well as preview or manipulate the creation of video effects. The Program Monitor has almost the same buttons and features as the Source Monitor, the difference is that the Program Monitor refers to sequences, not source material (see Figure 3.13). For example, the In Point, Out Point, Markers, and Edits buttons are applied to whatever active sequence is open in the Program Monitor, not to individual clips. Because of the button similarities, this section will cover only those transport buttons unique to the Program Monitor.

When you are making an edit from the Source Monitor to the timeline and you are using the editing buttons, the position of the CTI or the In point in the Program Monitor is where your edit will be performed. These windows work hand in hand, so it's important to pay attention to what you are doing in both windows.

Figure 3.13 The Program Monitor displays an open sequence, enabling you to navigate through the sequence and to make adjustments to specific areas of your edit.

If the last open sequence is closed in the Timeline window, the window will also close. To reopen the Timeline window, simply open another sequence (double-click on a sequence icon in the Project window) or create a new one.

What You Can Open

In the Program Monitor you can open any and all sequences in your project—whether the sequence is open in the timeline or not. Double-clicking on a sequence from your Project Monitor activates it in the timeline, as well as activating it in the Program Monitor. Whatever sequence is active in the Timeline window will also be active in the Program Monitor and vice-versa.

Window Layout

The window for the Program Monitor has of the same structure as the Source Monitor, but all the timecode data and information listed reflect the active sequence, as opposed to an active item of media. The CTI position reflects the location of the CTI within the boundaries of your sequence.

The tab area of the Program Monitor displays a tab for each sequence loaded in the Timeline window. When you toggle between sequences to bring one to the front of the stack and activate it, you click on the name of the sequence in the tab area. When there are more sequences than there is space to display their names, Premiere provides a special scroll bar to scroll through the sequences so that you can activate whichever one you choose. Because the Program Monitor is merely a monitor for sequences, activating a sequence opens it in the timeline, thus allowing you to playback, edit, and manipulate it. To close a sequence from the Program Monitor, click on the X next to its name in the tab area. This does not delete the sequence, it just closes it from view. Closing a sequence in the Timeline window also closes the associated tab listing in the Program Monitor.

Timecode and Time Navigation Controls

A sequence can have a total duration of 23 hours, 59 minutes, 59 seconds, and 29 frames, which is just enough time to use all the timecode values that exist. When you scrub within the Program Monitor's time ruler you will be scrubbing through whatever sequence is open in your Program Monitor. If you scrub in the timeline's time ruler, the CTI in your Program Monitor will update and scrub. The

Program Monitor's timecode field always displays the current value that the CTI is on in the active sequence.

Zooming in and out with Program Monitor's viewing area bar enables you to zoom in the Program Monitor only and not in the sequence in the Timeline window. This is a nice feature as your view does not update in the timeline when you want to zoom in for greater detail in the Program Monitor. The same goes for moving the viewing area bar to work in a different area of the sequence. In each of these instances, when you scrub in the new view or different area, the CTI updates in both windows.

Buttons and Transport Controls

Although the Program Monitor has buttons that perform the same tasks as those in the Source Monitor, it also has a few different ones. For example, the first and last buttons of the center group's top row are unique to the Source Monitor:

- **Go to Previous Edit Point** (shortcut key: Page Up). Enables you to snap the CTI to the left to the nearest edit or cut point. An edit point is considered any clip end or cut from one clip to the next.
- **Go to Next Edit Point** (shortcut key: Page Down). Snaps the CTI position to the nearest edit point to the right of the current CTI position.

The right group has three buttons only available in the Program Monitor. You'll find them on the button row, starting from the left:

- **Lift** (shortcut key: ;). The opposite of Overlay. If you have determined an In and Out point instance in your sequence and you would like to remove the material from that position, click Lift. Lift removes the material from the In/Out instance and preserves the space it took up.
- **Extract** (shortcut key: '). The opposite of Insert. Determine an In/Out instance in your sequence and choose Extract to remove the material *and* the space that the material took up in your timeline. For example, if you

choose a five-second section and click Extract, your overall sequence duration would be reduced by five seconds.

- **Trim** (shortcut keys: Ctrl+T). Opens the Trim window, which is a Monitor window used for viewing and adjusting edit points in the timeline. You can also open the Trim window from the Program Monitor's wing menu.

The Lift and Extract buttons are the basis for editing sequences in the Program Monitor.

Editing Functions

Used in conjunction with Insert and Overlay, Lift and Extract make up the powerful framework for performing complex edits with very simple keystrokes. As you work through the book, you will encounter these editing functions often. Be aware, however, that Program Monitor editing functions cannot be applied to every track of video at the same time. To lift or extract material you must first *target* the tracks that you wish to perform edits on, which is covered in depth Chapter 4, "The Timeline Window." You can target only one video and audio track at time, or you can target just video or just audio.

When I am editing with the Program Monitor, I often use it to navigate and snap to edits in the timeline. From these navigation points, I either move the clips physically or with keystrokes to modify my edit. If you have no In point or Out point selected in the Program Monitor, edits from the Source Monitor will be executed at the current position of the CTI.

Wing Menu Options

From the Program Monitor's wing menu (see Figure 3.14), you can gang Source to Program, adjust your monitor output, set the display quality, toggle to audio units, and choose the view mode for your monitor. There are also two choices that deserve a closer look:

Figure 3.14 The Program Monitor's wing menu adds three new choices—New Reference Monitor, Gang to Reference Monitor, and Playback Settings—to the familiar list.

- **New Reference Monitor.** To create a New Reference Monitor, simply select this option from the wing menu. When you open a new Reference Monitor you are creating a duplicate Monitor window from which you can view the active sequence. (See Figure 3.15.) You can then gang the Reference Monitor to the Program Monitor by selecting that option from the wing menu.

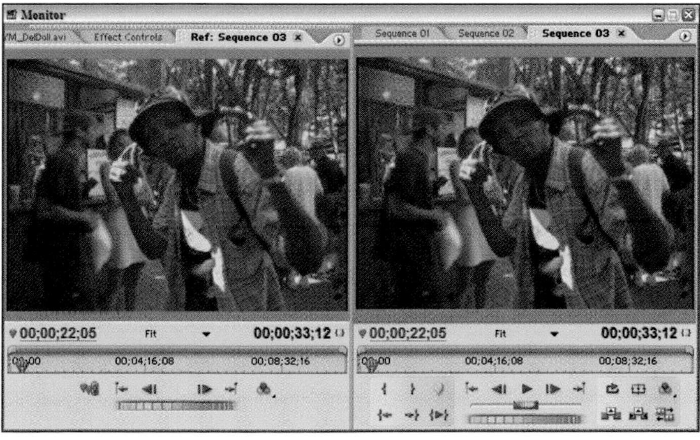

Figure 3.15 Opening a new Reference Monitor creates a new monitor that can reference whatever the active sequence was when the command was executed. Here you have Sequence 03 displayed in both the Program and Reference Monitor (which is docked in the Source Monitor area). This is useful for color correction: If you open the Reference Monitor and set the output mode to Waveform, you can monitor the literal waveform value adjustments in the Reference Monitor and the image being adjusted in the Program Monitor.

The Reference Monitor references only the active sequence when it is created. If you were to open another sequence or click on a different tab in the Program Monitor, the Reference Monitor would not update to display the active sequence, it would continue to reference the sequence with which it was opened. (More on Reference Monitors in Chapter 23, "Using the Color Corrector.")

- **Playback Settings.** The Playback Settings option is your wing menu shortcut to Project>Project Settings>General>Editing Mode>Playback Settings (see Figure 3.16). As discussed in Appendix C, the DV Playback Settings dialog is where you can toggle on or off the communication between Premiere Pro and your DV hardware for various playback circumstances.

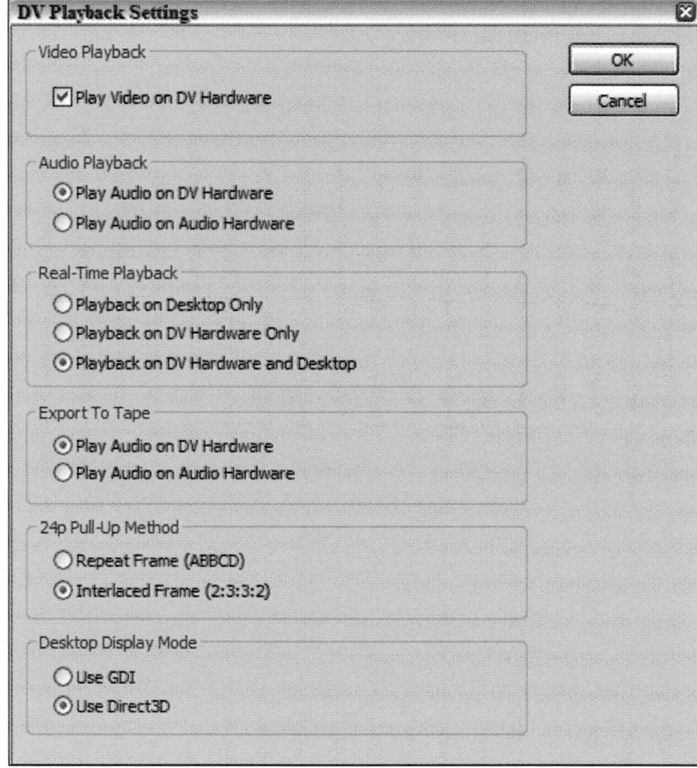

Figure 3.16 The DV Playback Settings dialog, which is accessible from the Program and Source Monitor wing menus, can help scale back the processing power needed to playback your video by toggling on or off communication with your connected DV device. The dialog also offers new settings for dealing with 24P playback.

Although the Reference Monitor is primarily used in very specific instances (color correction and track matting), having quick access to your Playback Settings can be very helpful when trying to focus your real-time playback performance to desktop only or DV only.

Effect Editing and the Program Monitor

The Program Monitor is also used in conjunction with the Effect Controls window. While you are assigning and adjusting effects, a preview of the effect will be displayed in the Program Monitor. The relationship between the Program Monitor and Effect Controls Window will be explored in Chapter 7, "Introduction to Effects."

Things to Remember

The easiest way to think about the Source and Program Monitors is: The Source Monitor views source material yet to be edited, and the Program Monitor views sequences and edited material. They both perform the same task of navigating through media, they just look to different places for media to view. The Source Monitor finds the clips and identifies the sections you want to add to your sequences. Picking the location to add the clips and then navigating through the edited sequence of clips is what the Program Monitor handles.

This chapter has focused on the specific features and functions of the Monitor window, but you have yet to explore the workflow for editing. To establish a workflow, you need to understand one more piece: the Timeline window. The next chapter will tackle that task, then Chapter 5, "The Editing Workflow," will unify these windows during a proper walk-through of the editing process.

CHAPTER

4

The Timeline Window

The Timeline window is where you will spend the most time in Adobe Premiere Pro. The Timeline window is the interface in which you can see your video clips and edit them together. I like to think of the Timeline window as a canvas or videotape, which slowly takes shape and definition as you work. For Premiere Pro, Adobe completely revamped not only the Timeline window's design, but also its editing functionality. (See Figure 4.1.) Perhaps the biggest advancement is support for multiple sequences.

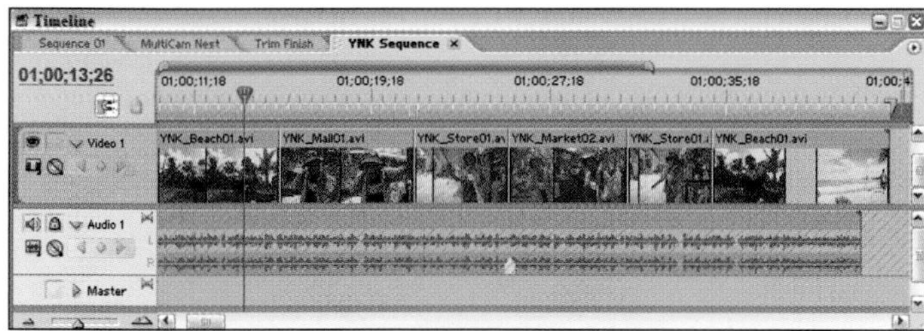

Figure 4.1 The Timeline window in Premiere Pro 1.5 supports a great editing workflow and a host of powerful features, such as multiple, nestable sequences.

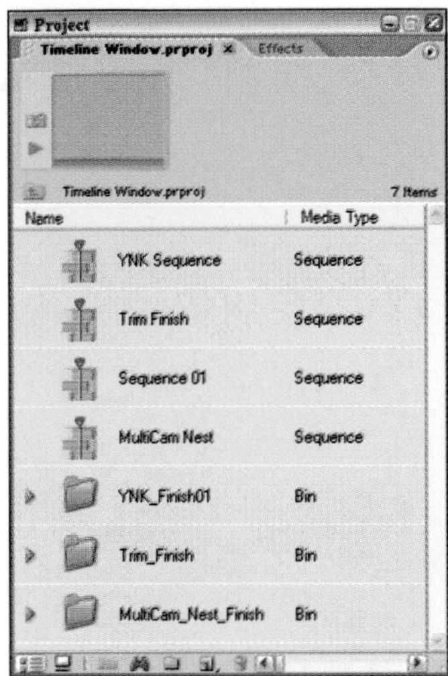

Figure 4.2 Notice that Figure 4.1's sequences have icons that reflect them in the Project window. Double-clicking a sequence icon opens the sequence in the Timeline window.

Sequences and Window Layout

In previous versions of Premiere, your Project window was tied directly to your Timeline window—one project meant one timeline. In Premiere Pro, the Project and Timeline windows are still related, but now both can open and support multiple sequences. (See Figure 4.2.)

To create a sequence, you select File>New Sequence or click on the Create Item>Sequence button in the Project window. To open a sequence in the Timeline window, you double-click on the icon from the Project window. (Ctrl+double-click to open the sequence in the Source Monitor.) When opened, the sequences load into the Timeline window, and each has a tab associated with it. The more sequences loaded, the more tabs visible in the Timeline window. If the number of tabs exceeds the visible space in the window, a slider bar appears at the top of the tab area enabling you to navigate to the other tabbed sequences.

By clicking on the tab for a loaded sequence, you bring it to the front of the view. Once a sequence is in view, you can edit and work inside of it. The active sequence in the Timeline window also will be the active sequence viewed in the Program Monitor and vice-versa. Although sequences may have varying numbers of total tracks, different track heights, and different master audio settings, the editing behavior of all sequences is the same.

If you click and drag a sequence out of the Timeline window and into empty space in your layout, you will create a new timeline with that sequence open inside it. As long as you have the screen real estate to display them, you can have multiple Timeline windows and multiple sequences open (see Figure 4.3).

Figure 4.3 By grabbing a sequence from its tab, you can pull it from its current timeline and drop it into blank space of the window where a new Timeline window will be created holding the sequence.

The Timeline window's real estate can be broken down into four main parts (see Figure 4.4):

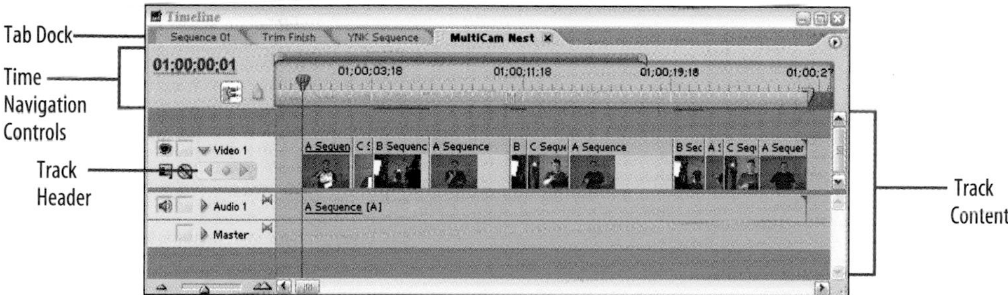

Figure 4.4 The Timeline window is made up of four primary areas.

- **Tab dock area.** Where you toggle between your loaded sequences.
- **Time navigation controls area.** Where you scrub the CTI, adjust the viewing area bar, get visual feedback for In points, Out points, markers, and selections, as well as decide the size and area of the timeline you wish to view.
- **Track header area.** Where you can decide what each track displays and the mode it is in. This space contains all the details for each track that is displayed in the track content area.

- **Track content area.** Where audio and video tracks are displayed at the settings and parameters you dictate in the track header.

The tab dock area's function should be clear, but the other sections of the window deserve a closer look.

Time Navigation Controls Area

The time navigation controls area is at the top of the track content area portion of the Timeline window. (See Figure 4.5.) It is composed of the:

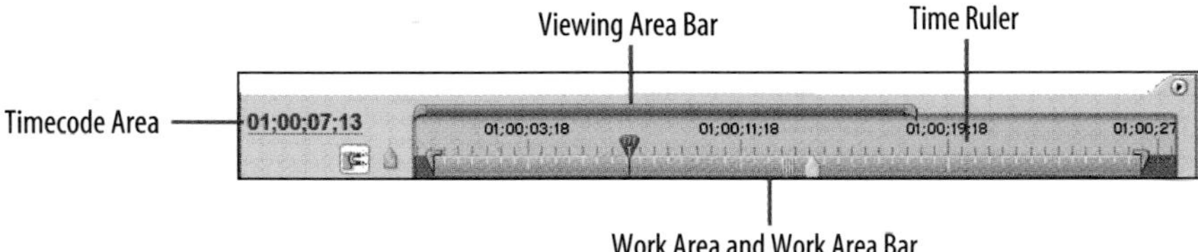

Figure 4.5 The time navigation controls area is made up of four components.

- Viewing area bar
- Time ruler
- Work area and work area bar
- Timecode area

Start at the top with the viewing area bar.

The Viewing Area Bar

The Timeline window's viewing area bar functions the same as the one in the Monitor window. By decreasing its size, you zoom in the timeline view. Expand the bar to zoom out. If the CTI is within the visible area of the Timeline window, adjusting the viewing area bar intelligently keeps the CTI centered within the window. You can also drag the bar left or right to focus on a particular portion of the timeline.

The Time Ruler

The time ruler is the gray bar delineated by tick marks that represent the timecode values for the active sequence. Clicking and scrubbing in this area activates the CTI to update and playback the video underneath the area being scrubbed. The timecode values displayed on the time ruler increase or decrease, respectively, when you zoom in or out your current view. In the time ruler, In points and Out points are shown as a dark gray point between brackets. You can assign In and Out points here, as well as view them.

Work Area and Work Area Bar

The work area is the dark gray area at the bottom of the time ruler. Here the lighter beige work area bar and the markers are visible. To assign markers, press the button at the top of the track header area. In the timeline, a marker will be assigned to whatever frame the CTI is on.

The work area bar dictates the area you want to preview, play, or export in the timeline. The work area bar helps you define smaller areas to preview and export as you can either export the entire sequence or just the work area.

Below the work area, you will see either a red or green stripe. The color tells you whether or not rendering preview files is necessary. (See Figure 4.6.) When you work in the timeline and apply an effect to a clip, a red bar displays above that clip signifying that its data must be re-processed and preview files need to be created in order to properly play the clip back with the effect. Using the work area bar, you define the areas over which you want preview files created. If you set the work area bar above the clip and press Enter, Premiere will render preview files for the clip. Once you create the preview file, the red bar turns green.

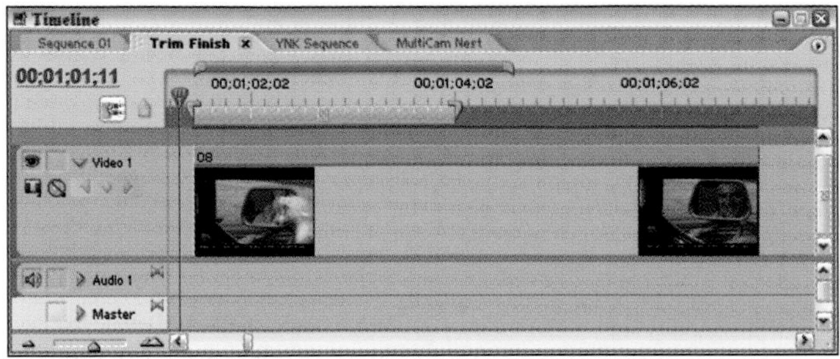

Figure 4.6 When you apply an effect applied to a clip, a purple line appears on it as an indicator (top). Above the track content area and below the work area bar, the red bar specifies that this clip needs rendering to playback at full resolution. When you press Enter, Premiere creates preview files for only the portion of the clip that is covered by the work area bar (bottom).

The important thing to remember is that the work area bar allows you to define specific areas to export or for which to build preview files.

Timecode Area

Next to the work area reside three important controls (see Figure 4.7):

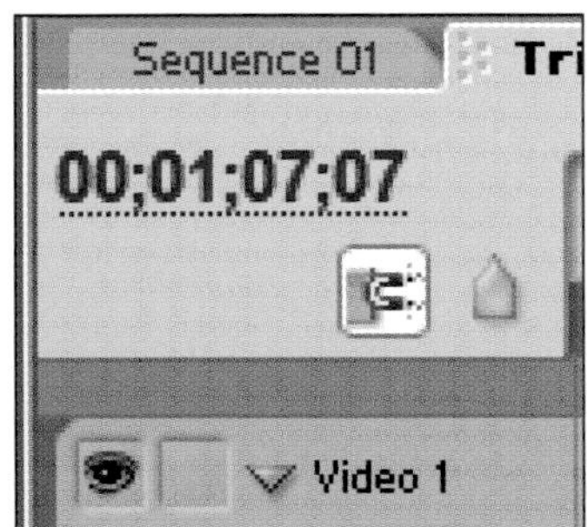

Figure 4.7 The Timecode area houses the timecode display (in blue), the Snapping button (left), and the Add Marker button (right).

- **Timecode display.** Shows the timecode number that corresponds to the position of the CTI in the timeline. Click in this hot text field, type a timecode value, and press Enter to snap to that position. If you type +5 and then press Enter, you will advance five frames to the right of your current CTI position. Typing a negative number moves you back the specified number of frames. You can use the hot text box to scrub through the timeline, as well.

- **Snapping button.** Toggles Snapping mode on and off. When Snapping is on (the default) and you move a clip in the timeline, the clip jumps to align to the nearest clip edge or marker. This is very helpful when you don't want any gaps or blank spaces created when you add clips to the timeline. Turning Snapping off enables you to drag and drop clips without them automatically moving to any edges. Snapping to an edge usually occurs when the clip being dragged is within about ten pixels of another clip edge or marker. If you are trying to make minor adjustment to the position of a clip that is within the snapping range, you will want to turn off Snapping and then make the move.
- **Add Marker button.** Adds a marker at the current position of the CTI. Double-clicking on a marker icon in the work area reveals the Marker dialog box, in which you can update a number of related fields with information regarding the marker (see Figure 4.8).

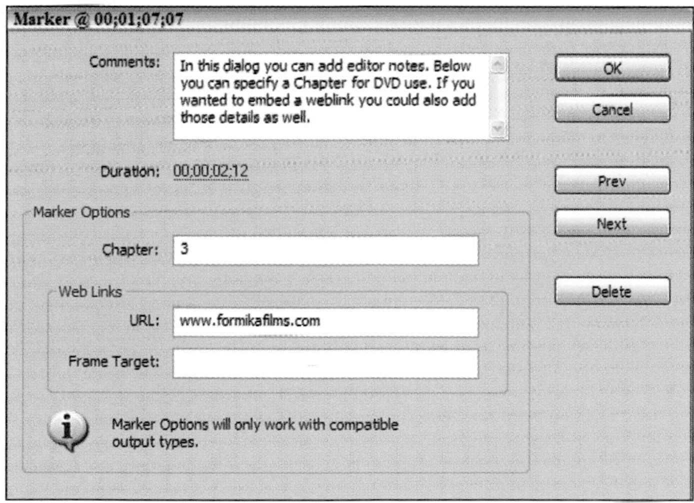

Figure 4.8 Double-click on a marker in the timeline to access the Marker dialog. Here you can add comments, assign duration, add chapter marks, and add web links to the selected marker.

You'll learn more about markers and Snapping mode in several lessons later in the book, as they are very helpful with lining up shots and arranging your edits with precision.

Track Header Area

At the left of the Timeline window, the track header area is where you toggle settings, display modes, and viewing modes for your tracks. Although you can drag and re-size the window as much as you like, the track header area cannot be made smaller than its default size.

Each track in the timeline has its own header with the track's name and track-related controls. You can rename a track by right-clicking anywhere in its header box and choosing Rename. Track headers come in two sizes: collapsed and expanded. You toggle between the two using the triangular icon next to the track's name. In their collapsed state (triangular icon points right), all track headers include an Output button and a Track Lock button. Audio tracks also have one extra icon, because mono, stereo, and 5.1 tracks look exactly the same. To tell the number of channels an audio track has, look for the icon of one speaker (mono), two speakers (stereo), or 5.1 (5.1) in the track header's top right corner (See Figure 4.9).

Figure 4.9 In the track header, you can you view and assign many different features to the content of the tracks. The Video 2 track is collapsed and locked, for example, and its output eyeball is clicked off. Video 1 is targeted (dark gray) and expanded. Audio 1 is an expanded stereo track. Also expanded, Audio 2 is a mono track and targeted (dark gray). Audio 3 is a collapsed 5.1 surround sound track. The Master track is collapsed and set to stereo.

Click the triangular icon to expand, or *twirl down*, an audio or video track header (the icon now points down), and you gain several more button controls: Display Style, Show Keyframes, Next Keyframe, and Previous Keyframe. Take a closer look.

Output Button

For both audio and video tracks, the Output button turns the track's output functions on and off. If there is an eye (for video) or speaker (for audio) shown in this box, then Output is turned on. If the box is empty, then the track will not be seen or heard when you play the sequence.

For example, you might toggle off output for a music track, while you edit other audio tracks, instead of trying to decipher them while the music is playing.

Track Lock

Clicking the Track Lock icon toggles the locking feature, which prohibits changes to the track. If you lock a track, hash marks appear within the boundaries of the track in the track content area. When the hash marks are visible, you are unable to click, select, or drag any media on to or off of the locked track. Locked tracks can be output with the rest of the sequence, however. To unlock a track, simply click the button again.

Locking is very helpful when you have placed items that you do not want to move, such as titles, music, or audio effects. Lock the track, and no matter what edits are made on other tracks, all your media will remain in the same place.

Display Style

Expanding a track gives you much more room to look at the track's contents. It also gives you additional controls, such as the Display Style icon, which lets you customize the track's look. Each video clip that is added to the timeline has associated with it frames that are played back in the Program Monitor. If you would like to get a sample of those frames within the boundaries of the clip in the track

If you set your display to Show Frames, zooming and navigating in your timeline may take a bit longer. The delay results from small preview frames being loaded into each view. These are needed to display all frames properly. Loading the frame is not instantaneous. Having additional RAM will help speed up this process, because the frames will be loaded into the RAM and accessed much quicker.

content area, click Set Display Style then choose: Show Head and Tail, Show Head Only, Show Frames, or Show Name Only. Most pro editors typically display the name only. When you are first learning Premiere Pro, however, Show Head and Tail is best, because it shows you the first frame and also the last frame of each clip. If you are zoomed into the timeline enough, the name of the clip will show between the first and last frame.

For audio tracks, Display Styles offers two choices: Show Waveform, which displays a graphic representation of your audio file, and Show Name Only.

Show Keyframes

In Premiere Pro, you can modify and add effect keyframes within the boundaries of a clip in the Timeline window. Say you want to zoom in on a video clip from your normal view, 100%, to 150%. To do this properly, you use the Motion tool, scale from 100% to 150%, and assign 100% and 150% values to certain frames (called *keyframes*) of the clip so that Premiere can calculate the difference between them. The result will be a dynamic zoom into your video clip, the speed of the zoom will be dictated by the time between the specified keyframes. The longer the time, the slower the zoom, and the shorter, the faster.

To add and adjust keyframes, you need to be in the display mode to view them. Click the Show Keyframes icon, then choose the mode you want.

Video Keyframes

For video tracks, the Show Keyframes icon offers three choices: Show Keyframes, Show Opacity Handles, or Hide Keyframes.

Show Keyframes enables you to see the keyframes associated with each clip in the timeline. It also gives you access to a drop-down keyframes menu in the body of a clip (see Figure 4.10). With it, you can switch between the various keyframes of a single clip.

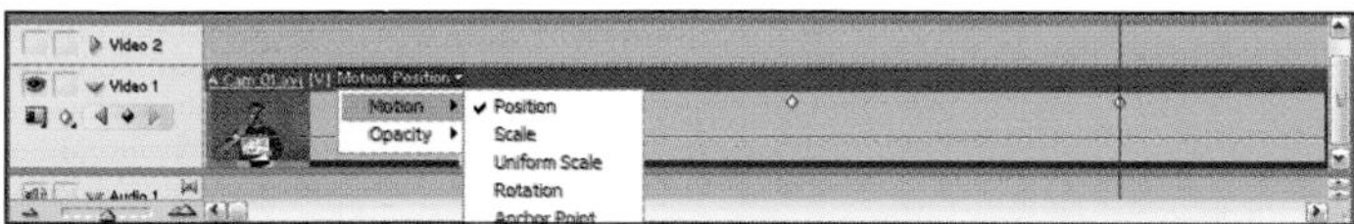

Figure 4.10 Having assigned position keyframes in the Motion effect for this selected clip, you can access and adjust those keyframes in the track area by putting the track in Keyframe Display mode then choosing Motion>Position. If you are zoomed in and cannot see the Effect drop-down menu, right-click on the clip with the keyframed effect. Remember that to view effect keyframes, you must first set the track to Show Keyframes in the track header.

Opacity is used to adjust and assign constant or varying transparency values for a clip in the timeline (see Figure 4.11). In former versions of Premiere, Opacity was used to fade a clip in or out. In Premiere Pro, you can use video transitions to easily fade a clip in or out on any video track. You just use the cross dissolve at the head or tail with no media on the other side.

Every video track has an Opacity value that is the transparency associated with the clip. A setting of 100% Opacity means that the file is completely visible with no transparency. A setting of 50% Opacity is half visibility. Set your display to Show Opacity Handles to be able to adjust keyframes for the Opacity value of each clip in the timeline.

Figure 4.11 Selecting Show Opacity Handles yields a yellow line that defines the Opacity value for each clip in the track. At the top of the clip, the line indicates 100% opacity. At the bottom, it indicates 0% opacity or complete transparency. To adjust Opacity, press the P key to access the Pen tool and drag the line up or down.

Hide Keyframes displays only the clip name and associated display style.

Audio

For audio tracks, Show Keyframe offers more options, because with these you can display two different keyframe properties: clip or track. Your choices are:

- Show Clip Keyframes
- Show Track Keyframes
- Show Clip Volume
- Show Track Volume
- Hide Keyframes

Premiere Pro supports both clip-based and track-based audio effects. Clip-based effects can be assigned to unique clip instances in the timeline. Track-based effects can be assigned to an entire track. A track-based effect affects all the media in the track in which it is assigned. Show Clip Keyframes displays the keyframes assigned for clip-based effects. Show Track Keyframes displays keyframes assigned for track-based effects. (See Figure 4.12.)

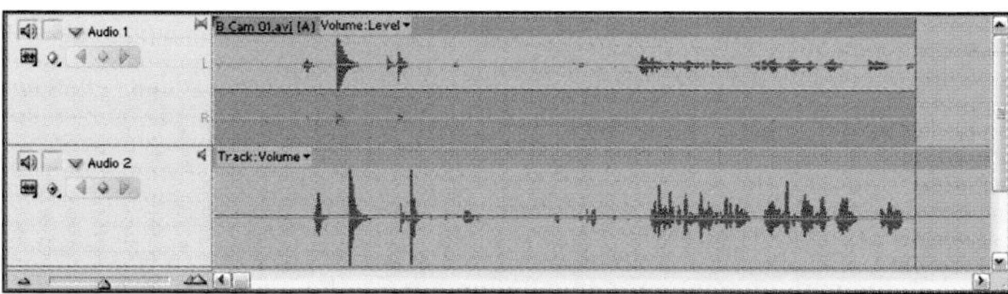

Figure 4.12 Audio 1 is set to display clip keyframes, and you can see the drop-down effect menu visible within the boundary of the clip. Audio 2 is set to display track keyframes, so the top of Audio 2's track content area is gray and its icon for the Show Keyframes mode has a small dot in the center of the keyframe.

Volume is the audio equivalent of video's opacity setting. With audio, if the volume is turned off, then you won't hear any sound; if a video track's opacity is zero, then you won't see any image. Toggling between Show Clip Volume and Show Track Volume displays the assigned values of either individual clips or the overall tracks.

Each of these parameters will be explored in later lessons. For now, just remember that individual audio clips have their own volume adjustments and effect settings. Plus, each individual track can have its own volume adjustments and effect settings. It is usually wise to first assign the clip adjustments, then make track adjustments when necessary.

Keyframe Navigation

While in a keyframe display mode, you can navigate through the assigned keyframes, using the Go To Previous and Go To Next Keyframe buttons. Go To Previous Keyframe moves the CTI backward one keyframe, and Go To Next Keyframe moves it forward one.

In the middle of the left and right pointing navigation buttons is the Add/Remove Keyframe button. To delete a keyframe, position the CTI's red Edit Line on it, then click the Add/Remove Keyframe button. If there is no keyframe under the Edit Line and you click the Add/Remove Keyframe button, Premiere adds a keyframe at that spot.

To navigate between clip keyframes, you must have a clip selected *and* have the CTI within the boundaries of the clip to go to the next or previous keyframe. This is not an issue when displaying track-based keyframes; the track keyframe area is for the entire track, not just one clip instance.

The red line that extends into the track content area from the CTI in the time ruler is commonly referred to as the Edit Line, because edit functions will occur at its position. When working in the timeline, keep in mind that the terms "CTI" and "Edit Line" are often used interchangeably.

Track Header Extras

Besides housing the control icons, the track header area has a few other important functions.

Targeting Tracks

When you are using the edit commands in the Source or Program Monitor, you must dictate which tracks the edits should be performed on. You must *target* the tracks. To target a track, click in any spot in the header that is not a box, button, or text field. Alternately, you can use keyboard shortcuts to target tracks:

- **Target Next Video Track Above: Ctrl+plus sign (+)**
- **Target Next Video Track Below: Ctrl+hyphen (-)**
- **Target Audio Above: Ctrl+Shift+plus sign (+)**
- **Target Audio Below: Ctrl+Shift+hyphen (-)**

A targeted track has a dark gray bracket on its left side and is a bit darker in color than the others listed (see Figure 4.13). Locked tracks cannot be targeted.

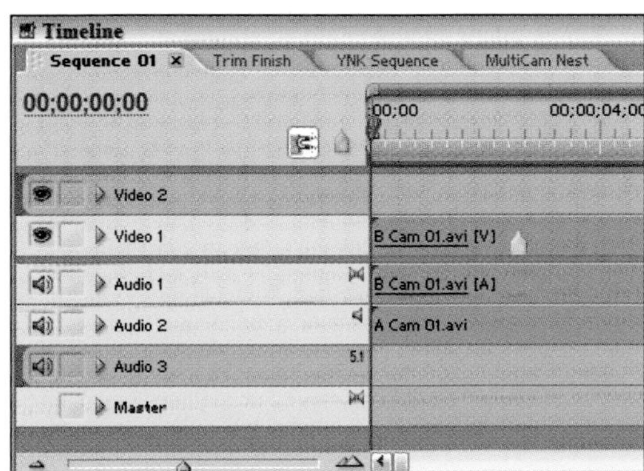

Figure 4.13 Video 2 and Audio 3 are the targeted tracks. Notice the dark gray color and the even darker gray bracket that is on the left edge of the track header. Targeting tracks is necessary for assigning edits with the Monitor window and applying default transitions.

In certain instances you will want to target audio only or video only. To turn targeting of a track off, click again within the boundaries of a targeted track.

Adding and Deleting Tracks

To create new tracks or delete existing tracks from your sequence, right-click within the track header area and choose the Add Tracks or Delete Tracks from the context menu.

Choosing Add Tracks from the context menu (or choosing Sequence>Add Tracks from the main menu bar) brings up the Add Tracks dialog. Here, you can specify whether to add video, audio, or audio submix tracks. You can specify the audio track type (mono, stereo, or 5.1), as well as its newly created placement in relation to the other tracks: before the first track, after the target track, or after the last track. (See Figure 4.14).

You can create new tracks by dragging and dropping a clip to the gray area (the pasteboard) just above the last video or audio tracks. Drag and drop a video clip to the pasteboard above the video tracks to create a new video track, or drag and drop an audio-only clip to the pasteboard just below the last audio track to create a new audio track.

When you choose Delete Tracks from the context or sequence menu, you get the Delete Tracks dialog, which presents the same three track types, just with slightly different criteria. (See Figure 4.15.) After you select the track type, you can choose to delete the target video track, all empty audio or video tracks, or all unassigned audio submix tracks.

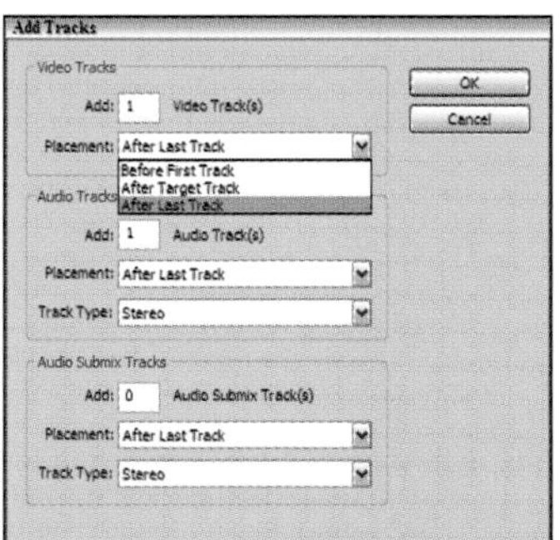

Figure 4.14 The Add Tracks dialog allows you to add video, audio, and audio submix tracks. You also can specify the track position of the new tracks.

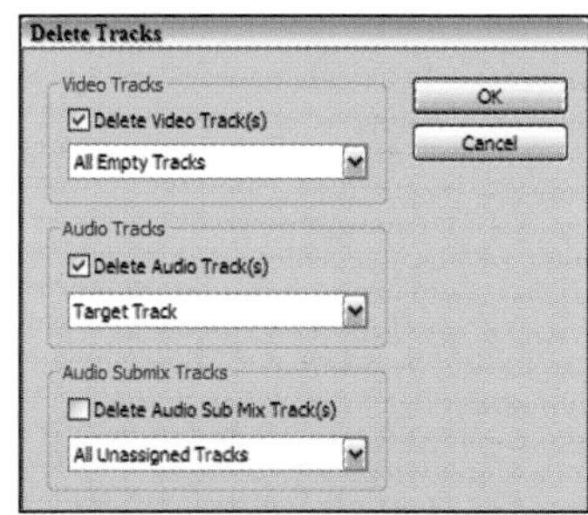

Figure 4.15 The Delete Tracks dialog lets you delete all of the separate track types in one dialog. You can either delete empty tracks or specific targeted tracks.

For example, if you wanted to get rid of an extra empty video track, you could delete it by targeting it, choosing Sequences>Delete Tracks, checking Delete Video Track(s), and selecting Target Track from the list box. To clean up a project once you are finished working in it, you can check Delete Video Track(s) and Delete Audio Track(s) in the Delete Tracks dialog, choosing All Empty Tracks from both drop-down menus.

Resizing Tracks

To customize your Timeline window, you can change the height of individual tracks. To adjust a video track, expand the track, position the pointer over the top edge of the track's header (the pointer transforms into the track height adjustment tool), then click and drag. For an audio track, click and drag the bottom. Once you find the right height, it will persist whenever you expanded the track. All tracks have the same collapsed size, but once they are expanded, every track can be its own unique size.

If you hold the Shift key down while making an adjustment to an expanded track's size, you automatically increase or decrease the size of all expanded tracks of the same type (see Figure 4.16). If you adjust an expanded video track, for example, only other expanded video tracks are affected. You would have to adjust the audio tracks separately. Collapsed tracks are not affected, either.

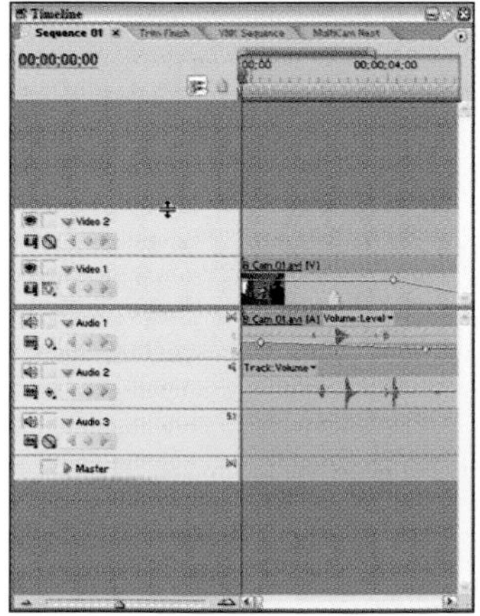

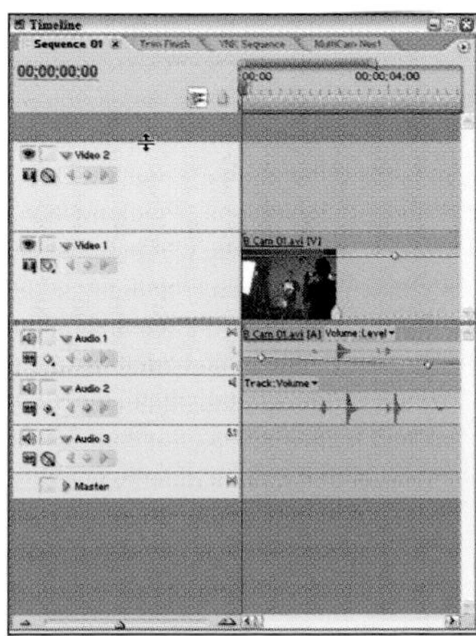

Figure 4.16 When you grab the outer edge of a track, the small track size adjustment tool appears (left). If you hold down the Shift key and increase the track's size, all expanded tracks of that type increase (right).

Adjusting Your Timeline Track View

If you want your Timeline window to emphasize audio tracks more than video tracks, you can click and drag the center line in the track header. The thick center line separates the audio and video tracks; clicking and dragging it automatically adjusts the balance between the displayed audio and video tracks.

Track Content Area

To the right of the track headers is the track content area, where all your editing work gets done. As you remember, the track header area determines how the track content area looks. Your video tracks are above the center gray line, and the audio tracks are below.

At the right edge of the timeline are two scroll bars—one for video and another for audio—so you can scroll your video and audio tracks separately. Below the tracks, the horizontal scroll bar helps you navigate to different points in your sequence. (See Figure 4.14.)

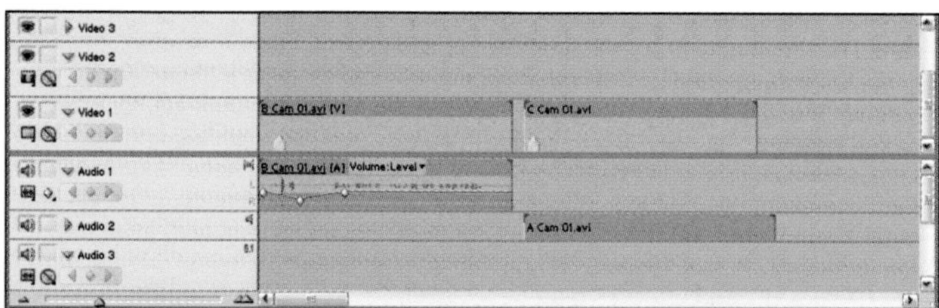

Figure 4.17 The track content area is surrounded by the horizontal scroll bar on the bottom, the vertical track scroll bars on the right, and the zoom controls just below the track header.

To zoom in or out of your tracks, use the zoom controls in the lower left corner of the Timeline window. Clicking on the small mountains zooms out, while clicking on the big mountains zooms in. Dragging the slider in the direction of either mountain achieves the same result. Pressing the + or – keys also zooms in and out, respectively. Every zoom keystroke updates the feedback of the zoom view, as well.

Now it's time to move into the primary content area of the Timeline window. The best place to start is with the behavior of video tracks.

Video Tracks

Your track view, display style, and keyframe viewing mode dictate what is seen in each video track. Figure 4.18 shows the results of different view settings.

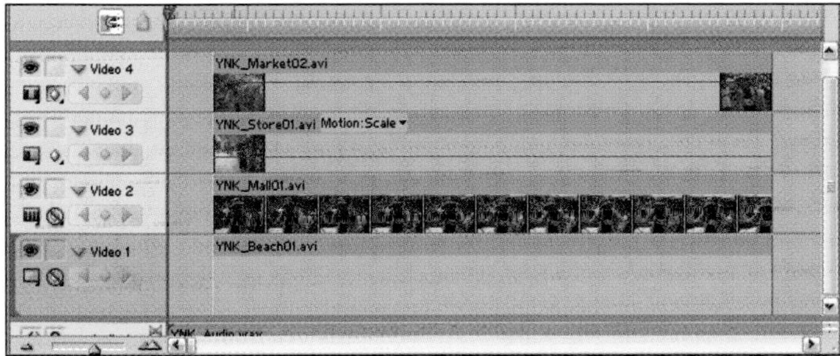

Figure 4.18 You can display your tracks in many different views. Video 1 displays the clip's name only. Video 2 displays frames. Video 3 is set to Head Only and Show Keyframes. Its keyframes are set to Motion:Scale. Video 4 has Show Head and Tail as well as Show Opacity turned on. In both Video 3 and Video 4, notice the orange wire indicating opacity and motion keyframes.

All video tracks have the same video properties with unique adjustable opacity and motion settings, which was not the case in previous versions of Premiere.

You can have unlimited video tracks in a sequence and the hierarchy of what's visible goes from the top of the stack down. This means that although the Video 1 track is your primary editing track, if you place a clip above Video 1 on the Video 2 track 2, it will cover the content on Video 1. Titles will go on Video 2, and the edited clips will be beneath the titles on Video 1. If you stack clips and wish to expose what's beneath, reduce the opacity of the top clips to reveal the lower ones. In Figure 4.18, only Video 4 is visible in the stack, because they are all on top of each other. If you were to reduce the opacity of Video 4, you would start to see Video 3 beneath it.

Another new track feature in Premiere Pro is the ability to add transitions to every track of audio and video. If you want to fade in a title on Video 2, you would place a one-sided cross dissolve transition on the head of the title. Because black is the blank space color of the timeline, if there is nothing beneath the title on Video 1, the title would fade up from black (see Figure 4.19). If there is a clip of media beneath the title, the title will fade up on top of the media.

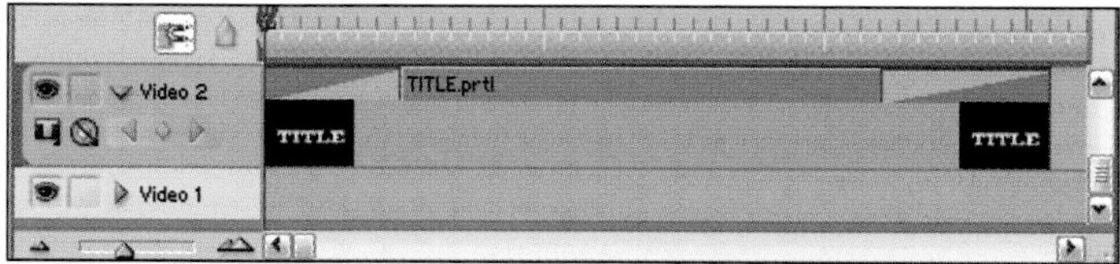

Figure 4.19 The title on Video 2 has two transitions: one at its head and one at its tail. With nothing beneath the title, the sequence will transition from black to the title then back to black at the end.

The look of a track in the content area can tell you a lot. The next sections examine a number of indicators found in the content area.

Locked Tracks

Locked tracks have a hash mark indicator throughout the entire track (see Figure 4.20). No media can be moved, selected, or added to a locked track.

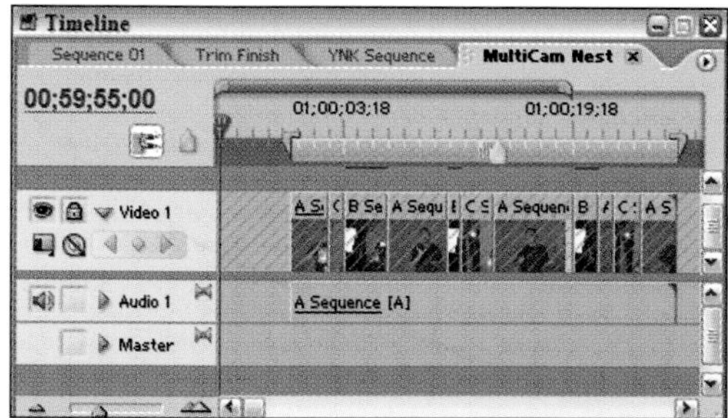

Figure 4.20 Video 1 is locked. You cannot apply edits to it, target it, or select or move clips in it.

Out of Sync

If the audio portion of an audio and video clip becomes shifted out of sync with the video portion (or vice-versa), a red indicator box appears in the corner of the clip (see Figure 4.21). The indicator box tells you how many seconds and frames out of sync the media is.

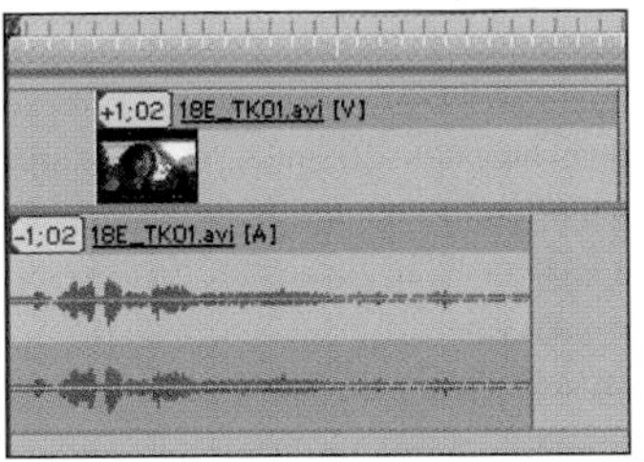

Figure 4.21 The red indicator for the linked audio and video states that the clips are out of sync by 1;02.

Right-click in the box to reveal two options: Move Into Sync and Slip Into Sync (see Figure 4.22). Moving into sync physically moves the clip back to the position where the media was originally. Slip into sync attempts to shift the media. Although the media will be offset physically still, Premiere updates the material in the audio and video so that it is back in sync but separated.

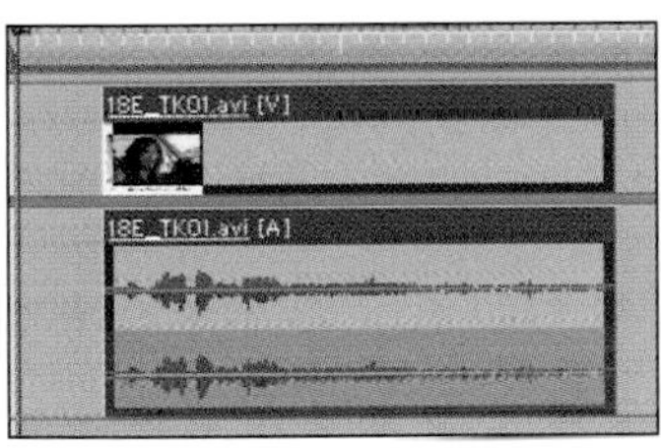

Figure 4.22 If you choose Move Into Sync, Premiere slides the media over to realign it and get back into sync (left). Choosing Slip Into Sync preserves the timeline postion (in this case a J cut) by slipping the source material in the clip into sync (right).

NOTES

When you capture a clip with both audio and video from your DV device, the clip plays back in the Source Monitor with both audio and video synchronously. When you drag an instance of the clip into the timeline using both the audio and video, the audio and video are "linked" together so that the audio is in sync with the video. You easily can find linked audio and video clips because the color of both clips is the same. If either the audio or video portion of the clip changes independently, then an icon displays revealing their sync status.

Clip Effect Keyframes

If you expand a track and turn on keyframe viewing, all clips will have a little drop-down Effects menu within the body of the clip. The drop-down menu displays the name of the selected effect parameter. This drop-down menu lets you toggle between the different effects and their parameters, so that you can decide which keyframes you want to view.

Because you can have multiple effects assigned to one clip, you navigate between the effects and their keyframable parameters from this menu.

All clips that have additional effects applied to them will have a purple line beneath the name area.

Clip Markers

Clip markers appear as upward arrows in the boundary of a clip when a track is expanded. When you are dragging clips in the Timeline window, clip markers will be identified as an edge that can be snapped to. This is very helpful when you are building your edit, as you can place markers in the exact positions where you want media added. When you add your media with Snapping on, you can place the media exactly where you initially determined.

You cannot double-click on clip markers in the timeline to assign marker settings; only timeline markers can have assigned comments, chapter numbers, and so on.

Media Boundaries

When you open a clip in the Source Monitor, it can have up to four defined parameters: Media In and Media Out, which are the first and last frames of the media, as well as Video In and Video Out, which correspond to assigned In and Out points. Sometimes your Media In and Video In will be the same value, because you started capturing at exactly the first frame you wanted to use in your edit.

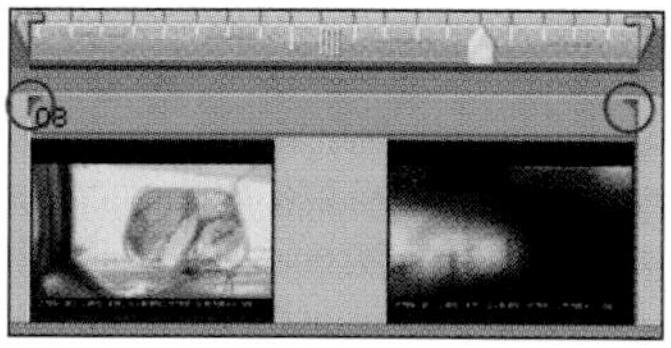

Figure 4.23 As the dog ears on the clip's head and tail indicate, this timeline clip instance is using the entire duration of the master clip it references.

In the track content area, a clip that begins at its Media In has a darkened upper-left edge. A clip that ends at its Media Out has a darkened upper-right edge. (See Figure 4.23.) These darkened edges are known as *dog ears*. The dog ears mean that you cannot extend or drag left or right to reveal more material from the clip because more material does not exist.

Audio Tracks

Audio tracks can be one of three different types: mono, stereo, and 5.1 surround. You can place audio files into a track with matching settings only. In other words, place only stereo clips in stereo tracks, mono in mono tracks, and 5.1 in 5.1 tracks. If you drop a mono clip into a project with only stereo tracks, you must drag it to the gray pasteboard area at the bottom of the window; Premiere will create a new mono track.

In regards to viewing audio track content, where video tracks display icons of video frames, audio tracks display the waveform values of the audio in the track.

Audio Display Modes

Audio tracks display the corresponding channel information of the clips they contain. Mono tracks reveal single-channel waveform files, stereo tracks show dual-channel files, and 5.1 surround has six-channel files. Because stereo and 5.1 require a lot of space to display their waveform information, you will often find yourself expanding these tracks and shifting the timeline view emphasis to focus more on audio. (See Figure 4.24.) You can accommodate this workflow quickly by creating a Workspace layout that moves your windows accordingly. Waveforms will either be on or off for your audio track.

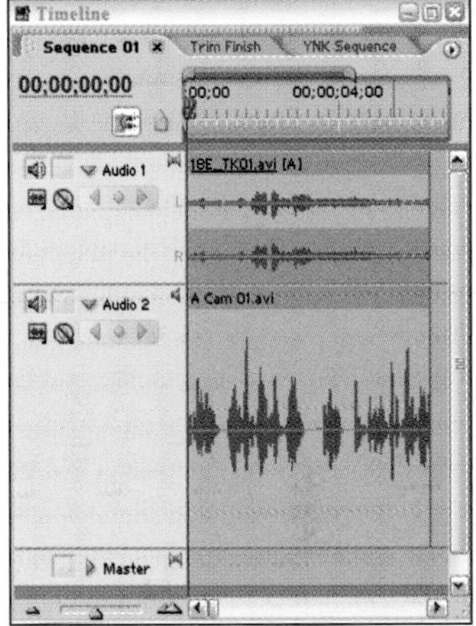

Figure 4.24 Just because audio tracks have only two display modes (waveforms on and off) doesn't mean that they can't be resized independently! It is far more appropriate to increase your audio track sizes and zoom in on each to get as much detail as possible from your waveform image.

Audio: Clip Versus Track

With audio tracks, you have the ability to look at clip effects and keyframes at either the clip level or the track level. Selecting Clip reveals the same drop-down effects menu as it does with video. Selecting track-based keyframes reveals a thick gray bar at the top of the track with a drop-down effect menu listing the parameters. The drop-down menu resides at the head of the track so you must navigate back to the beginning to define the parameter that you wish to view or adjust.

Audio Volume

The volume setting will be a thin orange wire that sits somewhere around the middle of your waveform. The wire sits in the middle because that is where the 0dB setting is. Raising the wire increases the volume, and lowering it reduces (see Figure 4.25). (More on editing and adjustable audio parameters in Section III, "Advanced Audio Techniques.")

Because transitions can be applied to all tracks of audio and video, you should use the audio cross fade transitions to fade your audio up and down. Instead of fiddling with volume keyframes, just drop the transition on the beginning or end of the clip and adjust its duration.

Figure 4.25 Audio 1 displays the clip volume; Audio 2 displays track volume. Because clip content cannot be added to the Master track, it also reveals an orange track volume wire.

Master Track

The audio Master track is not a track into which clips can be placed. The Master track is strictly for raising, lowering, or adding effects to the master mix down of your audio tracks. (See Figure 4.26.)

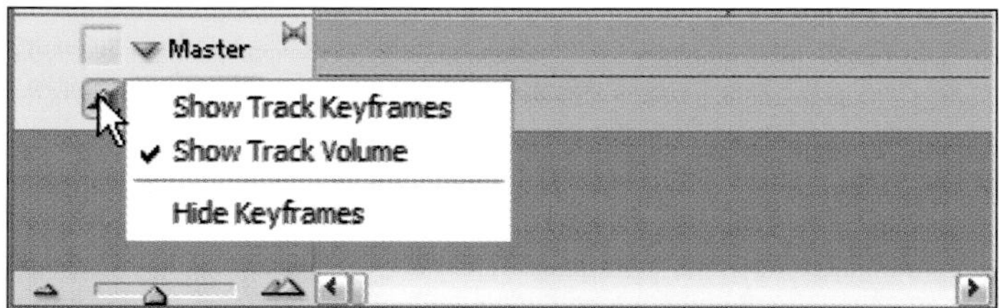

Figure 4.26 Because the Master track is track based, you can choose between viewing the track volume and the track (effect) keyframes.

If you expand the Master track, you will notice that it only allows you to display track-based keyframe parameters. Think of all your audio tracks as being funneled into the Master track that then turns things up, turns them down, and adds a reverb or any other effect. The final mix of your audio will pass through your Master track, which can always be monitored by looking at the levels in the VU Meters of the Audio Mixer window.

No matter what type of tracks your sequence contains—mono, stereo, or 5.1 surround—it will always be mixed down and played back in whatever the Master track is set to.

Wing Menu

The Timeline window's wing menu contains two important settings:

- **Audio Units.** Changes the counter setting from video frames to audio units. This feature functions the same as it does in the Monitor window, allowing greater zooming power and more detail from the audio files in the timeline. To remove clicks and pops or to make sure you are editing at the right spot, switch to Audio Units, zoom in, and find the proper place to make your edit (see Figure 4.27).

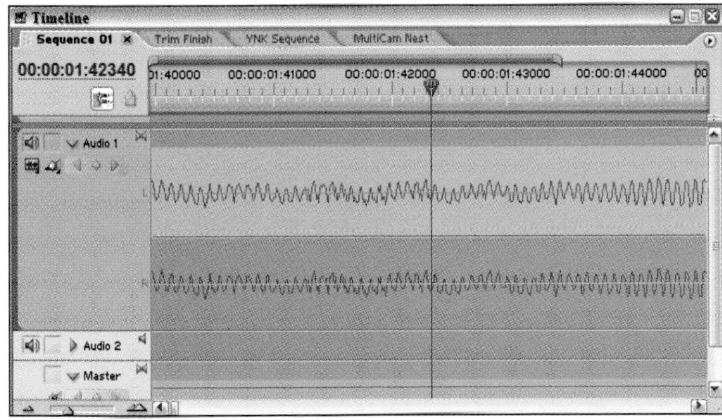

Figure 4.27 With the display set to Audio Units, you can zoom into the timeline at a subframe level. Doing this helps you extract more details from your audio file to clip out, remove, or cut on exact samples.

- **Sequence Zero Point.** Opens a dialog box that enables you to re-assign the starting timecode value of your current sequence. This is very helpful with multi-camera editing techniques (more on these later). It is also helpful if you are creating a project that matches back to another tape with its own specific timecode. Whatever value you enter will reflect the starting timecode value of frame 1 in your sequence. Even though these options are tucked away in a wing menu, they can still be assigned as keyboard shortcuts from Edit>Keyboard Customizations>Windows>Timeline Window>Timeline Window Menu.

Things to Remember

The most important things to remember in regards to the Timeline window are what you are viewing and which mode you are in. If you are editing audio clip keyframes and you are set to display track keyframes, you will start hitting your head against the wall! Don't do that, just look and see if the track has a gray bar on top. If it does, then you are working on the track level.

Let's say you find that your real-time preview responsiveness is not good enough when displaying a title that has motion and effects on top of a video clip that you are editing. In this case, you can turn off the output of the title track, tweak the edit beneath it, then, when you want to see the title, turn its track back on.

The last thing to remember is to use transitions to fade both audio and video in and out. Although it is a much different workflow than for former versions of Premiere, it makes the adjustments and workflow much faster to drop the cross dissolve and keep going.

The basics are behind you; now it's time to edit. In the next chapter, you will explore dragging, dropping, moving, and editing with the Monitor and Timeline windows.

CHAPTER

5

The Editing Workflow

Editing in Premiere Pro is far more intuitive and efficient than it has ever been. Whether you are using the Source Monitor to trim your clips or dropping all your clips to the timeline and then adjusting, Premiere Pro offers a lot of new tools and techniques to make the editing process less cumbersome.

I like to have a workflow when I edit, a structure and rhythm that I follow so that it is easy to make changes to what has been edited and so I can also decipher my work very clearly.

This chapter will guide you through a basic workflow and explain the new rules and new functions of editing in Premiere Pro. After a quick overview of the editing terms and basics, you will explore the program's functions within the context of a workflow.

Editing Basics

In former versions of Premiere, it was easy to get confused and accidentally change the flow of your timeline. Every editing task you perform in Premiere Pro, however, has some sort of interface response, so you know what you are doing. To understand what is going on, look at the cursor and the bottom of the application window. The cursor (Selection tool) updates and changes its appearance based on which tool you are using. (See Figure 5.1.) At the bottom of the application window, text suggestions will help guide you through your editing decisions. The text line offers ideas for tools and keystrokes that perform tasks associated with what you are doing. As you go through this chapter, pay attention to the feedback. Try to anticipate what it will say and what the results will be if you were to perform a suggested task.

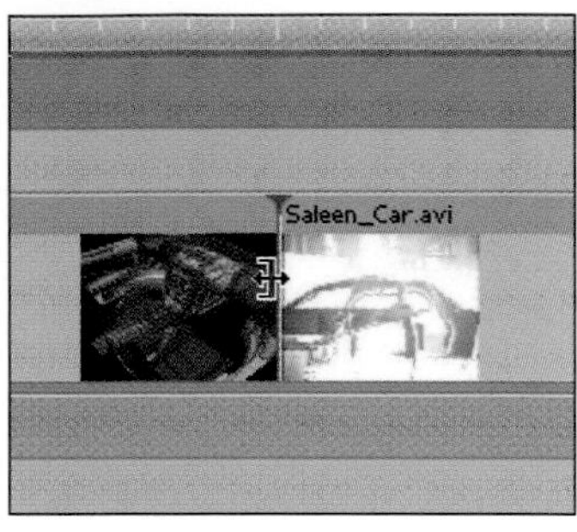

Figure 5.1 On the left, the Selection tool is hovering over a clip. As the tool gets near an edge of cut, it automatically turns into the edge trimming tool (right).

Six actions are the fundamentals of editing in the timeline:

- **Trim.** To adjust the In and Out points of media in the timeline.
- **Ripple.** To shift media to make room for added media or delete space created by removed media.
- **Insert.** To add media to the timeline by rippling and shifting media to make room for the added clips.
- **Overlay.** To add media to the timeline by placing the new clip on top of whatever media is beneath it in the track. Replaces the existing media with the new clip.
- **Lift.** To remove media from the timeline while preserving the space that the removed media occupied in the track. The opposite of Overlay.
- **Extract.** To remove media from the timeline by lifting the media, then rippling the surrounding media so that the space occupied by the removed clip is deleted. The opposite of Insert.

You'll hear these words often in this chapter. Your fingers also will become very familiar with two keys: Ctrl and Alt. These two keys are the modification keys that toggle not only the state of the selected tool, but also the editing mode when you are dragging and dropping media.

Because the Insert, Overlay, Lift, and Extract functions are just a modification key away, you can very easily perform complex edits. From shifting the order of edited shots to keeping your edit free of unnecessary gaps and empty spaces, the new editing functions are quite powerful.

Learn the rules, then expect results. This is the key to being comfortable with the new workflow. Knowing the tools and their exact behavior makes the editing process that much easier. You should also be aware of a major change from previous versions: Premiere Pro no longer supports A/B editing, in which the edit combines two subtracks of video into one Master track. Instead it offers single-track editing. This new approach may take some getting used to, but once you free your mind from its AB shackles and see the new light, it's beautiful!

Single-Track Editing

Because Premiere Pro is a single-track editing application, all of your edits between clips occur on a single video track in the timeline. (See Figure 5.2.) Because of the single-track design, Premiere Pro offers a number of tools to modify your clips after they have been placed. If you come from an AB background, you may have a few puzzling moments, but it's very likely that all of your problems can be solved by finding the right tool to use. When you get to the advanced editing techniques in Section IV, you will learn the proper tool for specific problems and explore various editing methods.

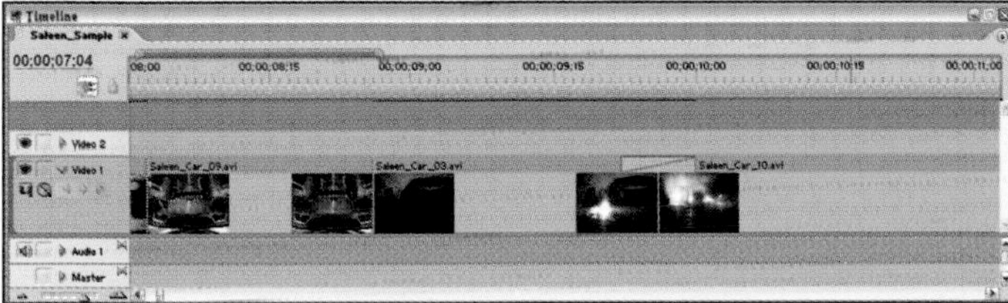

Figure 5.2 New for Premiere Pro is the single-track editing. No longer is there a visual A and B roll in Premiere Pro, only a single track of video where transitions appear as band-aids joining two clips together.

For example, the Ripple Edit tool enables you to easily trim In and Out points while keeping the surrounding clips adjacent to the adjusted clip. (See Figure 5.3.) The Slip tool is helpful because you can slide the In and Out points within the boundaries of the clip instance that is already placed in the timeline.

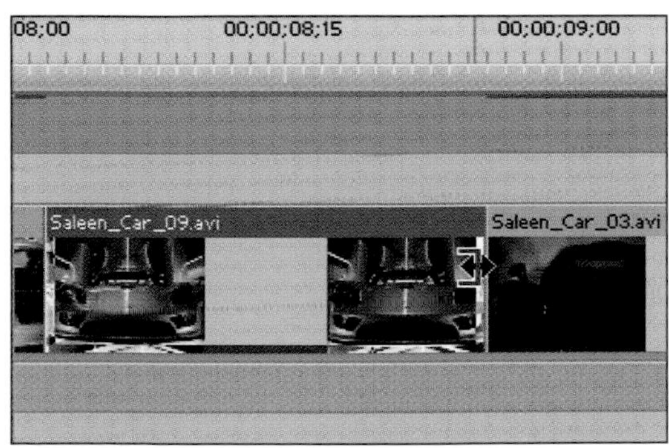

Figure 5.3 When you trim the tail of a clip with the Ripple Edit tool, the adjacent clip remains butted up against the newly adjusted clip. The Ripple Edit tool automatically deletes the blank space created by the edit and slides the media left so that there is no space between the cuts.

Editing with the Source Monitor

The most straightforward and intuitive way to start the editing workflow is to open a clip from the Project window into the Source Monitor. Once the clip is open in the Source Monitor, navigate through the clip and mark your In and Out points around the portion of the clip that you wish to use. Drag the clip down to the timeline and place it in its desired location. Of course, there's a little more to it than that.

Drag and Drop, Insert and Overlay

As long as your mouse button is pressed you have control of the clip and can move it. While holding the clip in the track that you want to add it to, find the downward arrow between two lines that's to the right of the cursor. This tells you the method in which the clip will be added to the timeline (see Figure 5.4).

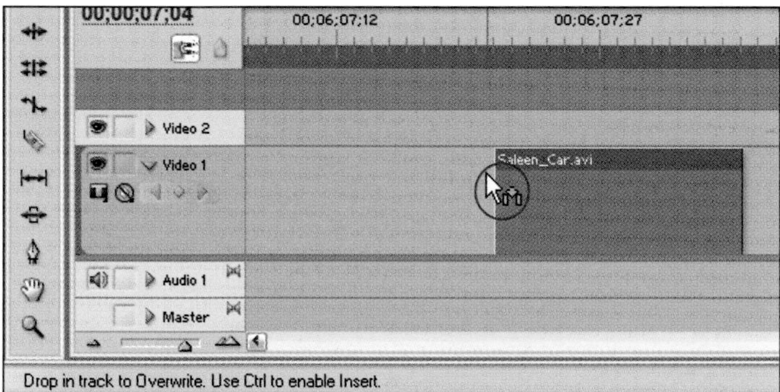

Figure 5.4 When you drag a clip or item into the timeline, Premiere will edit to the timeline in Overlay mode (the default). The cursor updates to indicate an Overlay edit as you drop the media. Notice the text in the bottom left corner of the screen that gives you additional tips and information.

A downward arrow means the default method, which is an Overlay edit for Premiere Pro (a change from earlier versions of the program). In an Overlay edit, the clip will be placed directly on top of and replace the material underneath when you drop it in the timeline. A right facing arrow means an Insert edit (more on these later).

Additionally, as you are editing there will be text feedback as to the mode you are editing in and the available keyboard modification keys. While you have a clip held, the bottom bar of the application displays helpful text.

Releasing the mouse releases the clip wherever your pointer is located, adding it to the timeline using your chosen method of placement: Overlay or Insert.

Overlay Edits

To better understand overlay edits, try a short exercise. You can use the Sample Project that came with Adobe Premiere Pro (the second Premiere Pro disk in the jewel case), or substitute another video clip.

1. Copy the Sample Project NTSC (or PAL, if you are in Europe) onto the desktop, and then double-click on the Sample_NTSC.prproj icon inside the folder to open the project.
2. Choose File>New>Sequence to create a new sequence in the project. Name the Sequence OVERLAY and assign it two video tracks and two stereo audio tracks. Double-click on the Sample Media folder in the Project window; you will use these clips to edit with.
3. Click on the menu bar of the Timeline window to make it active. Zoom in to the timeline by dragging the zoom toward the large mountains. In the timecode area, be sure that Snapping is turned on. (Clicking the Snap to Edges button or pressing S toggles Snapping on and off.) (See Figure 5.5.)
4. Select the clip Saleen_Car_01.avi from the Project window, drag it down into the timeline and slowly move it to the left toward the start of the timeline. Notice how it snaps to the far left side; this is the effect of Snapping mode (see Figure 5.6). When it's on, you can add media to the timeline without creating gaps or unwanted spaces. Also notice that the cursor icon indicates an Overlay edit.

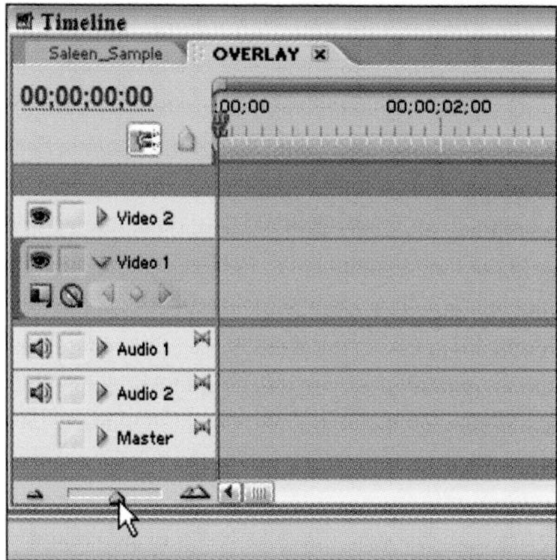

Figure 5.5 With the Timeline window active, notice the window bar is shiny silver instead of dull. The Snap to Edge button is turned on, and you are zoomed in about halfway through the zoom scale.

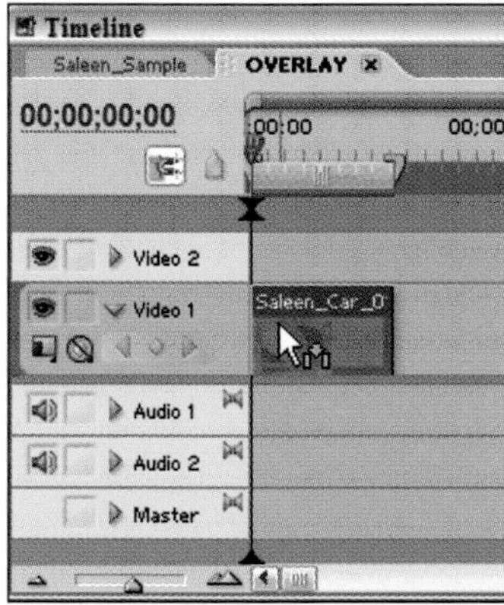

Figure 5.6 When Snapping is turned on, you see a thick black line with arrow on its top and bottom specifying where the clip will snap to. Here, the clip snaps to the head of the timeline in an Overlay edit.

5. Grab the Saleen_Car_02.avi clip, and place it immediately after the first clip on the same track. You should be able to easily drop this clip at the end of the other first clip, it should snap to the end. In fact, this clip can snap to either the start of the timeline or the Out-point edge of the first clip.

6. With two clips back to back in the timeline, drag the Saleen_Car_03.avi clip directly on top of Saleen_Car_02 (see Figure 5.7) so that it snaps to the cut between the two clips. When you release Saleen_Car_03, it will be added to the timeline in the position you determined, replacing the content that was beneath it.

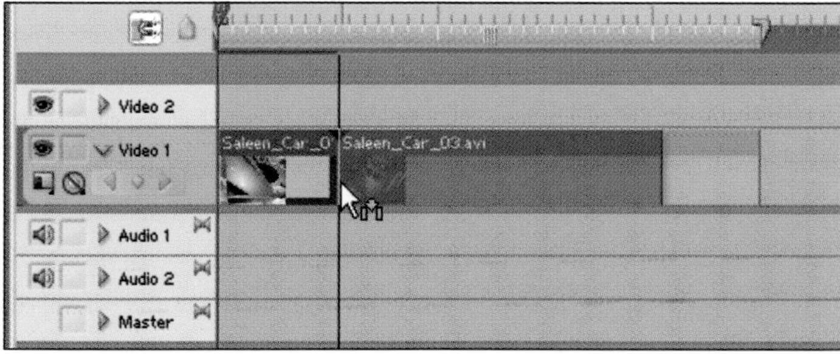

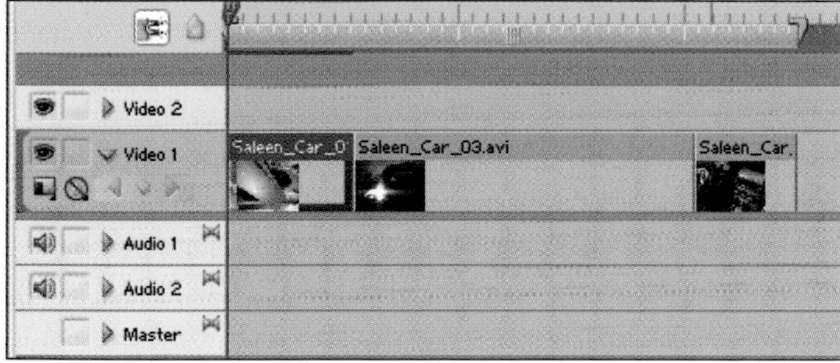

Figure 5.7 When you snap to the cut between the first two clips (top), notice how the Saleen_Car_03 clip is somewhat transparent, revealing what the Overlay edit will be replacing (the track instance of Saleen_Car_02) beneath it. Once the mouse is released (bottom), the Car_03 clip replaces the beginning of Car_02, leaving its tail after the end of the Car_03 instance.

When you add media to the timeline using an Overlay edit, it *replaces* whatever media was beneath it when you release the clip. The newly added clip replaces only the content that it covers. Because Saleen_Car_02 is longer than Saleen_Car_03, the remainder of Car_02 stays in the timeline. If you don't want the remainder of Car_02 in the timeline, you can select remaining instance of it and delete it. (If there is media to the right, say Saleen_Car_04, you can use the Ripple Delete command to delete the clip and the space it occupies.)

Don't like the way an edit turns out? Press Ctrl+Z to back up one step. The next short lesson looks at Insert edits. If you get confused by all of this, be sure to notice the feedback of the cursor and the text feedback in the bottom program bar. So, pay attention to the cursor icon and read the associated text.

Insert Edits and the Ctrl Key

Premiere Pro's second type of edit is the Insert edit. Instead of replacing and overlaying the content of the timeline, an Insert edit splits the content beneath the clip and inserts the clip in between.

Here's how it works.

1. Make a new sequence and name it INSERT. Arrange the Saleen_Car_01 and Saleen_Car_02 clips back to back in the Video 1 track of your new INSERT sequence. Remember to zoom in with the slider control or + key.
2. Click and drag Saleen_Car_03 from the Project window down to the same cut point that you edited it at in the last lesson. Snap the clip to the edit point and continue holding the mouse down.
3. Instead of releasing the clip as you did before, press the Ctrl key while holding your mouse. Notice that when you press the Ctrl key, the cursor changes from the downward arrow of an Overlay edit to the right arrow of an Insert edit. (See Figure 5.8.) Additionally, there will be right facing teeth marks that appear on your other tracks. These teeth marks signify which tracks the Insert edit will be applied to. Notice that the text in the bottom bar updates to confirm the Insert mode and its behavior.

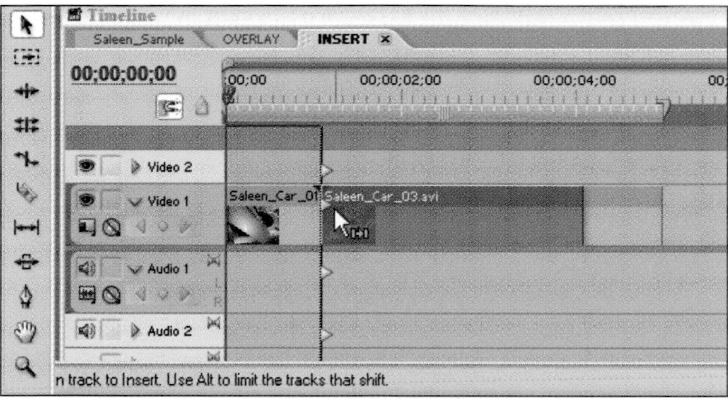

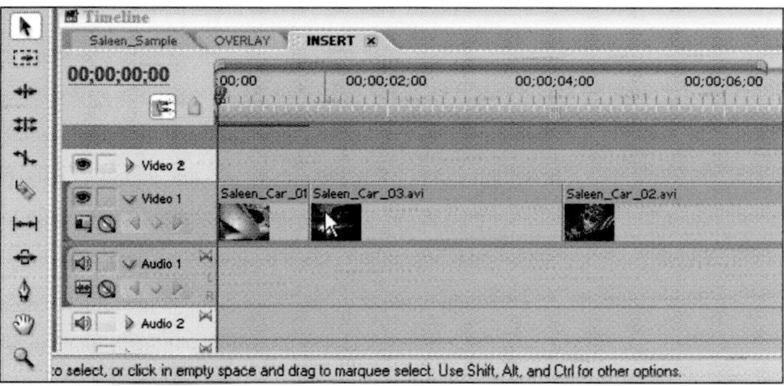

Figure 5.8 Press the Ctrl key while dragging and dropping a clip to toggle to Insert editing mode (top). The cursor icon updates to a right-pointing arrow, indicating that the clip will push the current media to the right to make room for itself in the timeline (bottom).

In an Insert edit, Premiere Pro "pushes" all the media to the right of your cursor position, leaving enough free space for the new clip. The new clip is inserted between the existing clips and nothing is overwritten. The Insert edit will occur on all those tracks displaying the teeth marks, meaning that space will be allocated for the selected clips on all those tracks. If a specific track is locked, it will not have an insert tooth and you cannot perform Insert edits on it.

4. With the Ctrl key pressed, release the mouse to drop the clip. Be sure not to release Ctrl before the mouse. Saleen_Car_03 inserts itself before Car_02 shifting the timeline material to the right.

5. Drag the clip Saleen_Car_04 from the Project window, and drop it onto Video 2 above the cut between Car_03 and Car_02.

6. Pressing Ctrl, drag Saleen_Car_05 from the Project window and drop it at the middle of Car_04 on Video 2 (See Figure 5.9). It splits the media in half on *both* Video 1 and Video 2, because insert editing by default makes space for the inserted clip on all tracks.

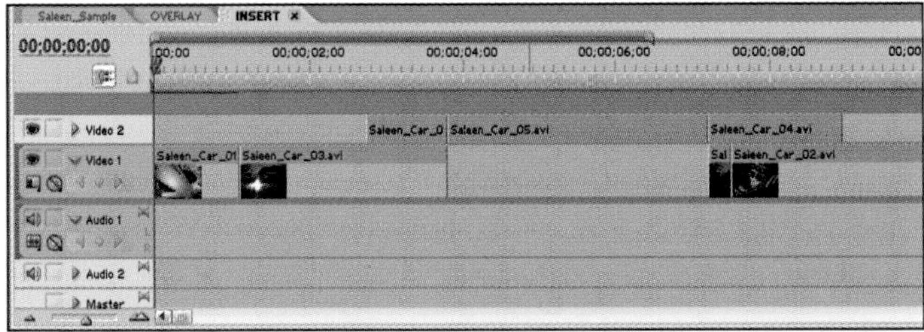

Figure 5.9 Inserting Saleen_Car_05 into Car_04 on Video 2 splits content of Video 1 in half as well.

7. Press Ctrl+Z to undo the last edit, then try another variation of the Insert edit. While pressing Ctrl and Alt, drag Saleen_Car_05 to the same cut point in as the last step, then release the mouse. (See Figure 5.10.) This edit is called an Insert Only on Target Track. Notice how it affects only the target track and there are no teeth marks on the tracks other than where your media is being added.

All Insert edits place the media based on the location of the inserted clip's first frame. To find this spot, look for the dotted line that displays as you hold down the Ctrl key. The dropped clip will begin at the point on the timeline under this dotted line. You can also set the Program Monitor to a two-up display that shows the start frame of the clip being added and the exact frame in the timeline where the clip will be edited.

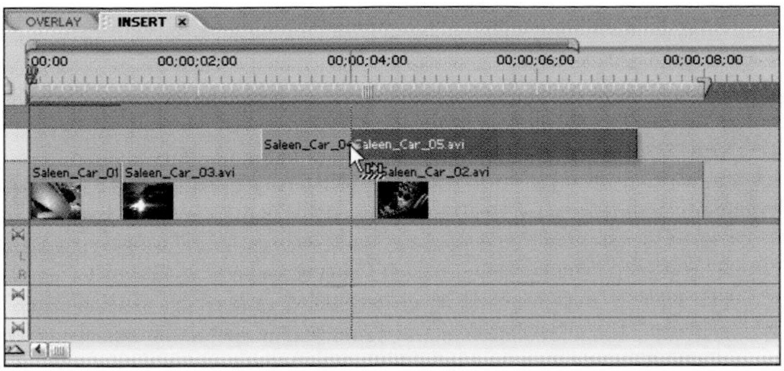

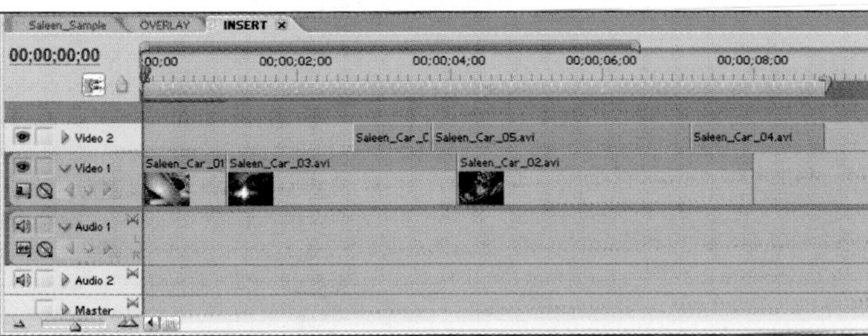

Figure 5.10 When you press Ctrl+Alt while dragging and dropping, the cursor indicates an Insert Only on Target Track edit (left). Now Premiere shifts only the media on Video 2; Video 1 remains intact (right).

When using Insert edits, remember that track items shift positions. Unless a track is locked, a standard Insert edit (Ctrl) inserts onto all tracks. An Insert on Target Track Only edit (Ctrl+Alt) limits the track shifting to only the track to which you are adding the media.

When assembling your initial edit, try adding all your clips to the timeline to establish the basic order of shots. If you open a clip that you want to add earlier in the cut, use an Insert edit (press the Ctrl key while dragging and dropping) to place the shot where you like.

When you drag and drop media from the Source Monitor to the timeline, Overlay and Insert editing functions similarly. The big difference is that the Source Monitor allows you to make adjustments to the In and Out points for your source material before adding the media to the timeline.

Edit Functions and the CTI

An alternative workflow for editing from the Source Monitor is to use the Insert and Overlay buttons with an open clip. Look in the right group of transport controls, bottom row. The Insert button depicts a clip being inserting into another that is separated; Overlay shows one clip being dropped directly on top of another. If you prefer keyboard shortcuts, use the comma (,) to insert and the period (.) to overlay.

Editing with the buttons or shortcuts is a bit more rigid than the freedom of dragging and dropping with your mouse. For example, there is no button to insert only on

To target video tracks you can use the keyboard shortcuts, as well. Ctrl+plus sign (+) targets the track above the current targeted track, and Ctrl+hyphen (-) targets the track below the currently targeted track. For audio tracks, use Ctrl+Shift+plus sign to target the audio track above (closest to bottom) or Ctrl+Shift+hyphen to target the track below (closer to the video tracks).

a target track, the equivalent of Ctrl+Alt. Dragging and dropping with the mouse allows you to drop your added media wherever you define in the timeline. Using the edit controls adds the media to the timeline in the location of either the CTI/Edit Line or an assigned In point from the Program Monitor.

To understand the edit buttons, try another method of editing the clips from Premiere Pro's Sample Project.

1. Create a new sequence, and name it SOURCE EDIT.
2. To edit properly from the Source Monitor, you need to specify the tracks on which you want your edit to occur by targeting your tracks. To target a track, click within the empty space of the track header area. The area around the track header when targeted will turn a darker gray and the left edge will become rounded.
3. Use the range select method (click and drag over the clips with the cursor) in the Project window to select two clips (Saleen_Car_01 and Saleen_Car_02). Drag them into the targeted track so that they start at the beginning of the timeline. Notice how the multi-selected clips are placed one immediately after the other in the track. You will most likely have to zoom in again, press the \ key to snap your zoom to fit the current clips within the boundary of the window.
4. Click and scrub in the time ruler area of the timeline to move the CTI/Edit Line to 02;12. With the CTI on this frame, press I to add an In point to the timeline at the position of the CTI.

   When you execute either the Insert or Overlay editing command using the buttons, Premiere first looks for an assigned In point at which to perform the edit. If no In point is assigned, Premiere performs the edit at the Edit Line's position.
5. Double-click on the Saleen_Car_03 clip from the Project window to open it in the Source Monitor. (Notice that clip has a previously assigned In/Out point. This is fine.) Press the Insert Edit button to insert the clip from the Source Monitor into the timeline at the In point you specified on the targeted track (see Figure 5.11).

Figure 5.11 Target Video 1, assign an In point at 02;12, then click the Source Monitor's Insert button to execute an Insert edit of the source material down into the timeline.

6. Press Ctrl+Z to undo, then press the Overlay button to see that an Overlay edit differs from an Insert edit. This time, the source material replaces the underlying clip material instead of pushing it out of the way to the right. Keep this sequence as it is; you will be using it for the next short lesson.

Using the editing commands is excellent for instances when you are either defining a specific region to which you want to edit (as in the three- and four-point editing techniques coming up), or if you have found an exact frame at which you want to insert or overlay. Instead of dragging and dropping, you just execute the desired edit at precisely the position you desire. It certainly insures position accuracy and used in conjunction with the Program Monitor's Timeline transport controls it can be a quick and efficient way to navigate and edit.

When you are dragging and dropping in the timeline or trimming the edges of a clip, watch the Program Monitor for feedback as to the frames you are editing. For example, when you are dropping a clip into the timeline, the Program Monitor shows you the last frame of the media before your inserted or overlaid shot and the first of media after the last frame of your inserted or overlaid shot. (See Figure 5.12.)

Timeline Editing

Once you have added clips to your timeline, Premiere Pro offers lots of features to help you organize and arrange them. When you are editing and rearranging in the Timeline window, you drag media from its current position and drop it where you want it to be. The same way you can choose to overlay or insert when you drop a clip, you can lift or extract a clip when you drag it. The opposite of overlaying, lifting is the default behavior. Extracting is the Ctrl-modified behavior, and it is the opposite of Inserting.

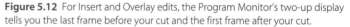

Figure 5.12 For Insert and Overlay edits, the Program Monitor's two-up display tells you the last frame before your cut and the first frame after your cut.

Lifting and Extracting

In addition to Overlay and Insert, which are functions for dropping media *in* the timeline, Premiere Pro has two unique functions for moving and dragging media *from* its timeline position: Lift and Extract. To understand how they work, continue working with the SOURCE EDIT sequence.

1. Select the center clip, Saleen_Car_02 and drag it up to Video 2 (see Figure 5.13).

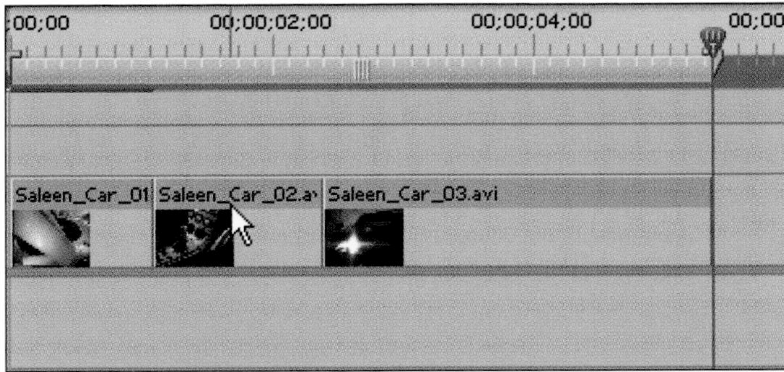

Figure 5.13 Premiere's default move for dragging clips is the Lift, which moves the clip from its current position and preserves the position of all other media in the timeline.

Notice that the space that Car_02 occupied on Video 1 is now empty. This is the default Lift behavior: You drag a clip from its position—lifting the media from its original spot—and the space defined by the clip's former boundaries remains open and preserved in the timeline. Like overlaying, lifting does not disturb or modify any elements surrounding the clips that you are lifting. Although Premiere does not give you any feedback to indicate you are in Lift mode, it is the default for dragging and moving a clip.

2. Press Ctrl+Z to undo your Lift edit so you can try an Extract edit.

3. Hold your mouse over Saleen_Car_02, then press and hold down the Ctrl key. To perform an Extract edit, you must hold down the Ctrl modifier *before* you click on a clip to select it (see Figure 5.14). With the Ctrl key pressed, the icon next to the cursor is now a left pointing arrow to indicate you're in Extract mode. The text in the bottom bar tells you as well.

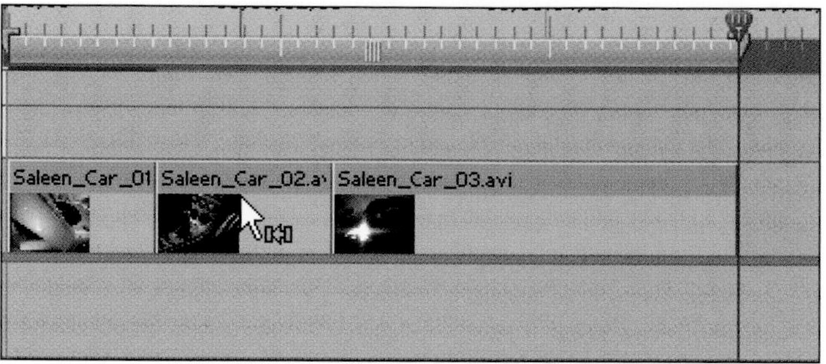

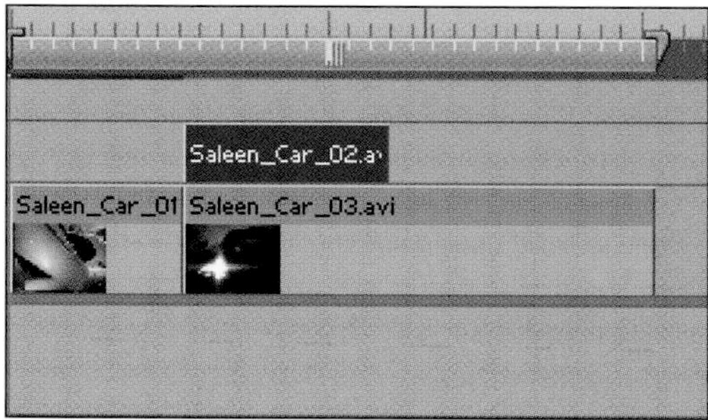

Figure 5.14 Before you click and move the clip from its current position, hold the Ctrl key down to put the cursor into Extract mode (top). Because this clip was extracted from Video 1 then overlaid on Video 2, the space it occupied on Video 1 is ripple deleted and the clip overlays above the other clips on Video 2 (bottom).

4. With the Ctrl key and mouse button held down, drag Car_02 to a new position on Video 2. First release the Ctrl key, *then* release the mouse. If you are still holding Ctrl when you release the clip after your move, you are immediately thrown into Insert mode. If you release Ctrl before the clip, you are in Overlay mode. Because you were in Overlay mode here, no shifting of track contents occurred.

These are the fundamental functions of dragging clips in the timeline. Use Lift to preserve the space the dragged media occupied and Extract to ripple delete the space that it occupied. When you link both the dragging (Lift and Extract) and dropping (Overlay and Insert) editing modes together, you will get a taste for what makes the editing workflow so powerful in Premiere Pro.

One Move, Four Choices

I want to take a few moments to re-iterate the last step of the last lesson. Once you decide the dragging method (Lift or Extract) for moving your clip from its current timeline position, you can choose not only a new location for the clip, but also how you want to drop it in (Insert or Overlay). Realizing this was my epiphany about the new power of Premiere Pro. Never before have Premiere's timeline editing tools offered such powerful options. Remember, as long as you hold down your mouse button while dragging a clip, you can decide whether to perform an Overlay edit or to press Ctrl to perform an Insert edit.

Consider a sequence of five clips arranged 1-2-3-4-5. Say you want to re-order the clips 4-1-2-3-5. In former versions of Premiere, you would have to perform about four steps to achieve what you can now do in one: Press the Ctrl key and drag Clip 4 from its current position (Extract) to the left. Your cursor snaps to the head (beginning) of the timeline with Clip 4 covering Clip 1. Press the Ctrl key and release the mouse and Clip 4 (Insert edit). Because you performed an Extract, Premiere closed the space formerly occupied by Clip 4, cutting Clip 3 directly to 5. Because you toggled to Insert mode, Premiere slides Clip 1 to the right to make room for Clip 4 at the beginning of the timeline before Clip 1. This is a monumental moment in the Premiere Pro editing experience. To see this editing move in action, check out the "Editing Three & Four Point Edits" video tutorial in the Fundamentals section on the accompanying DVD.

Editing with the Program Monitor

Overlay and Insert apply to source material, Lift and Extract apply to timeline material. Just as you can overlay and insert using buttons in the Source Monitor, you can also lift and extract in the Program Monitor using the Lift and Extract buttons or their keyboard shortcuts (; for Lift and ' for Extract). Give it a try.

1. Create a new sequence named PROGRAM EDIT, and arrange the Saleen_Car_01 through Saleen_Car_04 clips back to back on Video 1.

2. With Video 1 targeted, mark an In point at 02:28 and an Out point at 06;11 (see Figure 5.15). This space specifies in which portion of the timeline you want your edit to occur.

Figure 5.15 As with Source Monitor editing, the Program Monitor relies on targeting tracks and In/Out points to determine which portion of the timeline gets edited. Notice the In/Out instance in the Program Monitor and the blue highlight area in the Timeline window. This blue area indicates the track location where your Program Monitor edit will occur.

After you define your In and Out points, Premiere displays a dark gray instance surrounded by the In/Out brackets in the timeline's time ruler. Additionally, a light blue highlight/outline in the targeted track helps you identify the duration of the In/Out location specified for your edit.

3. Click the button for the type of edit you want. First, try the Lift button, which removes the material but leaves a gap in the timeline, preserving the space it took up. Press Ctrl+Z to undo, then click the Extract button to remove the material and close the gap that it occupied. (See Figure 5.16.)

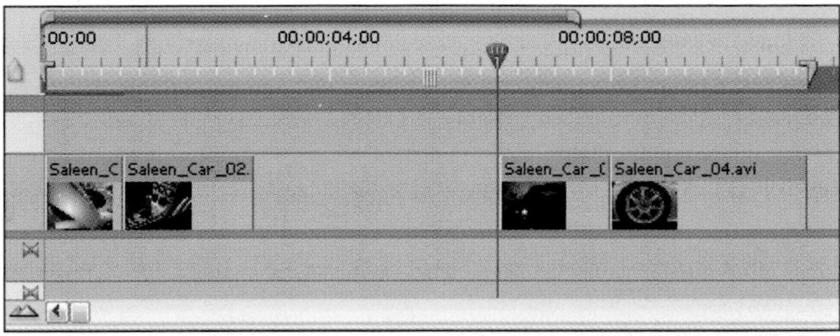

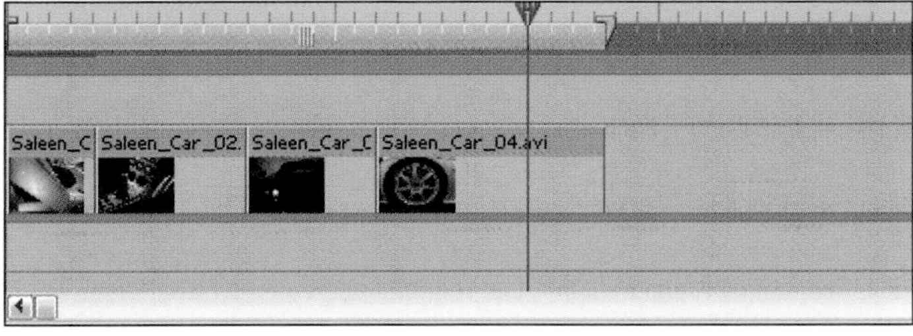

Figure 5.16 The Lift function (top) removes the material from the timeline entirely, leaving a gap at its former position. An Extract edit (bottom) removes the material and also closes the gap.

The primary benefit to using these Lift and Extract commands is that they remove the media from the timeline completely. Notice that when you lift or extract with the mouse, the selected material still has physical properties in the timeline and you have to decide where you want to put it. You can't just lift with the mouse and drag it out of the window to remove it; you have to find a new home for your dragged material. This is not the case with the Lift and Extract commands, which permanently remove the material from your timeline. Sounds mischievous, but it's really quite a practical alternative to the mouse moves.

Three- and Four-Point Editing

When the Program Monitor is used in conjunction with the Source Monitor, it can edit instances with exact precision thanks to three- and four-point editing.

Say your source clip has an In point and an Out point defined; that's two points. If you define an In point in your timeline with your Program Monitor, that's considered a third editing point. A three-point edit is any edit that uses a combination of three edit points. Because the Insert and Overlay commands execute their edits to any assigned In point in the timeline, you can pick an exact instance in a source clip and place it starting at an exact point in the timeline.

If your source material has an assigned In and Out point and the timeline also has a proper In and Out point, you have four points.

By now, you should know your way around creating a sequence and editing material together. Try following along with clips of your own choice. This technique universally applies to a variation of three-point edits:

1. Create a new sequence in your project and add four clips to Video Track 1.
2. Double-click on a new clip from the Project window to open it in the Source Monitor. Define an In point where you want the new clip to start and an Out point where you want the clip to end. That's two points.
3. In the Program Monitor, move the CTI to a specific location of the timeline where you want to add your open source clip. Once you are in position, press I or click the In point button to add an In point at the specified location. That's your third point.
4. Click either the Insert or Overlay button in the Source Monitor to add your exact source clip instance (two edit points) to the exact timeline position you assigned (one edit point). (See Figure 5.17.)

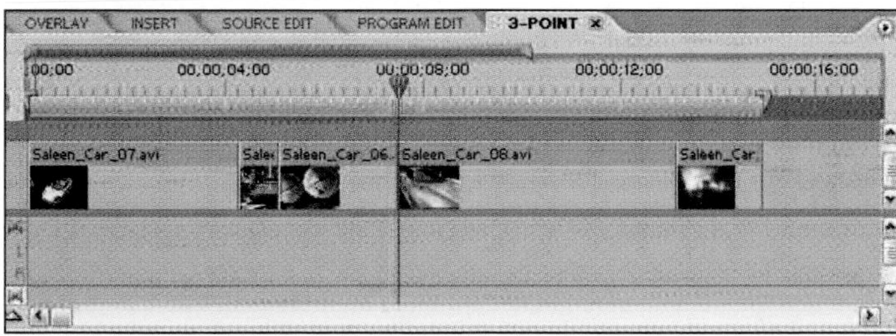

Figure 5.17 With an In point assigned in the timeline and source clip with both an In and Out point, clicking the Overlay button or (pressing the period key) executes a three-point Overlay edit starting at the marked timeline In point.

Congratulations, you have just performed a three-point edit. To try another variation, you need to isolate a portion of the timeline that you want filled with alternate material.

1. With the same sequence open, reposition the CTI in the Program Monitor and assign an In and Out point to a section of the timeline that you want to replace (two edit points). Be aware of which tracks are targeted.

Here you are creating an In/Out instance on Video Track 1 in which you defined the boundaries of your edit.

2. Open a new clip in the Source Monitor. This time, define just an In point where you want the clip to start when it is added to the timeline (one edit point).

   Look for a clip with content that can fill the space defined in step 1. The In point you set defines where you want the clip to start when you add it to the timeline. You do not need to assign an Out point for the source clip, because the timeline In/Out points define the boundaries that the clip will fill.

3. Be sure you are targeting the track in which the material that you wish to replace resides. Click the Overlay button. (See Figure 5.18.)

   If you were to click the Insert button, Premiere would insert the clip within the boundary and shift all the material to the right. By clicking Overlay, you are physically replacing the exact media defined by your three-point edit.

In a four-point edit, you define the boundaries of the timeline area you wish to edit (In/Out) and the exact source material (In/Out) that you wish to place between those boundaries. The primary difficulty with four-point edits is that the In/Out duration of the source clip must match the In/Out duration of the timeline boundaries, otherwise the Fit Clip dialog box will appear warning you of the mismatch and asking you to speed or slow the source clip when adding it to the timeline. If the source clip's In/Out duration is longer than the space you wish to fit it in, you must increase the speed of the clip so that when it is added to the timeline the defined In/Out points will still be respected. Choose to slow the clip speed to make the clip longer if there is not enough source content to reach the Out boundary.

To get a better understanding of four-point edits, watch the video tutorial "Editing Three & Four Point Edits," on the accompanying DVD.

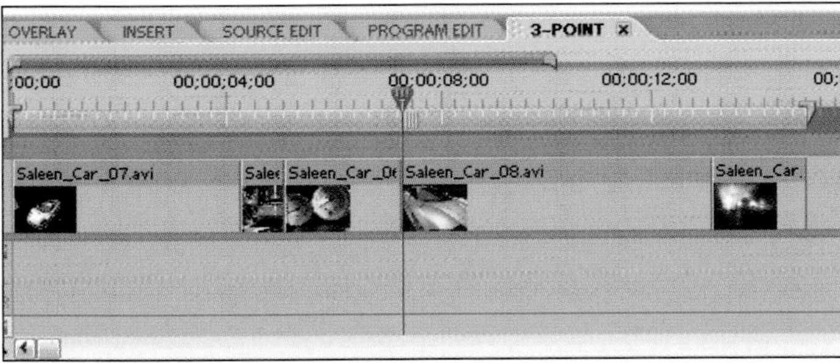

Figure 5.18 Working the opposite way, you filled a space in your timeline with specific source material, another three-point edit!

Three- and four-point edits are excellent when you want to fill a specific gap or fit certain content in an exact location. As you'll see later, three-point editing is particularly useful in multi-camera editing situations where you want the timecode of your source clip to match the timecode of your timeline. Four-point edits are useful when you are making an edit with a voice-over track and you need to insert a shot for an exact amount of time. If the speed of the shot is not an issue, you can pick exactly what you want to see and for exactly how much time.

When you are using the default cursor in the timeline (keyboard shortcut V), it updates to the Trim tool when placed near the head or tail of a clip in the timeline, as shown back in Figure 5.1.

Timeline Trimming

Although dragging and dropping lets you get your clips in place, other timeline tools enable you to fine tune and trim your edit into shape. The two you will use most often to edit your clips are the Trim tool and the Ripple Edit tool.

The Trim tool is used to shave off and remove unwanted portions of clips that exist in the timeline. By clicking either on the beginning or the end of a clip you can add or take away from the material shown in the timeline. A variation of the Trim tool, the Ripple Edit tool allows you to add or subtract from clip instances while at the same time preserving the adjacent material so that no gaps are created.

Sometimes you discover you want a little more or a little less of a clip after you've placed it in the timeline. You don't need to restart from scratch, just move your cursor and use it as the Trim tool instead.

To adjust a clip's In point, move your cursor over it in the timeline. The cursor will change into the Trim-in icon, a left bracket. Clicking and dragging to the right trims off the material at the head of the clip, reducing its duration and changing the In point. If you click and drag to the left, it increases the overall duration of the clip and updates you with a new In point. The Program Monitor displays whatever frame the tool is trimming past, so that you can see exactly what frame your modification is set to.

Move your cursor over a clip's Out point to access the Trim-out tool (a right bracket). Click and drag the Trim-out icon to change the location of the clip's Out point.

Limitations occur when you have a clip that is surrounded by two other clips. For example, Clip 2 resides between Clips 1 and 3. You want to change the In point of Clip 2 to earlier in the clip, but you want to cut to the same spot in Clip 3. In this case, you want to extend the beginning of Clip 2 to the left so that you can start the clip earlier in the shot. There is already a clip immediately to the left, however, and if you use the Trim tool you cannot drag past the boundary of another clip.

In this case, if you do not see the Media Start "dog ear" indicator in the top left corner, then you have additional material to the left of the current clip In point. While you can click and drag to the right to reduce the In point, if you are up against another clip you will not be able to use the Trim-in tool to adjust the In point of Clip 2 to the left. Adjusting the duration would require the media to the right of Clip 2 to be shifting to the right in order to make room for the extra material.

In former versions of Premiere, you would move Clips 2 and 3 to the right to make a gap between Clip 1 and 2, then extend the In point of Clip 2 to fill the gap so that the new material was added.

Premiere Pro offers a quick and better solution: Use the Ctrl modifier key to access the Ripple Edit tool. The Ripple Edit tool intelligently makes adjustments by extending or retracting In or Out points and shifting the surrounding media left or right to keep everything held together.

Ripple Editing

One of the features of Insert and Extract edits is the shifting of the media left (Insert) or right (Extract). This intelligent shifting of the media is termed *rippling*, like small waves in a bathtub. The idea of ripple edits is that all your adjustments preserve the direct proximity of the adjacent media.

Go back to the OVERLAY sequence of three clips, one right after the other: Car_01-Car_03-Car_02. This time you want to increase the duration of the clip Car_03 by revealing more material before its timeline In point:

1. Position the Selection tool (V) at the head of the Saleen_Car_03 clip instance so that the brackets face right. Before you grab the edge of the clip, hold down the Ctrl key to toggle the Trim-in tool into the Ripple-in tool, which looks bigger and thicker than the Trim-in tool (see Figure 5.19).

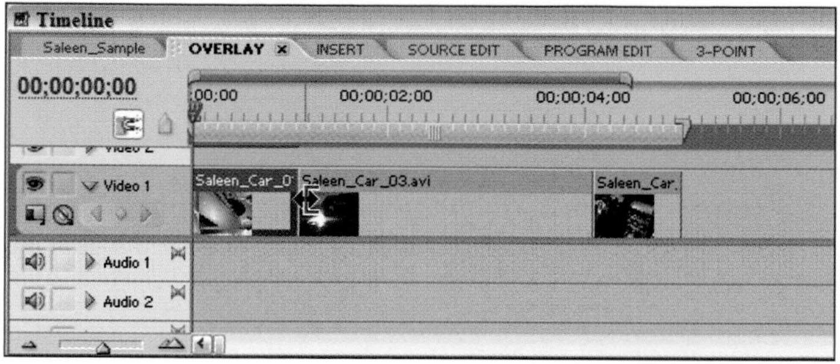

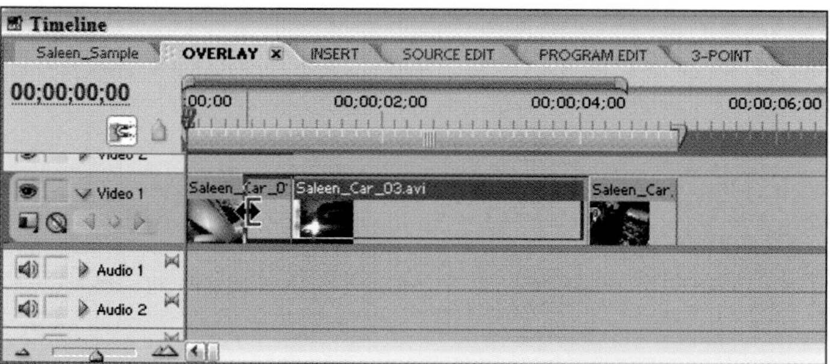

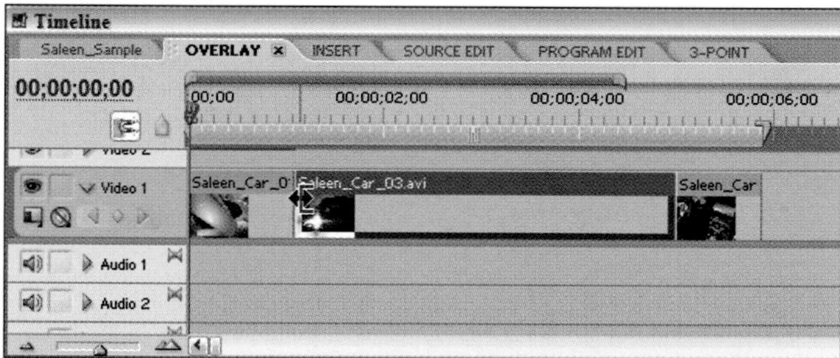

Figure 5.19 Push Ctrl to toggle the Trim tool to the Ripple Edit tool (top). Drag to the left with the Ripple Edit tool to reveal new material (middle). The final result (bottom): Car_01 is not adjusted at all, instead additional material is added to the head of Car_03, which ripples Car_02 further to the right down the timeline.

2. Continuing to hold down Ctrl, click and drag the In point left to reveal the new material and at the same time ripple (push) the material at the right of the edit down the timeline to the right. Using the Ripple Edit tool, you can trim and adjust the In and Out point of clip instances while at the same time preserving the cutting points of adjacent clips.

While you Ripple edit, the Program Monitor gives you a two-up display with the left frame revealing the last frame of Clip 1, before the cut, and the updating first frame of Clip 2, on the right, which you are dynamically changing as you continue to drag.

The Ripple-out tool works similarly on the tail end of clips. Although they may be hard to visualize, keeping four points in mind will help you master Ripple edits:

- Dragging the head of a clip left with Ripple-in lengthens the clip and pushes out (ripples) the material right.
- Dragging the head of a clip to the right with Ripple-in shortens the clip and takes in (ripples) material to the left.
- Dragging the tail of a clip right with Ripple-out increases the clip's duration and pushes out (ripples) material to the right.
- Dragging the tail of a clip to the left with Ripple-out reduces the duration and takes in (ripples) material left.

In all four of these examples, the cut points between the clip you are adjusting and its surrounding media will be preserved.

Ripple Delete

If you happen to have a blank gap or empty space in your timeline, you can right click within the boundaries of the gap and select Ripple Delete. This will delete the gap by rippling material on the right side of the gap (taking it in) to the left to close the gap.

Just like Insert edits that shift all tracks, Ripple edits and Ripple Delete ripple all tracks left or right depending on what you are adjusting. Locked tracks, however, are not affected or moved. If you finally have everything lined up in your timeline only to discover an empty gap on Video 1, you probably should unlock all locked tracks and ripple the edit (see Figure 5.20).

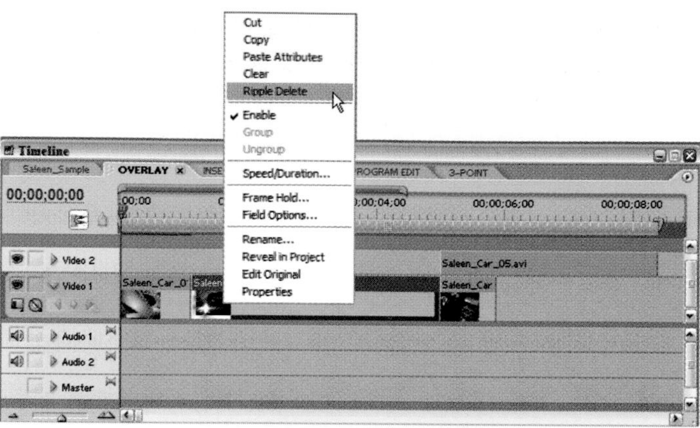

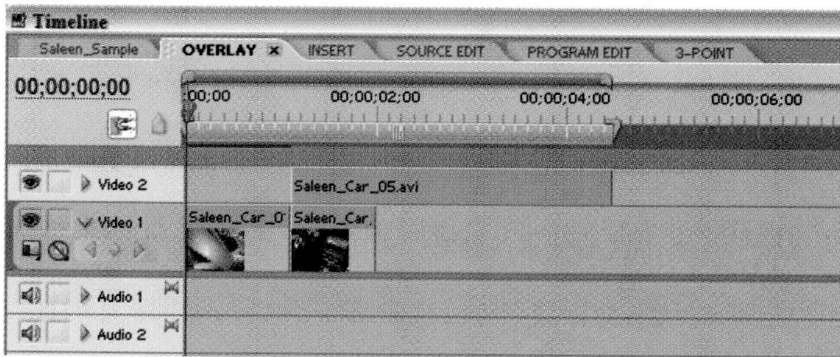

Figure 5.20 Whether ripple deleting an empty timeline space or clip, right-click on the selection and choose Ripple Delete from the context menu (top). At bottom, you can see that the ripple delete extracted the selected clip and shifted both tracks left to fill the space that the clip occupied.

Be warned, though, not all tracks may be able to ripple the amount you desire and the edit may not be performed. If you ripple the Out point of a clip left and there are items on other tracks that prohibit movement to the left, Premiere Pro will not execute the edit. Unfortunately, the program does not throw up a warning to tell what is wrong and where. You will have to deduce some of the symptoms from experience and a keen eye. In any case, locking tracks that do not have the space to ripple will allow the other tracks to ripple properly.

The Tool Palette

The Tool palette is your visual tool box from which you can click and choose tools that perform various powerful and helpful adjustments to your timeline. (See Figure 5.21.)

If you prefer not to click and select, each tool also has a keyboard shortcut. Once you have accessed a tool, your cursor updates with the appropriate icon for the selected tool. While a tool is selected, clicking and dragging in the timeline executes the tool's functions.

Figure 5.21 From the top, the Tool palette's tools are: Selection, Track Select, Ripple Edit, Rolling Edit, Rate Stretch, Razor, Slip, Slide, Pen, Hand, and Zoom.

The Tool palette has a number of tools for editing and re-arranging media in the Timeline window. From top to bottom they are:

- **Selection** (shortcut key: V). The standard cursor for selection. Press the Ctrl key to turn the Selection tool into the Ripple Edit tool.
- **Track Select** (shortcut key: M). Used to select all the content on one specific track. Pressing Shift turns this tool into the Multi-track Selection tool, which selects all tracks. Selection extends from where you click the tip of the tool to the right end of the timeline.
- **Ripple Edit** (shortcut key: B). Allows you to adjust the In or Out point of a clip instance in the timeline while rippling the media to its left or right, thus preserving the cuts.
- **Rolling Edit** (shortcut key: N). Enables you to dynamically roll the edit point between two clips, updating the Out point of the outgoing clip and the In point of the incoming clip at the same time.
- **Rate Stretch** (shortcut key: X). Lets you extend or reduce a clip's duration in the timeline by slowing down or increasing its speed, thus preserving its assigned In and Out points.
- **Razor** (shortcut key: C). Enables you to make incisions and cuts to individual media in the timeline. Holding the Shift key will make a cut through the entire timeline at the time position that you click.
- **Slip** (shortcut key: Y). Slides the visible media beneath the visible duration of the clip instance you are selecting, so that you can select a different portion of your clip to occupy the same space in the timeline. When you add a clip to the timeline, you may not be using all of the source material. If you were using only five seconds of a ten-second clip then there is still five unused

seconds somewhere beyond your In and Out points. Once a clip is edited into a sequence with adjacent material before and after it, use the Slip tool to shift the content of that clip within its timeline boundary. Slip the visible clip material left or right to display a different five-second section of the clip without altering its timeline boundary.

- **Slide** (shortcut key: U). Allows you to slide the visible duration and selected content of a clip over the surrounding media. If you slide to the right, the clip to the left of the sliding clip will have its Out point increased to display its content. The clip to the right would get covered by the slide (and vice-versa).
- **Pen** (shortcut key: P). Enables you to select and create keyframes in the Timeline window. Using the Ctrl key allows you to add keyframes. Using the Shift key allows you to click and select discontinuous keyframes and adjust them synchronously.
- **Hand** (shortcut key: H). An additional tool to click and drag the viewing area of the timeline left or right. It grabs at an anchor point where you click, and then moves left or right with your mouse.
- **Zoom** (shortcut key: Z). Zooms in and out of the timeline. Selecting and clicking zooms in. Holding Alt and clicking zooms out.

This brief overview of the editing tools for the timeline is intended to just whet your appetite. Section IV, "Advanced Editing Techniques," will serve up a full plate of details, presenting workflows for all the tools pointed out here.

Things to Remember

Don't be intimidated by the new timeline editing behavior. Keep practicing, and it will click. The primary points to remember are the Ctrl key and the ripple behavior. Whether you are rippling an edit point or rippling timeline material for an Insert or Extract, the Ctrl key is the modifier for all Ripple functions. You use the Ctrl key modifier for extracting when dragging and for inserting when dropping. In addition, the Ctrl key modifier turns the standard Selection tool into the Ripple Edit tool so that your cuts remain seamless.

As you edit, pay attention to which tracks are locked and why; try to create an intuitive order to the media in your timeline. If you build your primary edit on the Video 1 track and get it as tight as possible before you start adding titles and transitions, you will save yourself the headache of inserting and shifting media around when you don't want to.

I have found a structure for building my sequences that works quite well. It usually entails editing all of my main video and audio content on specific tracks. All my titles, graphics, music, and additional sound effects have their own tracks, which I rename accordingly. Being able to quickly identify what is what within your edit will help you better manage your sequences and content. With nested sequences I also find that breaking an edit into working sections helps the managing project's process. If it is logical to break your project down into smaller pieces and separate sections, create a new sequence for each part. All of this discussion and all of these ideas are thrown into motion in the lessons found in the book's advanced techniques sections; this is just a reminder to get you thinking about your own workflow and structure.

So, get that primary edit in shape, then prepare for adding transitions and using the Effect Controls window in the next chapter.

CHAPTER

6

Introduction to Transitions

A transition is a segue from one moment to another, a change that connects two different things. In digital video editing, a transition is the visual method used to switch from one shot to the next. The type of transition you choose—from a simple cut to a dissolve to more elaborate effects—can play a large role in the mood and feel of your project.

For example, dissolves and wipes help articulate the passage of time, while straight cuts quicken the pace of a sequence. In a scene where someone is taking the entire morning to study a race program and handicap horses for a day's races, dissolves and wipes help articulate the passage of time. When your character is watching the climactic horse race, however, dissolves or wipes may destroy the continuity of action. Cuts from the race to the character and back will keep the pace tight and tense.

Whenever you are editing and choosing transitions, ask yourself: What am I trying to say, and who am I saying this to? In some cases, standard wipes and dissolves may not give your project the right look or feel. This chapter will show you how Premiere Pro's transitions behave, so you can better decide which effect is right for your project.

Single-Track Transition Basics

Previous versions of Premiere used AB editing: Transitions could be added only to a special track between the A and B tracks.

With its single-track editing approach, Premiere Pro handles transitions in a more streamlined and flexible manner. (See Figure 6.1.) You can place a transition on a clip's head, a clip's tail, or any cut point between two adjacent clips. This means that if you put two clips right next to each other, you can drag a transition from the Effects window and drop it on the clips' cut point. Premiere Pro adds the appropriate media and uses it in the transition.

Check out the work of Japanese filmmaker Akira Kurosawa for some excellent examples of using wipes between shots to establish the passage of time between two moments.

Transitions can be placed between all media on all tracks, either audio or video. Finally, if you prefer the AB editing view, you can use the Effect Controls window to look at the AB relationship between your transitions, as well as to access custom transition controls.

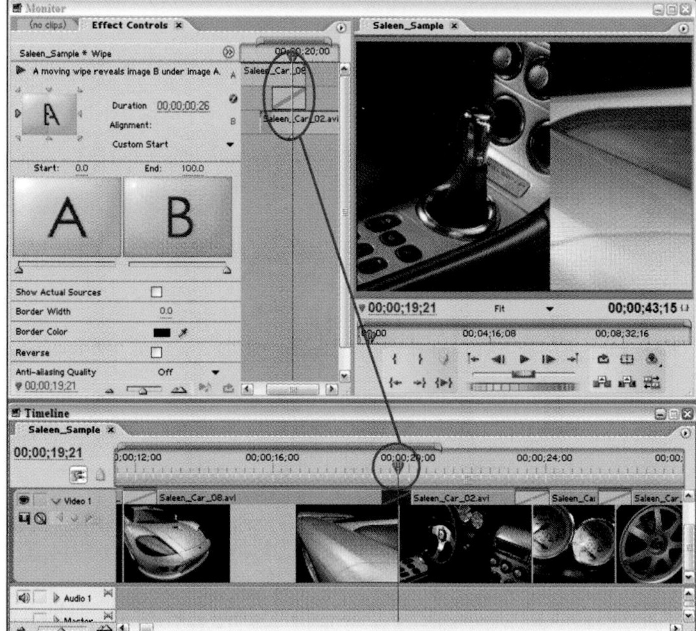

Figure 6.1 In Premiere Pro's single-track editing approach, small light purple transition "band-aids" connect adjacent clips on a single track in the timeline. When you click and select a transition, its properties and simulated AB roll appear in the Effect Controls window. Here, the selected transition is a wipe, as seen in the Program Monitor.

When you add a transition to media in the timeline, Premiere must render preview files for full-quality output of the transition instance. Red render bars appear over all instances of transitions until you render preview files by pressing Enter. Transitions on one or two DV clips should have no problem playing back in real time.

The Effects Window

The Effects window is where all your audio and video effects and transitions live. To access it, choose Window>Effects or click the Effects tab in the Project window. The window has four master folders:

- Audio Effects
- Audio Transitions
- Video Effects
- Video Transitions

Each contains subfolders in which effects or transitions are grouped by category. To find an effect, browse through the subfolders by twirling down their contents (see Figure 6.2) or use the Contains field at the top of the window to search by name. As you type in the Contains field, Premiere expands folders to show items matching the search criteria. As you type the word "dissolve," for example, Premiere first displays all transitions and effects with "d" in their names, then only those with "di," and so on until displaying on those with "dissolve" in their names. Deleting letters backs you up through the displays of search results.

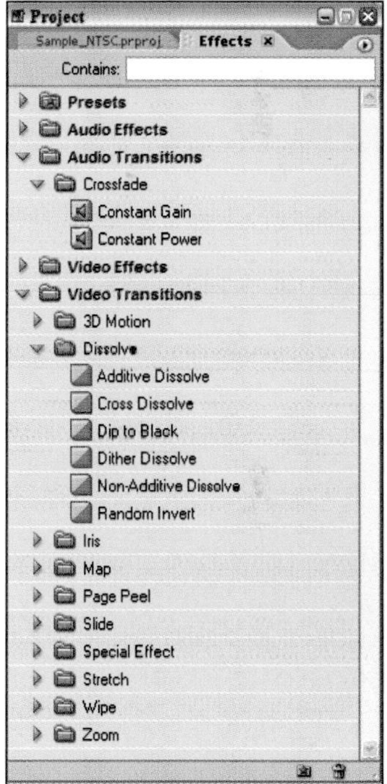

Figure 6.2 With both the Audio and Video Transitions folders expanded, you can see that your choice of audio transition boils down to two different fades. For video transitions, you have a lot more to choose from. Notice Constant Power and Cross Dissolve are the default transitions, as indicated by the red squares surrounding their icons.

As you browse through your transitions, one audio and one video transition will look slightly different as their icons are surrounded with red squares. These are your default transition. *Default transitions* are the transitions used for automated tasks and quick placement with the keyboard shortcuts. (Chapter 7, "Introduction to Effects," will discuss the contents of the Video and Audio Effects folders.)

Audio Transitions

The Audio Transitions folder contains a single subfolder called Crossfade, which contains two transitions: Constant Gain and Constant Power. Both transitions accommodate fading a clip up at its head, fading it down at its tail, and/or crossfading between two clips. The difference between Constant Gain and Constant Power is subtle but distinct. (See Figure 6.3.)

Constant Gain always fades in a straight, diagonal rising or falling direction. When using Constant Gain to fade your audio up at the head of a shot, the audio volume starts at 0% at frame 1 and reaches the 100% level at the end of the transition. Along the way, the volume (the gain) constantly rises in a uniform fashion, like a straight rising line.

Constant Power is a bit different. When fading up, Constant Power increases your audio from 0% to 100% in a steeper curve that quickly gets the volume up, then climbs more slowly to its 100% limit. Instead of being at 50% halfway through your transition, Constant Power would be closer to 75% and then it would slowly level off to 100% from there.

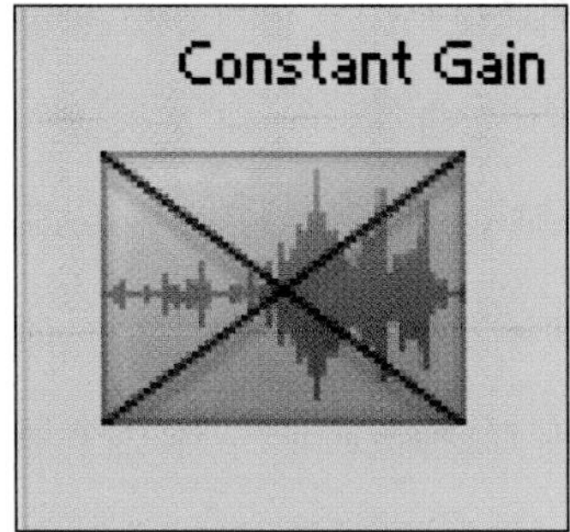

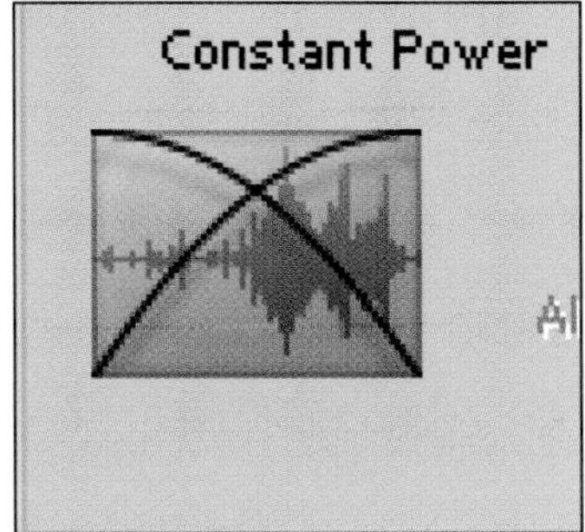

Figure 6.3 You can see the primary difference between the two audio transitions by comparing their icons: Constant Gain (left) increases volume uniformly, while Constant Power (right) adheres to more of a curve that rises faster to the full volume level.

Looking at the icon for each of these placed transitions will give you a good sense of how each works. For general fade purposes (fade in or out), I always use Constant Gain, which results in a progressive, simple fade. For cross-fades between two clips, I use Constant Power. With Constant Power transitioning two clips, instead of the audio dipping down halfway through the cross-dissolve the audio levels stay a bit higher and the sound level doesn't dip too low during the transition. In either case, you can quickly add the transition to your clips to fade their levels.

Video Transitions

The Video Transitions folder has ten subfolder categories:

- **3D Motion.** Contains transitions that have three-dimensional properties revealed over the course of the sequence. For example, a spinning cube with the first shot on one side and the second shot on a different side. (See Figure 6.4.)

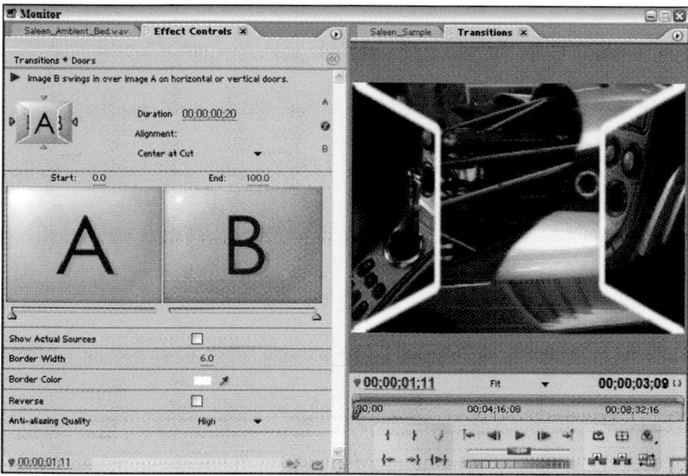

Figure 6.4 An example of a 3D Motion transition, the Doors transition opens or closes "doors" to reveal the incoming shot. Because the doors open or close, they allude to a third dimension or Z plane. You can add a border to the edge of the Doors effect and also anti-alias the border to make it more smooth.

- **Dissolve.** Contains methods of fading one shot into the other. This is the folder I draw from most often.
- **Iris.** Holds transitions that originate from an expanding centered shape, like the iris of a camera that dilates. (See Figure 6.5.)
- **Map.** Contains transitions that enable you to map certain image properties (luma and channel) to each other over the course of the transition. These transitions might be better termed as effects, because they overlap the two clips as opposed to creating a transition between the two. (See Figure 6.6.)

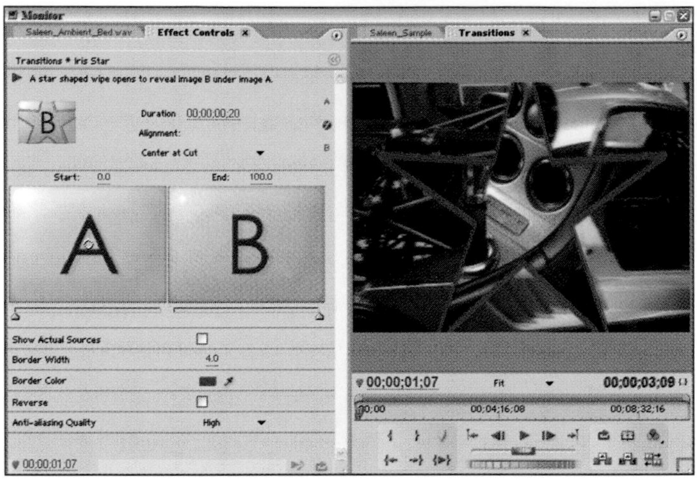

Figure 6.5 Using the Iris transitions you can pick from various shapes and have those shapes grow from nothing to reveal the incoming shot. Notice the description for this Iris Star transition in the top left of the Effect Controls window.

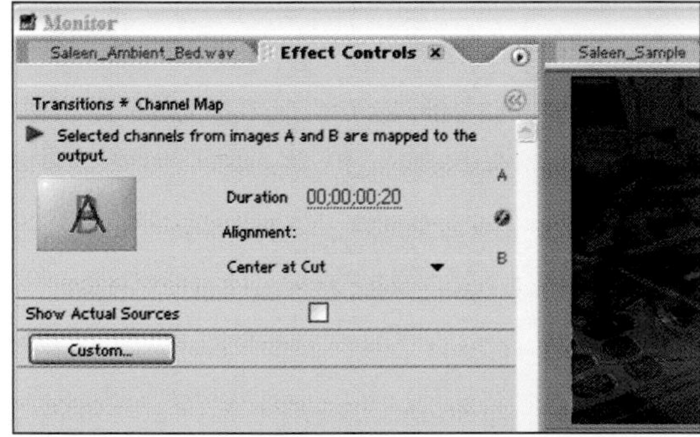

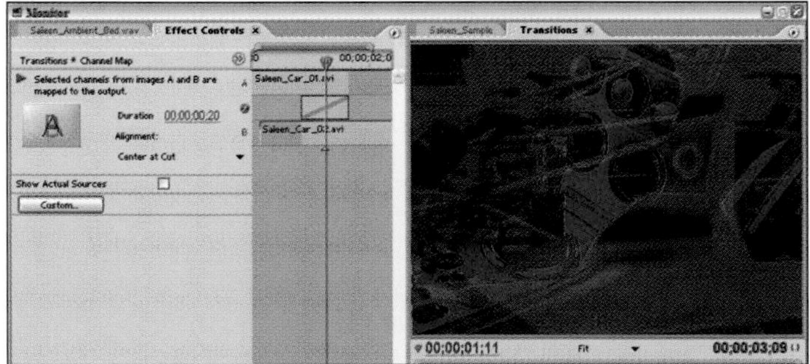

Figure 6.6 The Channel Map transition allows you to map specific color channels from one image to the channels of another image (top), causing them to show through. The result (bottom) can be an interesting effect, but not a useful transition.

- **Page Peel.** Includes transitions that peel away in different fashions, revealing another shot beneath.
- **Slide.** Holds transitions that slide one image on top of the other in various ways. There are also a number of band slides that look like strips of material that slide in separately and join together to make the new incoming shot.
- **Special Effect.** Contains more effect-like transitions. For example, Displace adds the image of the second shot to the first shot, not in a transitional way, but as an effect. Three-D maps the outgoing image to red and the incoming image to blue, like the effect of wearing red and blue 3D glasses. These are still considered transitions, because the effect requires two video sources. (See Figure 6.7.)

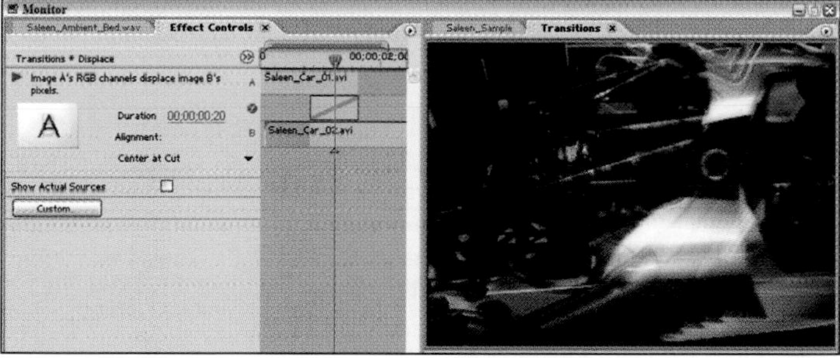

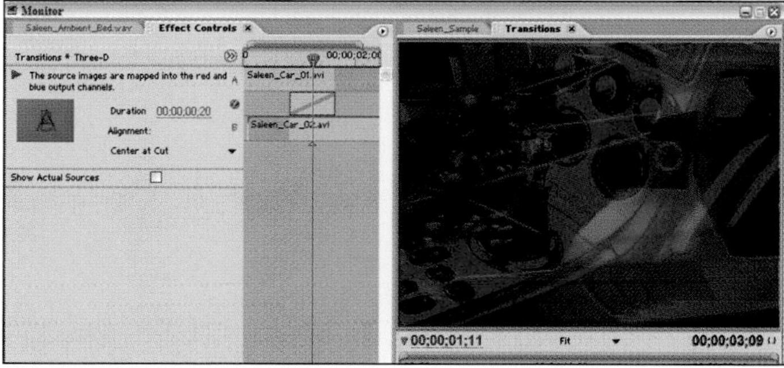

Figure 6.7 Displace (top) layers the two images, having the RGB color information of the outgoing clip A displace the pixels of the incoming clip B. The Three-D transition (bottom) produces a red/blue effect. In both cases these aren't really dynamic transitions, they are overlay effects.

- **Stretch.** Includes transitions in which the incoming images start at certain sizes and are stretched in different ways to reveal themselves.
- **Wipe.** Contains transitions that use the wiping technique of lines or shapes wiping in a set direction to reveal an incoming shot underneath. Wipes are another favorite of mine, because if you time a directional wipe with action that is moving in your shots, you can wipe with the action hiding the edit more efficiently.
- **Zoom.** Contains transitions that magnify into and out of your images as a means of hiding the cuts between the shots. Cross Zoom, for example, focuses in very tightly on your outgoing image, cuts to a close-up view of your incoming image, and quickly pulls back to reveal the full image. The result is quick zoom in and out where one shot becomes another.

While there are enough transitions here to get plenty of work done and have some creative choices, you can expand your transition options when you invest in a third-party capture card. Wedding and event videographers who need to have transitions with color, motion, and a bit more personality, for example, would benefit from more options than the standard transitions that come with Premiere Pro. Other editors, such as for film, TV, and music videos, and hobbyists certainly have enough transitions to choose from in Premiere Pro. Just be judicious in your selection of transitions, considering your audience and tone of the transition. A Star Iris Wipe might be flashier, for example, but perhaps a Cross Dissolve would better blend with your project's tone.

When editing in the timeline, if you reach the end of a shot that you would like to fade out or a cut where you want to apply a transition, it is only a keyboard shortcut away to add your default transition to the content at the current Edit Line position.

Default Transition

Out of the box, Premiere Pro's default video transition is Cross Dissolve, but perhaps you'd prefer another transition to be a keyboard shortcut away at all times. To choose or change the default transition, select the transition you want from the list in the Effects window. With the transition highlighted, choose Set Selected as Default Transition from the Effects window's wing menu (see Figure 6.8). The transition's icon now has a red border indicating it is assigned as your default. You can only have one audio and one video default transition.

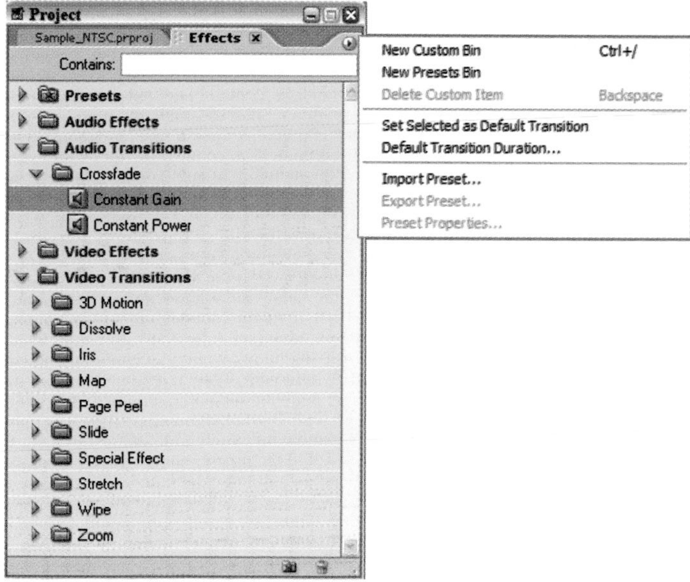

Figure 6.8 Set your default transition by selecting a transition in the folder and choosing Set Selected as Default Transition from the Effects window's wing menu.

You can quickly add the default audio and the default video transitions to the timeline using their keyboard shortcuts: Ctrl+D adds the default video transition, and Ctrl+Shift+D adds default audio transition. Once again, CTI position and targeted tracks are the keys to indicating where you want your transition added.

Default Durations

As discussed in Appendix D, "Workspaces and Preferences," you can set a default duration for your transitions while specifying your project's Preferences. Choose Edit>Preferences>General, then input the desired number of frames for Video Default Transition Duration and the desired number of seconds for Audio Default Transition Duration. (See Figure 6.9.) Whenever you add a transition to the timeline, it will automatically last the number of frames or seconds you specified.

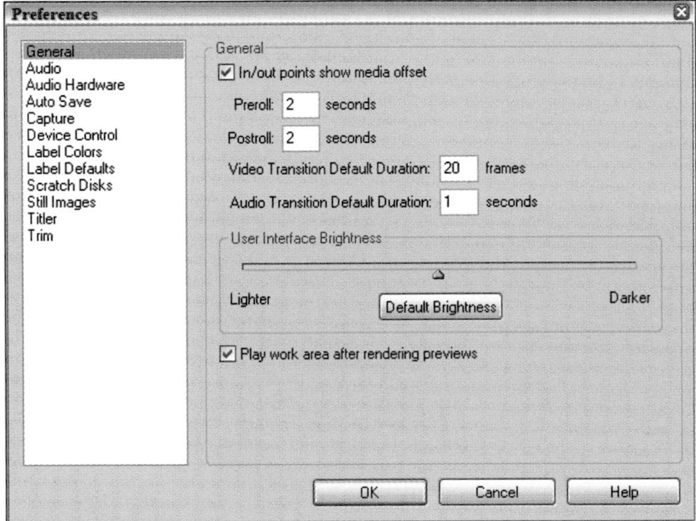

Figure 6.9 In the General Preferences dialog you can assign the default duration values for your video and audio transitions. Video transition durations are based on frames, while audio durations can be subframe-based. For example, 0.05 is a valid duration for a tiny audio transition.

If you need to change the setting while you work, choose Default Transition Duration from the Effects window's wing menu. When I am adding a lot of audio transitions between clips so that there are no straight cuts, for example, I usually shorten the Audio Transition Default Duration to a bit less than one second. Sometimes a 0.10 second transition gets rid of the abrupt pop that exists when one audio clip cuts directly to the next. For fading both audio and video clips in and out, I find one second is usually enough, but that's simply a matter of timing, tempo, and personal taste.

Custom Bins

If you find that you use a specific group of transitions and you hate navigating to them every time, you can create a new bin in the Effects window to hold your favorites. Choose New Custom Bin from the wing menu, or click the folder-shaped icon in the lower-right of the window.

Now you can drag the transitions or filters that you use most into the custom bin and rename it accordingly. Note that the transitions or effects do not move from their normal resting place; instead, Premiere places a shortcut to them in the custom folder for easy access. I recommend creating one custom bin for your favorite transitions and another for your favorite effects. Once you have your favorites organized for easy access, you're ready to drag and drop them into the timeline.

Dragging and Dropping Transitions

You can place transitions in the timeline in three different ways:

- Starting at the cut
- Ending at the cut
- Centered at the cut

The method used depends on the surrounding media and the mouse position when you release the transition.

Adding Transitions to a Single Clip

When you are working with a single clip, such as when you fade up a clip from black, you'll want to use the starting or ending at the cut methods. Starting at the cut means that when you drop a transition into the timeline, the transition will start from the cut point at which you inserted it.

For example, you want your project's first clip to fade up from black, so you need a transition to start at the cut—at the start of that initial clip (see Figure 6.10). Grab the Cross Dissolve (Video Transitions/Dissolve), and drag it to the head of that clip. Because there is no adjoining media to the left of the first clip, you see a blue line on the left, indicating the transition's start, and the transition icon to the right, indicating where the transition occurs. Notice the darkened area that appears when you hold the transition over the head of the shot. This shows you the transition's duration. Release the mouse to add the Cross Dissolve to the clip. The clip will now have the transition "band-aid" covering its head.

Figure 6.10 At left, a single-sided transition is being added to the head of the clip. Because there is no material before the shot, the cursor displays the transition icon for starting at the cut. The darkened overlay area represents the content that the transition will cover. On the right, you can see the results.

Ending at the cut is opposite of starting at the cut. To fade a clip out, for example, drag the transition to the right edge of the last clip (see Figure 6.11). This time the blue line is on the right and the transition icon on the left, indicating the transition ends at the cut point onto which you drop the transition.

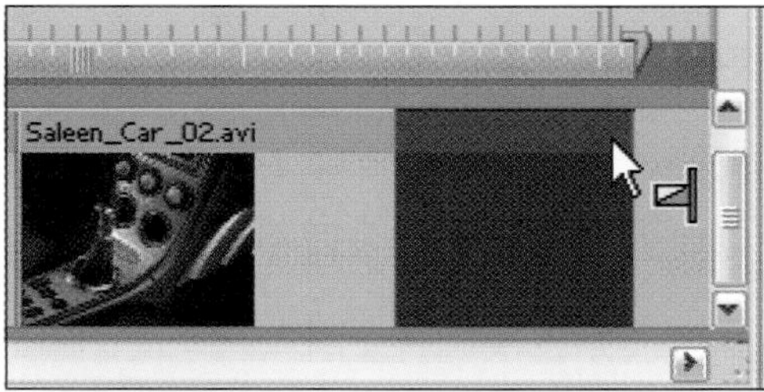

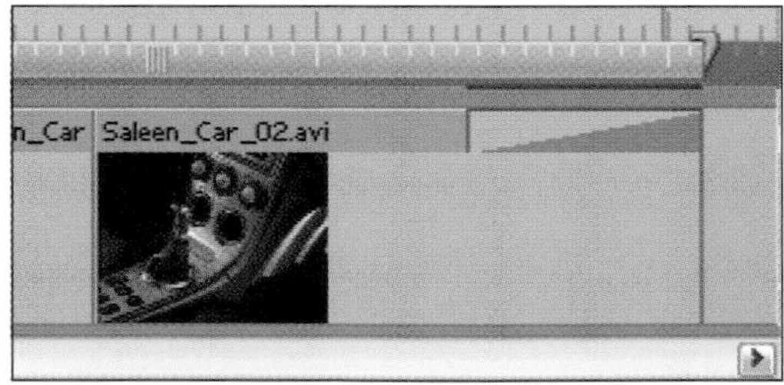

Figure 6.11 The opposite of Figure 6.10, this transition ends at the cut. The clip will fade down to the black empty space of the track.

Remember, to have a transition starting or ending at the cut, you cannot have any adjoining material near the clip. Any material directly to the left or right of the clip will be incorporated in the transition. For a clean starting or ending transition from or to black, for example, you need at least a one-frame gap of empty space to ensure the transition does not connect material.

Adding Transitions Between Two Shots

To create a balanced transition between two shots, center the transition at the cut. Centering is an option only when you are cutting between two shots. When you drag a transition over the cut point between two shots and hold the mouse directly over the center of the cut, the blue line appears in the middle of the transition icon. This means that the transition will have half of its duration on one side of the cut and half on the other. (See Figure 6.12.)

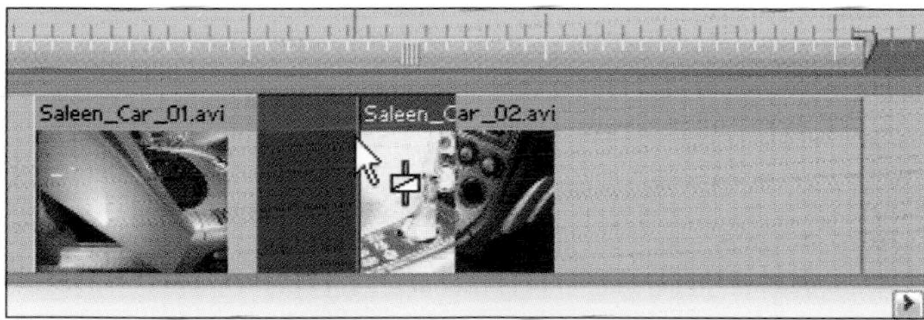

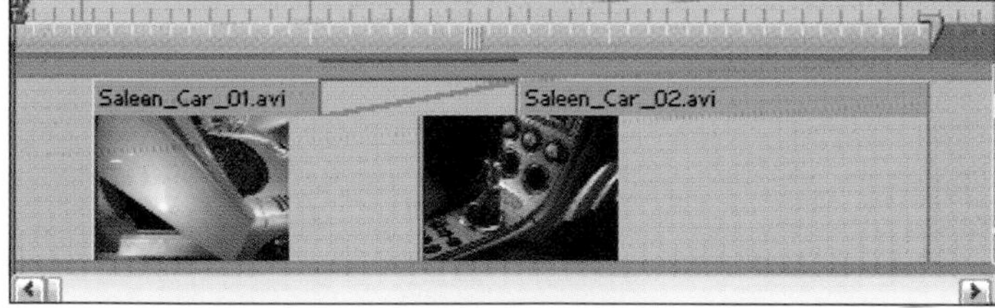

Figure 6.12 Drag and drop a transition directly over the cut point between two clips for a balanced, centered transition that connects the two shots.

Premiere uses an equal number of frames from each shot to display the transition properly. If you have a 30-frame transition centered on the cut between shots 1 and 2, Premiere needs 15 additional frames from the head of shot 2 and 15 frames from the tail of shot 1. If you only had 10 frames extra from shot 2, Premiere adjusts the transition duration to 20 frames and uses 10 extra frames from each shot to ensure the transition remains centered.

Sometimes you don't want or need such perfect symmetry in your transition, however, which brings us back to the techniques of starting and ending at the cut with two adjacent clips.

Drag a transition to the left side of a cut between two shots to get the icon for a transition that ends on the cut (see Figure 6.13). The current cut point between the shots will be the end of the transition when you add it to the timeline. Premiere adds additional material from the second shot so that the transition occurs properly. If you had a 30-frame transition ending on the cut from shot 1 to shot 2, for example, Premiere needs an additional 30 frames from the head of shot 2 for the transition to display properly. If there is not enough material, say you only had 20 frames, then Premiere assigns the transitions duration to be 20 frames instead.

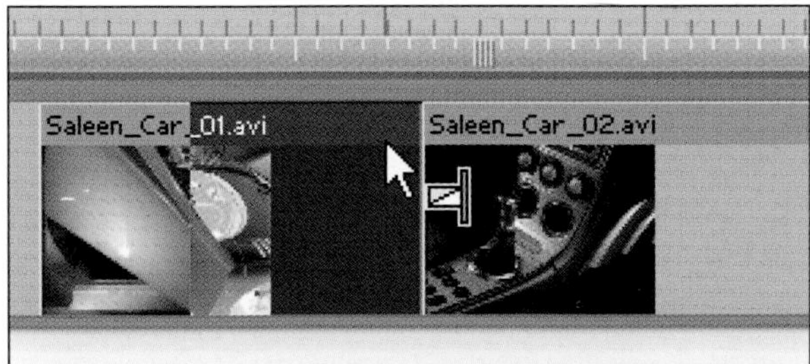

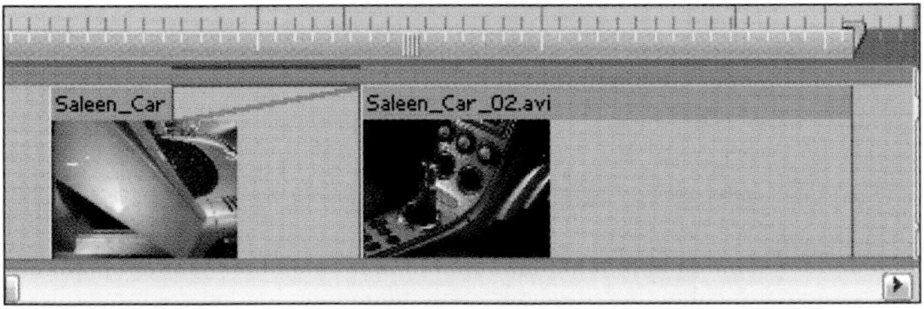

Figure 6.13 When you drag and drop a transition slightly to the left of the cut, you see the ending at the cut icon (top). The transition will be complete at the current cut point with the image entirely focused on the incoming shot.

Drag just to the right of the cut between shots 1 and 2 to get the icon for a transition that starts on the cut (see Figure 6.14). Using the default duration from the previous example, the transition would need 30 additional frames of tail material from shot 1 to start at the cut and transition to shot 2. Again, if fewer frames are available, Premiere will shorten the transition's duration accordingly.

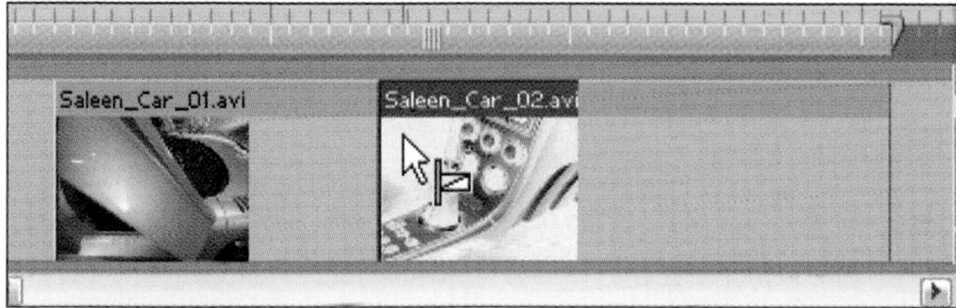

Figure 6.14 When you drag and drop just to the right of the cut between two clips, you see the icon for a transition that starts at the cut. With audio clips, transition placement functions the exact same way.

At some zoom magnifications, you may not have enough space to drag to the left or right of the cut to place a starting or ending at the cut transition. If you are zoomed out such that a few pixels are a few seconds, you will be able to target the center of the cut only. Not to worry, the Effect Controls window can very easily adjust the alignment of a transition that has already been placed.

Keyboard Shortcuts and Adding Your Default Transitions

If all this dragging and dropping of transitions has your mouse a bit tired, you can assign your default transitions to the timeline with a few simple keystrokes: Ctrl+D to add a video transition, Ctrl+Shift+D to add an audio transition.

To assign a default transition to the timeline, you must first target a track then identify the location of placement using the position of the Edit Line.

For a transition to be properly added, the Edit Line must be resting over clip content on the targeted track and in close proximity to or exactly at a cut point. You can apply default transitions to both audio and video clips in only three basic ways:

- Starting at the cut at the single-sided head of a clip
- Ending at the cut at the single-sided tail of a clip
- Centered at the cut between two adjacent clips

Using the keyboard shortcut to advance to the next edit point (Page Up and Page Down), you can quickly navigate to a cut point then press Ctrl+D to add a video transition or Ctrl+Shift+D to add an audio transition. Just pay attention to which tracks are targeted and where the Edit Line rests. Now that you know how to position transitions, take a look at the Effect Controls window where you can adjust transitions that are already in the timeline.

Effect Controls Window

You can adjust and assign all your effect and transition parameters in the Effect Controls window (see Figure 6.15). Double-click on a transition icon in the Timeline window, and the selected transition opens in the Effect Controls window for adjustments. You can also reach the Effect Controls window by choosing Windows>Effect Controls or by clicking the Effect Controls tab in the Monitor window.

The Effect Controls window is defined by two distinct areas: The left area is the Settings area and right area is the Navigation and Keyframe (for effects) area.

The Settings area (see Figure 6.16) displays the name of the sequence you are working in and the type of transition that is open. A description of the transition appears below with a Preview Play button. Click it to loop a thumbnail playback of the applied transition. By default, the Thumbnail Preview window shows only icons to preview the transition. To see what the video in the timeline looks like, you must click on the Show Actual Sources check box. The Duration hot text box enables you to dynamically scrub the value to either increase or decrease the duration of the transition. In the Alignment field, you choose a method of alignment from the drop-down list: Start at Cut, End at Cut, or Center at Cut. All three respect the original cut point that was assigned to your clips. The large Start and End preview windows allow you to customize the percentage value for which your transition will start from and end at, as well as reveal the flow of the transition, the A roll (start) to B roll (end) flow.

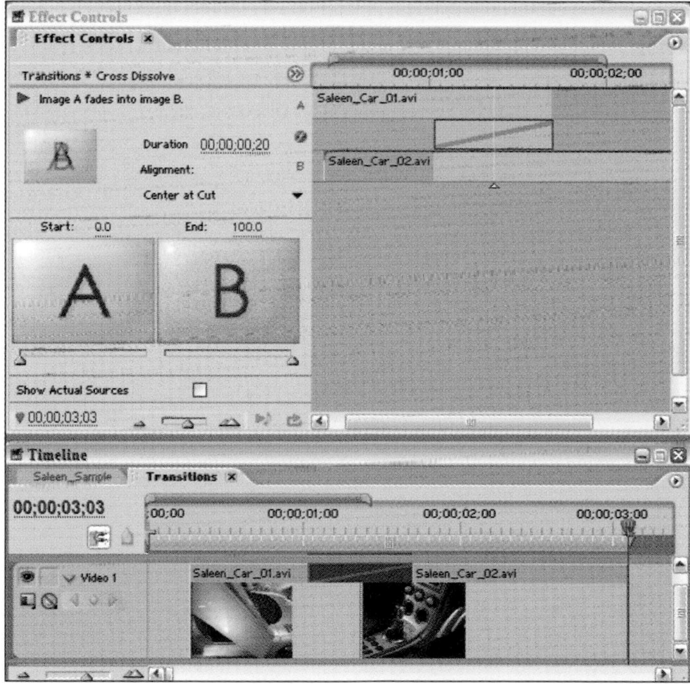

Figure 6.15 With a transition selected in the timeline, the Effect Controls window reveals transition settings, parameters, and an AB roll track preview. The outgoing clip in the transition, Saleen_Car_01, appears on track A, and the incoming clip, Saleen_Car_02, appears on track B. The transition is the center track area.

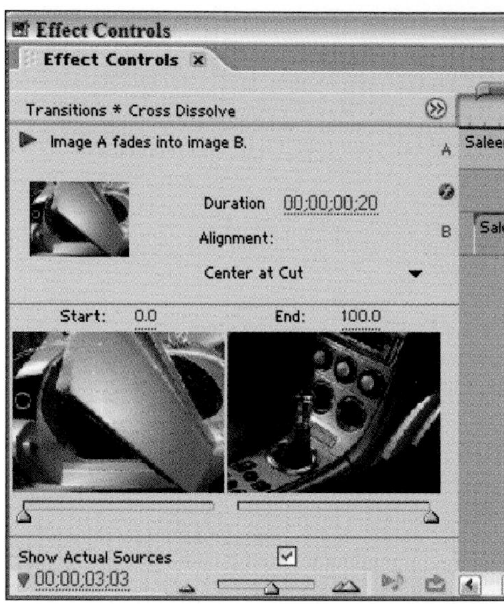

Figure 6.16 When you select a transition, the Settings area of the Effect Controls window displays the sequence and transition names, a short description of the transition, previews, settings for Duration and Alignment, as well as the option to show the actual source frames.

In the Navigation area to the right (see Figure 6.17), you get to see a display of your transition and the material it covers in an AB editing mode. The clip on the top is A (note the icon), B is the bottom track and the transition is in the middle. The bright colored portion of the clips signifies parts of the clips that are used and visible when playing back in the Timeline window. Additional unused material, if any, is displayed as darkened material either after the transition on track A or before the transition on track B. Being able to see if there is additional material gives you the option of knowing which adjustments you can make to the transition.

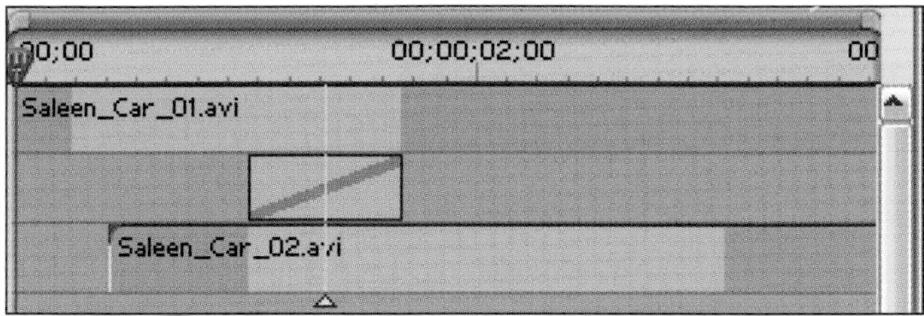

Figure 6.17 The entire Saleen_Car_01 clip is on the A track in the Navigation and Keyframe area of the Effect Controls window. Only the light blue portion of the clip, however, will be visible in the sequence. The dark blue areas reflect additional clip material that is beyond the timeline frame boundaries of the used instance. With this view you can easily determine whether you have extra material to draw from when extending or contracting your clip material.

The viewing area bar allows you to zoom in and out and navigate to different sections of your material. You can scrub the CTI from either the timeline or the Navigation area of the Effect Controls window. To make adjustments to your transition and clip material, click, drag, and move the transition or clip edges using the various editing tools that reveal themselves depending on where you hold your mouse (see Figure 6.18).

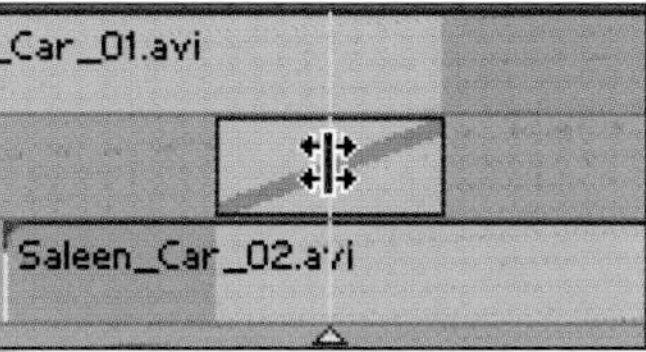

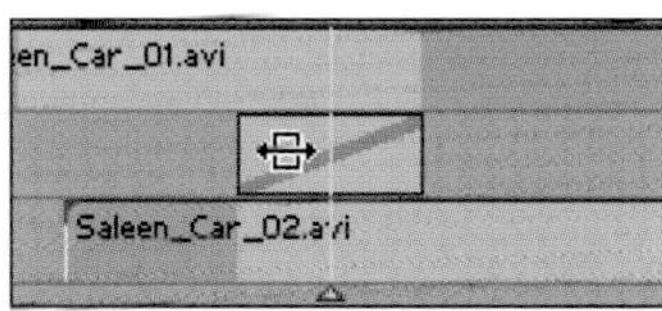

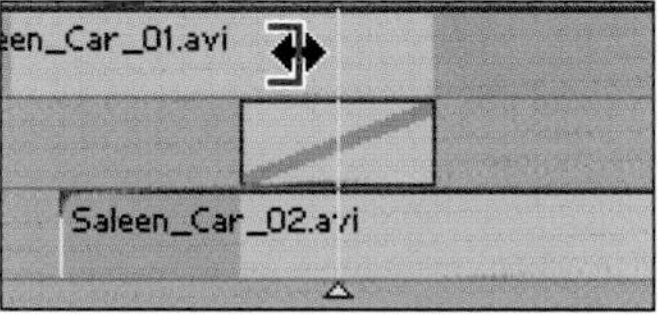

Figure 6.18 Hold your mouse over the exact cut point of the two clips to get the Rolling Edit tool (top), which enables you to roll the edit point between the two clips while also sliding the entire transition. Hold your mouse over the transition to get the Slide tool (middle), which allows you to preserve the cut point of the clips, but slide the transition in its exact duration to a different timeline position. Hold over either clip near the cut point to get the Ripple Edit tool (bottom), with which you can ripple edit the clip material, preserving the transition and the adjacent relationship of the clips.

Adjusting Your Transitions in the Effect Controls Window

The white line in the middle of the tracks (see Figure 6.19) signifies the original physical cut point between the two clips. If you toggle between Start at Cut, End at Cut, and Center at Cut, notice how the alignment of the transition is displayed in accordance with the cut point. To change your cut point, you can roll the white Edit Line back and forth. To properly change the cut point, hold the mouse over the Edit Line so that the cursor appears as the Rolling Edit tool. The Edit Line will update in the Timeline window and a two-up display in the Program Monitor will reveal your updating cut point frames. When you roll the Edit Line, it's also nice to see that the duration and alignment of the transition is preserved. While you roll your edit, the two-up display in the Program Monitor reveals the last frame of your A roll on the left and the first frame of your B roll on the right.

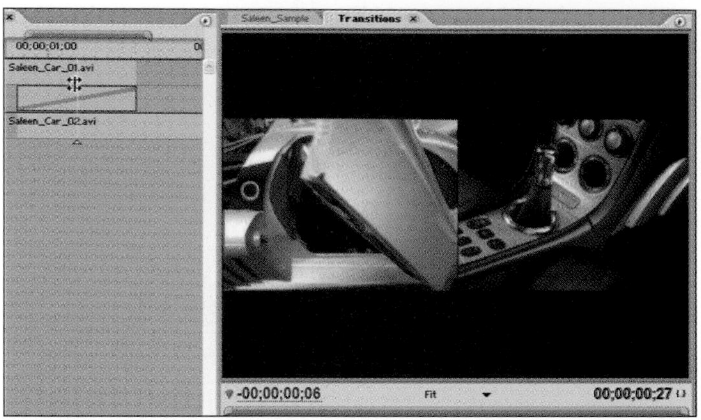

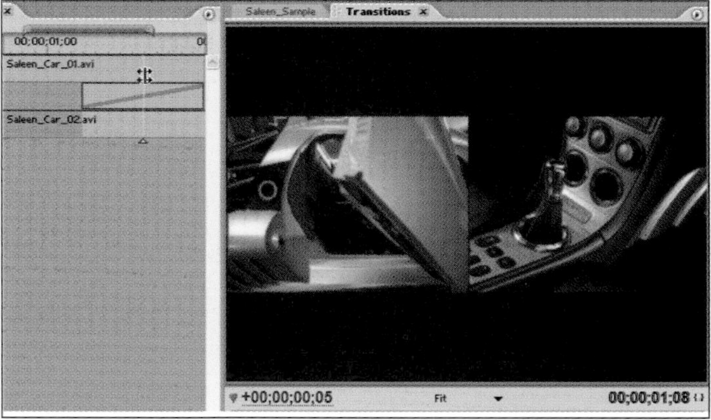

Figure 6.19 When you roll the edit point in the Transition view mode of the Effect Controls window, the Program Monitor provides a two-up display of the new cut point, showing the outgoing frame on the left and incoming frame on the right. The frame count number in the bottom left corner of the Program Monitor tells you how many frames you have moved the edit.

To update the position of the transition but preserve the original cut point, hold the mouse over the boundary of the transition so that the Slide tool icon appears. Now, slide the transition back and forth to move its entire position and preserve its duration. The two-up display shows the same last frame of A and first frame of B (see Figure 6.20).

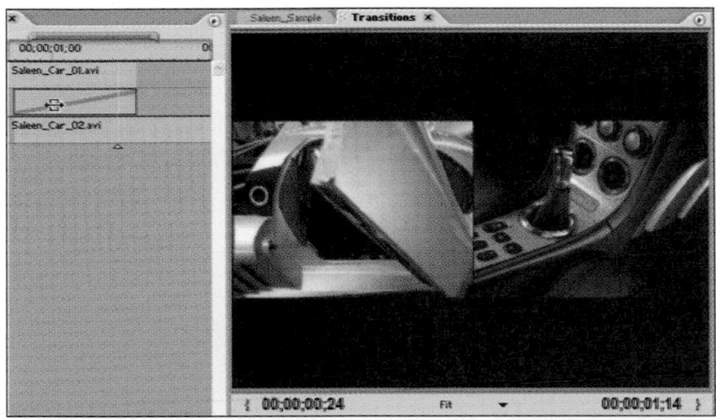

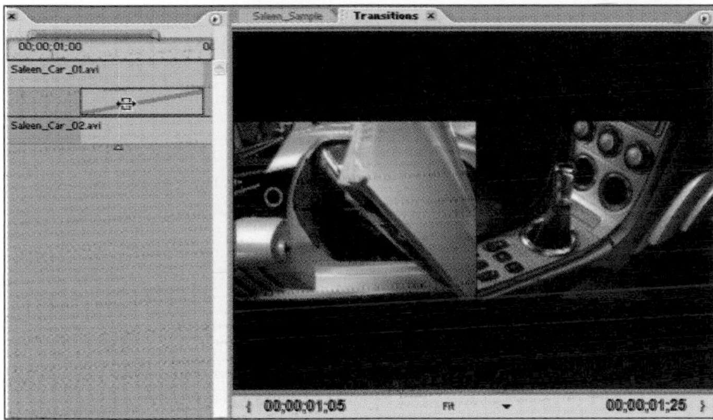

Figure 6.20 When you slide the transition itself, you get another two-up display that shows the first frame from the outgoing shot to be included in the transition on the left and the last frame of the incoming shot to be included on the right. The timecode feedback at the bottom of the Program Monitor shows the exact frame position of the sliding transition's In and Out points.

To extend either edge of the transition to make it longer or shorter, you need to hold the mouse over the edge of the transition so that you get the Edge Trim tool. Now, click and drag left or right to increase or reduce the duration of the transition. Dragging the right edge moves the incoming point from the B roll, so the right side of the two-up in the Program Monitor updates as you trim. Dragging the left edge updates the last frame of the A roll, so the left side of the Program Monitor's two-up updates.

To make ripple edits to clips under a transition, hold the mouse a tiny bit further inside the edge of the clip on A or B. Once you see the Thick Ripple Edit tool (see Figure 6.21), any adjustment will ripple that clip's In or Out point, thus shifting all tracks in the timeline left or right appropriately. The two-up display will reveal the edge frame that is being adjusted, A on the left and B on the right.

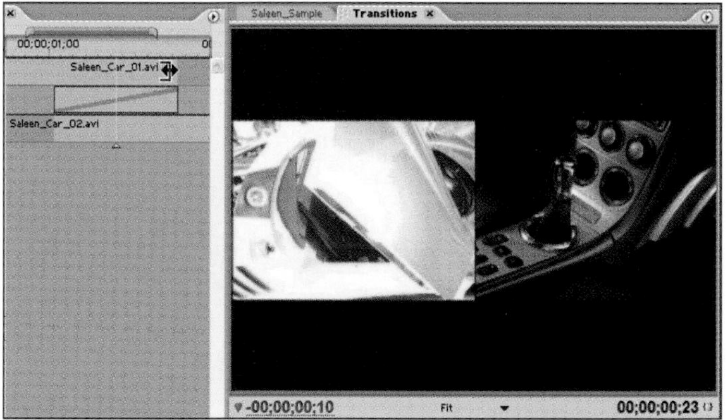

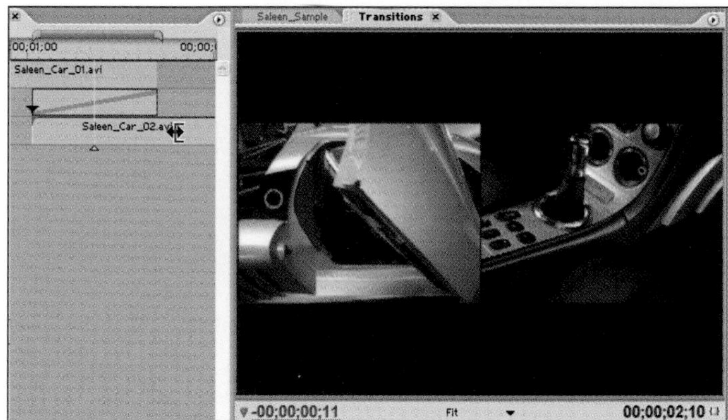

Figure 6.21 By dragging the outgoing shot to the right, I reduced its overall duration by 10 frames (as shown in the feedback of the top image's Program Monitor). In the image on the bottom, I added 11 frames of material by sliding the B clip to the right. Notice how you can snap the head of the source material to the cut point, and Premiere indicates that there is no additional material to the left of the clip's head (see the dog ear).

The power of all these tools and the strength of Premiere Pro's new transition architecture is that although a transition may cover an edit point, you can still make editing adjustments to that point.

For a video clip overview of how to adjust transition material in the Effect Control window, see the video tutorial, "Adjusting Transitions in the Effect Controls Window" in the Fundamentals section on the accompanying DVD.

Timeline Adjustments

Outside of the Effect Controls window you can still make adjustments to transitions in the Timeline window. If the track is collapsed, you only will be able to edge trim the duration of the transition and slide it to a different position between the clips.

When the track is expanded, the transition reveals itself in the upper portion of the track with the cut point of the clips below. To make modifications to the transition, click and adjust within the boundary of the transition band-aid. To make adjustments to the clip (ripple and rolling edits), select the appropriate tool or shortcut modifier then click and drag below the transition in the clip cut point area.

Although you don't lose functionality in the timeline adjustments, you do not get to see the additional available material. So if you are dragging a transition edge in the timeline and it won't go any further, double-click the transition and look in the Effect Controls window. You will find that there is no additional material to make up for the adjustment you want to apply.

Things to Remember

When you add a transition between two clips, you are defining a method through which one shot moves into another. Your transitions can start at, end at, or be centered on a cut point, plus they can be applied to all tracks. If there is content on Video 3 that can be enhanced by transitioning to another, then by all means exploit that. The ability to have six titles fading one into the other and not have them populate two separate tracks (as in former versions of Premiere) is an excellent preservation of timeline real estate.

Although you don't need to completely understand all the adjustment tools in the Effect Controls window just yet, I encourage you to watch the video clip and experiment with some adjustments. While you play, be sure to pay attention to the power and importance of the Ripple Edit tool, which is used to edge trim clip material when a transition is joining two clips together.

In the next chapter, you will explore the Effect Controls window in a different context: effect adjustments.

CHAPTER

7

Introduction to Effects

Working with Premiere Pro's many effects is similar to working with transitions. Like transitions, Premiere's Standard effects are grouped by type in the Effects window. As you did with transitions, you add Standard effects to media by dragging them from the Effects window and dropping them onto clips in the timeline. To fine-tune your effects, you use the Effect Controls window (see Figure 7.1). That's when Premiere Pro's power becomes evident.

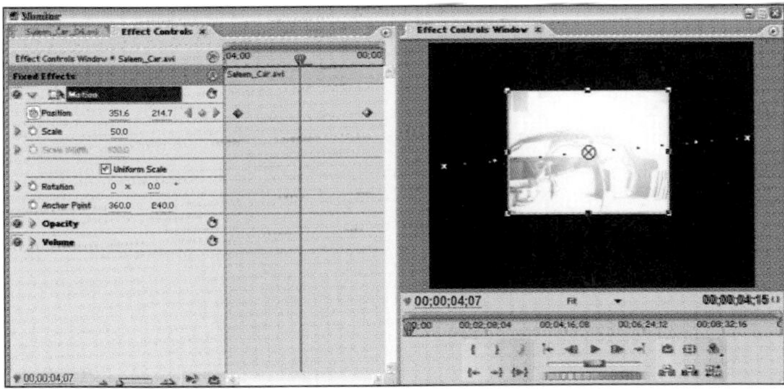

Figure 7.1 When a clip is selected from the timeline, the Effect Controls window provides its effect settings for adjustment. The Program Monitor displays a keyframed motion path that was assigned in the Effect Controls window.

If you're familiar with Adobe After Effects, the Effect Controls window's design and implementation may seem familiar to you. In designing Premiere Pro, Adobe tried to bridge the few gaps between After Effects and Premiere. Because Adobe designed a number of Premiere Pro features similar to their After Effects counterparts, if you're familiar with one program, you will be comfortable with effect work in both.

Standard Effects and Fixed Effects

Before you dive too deep into adjusting effects in the Effect Controls window, you need to understand the two types of effects you can adjust: Standard effects and Fixed effects.

Standard effects are the effects that Premiere provides in the Effects window's folders. You must manually apply them to your clips by dragging and dropping. *Fixed effects* are the basic properties that a clip has by default when it is placed on a track in the timeline. Video clips have two Fixed effects: Motion and Opacity. Audio clips have one: Volume. (See Figure 7.2.)

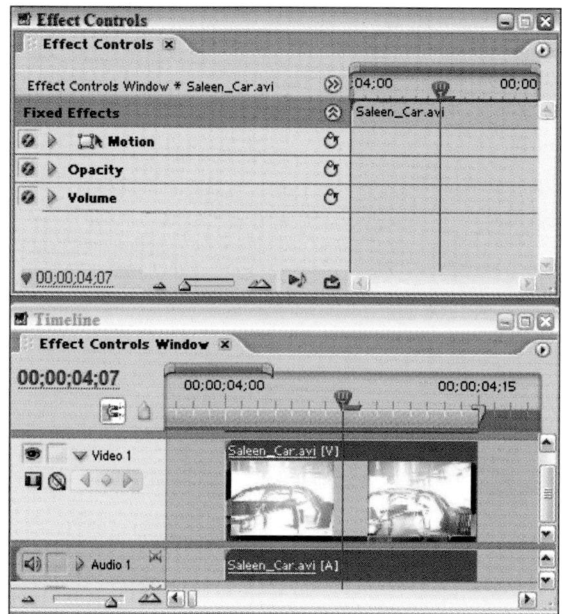

Figure 7.2 The selected clip has linked audio and video, so the three Fixed Effects—Motion, Opacity, and Volume—are immediately adjustable in the Effect Controls window. Notice how the name of the selected clip and the open sequence is visible in the Effect Controls window, as well as a display of the clip in the area to the right.

Video Fixed Effects: Motion

When you add a video clip in the timeline, you are placing it over a black, empty frame of space, whose size is defined by your Project Settings. You can use the Motion Fixed effect to reduce, enlarge, or move your clip within that frame of space. Combine the Motion effect with keyframes and you can pan and zoom around an image. The basic Motion parameters are:

- **Position.** The physical location of the image inside or outside the frame. You can adjust the clip's X axis value, which moves it right or left, and Y axis value, which moves it up or down. To "hide" a portion of your clip, adjust Position so part of the clip is outside the boundary of the frame. Only the portion within the frame boundary will be visible. (See Figure 7.3.)

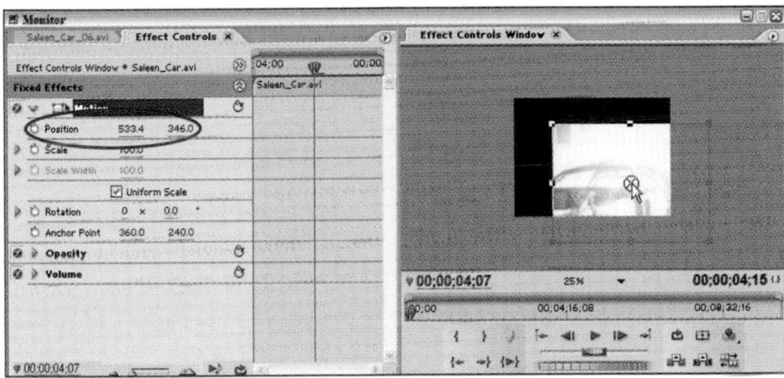

Figure 7.3 Clicking and dragging the clip updates its Position value in the Effect Controls window. You can also modify the X and Y values directly. With the Monitor set to 25% view, you can see the visible frame area (black square) and the boundary of the clip being re-positioned (wire-frame).

- **Scale.** The overall size of your selected clip. 100% is the normal default value. You can adjust the Scale Height and Scale Width of a clip separately if you click off the check box for Uniform Scale. Leaving Uniform Scale checked ensures that all scaling adjustments are equal with the height and width. (See Figure 7.4.)

Keyframing is a technique for which you assign changes in values to effect parameters at specific frames, called *keyframes*, in a clip. The job of the keyframes is to identify specific effect values at exact frames within the boundary of clip. For example, you set the first frame of your clip as a keyframe with the Scale effect set to 100%, and you set the last frame of the clip as a keyframe with Scale set to 200%. When Premiere plays back this clip, it dynamically increases the clip's scale from 100% to 200% over the duration of the clip, so the clip seems to smoothly zoom from 100% to 200%.

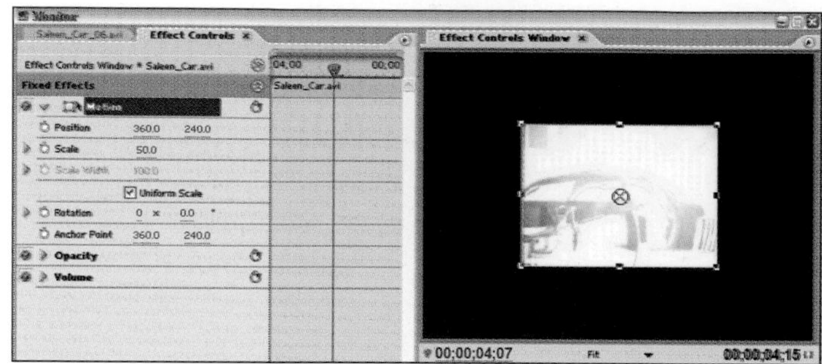

Figure 7.4 When you adjust the scale of your clip you can adjust the Height, the Width, or both together (Uniform). Here a 50% uniform scale adjustment results in the clip being half the size of its normal scale.

- **Rotation.** Defines the number of times (the left hot text) and angle at which (right hot text) a clip spins. If keyframing is not turned on, you can change the rotation angle. To make your image rotate you must turn keyframing on and set at least two keyframes with different Rotation values. The clip will spin from the first keyframe's Rotation setting to the second's. (See Figure 7.5.)

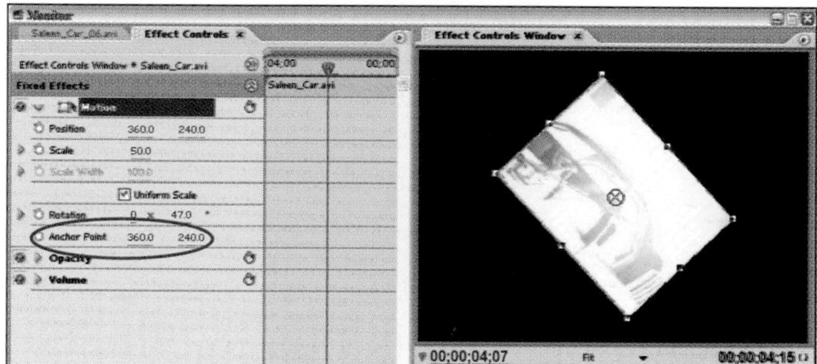

Figure 7.5 With the scale still at 50% it's easy to see a rotation adjustment applied to the clip. Here the Rotation value is 0 x 47. The first value reflects the number of rotations, the second value defines the angle.

- **Anchor Point.** The spot at which you choose to center your motion adjustments. Think of the Anchor Point as a tack through your image. If you move the Anchor Point to the bottom right corner, any rotation would spin from the corner, not the center of the image. (See Figure 7.6.)

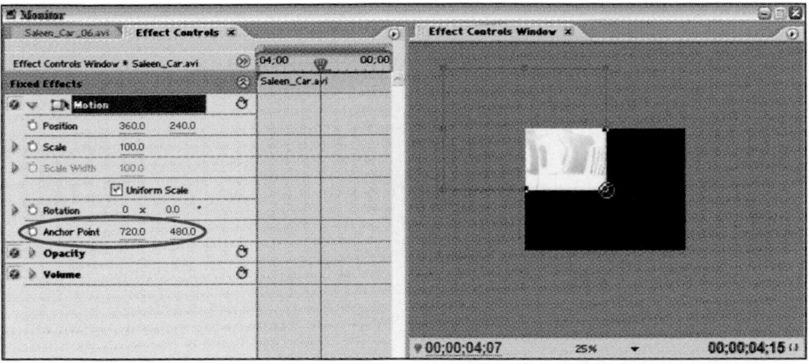

Figure 7.6 The anchor point here is defined as the lower-right corner of the frame, which has an exact coordinate value of 720×480. The Anchor Point defines the point where effects and adjusts will apply symmetrically. If you were to apply rotation with this Anchor Point, the clip would spin and rotate around the lower-right corner.

You can adjust the parameters for Motion, and other Fixed effects, in the Effect Controls window (more on this coming up).

Video Fixed Effects: Opacity

The Opacity effect enables you to adjust the transparency of a clip so that you can see through it to varying degrees. In previous versions, Opacity was used to fade up titles, graphics, stills, and video clips on any track other than Video 1. Because Premiere Pro can use transitions on all tracks to fade in and out, you can now use Opacity for custom fades and overall opacity adjustments. (See Figure 7.7.)

Audio Fixed Effects: Volume

The single Fixed effect for audio clips is Volume, which has two parameters: Level and Bypass. Level adjusts the actual level of your audio clip either increasing it or decreasing it. Bypass enables you to turn off your level adjustments and use the default volume of the audio clip.

Adjusting an audio clip's Volume parameters affects the dB rating of the clip instance in the timeline. When keyframing is turned off, you are adjusting the overall volume of the entire clip. Turn keyframing on to dynamically fade up and fade down the volume levels of your audio clip. (See Figure 7.8.)

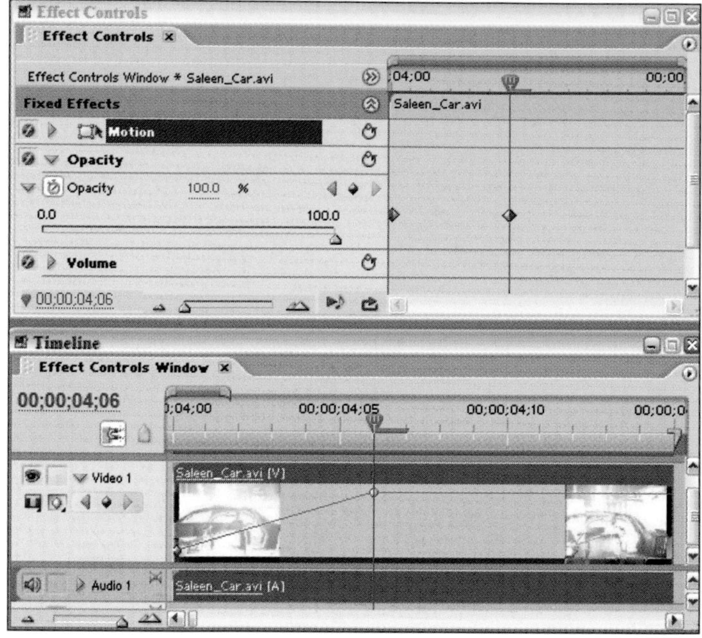

Figure 7.7 The two opacity keyframes assigned in the Effect Controls window are also visible in the timeline. Notice how the timeline keyframes have height positions that reflect their value going from 0 to 100% (a fade in), while the keyframes in the Effect Controls window are static on a single line. The keyframe value underneath the Edit Line in the Effect Controls window has a value of 100. That is the same keyframe and Edit Line position as in the timeline.

Figure 7.8 With the Edit Line on top of the first volume keyframe position, you can see that the start volume level is –oodB, which is no sound at all. The second keyframe is at –0dB, which is the default normal level. This is a simple volume fade. To bypass any keyframed fade and play the audio at its original volume, you can turn on the Bypass Volume parameter.

As you may remember, you can modify a clip's gain before adding it to the timeline. Because clip gain is separate from clip volume, you will not see an adjustment to the displayed clip volume if you have adjusted the clip gain.

Audio Standard Effects

The Audio Effects master folder in the Effects window contains separate Mono, Stereo, and 5.1 subfolders, all of which contain the same Standard effects, customized by channel type. When adding these effects to your timeline, be sure to use the proper audio channel type. For example, mono clips would need Mono effects, stereo clips need effects from the Stereo folder, and 5.1 clips need those from the 5.1 folder. If you are ever unable to drop an audio effect on a clip, most likely you are trying to add an effect type that doesn't match the clip type.

The Effect Controls Window

In the last chapter, you learned the power of the Effect Controls window for adjusting transitions. That window takes on a different look and feel, however, when you adjust and manipulate clip effects. To start customizing your effect parameters, choose Window>Effect Controls. When you select a clip in the timeline, the left side of the Effect Controls window lists the clip's Fixed and Standard effects and their parameters. The effects' associated keyframes appear on the right of the window in a timeline view. Only when a clip is selected can you make adjustments to the effect parameters in the Effect Controls window.

Depending on your preference, you can dock the Effect Controls window in the Project window or Source Monitor, or can leave It to float free as its own window. To move from one window state to the other, click and drag the Effect Controls window by its tab.

Effect Listings

Each effect listing has a twirl down triangle that enables you to expand the listing to reveal the effect's parameters or collapse it to view only the effect's name, on/off toggle, Reset button, and Direct Manipulation icon. (See Figure 7.9.)

The effect on/off toggle is at the far left of each listing. When the F is visible, the settings assigned within the effect will be applied to the selected clip. Click the F to turn off the effect for the selected clip. Turning an effect off deactivates it, but does not delete its parameters. This is useful when you're trying out multiple effects on the same clip. Disabling an effect also can improve real-time playback.

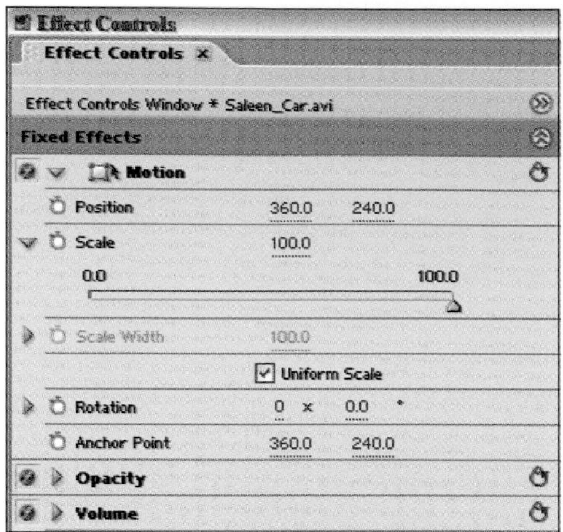

Figure 7.9 Twirling down the name of the effect reveals its effect parameters. Twirling down a parameter reveals, in most cases, an adjustment slider. To turn on keyframing for an individual parameter, click on the keyframe stopwatch for the parameter you want to adjust.

On the opposite edge of the effect listing you'll find the Reset button. Click it to return the effect's parameters to their original state. Unfortunately, you cannot reset individual parameters, only the entire listing. Use Reset with caution on effects with multiple parameters: You can lose a lot of work very quickly. The Undo command may be a better choice.

Some effects, such as Motion, have the Direct Manipulation icon (a square with a mouse pointer next to it) before their names (see Figure 7.10). Click on the effect name and the Program Monitor will display visible handles for you to grab and adjust. These handles directly manipulate a few specific parameters of the selected effect.

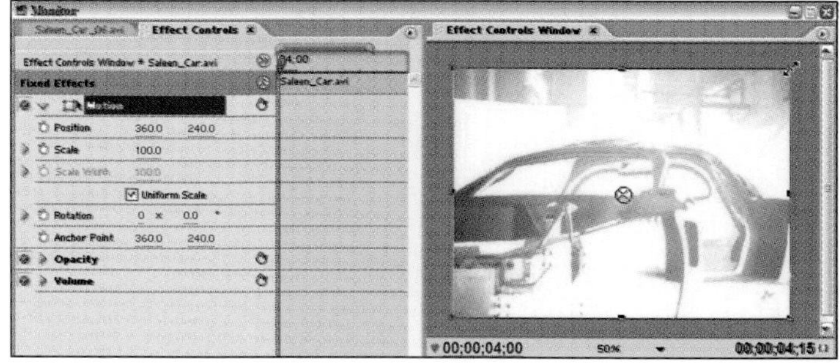

Figure 7.10 With direct manipulation turned on, you can click and drag from one of the corner handles to scale the selected clip. All your adjustments are dynamically updated into the settings area of the Effect Controls window.

Effect Parameters

To access an effect's parameters from the Effect Controls window, twirl down the effect's listing. To the left of each parameter name is the Toggle Animation icon (a little stopwatch). Click it to enable or disable keyframe adjustments (see Figure 7.11). When the stopwatch is empty, keyframe adjustment is disabled. When the stopwatch has a hand in it and a box around it, you can adjust keyframes. Once you set keyframes, clicking the stopwatch off will delete all assigned keyframes for the parameter. In some cases, such as the Color Corrector, this will delete the effect. Premiere Pro displays a warning dialog asking you to confirm your action before deleting the keyframes.

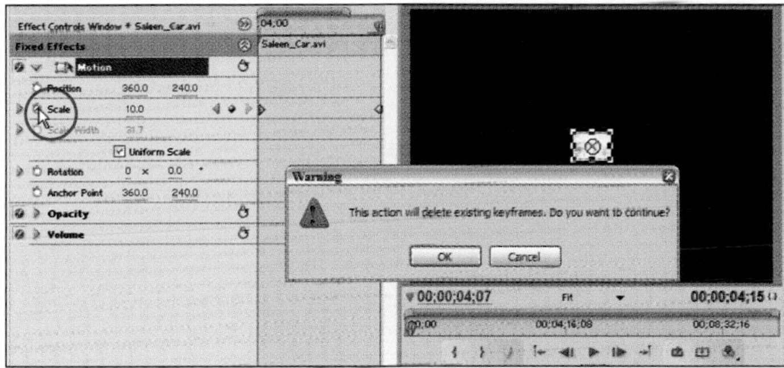

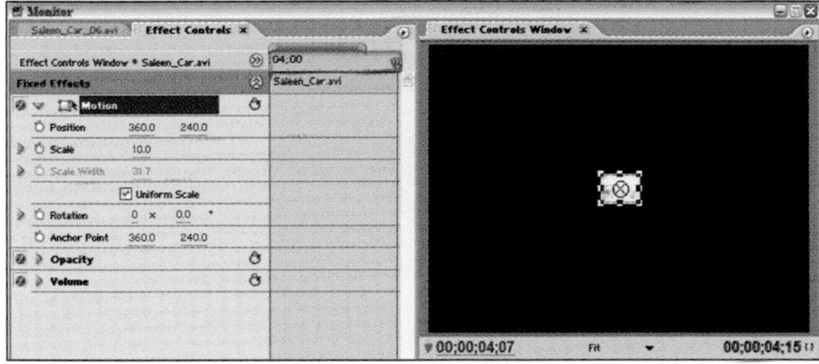

Figure 7.11 If you toggle the keyframing off, Premiere displays a warning (top), then deletes all keyframes (bottom). Notice that because the Edit Line was on top of the 10% scale keyframe when the keyframes were deleted, that became the static scale value.

You adjust the parameter using the hot text field to the right of its name. Scrub the field left or right to change its value. Holding down Ctrl while scrubbing adjusts the value at lower increments. Holding the Shift key and scrubbing adjusts the value at higher increments. Click in the hot text to manually enter the value you desire. If you prefer a more visual adjustment, click the twirl down triangle next to the parameter's name to access the slider control to change the parameter.

Docking the Effect Controls window in the Project window gives you a much wider window, meaning you have more screen real estate devoted to viewing and adjusting keyframes. If you're less concerned with keyframes and need to view all the effect listings and their parameters in one glance, resize the Effect Controls window to be very tall instead.

Timeline Viewing Area

The Effect Controls window timeline viewing area displays the effect keyframes associated with the selected clip. To check the accuracy of the effect and keyframe placements, you can zoom and navigate through the clip using the window's time ruler and viewing area bar. Scrubbing in the Effect Controls window reveals scrubbed frames in the Program Monitor.

By default, the boundaries of the Effect Controls window timeline viewing area are defined by the boundaries of the clip. Although this is the best view for most cases, you can extend the boundaries by toggling off Pin to Clip in the Effect Controls window wing menu. If you turn off Pin to Clip, you can adjust the viewing area bar so that you can see beyond the edges of the clip in the Effect Controls window timeline. (See Figure 7.12.) This view is not recommended unless subtle or advanced keyframing is required that starts beyond the boundary of the clip.

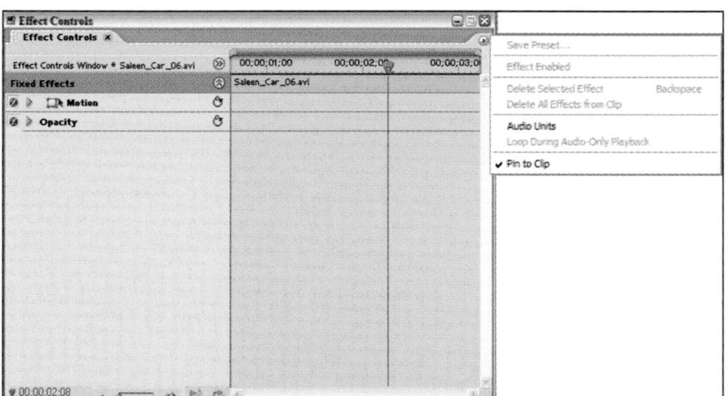

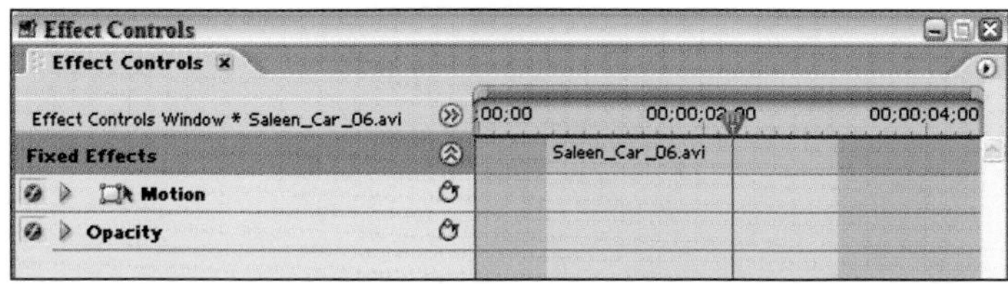

Figure 7.12 With Pin to Clip turned on (top) the boundaries of the Effect Controls window Keyframe Navigation area are pinned to the edge of the clip's timeline instance. If you turn Pin to Clip off, you can see beyond the edge of the clip instance (dark blue area) to assign additional keyframes in this area.

Turn Pin to Clip off to place an effect keyframe outside the boundary of your clip. With this "extra" keyframe in place, you later can adjust the duration or extend the edge of your clip toward that keyframe without reapplying the effect.

Working with Keyframes

Working with keyframes is an important part of applying effects in Premiere Pro, so learning how to manipulate them is vital.

When you are assigning keyframes for an effect, first make sure that the clip associated with that effect is selected in the timeline and that the CTI is positioned between that clip's boundaries. Next, click on the Toggle Animation button (the stopwatch) for the effect parameter that you wish to adjust or add keyframes (see Figure 7.13). Now, any adjustment to the parameter adds a keyframe at the CTI's position with the setting in the parameter's hot text. If the CTI is over an existing keyframe, changing a parameter's setting changes the value for that keyframe. Clicking the Previous or Next Keyframe buttons snaps the CTI backward or forward one keyframe for the current parameter. This works exactly the same as it did when you went through the same steps in the timeline tracks.

If you wish to add a keyframe and adjust it later, move your CTI to the desired spot and click the Add Keyframe button at the right of the parameter name. If the CTI is positioned on top of a keyframe, the Add Keyframe button turns a dark gray and clicking it removes the current keyframe for that parameter.

To move a keyframe to a new location, select it and drag it in the Effect Controls window timeline. Clicking and dragging a keyframe does not change its literal value, only its position. Using the Shift and Ctrl keys, you can select continuous or discontinuous keyframes to move them as a group. Clicking and dragging with the selection tool, you can marquee select a range of keyframes. (See Figure 7.14.)

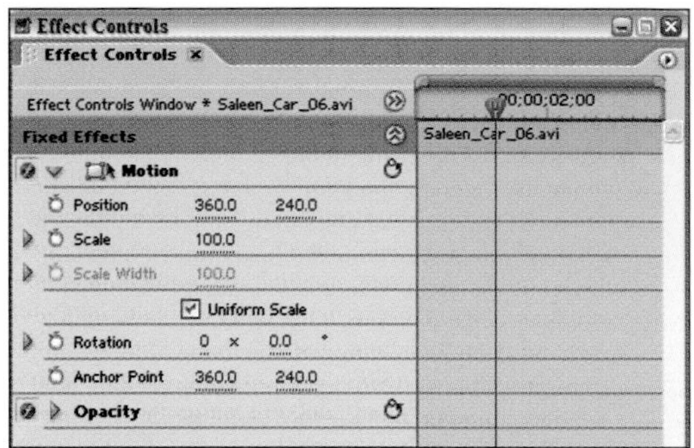

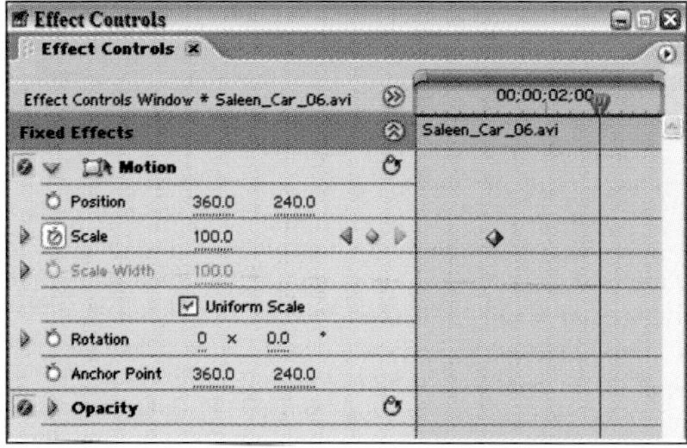

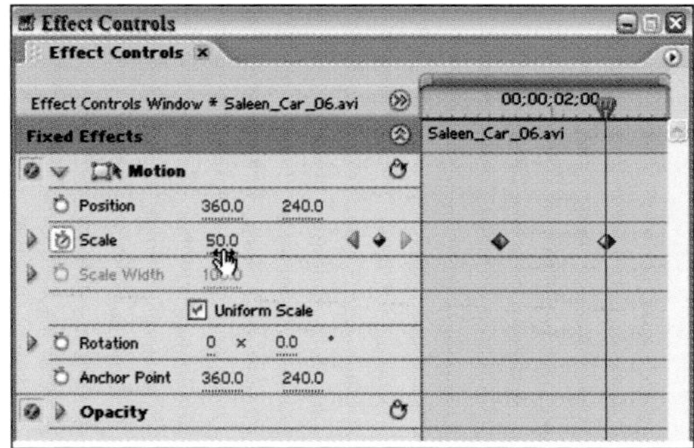

Figure 7.13 With the CTI positioned between the clip's boundary, turning on Toggle Animation (the keyframing stop-watch) assigns a start keyframe at the current Edit Line/CTI position. If the CTI is moved and the Scale is adjusted, a new keyframe is added at the new position to reflect the update.

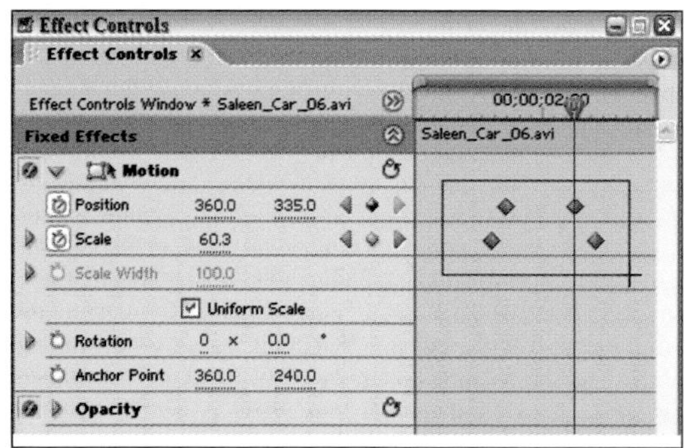

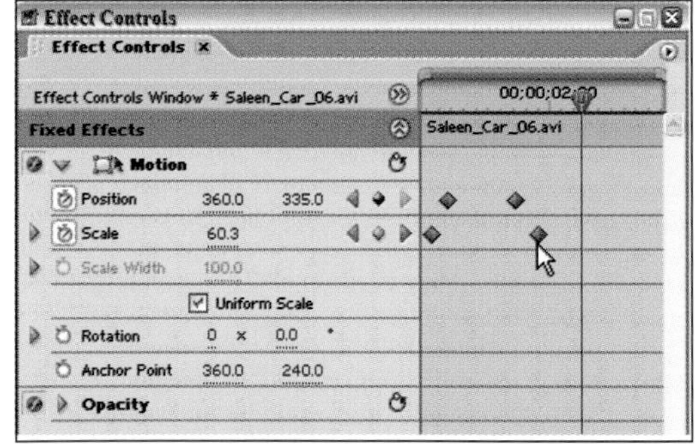

Figure 7.14 With the Selection tool, you can click and drag to marquee select multiple keyframes in the Effect Controls window. Once those keyframes are selected, not only can you copy and paste them to other clips, but you can also drag them as an entire group.

Be sure to stay aware of the CTI's position in the Effect Controls window as you work. As you scrub through a clip with multiple keyframes, the parameter values between keyframes update as you scrub. If you happen to park the CTI in a location without a keyframe and adjust a parameter that has Toggle Animation turned on, you will add a keyframe at that position. (See Figure 7.15.)

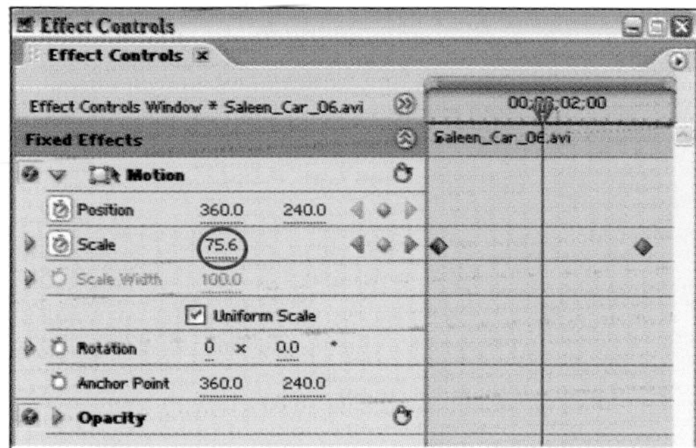

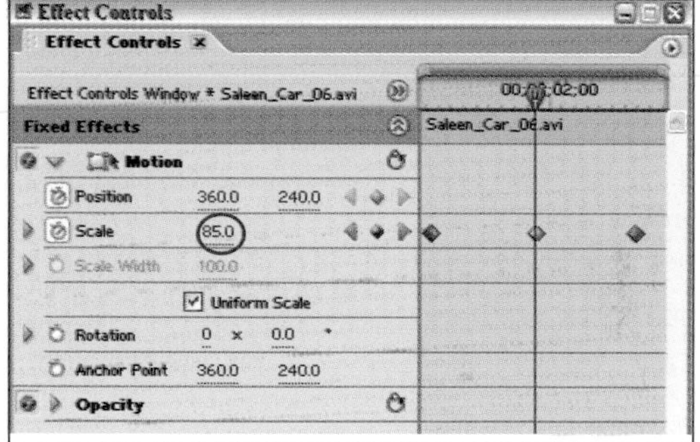

Figure 7.15 The left image shows a 50% Scale keyframe (left) and a 100% Scale keyframe (right). The current Scale value for the middle frame that the CTI is parked on is 75.6%. If you update that value to 85% (right image), you increase the amount of scaling for the same number of frames between the first and second keyframes and reduce the amount of scaling necessary to get from the second to the third keyframe. Therefore, the Scale effect is much faster from the first to the second keyframe, than it is from the second to the third.

Bezier Keyframes and Easing In and Out

New for Premiere Pro 1.5 is the support of Bezier curved keyframe handles. Bezier curves enable you to make smooth paths by adjusting and pulling handles associated with specific points on a path. In Premiere Pro, those points are the keyframes that you assign. Say you apply a position adjustment to a clip and want the line between the two points to be slightly curved. You would assign one of the keyframes to have a Bezier handle, then adjust the handle of that keyframe so that there is a curve from that point (see Figure 7.16). In the timeline, you can further navigate and manipulate all the keyframes and their handles that you set in the Effect Controls window.

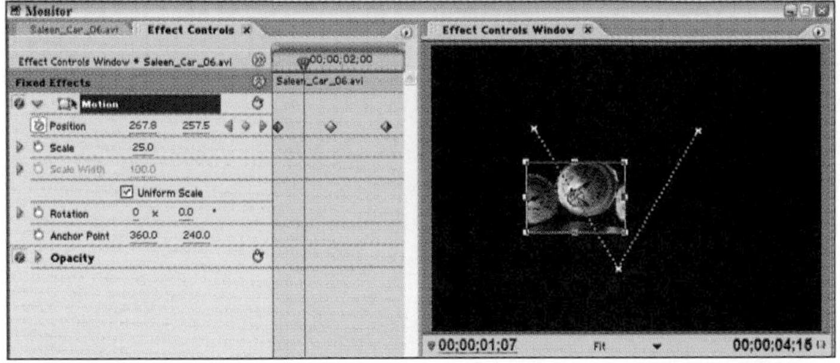

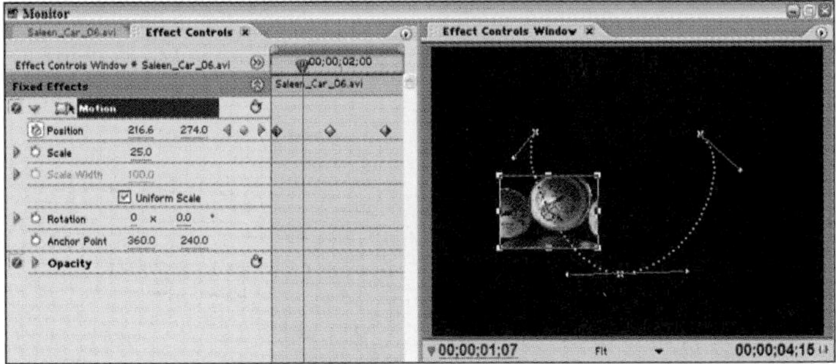

Figure 7.16 The initial motion path for this clip is a linear path (top). The bottom image shows the same path with Bezier handles to adjust the curves of the path.

One-dimension keyframes, such as Position (X and Y) and Anchor Points for Motion, cannot display bezier keyframe handles in the timeline, because their values cannot be reflected within the single track.

After you apply a keyframe, you can right-click on it and specify the type of handle or velocity setting that will be associated with its position. (See Figure 7.17.) You have two main choices: Temporal Interpolation and Spatial Interpolation. Temporal Interpolation addresses the velocity and timing of getting to a keyframe frame value. Spatial Interpolation addresses the curve and path definition for the keyframe.

For Temporal Interpolation, you have seven options: Linear, Bezier, Auto Bezier, Continuous Bezier, Hold, Ease In, and Ease Out. Ease In and Ease Out are the most practical and most often used for Temporal Interpolation. The eases affect the speed and velocity of the effect arriving to or leaving from that keyframe. (See Figure 7.18.)

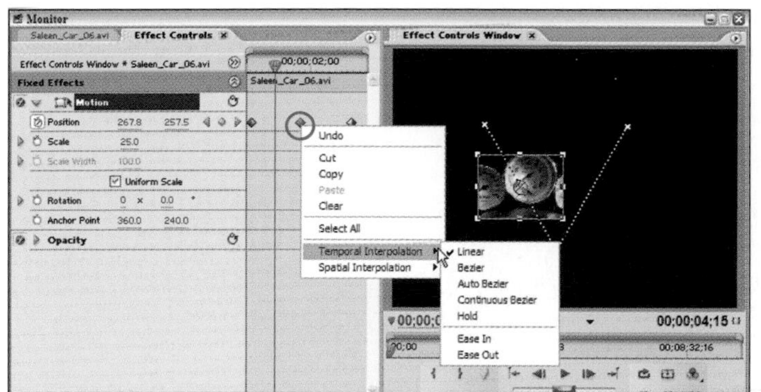

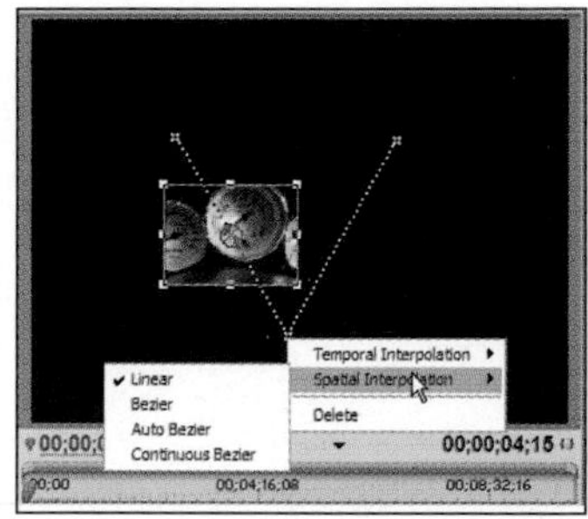

Figure 7.17 By right-clicking on the keyframe in the Effect Controls window or on the keyframe handle with direct manipulation turned on, you can access the Temporal and Spatial submenus to assign your desired interpolation value.

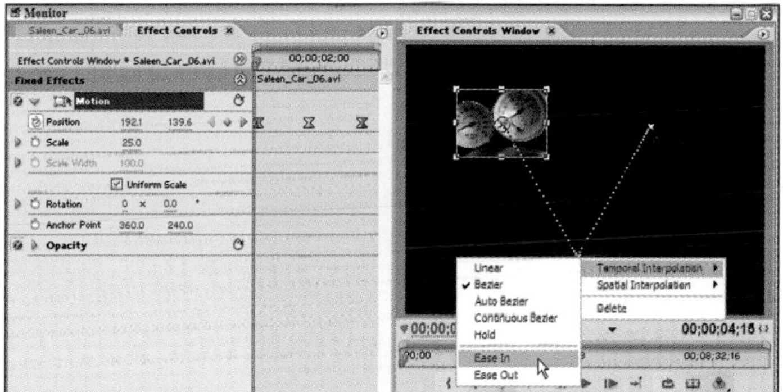

Figure 7.18 If you want a clip to slow slightly before arriving at a position keyframe, turn on Ease In for the selected keyframe. The tightness of the keyframe path dots reflects the velocity of the clip on the path.

To explore the various types of keyframe handles and how to properly adjust them, watch the "Adjusting Bezier Keyframes" video tutorial in the Fundamentals section on the accompanying DVD.

Viewing Keyframes in the Timeline

To view your keyframes in the Timeline window, choose Show Keyframes by clicking on the icon in the appropriate track header. A drop-down menu appears within the boundary of each clip. Click on the menu to see the effects associated with the clip. The submenus of each effect list all the associated parameters that make up your effect.

Select a parameter to display its associated keyframes within the boundary of the clip in the track (see Figure 7.19). The limitation of timeline keyframe viewing is that you can see only one keyframe parameter at a time.

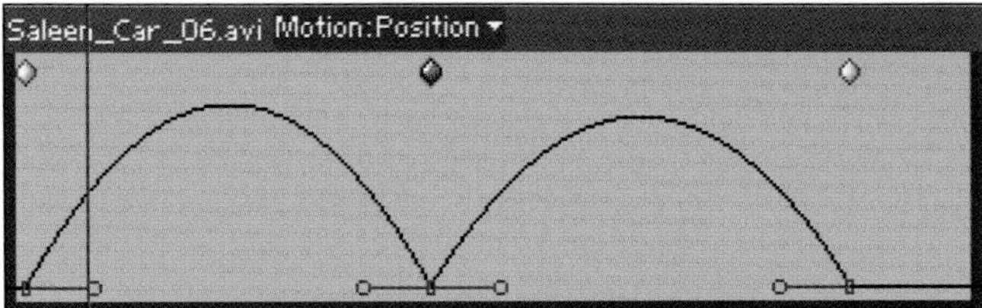

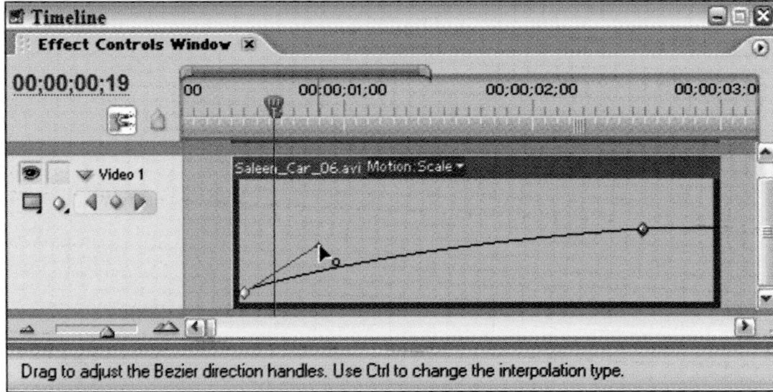

Figure 7.19 The top image shows the Position keyframes with their Temporal Interpolation value exhibited by the curved lines. Notice the keyframes are locked, because Position keyframes cannot be modified in the Timeline window. In the bottom image, you can see the keyframes for Scale, the Bezier handle associated with the first keyframe, and a bit of feedback as to what you can do to adjust the handle.

The Pen Tool

To make selections and adjustments to the keyframes displayed in the Timeline window, press P while the timeline is active to change your cursor into the Pen tool. Although you can make a few specific keyframe selections with the standard cursor tool, the Pen tool has many more important features.

To add keyframes to an effect parameter with the Pen tool, first make sure that the parameter has keyframing turned on in the Effect Controls window (the stopwatch has an arm). Back in the Timeline window, hold the Ctrl key and click the Pen tool on the displayed wire to add a keyframe to the displayed parameter (see Figure 7.20).

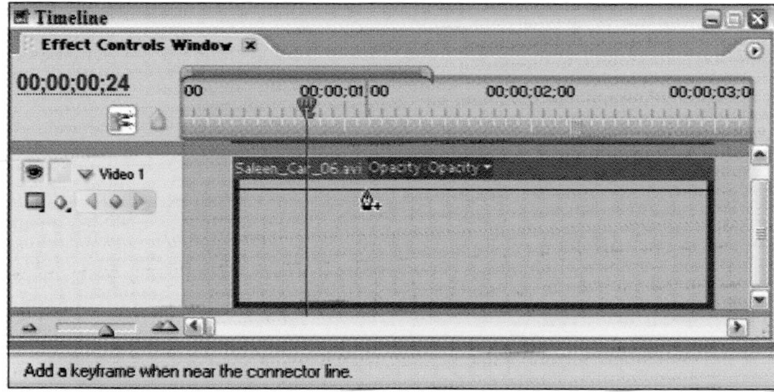

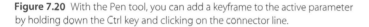

Figure 7.20 With the Pen tool, you can add a keyframe to the active parameter by holding down the Ctrl key and clicking on the connector line.

You also can modify displayed keyframes: Select the keyframe with the Pen tool and drag it up to increase the value of the parameter. Dragging the keyframe down reduces the parameter's value. Dragging a keyframe horizontally changes its position within the boundary of the clip.

Clicking and dragging over a group of keyframes with the Pen tool performs a range selection of the keyframes. With multiple keyframes selected, you can move or delete the entire selection. (See Figure 7.21.) Range selection is one of the Pen tool's most powerful features.

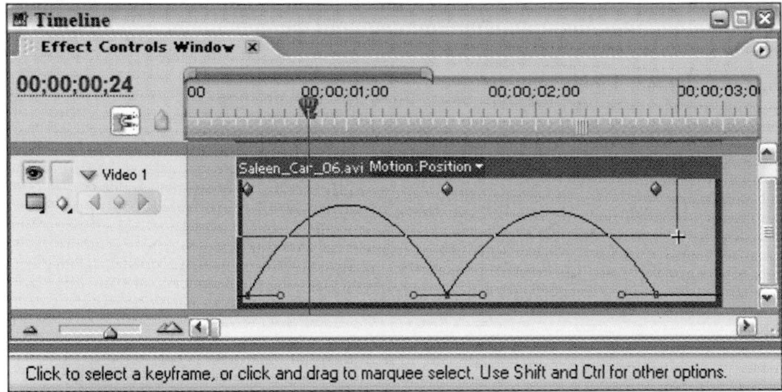

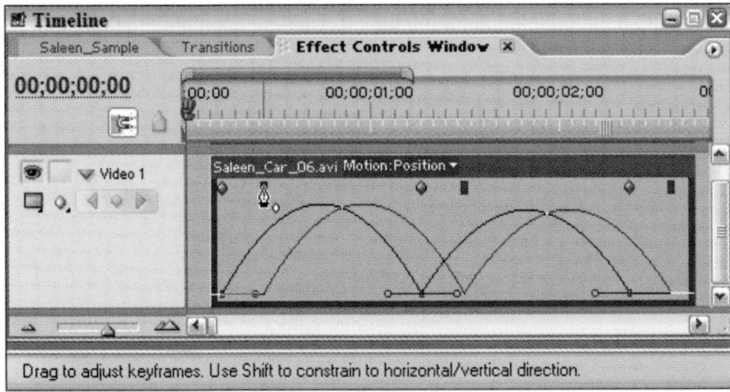

Figure 7.21 As you can in the Effect Controls window, you can marquee select in the timeline (left). You then can shift and move the selected group of keyframes (right).

Things to Remember

When adding and adjusting effects, always watch out for the keyframing states of the parameters and the position of the CTI. Often, if you are not paying close attention, you will get so involved in setting your parameters accurately that you will make three adjustments at different frames in your clip—but all will be moot because you forgot to turn on the keyframing stopwatch (the Toggle Animation button). Learn the rules, then expect results. Just as it is important for editing and viewing, the CTI position plays a vital role in the applying of effects.

The Effect Controls window is always active, even when it is underneath another window. The window always displays the effect attributes of whatever clip is selected in the timeline. If you have the screen real estate luxury of being able to have your Effect Controls window open at a big size, then by all means do it. The ease of jumping amongst your timeline, clips, and Effect Controls window helps build a healthy workflow for adding and adjusting any effect.

You are down the home stretch in getting a basic understanding of the application. The next chapter reviews some of the important audio rules and introduces the Audio Mixer window.

CHAPTER

8

How Audio Works in Premiere Pro

The way audio works in Premiere Pro is very different from the way it worked in previous versions. Adobe made three fundamental changes, all of which result in greater quality and better control over your audio. Premiere Pro supports:

- **A new audio mixer.** More powerful and practical than previous versions, the new audio mixer opens up the architecture to support both clip-based and track-based effects. (See Figure 8.1.) This means that you can apply audio effects to individual clips or the entire content of specific tracks. You can also accomplish standard mixing practices, such as stemming, sends, and automation. The support for live mixing automation enables you to adjust volume faders and levels as you play your sequence back and have those fade adjustments saved to the sequence after a single pass.
- **VST plug-ins.** With the advantage of clip and track effects comes new compatibility for VST plug-ins. Premiere Pro ships with several professional VST plug-ins that support mono, stereo, and 5.1 source material (see Figure 8.2), and many more of these audio effect plug-ins are available from third-party developers. (The VST plug-in format was originally developed for Steinberg's Cubase audio editing application.)

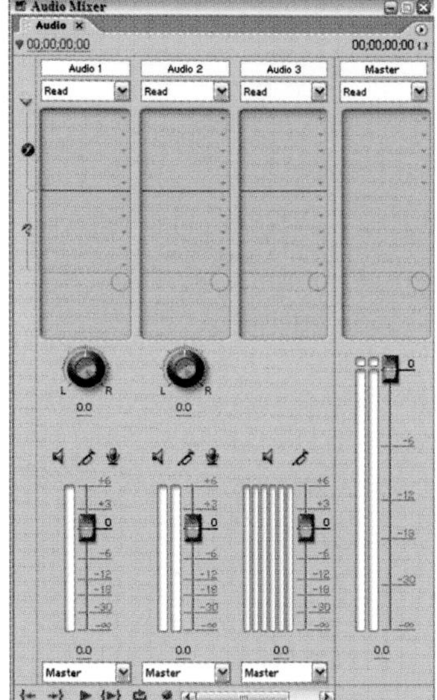

Figure 8.1 The full expanded Audio Mixer references the Audio sequence from the Timeline window and displays three tracks: Audio 1 (mono), Audio 2 (stereo), and Audio 3 (5.1 surround). Each track has its own pan knob and volume fader. The Master fader on the right controls the volume for the entire sequence.

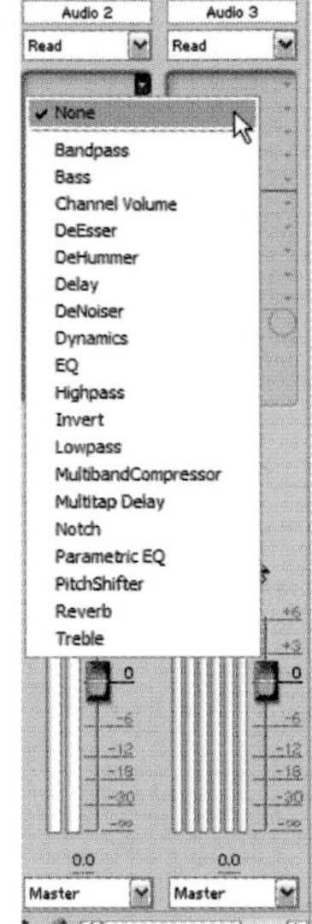

Figure 8.2 You access VST plug-ins from the Track Effects drop-down menu. DeEsser and DeHummer are new for Premiere Pro 1.5.

- **Creation of conformed audio files.** When you import and open files, Premiere Pro now automatically converts them into a proprietary format called conformed audio files. Having conformed audio files increases the detail that can be extracted from the audio waveform and allows Premiere Pro to communicate and process audio files more efficiently. Because the conformed files have an increased resolution, Premiere can more accurately assign and play back added audio effects and filters.

To better understand the importance of these changes, take a look at the flow of sound as it passes through Premiere Pro.

Importing and Conformed Audio Files

When you create a new project, one of the Project Settings you assign is the Sample Rate for audio—either 16-bit 48kHz or 12/16-bit 32kHz for standard DV. When you later import an audio file or an audio and video file, Premiere Pro looks at the audio's bit depth and sample rate and *conforms* it to match your project's settings. When the program creates conformed audio files, it increases the file to 32-bit resolution while increasing or decreasing the sample rate to match the project's kHz setting. Premiere then uses these conformed audio files to display the waveform information in the timeline and Source Monitor, to apply effects, and to play back the audio for the clip. Once you engage playback in Premiere Pro, if your DV camera is connected, the audio will always transmit at the proper bit and sample rate.

For the sake of drive performance and application responsiveness, keep your conformed audio files on a separate drive from your original source files. If your drive is slow, having to access both the source media and the conformed files from the same drive can create a bottleneck. You can specify your storage locations from Edit>Preferences>Scratch Disks.

Conformed files are temporal, meaning that deleting them does not corrupt or destroy your project. If Premiere does not detect conformed files when opening the project, it will create new ones. When you import a file with audio, watch the conforming progress bar update in the bottom-right corner of the application's window. Once the bar completes, the conformed file is created and ready to use anytime you play back the audio clip.

When you import a project that already has conformed files associated with it into another project, Premiere Pro 1.5 does not create new conformed files. Instead, Premiere Pro intelligently references the associated conformed files from the imported project.

Understanding Volume Levels

When you first record or import an audio clip, it has audio information that is measured in decibels (dBs) when played back. You can quickly see the waveform value for the audio or monitor the volume using the Audio Mixer's VU meters.

To monitor your audio clip with the waveform display, open the audio only clip in your Source Monitor. If the clip is a linked audio and video file, open it in the Source Monitor but toggle the Take Audio/Video button to Take Audio Only (see Figure 8.3) so that only the waveform is displayed. To view the waveform for your audio files in the timeline, expand the audio track and be sure that the track is set to Show Waveforms. When looking at the waveform, tall waveforms denote stronger sound with a higher dB, and short waveforms reflect quieter sound with a lower dB.

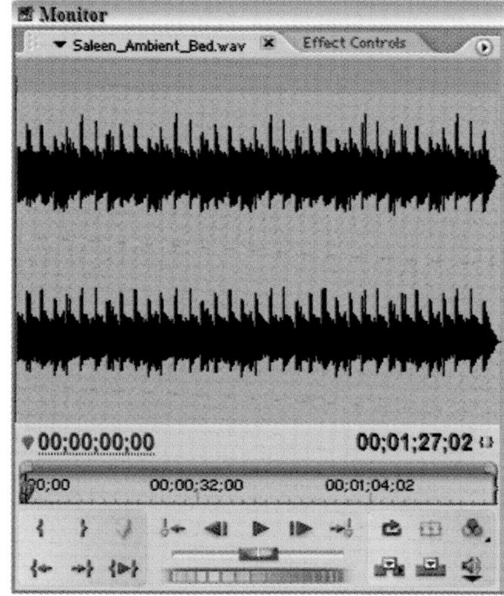

Figure 8.3 You can tell this audio clip is a stereo file, because the Source Monitor displays two waveform values.

Although the waveform is a nice visual representation, the VU meters give you more accuracy. To monitor your audio clip with VU meters, you must first add the clip to your sequence, then look at the VU meters registering in the Audio Mixer. If the Mixer is expanded, you can click on the wing menu and reduce its size to a small VU Meters window (see Figure 8.4).

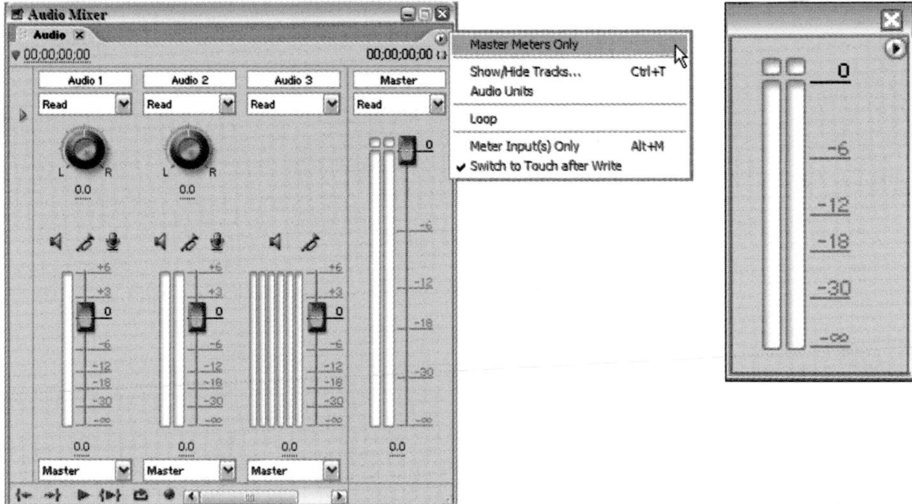

Figure 8.4 If you select Master Meters Only from the full Audio Mixer's wing menu (left), Premiere Pro displays the smaller VU meters only (right). To get back to the full mixer, click on the wing menu again and select Audio Mixer.

Loud audio registers close to 0dB, and quiet audio registers down around –18dB. The VU meters are essential for monitoring your audio levels so that they do not exceed their ceiling and begin to distort or degrade. If your audio is too loud (shown by red ticks in the VU meters), it will play back with clicks, pops, and other artifacts.

If your clip is too quiet, you might get your first clue in the waveform display: The clip doesn't have tall waveforms. When you monitor the clip more closely in the Audio Mixer's VU meters, you can see its exact dynamic dB levels as it plays back.

So, what do you do if your clip is too loud or too soft? You can alter the playback volume level from three controls:

- **Clip Gain.** For use on clips before adding them to a sequence. Gain adjustments are assigned to the master clip; whenever you use the clip the adjustments are preserved.

- **Clip Volume.** For use on clips already in a sequence. These adjustments stay with the clip even if it is moved to different tracks or copied from one sequence to another.
- **Track Volume.** For use on all clips in a single track. The volume adjustments are track specific and have no relation to specific clips in the track.

Keep in mind that when you make a Clip Volume or Clip Gain adjustment, Premiere does not alter the display of the file's waveform. Although your audio sounds louder after you adjust Clip Volume or Clip Gain, its waveform does not look any larger than it originally did. That's just how Premiere Pro works for version 1.5.

When normalizing a clip with dB levels that exceed 0dB, the Clip Gain dialog yields negative gain adjustment values so that you can reduce the strength of the signal. Remember that if your audio does exceed the 0dB ceiling, the source file probably is clipped and has some added artifacts. In these cases, lowering the volume doesn't make it sound better, just less noticeable. If you have damaged audio files, you can do a lot of fixing and adjusting in Adobe Audition.

Clip Gain and Normalizing your Audio

Before you add an audio clip to your sequence you can increase or reduce its volume by adjusting the Clip Gain. Say you import a quiet audio clip. Select the clip in the Project window, then choose Clip>Audio Options>Audio Gain to access the Clip Gain dialog (see Figure 8.5). For your quiet clip, increasing the dB setting (the Gain) boosts its audio signal accordingly. Setting the dialog's hot text to 5.0dB boosts the audio signal by 5.0dB. Clicking and dragging the hot text to the left reduces the Gain and trims audio levels by whatever negative value you assign. To apply your setting to the clip, click OK.

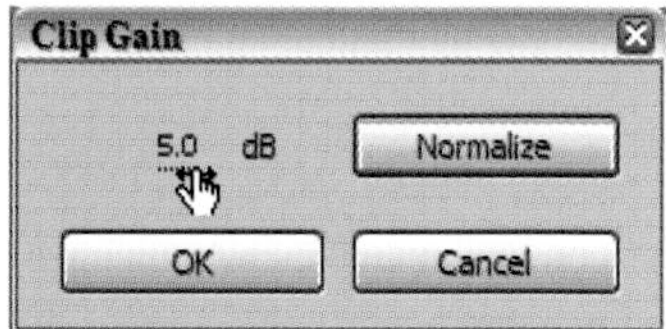

Figure 8.5 In the Clip Gain dialog, you can assign a positive or negative Gain value by adjusting the hot-text dB value. You can also apply an "intelligent gain" by clicking the Normalize button.

Clicking the Clip Gain dialog's Normalize button achieves a very useful result: Premiere Pro provides a recommended Gain value for your clip. Premiere examines the entire dB value for the audio file selected, and it determines how much it can increase or decrease the dB so that the strongest signal does not peak or exceed the ceiling level (0dB) in any portion of the clip. Once you click Normalize, Premiere updates the Gain value in the hot-text field with a recommended value for proper adjustment. Clicking OK applies the Gain value to the clip.

Although you can access the Clip Gain dialog when a clip is selected in the timeline, there is a major benefit to making Gain adjustments to the master clips in the Project window. When you adjust the Clip Gain of the master clip, Premiere adheres to and respects that adjustment every time you add an instance of the clip to the timeline. Normalize your audio clips in the Project window *before* adding them to the timeline. If you already have instances of a clip in the timeline and you adjust the master clip in the Project window, the Gain value of the clips in the timeline does *not* update.

In Premiere Pro 1.5, hold your mouse over a clip in your sequence to display that clip's information in the tool tip window. If gain adjustments have been made, you can see that information when holding the mouse over an audio clip in your active Timeline window.

Clip Volume

Say you need a track of bird sounds to accompany video of a flock of birds flying across a field to land around your actor. Your field recording came out at a low level, and when you import the clip into Premiere the birds sound as if they're miles away. To fix this, you first boost the Gain to increase the signal strength. Now when you add the clip to your sequence, you can lower the Clip Volume at the start of the sequence (so the birds sound as if they are at the far end of the field) and increase it at the end (so they sound as if they surround the viewer as well as the actor). These adjustments can be made by tweaking the clips' volume handles Timeline window. (See Figure 8.6.)

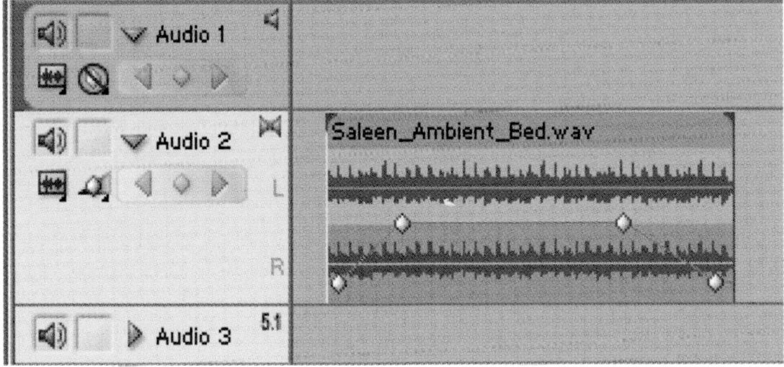

Figure 8.6 With the Audio 2 track set to Show Clip Volume, the yellow volume line reflects the assigned levels. Using the Pen tool, you can click and add handles to the level to adjust the clip volume dynamically. Here the clip fades in to its normal 0dB clip volume then fades out.

To review, Gain adjustments boost or reduce the basic signal level of your audio file, before and sometimes after it has been added to a sequence. Clip Volume is the means by which you adjust the volume level of a specific clip instance in a sequence.

Clip Gain is independent from the Clip Volume so Clip Gain adjustments do not affect a clip's Clip Volume setting. No matter what Gain settings you apply, a clip's Volume displays at the default of 0dB until you adjust the Clip Volume setting. This independence also means, for example, you could increase the Gain to add strength to the audio signal then bring the Volume down just a little.

Empty space on a video track is displayed as pure black. Empty space on an audio track registers as complete silence or –oodB. The same way adding a cross dissolve to the head of a video clip fades it up from black, adding an audio dissolve to the head of an audio clip fades the audio up from complete silence to its assigned clip volume.

One way to increase the Volume of an audio clip in a sequence is to select the clip in the Timeline window and open the Effect Controls window. As you remember from Chapter 7, "Introduction to Effects," Volume is a Fixed effect for audio clips. When you adjust the volume properties of a clip in the Effect Controls window, position the CTI where you wish to make the change and twirl down the Level slider for volume. (See Figure 8.7.) To increase the entire clip's volume, make sure Toggle Animation (the stopwatch icon) is off, then make your adjustment. To keyframe volume fades and adjustments, turn Toggle Animation on and then assign keyframes with the desired Volume levels at the appropriate points in the clip's boundary.

If you prefer, you can adjust a clip's Volume in the Timeline window with the Pen tool (press P with the timeline active). (See Figure 8.8.) First, toggle the audio track display to Show Clip Volume, and Premiere will display every clip's volume in that track. To adjust a static level, you can click and drag when the Pen tool displays the horizontal volume line. Dragging upward increases the volume and downward decreases. If you want to add keyframes with different level values, press the Ctrl key and click the Pen tool on the volume line to add a keyframe handle at the assigned position. Click on the keyframe, and drag it up or down to raise and lower the volume. Adjusting the Clip Volume level is useful for removing specific sections or unwanted sounds.

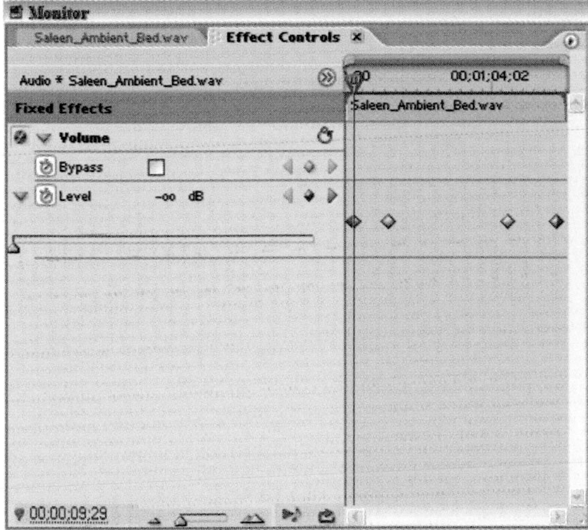

Figure 8.7 With the adjusted clip from Figure 8.6 selected from the timeline, its effects properties become available in the Effect Controls window. Because the volume level has a number of different handles with different values, the Toggle Animation button is active. With the CTI on top of the first keyframe handle, you can see that it has a value of –oodB which is complete silence.

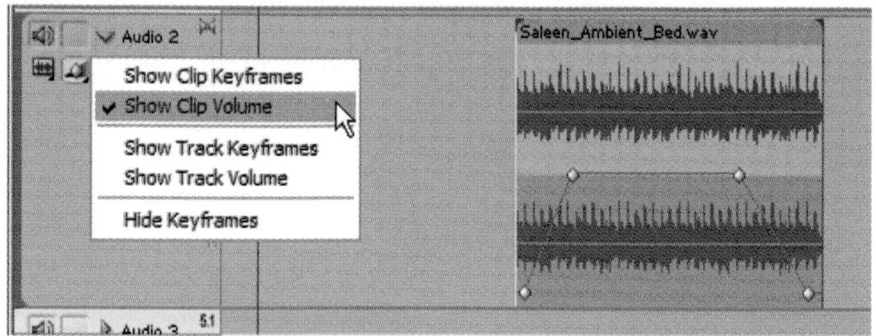

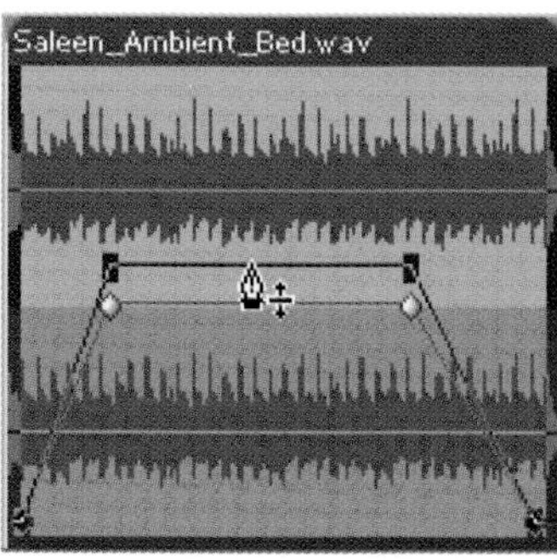

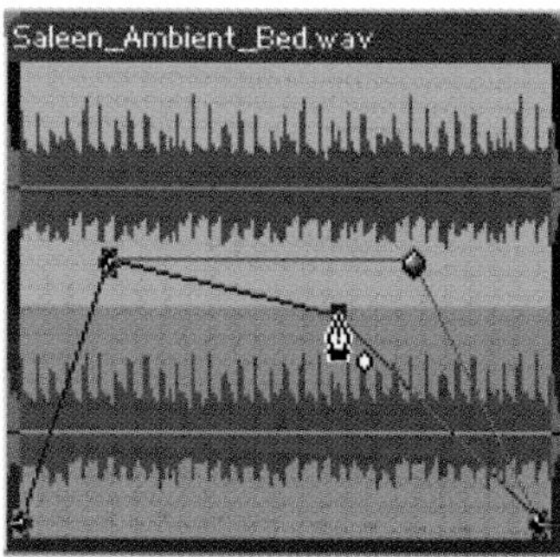

Figure 8.8 Set the track to display clip volume (top), then you can use the Pen tool to raise a static value between two volume handles (bottom left) or click and modify a single keyframe handle (bottom right).

Automation is the equivalent of keyframing effects, only it is done live as the audio tracks play. To fade the volume at specific points, switch the track into one of three Automation modes and press Play. Now, when the timeline plays back, you can make live adjustments to the audio track's parameters. Premiere saves these adjustments, writing them as keyframes to the adjusted parameter. Automation is very powerful as you can watch, listen, and make adjustments at the same time. You'll learn more about it in Chapter 18, "Mixing Your Audio."

In the "Advanced Audio Techniques" section, Chapters 14 to 18, you will explore clip volume adjustments and much more.

Track Volume

Clip Gain and Clip Volume are specific to individual clips, but Track Volume adjusts the volume level of an entire track. You can adjust Track Volume from its default of 0dB in the Audio Mixer window or the timeline. In the Audio Mixer window, use the volume faders at the bottom of each track panel. The position of the fader reflects the level of the associated track. For a static adjustment, turn the Automation mode Off and then drag the fader up or down to increase or decrease the dB level. (See Figure 8.9.) Be careful: If you performed any Automation or if you keyframed track volume or effect values, setting the Automation mode to Off deletes all of the keyframes for the entire track.

To make adjustments to the track in the Timeline window, toggle your audio track display to Show Track Volume or Show Track Keyframes and adjust accordingly with the Pen tool. Raising values above the center volume line increases the dB, and dragging below it decreases dB.

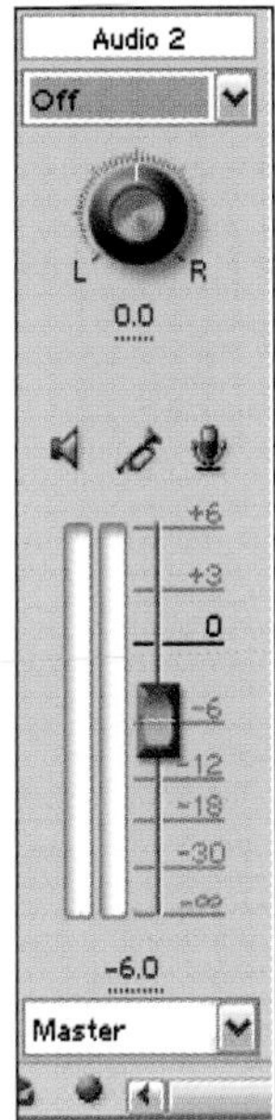

Figure 8.9 With the Automation mode for Audio 2 set to Off, you can make uniform track volume or panning adjustments that affect the entire track. Here the track volume for Audio 2 was turned down by 6dB, meaning all the audio in Audio 2, no matter how loud, was reduced by 6.0dB.

Audio Tracks

As mentioned earlier, you can have up to 99 audio tracks, including submix tracks, in any combination of mono, stereo, and 5.1 surround tracks. All of these 99 tracks get mixed together when you play back your sequence and their volume values are displayed in the VU meters of the Master track. By having all of your tracks mix down and then play out through the single Master track, you enable an added level of control for reducing, filtering, or adjusting the entire mix of your audio in one single track. (See Figure 8.10.)

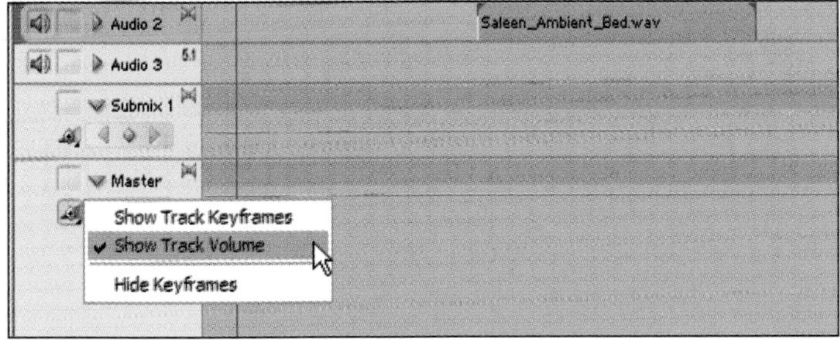

Figure 8.10 The Master track displays at the bottom of the sequence and has only track-based display properties. The Master track does not contain specific clip information and it is always on. Notice that there is no Output button to mute the track.

Master Track

When creating sequences, you have the ability to define your audio Master track as being mono, stereo, or 5.1. When you open the sequence, the Master track appears at the very bottom and cannot contain any clip information. In the Audio Mixer it is the track to the far right.

Panning is the moving of sound from one speaker channel to another. If you were to mix your sound so that it was only heard on the right speaker, that would be referred to as panning right.

Think of the Master track as a siphon or a funnel. Although you may have all sorts of audio tracks in a sequence, they ultimately must be funneled down through the Master track and distributed accordingly. If you have a mono track (with one channel of information) in a sequence with a stereo Master track (with a left and a right channel), the mono track would, by default, play back equally on each of the two stereo channels. By placing a mono track in a stereo master, you gain a stereo mix down, which opens the possibilities of panning your mono audio to either the left or right channel or keeping it centered equally to both. If you place a stereo track in a sequence with a mono Master track, you lose the panning properties of the stereo track: The mix down would be to a single mono channel.

Because all of your sound is funneled through the Master track, adjusting the Master track's settings and parameters affects the overall sound of your sequence. For example, to reduce the volume for your entire sequence, simply turn down the Master volume slider in either the Audio Mixer or the track (displaying Track Volume). Similarly, to add a reverb effect to your entire sequence, add the reverb effect to the Master track. (See Figure 8.11.)

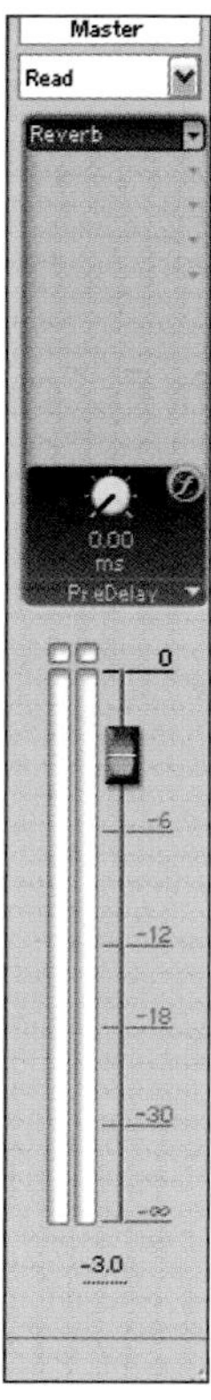

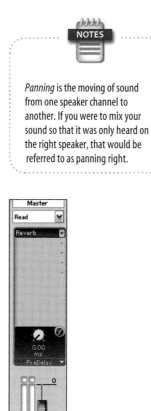

Figure 8.11 The Master Track has a Reverb effect applied from one of the Effects drop-down menus. You can also see that the Volume fader has been reduced to –3.0dB. These two adjustments will affect the entire mix and output of the sequence, so that all the audio has a reverb and a volume lowered by –3.0dB.

Sub-Mix Tracks

As for the Master track, no clip content can physically be added or dragged onto submix tracks; you only can apply effects and make volume or pan adjustments. Similar to Master tracks, submix tracks act as pipelines. The workflow with submix tracks is to *send* a normal track to be processed through a submix track. This ability is especially useful when you want to apply the same effect to multiple tracks. When you apply one effect to a submix track and send multiple tracks to that submix track, all those tracks get processed with the effect from the submix. (See Figure 8.12.)

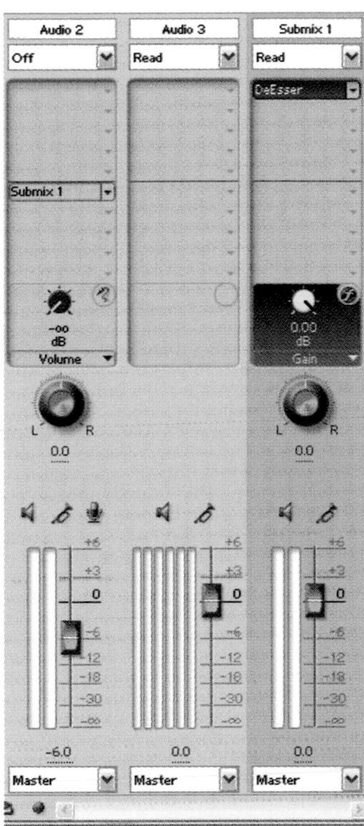

Figure 8.12 Here Audio 2 is sent to Submix 1. The Sends area is just below the Effects area of the Mixer window. The DeEsser effect is assigned on Submix 1 and will be processed to the content of Audio 2, which is being sent to the submix track.

For more on how submix tracks work, try the lessons in Chapter 18.

Clip Versus Track Effects

In Premiere Pro, you can apply audio effects at the clip or track level, just as you can assign clip and track volume. Like clip volume adjustments, clip effects apply to only one clip. Track effects, like track volume adjustments, apply to a specific track and not the individual track content. To add audio clip effects, you follow the exact same workflow as video effects, with one exception. To decide which effect you want to use, you need to identify the type of clip you are adding the effect to: mono, stereo, or 5.1.

Clip Effects

As mentioned in Chapter 7, you must choose the proper type of clip Standard effect—Mono, Stereo, or 5.1—to match the clip to which you are applying it. As with video effects, you can adjust an audio effect by selecting a clip in the timeline and placing the CTI over the clip boundary. The clip's properties will appear in the Effect Controls window. (See Figure 8.13.)

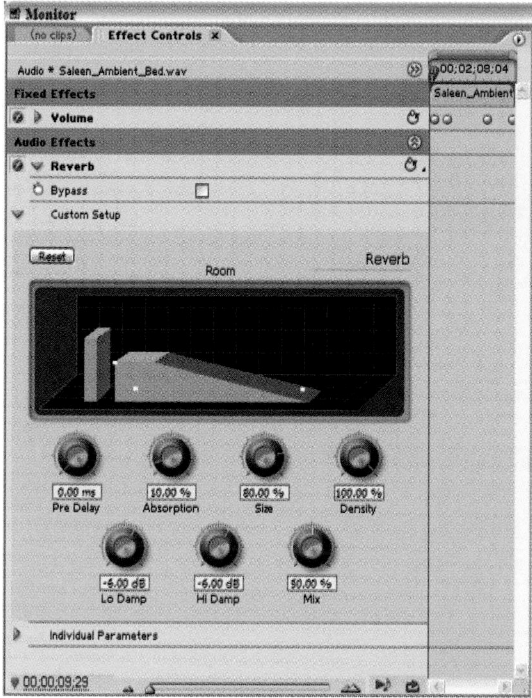

Figure 8.13 The Audio Effects listing is below the Fixed Effects listing in the Effect Controls window. Here the Reverb effect listing has been expanded. Expanding the Custom Setup listing reveals a graphic interface that enables you to manipulate and adjust the reverb value.

A number of effects have the standard twirl down slider to adjust settings, but for others you must twirl down to access a custom setup display with a nice visually interactive adjustment area. As for video effects, you can add keyframes for audio effects only when the Toggle Animation button is switched on. When you move a clip with a keyframed effect applied, the keyframes preserve their position as the clip defines their boundary. Again as for video effects, you can view audio effects and their keyframes in the track area by setting the track display to Show Clip Keyframes.

Track Effects

Clip effects adjust only the clip instance, as it is visible in the sequence. Track effects are a means of adding effects to an *entire* track. Although you might want to change the pitch of one specific clip (using the PitchShifter clip effect), you may also want to add a reverb to an entire track.

Using the Audio Mixer, adding and adjusting track effects is quite simple. With the Audio Mixer open, you can view all of the tracks in your sequence; each has a unique panel in the mixer. Each panel has a name that corresponds to the associated track in the sequence. To add an effect to a track, you click on the top drop-down menu and select the effect from the list. (See Figure 8.14.) Once you select your effect, double-clicking on it brings up a dialog with visual parameters that you can adjust. (See Figure 8.15.) Right-clicking on the effect name reveals a drop-down menu of presets for that effect. (See Figure 8.16.)

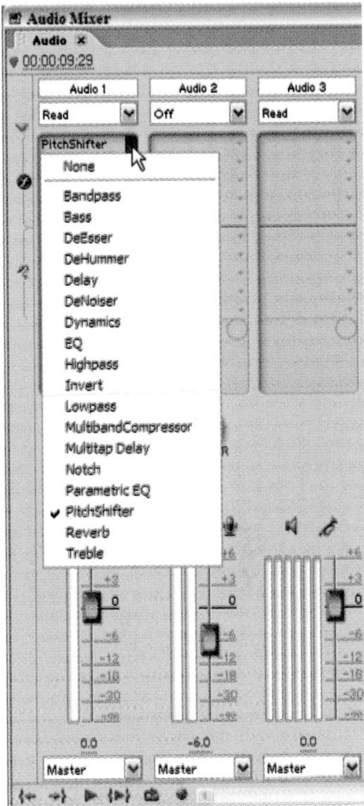

Figure 8.14 To assign a track effect in the Audio Mixer, click the Effects area of the desired track and select the effect from the drop-down menu.

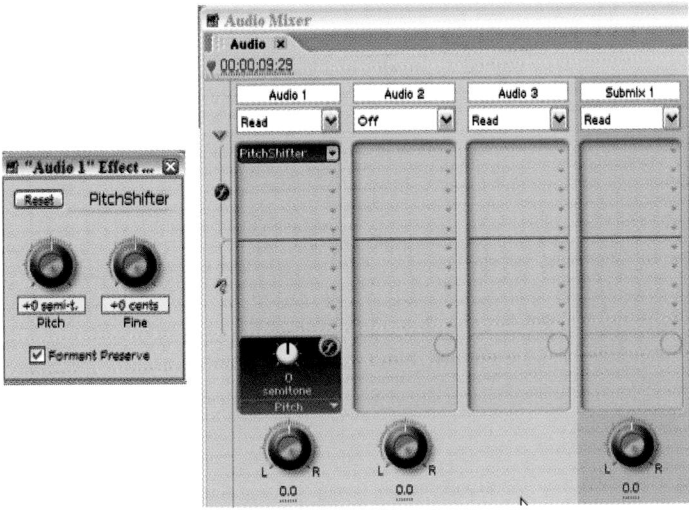

Figure 8.15 Double-click on the PitchShifter, or any effect listing, to open its dialog and visually manipulate it. At the bottom of the Sends area, notice the control knob that reveals one of the PitchShifter's effect parameters.

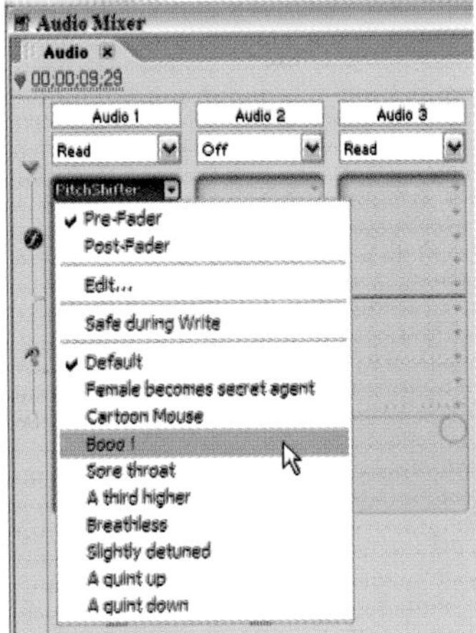

Figure 8.16 To access a custom preset, right-click on the effect and select the preset from the drop-down menu.

Clip effect manipulation in the Audio Mixer leaves some features to be desired, because some audio effects do not have a visual display in which you can make adjustments. For these, you can make adjustments in a small area of the Audio Mixer's track panel (see Figure 8.15). Highlight the added effect and a drop-down list with the effect's name appears just above the radio buttons. Click on that drop-down list to reveal all of the parameters that you can adjust for the effect. To adjust the parameters, modify their value in the little box that appears above the list. With no keyframes or Automation applied, any effect adjustment will be static for the entire track. To apply effects, you can click and use the Pen tool in the timeline with Show Track Keyframes turned on or you can set your track into an Automation mode and start adjusting.

With track-based effects (and mixing), keyframes have nothing to do with clip position and everything to do with track position. A track volume fade from 0dB to 4dB at 5 seconds into your timeline will persist no matter if there is clip media underneath the keyframes or not. If you have automated or added track-based keyframes, you may want to lock your track so that the mixing properties are preserved with the audio clips underneath.

You'll learn more about effects in the chapters of the "Advanced Audio Techniques" section.

Previewing and Playback

Depending on the effects and adjustments being made, Premiere Pro does not always need to create audio preview files. If you add a number of effects, however, Premiere Pro will render audio files when you press Enter to play your sequence back. To learn about nesting sequences and creating audio preview files, watch the video tutorial "Neting Sequences and Rendering Audio" in the Fundamentals section on the accompanying DVD.

Things to Remember

At the end of the day you need your project to sound as good (or better) than it looks. Getting your audio to sound just right can go a long way toward enhancing the production value of your projects. Because you now know how to monitor your audio and because you know the three different ways to adjust it, your audio levels should now be in much better shape. Keep the overall levels of your tracks' audio adjusted so that the sound is loud enough, but not too loud.

It may help you to set your timeline to Audio Units display mode, which shows audio samples instead of video frames. The Audio Units display can help you zoom into your waveform in the monitors or timeline to see better what information is revealed.

Because you can assign clip and track effects separately, you can add more depth and diversity to the sound in your timeline.

The next chapter, on the other hand, will help you add more depth to your titles and graphics elements by introducing the Adobe Title Designer.

CHAPTER

9

The Adobe Title Designer

Inside Premiere Pro is an incredibly useful titling tool: the Adobe Title Designer. The Title Designer's straightforward and easy-to-use controls help make title creation quite simple. If you know Adobe Illustrator, some of Title Designer's tools, such as those for stacking and positioning items, will seem familiar. In this chapter, you will learn the basics of creating and using title styles, moving and arranging text and objects, as well as loading and saving templates.

Window Overview

To open the Adobe Title Designer, press F9 or select File>New>Title. (See Figure 9.1.) The top row of control holds a number of function buttons for accessing templates, font types, and specifying the type of title you want to create (still, roll, or crawl). You add objects and text to the drawing area (center section) with the tools palette. The Object Style and Transform panels allow you to manipulate the text and object style, as well as adjust the position of the text or objects. From the Styles Library, you can add, select, and apply custom or default styles to objects and text.

When the Adobe Title Designer is open, you have access to the Title menu in the main menu bar, as well (see Figure 9.2). The Title menu contains shortcuts and items that help arrange and adjust the open title or selection. You can assign keyboard shortcuts for most of the listed Title menu items.

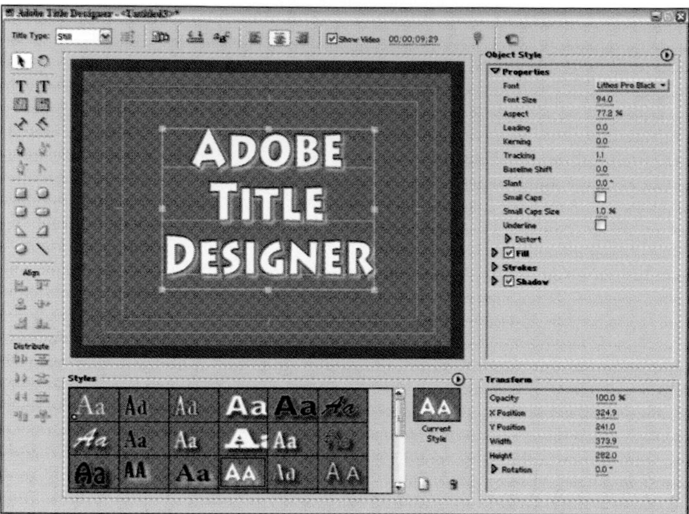

Figure 9.1 The Adobe Title Designer is composed of the tools palette (left side vertical), a top row of controls, the Object Style panel, the Transform panel, the Styles Library, and the drawing area.

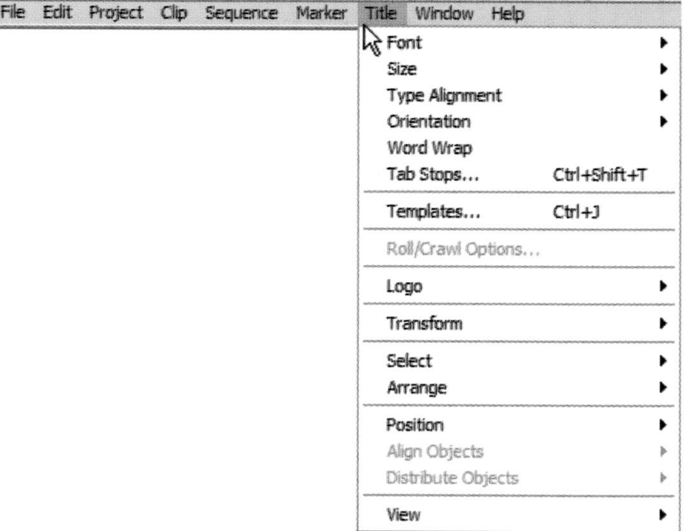

Figure 9.2 Some controls, such as Word Wrap, are available only from the Title menu. You can access a subset of the full Title menu by right-clicking in empty space of the drawing area.

Top Row Controls

The top row of controls in the Title Designer (see Figure 9.3) begins with the Title Type drop-down menu. Here you specify the type of title you are creating:

- **Still.** A static title that doesn't move.
- **Roll.** A vertically moving, or rolling, title.
- **Crawl.** A horizontally scrolling title.

When you choose Roll or Crawl, you can access the Roll/Crawl Options dialog by clicking the icon next to the Title Type menu. If you want your roll or crawl to start or end with the entire title off screen, check the appropriate box in the dialog. (See Figure 9.4.) You then can assign frame values for how long you want the title to be off screen before it comes on (Preroll), how long you want it to take to move to its center position (Ease-In), how long you want it to take to get back off screen (Ease-Out), and finally how long you want it to hold off screen (Postroll).

Figure 9.3 The top row of controls contains the Title Type drop-down, Roll/Crawl options, the Templates button, the Tab Stop button, the Font Browser, three Type Alignment buttons, the Show Video check box, a hot-text field for the background video timecode, the Sync to Timeline Timecode button, and the Send Frame to External Monitor button.

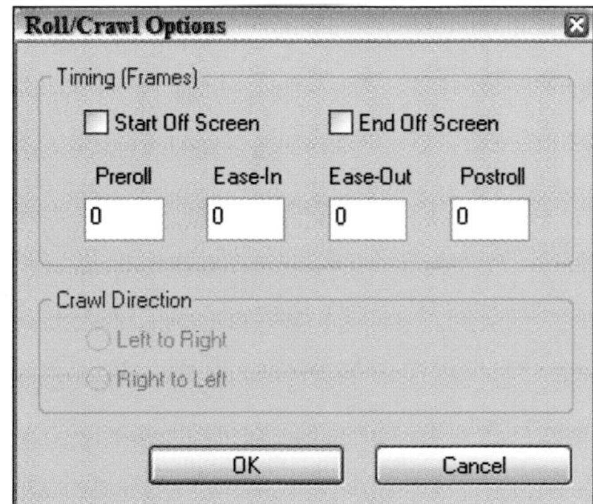

Figure 9.4 Clicking the Start Off Screen and End Off Screen check boxes allows your rolling or crawling title to start completely out of view then roll (vertically) or crawl (horizontally) on and off screen.

If it is important for you to preview specific characters in the Font Browser, go to Edit>Preferences>Titler. In the Titler Preferences window, you can specify exactly which characters are displayed in the Font Browser.

Next to the Roll/Crawl Options button is the Template button. Click this to access a host of ready-made templates and load them into the Title Designer. You can use them as is, or modify them (more on this at the end of the chapter).

The Tab Stop button (Ctrl+Shift+T) becomes active when you select text. Tab stops are very helpful for creating a credit roll, as you will see in Chapter 13, "Advanced Titling: Templates."

Next is the Font Browser button. Select any text, click this button, and you can scroll through a list of font choices (see Figure 9.5). Click on a font, and Premiere updates your text in a preview of the selected font. You also can use the Up and Down arrows to navigate to the next and previous fonts quickly. I really like the Font Browser, because it gives you an exact image of what each font looks like. From the enormous default list, you can see that Premiere Pro installs a ton of fonts for you.

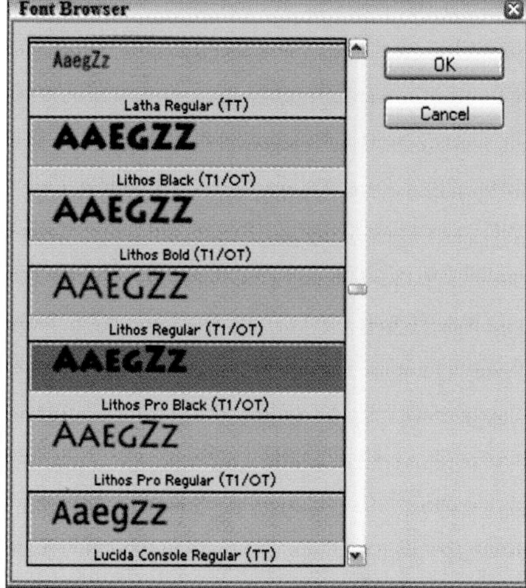

Figure 9.5 The Font Browser is a great interface for previewing what a font looks like and applying the font to your text.

The next three buttons are for assigning type alignment justification: Left, Center, and Right. With any paragraph or text item selected, clicking an alignment button will align the text to that setting.

The Show Video check box toggles on or off the Video Frame display from the open sequence. If the box is checked, you will see the associated video frame beneath your title. The hot text box to the right is tied to the timecode value in the open sequence. If you enter a timecode value or scrub the hot-text value, the displayed video frame updates to the frame in that timecode position. This is very helpful when you want to determine the exact positioning or proper color choices for a title. Checking Show Video and navigating with the timecode hot text enables you to see what your title looks like over any frame in your sequence.

If you want the displayed video frame to snap back to a special point in the sequence, position the CTI there. Now, click the Sync to Timeline Timecode button to move the title-over-video display to the CTI's position in the sequence.

The last button along the top row, Send Frame to External Monitor, sends the current displayed frame in your drawing area out to your connected DV device. If you click the Send Frame to External Monitor button (or press Ctrl+E), Premiere sends the active frame to your device via FireWire, whether video is showing or not. This is helpful for seeing how the final title will look on a proper video monitor, as opposed to your computer desktop.

Object Style and Transform Panels

The Object Style panel houses all of the adjustable style properties for both text and objects. Select any item created in the Title Designer to see its editable properties displayed in this panel. (See Figure 9.6.)

A *style* is a saved set of object properties (color, font, size, and so on) that you can use on any subsequent object or text item.

Just below the Object Style panel is the Transform panel. Here you can move and adjust the position, rotation, and opacity for selected items in the Title Designer. You will learn more about the Transform panel's controls later in the chapter.

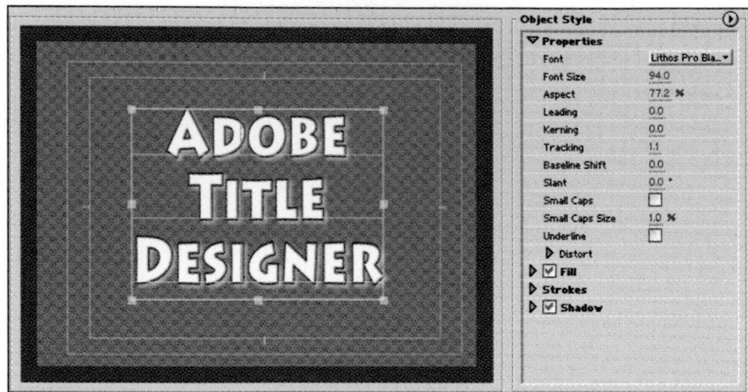

Figure 9.6 With text selected in the drawing area, the fields of the Object Style panel reflect all the settings associated with that text. Adjusting any of these fields dynamically updates the selection in the drawing area.

Text and Object Creation Tools Palette

The Title Designer's tools palette houses text and object creation tools (see Figure 9.7). From the top, left to right the tools are:

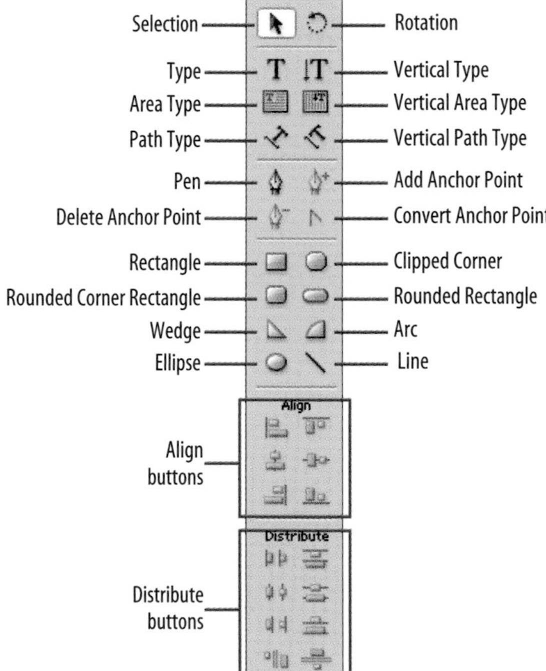

Figure 9.7 The tools palette holds the Title Designer's object and text creation tools.

- **Selection** (shortcut key: V). For selecting, moving, and adjusting objects.
- **Rotation** (shortcut key: O). For grabbing and rotating text or objects.
- **Type** (shortcut key: T). For creating text.
- **Vertical Type** (shortcut key: C). For creating vertical text.
- **Area Type.** For defining a box in which to add horizontally oriented text. You specify the box size. Think of it as the text-in-a-box tool.
- **Vertical Area Type.** For defining a box in which to add vertically oriented text. Again, you specify the box size.
- **Path Type.** For writing text on a defined path.
- **Vertical Path Type.** For writing vertical text on a path.

Below the path type tools are the path adjustment tools:

- **Pen** (shortcut key: P). For creating and adjusting anchor points.
- **Add Anchor Point.** For adding anchor points on a path.
- **Delete Anchor Point.** For deleting or removing an anchor point on a path.
- **Convert Anchor Point.** For converting an anchor point into a smooth curve. Think of it as the Bezier-adjustment tool.

The last group in the tools palette is the object creation tools, which are pretty self-explanatory:

- Rectangle (shortcut key: R)
- Clipped Corner
- Two Rounded Corner Rectangles with different levels of curves with the corners.
- Wedge (shortcut key: W)
- Arc (shortcut key: A)
- Ellipse (shortcut key: E)
- Line (shortcut key: L)

Below these tools are the Align and Distribute buttons, which enable you to align and distribute multiple selected objects. These buttons are active only when more than one title element is selected. If you want to align three items horizontally, for example, click and select the three objects then choose the button for horizontal center alignment.

The Styles Library

The Styles Library at the very bottom of the Title Designer is where you can load, save, and apply styles to selected objects and text in the drawing area (see Figure 9.8). A small icon, or *swatch,* displays for each available style. You can also load additional styles from the Styles folder in your Program Files/Adobe/Premiere Pro/Presets directory.

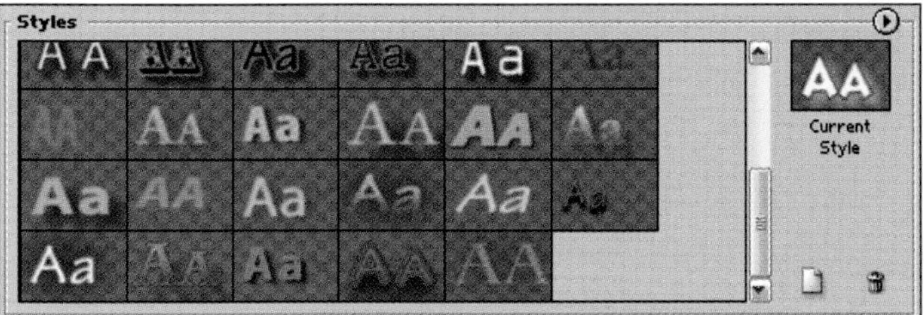

Figure 9.8 Preview the look of a style in the Style library, then click on the style to apply it to the selected items in your drawing area.

When you create text or an object in the drawing area, Premiere automatically applies the default style to it. Identified by a small diamond on the swatch, the default style swatch appears in the first position of the library (upper-left corner). To set a new style as the default style, right-click on the new style and choose Set Style as Default from the context menu. To change the style of text or an object, select it in the drawing area and click a style swatch to apply the associated style attributes to it. Although the style swatches that come with Premiere Pro are specifically designed for text, they can be applied to both text and objects.

To better understand style attributes, take a closer look at the details of creating and using styles with objects and text.

Creating an Object

To create an object, select an object creation tool, such as Rectangle, from the tools palette, then click and drag in the drawing area. The farther you drag from the first click point, the larger your object. To conform the object to a 1:1 ratio, hold down Shift as you drag. If you want to make a perfect circle, for example, select the Ellipse tool, hold down the Shift key, and drag. (See Figure 9.9.)

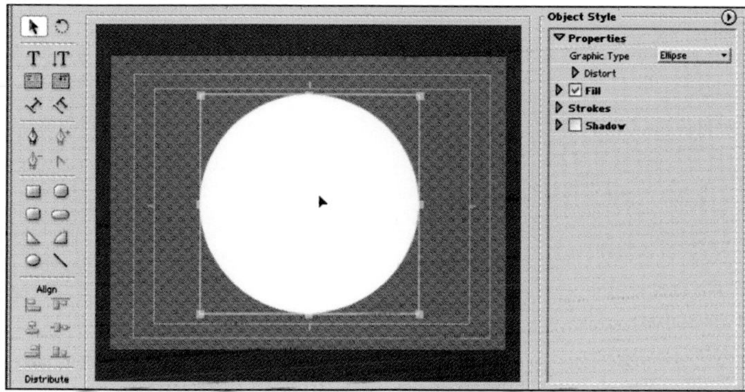

Figure 9.9 This 1:1 circle was created using the Ellipse tool. Its default style is solid white, as shown in the Object Style panel.

When your cursor is in a Tool mode (one of the 15 text or object tools), its only function is to create the item associated with the tool. If you want to modify an object's dimensions, you must switch to the Selection tool (press V or click it in the tools palette). With the Selection tool, you can click and drag the objects to move them. Pressing Alt while dragging duplicates an object.

Editing an Object's Physical Dimensions

Create a square or any object, then click on the Selection tool to activate it; you will see eight adjustment handles with which you can modify the object's dimensions. Clicking and dragging on the corner handles increases the object's size from the selected corner. Clicking and dragging from the side handle points adjusts the size of the object on the side that you are dragging. In both cases, holding the Shift key while dragging preserves the object's aspect ratio, meaning the object's size will increase or decrease uniformly. Hover over one of the corner handles, the cursor switches to the Rotation tool; grab the handles to rotate the selected item. Holding down the Shift key constrains rotation to exact 45-degree increments. (See Figure 9.10.)

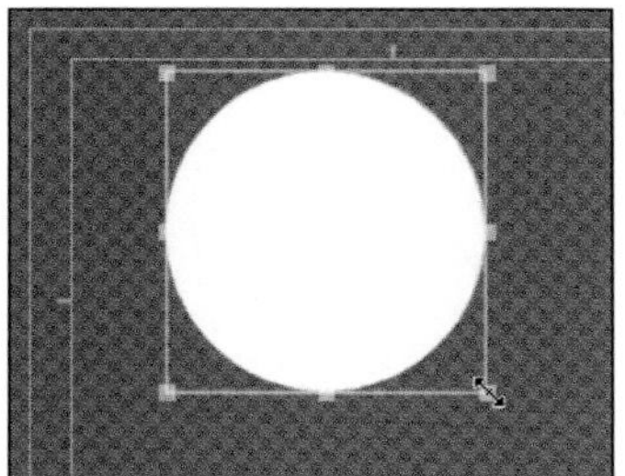

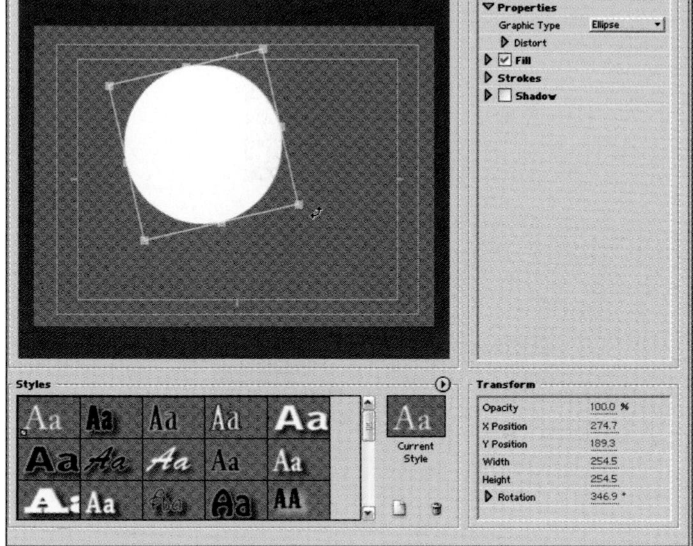

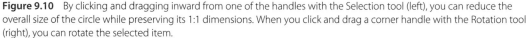

Figure 9.10 By clicking and dragging inward from one of the handles with the Selection tool (left), you can reduce the overall size of the circle while preserving its 1:1 dimensions. When you click and drag a corner handle with the Rotation tool (right), you can rotate the selected item.

For more detailed adjustments to specific dimensions, select the object and adjust it using the controls in the Transform panel (see Figure 9.11). Here, you can adjust the object's location by specifying coordinates for X Position and Y Position, as well as set exact values for the object's Width and Height. You can also adjust the Opacity parameter, which determines the transparency of the object, and Rotation, which turns the object the number of degrees you specify, up to 360.

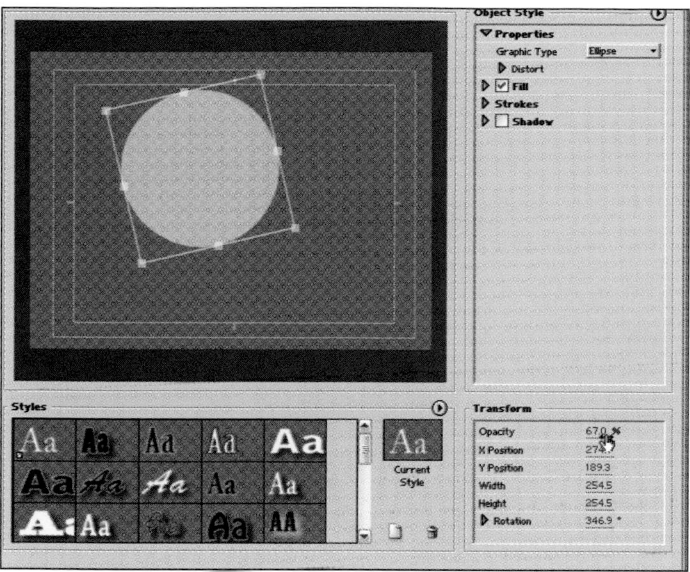

Figure 9.11 The Transform panel displays the exact Opacity, Position, Size, and Rotation values for the selected item. Because all of these fields are hot text, you can easily adjust any of them to exact settings.

Object Styles

Although you can change an object's style simply by clicking on a different swatch in the Styles Library, the Object Style panel provides more details about and adjustments for the chosen style. Four twirl down menus give you access to the necessary parameters: Properties, Fill, Strokes, and Shadow.

Properties

Select your object, then twirl down the Object Style panel's Properties menu (see Figure 9.12). The resulting Graphic Type drop-down menu lists the current object type and enables you to switch to a new type of object with the same dimensions as the original. Twirl down the Distort menu and adjust the X and Y values to add some x- and y-axis bending or distortion to your object. If you have text selected, an expanded drop-down menu appears revealing additional text-specific adjustment fields.

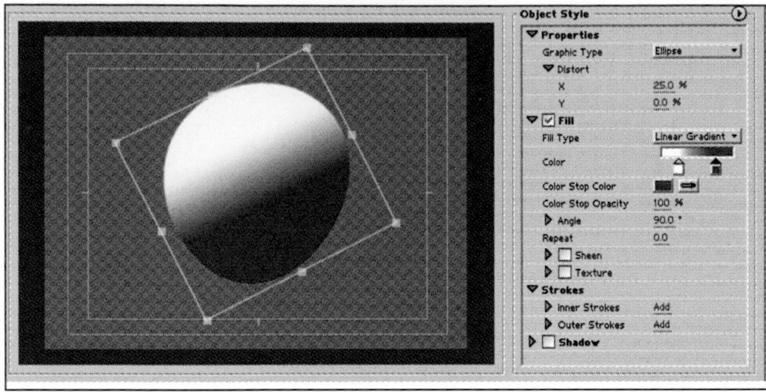

Figure 9.12 The Object Style reveals the style details associated with the selected ellipse. Notice that the X axis distortion has altered the shape of the circle and that the active Fill is using a linear gradient with the color split at a 90 degree angle. The dark arrow above the red color box for the gradient means that you can adjust and assign that color using the color stop color controls below.

Fill

The Fill twirl down houses controls for adjusting the object's fill type, color, and more. For a transparent object, make sure the Fill check box is empty. Click the Fill check box on to access its controls. For example, the Fill Type drop-down menu enables you to specify the kind of fill you want: one solid color, two colors in a linear or radial gradient, four colors in a gradient, a bevel, Eliminate, which makes both an object's fill and shadow transparent, or Ghost, which removes the fill, but keeps the shadow. You can specify the fill color two different ways: Click in the color box to access the Color Picker, or click and drag the eye-dropper over any color in your desktop window, then click again to set that color.

If you are assigning colors to a gradient, each color in the gradient has a box associated with it and an arrow pointing to where the color exists at its full value. To assign a color, click the box for the color that you want to change. The arrow above the box will turn black, and any adjustment you make using the eye-dropper or Color Picker will update the selected gradient color. Clicking and dragging the boxes, you can increase or decrease the distance and positioning of the two colors.

Whether you are assigning one, two, or four fill colors, each fill color has an Opacity parameter that you can adjust. If you want one color of your two-color gradient to be a little bit transparent, select that color (by clicking the box) then adjust its Opacity value.

Sheen

Your fill can also have a *sheen*, which emulates a highlight on a shiny surface, like a chrome effect. To add a sheen to your object, click the Sheen check box and twirl down its parameters. (See Figure 9.13.) A sheen's Color and Opacity settings work the same as those for a basic fill, and the rest of the sheen parameters are pretty self explanatory. If you want a thin diagonal white stripe, for example, set Color to white, Size to 10, and Angle to 135. If you do not want the stripe centered, adjust Offset to shift it up or down. Chapter 12, "Advanced Titling: Styles" uses a sheen to help accentuate the shiny look of a lower third title.

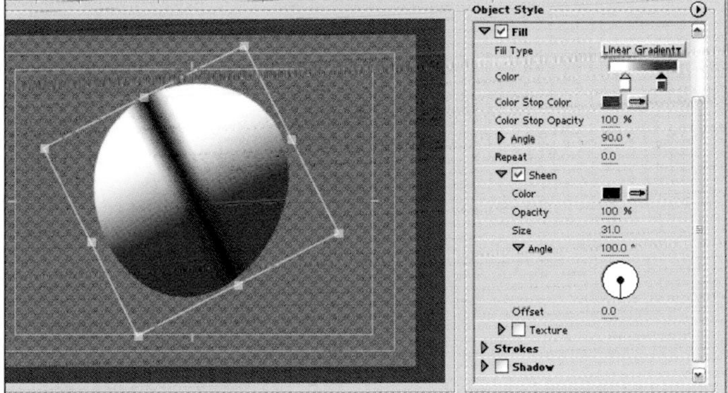

Figure 9.13 With the Sheen check box on in the Object Style panel, you can adjust the color, opacity, size, angle, and offset of this black sheen.

Texture

Click the Texture check box on and twirl down its parameters to specify an external graphic to fill your text or object. Click inside the Texture box, and choose an image to load. Premiere automatically inserts it inside your object's fill area. Using the Flip with Object and Rotate with Object check boxes, you can lock the orientation of the fill image (texture) to that of the object, so that if the object is flipped or rotated, then the texture flips or rotates accordingly.

The Scaling twirl down menu enables you to scale the size of the texture inside the object, while the Alignment twirl down lets you change the alignment of the texture image, moving it left or right, up or down inside the fill. Twirl down Blending to blend the texture with the fill color and more.

Strokes

Strokes are basically outlines (see Figure 9.14). They are not called outlines, because there are two types of strokes: inner strokes and outer strokes. An inner stroke is a line inside the defined edge of your object. When you increase the size of an inner stroke, it grows inward, closer to the center of your object. An outer stroke uses the edge of the object as its starting boundary and grows outward when you increase its size.

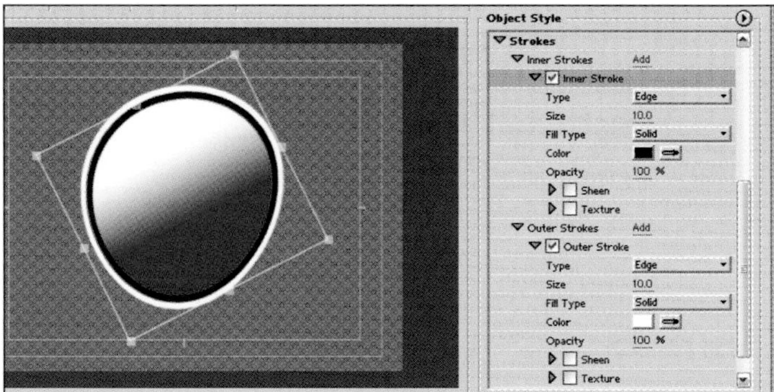

Figure 9.14 This object has both an inner stroke (black) and outer stroke (white). In addition to adjusting the stroke's default values, you can add a sheen or texture to the fill of the stroke.

To add and adjust an inner or outer stroke, twirl down the Strokes menu and click Add for the stroke you wish to create. You can create several inner and outer strokes, so get used to twirling down quite a bit to reveal the properties of each stroke.

Strokes can be one of three types:

- **Edge.** A basic line; the default type.
- **Depth.** An angled edge on one side of your object that appears to add depth to the object. (See Figure 9.15.)

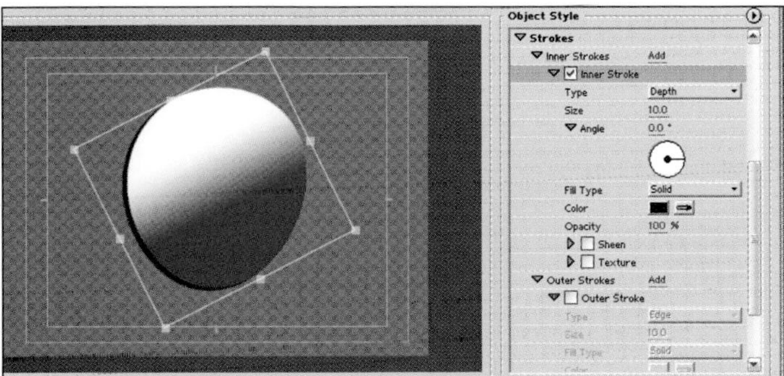

Figure 9.15 This time the object has Depth inner stroke. Notice how the depth appears on one side of the object, as if the object was viewed at an angle.

- **Drop Face.** A copy of the object's size and dimensions that you can shift inside the object's boundaries for an inner stroke or outside for an outer stroke.

Each stroke type has its own adjustments. For Edge strokes, you can set the line's size. For Depth strokes, you can adjust the angle and size. For Drop Face strokes, you can adjust the angle and magnitude of the stroke. The magnitude is the amount of shifting applied to the drop face of the object.

The controls for specifying fill type, choosing a color, setting opacity, and adding a Sheen or Texture mirror those for the Fill parameters.

Shadow

The final style attribute is Shadow. Click the check box and twirl down to access the Shadow parameters: Color, Opacity, Angle, Distance, Size, and Spread. Color and Opacity operate as they do for Fill and Strokes. Angle dictates the angle from which the shadow falls. Distance measures the space between the object and the shadow—how close or how far away the shadow is from the object. Size adjusts the shadow's overall size in accordance with the object: A value of 0.0 creates a shadow of equal size to the object, negative values create smaller shadows, and positive values result in larger shadows. Spread dithers or softens the edge of the shadow's color. Increasing the Spread value softens the shadows edges and gives the illusion of them disappearing into the other color, as opposed to dropping off.

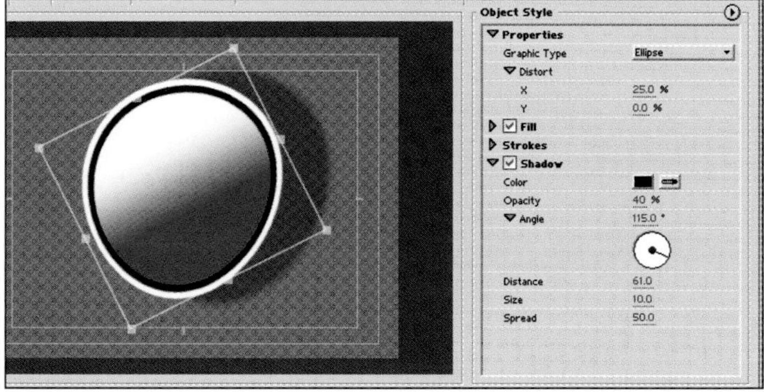

Figure 9.16 This shadow is a bit larger than its object (Size set to 10) and has a soft end edge (Spread set to 50).

Creating Text

Creating text is as simple as creating objects, with a few more functions and details thrown in. Decide on the orientation of your text—horizontal versus vertical, inside of a box or on a path—and click the associated text creation tool: Type, Vertical Type, Area Type, Vertical Area Type, Path Type, or Vertical Path Type. Click in the drawing area to create an instance for text to be added and begin typing. As you type, the text appears in the default style. (See Figure 9.17.)

Text creation tools have two states: Create mode and Edit mode. Select a text creation tool and mouse over blank space in the drawing area. See the little dotted lines around the tool? These dotted lines tell you that when you click you will create a new instance where you can add text. With the same text tool selected, mouse over existing text: The dotted lines are gone. Click within the boundaries of existing text to select a specific character position to modify or add to. To select multiple words or characters, you need to click and drag inside the text area.

If you want to move text, either switch to the Selection tool and drag it or with the current text active and the text tool still selected, move and adjust the text's position properties in the Transform panel. (See Figure 9.18.)

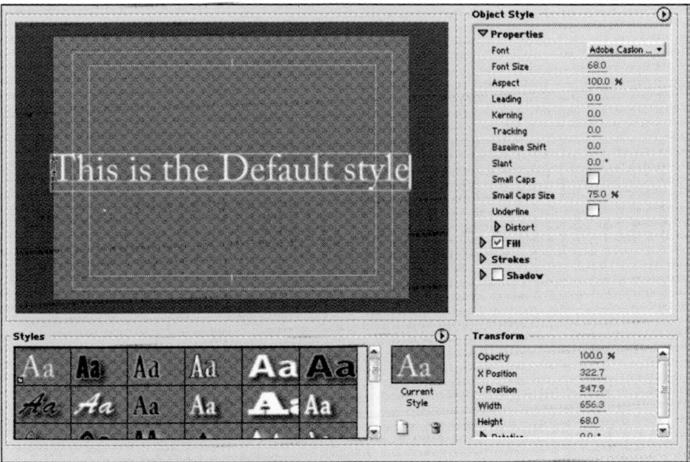

Figure 9.17 Using the Type tool, you can enter text in the drawing area by clicking with the tool and then typing. Notice that the text uses the default style, which is the swatch marked with the small diamond in the Styles Library.

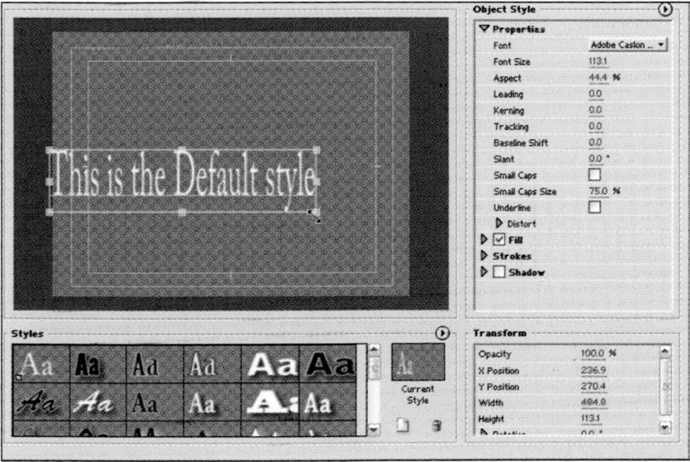

Figure 9.18 Use the Selection tool to select, resize, rotate, or move text. Hold down the Shift key and adjust the text's scale to change the font size dynamically.

If you click on the Selection tool and select a text element, a box with handles appears around that text. Pulling the side or corner handles makes the same alterations as for objects. Holding the Shift key constrains the adjustment so that the text does not distort as you enlarge or shrink it.

Type Alignment

When entering text, you can specify how you would like it aligned: centered, left justified, or right justified. You can do this in a few different ways: Select the text box, and choose Title>Type Alignment from the main menu bar, then pick your alignment format (Left, Center, or Right). You can also right-click on a text selection and choose Type Alignment from the context menu that appears. Or, simply click one of the alignment buttons from the top row of controls.

Text Styles

You can apply styles to text by clicking a swatch in the Styles Library. Once the style is activated for the selected text, you can fine-tune that style by adjusting the listed parameters in the Object Style panel. A key feature of applying styles to text is that you can select either entire words or individual letters and apply different styles. (See Figure 9.19.)

The Object Style panel's Fill, Strokes, and Shadow twirl downs for text are the same as for objects. The Properties twirl down for text, however, has 11 additional attributes to adjust. The first is the Font drop-down menu. To specify your text's font, choose one from the menu's list or choose Browse to access the Font Browser. The text automatically updates to display the new font. Clicking and dragging the Font Size hot-text box dynamically and visually adjusts the size of the font. This is where I get jazzed about the Title Designer; most titlers force you to enter specific number values for text properties, then you have to wait for a preview of the property after you enter the value.

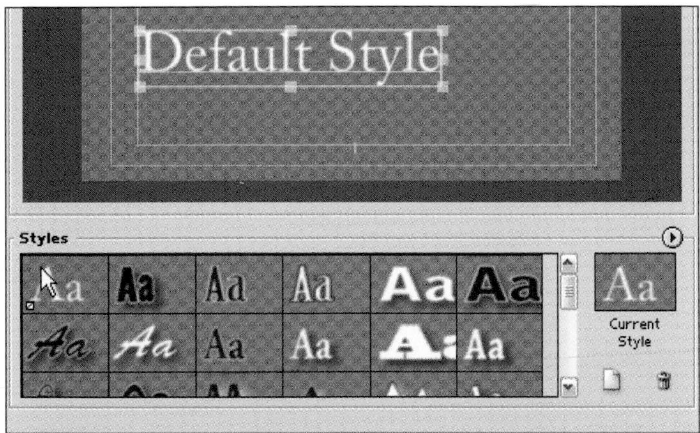

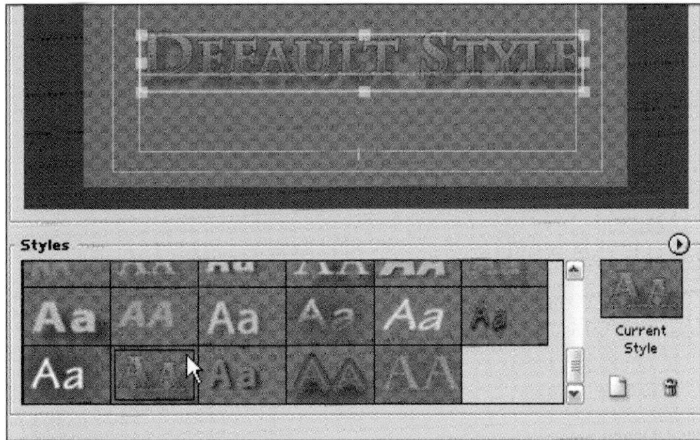

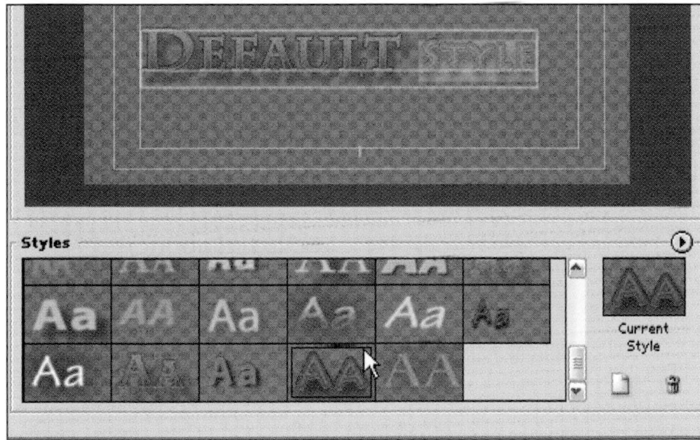

Figure 9.19 When you first add text to the drawing area, it appears in the default style (top). Select all the text and click a swatch in the Styles Library to apply a new style (middle), or select only a portion of the text and apply a new style to that (bottom).

With the Aspect parameter, you can adjust the stretch of your text. Settings above 100% pull the text from its first character's position; settings below 100% squish the text closer together.

The Leading attribute adjusts the space between lines of text. Adding to the value creates more space between lines, and reducing brings the lines closer together. (See Figure 9.20.)

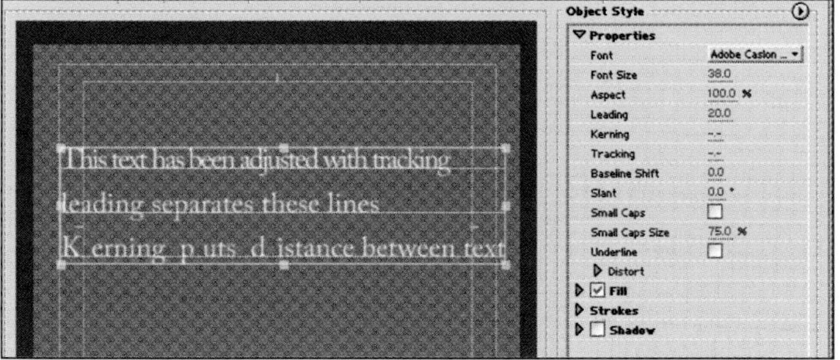

Figure 9.20 Reducing Tracking for the first line brought all the letters closer together. The extra spaces on the third line were created by clicking between pairs of characters and increasing Kerning. The Leading setting determined the distance between the lines.

To change the space between individual characters, use Kerning. Say you want a comma to fit more snugly next to the character on its left. With the Type tool, you would click between the letter and the comma, then change the Kerning setting to a negative value to bring the characters closer together. Positive Kerning values move characters farther apart. (See Figure 9.20.)

The Tracking setting enables you to adjust the kerning for all characters equally. To add more space between every character of text, slide the Tracking hot text value to the right into positive numbers. Sliding left into negative numbers reduces the space between all characters. (See Figure 9.20.)

The invisible line on which all your text is written is referred to as the *baseline*. To move the entire text or a specific character above or below the baseline, increase or decrease the Baseline Shift value, respectively. If you want something more creative than a flat horizontal line, use the Path Type tool or Vertical Path Type tool to define the line. Combining Kerning and Baseline Shift, you could very easily move that example comma closer to the character on its left and then up or down to an even better position.

The Slant attributes give you a pseudo italics look, slanting your characters based on the angle you choose.

The next attribute is very cool. The Small Caps check box enables you to convert all of your text to capital letters in one click (see Figure 9.21). By keeping Small Caps Size set to less than 100%, you can preserve the text's original hierarchy of lowercase to capital letters. The default Small Caps Size is 75%, meaning that lowercase letters will be capitalized but their size will be 75% of the full size. Of course, your font must support lowercase letters for this to be most effective.

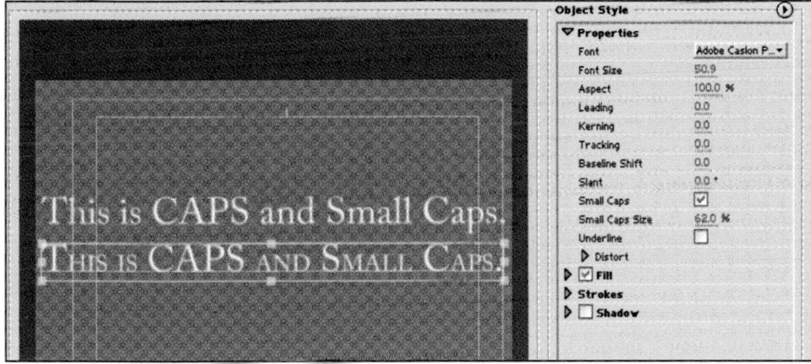

Figure 9.21 The second line of text is a duplicate of the first, but with Small Caps turned on and Small Caps Size set to 62%. Notice how Small Caps keeps the same proportions as in the sentence with both upper- and lowercase letters.

The last unique text property is Underline. Clicking on the Underline check box adds an underline beneath your text. The underline always respects the bottom of the character. In other words, if you add a baseline shift, the underline adheres to the bottom of the text, not the default baseline.

Although they apply distortion based on the X and Y axis for text as they do for objects, the Distort hot-text boxes are worth a mention. Although you can easily see distortion on large objects, the result is often very subtle on text. Playing with the Distort settings, however, can result in cool-looking characters. I encourage you to tinker with these, as well as fills, shadows, and strokes. Chapter 12, "Advanced Titling: Styles," will guide you through some creative alterations on the way to making a custom style.

Moving and Arranging Text and Objects

Once you have items within the boundaries of your drawing area, you can select them using the click-and-drag method (Shift-click to select multiple items). After selecting items, you can move them around.

Using the Transform panel, you can adjust an item's opacity, position, overall size, and rotation. If you have multiple items selected and are using the Selection tool, the cursor will update to illustrate whether you are making a position (arrow) adjustment or rotation (Rotation tool) adjustment. This is the same as the selection behavior for modifying selected text or objects.

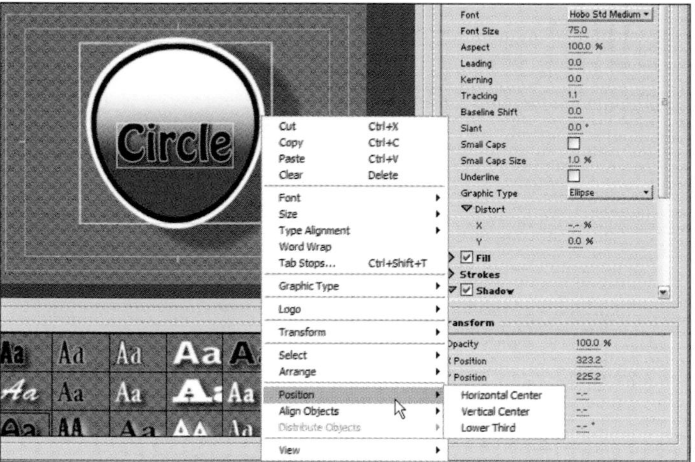

Figure 9.22 With both the text and object selected, you can still resize, rotate, and reposition the selected items as if they were one. Additionally, you can right-click on the selection to change the position of the selection within the drawing area.

With one or more items selected, you can right-click on the selection and access the Position submenu's three options:

- **Horizontal Center.** Leaves the vertical position of your selection the same but centers the selection horizontally.
- **Vertical Center.** Preserves the horizontal position of your selection and centers the selection vertically.
- **Lower Third.** Preserves the horizontal position of your selection and moves the selection down to the lower third of the frame.

Lower third refers to the lower-third portion of your frame. Typically news casts include a title that introduces a person with their name. This title resides in the lower third of the frame.

If you have two items created on top of each other or you have text that you want to appear on top of an object, you may need to change the stacking order of these items. Right-click the item and choose Arrange>Send to Back to send it to the bottom of the stack, or right-click and choose Arrange>Bring to Front to bring it to the top of the stack. To bring an item forward (closer to the top) by one position, right-click and select Arrange>Bring Forward. To send an item backward one level (farther from the top), right-click and select Arrange>Send Backward. If you prefer working with the Title menu, select the item, then choose Title>Arrange and the direction you want to go.

If all of the manipulating, shifting, and adjusting is too much, the Adobe Title Designer does offer some helpful ready-made templates that you can load and modify in a few simple steps.

Using Templates

Templates are pre-made title layouts that you can load and modify. Whether you're working on a video for your child's birthday, your family vacation, or another event, the odds are likely Premiere Pro offers a title template suited to your project. Templates provide integrated text and graphic elements that you can load and modify to add a bit more visual spice to your edited project. (See Figure 9.23.)

All of Premiere's built-in templates were created using the Adobe Title Designer. If you want to examine some title-making techniques, select a template and explore the Object Style and Transform panel settings for all the template's elements.

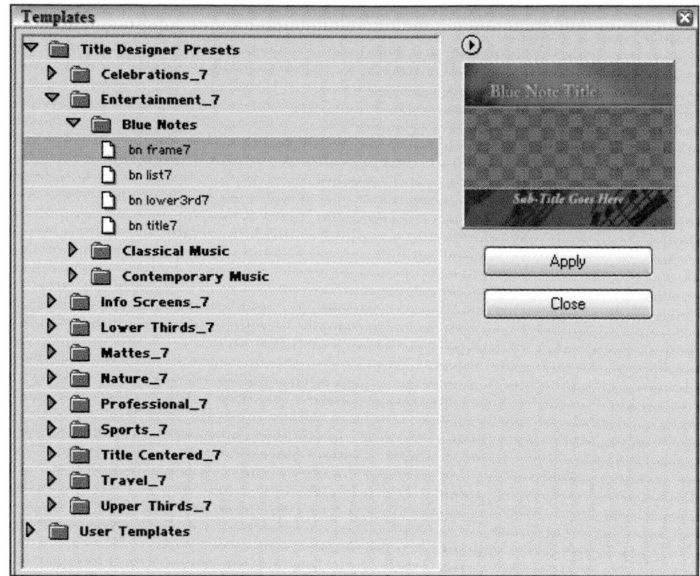

Figure 9.23 From the Templates dialog, you can select and load ready-made title templates.

To load a template, click on the Templates button in the Title Designer's top row of commands, then select a template from the cascade of expanding folders in the Templates dialog. The dialog's right panel displays a preview of the selected template. Click OK to open the selected template inside of your drawing area. Be careful, however: When you load a template, it overwrites whatever items exist in your drawing area.

Modifying a Template

Once loaded, templates are pretty simple to modify. To modify a template or personalize it for your titling needs, select the Type tool and click within the boundaries of the text that you want to alter. (See Figure 9.24.) Making sure you do not see the dotted lines, click and select the text you want to change, then retype the text as you wish.

If you want to make your newly added text a little bit bigger or a different color, adjust the Object Style panel attributes as you see fit. Likewise, you can click and select any object in the template to modify it.

Figure 9.24 In the top image, the Type tool displays as if it is going to add new text. In the bottom image, a template is loaded and the Type tool is hovering over a text element. Note how the text gets highlighted with a box and the Type tool displays without the dotted lines. Clicking would allow you select and modify the highlighted text.

Saving Templates

You can save any custom text or object layout as a template for future use. The first step is to access the Templates dialog (click the Templates button in the top row of commands or press Ctrl+J). In the wing menu of the Templates dialog, choose Save <Titlename> as Template. You will be prompted to then name your custom template. Clicking OK saves a copy of the current layout in your Templates folder (on your root disk) with the name you specify, plus adds an instance of it into your User Templates folder in the Template dialog's left panel. It's pretty easy and incredibly useful to create your own library of templates to suit unique project needs.

Chapter 13 will add a few helpful templates to this folder.

Things to Remember

If you are feeling unsure about your title creation skills, I highly recommend loading some templates and modifying them to suit your needs. To create a simple new look, I typically load a lower-third template then change the shape and color of the object, as well as the text's size and font. If I am happy with the results, I save the modified template as a new custom template.

As you make your adjustments, remember that with text you can make every property adjustment to either individual characters or entire text selections. If you want a word with a different font for each letter, for example, simply select each letter in turn, changing the font each time. The same goes for adjusting color, strokes, and shadows. With this in mind, you can create a diverse selection of titles and explore some wacky, but cool options.

This chapter marks the end of the introductory section for *Adobe Premiere Pro Studio Techniques*. From here, the book dives head first into techniques, workflow, and practical working examples of how to use Premiere Pro to its fullest potential.

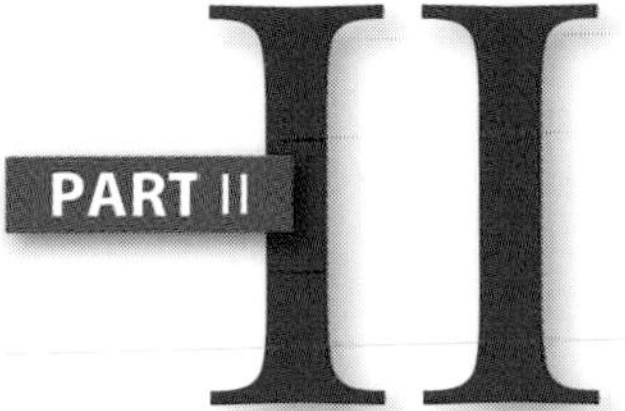

Advanced Graphics and Titles

CHAPTER

10

Working with Photoshop Files and Nesting Sequences

One of the most welcome features of Adobe Premiere Pro is its ability to import a layered Photoshop file. Importing all those layers, however, can significantly increase the number of files in your final sequence.

To reap the benefit of this new feature without the added cost, use nesting. *Nesting* is the process of consolidating multiple files into a single sequence that represents the entire group. Not only is nesting a powerful way of minimizing clutter in sequences, it is also an efficient way to group clips for better control of effect placement.

In this chapter, you will learn how to nest groups of layers to add motion and effects to individual layers without altering the integrity of the original Photoshop file. The first lesson will teach basic nesting by creating a graphic opening for a photo montage. You will then apply motion and some transitions to the elements of that nested sequence in the second lesson.

Nesting Sequences

Using nesting techniques, you can create effects that are much easier to control and adjust. Here you will import a nine-layer Photoshop file and reduce it down to four sequence files, each consisting of grouped layers.

The photo montage itself is the subject of Chapter 11, "Working with Still Images."

To import a single layer from a Photoshop file, set Import As to Footage and select the layer you want to import from the Choose Layer drop-down menu.

The Photoshop file for the example project maps three cities in Italy and will become the intro to a photo montage. Each of the city's names will fade in and enlarge, then the scene will cut to photographs of the named city. To adjust the different city names separately, you will need to nest specific cities together. This lesson preps the framework for the files so that you can create the desired effect with a greater amount of control in the next lesson.

1. Open the Nest_Start.prproj file from the APPST Lesson Files/Chapter 10 folder. Select File>Import, and open Italy_MapDV.psd from the same folder. From the resulting Import Layered File dialog, select Sequence from the Import As drop-down menu, and click OK. (See Figure 10.1.)

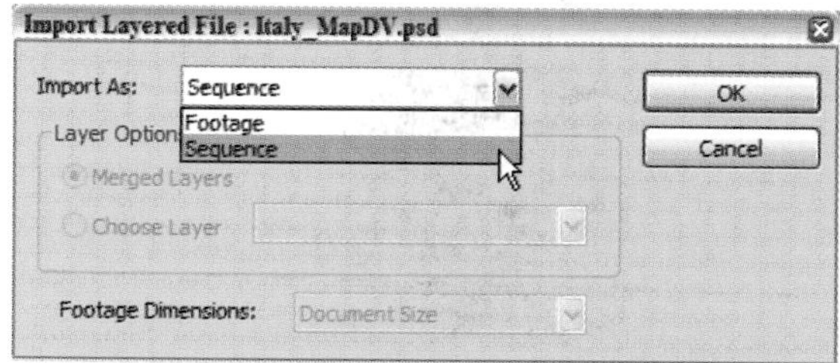

Figure 10.1 When you open a Photoshop file, you can import single layers or the entire document as a flattened still (Footage) or import all of the layers as a sequence.

This step imports the Photoshop file as a unique sequence that properly reflects the Photoshop document's stacking order. Each layer becomes a separate still in its own track. (See Figures 10.2 and 10.3.) Transfer modes, such as Darken, Difference, and Exclusion, are not supported when importing into Premiere Pro.

Figure 10.2 The original document in Photoshop. Notice the name of each layer and the order in which the layers are stacked.

Figure 10.3 Importing the layered Photoshop file into Premiere Pro creates this sequence. Notice that the stacking order and layer names duplicate those of the original and that the image looks the same in the Program Monitor as it did in Photoshop.

When you import, Premiere creates in a new folder: Italy_MapDV. Inside are nine still images and a single sequence. Each still image reflects an individual layer from the Photoshop file. The sequence, named exactly for the Photoshop file, contains all the stills stacked above each other in the same order as the original Photoshop file. These nine files make up the image that displays in the Program Monitor when you scrub over their timeline position.

Figure 10.4 With the Edit Line over the two tracks, the Program Monitor displays the result of the two Rome layers, the name and the button. Because the layers were created in Photoshop, the black space around the letters is attributed to the alpha channel; this means that it is transparent or keyed out when you place it on top of other content.

2. Select Project>Projects Settings>Default Sequence. Set Video Tracks to 2 and Audio Master to Stereo with 1 Stereo Track. Click OK out of this dialog, then create five new sequences and name them: Rome, Florence, Portofino, Italy Map, and Map Comp.

   Adjusting the default sequence value lets you quickly create sequences with a specific track number. The five unique sequences you created later will house, respectively, the three city layers, the map layers, and the final composition of the four sequences.

3. Click on the Rome tab in the Timeline window to open the Rome sequence. Open the Italy_MapDV folder, and drag and drop the Rome Button/Italy_MapDV.psd file onto the Video 1 track of the Rome sequence. Drag and drop the Roma/Italy_MapDV.psd file onto the Video 2 track directly above the instance on Video 1. (See Figure 10.4.) Open the Florence sequence. Drag and drop the Florence Button/Italy_MapDV.psd file to Video 1 and Firenze/Italy_MapDV.psd to Video 2. Finally, open the Portofino sequence, drop the Button layer to Video 1 and the Name layer to Video 2.

   Because you want to control the city name and the button for the city independently, both layers need to be nested into their own sequence. Putting the button on Video 1 and city name on Video 2 ensures that the city name remains on top of the button when it is resized or repositioned. Each single city sequence now reflects the result of the two layers inside of it.

4. Click on the Italy Map tab in the Timeline window to open the sequence. Drag and drop the Pattern Fill/Italy_MapDV.psd to Video 1. Drag and drop the Color Layer/Italy_MapDV.psd to Video 2 directly on top of the file on Video 1. Drag and drop the Outline/Italy_MapDV.psd file into the gray space above Video 2, snapping to the head of the timeline directly on top of the files below.

As you did for the city names, here you created a single sequence to display the map layers. Because there were only two tracks available for adding content, you created a third by dragging and dropping to the empty gray space above Video 2.

Although you won't be applying an effect to the Map layers, one file will be easier to manage than three in the final composition.

5. Click on the Map Comp tab in the Timeline window to open the Map Comp sequence. Locate the five sequences you created in the Project window. Hold down the Ctrl key, and double-click on the Italy Map sequence in the Project window to load it in the Source Monitor. Toggle the Take Audio/Video button to Video Only. Drag and drop the Source Monitor sequence into the Video 1 track of the Map Comp sequence. (See Figure 10.5.)

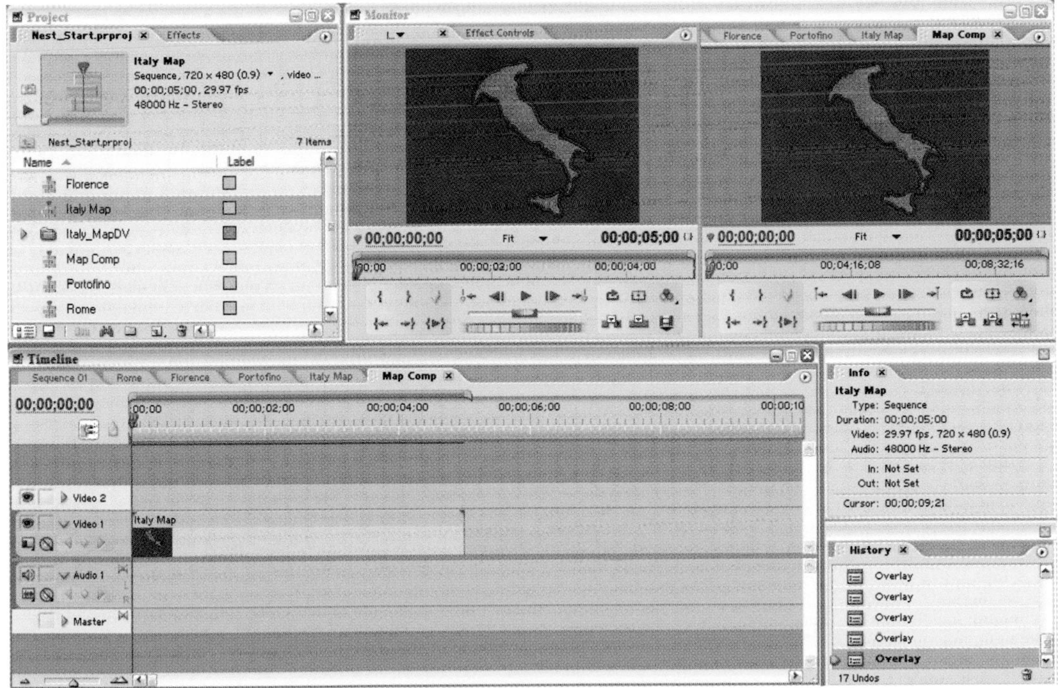

Figure 10.5 The Italy Map Sequence was opened as if it were a clip in the Source Monitor. Take Audio/Video is set to Video Only, and the result of the drag and drop to the timeline is a single clip on the Video 1 track. Notice that the clip name is the same as the name of the sequence that it represents. Double-clicking on this clip, which is now a **nested sequence**, In Video 1 opens the Italy Map sequence in the Timeline window.

Because you are not going to use any of the audio tracks from the individual sequences, you turned off their audio before nesting them into the final composition. Nesting the Italy Map on Video 1 ensured that the map is beneath all the other layers. Now you can finish nesting the rest of the sequences.

6. Open the three remaining city sequences in the Source Monitor, turn off their audio, and add them to the Map Comp sequence with Florence on Video 2, Portofino on Video 3, and Rome on Video 4. (See Figure 10.6.)

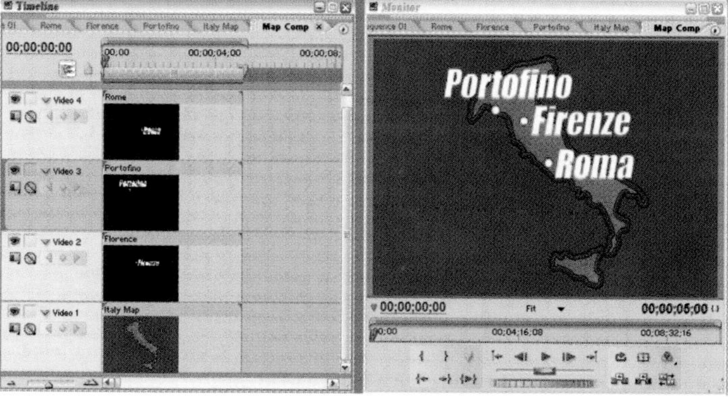

Figure 10.6 The final result of your nesting work. Here you can see all four of the nested sequences stacked one on top of the other with the result displayed in the Program Monitor. Notice how the icon for the nested sequence in the Timeline window displays a snapshot of the content of the sequence. Even when nesting, the alpha channel for the files in the city name sequences is preserved and used to display the city names on top of each other and the map.

Compared to the original nine-layer sequence, the Map Comp sequence is now quite manageable with fewer files, revealing the benefits of nesting. Say you want to fade up the Rome name and Rome button. In the original sequence, you would have dropped transitions on both files, whereas in the nested sequence you can drop a transition on only the single nested sequence for Rome. If you want to create a motion path for the Rome Name and Button layers, instead of creating the same path twice, you could apply the motion path to the nested sequence. To look at the final results I came up with, open Nest_Finish.prproj in the APPST Lesson Files/Chapter 10 folder.

All of the work in this first lesson builds the proper framework and structure from which you can independently adjust groups of layers without affecting the entire document. To take this even further, you can open any of your nested sequences and apply effects to the individual tracks in the sequence. Any effect applied to the contents of the nested sequence will be revealed any place the sequence is nested. This next lesson demonstrates the power and benefits of this feature.

To open the source sequence for any nested sequence, simply double-click on the nested sequence; the source sequence opens inside the Timeline window. Alternately, you can target the video track that holds the nested sequence, and with the Edit Line positioned over the nested sequence that you want to open, press Shift+T. This action is called Match Frame.

If you want to open a nested sequence in the Source Monitor, just Ctrl+double-click on the nested sequence.

Adding Effects to Nested Sequences

With all the layers properly nested into separate sequences, you're ready to try applying effects to the nested sequence material. For this lesson, you will be fading in and enlarging the Rome name, alluding to the fact that the Rome photo montage will appear next.

1. Open Nest_Effects_Start.prproj from the APPST Lesson Files/Chapter 10 folder. Open the Map Comp sequence in the Timeline window, and click on the Florence clip in the Video 2 track. From the Video 2 track header, select Show Opacity Handles from the Show Keyframe button menu. Press the P key to activate the Pen tool. With the Pen tool, click on the Opacity line for the Florence clip and drag downward so that Opacity is 50%. (See Figure 10.7.)

   Instead of using the Effect Controls window in this step, you displayed and adjusted keyframes in the Timeline window. Setting Opacity to 50% made the entire Florence name clip somewhat transparent. Next, you will assign a simple fade out of the Opacity setting.

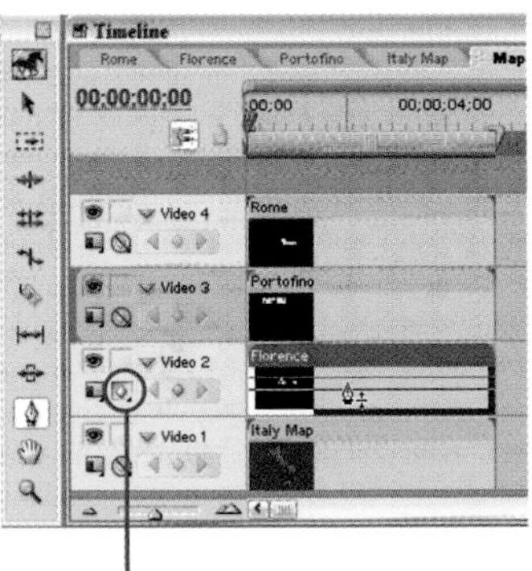

Figure 10.7 Using the Pen tool, you can adjust individual keyframes or constant values for displayed effects in all audio and video tracks. Adjusting a constant effect value yields a small line with two arrows next to the Pen tool's icon. Here, the adjustment reduces the Opacity of the entire clip to a constant 50% value.

2. Position the Edit Line at 02;00 in the timeline. In the Video 2 track header, press the Add Keyframe button to add a keyframe handle to the current position. Move the Edit Line to 03;00 in the timeline, and add another keyframe. With the Pen tool selected, click and drag the second keyframe to the bottom of the track, making Opacity 0%. (See Figure 10.8.)

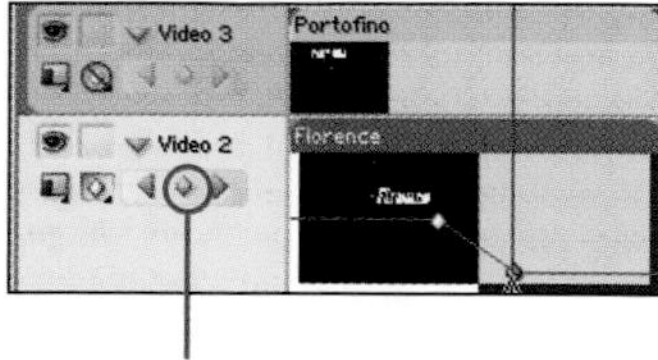

Figure 10.8 Two newly created keyframes. Lowered to the bottom of the track, the second keyframe reflects an Opacity value of 0%, complete transparency. To add a keyframe to the current Edit Line position, simply press the Add/Remove Keyframe button in the track header. Clicking the same button when the Edit Line is on top of a keyframe removes that keyframe.

This step introduced a method for creating a custom opacity fade: You created two keyframes to anchor the starting (50%) and ending (0%) opacity values of the fade. Now the clip starts at 50% opacity for two seconds and has a one-second fade out to 0%. Because you want all the city names to start opaque and fade together, in the next step you will copy the opacity keyframes from the Florence clip into the other city clips.

3. Using the Pen tool, hold down the Shift key and click each of the opacity keyframes that you created. With both keyframes selected (yellow), right-click on one of the two and select Continuous Bezier from the menu that appears. (See Figure 10.9.)

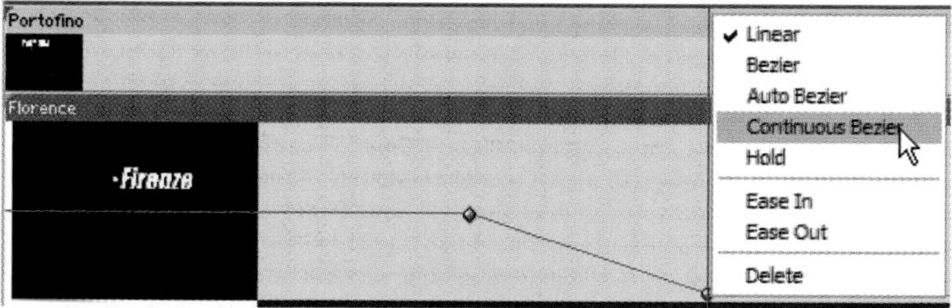

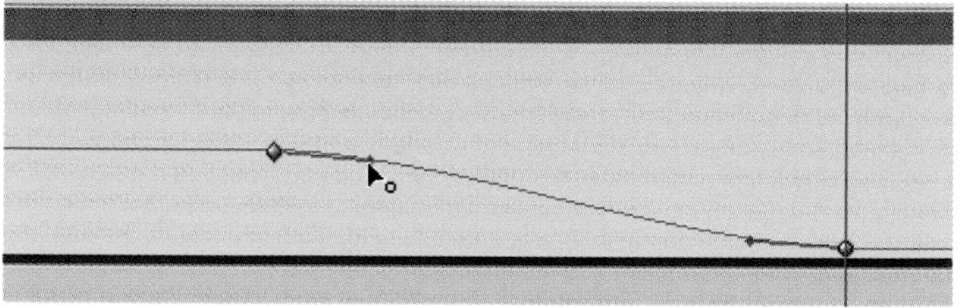

Figure 10.9 When you are assigning keyframes within your video track, you can adjust and create curves between the keyframes. The first image shows the options for creating the curve. To adjust the curve once it is assigned, you can click on and adjust the Bezier handle associated with each individual keyframe. In the second image, the Bezier handle appears as the short blue line.

When you first created the keyframes to assign the fade, a straight line joined the two. To create a smooth fade from one to the other, you assigned Continuous Bezier. If you want a smooth curve between multiple keyframes, you can select all the keyframes that you want to adjust the line for and select Continuous Bezier.

4. Select Window>Workspace>Effects. Click on the Florence clip in the Map Comp sequence. Right-click on the Opacity listing in the Effect Controls window, and choose Copy (see Figure 10.10). Select the Portofino clip in the Map Comp sequence, right-click in the blank space of the Effect Controls window, and choose Paste. Click on the Rome clip, and again paste into the Effect Controls window. Set the Video 2 and 3 tracks to Show Opacity Keyframes.

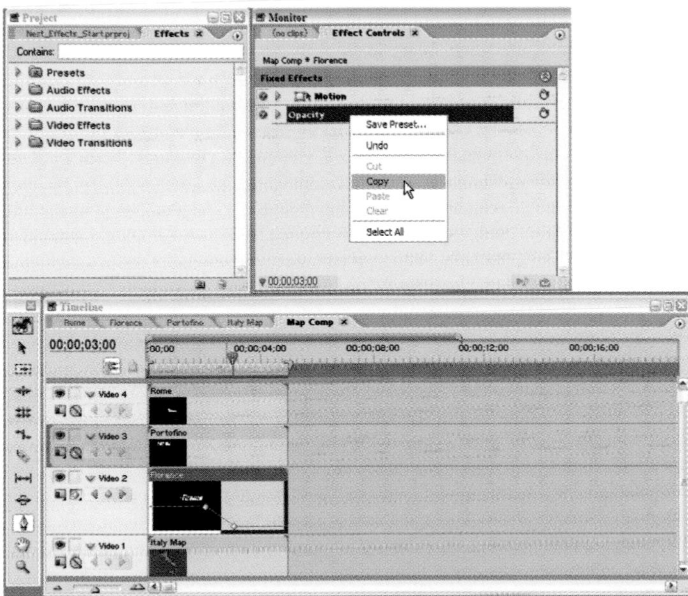

Figure 10.10 Select the Florence clip in the Timeline window to display its effect parameters in the Effect Controls window. By selecting an individual effect listing, Opacity in this case, you can right-click and copy the effect to your clipboard. Selecting other clips in the timeline, you can paste the Opacity selection back into the Effect Controls window for them.

Copying and pasting effect listings in the Effect Controls window is a quick way to apply the same effect and keyframes to multiple clips. Keep in mind that you would have done about three times more work if the sequences had not been nested.

Although you originally made the opacity adjustments in the timeline, you can view and manipulate the entire effect parameters for each individual clip in the Effect Controls window. Anytime a clip is selected, you can view its effect parameters in the Effect Controls window.

5. Continuing in the Effects Workspace mode, select the Rome clip in the timeline. Position the Edit Line at 03;00. In the Effect Controls window, twirl down the Opacity listing and change the value of the current Opacity keyframe to 100%. (See Figure 10.11.)

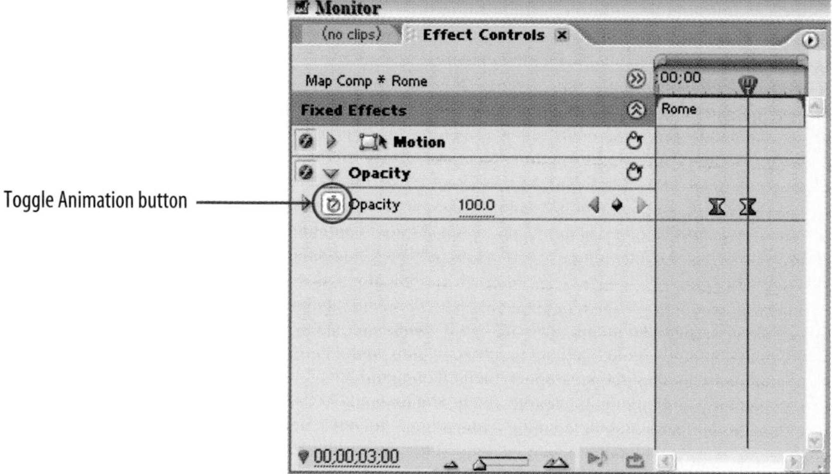

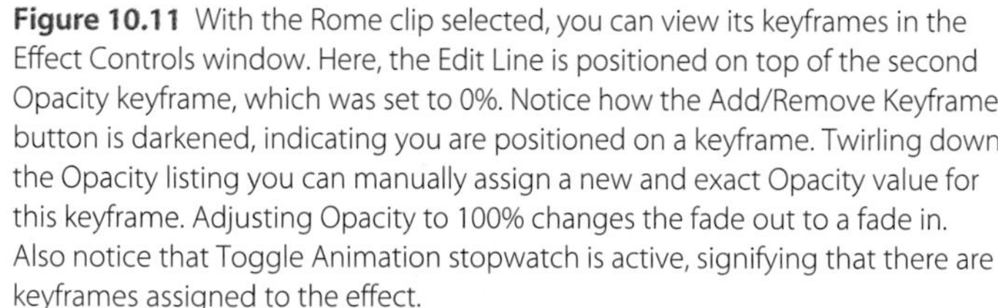

Figure 10.11 With the Rome clip selected, you can view its keyframes in the Effect Controls window. Here, the Edit Line is positioned on top of the second Opacity keyframe, which was set to 0%. Notice how the Add/Remove Keyframe button is darkened, indicating you are positioned on a keyframe. Twirling down the Opacity listing you can manually assign a new and exact Opacity value for this keyframe. Adjusting Opacity to 100% changes the fade out to a fade in. Also notice that Toggle Animation stopwatch is active, signifying that there are keyframes assigned to the effect.

NOTES

When you want to adjust an exact keyframe, the Edit Line must be positioned directly on top of it. To make sure you are on top of an exact keyframe, use the Go to Next/Previous Keyframe buttons for the keyframed effect's listing.

You can easily modify keyframes directly in the Effect Controls window. Here you changed Opacity to create a fade in for the Rome clip. (You'll need it in the next chapter when you build the Rome photo montage.) Next, you will apply a gradual size increase that occurs as the word "Rome" fades in.

6. Double-click on the nested Rome clip in the Map Comp sequence to open it in its own Timeline window. Select Roma/Italy_MapDV.psd on the Video 2 track. In the Effect Controls window, twirl down the Motion listing. Position the Edit Line at 02;00. Click the Toggle Animation button on for Scale. Reposition the Edit Line to 05;00. Adjust the Scale value to 175.0. Select both of the keyframes you just added, right-click on one, and select Continuous Bezier from the context menu. (See Figure 10.12.) Press Enter to preview your results. Click on the Map Comp sequence tab, and press Enter to preview the results of the entire sequence.

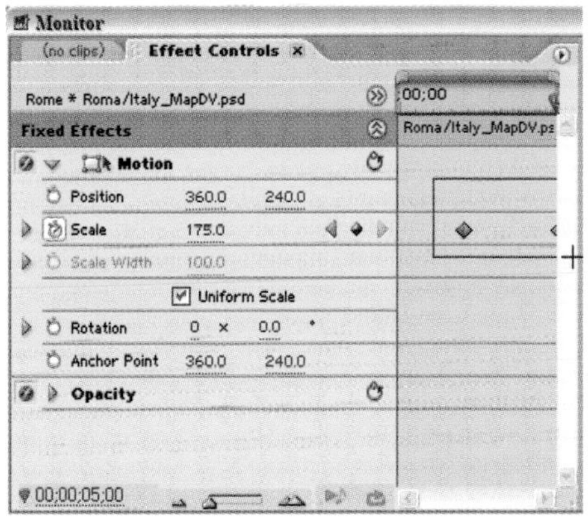

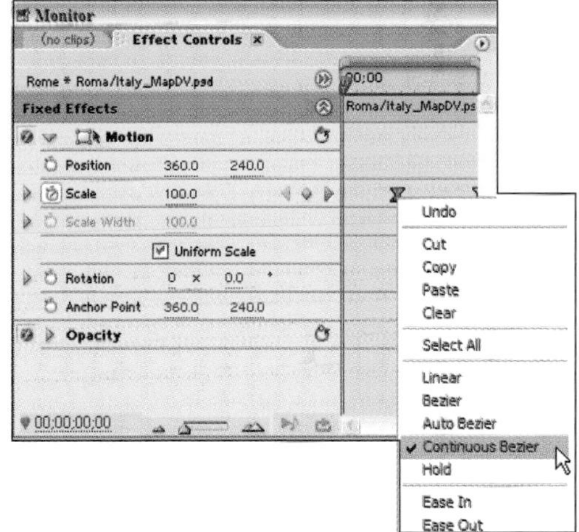

Figure 10.12 You can marquee select two Scale keyframes (top left), and set the Continuous Bezier option for interpolating a curved line between them (top right). The resulting curved value for Scale appears in the video track (bottom). The result is a smooth scaling increase from 100% to 175%.

To emphasize only the city name, you navigated into the original Rome sequence and applied a Scale adjustment to the city name layer only. Turning on Toggle Animation assigns a keyframe at the current Edit Line position with the current value for the parameter being animated. In this case, 100% Scale was assigned at the 2;00 keyframe. With keyframe animation turned on, if you reposition the Edit Line and modify an effect parameter, Premiere will create a new keyframe to reflect the adjustment. Here, a keyframe for 175% Scale was created at 5;00. You also made sure that the Scale was a smooth curved value between 100% and 175%.

This step articulates the power and control of nesting. The result of the two keyframes is a dynamic scaling of the single layer from 100% to 175%. Because this sequence is nested into the Map Comp, the scaling adjustments are seen along with the Opacity adjustment made to the nested sequence itself.

7. Create a new sequence and name it Photo Montage. Holding the Ctrl key, double-click on the Map Comp sequence from the Project window to open it in the Source Monitor. Toggle Take Audio/Video to Take Video Only. Drag and drop the Map Comp sequence into Video 1. With the Edit Line positioned at the head of the timeline, press Ctrl+D. (See Figure 10.13.) Now you are ready for the next chapter!

   Here's to redundancy! This step nested the Map Comp sequence inside a new sequence, which you will use in the next chapter to build your final photo montage. If any changes need to be made to the Map Comp, you can tweak any of the nested sequence settings in the Map Comp sequence or the individual layers in the original city name or map image sequences.

   By properly nesting the Map Comp into the Photo Montage sequence, any and all changes to the sequences and layers it references will be revealed in the final nested instance. To see my final results, open the file Nest_Effects_Finish.prproj from the APPST Lesson Files/Chapter 10 folder.

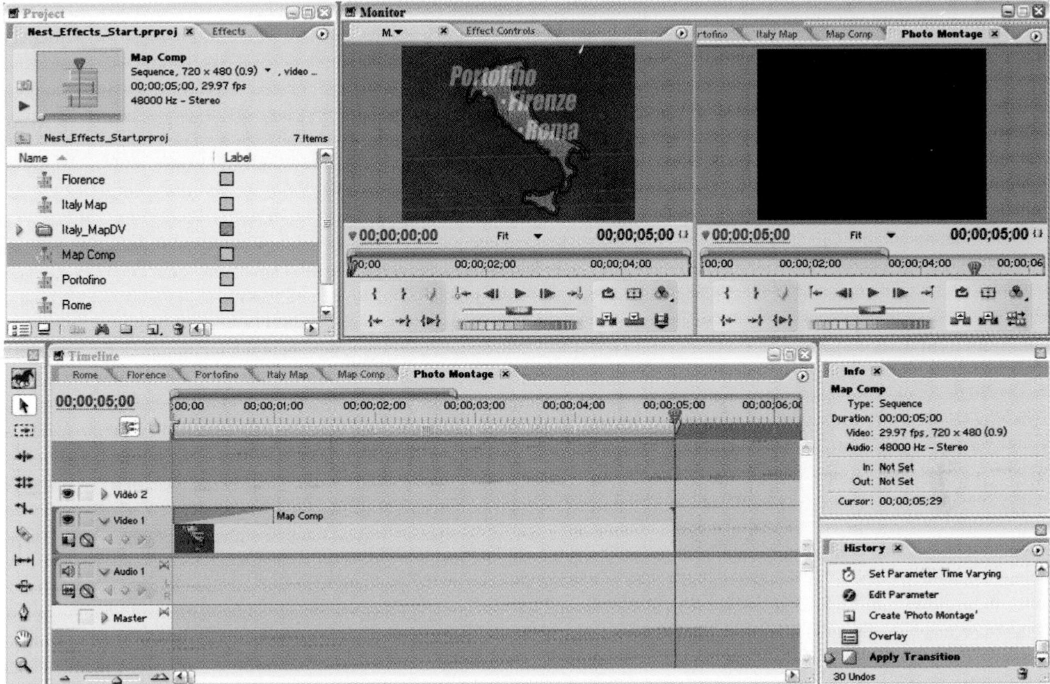

Figure 10.13 Compared to the original nine layers, this final nested sequence is much easier to manage. Because this nested sequence references numerous sequences and source files with specific settings, the results show through in the current nested view.

As you can see, using a nested structure has definite advantages. By separating individual layers and sequences, and thus controlling them separately, you can more easily modify and change any of the nested elements. So, not only can you easily apply changes to an entire sequence in one step, you can also quickly adjust any single element. From reducing clutter to controlling separate layers, there are numerous uses for nesting.

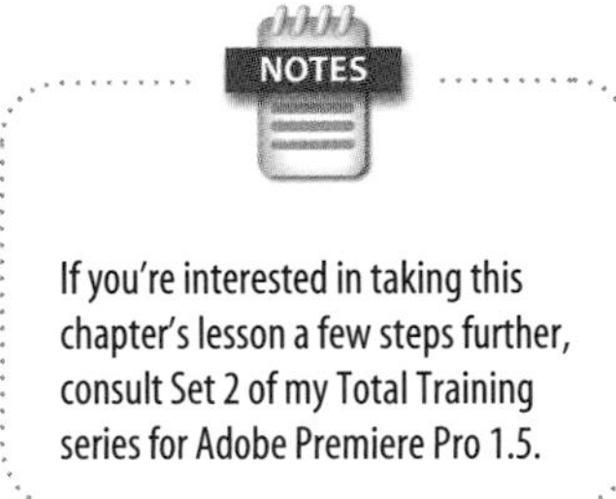

If you're interested in taking this chapter's lesson a few steps further, consult Set 2 of my Total Training series for Adobe Premiere Pro 1.5.

Things to Remember

Premiere Pro works hand-in-hand with Adobe Photoshop's layering capabilities, enabling you to import Photoshop files with each layer in a separate sequence.

Using the nesting technique, you then can group specific layers in one sequence to apply effects to the entire group. If you want to vary the effect within the group, you just simply go into the original nested sequence and adjust the layer/track directly. Throughout the course of this book, you will see the nesting concept referenced again and again; in many instances, nesting is a highly practical and valuable technique.

In the next chapter, you will create a photo montage, integrating a still image sequence with the map sequence that you just created. Using custom presets, you will add your own motion adjustments to create beautiful and precise image pans to your still image files.

CHAPTER

11

Working with Still Images

With Premiere Pro, the overall quality of still images has increased dramatically. Instead of re-sampling and reducing the resolution of imported still files, Premiere Pro now processes the full resolution of the still files, rendering the final result to your output video settings.

In former Premiere versions and in competitive nonlinear editors, when you imported a 1600×1200 still image, the still is automatically resized to 720×480 or your project dimensions. If you wanted to zoom in on the image, you were no longer zooming in on your 1600×1200 image, instead you were zooming in the resized 720×480 which yielded lesser quality results. With Premiere Pro, this is no longer a worry.

This chapter aims to help you understand how to properly prep your images, import individual stills or groups of images with ease, and then create smooth and dynamic image pans like those Ken Burns used in *The Civil War* and *Baseball*. Along the way, you'll learn some good guidelines for working with still images, as well as how to save the image pans as re-usable custom effect presets.

Importing, Image Size, and Auto-Scaling

Print and video images inherently have different requirements: Video has a set screen resolution of 72 dots per inch (dpi) and a standard frame size of 720×480 (DV), while much higher dpi counts and image sizes are often used for printing. In past versions of Premiere, importing still images with these larger resolutions resulted in a compromise where the image was converted to a smaller size and this resulted in a loss of image quality. Premiere Pro, however, takes a new approach that accurately processes stills and preserves their true resolution. In Premiere Pro you have a choice: Do you want to add stills to the timeline at their original full size or have Premiere Pro automatically scale them to fit in the video frame? Even when Premiere Pro auto-scales an image, it still references the image's full resolution; the image is not permanently converted to a smaller size.

If you want to zoom in on or pan on the image, I recommend leaving the frame size as large as you can. Make sure the horizontal width is at least 1000 pixels for landscape-oriented stills, and the vertical height is at least 1000 for portrait images. If you plan on zooming up to 200%, then make sure the still is at least double the size of a standard video frame.

PAR: Square Pixels versus Non-Square Pixels

A video frame, like all computer graphics, is made up of pixels. Most pixels are exact 1:1 squares, meaning they have a 1:1 *pixel aspect ratio* (PAR). The pixels that make up an NTSC DV video frame, however, are 1:0.9 and, thus, non-square.

The easiest way to see the results of how square pixels are distorted in DV space is to create a still image of a perfectly round circle in Photoshop with square pixels. When you import the file into Premiere Pro and add it to a DV sequence, the PAR for DV shifts the circle to become an oval.

Photoshop CS can now work with and tag images properly for non-square pixels. Premiere Pro can recognize the tag and preserves the integrity of the image when it is imported so that there is no distortion. If you are prepping images in Photoshop and you want to use them in a DV project, use the Non-Square Pixel for DV (720×480) setting when creating your still.

If you want to create a square pixel document in Photoshop for use with an NTSC DV project and you want to retain the integrity of the image when you bring it into Premiere Pro, you should save the image at 720×534. When Premiere Pro imports the image and incorporates it into the timeline, the shift of the PAR is compensated for by the additional 154 extra pixels.

If you don't plan any zooms or pans, try Premiere Pro's automatic scaling. When this option is on and you import a still image at a frame size of 1600×1200, Premiere Pro then automatically applies a Motion/Scale adjustment to resize the image so that it fits snug within your project's video frame. If you wanted to zoom back into the image at a later point, you could just animate the Motion/Scale effect listing.

In this lesson, you'll examine the benefits of both approaches, as well as learn how to assign a default duration to all still images that you import.

When opening the different projects for each lesson, keep in mind that you will sometimes have to locate certain files associated with the project. For example, the PSD file (Italy_MapDV.psd) that this project is looking for is in the Chapter 10 folder used for the last chapter.

1. Open Still_Import_Start.prproj from the APPST Lesson Files/Chapter 11 folder.

   This lesson starts where you left off in the last chapter, adding a photo montage to the opening graphic you created.

2. Create a new bin in your Project window, and name it Rome Stills. Create a new sequence within this bin (one video track and one stereo audio track), and give it the same name.

   Continuing to emphasize the idea of nesting, you are structuring this project so that all the individual elements are contained within their own sequences. Because you want the final photo montage to be accessible as a single clip, you will assemble all the Rome stills in a sequence of the same name.

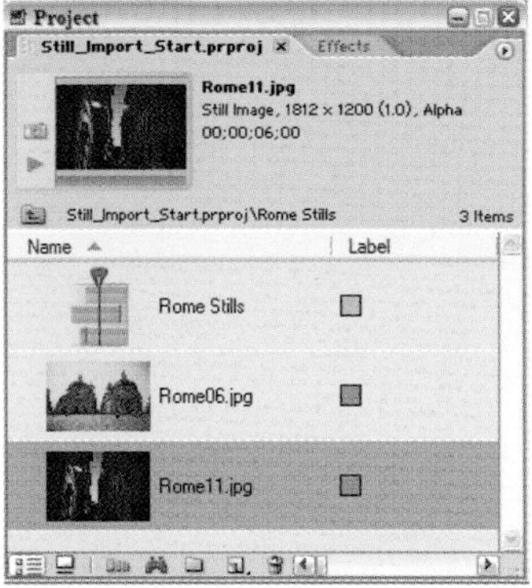

Figure 11.1 Clicking on a file in the Project window reveals its properties in the Project Preview area. Here you can see the frame size for the imported image, its pixel aspect ratio (PAR), whether the image contains an alpha channel, and its assigned duration.

3. From the Edit menu, select Preferences>Still Image. In the Still Image Preferences pane, change Default Duration to 180 frames and click OK. Click on the Rome Stills bin in the Project window. Press Ctrl+I to access the Import dialog. From the Rome subfolder in the APPST Lesson Files/Chapter 11 folder, select Rome06.jpg and Rome11.jpg, and click Open. In the Project window, click on the images to view their properties. (See Figure 11.1.)

   Because still images can be an infinite duration, assigning a default duration for all imported stills streamlines your workflow, especially if you are importing several images. You assigned the Default Duration for these two stills to be 180 frames (6 seconds), because they are the first and last images of the montage. Later, you will fade the montage in and out, therefore, need some extra frames to play with.

4. Choose Edit>Preferences>Still Image, and set Default Duration to 150 frames (5 seconds). Import the remaining files in the folder (select all except Rome06 and Rome11). Click on the newly imported stills individually, and view their properties in the Project Preview area to see their change in duration.

   The second batch of imported stills does not need extra frames for transitions, so you lowered Default Duration to 150. Now the Project Preview area reports the stills are only five seconds long.

5. From the Project menu, select Project Settings>General. Click the check box for Scale Clips to Project Dimensions When Adding to Sequence. (See Figure 11.2.) Click OK. In the Project window, select Rome11.jpg and insert it onto the Video 1 track at the head of the timeline. Open the Effect Controls window and expand the Motion effect listing. (See Figure 11.3.)

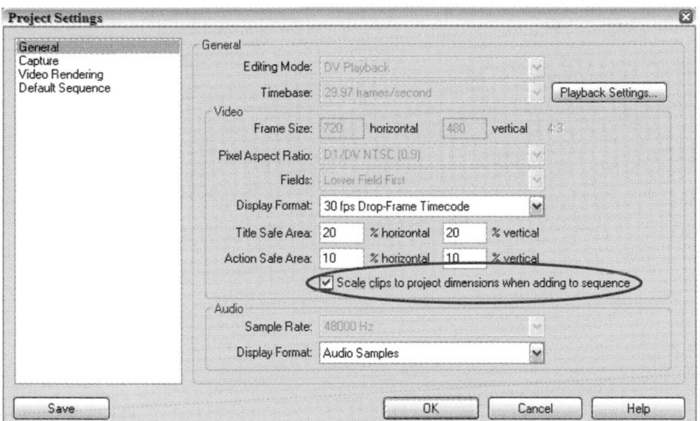

Figure 11.2 When Scale Clips to Project Dimensions When Adding to Sequence is on, Premiere Pro increases or decreases the scale of clips added to the timeline so that they fit exactly to the edge of your project's frame.

Figure 11.3 Rome11.jpg file was added to the timeline on Video 1. In the Effect Controls window, you can see that Premiere reduced the height and width equally; Scale Height and Scale Width are both 35.8. Now the original 1812×1200 frame fits inside the 720×480 frame. Because the original file's aspect ratio was not 4×3, the Program Monitor displays a slight black letterbox around the image.

When you check the Scale Clips check box, Premiere Pro automatically adjusts the Scale Height and Scale Width of the added file so that the entire image fits within the confines of the 720×480 video frame. This image is the last still in the montage; later you will create a slow zoom into the night sky as a fade out from the montage.

Whether you import a Photoshop file, create a new title, or create a color matte, these items are considered stills and adhere to the Default Duration value you set in your Still Images Preferences. When you open a layered Photoshop file as a sequence, all the layers that make up the sequence adhere to the same default duration.

Take note that when you import a still that does not have a 4×3 aspect ratio, such as 1280×720, when the file is automatically scaled to fit the 720×480 frame, it yields empty space where the aspect ratio is different. The example image would have empty black space at the top and bottom of the image, much like a letterbox for a widescreen film transferred to video. If you don't want the black space, simply adjust the scale to find the right size.

If you plan a zoom effect for an image, you can quickly add the image to your sequence with Scale Clip turned on. This way, the images automatically scale to a size at which they fit snug within the frame. If you want to zoom in, position the Edit Line at the beginning of the clip and turn on keyframing (click Toggle Animation) for Scale, then reposition the Edit Line at the end of the clip and adjust the Scale to the zoom you want. To zoom out, do the opposite: Turn on keyframing with the Edit Line at the end of the clip, then adjust the Scale at the beginning. The benefit of this workflow is that the automatic scaling selects a perfect scale value without your doing the calculations. Remember, when keyframing is turned on for any effect parameter it assigns a keyframe for the current value at the position of the Edit Line.

6. Choose Project>Project Settings>General, and turn off the Scale Clips option. Select the Rome06.jpg file from the Project window, and while holding the Ctrl key down, drag and drop it at the beginning of the timeline before Rome11. Select the file in the timeline, and open the Effect Controls window. Place the Edit Line over the selected clip and twirl down the Motion settings in the Effect Controls window. Click the Motion effect name to turn on direct manipulation. (See Figure 11.4.)

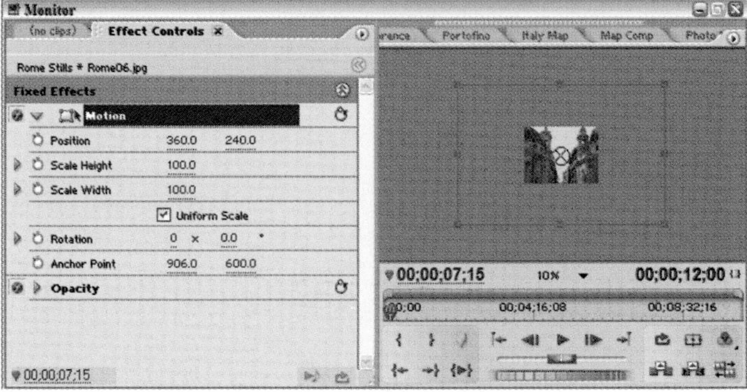

Figure 11.4 Here, the effect properties for Rome06.jpg are active in the Effect Controls window and direct manipulation is turned on. You can see the actual size of the still's frame (the wireframe) in relation to what is visible in the 720×480 video frame. Notice that the scale of the Program Monitor view has been reduced to 10% in order to see the entire frame.

Importing Rome06 at 100 for Scale Height and Scale Width means that you cannot see the entire image: Its frame size is more than twice as large as your video frame.

This lesson laid a foundation of basic settings for importing stills. In the next lesson, you will build on it and learn to use Premiere Pro's Automate to Sequence feature.

Automate to Sequence

The Automate to Sequence feature allows you to select a group of files from the Project window and add them to the timeline. You can add them sequentially or in a custom order, and even instruct Premiere to place transitions between the clips automatically.

In this short lesson, you will use Automate to Sequence to create the skeleton for your photo montage by quickly adding a group of stills to the timeline.

1. Open Automate_Start.prproj from the APPST Lesson Files/Chapter 11 folder. Expand your Project window so that you can see all the files and columns, then rearrange the column order to read: Comment/Good/Video Info. For every vertical (portrait) image, click the Good check box. (See Figure 11.5.)

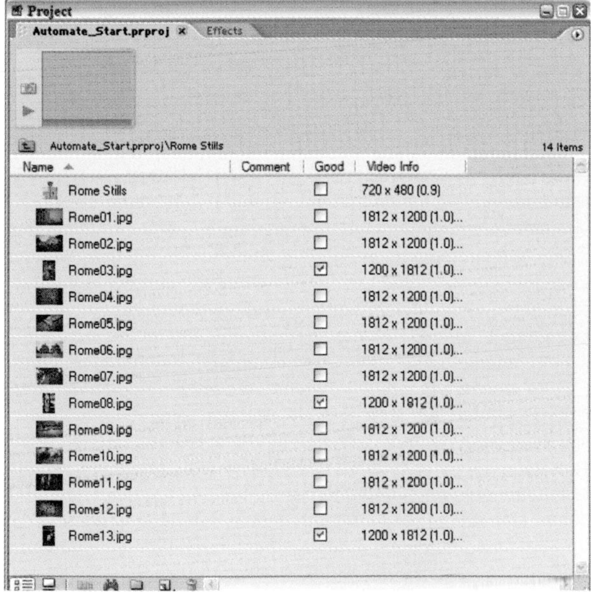

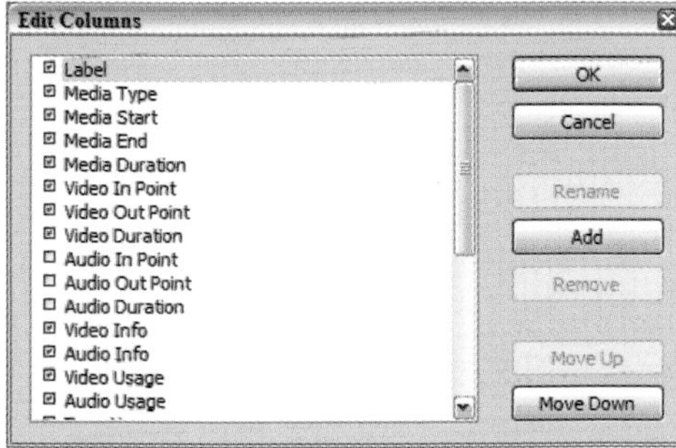

Figure 11.5 Drag a column by its heading to change its position in the Project window. The column order will persist when you open other bins in your project. You can add or remove columns by checking or unchecking the boxes associated with the columns in the Edit Columns dialog box, accessed from the Project window wing menu.

Because a folder full of still images can take up a lot of screen real estate when scrolling through and selecting images, you can rearrange and use specific columns to tag files and quickly adjust their order. Checking the Good box gives you the option of seeing which images are desirable (in this case, desirable means vertically aligned) if the file thumbnail is turned off.

2. Double-click the Comment column for Rome06.jpg, and enter a 1. Enter a 2 in the Comment column for Rome11.jpg. Click on the Comment column header to change the sort order to ascending (the arrow points up). Select the images Rome01 through Rome13, excluding Rome06 and Rome11 at the bottom. (See Figure 11.6.)

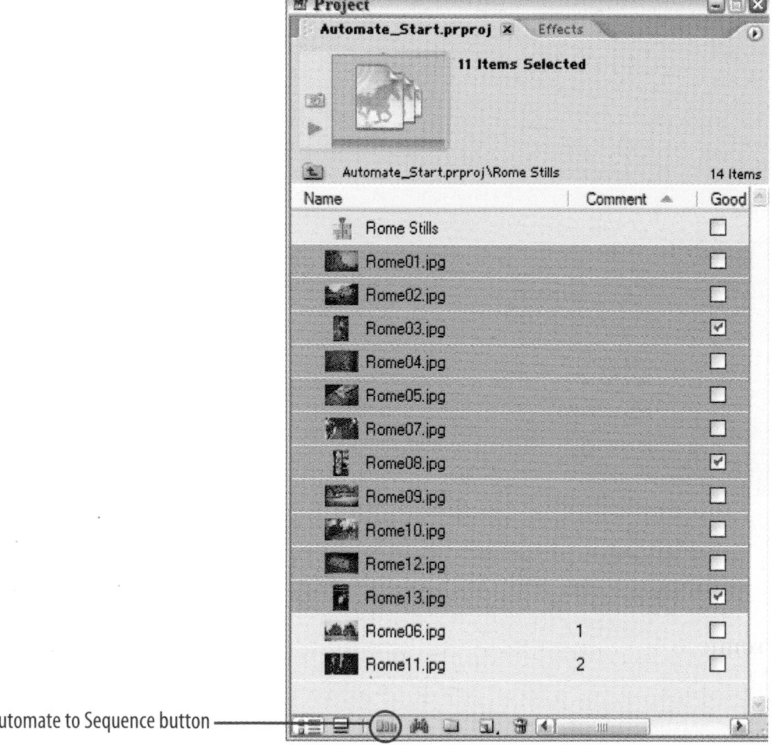

Figure 11.6 With metadata entered into the Comment column and the sort order ascending, all the images with empty comments appear before the images with data added. This enables you to select the remaining files you need to add in the order that they were named. With the files selected, the button for Automate to Sequence becomes active.

You can enter alpha/numeric data in the Comment column, then sort based on that data. Here you used the technique to group the images in numeric order and exclude the two stills previously added to the timeline. The Automate to Sequence feature sends your files to the timeline based on the sort or selection order you define.

3. With the 11 stills selected in the Project window, activate the Timeline window and press Page Down to position the Edit Line at the cut point between Rome06.jpg and Rome11.jpg in Video 1. Activate the Project window, and click the Automate to Sequence button. In the Automate to Sequence dialog, make the following settings and click OK (see Figure 11.7):

   Ordering: **Sort Order**
   Placement: **Sequentially**
   Method: **Insert Edit**
   Clip Overlap: **30 Frames**
   Apply Default Video Transition: **On**

   First you need to tell Premiere where to automatically add your stills, then you tell the program how to add them. Here, you placed the Edit Line at the cut point where you wanted to add the new images—between Rome06 and Rome11. In the Automate to Sequence dialog, you then told Premiere to add the images sequentially based on their sort method, using an Insert edit, with a 30-frame overlap duration for the transitions. Because of the current default transition setting, Premiere will add cross dissolves.

   When assigning the Clip Overlap value, remember that the value is not added to the existing stills, but used from their default duration. For each of these five-second stills, Premiere would use one second for its dissolve in and one second for its dissolve out, leaving three seconds as its unobstructed display time.

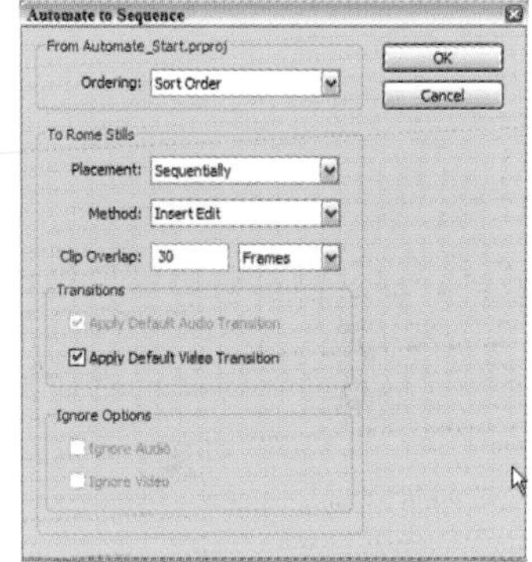

Figure 11.7 The Automate to Sequence dialog tells you the origin of the clips being added, as well as the name of sequence to which Premiere will add them. The most visible benefit of the Automate to Sequence feature is the ability to add audio and video transitions to every cut in the sequence.

4. For the final step, add cross dissolves centered on the cuts between the first and second shot, as well as between the last and next to last shots. With Video 1 targeted, position the Edit Line at each of the cut points and press Ctrl+D to add a default transition to the cut on the targeted track.

For a short video tutorial on Automate to Sequence and Custom Columns, consult the training on the accompanying DVD. In the Advanced Techniques section, the "Custom Columns, Automate to Sequence" tutorial covers creating custom columns and other aspects of the Automate to Sequence feature.

Although Automate to Sequence places transitions between the files it is adding, it does not apply transitions to the clips at the cuts in which the edit occurred. To streamline the entire sequence, you put transitions between all your shots. Now you are ready to add some motion.

The Automate to Sequence feature offers a means of quickly getting your edit into shape. Because the Scale Clips to Project Dimensions When Adding to Sequence check box was turned off, all the stills were added to the timeline at 100%. In the next lesson, you will adjust those settings and add clean motion and scaling effects to create fluid image pans and zooms with your still images.

Image Panning and Creating Custom Effect Presets

Incorporating motion can make the difference between a boring photo montage and one that holds your attention. By slowly revealing elements of the picture or focusing on a particular area of the photograph, still images become dynamic and thus come to life. To add some life into the Rome montage, you will add some crisp and clean motion effects to scale and pan on the stills. Specifically, in this lesson you will create four motion settings that incorporate keyframe animation. You will also learn how to save these motion settings as custom effect presets for use on other projects.

1. Open Still_Effects_Start.prproj from the APPST Lesson Files/Chapter 11 folder. Using the Effects Workspace, select the first still (Rome06.jpg) in the Timeline window. Press the Home key to position the Edit Line at 00;00;00;00. In the Effect Controls window, click the Motion effect listing to turn on direct manipulation. Adjust the clip's Anchor Point to be 906.0×800. Check the box for Uniform Scale, and increase Scale Height to 125. Turn keyframing on by clicking the Toggle Animation button, and set a keyframe for Position and one for Scale Height. (See Figure 11.8.)

Figure 11.8 Select the Rome06.jpg clip to view its effect properties in the Effect Controls window. Based on the position of the Edit Line, you can add animated keyframes for any of the effect parameters that have Toggle Animation (the stopwatch icon) turned on.

Once you turn direct manipulation on, you can see the various handles associated with the selected clip. The center cross reflects the anchor point, which is like a thumbtack through the image. Just as a piece of paper moves around the point where it's tacked, your moves are based on the image's anchor point. For example, as you scale the image out, the zoom will originate from the anchor point, assigned here in the bottom center of the image. Although direct manipulation offers a lot of adjustment points, you can modify the anchor point only from its field in the Effect Controls window.

To dynamically scale and move the image, you assigned two keyframes at beginning of the clip (Edit Line position 00;00;00;00). To properly animate the keyframe settings, you will need to reposition the Edit Line in the next step and modify the value of the keyframes.

2. With the Timeline window active, press Page Down to advance the Edit Line to the cut point of the next clip. With the Rome06 file still selected in the Effect Controls window, enter 360×333 for Position and 45 for Scale Height. Premiere creates two keyframes. Shift-click or marquee select these two keyframes, and drag them to the very end of the selected clip (see Figure 11.9). Click at the beginning of the sequence and press Play to preview the image zoom that you just created.

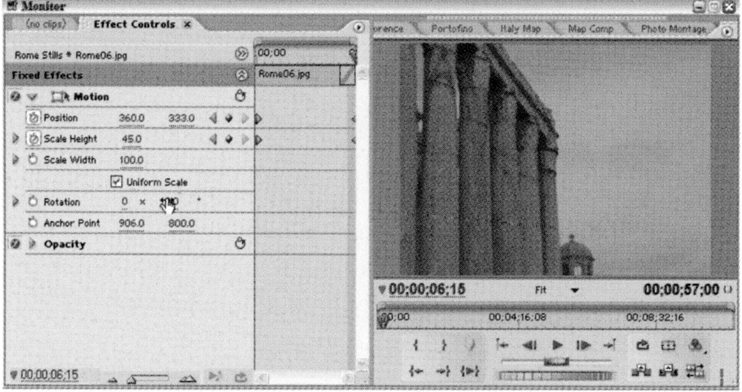

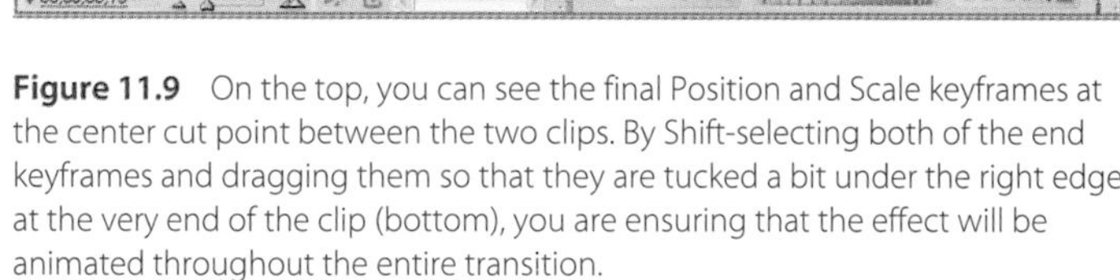

Figure 11.9 On the top, you can see the final Position and Scale keyframes at the center cut point between the two clips. By Shift-selecting both of the end keyframes and dragging them so that they are tucked a bit under the right edge at the very end of the clip (bottom), you are ensuring that the effect will be animated throughout the entire transition.

For smooth scaling and position changes, select all four keyframes for Scale and Position, right-click on one, and choose Temporal Interpolation>Continuous Bezier. This creates a curved rate of change between the values as opposed to a straight line.

The video tutorial "Adjusting Bezier Keyframes," from the Fundamentals section of the DVD shows you how to use Bezier curves and ease adjustments with individual keyframes. Bezier curves can adjust the Spatial or Temporal Interpolation values between effect keyframes. In plain terms, they can curve your motion path lines (Spatial) or simply smooth and adjust the velocity and acceleration (Temporal) of an adjustment between multiple keyframes.

Because the end of the Rome06 clip instance is covered by a transition, you cannot see its last frame. The final frame of Rome06 has completely dissolved into the file Rome01. By navigating to the cut point, which is nearly the end of the clip, you can see Rome06 in relation to the shot that will next appear, as well as see your adjusted effect values and create two keyframes. You can then select the keyframes and drag them to their final position at the end of the timeline view for the Rome06.jpg. The result of this first animation is very clean: a simple zoom that emphasizes the idea of motion from the beginning to the end of the clip.

3. With the Rome06.jpg file still selected and active in the Effect Controls window, right-click on its Motion listing and select Save Preset. Rename the preset Rome Zoom Out 01. Click Scale for Type, and add the brief description "Horizontal Zoom Out, Position and Scale KF." (See Figure 11.10.)

   Saving the effect as a custom preset enables you to reuse it for the other stills in this sequence and beyond. Because this effect has a start and end keyframe, you chose Scale as the type of preset. Choosing Scale allows you to apply an effect to a new clip of different duration. Scale applies the effect proportionally across the duration of the clip; a shorter clip means a faster effect. Anchor to In Point keeps the exact timing and pacing of the animation but starts it at the clip's In point. Anchor to Out Point keeps the exact timing and pacing of the animation, but it starts at a calculated time and ends exactly at the Out point.

4. Select the second clip in the Rome01 Sequence. Position the Edit Line at 7;04. Activate direct manipulation for the Motion of this clip. Set Anchor Point to 0.0×1200.0, and Position to 0.0×480.0. Turn on keyframing (Toggle Animation) for Scale and Position. Reposition the Edit Line at 8;11. Adjust the Position to –97×480 and Scale Height to 41. Select both keyframe groups, and reposition the right keyframes at the head of the clip and left keyframes at the tail.

   For the second clip, you anchored the image in the lower-left corner and then repositioned it so that the image scaled with a slight panning move from the lower-left corner outward. Because both sides of this clip have transitions, you created your start and end position keyframe groups in the center of the clip and then dragged each group outward to its corresponding edge.

5. Save this effect as a custom preset with Type set to Scale and name it Rome Zoom Out Anchored LL. In the Description, note that the effect was created for a horizontal clip. Position the Edit Line at the head of the timeline, and play back the two clips to see your results.

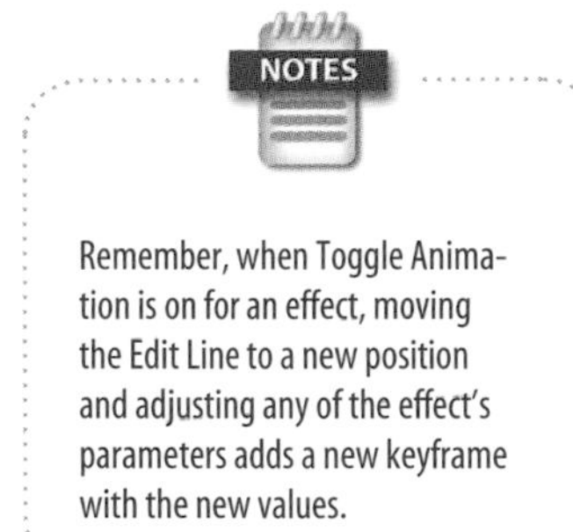

Remember, when Toggle Animation is on for an effect, moving the Edit Line to a new position and adjusting any of the effect's parameters adds a new keyframe with the new values.

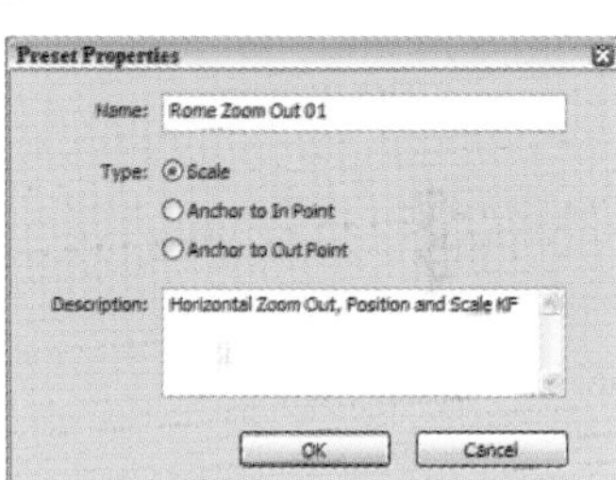

Figure 11.10 One of the most cherished new features of Premiere Pro 1.5 is the ability to save effect settings as individual custom presets to be reused at any time.

If you create a zoom-in effect and want to quickly make the effect zoom out, simply swap the position of the Scale keyframes. Because the individual keyframes have a specific effect value embedded in them, adjusting their position preserves their original settings.

6. Select the third clip in the timeline, Rome02. For this clip, a simple Scale adjustment will do. Position the Edit Line at 12;13. Set Scale Height to 44.0 and Position to 412.0×240.0. Click on the Toggle Animation button for Scale Height. Reposition this keyframe at the end of the clip instance in the Effect Controls window. With the clip still selected, reposition the Edit Line to the beginning of the clip instance in the Effect Controls window (approximately 10;00). Adjust Scale Height to 110. Save this effect as a custom preset named Rome Zoom Out 02. In the Preset Properties dialog, choose Scale and add a description specifying a horizontal image.

   Resizing this image helped you find the optimum scale at which you could see the entire image. With Scale at 44, the frame was slightly shifted so you readjusted the position of the clip. Because this is a simple zoom out, you only animated the keyframes for scale. Again, you can use Temporal Interpolation>Continuous Bezier to smooth the scale between the keyframes.

7. Select the fourth clip, Rome03.jpg. Position the Edit Line at approximately 16;06. Expand the Motion settings and click on the Motion effect name to activate direct manipulation. In the Program Monitor, adjust the zoom view to a percentage value that reveals the entire wireframe for the selected image. (See Figure 11.11.)

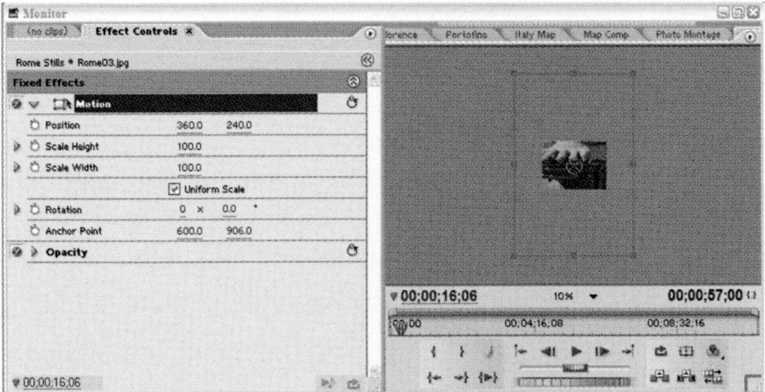

Figure 11.11 To see an entire vertical image larger than the frame, activate direct manipulation and reduce the size of the Program Monitor zoom. Now you can adjust and manipulate the image by dragging it in the Program Monitor window.

To create the vertical pan of this image, you will need to resize the image to fit snugly to the edge of your video frame. In order to later resize and reposition it, here you activated direct manipulation to display the wireframe for the entire image. With direct manipulation turned on, you can click on the handles in the Program Monitor window to resize or reposition the image.

Dragging an image handle changes the Scale parameters, but dragging the entire image changes the Position parameters.

8. Grab the side handle of the wireframe, and drag it inward to scale the width to 54. (See Figure 11.12.) Grab in the center of the image, and drag upward so that the bottom of the image is in the frame. (See Figure 11.13.) A Position value of 360×120.0 should be perfect. Turn on keyframing (Toggle Animation) for Position only.

Figure 11.12 Grab and move any of the eight image handles to scale the image. Because this clip has Uniform Scale turned on, adjusting the horizontal handles adjusts both horizontal and vertical scale values.

Figure 11.13 Hold down the Shift key when repositioning the center position to lock the alternate position coordinate. Here, holding Shift while you drag downward locks the horizontal position of 360.

After finding the image's proper scale and position, you assigned a keyframe for Scale to achieve a vertical pan from the bottom of the image to its top. In the next step, you'll find the end keyframe.

9. With clip Rome03 still selected and direct manipulation active, reposition the Edit Line to 17;13. In the Effect Controls window, adjust the Position value to 360×480. (See Figure 11.14.) Move the respective keyframes to the head and tail of the selected clip. Save this Motion effect as a custom preset named Rome Vert Pan Up, and click Scale for Type.

   Modifying the vertical Position value revealed the motion path for the selected clip. Because you modified the Position value, Premiere created a new keyframe at the current frame. Notice that when direct manipulation is turned on, all path adjustments and keyframe positions are visible.

Figure 11.14 The motion path created by the two Position keyframes is visible as the dotted line between the two points.

10. Drag and drop the Rome Zoom Out 01 custom effect preset onto the last clip in the sequence, Rome11.jpg. Select this clip, and open the Effect Controls window to reveal the keyframe properties. Position the Edit Line in the middle of the clip at 54;08. Selecting each group of start and end keyframes, swap their position to reverse the effect. In the Scale effect listing, click the Go to Next Keyframe button if the Edit Line is before the last keyframe of the scale effect. If the Edit Line is past the last keyframe, click the Go to Previous Keyframe button to snap the Edit Line to the last Scale keyframe. Adjust the Scale value to 100. (See Figure 11.15.)

Once you apply a custom effect preset to a selected clip, you can then easily modify the assigned keyframe values. The only rule is that the Edit Line must be on top of the keyframe that you want to adjust. To perfectly position the Edit Line on a keyframe, use the Go to Next or Go to Previous Keyframe buttons for the desired effect in the Effect Controls window. It is a good practice to always use the Go to Next/Previous Keyframe buttons, because if you are off by even one frame, a new keyframe will be created and it may cause undesirable effects.

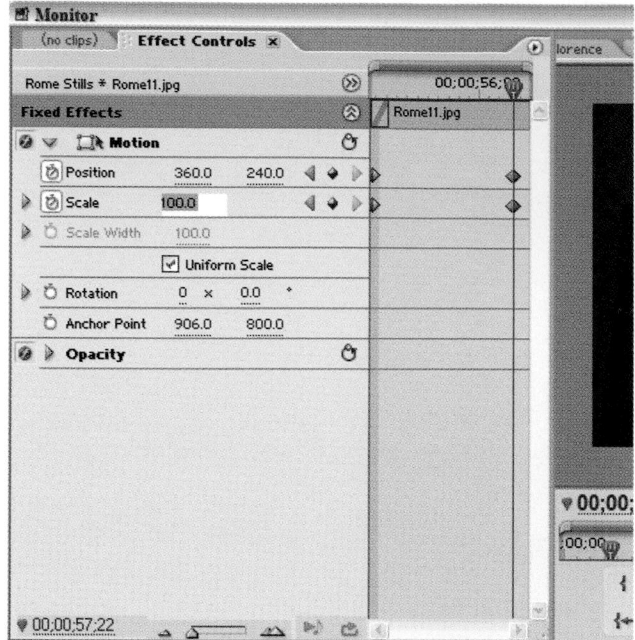

Figure 11.15 Clicking on the Go to Next Keyframe button for the Scale parameter snapped the Edit Line to the last Scale keyframe. Because there are no more keyframes to the right of the current keyframe, the Go to Next Keyframe button is now dimmed. When the Edit Line is positioned over a keyframe, you can adjust parameter settings for that keyframe. To delete the keyframe, click the Add/Remove Keyframe button.

11. Using the workflow you just learned, create your own custom motion settings, or add and modify your newly created custom presets to the remaining images in the sequence. To take a shortcut to the final step, simply open Still_Effects_Finish.prproj from the APPST Lesson Files/Chapter 11 folder and examine the remaining effects.

12. Open the Photo Montage sequence in the Timeline window, and position the Edit Line at 4;00. From the Rome Stills folder, drag and drop the Rome Stills sequence starting at the current Edit Line position. From the Effect Controls window, drag and drop the Cross Dissolve transition so that it is starting at the cut between the two shots (see Figure 11.16). Add another cross dissolve to the end of the Rome Stills sequence, then press Enter to render the work area and view the final, full-resolution version of the montage.

Figure 11.16 With the Rome Stills sequence overlaid at 4;00 in the timeline, hold the Cross Dissolve transition just right of the cut point to add it with Starting at the Cut alignment. Using this technique makes sure that the entire last second of the Map Comp graphic is used for the transition.

If you can't get enough of this photo montage example, the Premiere Pro video training series from Total Training goes into great depth about creating additional Motion effects, as well as adding music to the montage. My "Tips & Tricks" series covers more photo montage effects, while the "What's New for Adobe Premiere Pro 1.5" set covers Bezier keyframes inside and out.

For the last step, you nested the Rome Stills sequence into the Photo Montage sequence. Because the opening graphic is five seconds long and it should fade up while the graphic is still visible, you overlaid the Rome Stills sequence on top of the last 30 frames of the Map Comp. Dropping a transition that starts at the cut used those last 30 frames for the transition, as well as the first 30 frames of the Rome Stills sequence. You can now add your own music track to give the piece a little more personality.

This lesson lays the ground work for Motion effects, but there is a lot left to cover. With the foundation established and a handful of presets, you should be able to tweak, adjust, and then come up with your own version of the perfect image pan or zoom presets.

Things to Remember

When working with stills, proper management of the imported image's resolution and frame size is vital. You can speed up processing, for example, by reducing the still image to 72dpi before you import it into Premiere Pro. As for the frame size, you can pre-define what size you wish your images to be. If you plan on zooming at levels between 150% and 200%, be sure that the frame size of your image is at least double that of your video frame; a 720×480 video frame, for example, would need a 1440×960 picture frame.

Because you can't range select and adjust the duration of an entire group of stills, you will want to adjust your default still duration value before you import groups of stills. Whatever the current duration is will be assigned to your images when they are imported.

After you import your images, you still have resizing options. When adding stills to your sequence, remember that you can add them at their normal frame size or you can instruct Premiere to automatically resize them to fit entirely within the video frame.

Finally, consider using custom effect presets. With Premiere Pro 1.5, you can create and re-use effect presets. You can also export and import presets to and from other Premiere Pro 1.5 users. All of the presets that were created for this lesson can be imported individually. Just choose Import Preset from the Effects window wing menu, and select the presets from the APPST Lesson Files/Chapter 11/Custom Presets folder, and use them as much as you like.

The next chapter switches gears a bit to look at another type of graphic: titles. You will explore some of the features of the Adobe Title Designer. With this very practical tool, you quickly and efficiently can create your own custom titles, styles, and templates.

CHAPTER

12

Advanced Titling: Styles

Adobe Title Designer combines the power to create unique, attractive titles with the ability to save the style and design of the title's text and objects. With the Title Designer, you can create and save custom personalized titles and templates that you then can use over and over for multiple projects. Creating custom templates allows you to quickly load a title and update its text to reflect what is unique in its current application. If you produce wedding or corporate videos, for example, you have the option to streamline and customize the titles that appear in your videos.

This chapter focuses on creating styles—the way text appears, that particular shine on a box edge. You will first create a geometric object with a custom style, and then you will create custom text that fits into the object. The result will be a lower-third title template that you can use for future projects. Along the way, you will learn about all the properties that make up the style of the text or object.

Creating a Style from an Object

The easiest way to understand style properties is to apply them to an object.

1. Open Title_Style_Start.prproj from the APPST Lesson Files/Chapter 12 folder.
2. Choose File>New>Title, or press F9 to open the Title Designer. From the Tool palette, select the Rounded Rectangle tool and create a rectangle in the center of your Title window with a Width of 325 and a Height of 80. (See Figure 12.1.)

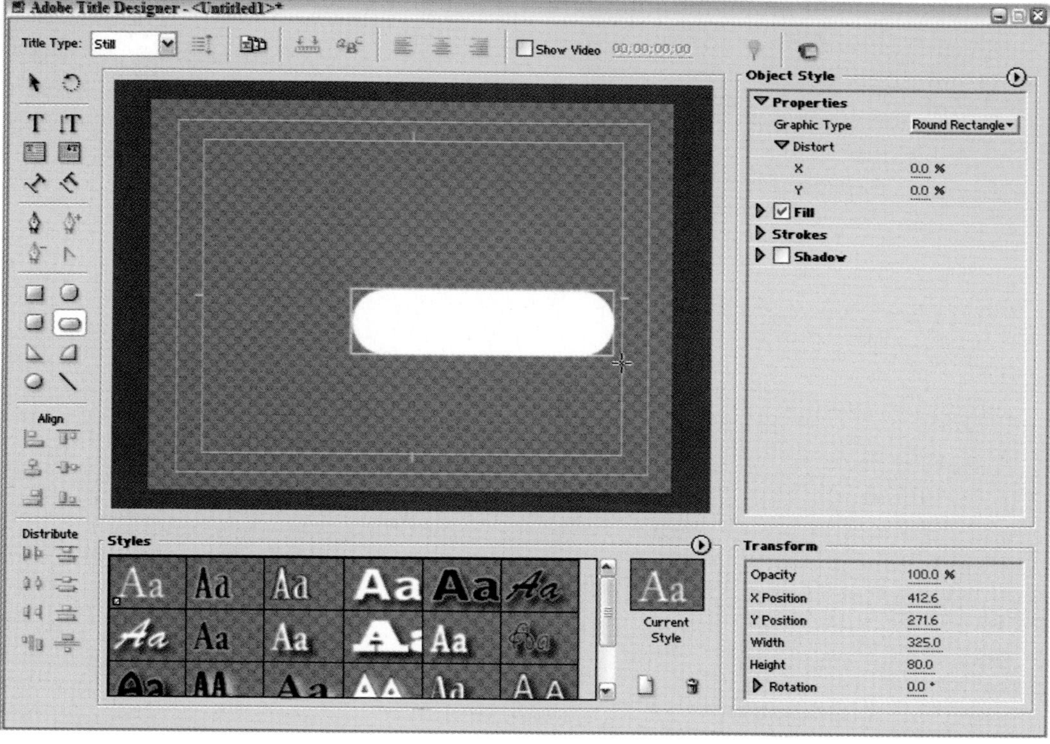

Figure 12.1 To create an object, click and drag using the object creation tool of your choice. The range of your drag determines the size of the object. If you want your object to have an exact width and height, be sure the object is selected and adjust the two parameters in the Title Designer's Transform section. Notice Width is manually set to 325 and Height to 80.

For this title, you need a simple, but striking object that can be centered in the lower third of the frame and fit text. With a little bit of distortion, you will alter the dimensions of this object to look more stylish.

3. With the new object selected, twirl down the Properties listing in the Style Palette and then twirl down Distort. Assign 20% to X and 30% to Y.

   The Distort values pinch the selected object on its X and Y axes. To distort the opposite direction, use a negative Distort value.

4. With the Fill check box checked, twirl down the Fill listing. For Fill Type, select 4 Color Gradient. Click on the upper-left square of the Gradient display so that the black arrow appears beneath it. Click the color swatch next to Color Stop Color to open the Color Picker. (See Figure 12.2.) Select the values R0, G138, B0, and click OK. Click to select the lower-right square of the gradient, and assign that position the same color value.

   The Fill listing determines the coloring that fills your selected text or object. Of the several choices in the drop-down menu, I think the 4 Color Gradient offers a good method of creating a professional looking title.

   Your 4 Color Gradient is now diagonally green from northwest to southeast and diagonally white from northeast to southwest. For this step, you just assigned a basic color for the object. You can easily change the color for your subsequent projects.

5. Click the Sheen check box, and twirl down the Sheen listing. Click the Color Picker, and assign a darker green (R0, G102, B0). Click OK. Set Size to 35, and leave Angle at 90 degrees. (See Figure 12.3.)

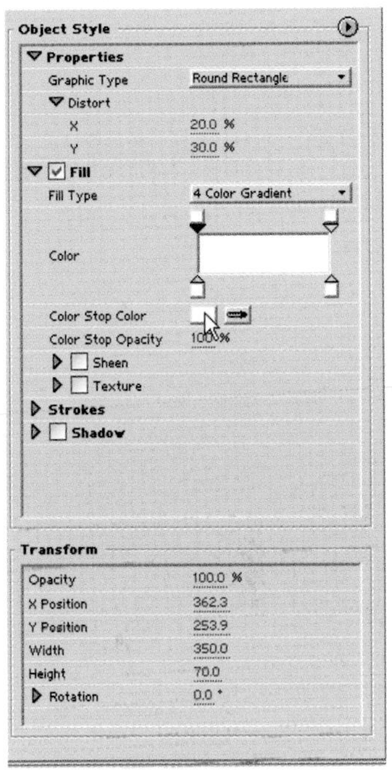

Figure 12.2 When you assign colors to a gradient, you must first click the color box for the position that you want to assign. The selected position will have a black arrow pointing downward below the color box. To assign a specific color to that position, click the Color Picker box shown here beneath the mouse. Additionally, you can assign color using the Eye Dropper, which allows you to pick a color from any region of the desktop. This is very helpful for picking a color that is a part of your video frame, but may be difficult to identify in the color picker.

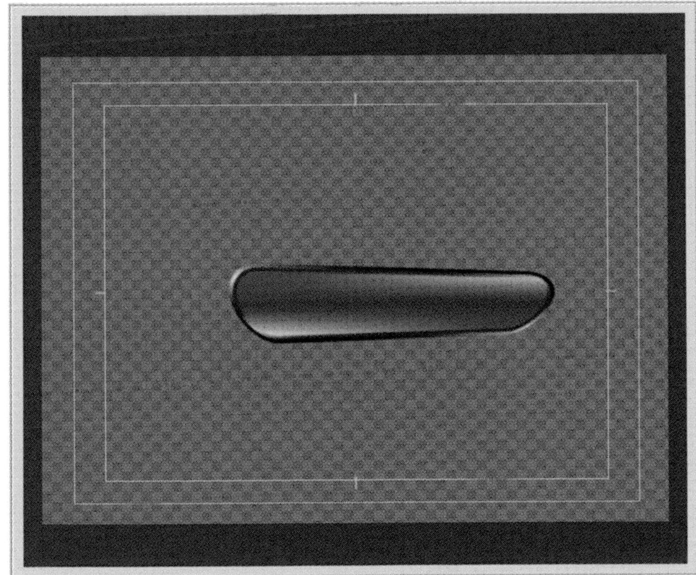

Figure 12.3 Sheens are an integral part of adding subtle depth, gloss, and elegance to a title object. In this image, you can see how much better the object's coloring looks with the white sheen on the black edge of the object and the dark green sheen in the middle.

A *sheen* is essentially a line that appears in the fill coloring of your object. Using the Size, Angle, and Offset parameters, you can position that line wherever you want within the boundaries of the object. While you based your initial object coloring on a green value, the sheen is dark green, so that when applied it almost looks like the color starts dark in the center and in two corners it gets a little bit lighter. If you are using a different color than green, guideline is for the gradient to have the base color and the sheen to be the same color, only darker.

6. Twirl up the Fill listing, then twirl down the Stroke listing. Click the Add button next to Outer Strokes, and twirl down the Outer Strokes listing. Twirl down the newly checked Outer Strokes listing, and assign the following values:

   Type: **Edge**
   Size: **4**
   Fill Type: **Solid**
   Color: **R0, G60, B0**

   Outer strokes are outlines that begin on the edge of the object and grow outward as their size increases. You first added an outer stroke, then you defined the size and color of the stroke. The guideline for the first outer stroke color was an even darker green than the fill's sheen. In the same way that the fill can have its own sheen, individual strokes can have a sheen applied to them. For this lesson, the combination of multiple outer strokes with different sheens create a great looking object.

Inner strokes are lines that trace the inner contours of the object or text and that stack and expand inward.

7. Click the Sheen check box for the first Outer Stroke, and twirl down the Sheen listing. Enter the following values, then twirl up the Outer Stroke listing (See Figure 12.4):

   Color: **R229, G255, B196**
   Size: **25**
   Angle: **260**

For the first outer stroke sheen, you chose a light green/yellow color that is closer to the corner white than the corner green. Adjusting its angle, you positioned the sheen near the curves of the object. This positioning gives the illusion of added dimension to the object. The slight change in color makes a distinction between the fill and the stroke. To add the finishing touches on the object, add another outer stroke.

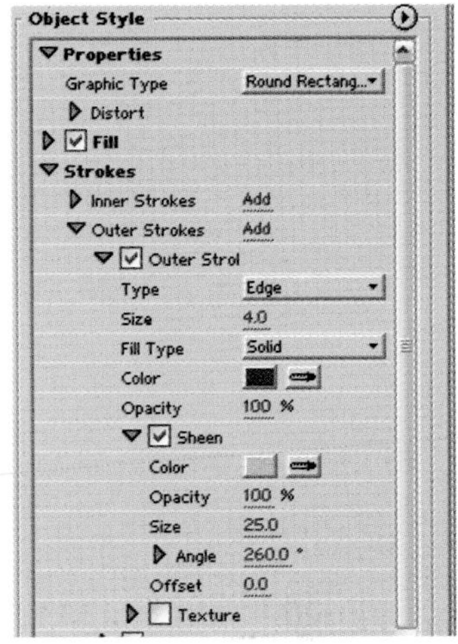

Figure 12.4 You can apply an outer stroke, then add a sheen within that single stroke. Because the sheen affects the single stroke only, it further enhances the illusion of shine and depth to the edge of the object.

8. Add a second outer stroke, and assign the values:

   Type: **Edge**
   Size: **4**
   Fill Type: **Solid**
   Color: **Default Black**
   Opacity: **100%**

9. Click the Sheen check box to add a sheen. Assign the values:

   Color: **Default White**
   Opacity: **100%**
   Size: **40**
   Angle: **100**
   Offset: **0.0**

   Each additional stroke is applied to the edge of the previous stroke, not the edge of the initial object. For this step, you added a final black outer stroke and used the same sheen technique to give it the appearance of depth. (See Figure 12.5.) The black outer stroke gives the object a definitive outer edge and completes its design.

10. With the object selected, click the Styles Library wing menu and select New Style. Name the style Green Object. Click OK. (See Figure 12.6.)

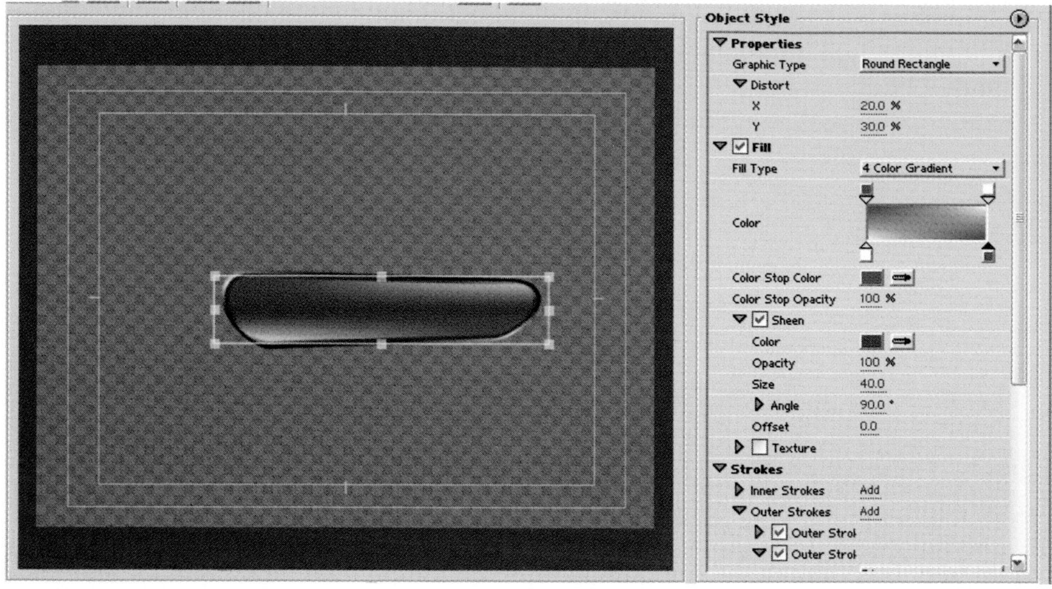

Figure 12.5 With two outer strokes, each with a slightly different sheen color and sheen position, you can easily create the illusion of depth for any object created in the Title Designer. Here the edge looks metallic as if there was light shining on it.

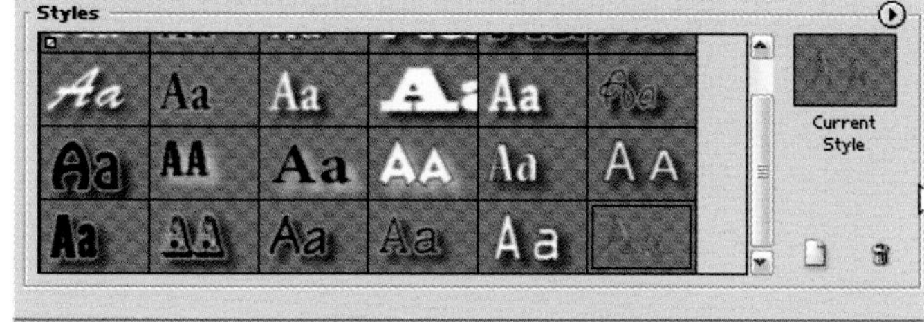

Figure 12.6 Once a new style has been created, it becomes available for re-use in your Styles Library. Clicking on an object, then clicking on a Style Library swatch, assigns those style properties to the object.

To change styles for text, select the text element and click the new style swatch. Premiere updates the text with the style of the selected swatch. To update a text element's fill, strokes, and shadow properties, but not its text properties, hold down the Ctrl key while you click another style swatch. With the Ctrl key held down, the original text properties remain intact but the fill, strokes, and shadow update.

In your Styles Library, Premiere Pro creates a new swatch that reflects the entire object style properties for the object you just created. Whenever you create a new style, the style will be added as the last swatch in the Styles Library.

11. Select the Rectangle tool, and create a new object in your Title window. With the new object created and selected, click the last thumbnail that you just added in the Styles palette.

    By creating a thumbnail for the object style properties, you now have the ability to apply custom styles to multiple, different types of objects or text.

The final and most important element of this lesson is to emphasize the ease in which you can save and apply a customized style. Using this workflow, you can create your own title elements and save them for future work so that you don't waste time repeating the same design steps.

To see some final title objects, open the file Title_Style_Finish.prproj and open the Objects title. You can then look at how I adjusted individual parameters, increasing the fill sheen for certain objects and shifting the position and size of the stroke sheen in other objects. To further understand the technique of creating good looking object styles, you can open any of the title templates and select an object element from the template. Its style properties will be active and easy for you to browse in the Object Style palette.

Creating a Custom Text Style

Creating a custom text style is quite similar to creating a custom object style. The main difference is that working with text enables you to define several additional text-specific parameters, as well. You'll investigate adding styles to text in the steps that follow. By the end of the lesson, you will combine the text with the object you created earlier to produce a good looking, lower-third title template.

1. Open the project file Text_Style_Start.prproj from the APPST Lesson Files/Chapter 12 folder. Double-click on the Style.prtl title file in the Project window to open the title in the Adobe Title Designer.
2. Using the Type tool, click in the title frame and enter:

    First Lastname

    Use upper- and lowercase as shown. In the Object Style Properties for the active text, select Eras Demi ITC font from the drop-down Font menu. Change the Font Size to 46. Click the check box for Small Caps and change the Small Caps Size to 80%. (See Figure 12.7.)

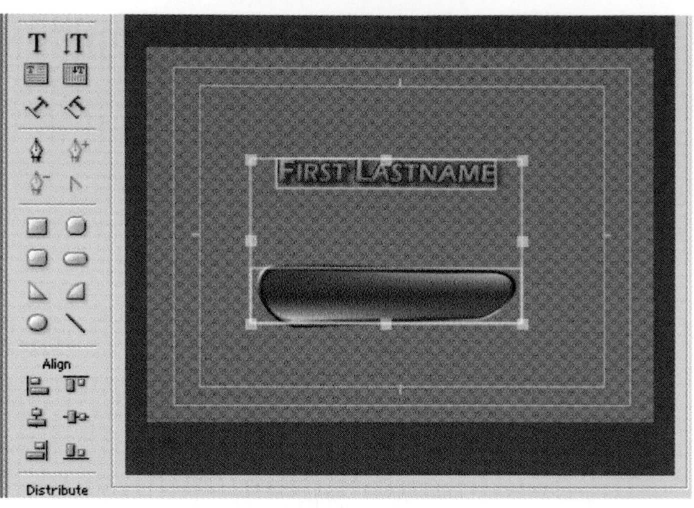

Figure 12.7 With a text element selected, consult the Object Style area to see and adjust its font name, font size, Small Caps status, and Small Caps Size.

NOTES

An enhancement for Premiere Pro 1.5 is support of True Type font sizes. When you use a True Type font in Photoshop with a size of 38, the same font at the same size will be exactly the same in Premiere Pro. In previous versions, Title Designer's font sizes were a bit bigger. The titles you created in version 1.0 of Premiere Pro should automatically convert to a new size when you open them in 1.5 so as to not appear different.

With text selected, you can change the displayed font from the drop-down menu. The font browser (look up in the Font drop-down menu) shows you a preview of the font, as well as its name. Adjusting the size of the text was necessary to fit it into your object. Turning on Small Caps switches every character into capital letters. Adjusting the Small Caps Size enables you to preserve the relationship of the upper- and lowercase letters by reducing the size of the letters originally typed in lowercase. (For more on the remaining text parameters, see Chapter 13, "Advanced Titling: Templates.")

3. Twirl up the Properties listing, and twirl down the Fill listing. For the selected text, assign 4 Color Gradient as the Fill Type. Assign the following color values for the gradient (see Figure 12.8):

   Top Left corner box: **R255, G255, B191**
   Top Right: **R255, G255, B148**
   Bottom Left: **R247, G247, B89**
   Bottom Right: **R242, G223, B78**

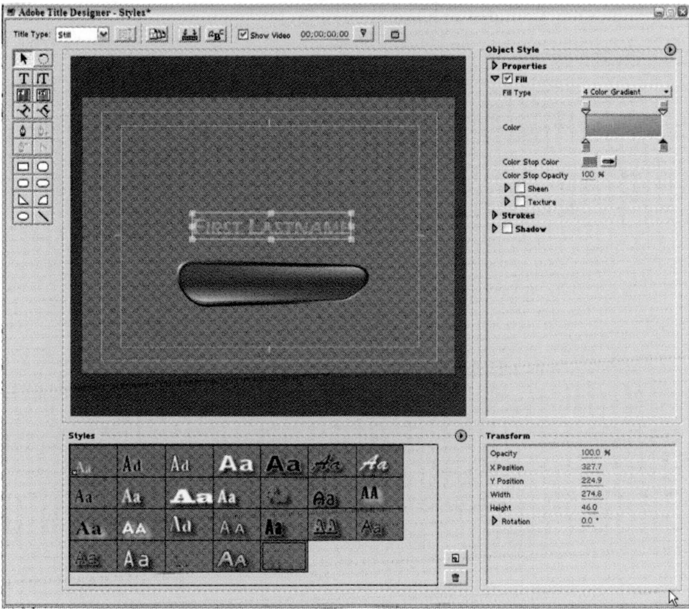

Figure 12.8 For the 4 Color Gradient fill of the text, the yellow's intensity increases over the course of the gradient. Using yellow for text is recommended in certain titles, because pure white can tend to be too bright. This light subtle yellow color will be easy to read on top of the object's green gradient.

Instead of having two colors in this gradient as you did for the object, you set each corner of the gradient to gradually increase the intensity of yellow.

4. Twirl up the Fill listing, and twirl down the Stroke listing. Add one outer stroke, and assign the values:

   Type: **Edge**
   Size: **14**
   Fill Type: **Solid**
   Color: **Default Black**
   Opacity: **100%**

5. Click the Sheen check box for the outer stroke, and enter the values:

   Color: **R255, G255, B168**
   Opacity: **60%**
   Size: **60**
   Angle: **65**

As you learned with the object, adding a sheen can create a subtle illusion of depth. For the first stroke, you added a sheen similar in color to the fill color. At first glance, this sheen looked far too strong, but once you reduced its opacity, it blended in with the stroke. When you close the text style by adding another black outer stroke, it will look great.

6. Twirl up the current outer stroke, and click Add to create a second outer stroke. Twirl down the second Outer Stroke listing, and assign the values:

   Type: **Edge**
   Size: **14**
   Fill Type: **Solid**
   Color: **Default Black**
   Opacity: **100%**

   Adding the second outer stroke gives a final outline that properly defines the visible text.

7. Twirl up the Outer Strokes listing, then click the Shadow check box and twirl down the Shadow listing. Enter the following Shadow values:

   Color: **Default Black**
   Opacity: **50%**
   Angle: **122**
   Distance: **10**
   Size: **0**
   Spread: **35**

   While Opacity controls the transparency of the shadow, Spread gently increases its size and thins out the emphasis of the color. For this adjustment, you want a shadow that is reasonably close to the text with a spread that still emphasizes the shape of the text. (See Figure 12.9.)

8. With the text selected in the Title window, click on the New Style button (next to the Trashcan in the Styles Library area). Name the new style Custom Yellow Text, and click OK.

   Saving and preserving a custom style for text works the same as for an object.

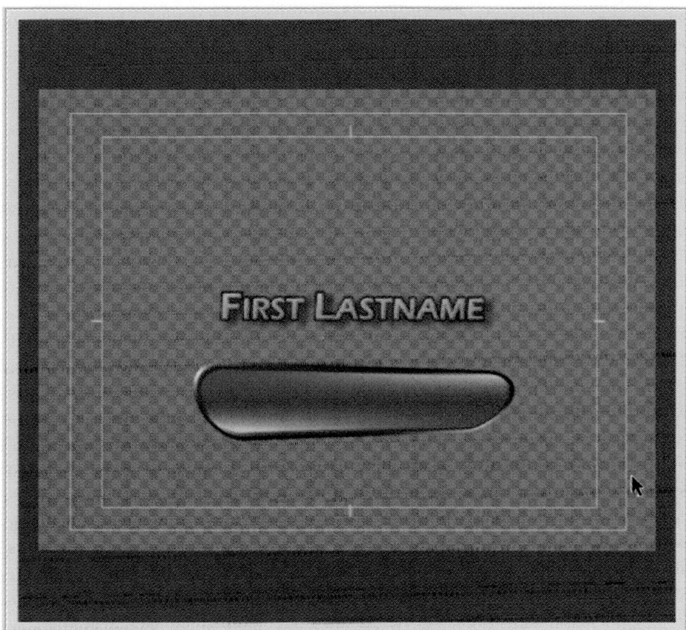

Figure 12.9 The result of your style adjustments is a very clean looking text element that will stand out on top of another object.

9. Using the Selection tool, choose the text and object (Shift-click each, or drag and marquee select them both). With both selected, click the Alignment button for Horizontal Center, then click the Alignment button for Vertical Center. With the objects still selected on top of each other, right-click and select Position>Horizontal Center then finally right-click again Position>Lower Third. (See Figures 12.10 and 12.11.)

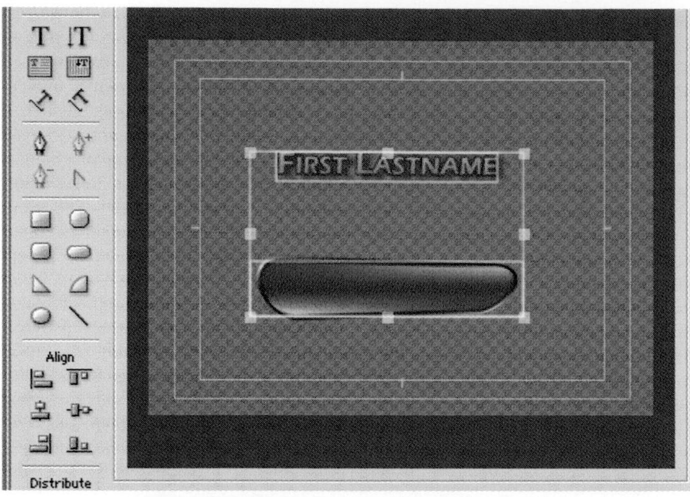

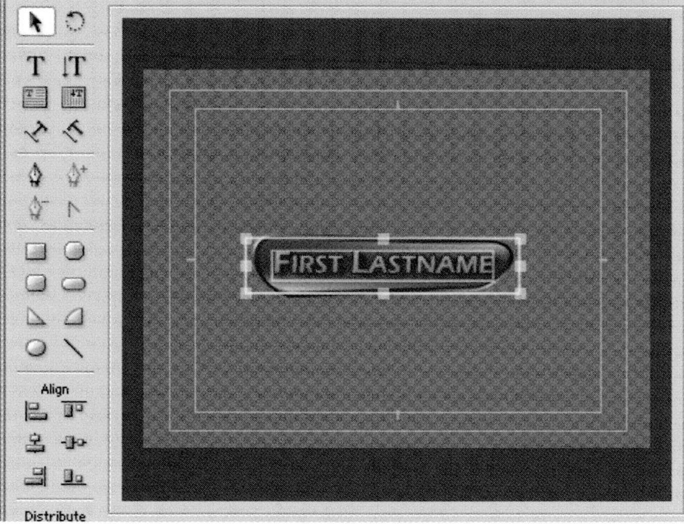

Figure 12.10 The Alignment buttons enable you to adjust the alignment of multiple selected objects. First the elements are aligned horizontally (top), then vertically (bottom) so that they fit exactly within each other.

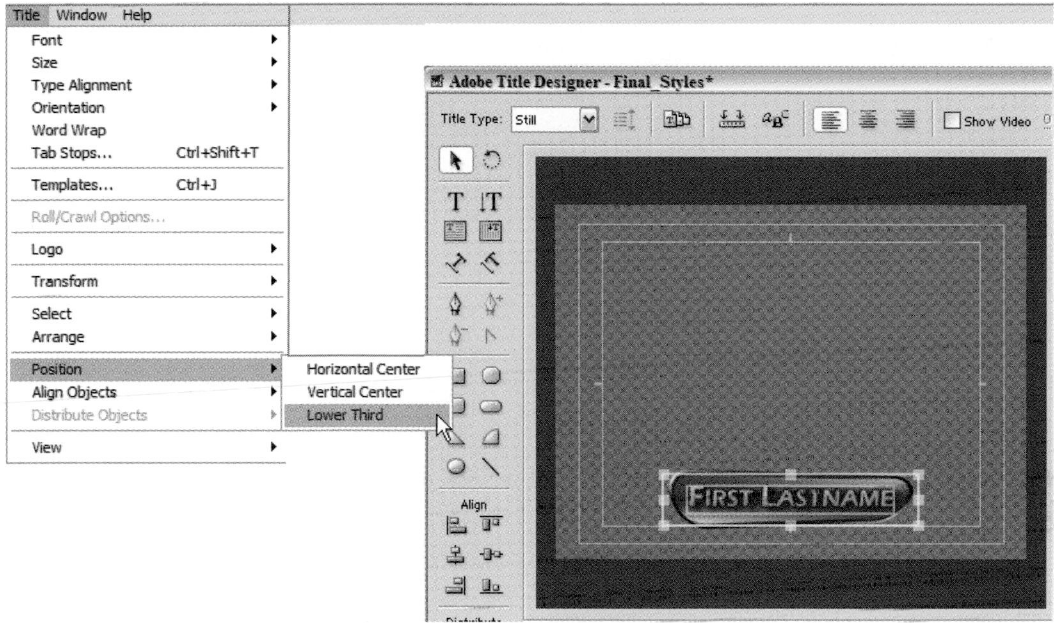

Figure 12.11 Once the elements are placed perfectly together, you can reposition them to the proper location on the screen by accessing the position shortcuts from the right-click or Title>Position menu.

You aligned the two elements horizontally first so that the text was in the horizontal center of the object. Aligning them vertically ensures the text will fit properly inside the absolute center of the object.

Next, you centered the selection horizontally so that it appeared in the absolute center of the frame, then you re-positioned it to the lower-third region for later use as a title template to introduce people in your video. (See Figure 12.12.)

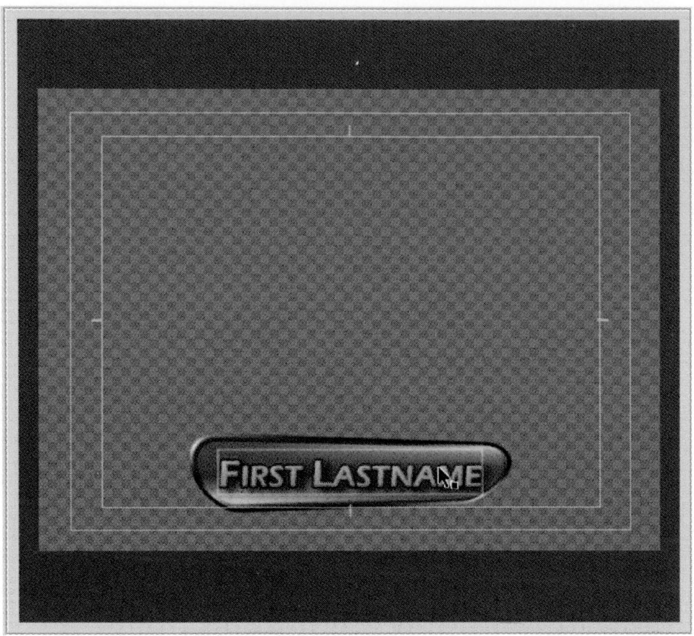

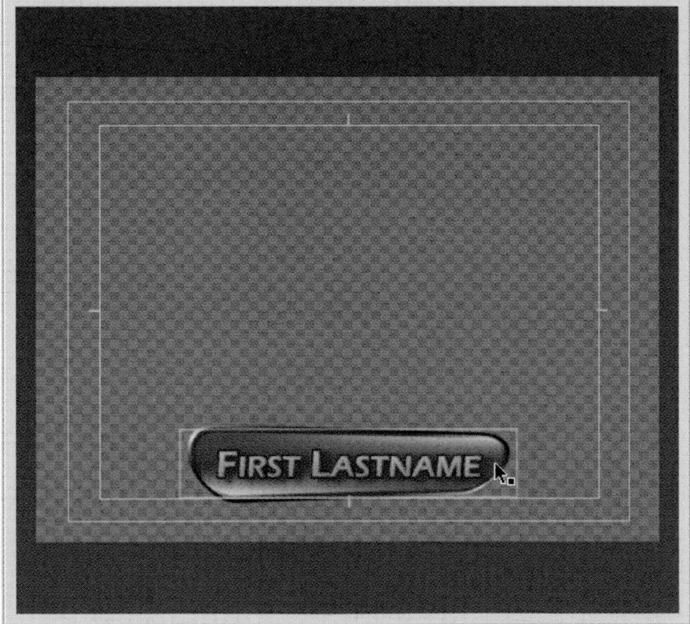

Figure 12.12 When you position the Selection tool on top of an area that only the object occupies, Premiere surrounds the object in a transparent box. Clicking when the transparent box appears selects the element that the box surrounds.

10. From the File menu, choose Save As and name this file Merged Styles.

You will begin the next chapter's lesson by creating a template using this saved title. If you do not save the file, it will still be there waiting for you when you open the next project: Open Text_Style_Finish.prproj from the APPST Lesson Files/Chapter 12 folder, then open Final Styles.prtl to see my final title.

Using the foundation from creating an object style, you applied a similar method to the text with some slight variations. Because text letters vary in shape, the sheen technique for adding depth might not always be appropriate; some letters might not have the proper angles for the sheen to work on. To get around this, reduce the sheen's opacity to produce a more subtle effect. By the same token, instead of two diagonal colors in the four-color gradient, you focused on gradually emphasizing one color. This way the letters, which consist of all shapes, have the same general color tone. Once again, the end result was a new style in your Styles Library that you can use again and again in future projects.

Things to Remember

This workflow can be duplicated on a project-by-project basis, creating unique objects and text styles according to the tone of the piece you are working on.

The fundamental things to remember are that objects and text have the exact same fill, stroke, and shadow properties, the only differences being the text parameters for text elements and the differing geometric shapes for the object elements. If you happen to create a unique text style that you want to add to an object, you can create an object and apply that same style to the object. The object will not convert to text; it will just assume the fill, stroke, and shadow properties of the applied style. The same rules apply when applying an object style to text, except for the fact that object styles will use the default text parameters.

Filling and coloring the elements is by far the most important attribute of the titling process (aside from your choice of fonts for the text). While the example used strokes of single solid colors, you can fill a stroke with a four-color gradient just as you can an object or text. If at any point while you experiment, you want to save the current style, simply create a new style with the element selected in the Title window.

In the next chapter you will explore creating, modifying, and saving title templates. Although you now can create and save custom styles, templates can be even more powerful—especially pre-existing templates, as you'll find out next.

CHAPTER

13

Advanced Titling: Templates

Some of the most practical and simple aspects of the Adobe Title Designer are its template functions. Templates are ready-made titles with text and objects that you can replace and modify on a project-by-project basis, without altering the original. You can build your own custom title templates, modify the templates included with the Title Designer, or use the built-in designs as is.

In this chapter, you will:

- Save the lower-third title you created in Chapter 12, "Advanced Titling: Styles," as a new template
- Modify a ready-made template and resave it as a custom template
- Create a credit roll template, which is very valuable for most production work

The first two lessons rely on such basic title functions as selecting, moving, and modifying the properties of existing objects in the title template. The third lesson goes a bit further, exploring Tab Stops, Roll/Crawl Options, and Properties settings for text.

Creating a Custom Template

Creating your own template is quite simple. From any open title you can save a custom template comprised of all the title's elements and their properties. After you save a title as a custom template, that title file resides in the Custom Template folder managed by Premiere Pro—even if you delete the title the template was based on. You then can load the title anytime you want by clicking the Templates button and choosing the custom template, as opposed to importing a file.

1. Open Template01_Start.prproj from the APPST Lesson Files/Chapter 13 folder. Double-click on the Final_Styles title in the Project window. Click the Templates button (see Figure 13.1) or press Ctrl+J to access the Templates dialog.

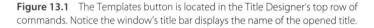

Figure 13.1 The Templates button is located in the Title Designer's top row of commands. Notice the window's title bar displays the name of the opened title.

2. In the Template dialog's wing menu, select Save Final_Styles as Template (see Figure 13.2), and type Custom Lower Third for the name when prompted. Click OK.

   When you save your current title as a template, you can assign it a custom name. Premiere saves the newly created template into the User Templates folder.

3. With the Templates window still open, twirl down the User Templates listing and select Custom Lower Third (see Figure 13.3). Click on the wing menu to view your options (see Figure 13.4). Select Set Template as Default. Close the Templates window, then close the Title Designer.

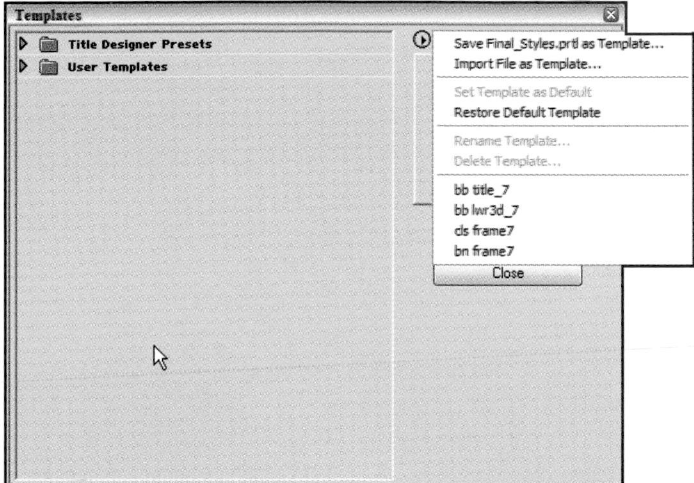

Figure 13.2 Premiere Pro inserts the name of your title in the Save as Template wing menu option. When you build a title from scratch, <Untitled> appears instead. Remember that when you save your open title as a template, Premiere duplicates the title's entire state and layer ordering when making the template.

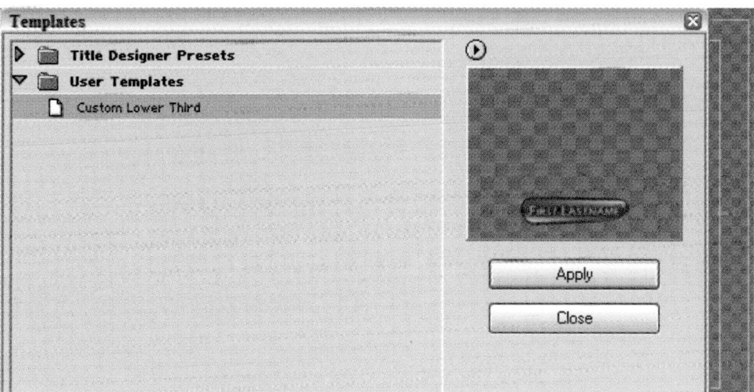

Figure 13.3 Selecting an item in the User Templates listing shows the preview image at right.

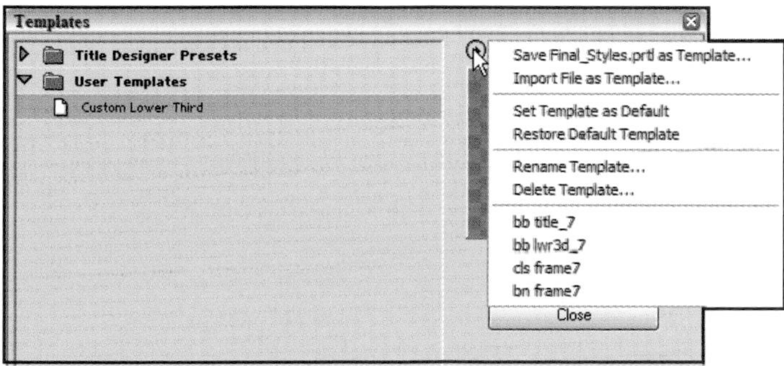

Figure 13.4 A few additional options are available from the wing menu when a template is selected. Note you can now choose Set Template as Default, Rename Template, or Delete Template.

After creating your own custom template, you can change its name, delete it, or assign the selected template to be your default title template. Premiere Pro automatically loads the default title template into the Title Designer's drawing area when you create a new title.

4. Select File>New>Title.

   When you open a new title, Premiere Pro automatically loads your default title template. Because you set your lower-third template as the default, you can easily create any number of titles in this format: Just open a new title, enter the appropriate text, and save the title with a unique name. To turn off the modified default title template, open the Template dialog and select Restore Default Template from the wing menu.

This first lesson illustrates how easy it is to create custom templates and how they can expedite and streamline your title creation workflow.

Adding Logos and Modifying Pre-Made Templates

When you want help refining the style and eloquence of your titles, the best place to look is the Templates dialog. You very easily can load one of the more than 100 built-in templates, then alter its elements to suit your project needs. In this lesson, which assumes you're putting together a DVD of a baby's first birthday, you'll learn how to alter a template and save the adjustments as a new template.

You will open one of the templates in the Celebrations folder and add a picture to personalize the title. Just in case your family has a baby boom, you will save the modified template as a custom template. An important element of this lesson is incorporating pictures or graphic file elements to your title document: You will explore adding a logo as well as using an image for a fill texture.

1. Open the Template02_Start.prproj file from the APPST Lesson Files/Chapter 13 folder.

BdayBoy.jpg, which is located in the same folder, is the primary image (logo) that you will incorporate into the title template.

2. Select File>New>Title or press F9 to open the Adobe Title Designer. Click the Templates button, and in the Templates dialog, go to Title Designer Presets> Celebrations>Baby Boy. Select bb frame_7, and click Apply to load the template.

   Once the template is loaded, you can modify and manipulate any of the title elements without affecting the original template. For this template, you want to replace the image of the rattle with a picture of the birthday boy.

3. Select the rattle graphic in the lower-left corner, and delete it. To do this, hold the mouse directly over the graphic, right-click, and then select Clear. Otherwise, you can select the single object and press the Delete key. Right-click again, select Logo>Insert Logo, and choose the BdayBoy.jpg file from the APPST Lesson Files/Chapter 13 folder. (See Figure 13.5.)

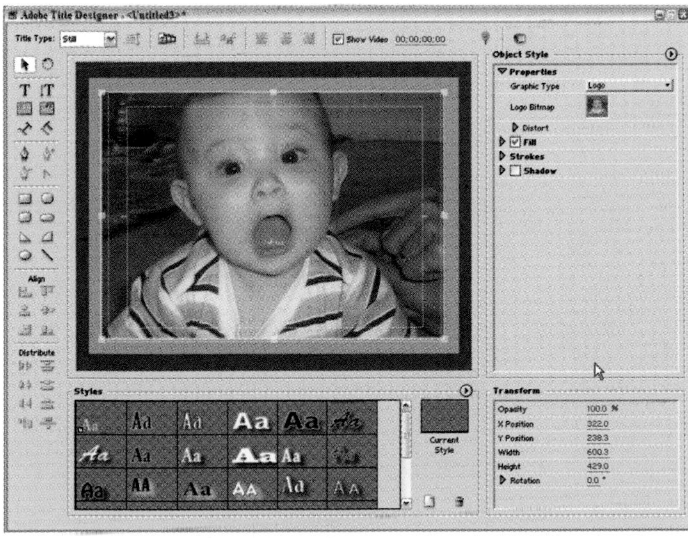

Figure 13.5 When you import a picture or graphic as a logo, it opens at the full frame size and dimensions of the original document. It is not scaled. Also, notice Logo is listed for Graphics Type in the Properties twirl down of the Object Style panel and a sample of the image is shown next to Logo Bitmap.

Because Premiere Pro can insert a logo or a texture, let me clarify the difference. A *logo* is the type of identifying graphic for which people and companies pay a lot of money. They are very client-oriented, professional graphics meant to be used as delivered. The logo tools manage the size and aspect ratios of logos, providing minimal support for altering them artistically. *Textures*, on the other hand, are all about the art and adding mood, depth, and feeling to your graphics and titles.
So, if you want to preserve the aspect ratio of a graphic, you can insert it as a logo and reduce the adjustments that can be applied to the image. If you want to blend the graphic with other title elements, then insert it as a texture.

Inserting a logo is one of the methods by which you can add a picture or graphic file into the Title Designer's drawing area. To adjust the size and position, simply drag the image's handles.

4. Hold down the Shift key and drag the upper-right handle down and to the left, so that the graphic gets to a size closer to that of the rattle. If the picture still covers the text "Baby Boy's Name," use the Selection tool to slide the text a few pixels to the right. (See Figure 13.6.)

   To avoid distortion and preserve the original aspect ratio of an inserted graphic when you resize it, hold down the Shift key while you drag the adjustment handles.

5. Click and select the picture of the boy. From the Object Style panel's Properties twirl down, expand Strokes and then expand Outer Strokes. Add an outer stroke with the settings:

   Type: **Depth**
   Size: **9**
   Angle: **315**
   Fill Type: **Solid**
   Color: **Black**
   Opacity: **70%**

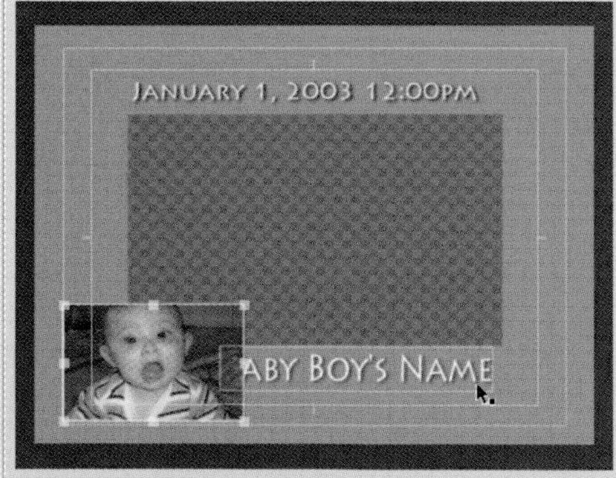

Figure 13.6 If your new picture covers the template's text, click on the text with the Selection tool (left) and drag it a few pixels to the right (right).

Imported graphic and picture files have the same style properties as any object explored thus far in the book. You can easily add inner or outer strokes, as well as fills, sheens, and shadows.

You now have a picture, but you would prefer it in an oval like the rattle graphic. The only limitation of using the Insert Logo feature is that the original shape and dimensions of the file will be adhered to in the title. If the picture is a square, you can't just change it to a circle. You can, however, work around this limitation.

6. Right-click on the baby picture, and clear the file from the title. Press the E key to select the Ellipse tool, and make a circle in the bottom-left corner of the title frame. Click the default style swatch in the first position of the Styles Library to give the object a default white fill. The circle should be approximately 180×180.

   Instead of using the square image of the baby, you created a circular object in which you will use the baby picture as a texture fill.

7. With the newly created circle selected, twirl down the Fill listing in the Object Style panel. Check the box for Texture, and twirl it down. Click in the blank gray box to the right of the word "Texture," and select the BdayBoy.jpg file from the Choose a Texture Image dialog box. Click Open. (See Figure 13.7.)

   To add a picture, graphic, or grayscale texture to any object, activate the Texture Fill and select your desired texture file. With the texture in place, you can modify it a number of ways.

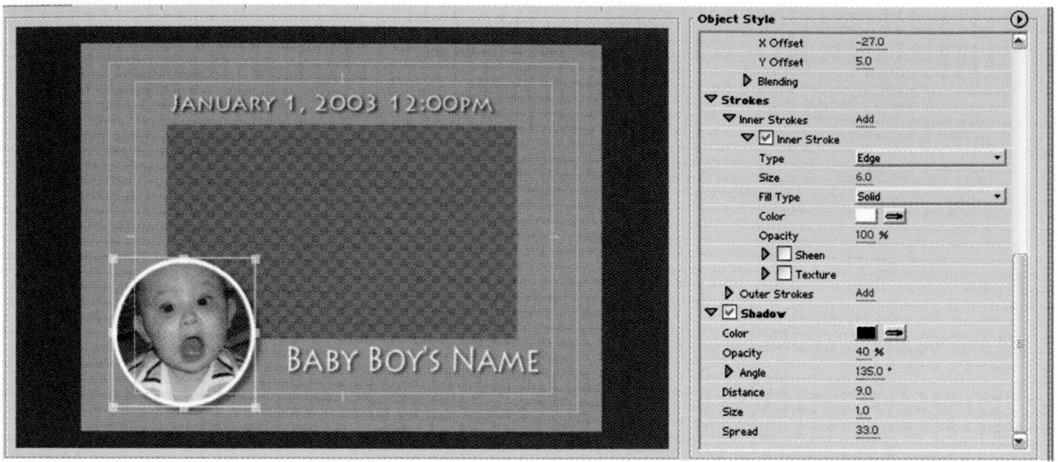

Figure 13.7 No matter what type of object you create, you can fill it not only with gradients and colors, but also with textures or graphic images. Here you can see the selected texture in a small preview area and the circle now filled with the image of the boy.

8. Continuing in the Object Style panel, twirl down Fill, then Texture, then Scaling, and set Object X and Object Y both to Face from the drop-down menus. Set Horizontal to 140%. Next, twirl down Alignment, and set Object X and Object Y both to Face. Change X Offset to –27.0 and Y Offset to 5.0.

   When you are working with a texture fill, you need to keep in mind some scaling and alignment rules for the texture that is filling the object. In terms of scaling, Clipped Face and Face resize the graphic to fit within the boundaries of the object it is filling. Texture uses the graphic's default size as the dimensions of the fill image. Because the circle has more of a squared 1:1 boundary than a rectangular one, adjusting the Horizontal scale of the image made it wider.

   If you reduced the size of the texture to be smaller than the boundaries of the object shape, the Tile check boxes allow the image to tile vertically and horizontally in order to fill the object. Without tile, there would be black space around the image where it did not fill the object.

Once the image is scaled and placed within the boundaries of the object, Alignment lets you offset or slightly nudge the image horizontally or vertically. Here, shifting the image a bit to the left centered it within the object.

When the Alignment Rule X is set to Left, the texture locks to the left edge and it grows to the right. Offsetting the X value by –27 moves that left edge a value of 27 to the left; it is offset. Rule Y is set to Top, this means it is locked to the top edge and grows downward. With a Y Offset of 5, you push the image five pixels down from the top. In order for no black space to appear in the area above the image where it was pushed down, tiling is turned on. Tiling repeats the texture from all edges.

9. Add an inner stroke to the selected object:

   Type: **Edge**
   Size: **6.0**
   Fill Type: **Solid**
   Color: **White**
   Opacity: **100%**

10. Add a shadow with the settings (see Figure 13.8):

    Color: **Black**
    Opacity: **40%**
    Angle: **135**
    Distance: **9**
    Size: **1**
    Spread: **33**

    The small inner stroke and shadow unify the look of the added object with the look of the title's other objects. Now that the title is complete, you can save it as a template for continued use.

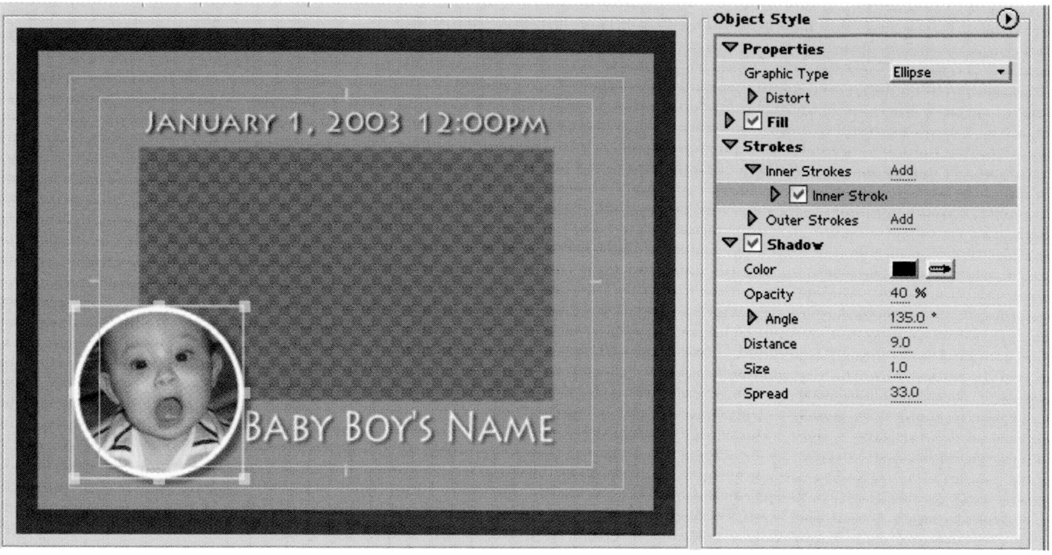

Figure 13.8 The new graphic is now unified with the other object to match color and shadowing with a far better look and feel than the square image that you originally inserted. If a general logo insert doesn't give you the result you want, consider using an image as a texture within a custom object instead.

11. Finally, select and change each of the text elements in the title (Baby Boy's Name and January 1, 2003 12:00 PM) to information relevant to your project. If you like, you now can open the Templates dialog, select Save <UntitledXX> as Template from the wing menu, and name the template. I saved it as New_Baby_Template.

I encourage you to use your own graphics and images in the titles that you create and templates that you modify. Although logos have less flexibility and adjustment qualities (for good reason), you can always add an image or graphic into your title as a texture fill. Design-wise, if you don't feel like you have a good sense of how a title should look, simply load a template and modify it to suit your needs.

Creating a Custom Credit Roll Template

To provide you with more experience working with text and moving titles, the final lesson of this chapter will guide you through creating your own custom credit roll. Although your font taste and spacing may deviate from the example, the most important things to learn are the basic settings and adjustments needed for a simple, clean credit roll. With that in mind, you will focus on text spacing and tab stops.

1. Open Rolling_Title_Start.prproj from the APPST Lesson Files/Chapter 13 folder. Press F9 to create a new title. From the Title Designer's top row of controls, choose Roll from the Title Type drop-down. Select the Area Type tool from the Tool palette, then click and drag from the top-left corner of the inner title-safe boundary down and to the right just out of frame with the right side of the tool on the edge of right title-safe boundary. Grab the Selection tool, and pull the top of the newly created square above the top of the title frame. (See Figure 13.9.)

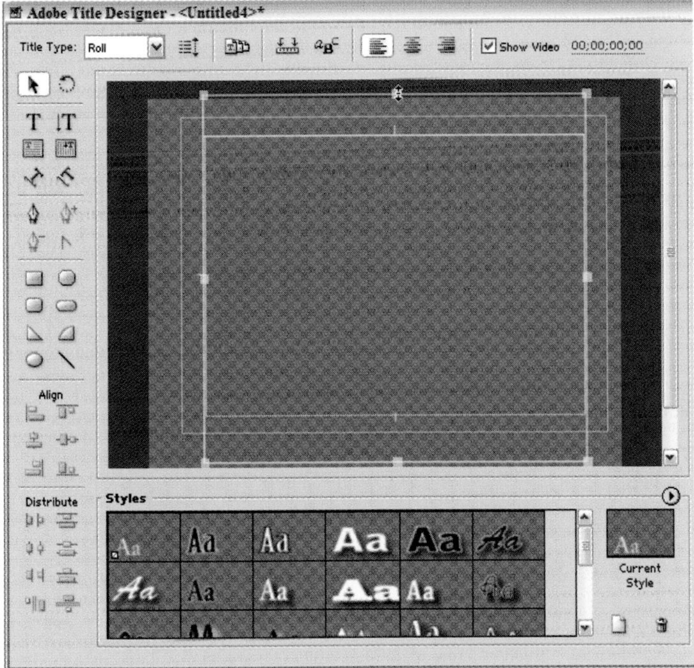

Figure 13.9 The square starts on the edge of the inner title-safe boundary and follows both sides of its horizontal boundaries with the bottom of the square outside the frame area. For your credits to roll from below the frame up and off the top of the frame, you must extend the top edge of the square above the top of the frame.

This step defines the area in which the rolling text will be written and roll from. The area you defined is the absolute boundary in which your text can roll. By defining the top and bottom of the area text to be outside the visible frame (as delineated by the title-safe boundaries), you ensured that your credit will roll up and then out as if it came from below the image and disappeared above the image. If you instead created a square that fit inside the title-safe boundary, the rolling text would appear rolling up in the lower-third portion of the frame and disappear as it reached the upper-third portion of the frame.

2. From the Title menu, select View and turn on Tab Markers. Click the Tab Stops button in the top row of controls to open the Tab Stops dialog. Click in the white space above the ruler bar to add a tab stop. Position the tab stop so that it rests in the center of the drawing area on top of the center hash mark in the title-safe boundary. Click the Centered Tab button to make this tab a center justified tab stop. Add a second tab stop just to the right of the left edge, and click the Left Justified button. Add a third and final tab stop just to the left of the right edge, and click the Right Justified button. Click OK. (See Figure 13.10.)

   If you haven't worked with Tab Stops, I encourage you to watch "Assigning Tab Stops," the video file associated with this step, which can be found in the accompanying DVD's Advanced Techniques section. When you tab to the stops you set, the text you add will assume the right, left, or center justification that the tab stop represents. Try adding some text to see how it looks.

3. Select the Type tool, and press the Tab key twice to navigate to the center tab stop. Type the word "Group." In the Object Style panel, twirl down Properties and set Courier New>Bold for Font. Set Font Size to 30 and Leading to 8.2. Back in the drawing area, press Enter to create a new line. Press the Tab key once, and type the word "Position." Press the Tab key twice, and type First

Lastname. Select the second and now third line of text from the word “Position” to “Lastname.” As shown in Figure 13.11, set:

Font Size: **21.8**
Leading: **8.2%**
Tracking: **–5**

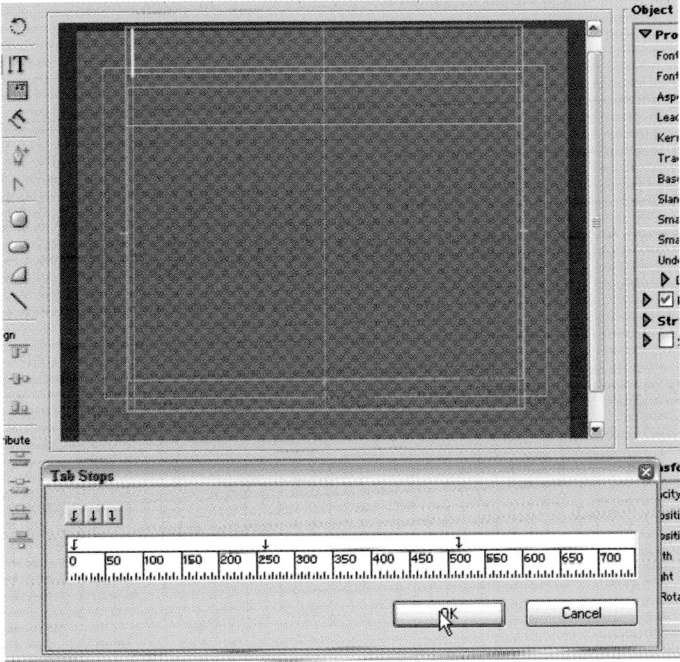

Figure 13.10 The center tab stop is center justified, the left tab is left justified, and the right tab stop is right justified.

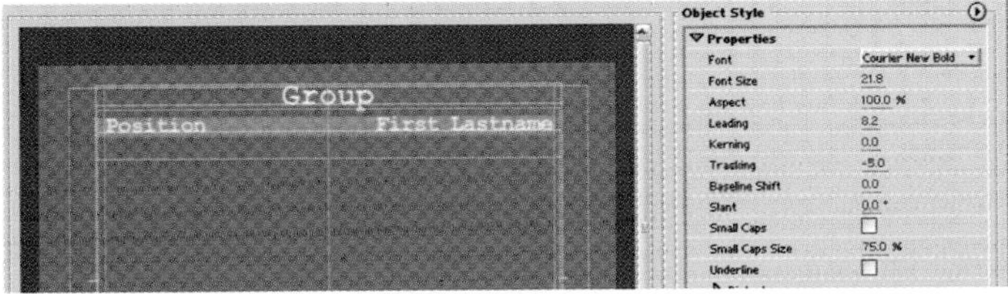

Figure 13.11 By selecting a group of words, you can alter the font size and all the styles properties of the selection separate from that of the other text in the square.

First, you center the main heading for the group of credits to follow. You could change the word “Group” to “Cast” later, for example, if the first section of credits is for the cast of your project. The second line of text creates two listings, one for the cast position and the other for the individual's name. The second line's reduced font size enables more text to fit, and the reduced tracking tightens the space between each letter on a uniform scale. Reducing the leading closes the overall space between the first and second line.

4. With the second line of text still selected, press Ctrl+C to copy it. Click after the letter "e" in lastname, and position the cursor at the end of the text on the right tab stop. Press Enter to create a new line. Paste the text onto the second line (Ctrl+V). Repeat this step twice more to create four listing lines. Select these four lines, and reduce their leading to 6. (See Figure 13.12.)

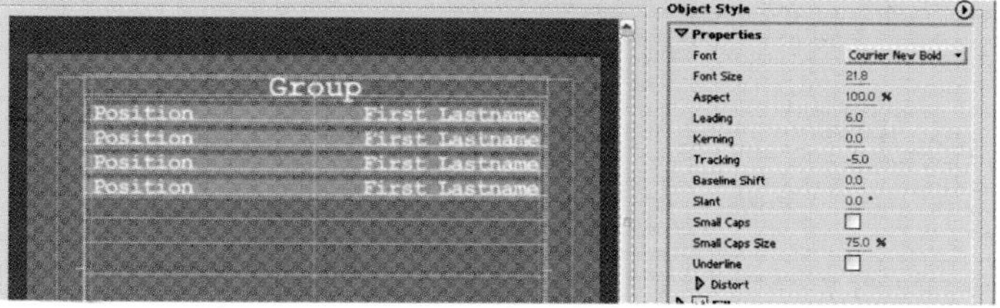

Figure 13.12 By selecting and adjusting the leading of these four lines, you make them appear tighter together and more as their own group.

Notice that instead of pasting at the first tab stop, you paste at the left edge of the square. The selection for the text recognizes that the first word has a tab stop value of 1 and the second set of words has a tab stop value of 3, so Premiere pastes them accordingly.

5. With the Type tool still selected and the cursor blinking after the last Lastname, press Ctrl+A to select all the text. Copy it (Ctrl+C), deselect the text by clicking after the last Lastname, and then press Enter three times to create three lines of spacing. Paste (Ctrl+V) the text at the current cursor position. Press Enter three more times, and paste again.

Although the last copied text group is technically off-screen, you can still scroll down through the text and modify the information. In these five steps, you created a custom credit roll with groups of text that you can fill on a project-by-project basis. Now it's time to assign the Roll/Crawl Options and save the template.

6. Click on the Roll/Crawl Options buttons in the Title Designer's top row of controls. In the resulting dialog, click the check boxes for Start Off Screen and End Off Screen. Click OK. Click the Templates button to open the Templates dialog. From the wing menu, select Save <UntitledXX> as Custom Template. Name the title Custom Roll, and click OK.

   Choosing to start and end your title off screen means that even if you have text at the top of the frame, your titles will start blank and roll the text of your title into frame, then end by rolling the text completely out of frame. The Ease-In and Ease-Out settings slow the title when it first rolls in and when the title ends and rolls out.

The speed of a rolling or crawling title depends on the duration you assign to the title when it is added to the timeline. When added to the timeline, the title file must complete from top to bottom or side to side within the duration it is assigned. If you have 200 lines of text in a rolling title and the title has a duration of only five seconds, for example, the text will fly by in order to get from the top to the bottom in that amount of time. To slow a rolling or crawling title, extend its duration; decrease its duration to speed it up.

To see the title I came up with and how different durations affect the speed at which the title rolls, open Rolling_Title_Finished.prproj from the APPST Lesson Files/Chapter 13 folder. You can take a number of clues and tips from this lesson and switch them up to customize your tabs stops, font, font size, and line spacing to create your own custom credit template or title with text.

Things to Remember

All the clues to making an attractive title reside in the properties of the title templates that you like best. If you find a particular template that you really like, simply click on the individual elements that make up the title and scour over all of the settings in the Object Style panel, especially the Properties twirl down. With an object selected you can see the technique used for filling, adding strokes, and creating more depth to the elements in the title. You can find an object with a sheen, for example, and click the sheen off to see the difference. The more you investigate, the more you'll understand why your favorite templates look the way they do.

Remember, too, that you can change specific text properties of individual text elements in a large group of text. If you want every line to have different leading, fonts, and tracking, for example, select each line and make the adjustments on a line by line basis.

Fiddle with the Title Designer whenever you have spare time. You'll find that you very easily can create customized templates that will save you time on many later projects. On the other hand, if you create a unique title for a project, consider saving the title as a template. You never know when it will come in handy.

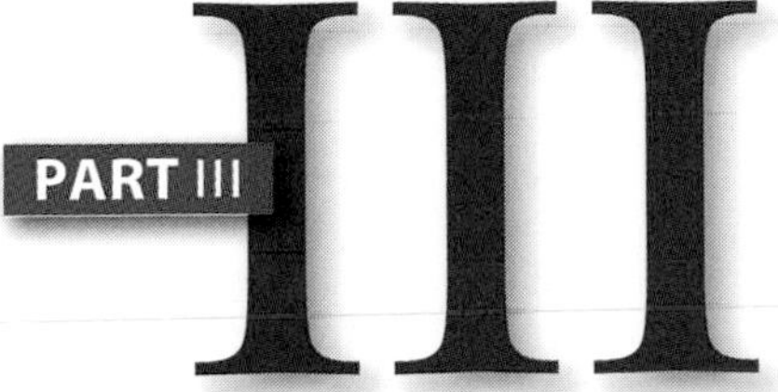

PART III

Advanced Audio Techniques

CHAPTER

14

Using Your Audio Hardware

As you know by now, Premiere Pro has some powerful and professional audio features. To make the most of them, however, you may need to customize your audio hardware and its parameters. For example, upgrading your system's default audio hardware with a third-party audio interface can provide better recording quality, more accurate playback acoustics, and a dynamic 5.1 surround mix environment. If a new audio interface isn't in your budget, a high-quality microphone can help you get the most from your existing system when recording. Of course, no matter what hardware you have, proper parameter settings can make or break your projects.

This chapter covers a lot of ground to help you understand a handful of facets relating to setting up, recording, and playing back the best quality audio possible. Whether you are using an additional audio interface or not, many system settings and Premiere settings can help you maximize the quality of the audio coming in and playing out.

Audio Interfaces

Most base-level audio cards that come with Windows systems record in from the microphone port (usually a 1/8" stereo plug) at 16 bits, stereo at a sample rate of 44kHz. They usually playback to the speaker port (another 1/8" stereo plug) at 16 bits, stereo, 44kHz. These settings are fine for most, if not all, general usage.

NOTES

Developed by Steinberg for its VST product line, ASIO (Audio Stream Input Output) is an audio communication standard that can access one or more devices (interfaces) to record or play audio through. The benefit of the ASIO communication method is that there is an immediate response when playing or recording high quality audio. By supporting ASIO devices, Premiere Pro assumes the features of high quality and instantaneous audio recording and playback with a ton of professional devices (interfaces).

For my laptop system, the default audio interface is the Avance AC97. For surround sound playback, I use an ASIO-certified emagic A26 interface that has two input ports and six output ports. If I connect the six output ports to the six speakers that make up a surround sound system—left, center, right, surround left, surround right, and LFE (low frequency)—I can properly play back from Premiere Pro in surround sound. On top of that, the device gives me the opportunity to record at a bit depth of 16 or 24 bits and a sample rate of 44, 48, or 96kHz.

To capture at a higher bit depth and sample rate, however, say at 24 bits and 96kHz, then you need to invest in a more robust audio card, also called an *audio interface*. Capturing and working at higher rates increases the quality and detail of the sound you are recording and playing. To accurately work in and playback 5.1 surround sound audio, you will also need to add an additional *audio interface*. Default stereo devices have only two speaker outputs (two channels); to accurately play surround sound sequences you need an interface with six separate output channels. (See Figure 14.1.) Because Premiere Pro supports ASIO devices, however, making the jump to a more powerful interface is quite easy.

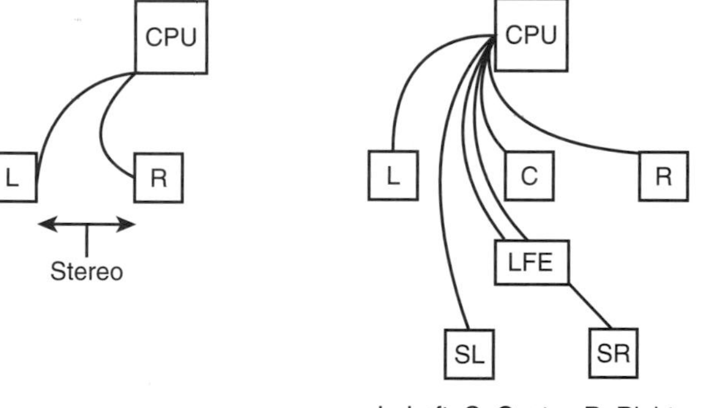

Figure 14.1 The standard stereo speaker setup (left) has a left speaker and right speaker that can connect to the default stereo output of your computer. To support six surround sound speakers (right), you need an audio interface with six output channels, each routed to the proper speaker.

If you want surround sound playback, be sure to pick up an interface with at least six output ports. In general, get a card that supports at least 16 bit, 48kHz recording and playback. Of course, 24 bit, 96kHz would be optimum.

For desktop PCs, most ASIO devices will be a PCI card installed inside your machine. The back of the PCI card may feature plugs where you can insert your speaker and microphone cable or it may have a breakout box. Sometimes called a rat tail, or B.O.B, it connects to the card on one end and has female insertion points for speakers and microphones on the other.

To upgrade a laptop PC, you'll need to purchase an external audio interface that connects via a USB or FireWire cable. These breakout boxes may come with various numbers of input or output ports. If you want true 5.1 support, be sure your new interface has at least six outputs.

After your new audio interface is installed, you'll need to set its properties. The exact process and options depend on your card, but at a minimum you'll probably have to set the sample rate. Figure 14.2 shows the Device Options dialog for my emagic A26.

M-Audio has an excellent line of FireWire interfaces that support ASIO. You can use them confidently with both laptop and desktop PCs, and they are highly portable. M-Audio also has very reasonably priced surround sound ASIO PCI interfaces.

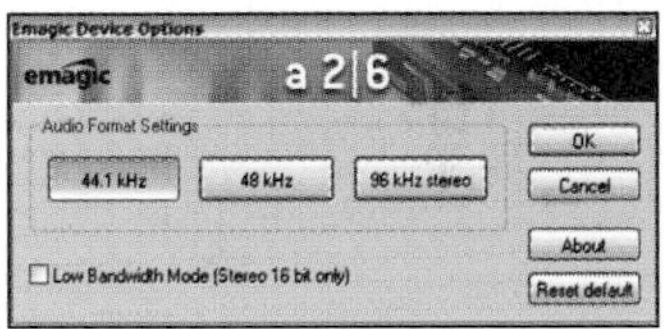

Figure 14.2 After installation, be sure to adjust the proprietary settings for your additional audio interface. Your Device Options dialog may differ from mine shown here.

Adjusting Audio Settings

No matter which audio interface you use, when you set up your system to record, you need to verify that the input volume level for your microphone is at the proper level. Additionally, when you play back to your speakers, you need to make sure that the speaker output volume is also adequate. For both of these adjustments, go to the Windows XP Sounds and Audio Devices Control Panel (Control Panels>Sounds, Speech, and Audio Devices>Sounds and Audio Devices). (See Figure 14.3.) The tabs you'll use most are:

- **Volume.** For setting your device volume level
- **Audio.** For specifying input and output device levels
- **Voice.** For helping to get your voice recording levels to the right point
- **Hardware.** For verifying and troubleshooting issues with audio in your system

In each tab, be sure to select the device for which you are adusting settings—your default card or ASIO interface (see Figure 14.4).

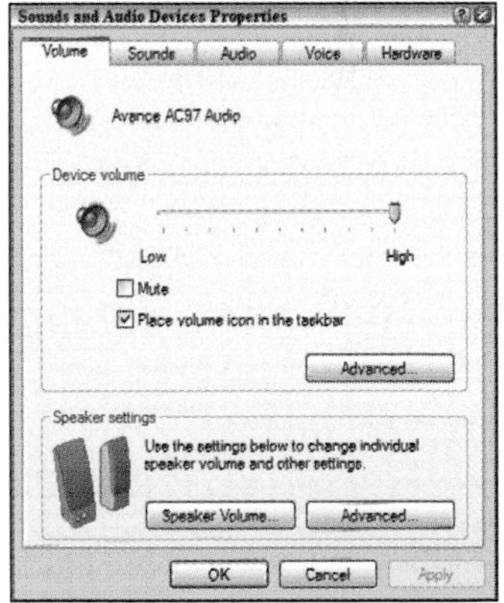

Figure 14.3 From the Sounds and Audio Devices Properties Control Panel, you can access all your system settings associated with audio input, output, and attached hardware.

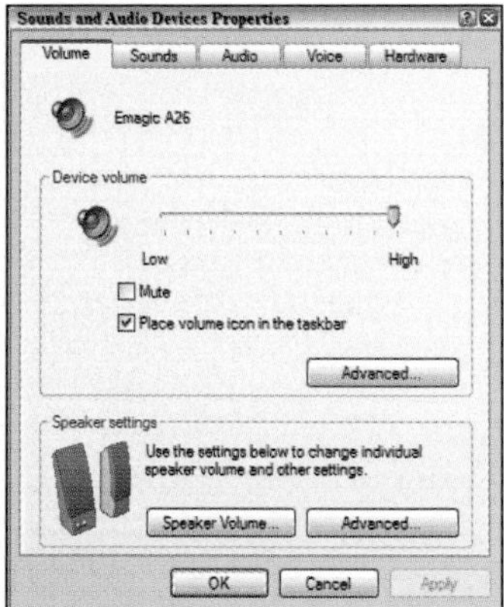

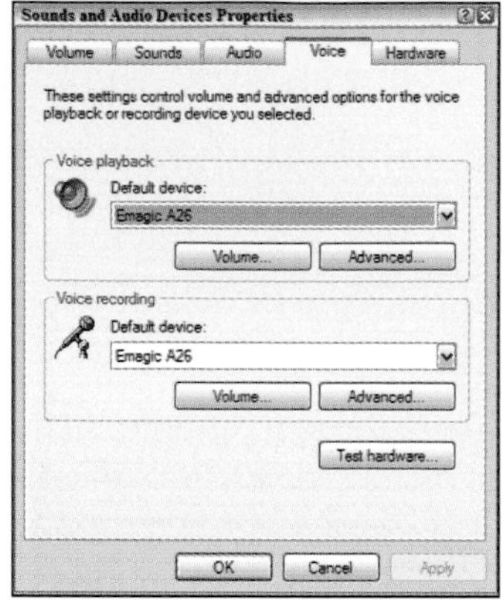

Figure 14.4 Notice how in each tab, I have selected my ASIO device, the emagic A26. When switching from the default device to your secondary audio device, be sure to click Apply so that your changes update the system settings.

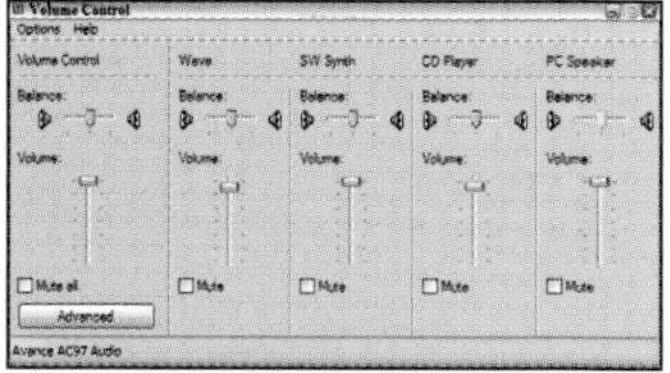

Figure 14.5 In the Volume Control dialog, you can see and assign volume levels for the devices or interfaces on your system. Be sure the Volume Control fader is not muted, because it adjusts the overall system volume.

The Volume Tab

The Volume tab allows you to control the *overall* output volume for your system (see Figure 14.3). Clicking Advanced opens the Volume Control dialog where you can adjust the output volume for *individual* components of your system (see Figure 14.5). If you are not hearing any audio when you play back, the Volume Control dialog is the first place to troubleshoot and check that your levels are properly set.

The Audio Tab

The Audio tab is the control area where you can switch between devices for different tasks (see Figure 14.6). If you want to playback through your ASIO interface and record using your default interface, for example, use the drop-down menus to assign Sound Playback to the ASIO device and Sound Recording to your default device.

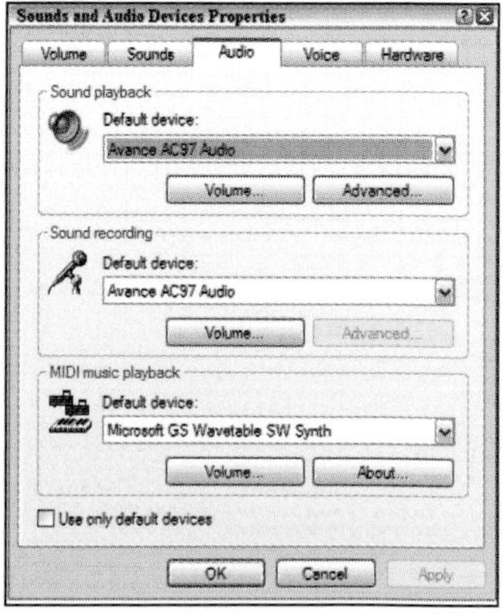

Figure 14.6 The Audio tab offers you drop-down menus for selecting which device you are using for playback, recording, and MIDI playback.

Clicking the Volume in the Sound Playback area opens the Volume Control panel (see Figure 14.5). Clicking the Volume in the Sound Recording area opens the Recording Control panel (see Figure 14.7). When recording from the microphone input, for example, you adjust the incoming volume with the Recording Control panel's Microphone slider. Also note that you can select from which device you would like to record by clicking the check box under the appropriate slider: CD Player, Microphone, or Phone Line.

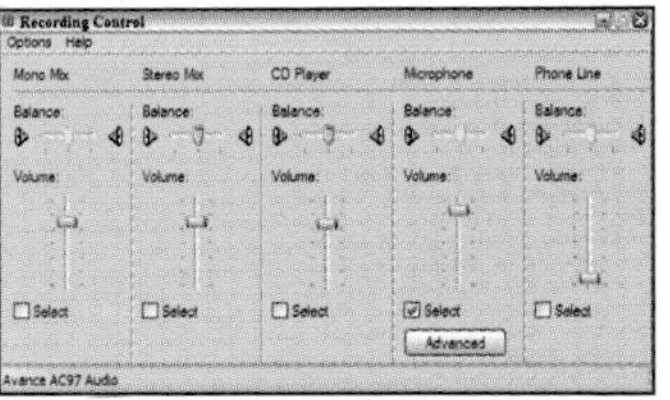

Figure 14.7 The Recording Control dialog allows you to adjust your recording volume. In this image, I selected the Microphone as the input device.

Click the Advanced button under the Microphone Volume slider to access the Advanced Controls for Microphone panel to fine-tune the incoming audio (see Figure 14.8). When your microphone needs an additional boost, click the Mic Boost check box. These settings will vary from system to system and microphone to microphone, so you may have to fiddle with it to get the best level.

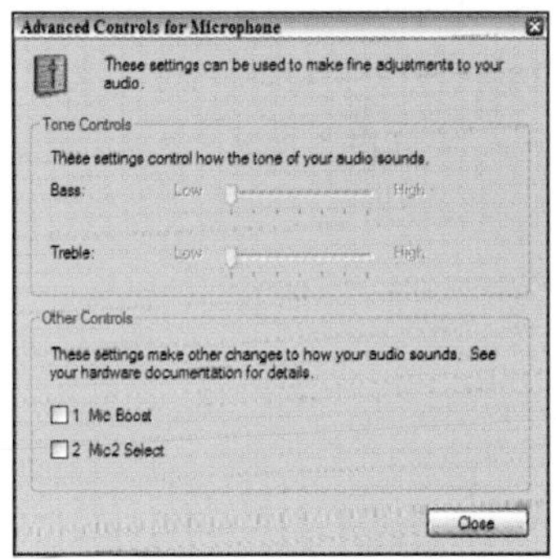

Figure 14.8 The Advanced Controls for Microphone allow you to adjust setting associated with the Microphone input. If your incoming signal is too low, you can click the 1 Mic Boost check box to gain step the incoming signal so that it is stronger.

The Voice Tab

The Voice tab verifies the input and output device for voice recording (see Figure 14.9). If you are having trouble configuring and optimizing your recording and playback levels, you can press Test Hardware to use the Sound Hardware test wizard. Before you do, make sure your microphone is properly plugged in and you have speakers or headphones for listening. The wizard asks you to speak aloud and then analyzes the results to make adjustments to your volume settings.

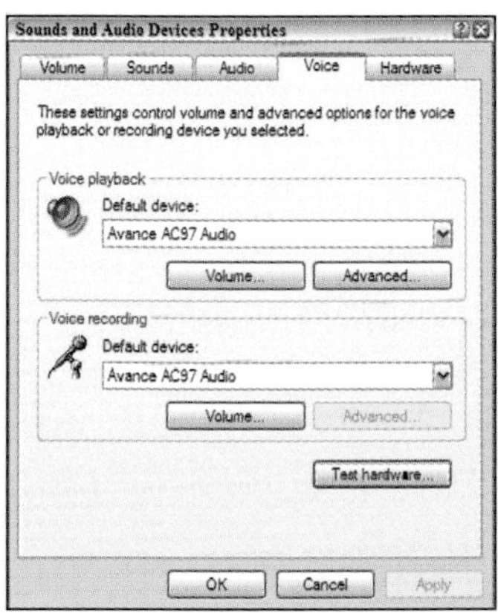

Figure 14.9 You can change your selected playback and recording device from the Voice tab. If you want to record from a secondary audio interface, select it from the Default Device drop-down menu under Voice Recording. If you are having difficulty configuring your microphone, click the Test Hardware button to run the hardware wizard, which walks you through steps to verify that your input and output for recording is configured.

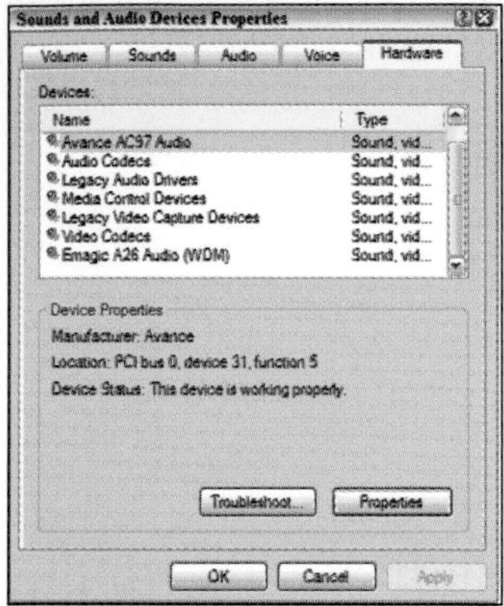

Figure 14.10 If you are experiencing trouble with sound from any attached device, you can click the Hardware tab to access a list of the sound devices associated with your system. With a device selected, click Troubleshoot or Properties to get more information and to troubleshoot the status of the device.

The Hardware Tab

From the Hardware tab, you can view, select, and analyze the status of your connected devices and drivers (see Figure 14.10). If you have a problem playing back with an additional audio interface, select the card from the Devices list to see if it is functioning properly. With the device selected, click Properties to reveal General, Properties, and Driver information. Additionally, you can run a troubleshooting wizard to help identify any current problems with your hardware devices.

Premiere's Audio Hardware Preferences

Once you get inside of Premiere Pro, you need to assign some additional audio hardware settings to map output channels and customize your ASIO device. Even if you are using your default audio device, it is helpful to understand what these controls do and how to adjust them.

Output Channel Mapping

After you designate your input and output devices, head over to your Audio Hardware Preferences (Edit>Preferences>Audio Hardware). The Output Channel Mappings area reveals all the output channels associated with your chosen device and lets you rearrange which channel plays what. For example, for your Adobe Default Windows Sound option, Output Channel Mappings lists two channels for stereo output (see Figure 14.11). Dragging the left and right speaker icons from one channel to the other swaps which channel plays the left and which channel plays the right.

When you select a six-channel ASIO device for output, the list gets more crowded. Figure 14.12 shows all six output channels associated with my ASIO card. To route the channels for my 5.1 surround system, it is just a matter of matching the icons for the channels to where the speakers are plugged in. For example, the LFE is plugged into output port number 6, so the LFE icon in the output channel mappings should be in output 6.

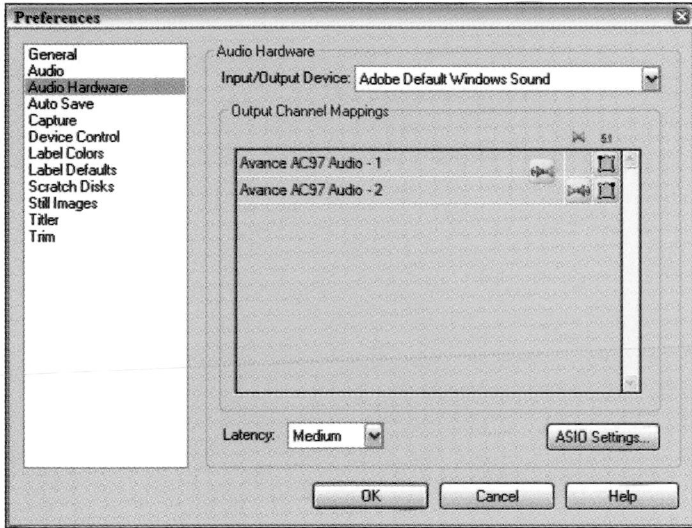

Figure 14.11 In the Output Channel Mappings area of Audio Hardware Preferences, drag the speaker icons to assign them to an output channel.

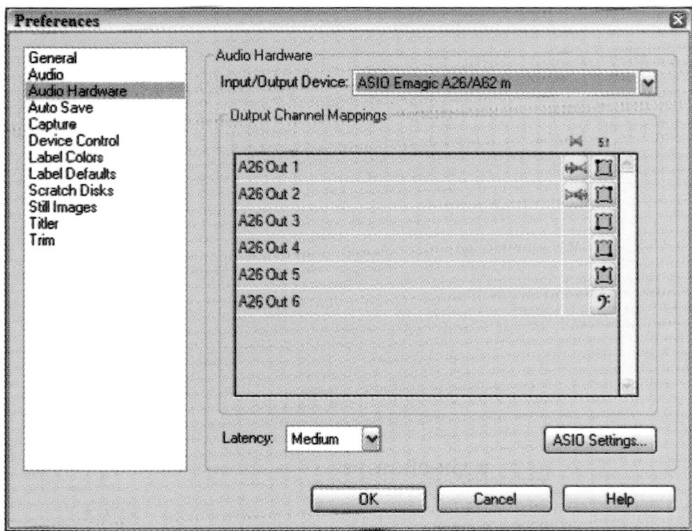

Figure 14.12 The Output Channel Mappings listing for an interface with six output channels contains icons for every speaker of a 5.1 surround system. The icon with the ear and the colon is for the LFE.

Figure 14.13 When you click the ASIO Settings button in Audio Hardware Preferences, the resulting dialog will be specific to the installed device and will dictate its playback and recording parameters. The pictured dialog is for an emagic A26.

ASIO Settings for External Device

Although each ASIO device has its own settings and dialog box, Premiere Pro offers a single route to access them. In the Audio Hardware Preferences window, click the ASIO Settings button to open a settings dialog specific to your audio interface.

For example, Figure 14.13 shows the dialog for my emagic device. The Driver Latency setting increases or decreases the latency period when playing back with the device. The latency value is milliseconds over the assigned sample rate. Here the card is assigned to play at 44.1kHz. Increasing Driver Latency produces improved performance, because it allows the device a bit more time to do its processing. Decreasing the setting demands more from the device. The remaining fields toggle the card's playback and recording bit depths: 16 or 24 bits. Increasing the bit depth for input enhances the quality of audio being recorded.

Input: Picking a Microphone

You configured and adjusted your input, but what about your input device? In many audio recording situations, the size of the input jack and type of audio card are not nearly as important as the microphone that you are using. If you have a good microphone and recording settings of at least 16 bit, stereo, 44kHz, then you should achieve an adequate recording. (Keep in mind that the standard for CD audio is 16 bit, 44.1kHz, but DV is 16 bit 48kHz.) To pick a good microphone, you need to consider a few factors.

Power and Pre-Amps

Some microphones, called *active microphones*, use batteries in their bodies to give them power, other mics require a separate device to provide power, and a third group requires no additional power, only a pre-amp to amplify the mic's signal.

Microphones requiring separate power are known as *phantom microphones* or *condensers*. They must be plugged into a port that not only takes in their signal, but also provides power. If the input port of your audio card does not provide phantom power for your microphone, then you must purchase a phantom power box that accepts the microphone input on one side, provides it power, and connects to your recording device with the powered signal on the other side. When you purchase or order your microphone, be sure to identify whether it is phantom or self-powering. Higher quality and expensive microphones commonly require either phantom power or a pre-amp.

Microphones that don't need power may, however, require a *pre-amp*, which is a small box that acts as a go between from your microphone to your recording device. The microphone plugs into the pre-amp, which plugs into the recording device. The benefit of having a pre-amp is that it can *gain stage*, or boost, the incoming signal from the mic to give you a stronger incoming audio level. Some phantom boxes also come with a built-in pre-amp. Using the pre-amp's dial, you can increase or decrease the strength of the signal coming out of the microphone. Conveniently, the 1/8" stereo jack on your default Windows audio card has a built-in pre-amp, making it easy to use basic webcam voice microphones and other basic microphones without having to worry about any additional devices.

Microphone Classifications

The next factor to consider when shopping for a microphone is which type will be best for your projects. Microphones are specified in three groups:

- **Dynamic microphones.** The type of mics that you typically see on a desk at a press conference or near the drums of a rock concert. Shaped like ice cream cones, they are very durable, are self-powered, and can handle a very high range of noise, from loud crashes to whispers. These mics are usually not too expensive (around $100) and are perfect for the home recording of voiceovers. Dynamic mics that don't require power are commonly referred to as *passive*.

- **Condenser microphones.** Typically either phantom or battery-powered microphones. They have a better range and clarity level than dynamic mics; they also respond better to different frequencies. Condenser microphones break down into further categories, but for now it is important simply to know that condenser microphones are useful for recording professional voiceover content or the voice of a singer.
- **Ribbon microphones.** Very expensive and very delicate microphones that cannot handle high sound pressure levels (loud noises) well. Like dynamic mics, they do not require additional power. Ribbon microphones are perfect for recording ambient noises and natural sounds, because the character of the metallic ribbon's response to sound produces very warm, natural recordings. Related to ribbon microphones are PZMs (pressure zone microphone). Typically flat, plate-like devices, PZMs are omni-directional microphones that can be placed on a wall to record the sounds and ambient atmosphere of an entire room. If you need to record atmospheres and ambient noises for a film or other project, you could rent a ribbon microphone.

Each type of microphone can either be omni-directional or uni-directional. For *omni-directional* mics, the field of recording sound comes from all directions. In *uni-directional* mics, the pickup pattern is emphasized in one focused direction and sounds that do not fall within the pickup pattern are rejected. In other words, the recording comes from one specific direction. Uni-directional microphones vary in their degree of sensitivity much like the angle and diameter of a spotlight (see Figure 14.14).

For example, *shotgun* microphones are uni-directional microphones that are always pointed toward the mouth of the character who is speaking. On film sets, you see these microphones being held on a long stick (*boom*) above the actors' heads during filming. The boom operator is the person who gets the microphone close enough to record, but out of the view of what's being filmed. The real benefit of the shotgun mic is that it captures the actor's voice only, while rejecting most of the production sound and noise coming from behind or above.

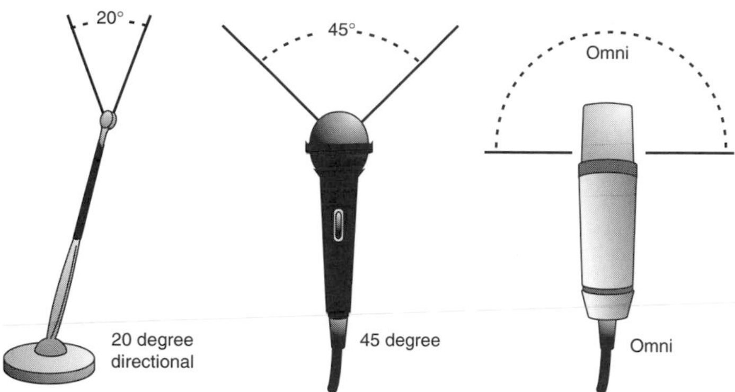

Figure 14.14 Common for film production, 20-degree directional mics (left) are pointed directly at the mouth of a character so as to not pick up other sounds. A 45-degree mic (middle) picks up sounds from a wider range. Omni-directional mics (right) are useful for picking up a full range of natural sounds coming from all directions.

Depending on your budget and intended use, you can explore a simple dynamic directional mic or a condenser mic for recording live audio.

Recording Live Audio

When recording from your default audio microphone jack or from the inputs on your additional audio device, you use the Premiere Pro Audio Mixer to determine which inputs to record from. These inputs directly relate to what was selected in your Audio Hardware Preferences.

Choosing an Input

Depending on which input/output device you have selected in Premiere Pro's Audio Hardware Preferences, you can easily choose which input channel to record from in the Audio Mixer. Select the track you wish to record into by clicking the Microphone Record toggle button. With the button on, you can select the recording input channel from the drop-down menu above the button (see Figure 14.15).

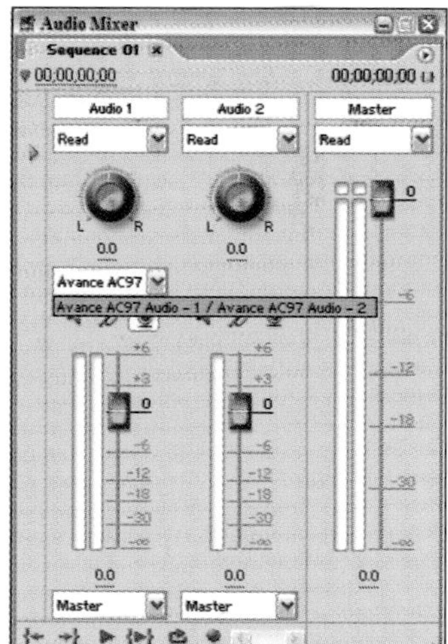

Figure 14.15 Turn on a track for recording, then use the drop-down menu in that track's Audio Mixer column to specify an input port for recording. Using the default stereo input from my default Windows Audio setting, I get to record both channels into my stereo track.

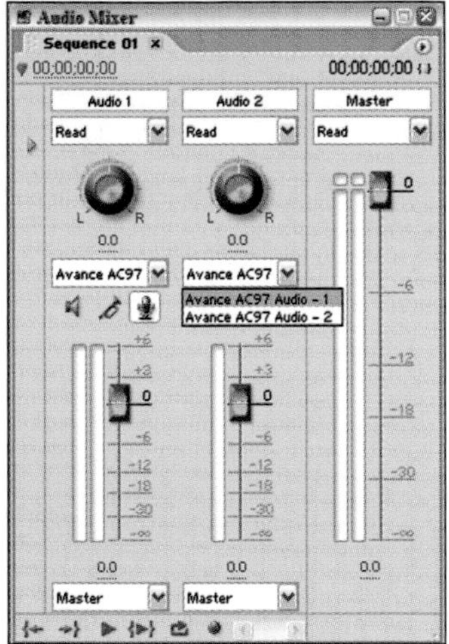

Figure 14.16 Using the same default Audio setting, notice how Audio 2, which is mono, allows me to select either channel 1 or channel 2. Although the input still may be stereo, you can record only mono (single channel) into a mono track.

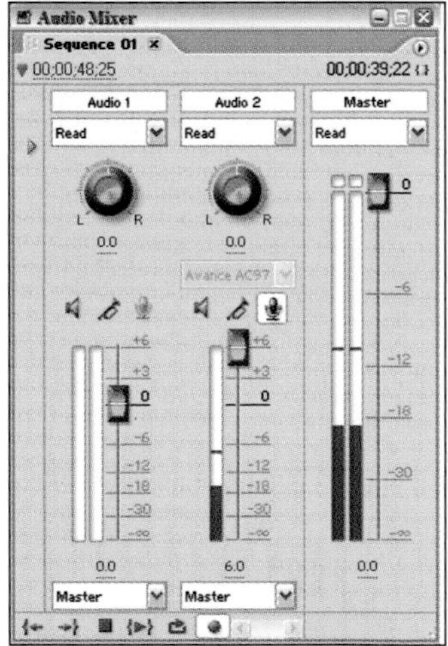

Figure 14.17 When you raise the slider above 0dB, you boost or add gain to the incoming signal, making the audio louder.

When recording, the track type that you are recording into is a critical choice (see Figure 14.16). If you activate a stereo track for recording, Premiere creates a stereo file; activating a mono track results in a mono file. For a live voiceover recording, for example, recording a single channel, mono file is best, because you can mix down and pan your voiceover in a stereo or surround sequence later.

Live Level Adjustments

With your track selected, put the Audio Mixer into record mode by clicking the red record circle in the bottom of the Mixer window. Once you begin recording, you can either increase or reduce the incoming audio's volume by moving the Track Volume slider up or down. (See Figure 14.17.) Of course, after you finish recording you can normalize the audio file so that it achieves its optimum volume. Getting a solid recording the first time around, however, is very important.

To further adjust or change the levels coming into your microphone port, you can revisit the Advanced Controls for Microphone dialog in your Windows XP Sound Control Panel. (See Figure 14.8.)

Output: Speakers and Headphones

As you play back and mix your audio, you can listen to it with speakers and headphones. You can connect as many speakers as you need, or, you can purchase six-channel surround sound headphones (although they aren't quite the best way to properly listen to a 5.1 mix in surround sound).

If you are serious about your audio work in Premiere Pro, I recommend using both speakers and headphones, because of the amount of low and high frequency noise that can go undetected with most speakers, especially small computer speakers. Having big snug headphones wrapped around your ears completely immerses you in the world of sound, and when you work with sound it should be all consuming. A good pair of headphones that reduces or blocks out external noises is worth a few extra dollars. As for speakers, dollar amount still equals quality and that goes double for surround sound systems. Expensive speakers are likely to have a better dynamic ability to accurately play a higher range of frequencies.

To hear anything through either, however, you need to make sure all your levels are set up properly.

Mixing and Monitoring

As you remember, you can set the overall system volume level that is routed to the speakers on your system. It is always a good idea to keep this volume on the higher side and to reduce the volume on the individual speakers if it is too loud.

Although Premiere Pro's mixer accurately displays the exact dB level of your audio while it plays, if the sound output volume of your system is too low, you may not be able to distinguish distorted or garbled audio. If the volume is not loud enough, you also won't be able to hear the clicks, pops, and other noises that need to be removed.

Keep in mind that adjustments to the volume sliders in the Audio Mixer affect the audio levels in adjusted track. Adjustments to the Master Volume slider affect the level of the sequence's entire mixdown. Adjustments to the sound out, headphone out, or speaker volume from the audio card will affect the loudness at which you hear the audio from Premiere Pro.

Things to Remember

There are a number of points to take away from this chapter regarding setting up, recording in, and playing out audio with Premiere Pro.

When setting up, use the Sound and Audio Devices Properties to adjust the incoming and outgoing volume levels for the default audio and additional audio interfaces with your system. If you are trying to use a 5.1 multi-channel surround sound system, be sure the interface supports ASIO and be sure you have properly mapped your speakers in the Audio Hardware Preferences dialog. In the same dialog, to access additional settings proprietary to the device, click the ASIO settings with the device selected as the Input/Output device.

If you are doing voiceovers for home videos and your own projects, there is no need to shell out $1000 for a condenser microphone. A dynamic microphone from your local music store (or the web) is totally reasonable. When purchasing your microphone, check if it requires a pre-amp. If it does, see if you can get the mic with a 1/8" plug adapter; that way you can use the pre-amp of your default audio device.

If you want to record higher quality audio or have a specific task in mind, research the condenser or ribbon options. At the end of the day, if you only need to record a few things, you can always rent a good microphone and return it once your work is complete. Again, verify the pre-amp, phantom, and battery power needs for each microphone.

When listening to your audio, have the best and worst scenarios readily available. For example, I have a television with a mono speaker as my worst listening environment. On the flip side, a sensitive pair of big snug headphones allows me to block out all other sound and focus on the audio. For the best in speakers, I have surround speakers properly placed and positioned so that the sound is accurately distributed. At the end of the day, not all of us can afford a sound-tight room and precise JBL speakers, but given the portability of Premiere Pro, you could achieve a decent amount of work at home then bring your project into a professional studio to finish the job.

Finally, one last thing my mentor always said was that the audio coming out of your system can only be as good as the audio coming into it. Meaning, if you have a poor quality recording, there's a lot you can do to fix it, but it will never compare to a crisp, clear and full-bodied original recording.

In the next chapter, you will dive into recording an actual voiceover. In later chapters, you will cut it up, clean it up, and then fix it up to make it sound as good as possible.

CHAPTER

15

Recording a Voiceover

Whether you are creating a commercial for broadcast or a family vacation video, voiceover narration can add a substantial amount of context and information to your piece.

This chapter will walk you through setting up your project for recording a voiceover, properly setting your input levels, arranging your sequence to better suit a recording environment, and the actual recording itself. In the next chapter, you edit your voiceover, cut it up, add subtle transitions, and remove unwanted breaths. For both these lessons, you'll add a voiceover file to the Saleen sample project that came with Premiere Pro.

If you haven't used the sample project already, I recommend that you copy the Sample Project NTSC folder from the Sample Project disc that came with Premiere Pro. The Premiere Pro installer came in a CD-ROM jewel case, and it included two discs. The first disc is the installer, the second holds the sample files. To use the sample file for the upcoming lessons, insert the disc and open it in Windows Explorer. Copy the Sample Project NTSC folder, and paste it onto your desktop or secondary drive. When instructed by the lesson, open the Sample Project in the folder and follow the steps.

When I edited the sample project for Adobe, I tried to make a short and sweet montage of clips integrated with transitions on two tracks each for audio and video, as well as an animated Photoshop file to highlight that feature. For the audio section, you will treat the montage as if it were a Saleen commercial.

Two Schools for Voiceover

Traditionally, there are two schools for voiceover work. School One is to write your script first, edit the voiceover, and then add the video where it needs to be placed. School Two is to edit the video first and then narrate and add your voiceover to color the video. Neither is right or wrong, but sometimes one approach is better suited to your material than the other. What's most important in your project? Audio and text are the foundations for School One (script first, video second), whereas video and visuals are the foundations for School Two (video editing first, narration second).

If I am working on a family video, photo montage, or DVD commentary, I edit the clips first, then narrate and add the voiceover—School Two. If I am editing a commercial or putting together a project with a defined length, I follow School One. I record and edit the voiceover first to ensure that I am at the proper length, then I edit the video and make small adjustments to the voiceover where it's necessary. If a piece needs to convey certain verbal messages, slogans, or descriptions, it's important to write, record, and edit the entire voiceover so that you know it fits within the duration you have for your completed edit.

To reduce the preparatory video editing steps, you'll use the completed Saleen project and follow School Two this time. To help you out, I have put together a brief script that echoes the visual emphasis of the edit. Time to get started.

Recording Preparations

To begin recording a voiceover, you have to have a sequence open and available to record into.

1. Open the Recording_Start project from APPST Lesson Files/Chapter 15 folder. To load the project properly, link to the media in the Sample Project NTSC folder when prompted.

When opening the Voiceover_Start.prproj file, you need to link the files in this project to the sample files that came on the second sample files installation disc with Adobe Premiere Pro.

2. Right-click in the track header of the open sequence, and select Add Tracks. In the resulting Add Tracks dialog, make the following settings in the Audio Tracks area:

   Add: **1**
   Placement: **Before First Track**
   Track Type: **Mono**

   Click OK to accept. (See Figure 15.1.) Right-click in the track header of the newly created Audio 1 track, and select Rename. After the text highlights, change the track name to VO (for voiceover).

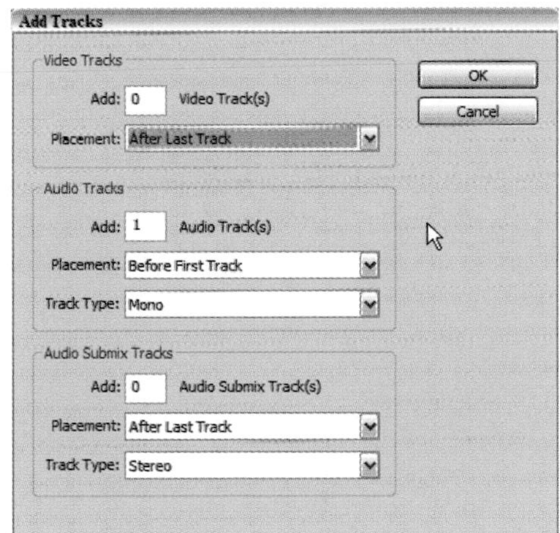

Figure 15.1 In the Add Tracks dialog, you can add three separate track types in one action, Video, Audio, and Audio Submix. For this lesson, you need to add just one mono track.

Because you want the voiceover to be a single-channel file, you select Mono for Track Type. By specifying Before First Track for Placement, you ensure Premiere creates the track before the current track (the music track). I typically put my music track at the very bottom of my sound mix with the other tracks above. I also rename the track something specific to the content that will be in the track. Labeling your voiceover track VO enables you to easily verify what's in the track when your mixer is open and you can't see the physical content of the track.

3. To better equip the timeline for recording the voiceover, create a new Universal Countdown Leader (UCL) and insert it at the head of the current sequence on the Video 1 track. Select File>New>Universal Counting Leader, and drag the UCL from your Project window to the beginning of Video 1. Hold down the Ctrl key before you release the clip, so that it is inserted before the current material in the timeline (see Figure 15.2). After adding the UCL, hold down the Alt key and select only the audio portion of the UCL. Press Delete to delete its audio from the sequence.

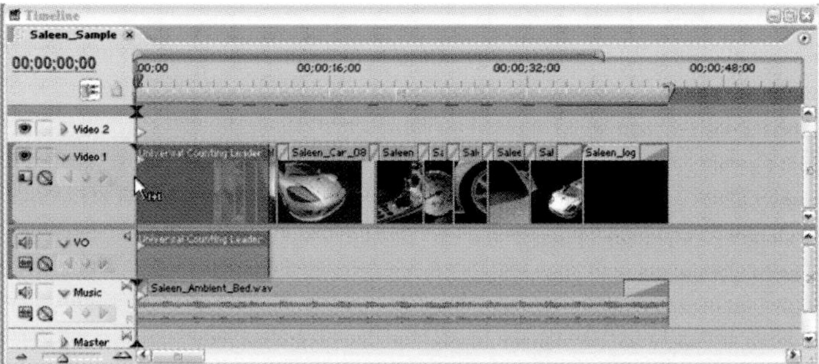

Figure 15.2 Holding down the Ctrl key toggles you into Insert editing mode, thus rippling the current media on all tracks to the right to make room for the inserted UCL file. Holding down Ctrl+Shift enables you to insert and ripple the content onto only the tracks where the edited media is added.

Because your voiceover recording begins at the moment you play back your sequence from the mixer in record mode, it is good to have a few seconds (or more) of pre-roll time to step back from the computer and begin your voiceover at the start of your edit. Adding a UCL to the timeline is a trick that buys you that time.

4. Select Edit>Preferences>Audio Hardware. In the Audio Hardware Preferences, verify the Input/Output device that you are using to record your audio. Your choices will be the Adobe Default Windows Sound 1.5 or any additional audio interface installed on your system.

This step verifies which device you are using to capture your audio. If you have a two-channel ASIO device, for example, you can select that device from the Input/Output listings and then record from the inputs on the device. For the default windows setting, you will most likely be recording from your 1/8" microphone input jack.

If you are having trouble configuring your device, consult Chapter 14, "Using Your Audio Hardware" to review the setup process.

5. From your Window menu, select Workspace>Audio. The Audio Mixer will open; double-check that it is expanded to show the full mixer. From the Audio Mixer's wing menu, choose Meter Input(s) Only.

   Adjusting your workspace is a quick and simple way to have access to certain windows. The Audio Workspace always has the Audio Mixer open in its layout. Selecting the Meter Input(s) Only option puts the mixer into a mode that displays the dB volume level of any incoming signal.

6. In the Audio Mixer, click the Microphone Toggle button in the VO track to enable the track for recording. From the drop-down menu above the icon, select the appropriate input channel (see Figure 15.3).

   This step ensures you will be able to view and record the levels coming in from your microphone input during recording.

Figure 15.3 The mixer is set to monitor inputs only and the VO track is enabled for recording with an input channel selected. Notice how the VU meters register about –30dB of sound coming from my plugged in microphone.

Because there's more to recording quality than the input line, give some thought now to your recording environment.

Room Acoustics

Where you record can have a big effect on your results. Although not all of us can afford to sound proof a room to eliminate echo and reverberation, you can do a few simple things to reduce and diminish potential unwanted noises.

Be sure that you are not recording near any appliances that produce a low frequency hum (a refrigerator or certain light fixtures on dimmers). Although you can remove these hums with the Notch filter, avoiding them makes for one less element of noise. Similarly, placing your microphone near the computer potentially can pick up the noises of your computer and nearby devices.

Try not to stand in the center of the room. Recording from a corner with your back to the wall can reduce some immediate reverberation from your voice. Particularly if you have a dynamic directional mic pointing toward you and the corner, you won't have such a dramatic echo coming from behind.

Remember, too, that carpets absorb sound, whereas hardwood floors echo it.

At the end of the day, a little noise isn't the end of the world. Feedback, static, and poor volume levels (either too high or too low) can be far more damaging to your recording.

Recording Your Voice

Having prepped your timeline and set it up for recording, it's time to press Record and lay down your voice track. For this series of steps, make sure that your voice registers at a healthy level and does not peak or exceed the 0dB ceiling.

1. Practice speaking the voiceover script (see Note) into the microphone at a normal room speaking level. Be sure that you see your VU meters responding to your vocal level as you are speaking.

   As you speak into the microphone, the volume level coming from the microphone input should never exceed the dark black 0dB line. You will want to be somewhere between –12dB and just above –6dB.

   Find the optimum distance and relative position that the microphone should be from your mouth so that your voice is not too loud or too soft. After you are comfortable with your practice, move on to the next step. If you still have low levels, refer to the sidebar or see the previous chapter's "Adjusting Your Audio Settings" section.

Sample Project Voiceover Script: "A dream comes to life. The Saleen S7 is a breathtaking sports car that blurs the line between science and art. From its sleek aerodynamic shape to its luxurious interior, the S7 is the premiere sports car for the twenty-first century. Built from the most solid materials and weighing under 2000 pounds, the Saleen S7 is truly a dream come true."
Disclaimer:
"This voiceover is not intended to endorse or represent Saleen and should only be used for instructional purposes. Thank You."

Troubleshooting Your Input Levels

From Windows, open the Sounds and Audio Devices Properties Control Panel. Select the Audio tab, and click the Volume button for Sound Recording. In the Recording Control Panel, be sure that Microphone is the selected Recording Device and that its volume level isn't too low. (See Figure 15.4.)

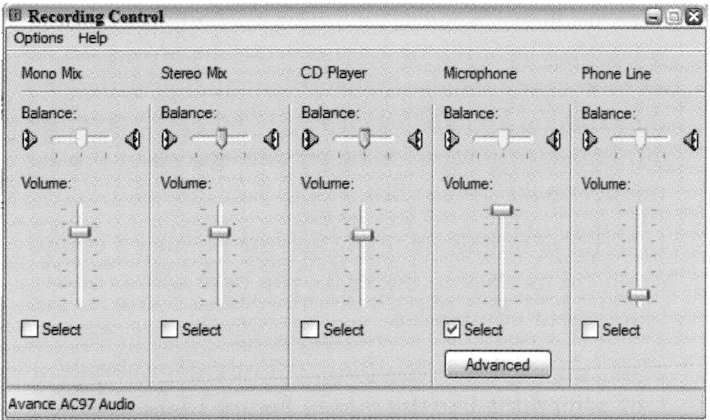

Figure 15.4 Clicking the Advanced button opens an additional dialog where you can add a boost to the incoming levels from your microphone. Notice that Select is checked under Microphone, indicating your mic is the Incoming device.

As discussed in the previous chapter, you can set and configure your input and output levels in this Control Panel as well as raise the volume level of your microphone.

If you are using a pre-amp with your mic, you can adjust the amp level to make your voice louder or softer. As you speak and adjust your amp, the levels will update live in the Audio Mixer window.

2. With the volume input level set and your rehearsal complete, click the Solo Track button (the horn button) in the VO track of the Audio Mixer. (See Figure 15.5)

   Clicking the Solo Track button mutes the Music track so that the music does not play back as you record. Regardless of whether you turn on Meter Input(s) Only, you will want to solo whichever track you are recording into at the time.

3. Select the Timeline window, and press the Home key to position the CTI at the head of the timeline. In the Audio Mixer, click the red Record button to arm the Audio Mixer for recording. When you are ready to record, press Play.

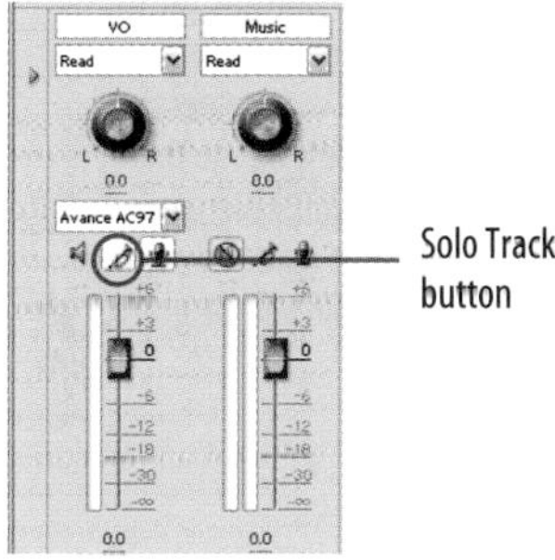

Figure 15.5 Clicking the Solo Track button automatically mutes the other tracks in the sequence so that the only audio you hear is that of the specified track.

Things to Remember

With voiceover recording, less can be more when it comes to channels. Record a stereo voiceover only if you are certain that is exactly what you need. The disadvantage to a stereo voiceover is that your voice may not be equally balanced between the left and right channels. A mono voiceover file, when added to a stereo or surround sound sequence, will have an equal value on all channels. Furthermore, you have greater control adjusting or panning from left to right with a mono file. Finally, I recommend that you record your voiceover, listen to it, and decide whether you want to keep it or not. If it's a keeper, export it, rename it, and if you want to record again, overwrite the file in the timeline and keep at it.

Even if you don't have a million dollar microphone or recording environment, the techniques you'll learn in the next chapters will help you edit, clean up, and create an even better sounding audio file.

CHAPTER

16

Editing Your Voiceover

After you successfully record your voiceover narration, you can do a lot to the file to clean it up and get it flowing and sounding better than the original recording. In this chapter, you will edit the voiceover you created in Chapter 15 to match the flow of the video. You will add transitions to the head and tail of each clip so that there are no abrupt or excess noises. Finally, you will learn a new technique for removing unwanted breaths or noises in the spaces between words.

Cutting Your Voiceover

Editing the voiceover file is the first step to getting it into shape. Once you normalize the volume level, you will cut the voiceover into smaller pieces and adjust the timing with the flow of the video. By spacing out the words and sentences you will create timing that is different than in the original recording.

1. Open the VO_Editing_Start.prproj file from the APPST Lesson Files/Chapter 16 folder. Press Ctrl+I to access the Import File dialog, and import the file Saleen_VO.wav from the same APPST Lesson Files/Chapter 16 folder. The imported file will appear selected in the Project window. Choose Clip>Audio Options>Audio Gain (see Figure 16.1), and in the resulting Clip Gain dialog, click Normalize.

   This voiceover file does not require any gain adjustments, and the result from Normalize is 0dB. This is because the pre-amp that I used for recording properly adjusted the incoming signal so that the levels were as strong as possible without exceeding the ceiling. I strongly recommend always starting your workflow with normalization of the audio, because you may often have a less than perfectly recorded file.

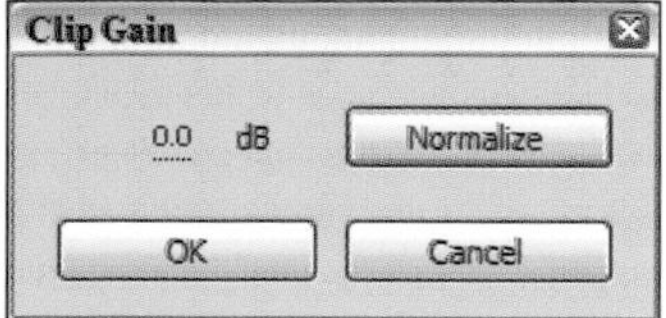

Figure 16.1 When you normalize the master file selected in the Project window, all subsequent instances and uses from the master clip will use the adjusted Gain value. The first and most important step before cutting up your file is to Normalize its volume level.

2. Double-click the Saleen_VO.wav file in the Project window to open it in the Source Monitor. Adjust the viewing area bar so that you are zoomed into the details of the file. (See Figure 16.2.)

   To begin cutting up the voiceover file, you want to be zoomed in tight enough to the source material so that your In points and Out points don't include a lot of extraneous material.

   The next step is to edit out all the mistakes and empty spaces between the important words and phrases that will make up your final voiceover edit. I'll walk you through cutting up the first element and then identify the rest of the cuts for you to finish later.

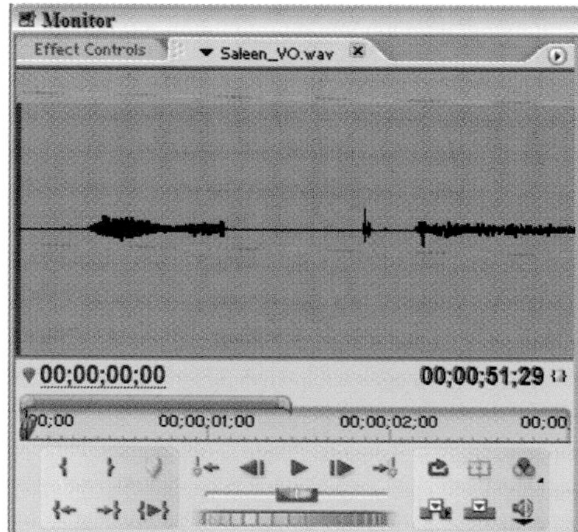

Figures 16.2 The clip as it is first revealed in its entirety (left) and with the viewing area bar reduced to zoom in tighter to the open clip (right). When editing audio, not only can you use the viewing area bar to zoom in, but you can also toggle your display to audio units so that you can zoom to the subframe level.

3. Make sure you are displaying video frames in your Source Monitor and not audio units. Click to select the current frame's timecode value in the lower-left corner of the Source Monitor, type the value 412, and press Enter. Your CTI should snap to the timecode value of 04;12, just before the first phrase, "A Dream." Press I to mark an In point. Select the current frame timecode value again, type 511, and press Enter. Your CTI should

snap to 05;11, which is right after the phrase "A Dream." Press O to set an Out point. Click and drag the In/Out instance from the Source Monitor, releasing it onto the VO track at the 0 numbered marker in the timeline (see Figure 16.3).

You identified a section of the audio file and determined precise In and Out points so that there was no extra material. Once you made your selection, you added the subclip into a predetermined position in the sequence.

Figure 16.3 By creating a small In/Out instance from the master clip, you have a unique subclip that contains only the duration specified from the Source Monitor. Because Snapping is on, if you drag the subclip near any of the numbered markers, you can automatically snap to their position and release the subclip in that place. Notice that because you are dropping the subclip using no modification keys, the Overlay icon displays and no elements of the timeline are shifted when you release the clip. Finally, notice how the black Snapping line has an arrow point up at the top of the timeline, this indicates that it is snapping to a timeline marker.

4. To make the next subclip, simply create a new In/Out instance and drag the subclip to the next marker position in the timeline. Table 16.1 lists the remaining In/Out instances and the phrases that each contains. After you have cut each up, your edit should look something like Figure 16.4.

Table 16.1: Voiceover In/Out Instances for Cutting

Timecode Range	Phrase	Marker Number
05;21–6;29	"Comes to life."	1
11;26–18;02	"The Saleen S7...art."	2
18;16–20;27	"From its sleek aerodynamic shape..."	3
21;01–23;02	"To its luxurious interior..."	4
28;17–32;21	"The S7 is...century."	5
33;03–41;18	"Built...dream come true."	6
42;00–49;09	"This...Thank you."	7

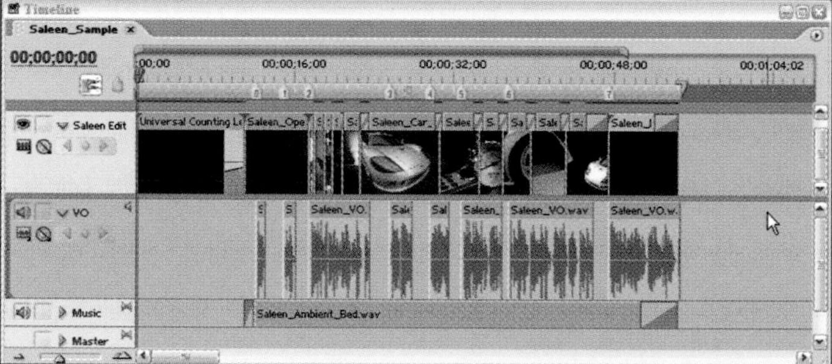

Figure 16.4 The markers make an easy guide for placing each subclip, but feel free to take some liberties if you want to change their position. Remember that if you do want to move the clips within a small range, you can toggle off Snapping ("S") so that every slight move doesn't snap to the next potential snapping point.

Once the pieces of the voiceover are separated, you can put certain elements farther apart or closer together. It's up to you to feel the rhythm and flow, deciding where exactly everything should line up. Because there is a music track, don't worry too much about the dead air between clips.

5. Open Edit>Preferences>General, and assign a value of 0.15 seconds for your Audio Transition Default Duration. Click in the VO track header to make sure that track is targeted (the track header will become dark gray). With no clips selected, press the Home key to snap the CTI to the beginning of the timeline. Press the Page Down key until your CTI is snapped to the head of your first voiceover subclip. Press Ctrl+Shift+D to add a default transition to the head of the subclip. Press Page Down to snap the CTI to the tail of the first subclip, and press Ctrl+Shift+D to place a default transition at its tail. Your first clip should look like Figure 16.5.

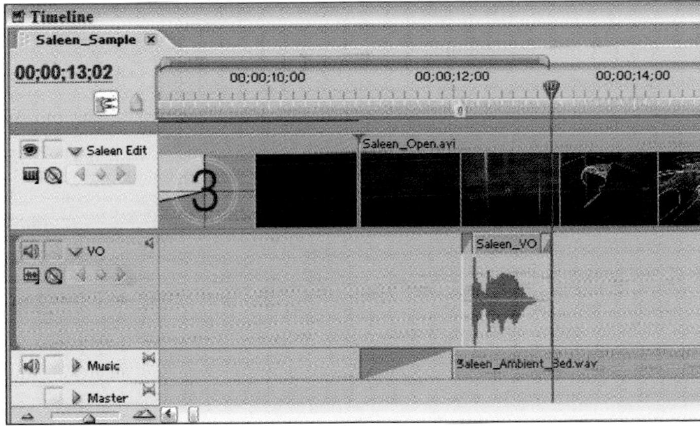

Figure 16.5 A one-sided transition was added to both the head and tail, creating a smooth volume fade from the empty space of the timeline to the audio of the subclip and then back to the empty space of the timeline. If your audio levels pop up in volume while you play the cuts of your inserted subclips, you can add transitions at the head and tail of each subclip to smooth the increase in volume.

It may be necessary to zoom into your timeline to see the placed transitions because their size is 15/100ths of a second. You can vary the size of the transition to create a longer or shorter fade in and out.

6. Step through the rest of the sequence adding transitions to the heads and tails of all the subclips. If you overshoot an edit point, Page Up snaps the CTI/Edit Line backward to the previous cut point. Once you have placed a transition, if you want to increase its duration, zoom in tight enough to grab its inner edge and

pull the edge toward the center of the clip. Alternatively, if you double-click on a transition, you can modify its properties in the Effect Controls window.

Once you have placed your transitions, your edit should be in perfect shape to continue with the adjustments.

Speed Adjustments and Pitch Shifting

For the final disclaimer that is placed underneath the Saleen logo at the end of the edit, try picking up the pace, much like those rapid-fire disclaimers on certain television commercials.

To do this, select the clip you want to adjust in the timeline and press Ctrl+R (or choose Clip>Speed/Duration) to open the Speed/Duration dialog box. In this dialog, adjust the speed of the clip to 120% and click the check box for Maintain Pitch. When you choose to maintain pitch, Premiere Pro dynamically adjusts the pitch of the sped up audio so that it does not sound squeaky like a mouse, instead like a normal voice. The result is audio that is sped up to reduce its duration but without a distorted high pitched sound.

Using this method in Premiere Pro, you can achieve the effect, but with some audible artifacts. Listen to the file Disclaimer_PP_120.wav as an example (APPST Lesson Files/ Chapter 16). Notice that although I was able to increase the speed and maintain a pretty similar vocal pitch, the file still has a slight electronic feel.

For comparison, I loaded the same file into Adobe Audition and used its Speed and Pitch tools to make the same speed adjustment while preserving the pitch. Listen to the file Disclaimer_AUD_120.wav (APPST Lesson Files/ Chapter 16) to hear the dramatic difference in quality.

As you can see—or hear—it is possible to expand or reduce the size of individual clips while keeping the proper pitch and sound of the voiceover intact. Although Premiere Pro has excellent audio processing capabilities, consider using Adobe Audition to take things to the next level.

Breath Removal

Some expendable elements that you can edit out of recorded speech are the subtle breaths and empty spaces between words. Particularly with voiceover narration, you don't want to hear any room tone or breaths between words and phrases. The effect is better when the only vocal sound comes when words are spoken, the rest of the track should be empty. Because your music will fill in the blanks, you want your voiceover to be as solid as possible for the elements that you want to hear. You can fine-tune and hone the audio a bit more with this technique for quick removal of smaller breaths or noises.

1. Open the file Breath_Removal_Start.prproj from the APPST Lesson Files/Chapter 16 folder. The second to last subclip of voiceover, positioned at Marker 6, starts with the words "built from the most." Between the words "pounds" and "the Saleen" (approximately 41;25), there is a little breath that you can easily clip out using the following keyframe adjustment method.

2. Click on the Toggle Track Output button for your Music track to turn the speaker off. In your VO track, select Show Clip Volume from your Show Keyframes drop-down list.

   Because you turned off the output of the Music track, the only sound you'll hear while playing back will be the VO track. By setting Show Keyframes in the VO track to Show Clip Volume, you activate the visual display and interface for directly adjusting the volume of the individual subclip instances.

3. Move your CTI to 41;18 in the timeline. Switch your timeline counter to Audio Units from the Timeline window wing menu, and zoom into your timeline at the current position. With your speaker or, preferably, headphone volume turned up, scrub the edit line between the end of the "sss" sound and the beginning of the "thhhh" sound—approximately 41:27000 to 41:44000. (See Figure 16.6.)

If you do not hear audio when you scrub, be sure that you have Play Audio While Scrubbing checked in your Preferences>Audio dialog.

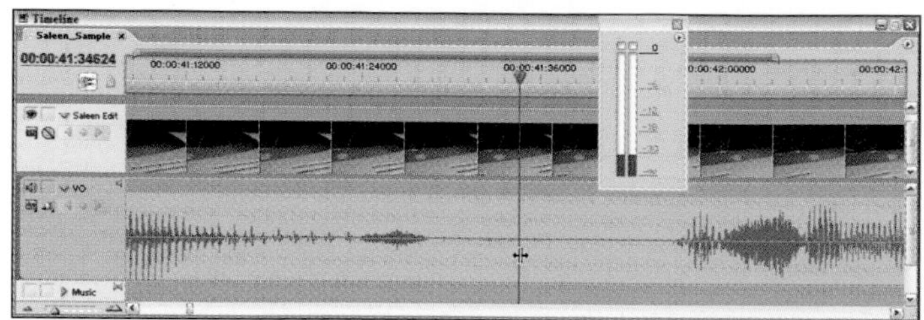

Figure 16.6 Notice that the breath does register a small waveform value where the Edit Line is scrubbing. Also, notice how even while scrubbing, the VU meters properly display the dB levels for the area being scrubbed. For this section, the volume level is about –30dB. Although this is not a particularly loud breath, it does register. By keyframing the overall volume levels in the section where the breath exists, you can easily get it out of your final edit.

Because of the subframe sample level display, it is quick and easy to display your subframe waveform and scrub at the subframe level. By doing this, you can have greater accuracy in isolating and then removing unwanted sound elements.

4. With the Timeline window active, press the P key to change your cursor into the Pen tool. Using the Pen tool, hold down the Ctrl key and add four keyframes starting from the end of the "sss" sound and ending at the beginning of the "thhh" sound (see Figure 16.7).

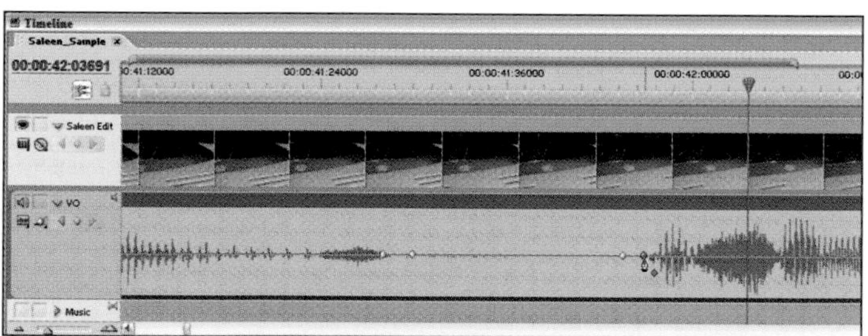

Figure 16.7 I have strategically placed the keyframes close together on each side. The first keyframe is placed at the end of the "ssss" sound with an accompanying keyframe just after. The fourth keyframe is created at the beginning of the "thhh" sound with an accompanying keyframe just before.

The Pen tool is your tool for adding, selecting, and adjusting keyframes. Holding down the Ctrl key toggles the Pen tool into a mode in which every click adds a new keyframe handle. The orange line displays the clip volume level, and now that you have added keyframes to that line you can adjust its value dynamically.

5. Continuing with the Pen tool, click and drag down the volume line between the two inner keyframes so that the volume line reads –oodB. (See Figure 16.8.)

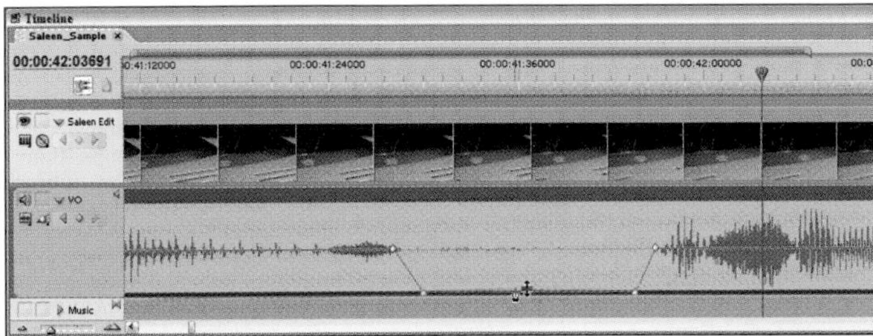

Figure 16.8 When the Pen tool is held between two equal keyframe handles, it displays a horizontal bar with upward and downward pointing arrows. The function of the tool in this circumstance is to move the entire value between the two handles up or down in unison. Because it affects only the value between two handles, the outer keyframe handles preserve their current value. The inner two are adjusted to whatever you determine, in this case 0dB or no volume.

By dragging the center line down between the two inner keyframes, you have created a dip in the volume level of the subclip. The outer keyframe handles become the anchor points for the current volume level. The inner keyframe handles become the anchor points for the muted volume level.

With your adjustment, the volume is at its normal level of 0dB until the end of the "ssss" sound. After the first keyframe handle, the volume fades down to –oodB, which is essentially muted. The volume remains muted until it hits the next –oodB keyframe handle, from which point the volume fades back up to the normal –0dB.

6. Click on the second keyframe with the Pen tool, and move it slightly closer to the first keyframe by gently dragging it left. This should make the line between the first two keyframes steeper. Click and drag the third keyframe closer to the fourth to make that angle steeper as well.

By moving the keyframes closer together, you are causing the fade between volume levels to occur faster and less noticeably.

7. With the Pen tool still active, click and marquee select all four keyframes. (See Figure 16.9.) Right-click on one of the keyframes, and select Continuous Bezier from the drop-down menu.

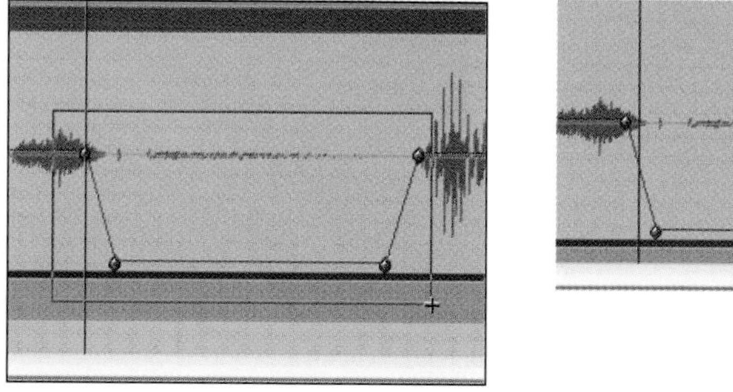

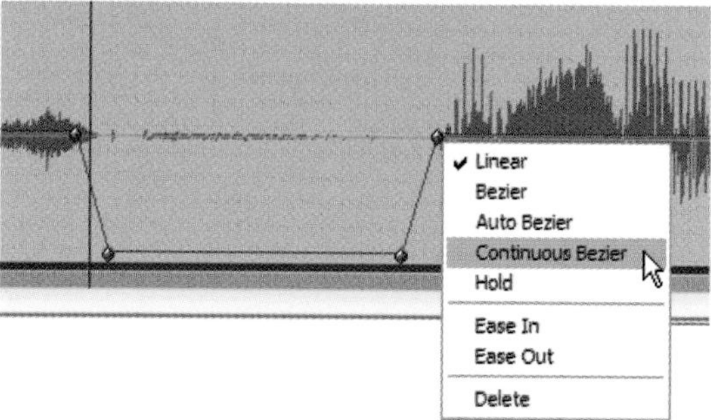

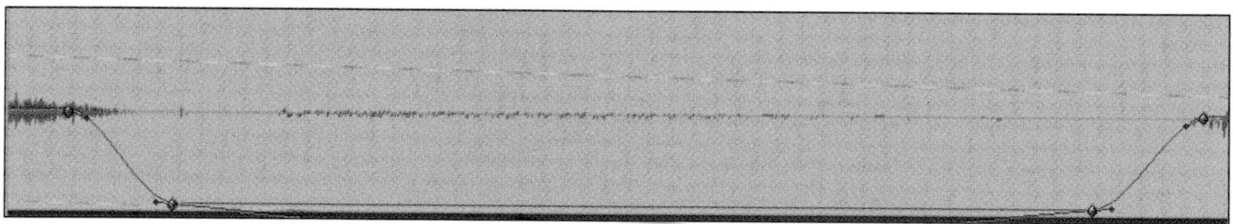

Figure 16.9 By clicking and dragging over the keyframes you can select them all (top left). After the keyframes are selected (yellow), you can right-click on any of them and change the straight lines that connect them into Continuous Bezier curved lines (top right). The result of the curved line connecting the keyframes is subtle but effective (bottom). Notice the Blue keyframe handles that can be adjusted to change the curve.

By choosing Continuous Bezier for the keyframe interpolation, you created smooth volume curves, as opposed to straight linear lines. Now, the audio smoothly fades out, then smoothly fades back up.

8. Using the Pen tool, and with the keyframes still selected (see Figure 16.10), press Ctrl+C to copy the selected keyframes.

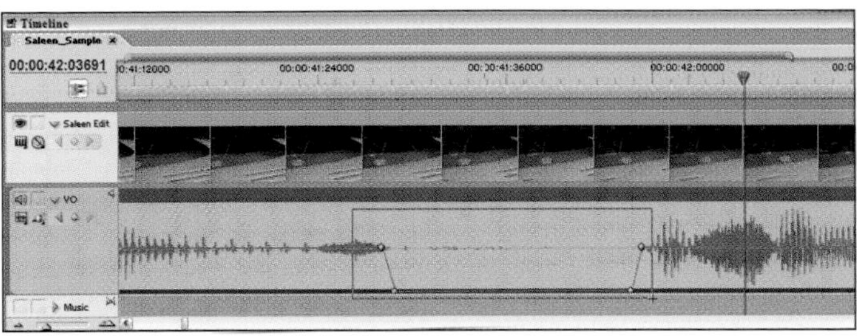

Figure 16.10 Just as in the last step, the Pen tool can range-select a group of keyframes. Simply click the mouse down and drag the Pen tool past a group of keyframes. The selected keyframes turn yellow. Pressing Ctrl+C copies the selected keyframe values and spatial positioning to your clipboard. You can then paste those exact keyframe values into the clip volume level of another subclip.

To copy and paste keyframes from one clip to another, the clip that the keyframes are being pasted into must be selected. Keyframes always are pasted starting from the position of the Edit Line.

9. Position the Edit Line at 51:05000 (approximately), and click within the clip boundary of the Disclaimer subclip to select that clip in the timeline. Press Ctrl+V to paste the copied keyframes into the Disclaimer subclip, starting from the current Edit Line position.

   Notice that the keyframes are copied exactly into the new clip adhering to their copied parameters. From this point, all you need to do is use the Pen tool to range-select one side of the pasted keyframes and adjust them in unison.

10. Zoom into your timeline, and move the Edit Line to approximately 51:2100. With the Pen tool, range-select the two right keyframes and slide them left so that the last keyframe lines up with the Edit Line (see Figure 16.11).

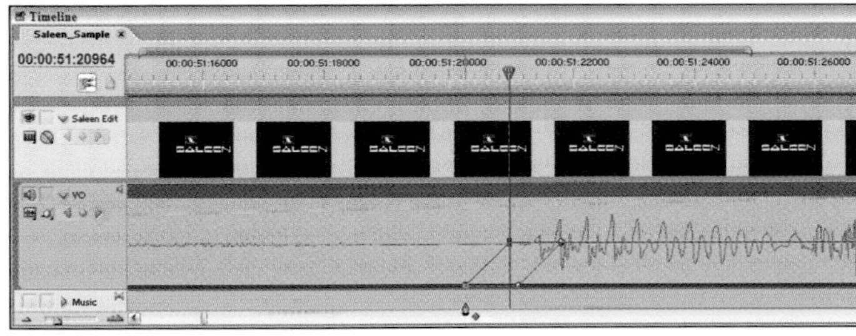

Figure 16.11 By first positioning the Edit Line exactly where you want your volume to be back at its normal level, all you need to do is range-select the two keyframes and slide them left accordingly. This picture was taken "in action" and the darkened keyframes reflect the new position to which the two keyframes are being moved.

You have now created a very simple keyframed volume adjustment that mutes a portion of your clip's volume between two points. Using the copy and paste function, you can apply and easily adjust keyframes to remove any unwanted small breathes and sounds.

This technique is very powerful because once you create the first four keyframes with their volume adjustment, all you have to do is paste them into a new position to re-use them.

Things to Remember

The important things to remember from these lessons are the simple facts about the value of clean sound without any unwanted noises. Although some audio work seems a bit tedious and highly detail oriented, I have been quite inspired by the depths in which Premiere Pro allows access to make important adjustments.

Zooming in to the sample level and assigning keyframes to precise positions in order to remove small noises and breaths is invaluable to a professional workflow. Although there are many filters and effects that can do this for you, by creating one keyframed breath removal instance, you can copy, paste, and slightly adjust the keyframes to accommodate any other removal in the volume of any clip in any sequence in your project.

Although this chapter shined a bit of a light onto Adobe Audition for professional processing and adjustments to your audio files, Premiere Pro has a number of very effective professional filters to help make your audio sound better. In the next chapter, we will explore a number of those filters as you learn about clip-based and track-based audio effects.

CHAPTER

17

Audio Clip and Track Effects

Recordings rarely come out perfect, but Premiere Pro offers some help. Several audio clip effect and track effect filters can help you clean up and further refine the sound of your recording. For example, you can use EQ, Pitch Shift, Reverb, and Delay to boost parts of your sound and adjust it, giving it more spatial and tonal personality.

In this chapter, you will apply clip and track effects to refine and add personality to the voiceover narration you recorded in Chapter 15. Clip-based effects alter an individual clip, while track-based effects alter an entire track, affecting all the clips contained in that track. By exploring both clip and track effects, you will understand the proper use for each while becoming more comfortable with using the audio mixer.

Applying Clip Effects

Once you have your voiceover, you can start playing with different effects as a means of creating a richer, more vibrant, and better sounding file.

For this lesson, you will use several effects to increase the quality and strength of the voiceover track's sound and tone. The most dramatic and effective adjustments can be done with the EQ effect, but you will get to that in a minute, the basic idea is to refine the sound into something better and clearer than what you began with.

1. Open Clip_FX_Start.prproj from the APPST Lesson Files/Chapter 17 folder. Be sure to link to the appropriate Sample Project video files and to link Saleen_VO.wav from the same folder that the project originates. With the project open, select Window> Workspace>Effects. Adjust your workspace so that you have direct access to the Effects window and the Effect Controls window. Position your Edit Line near timeline marker 2.

Premiere Pro supports its own and third-party VST plug-ins. VST plug-ins are professional quality plug-ins that offer a wide variety of processing functionality. Common plug-ins for adjusting a voiceover file range from EQ to Pitch, Reverb, and Delay; occasionally there are other effects, but you can get a better taste for those in a book that covers working with audio. Additionally, note that you can clip out unwanted noises and frequencies using a Noise Gate in the Compressor effect. For this project, however, the results are far too dramatic and unnecessary.

You now have direct access to the windows you will use most. When working with audio effects in particular, I recommend increasing the size of your Effect Controls window, as the VST plug-in controls have custom controls that can be quite large.

In the timeline, identify the audio clip instance that begins at timeline marker 2, this is the clip that you will be applying your effects to.

2. In the Effects window, select Audio Effects>Mono>EQ. Drag and drop this effect onto the subclip at timeline marker 2 in the VO track. Click on the subclip to activate its properties in the Effect Controls window. Twirl down the EQ effect listing in the Effect Controls window, and then twirl down Custom Setup to reveal the EQ interface. (See Figure 17.1.)

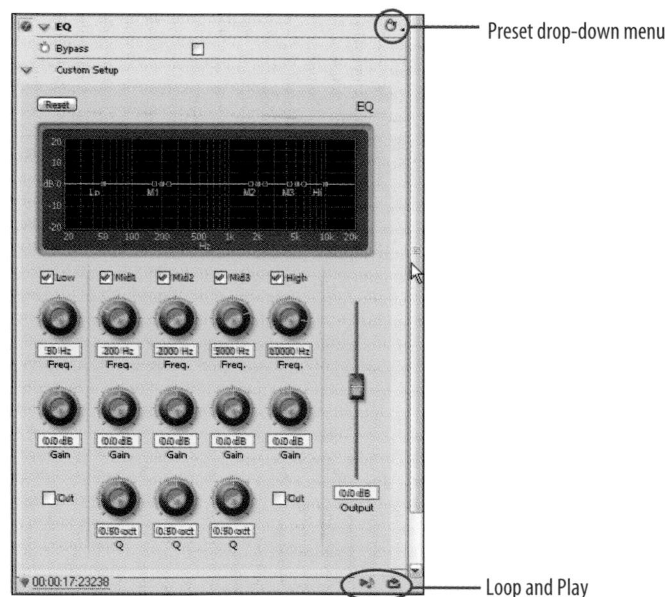

Figure 17.1 The EQ effect dialog houses five frequency ranges: Low, Mid1, Mid2, Mid3, and High. Each column has a correlating grid position, so that while you manually adjust the exact value, you have a visual representation of the adjustments being made. The Output volume slider increases or decreases the gain of the overall audio being processed by the EQ. Also, notice the Loop and Play Audio buttons in the lower-right corner of the Effect Controls window. The Preset drop-down menu enables you to access presets associated with the effect; choosing Default would essentially reset the effect.

The EQ plug-in is a frequency equalizer, which enables you to add or reduce volume gain levels within specific frequency ranges. If you had a loud low frequency hum, for example, you could lower the gain in that low frequency area as a means of reducing the overall presence of the hum. To get a good idea as to the type of adjustments the EQ can make, click on the Preset drop-down menu in the upper-right corner of the effect listing in the Effect Controls window where the Reset button is located (see Figure 17.1). Notice the adjustments that each preset makes to the controls in the interface.

Because the subclips in the VO track are mono, remember to drag and drop mono effects onto each of the subclips to which you want to apply effects. For stereo tracks and clips, use the stereo effects, and use 5.1 surround effects for 5.1 clips.

In the next step, you'll make an EQ adjustment to help reduce some low frequency noise and then to increase some of the high frequency elements to make the voice sound a bit more crisp.

3. In the EQ custom setup, check the Low Frequency check box and set the frequency to 37Hz. Click the Cut check box. Adjust the following frequencies:

   Mid1: **Reduce Gain by –3 to –5.0dB in the 250 to 325Hz frequency**

   Mid2: **Reduce Gain by –3.0dB in the 1250 to 1500Hz frequency**

   Mid3: **Increase Gain by 1 to 3dB in the 3200 to 3700Hz frequency**

   High: **Increase Gain by 2 to 4dB in the 7500 to 9000Hz frequency**

   For comparison, Figure 17.2 shows the exact settings that I used. For the next step, you can put playback into a looping mode so that you can do live adjustments to the effect while the audio continues to play back.

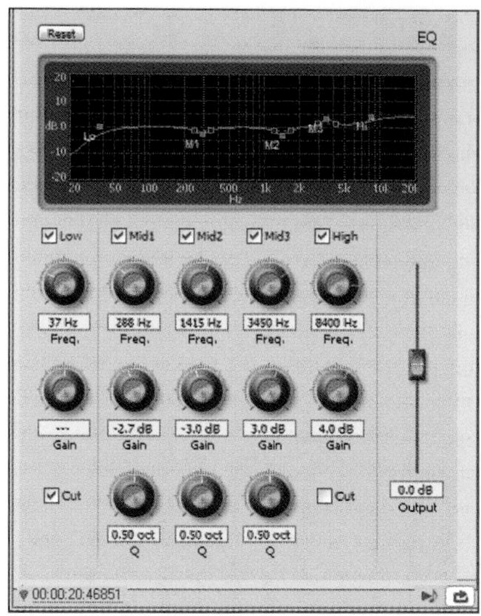

Figure 17.2 Cutting the low frequency at 37Hz, as shown here, means nothing below 37Hz will be heard. Depending on the amount of low frequency noise in your voiceover, you can cut your Low accordingly. The rest of the levels reflect a subtle but calculated adjustment. You can use the five listed adjustment ranges as potential choices to explore with your own voiceover file.

To hear the kind of drastic adjustments you can make using the EQ, try twirling the Gain knob for the high frequency from one end to the other while the audio loops.

4. With the subclip still selected, activate the Loop button in the lower-right corner of the Effect Controls window, and then press the Play Audio button to its left.

   When you are setting and previewing audio effects using the Effect Controls window, clicking the Loop and Play Audio (Play only the audio for this clip) buttons loops the entire selected clip instance until you press Stop. The power of looping is that your audio plays continuously while being updated with the live effect adjustments that you apply.

   Having adjusted the EQ, it's time to add some more noticeable effects to help change the vocal tone. Perhaps you are not entirely satisfied with the tone or pitch of the voice; in the next step you will make a slight adjustment using the PitchShifter.

5. Collapse the EQ effect listing in the Effect Controls window. Grab the Mono PitchShifter effect, and drop it into the Effect Controls window below the EQ effect listing. Twirl down the PitchShifter and its Custom

Setup. Set the Pitch to –1 Semi-t and the Fine to 30 cents, click off the check box for Formant Preserve. Click Play Audio to hear your adjustment. Figure 17.3 explores the PitchShifter knobs and settings.

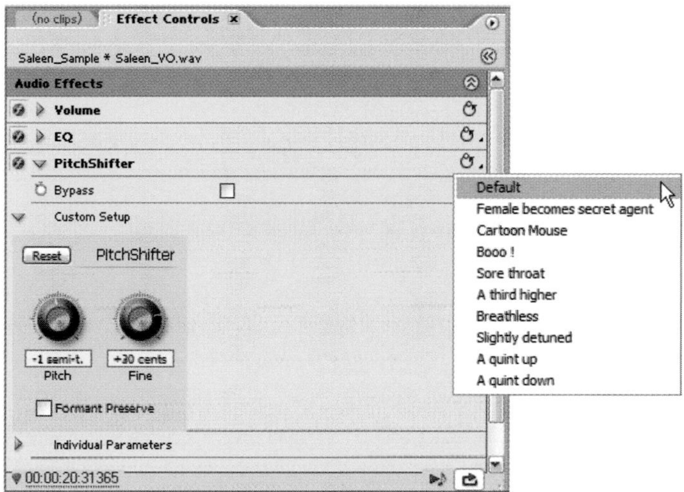

Figure 17.3 The PitchShifter has presets you can load and apply to achieve specific sound adjustments. Pitch adjusts the pitch; positive values go higher and negative values go lower. Fine determines the detail of tuning in the adjustment for Pitch. The more fine, the better the Pitch adjustment. The Formant Preserve check box enables you to turn on or off the preserving of formants from shifting. When formants shift, the sound will become more cartoonish. An excellent way to illustrate this is to play the Cartoon Mouse preset, then turn on Formant Preserve and play it again. If you turn on Formant Preserve you will be avoiding pitch shifts that sound dramatically different from the original pitch.

The PitchShifter is a VST plug-in that dynamically increases or reduces the pitch of the audio being processed. Reducing the pitch value makes the voice sound as if it is speaking slower, while increasing the pitch makes the voice sound like a chipmunk. Using the PitchShifter to make slight adjustments can result in a more masculine or feminine sounding voice. Increasing Fine helps increase the quality and precision of the pitch adjustment, and decreasing Fine reduces it. When the formants in your audio clip shift, the pitch of the audio radically changes. Turning on Formant Preserve attempts to preserve the Formants so the pitch stays the same. When you speed up an audio clip and want the pitch to be the same, Formant Preserve is activated.

You can expand or collapse all your effect listings and their individual parameters by holding down the ALT key and either twirling down (to expand) or twirling up (to collapse) an effect.

Two effect choices offer somewhat similar processing results: Reverb and Delays. A reverb adds spatial properties to your sound, whereas a delay adds depth and strength. A large sounding reverb can make your voice sound as if it was recorded in a cathedral. A very minor 20 millisecond delay can make your voice immediately sound stronger. Delays of 0.02 or 0.04 seconds are typical in radio advertisements, think: "Sunday, Sunday, Sunday at the Monster Truck extravaganza!"

Now that you have added a slight Pitch effect and cleaned up the file using the EQ, it's time to add some spatial properties to the voiceover.

6. Collapse the PitchShifter effect listing in the Effect Controls window, and click off its Effect toggle. Drag and drop the Mono Reverb Effect into the Effect Controls window below the PitchShifter listing. Twirl down the Reverb listing, then twirl down its Custom Setup to reveal its interface.

In the language of reverb there are two words that you need to know: bright and dark. *Bright* indicates more of an echo, *dark* is less of an echo. If you imagine the reverb sound of different rooms, bright would be wooden or marble floors, dark would be carpeted floors. Reverb refers to the reverberation of sound off of the walls and floors. The reverb is based on the size of the room, the distance you stand from the walls and the brightness or darkness of the room. See Figures 17.4, 17.5, and 17.6 to understand the visual difference between two different sounding rooms.

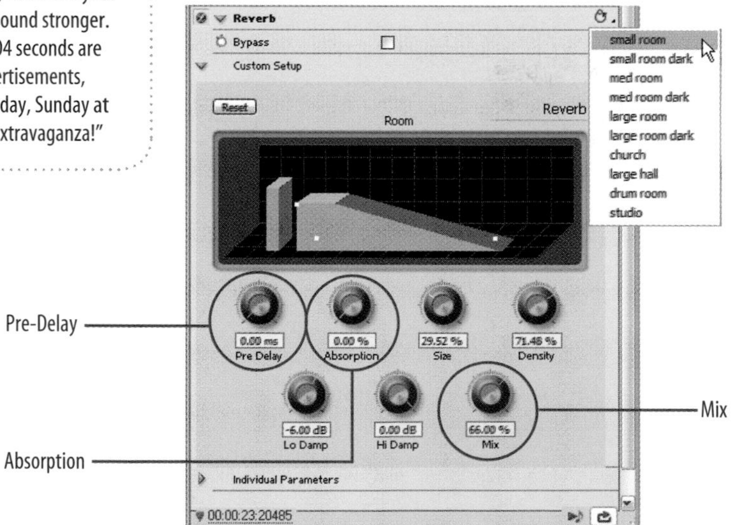

Figure 17.4 Click the Reverb Preset button to switch between different Reverb presets. This image shows what the Reverb interface looks like when it simulates a small room. Because the room is small, there is no Pre Delay for the sound. This preset is also bright and has an echo quality because there is also no absorption.

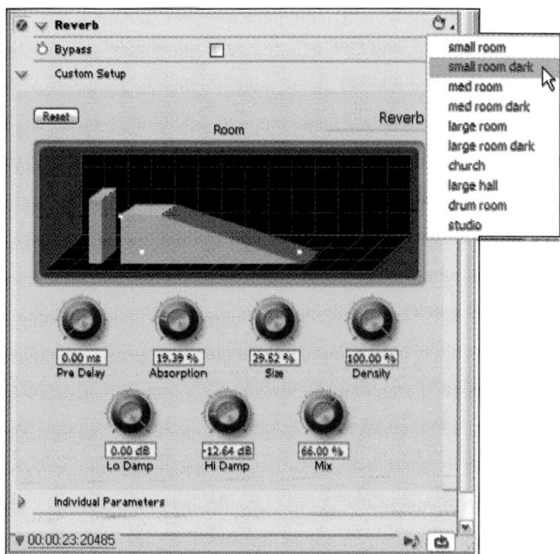

Figure 17.5 By contrast, this is the Reverb interface that simulates a small room, dark. Notice the increase in the Absorption, Density, and Hi Damp values. Also notice that the size of the room and the mix changed.

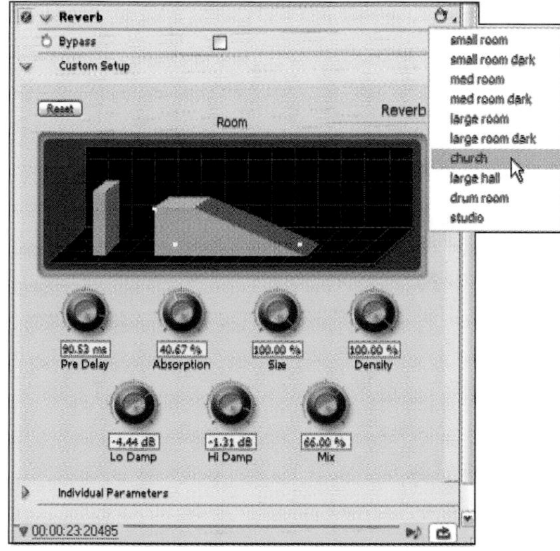

Figure 17.6 This preset shows the reverb qualities of the Church preset. Notice the drastic change in Pre Delay and Size, these two greatly increase the presence of the echo. The Absorption also has an increased value so the echo doesn't linger too noticeably. If you turn the Absorption back to 0, you can hear the "ssss" noises and other small sounds linger longer as the voice speaks.

The Reverb interface attempts to display a room and the potential echo reverb properties. Imagine the sound originating from the left rectangle and into the right reverb object. The longer the object (pulling from the left white control point), the less absorption and the brighter the sound. This is why adjusting absorption adjusts the length of the object. The farther the object is from the rectangle, the greater the delay and the more apparent the echo. Clicking from the center of the object and dragging it to the right creates a more present echo. Finally, in terms of physical adjustments, the third and top-right white control point allows you to adjust and determine the height of the object. The height directly relates with the mix, and the taller the object, the more affected the sound will become.

7. Using these three basic properties, play around with the reverb by manipulating the different control points and then listening to your results. To fine-tune your results, you can reduce or increase the Size, Density, and Hi/Lo Damp settings.

8. Set the reverb values as follows:

   Pre-Delay: **0.00**
   Absorption: **83.5**
   Size: **59**
   Density: **27.5**
   Lo Damp: **–15**
   Hi Damp: **–15**
   Mix: **7**

   Although these settings are subtle, the voiceover has no need for a dramatic reverb. Add just enough to give it some personality and to give the voice a slight spatial quality. Remember, after you finish with your effects, you will mix the music, so some of these adjustments will sound better when mixed with the music.

9. Collapse the Reverb effect listing, click it off, and drag in the Mono Delay effect into the Effect Controls window just above the Reverb listing below the PitchShifter. Expand the Delay effect and its three expandable settings: Delay, Feedback, and Mix. Set:

Delay: **0.02 seconds**
Feedback: +/–**15%**
Mix: +/–**35%**

As mentioned earlier, delays can be very effective for enhancing the vocal presence. There is a very fine line, however, between a minor delay and an over exaggerated doubling-up of sound. That difference is about 40 milliseconds.

By placing the Delay above the Reverb effect you would be delaying the result of the EQ and PitchShifter; that delayed result would then be processed by the Reverb. Because you don't want to double up and delay the Reverb result, you place the effects in the order in which you want them processed.

Essentially, all the Delay effect is doing is doubling up the audio with a slight offset delay. The Delay value allows you to set the amount of time that exists between the original audio and its delay. For most voiceover work, a value between 0.01 and 0.06 seconds is effective, anything above that sounds like the echoing voice on the loudspeaker at the motor speedway.

The feedback setting takes the delayed audio and signal and simulates the feedback of that signal on top of itself. Experimenting with Feedback can create a much more techno-cyber effect.

Finally, the Mix setting allows you to adjust the mix emphasis between the originating sound (0%) and the delayed sound (100%). A Mix setting of 50% has an equal emphasis on the original sound and the delay.

10. Collapse Delay, and turn off its toggle. Turn on the Toggle Audio buttons for the EQ, PitchShifter, and Reverb; these are the effects that you want to process together. Holding down the Ctrl key, click and select these three effect listings in the Effect Controls window. Press Ctrl+C to copy these three effects.

Delay was added merely to illustrate the effect; it is too much for the tone of this commercial.

When you select and copy effect listings from the Effect Controls window into your clipboard, you can then paste the effects into the Effect Controls window of individual or multiple selected clips of the same format. Audio effects to audio clips, video effects to video clips.
Also, you can save any assigned effect as its own custom preset; this workflow was covered in the second half of Chapter 11, "Working with Still Images."

11. In the timeline, Shift-click the seven other subclip instances that do not have any added effect settings. (Be sure that the clip from which you copied the effects is not selected.) Press Ctrl+V to paste the copied effects onto each selected clip.

    The result is that the other selected clips now have the same individual audio clip effect settings as the original adjusted subclip. This is one technique for creating a unique stack of effects and sharing them with a group of clips.

In Premiere Pro, there's often two routes to the same goal. Next you'll use the Audio Mixer and its effect interface to achieve the same result with less copying and pasting.

Render and Replace

After you apply audio clip or speed effects, Premiere Pro must render audio files before playing back your timeline. While rendering, the application processes the audio files with effects by creating preview files. Premiere then uses these preview files to play the effects accurately.

You can choose to permanently process a file with effects or speed adjustments applied. Select the file in the timeline, in this case the sped up disclaimer, and choose Clip>Audio Options>Render and Replace.

Premiere Pro then automatically creates a unique clip that is the same duration and has the same effects as the selected clip and saves that file to your disk. Next, Premiere Pro immediately replaces your original file with the newly created processed file.

This entire process is beneficial for exporting a single effect-enhanced audio file from your sequence. It also is helpful when you apply speed changes to a master clip, cut it up numerous times, and then add audio effects. To reduce the overall processing time, you can render and replace a clip, and then apply the effects on top of the replaced version.

Exporting and Consolidating Your Voiceover Track

After you apply your clip effects to all the clips in the VO track, you have the option to export and consolidate the edited voiceover with effects into a unique processed file. You later can archive the file or pass it off as a deliverable to send to a client who wants to hear the audio only.

To do this, you need to turn off the sound for the Music track by clicking off the speaker in that track's track header area. With the timeline active and the speaker off for the Music track but on for the VO track, choose File>Export>Audio.

In the resulting dialog box, verify the Windows WAV format 48kHz, 16 bit mono file format settings. Name the file Saleen_VO_Final_FX.wav. At this point, you can use this one processed audio file as opposed to its smaller pieces.

Applying Track-Based Effects

Clip-based effects are excellent to use when individual clips need alternate adjustments and differing effects. If you need to apply a range of effects to an entire track full of clips, however, track-based effects are an intuitive solution.

Because track effects have the same parameters as their clip-based cousins, this lesson will spend less time on what to tweak and more time on how to interact with and apply track effects. You will do that in the expanded Audio Mixer.

1. Open the Track_FX_Start.prproj file from the APPST Lesson Files/Chapter 17 folder, and review the edit. Adjust your workspace to Workspace>Audio.

   I have already saved the project with the Audio Mixer opened entirely. I suggest you rework your workspace layout, however, so that the Mixer, Timeline, and Monitor windows are at a reasonable size for your desktop. Choosing the Audio Workspace resizes the windows accordingly so that you can see the Monitor window, Timeline window, and full Audio Mixer.

2. In the Effects area of the VO track of the Audio Mixer, click the top empty effects drop-down menu and select EQ from the listed effects. Double-click the EQ listing to open the effect interface. (See Figure 17.7.)

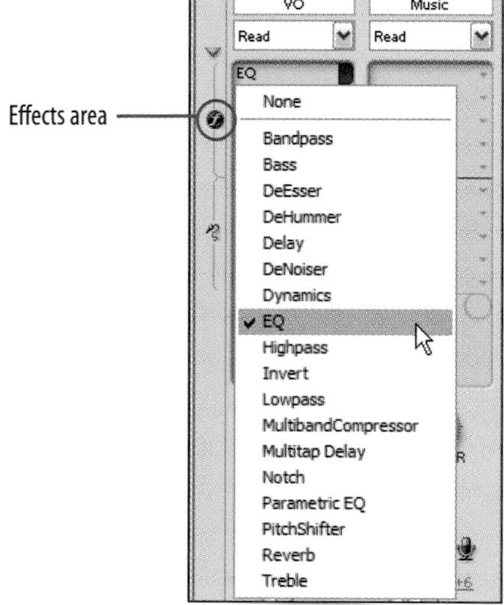

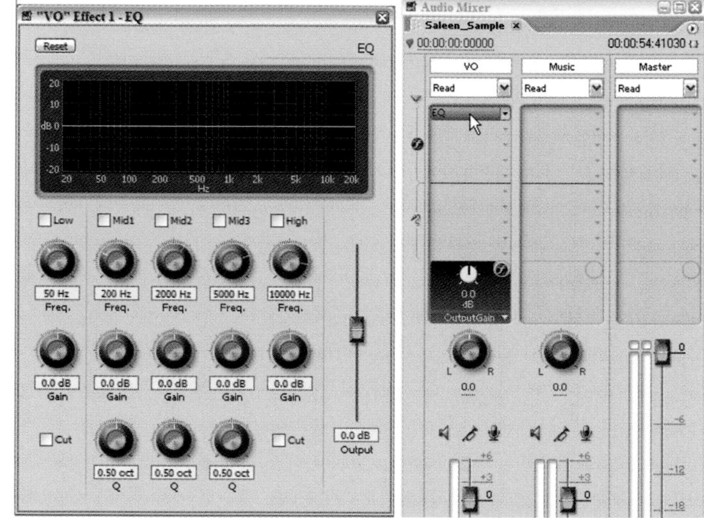

Figure 17.7 The top expanded area of each audio track in the Audio Mixer is known as the Effects area. Clicking on a blank field yields a drop-down menu with effects that you can activate and select for the track. Double-clicking on the effect listing opens its associated dialog box.

Instead of dragging and dropping as for clip effects, you simply select the desired track effect from the menu listing in the Effects area. You can have up to five effects per track. Notice the interface for the EQ matches the interface you learned from the EQ clip effects custom setup.

3. Check the Low Frequency check box, and set the frequency to 37Hz. Click the Cut check box. Assign the following EQ values:

   Mid1: **Reduce Gain by –3 to –5.0dB in the 250 to 325Hz frequency**

   Mid2: **Reduce Gain by –3.0dB in the 1250 to 1500Hz frequency**

   Mid3: **Increase Gain by 1 to 3dB in the 3200 to 3700Hz frequency**

High: **Increase Gain by 2 to 4dB in the 7500 to 9000Hz frequency**

For each selected effect in the Audio Mixer, there is a small knob and adjustment area at the bottom of the Effects/Sends area. If you want to make adjustments without opening the EQ interface window, select each knob from the drop-down at the bottom of the Effects/Sends area. With a specific parameter selected, the knob updates its value. In Figure 17.8, adjusting the knob for Output Gain achieves the same result as adjusting the Output slider in the EQ interface.

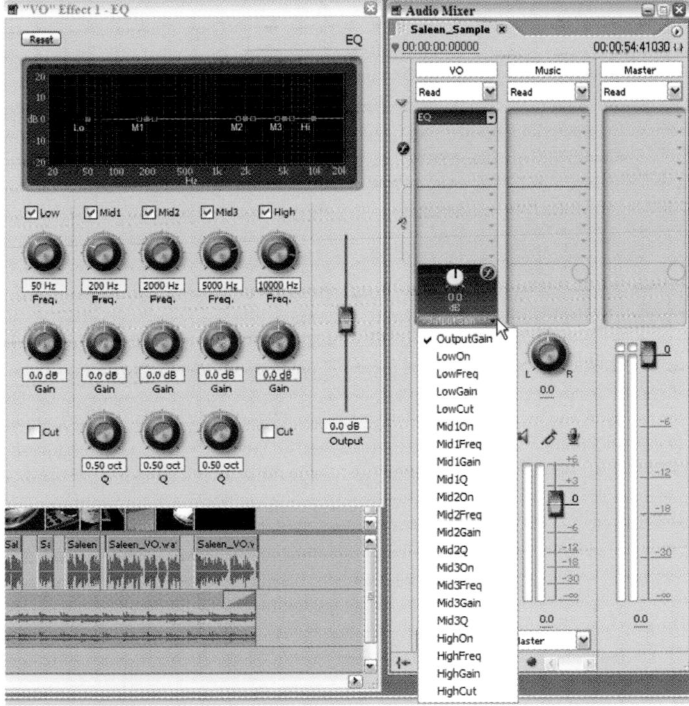

Figure 17.8 The EQ effect interface on the left contains all the controls and knobs for adjusting each associated effect parameter.

4. Select PitchShifter from the empty effect listing below the EQ track effect. Instead of double-clicking to open the effect interface, set the following values for the parameters in the adjustment area:

   Semitone: **–1**
   FineTune: **+30 cents**
   Formant Preserve: **Twist left to turn off**

Although you can enter values in the adjustment area for the selected effect parameter, it is sometimes difficult to use the knob when trying to enter precise values. In that case, you can open the effect interface and enter the information in the selected parameter using your keyboard.

5. From the empty effect listing below PitchShifter, click and select Reverb from the drop-down list. Double-click on the Reverb effect to open its interface and enter the following values:

   Pre-Delay: **0.00**
   Absorption: **83.5**
   Size: **59**
   Density: **27.5**
   Lo Damp: **–15**
   Hi Damp: **–15**
   Mix: **7**

6. Play back your sequence so that you can hear the voiceover with effects and music at the same time. Click the Solo Horn toggle for the VO track, and play back the timeline to hear only the voiceover.

   Like the Effect Controls window, the Audio Mixer has looping and playback buttons. Pressing Loop and then Play puts the mixer into a looping mode that continues until you press Stop. To loop an individual section of the sequence, place an In point at the beginning of the section you want to loop and an Out point at the end of the section you want to loop. With sequence In and Out points assigned, Premiere loops between the assigned In and Out points.

7. In the VO track header, switch the timeline keyframe display drop-down list to Track Keyframes. Click the Track Effect drop-down menu to reveal the effect display options (see Figure 17.9). Select PitchShifter>Pitch.

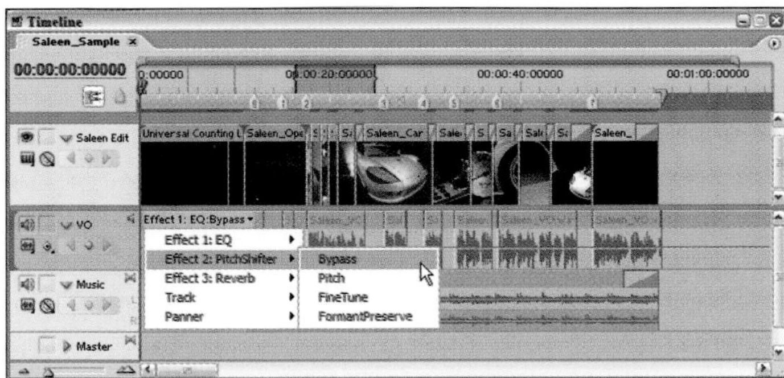

Figure 17.9 Setting your track display to Track Keyframes puts the track display into a mode in which you can add and manipulate keyframe values for specific effect parameters. The Effect drop-down menu for the track will be at the beginning of the track and it will list all the associated track effects and their parameters. Selecting a specific parameter updates the track display with its keyframe settings.

The same way you used keyframes to adjust the clip volume to remove breaths in Chapter 16, "Editing Your Voiceover," you can also adjust exact track effect values using keyframes. To use keyframes to adjust a track effect, select the effect you want to adjust when the track is in Show Track Keyframes mode.

8. Position the Edit Line just before timeline marker 7. Press P to change your cursor to the Pen tool. Press Ctrl, and create two new keyframe handles just before the start of the voiceover clip at the marker. Click and drag the second keyframe handle upward so that the Tool Tip window reveals a value of 5 semitones as opposed to the current –1. (See Figure 17.10.)

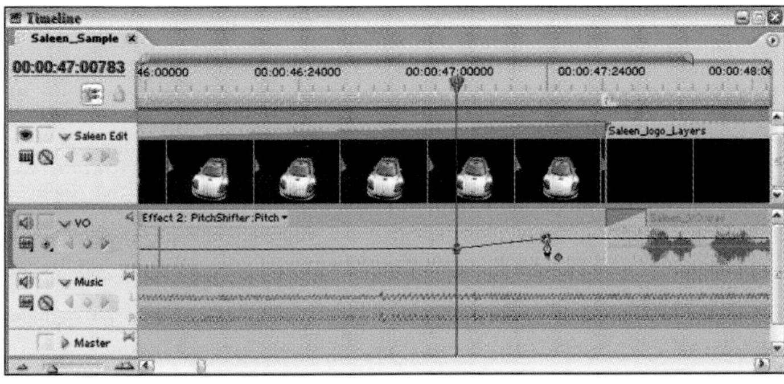

Figure 17.10 After you select the track effect parameter to display, the height positioning of keyframes within the track reflects an increase (upward) or decrease (downward) in the value for the selected parameter. In this case, you change the pitch such that it will increase from –1 semitones to 5 semitones. The voice will sound a bit more cartoonish and mouse-like.

Although the 5 semitones are a bit high pitched, you can use the Pen tool to grab the 5 semitone line and uniformly reduce it down to 1 semitone. Because you have anchored the previous –1 semitone value with the first keyframe, the spatial positioning and height of the second keyframe dictates the speed of increase and point at which the exact new semitone value is reached. As you can see, you have timing control within a track for adjusting the applied track effects.

9. Switch your Track Keyframe Display to Show Track Volume, and using the Pen tool, drag the track volume down somewhere between –3 and –4dB. Switching over to the Audio Mixer, click and drag the hot-text box below the Track Volume fader so that its value is –2.0dB.

   Notice how after you adjusted your track volume in the physical track, the Track Volume fader in the Audio Mixer updated to reflect the same settings and vice-versa.

   This step shows that you can work in different areas of the application to get similar results. If you like working with keyframes, you can do so. If you want a precise value, however, you can literally enter the value to the fader in the mixer.

10. Click off the Solo Horn for your VO track (if it is still active), and listen to your voiceover and music together.

    In general, the voiceover sounds better with the music behind it. This is usually the case, and often you will have to mix the two to find the perfect value, which is exactly what you will do in the next chapter.

Using track effects was certainly a faster and more efficient method for adding effects to a cut-up voiceover file. Using this basic workflow, you can add or reduce track effects to achieve a result that works best for the audio file that you have. Although you dabbled a tiny bit in adjusting track effect keyframes here, the next chapter will dive much deeper into mixing your audio tracks.

Things to Remember

To enhance the sound of a voiceover narration, try using EQ, Reverb, PitchShifter, and, if appropriate, Delay. With each of these effects, you can save and load your own custom presets or try a few of the presets provided as a means of exploring the various possible adjustments to be made. A lot of what goes into making a voiceover file sound better is finding a few detailed effects or a particular pattern of effects to apply. Once you do this a couple of times, you will have a pretty good idea of where to go and what to adjust the next time around.

I hope this lesson gave you a little epiphany regarding audio effects—not only how to organize audio within tracks, but also how to decide when to use a clip effect or a track effect.

The next step in the sound process is to integrate the voiceover track with the music track, which you'll tackle in the next chapter. Finally, Chapter 18 will cover *automation*, the live mixing of the volume levels between the voiceover and music track.

Adobe Audition is far superior and focused in filtering and audio effects processing. You can reference the integration chapter later in this book to understand how much farther you can take your audio files with Audition.

CHAPTER

18

Mixing Your Audio

Creating a sound mix could possibly be the most difficult production task to put down onto paper. Mixing sound is based on nuance, tiny details, and a feeling you get (or don't get) while you are watching pieces of your project come together. Premiere Pro offers two powerful features to help you with this process: submixing and automation.

In this chapter, you will learn how to use submixing to share common effects and arrange sound elements in your sequence. You will also investigate using automation techniques for live mixing and adjusting of the audio in your sequence. Because so much of sound mixing is in the hearing, I encourage you, after reading, to practice and hone your mixing technique with your own material.

Creating Your Mix

To create a good sound mix with some layered effects, you are going to add a few sound effects files into the overall mix with the voiceover and music you have been working on in the last few chapters.

1. Open the Submix_Start.prproj from the APPST Lesson Files/Chapter 18 folder. Organize your workspace so that you have a good amount of space for a tall timeline and a wide Audio Mixer.

It's important to allocate enough space for the Audio Mixer and the audio track portion of your timeline. In my default workspace for this project, I collapsed one video and two audio tracks that weren't going to be manipulated during the lesson.

2. Choose File>Import, browse to APPST Lesson Files/Chapter 18/SFX, and click Import Folder. Once the folder is imported, double-click and open the SFX subfolder in the Project window. For each clip in the Project window, choose Clip>Audio Options>Audio Gain, then click Normalize in the resulting dialog. Adjust the Gain value hot-text field based on these recommendations:

   Chains: **6.6dB**
   Clank: **0.9dB**
   Drill: **12.2dB**
   Electric Motor: **7.7dB**
   Fairy Dust: **8.0dB**
   WaterCrash: **–1.2dB**

   First, you import the desired files, then you get their individual Gain levels up so that you have a nice strong signal. The Chains file has one instance where the audio exceeds 0dB, so Premiere recommends you normalize it at 0dB. Because you are not going to use a section that is too loud, you will still want to bring up the Gain to 6.6dB.

3. Toggle the Track Output off for both the VO track and the Music track. Drag and drop the WaterCrash.mp3 file into the gray area below the audio tracks to create a new track for the clip. Position it at timeline marker 1 (see Figure 18.1). Right-click in the new track's header area, and rename the track FX Smoke.

   By turning off the other audio tracks, you can focus solely on the new effect's sound and position. I previously identified this clip position, but as you proceed, you can take liberties shifting it to better suit the edit.

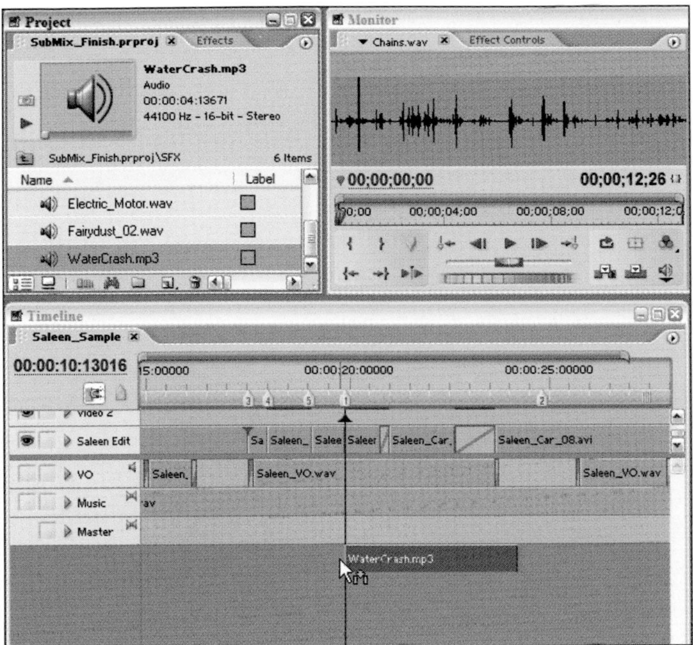

Figure 18.1 With Snapping turned on in the timeline, you can drag an added file into the timeline and still position it exactly where you want it to be placed when the new track is created. The upward snapping arrow indicates snapping to the marker position.

4. Add an effect to the WaterCrash clip. Open the Effects window, and from the Audio Effects/Stereo folder, drag and drop the EQ effect onto the WaterCrash.mp3 instance in the timeline. Select the clip instance in the timeline, and open the Effect Controls window. From the Custom Setup for the EQ effect listing, enter the following values:

   Low: **52Hz, –20dB, Cut Off**
   Mid1: **91Hz, 10.2dB**
   Mid2: **775Hz, 6.8dB**
   Mid3: **918Hz, 7.2dB**
   High: **3801Hz, –20dB, Cut Off**
   Output: **–6.6dB**

   You will be doing track mixing later, but at times like this a clip effect does the job quickly and easily. The sound of the water crashing needs to resemble a sound that emphasizes the car passing through the cloud of smoke. Although this is slightly exaggerated by the water sound, it does the trick once the EQ has been tweaked.

The goal was to take a sound that resembles the idea being explored and then manipulate it with a filter or two, to get it sounding more appropriate. With the effect, the WaterCrash clip no longer sounds like water, taking on a new personality instead. Setting the Output level in the EQ Custom Setup reduces the overall volume of the clip instance.

5. Drag and drop the Fairydust_2.wav file into a new track at timeline marker 2. Rename the new track FX FAIRY. Right-click on the Fairydust_2 instance in the timeline, and select Speed/Duration. Slow down the speed of the clip to 80%, and click Maintain Pitch. With the Fairydust_2 clip instance in the timeline selected, choose Clip>Audio Options>Render and Replace (see Figure 18.2).

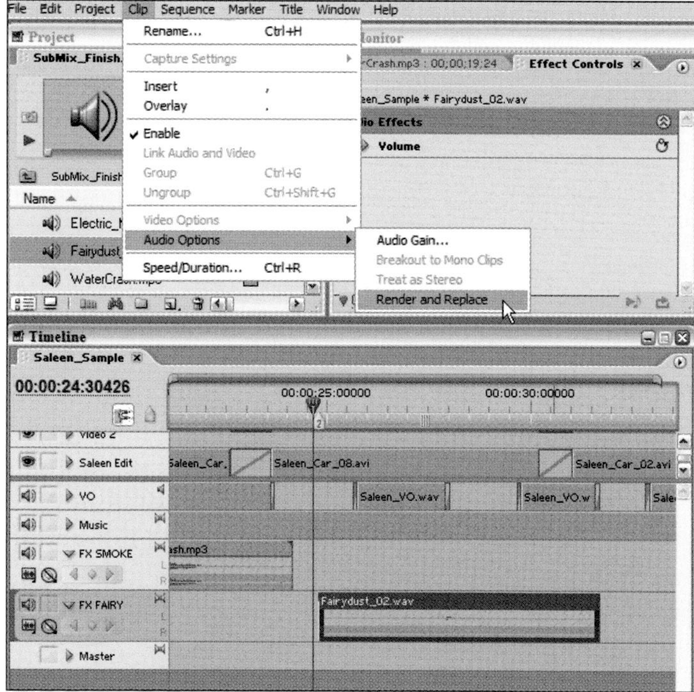

Figure 18.2 With the Fairydust_2 clip selected after the speed change has been applied, choosing Render and Replace processes the speed change of the clip and creates a new clip instance that does not require processing.

Because you are going to apply an effect on top of the Fairydust_2 clip after you have adjusted its speed, every time you want to play back and preview with effect adjustments you will have to render the audio. By selecting to render and replace the speed-changed Fairydust_2 clip, you are creating a new clip instance that is processed already at the adjusted speed. This means that applying and adjusting effects to the replaced clip will be played back in real time.

6. Apply the stereo Delay effect to the new replaced FX FAIRY_Fairydust_02.wav in the timeline. Use the default setting, adjusting only the Feedback to 50%. Delays should be 1.00 seconds and Mix 50%.

   Adding the Delay effect further enhances and alters the fairy dust effect. While it seems a bit too loud and a bit obtuse, you will shape its panning and fading in the next lesson.

7. Right-click in the track header area, and add four mono tracks and one mono submix track. Rename the mono tracks FX Shop1, FX Shop2, FX Shop3, FX Shop4, and rename the submix track Sub Shop. Next, follow Table 18.1 to add the clips into the proper positions. Your sequence should look similar to Figure 18.3.

Table 18.1: Mono Tracks to Add

Track	File	In Point	Out Point	Timeline Marker
FX Shop1	Chains.wav	02;17	03;09	3
FX Shop2	Electric_Motor.wav	04;00	04;28	4
FX Shop3	Clank.wav	01;02	02;04	4
FX Shop4	Drill.wav	04;13	05;08	5

Although you may take a few liberties with shifting the In and Out points and placement of the subclips, it is first important to label all the tracks in your audio mix so that when you work in the Audio Mixer you can easily distinguish between the tracks. Because there are four sound effects placed in close proximity, it is wise to keep each sound effect on a different track, not only

Sending tracks to a submix track is a very easy way of ganging together clips with effects and controlling them with one easy slider.

for spatial position, but in terms of mixing flexibility. By having each effect on its own track, you have greater control and fewer adjustments if each track accommodates one specific effect type. This is obviously the case with the voiceover file cut up on its own track.

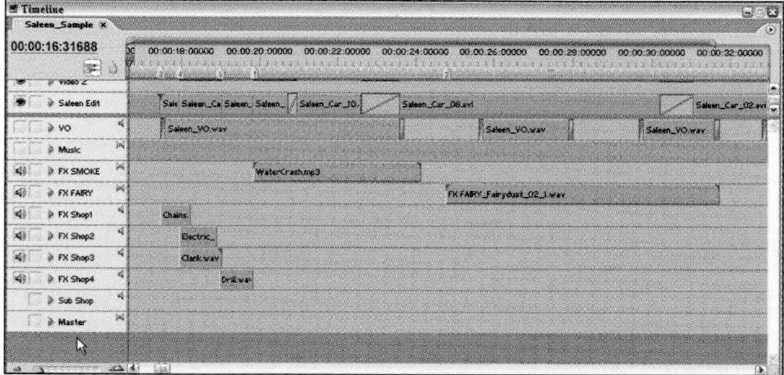

Figure 18.3 Both the Fairydust and WaterCrash clips display the purple clip effect line, which means effects are applied to those individual clips. At the marker positions 3, 4, and 5 the FX Shop tracks clearly display the stacked effects that make up some ambient shop noises.

8. Expand your Audio Mixer so that you can see the Effects/Sends area. In each of the four new Mono FX tracks, click in the top blank drop-down menu in the Sends area and select Sub Shop from the list that appears. (See Figure 18.4.)

   This step redirects the processing of the new Mono tracks through the submix track. Now if you apply one effect to the Sub Shop Submix track, all the Mono FX tracks will be processed with that effect.

9. In the Sub Shop submix track, apply the track-based Reverb effect. Right-click on the Reverb effect listing, and select the Church preset. In each of the FX Shop tracks, set the Send Volume value to 0.00dB (see Figure 18.5).

Figure 18.4 The bottom half of the Effects and Sends area of the Audio Mixer allows you to send the signal from one track to be processed by another track. Using the drop-down menu, you can send to a submix track (such as Sub Shop, chosen here) or your Master track, or you can create a new submix track.

Figure 18.5 Increasing or decreasing the Send Volume affects the overall level of the track volume being processed by the submix track. If you want one track to be a bit lower in the mix, for example, reduce the Send Volume. Keep in mind, the default Send Volume is always oodB when you first send a track to a submix track; you must manually adjust each track to your desired volume.

Here's a tip on how to quickly preview and loop specific sections of your timeline with the Audio Mixer: Create two timeline In and Out points, one at the beginning of the area you want to preview and one at the end. (Position the Edit Line, and press I to set the In point, then reposition and press O for an Out point.) Click the Loop button in the Audio Mixer, and then click Play. Because you have a defined timeline In/Out instance, looping will occur within those boundaries. When tweaking track effects in their effect interface, you can get live looping playback of your adjustments when you are in this mode.

Because all four FX Shop tracks are being sent to the submix Sub Shop track, they will be processed with whatever effects are applied to the Sub Shop track. The volume level of the individual tracks will be based on the value of the Send Volume in each of the sent tracks. To give the sound effects a good spatial sound (as if they occurred in a large bright car shop), you can select the Church preset. Once all of the tracks are being sent with a solid volume level, the group of clips takes on a new shape in the mix.

10. For each FX Shop track, make the following volume adjustment below each of the associated volume faders:

FX Shop1: **–3.7dB**
FX Shop2: **–3.4dB**
FX Shop3: **0.6dB**
FX Shop4: **–2.8dB**

Then, in each of the FX Shop tracks, change their Output controls from Master to Sub Shop. (See Figure 18.6.)

Figure 18.6 The VU meter lines reflect the ceiling of the audio being played back. As you can see, the audio is under the 0dB mark in the master mixer and the color is in the safe green range. (Yellow indicates safe but loud audio, but red is too loud.) Assigning the Output controls for each of the Shop effect tracks to the submix track allows you to control their panning properties and overall volume with one slider and one panning knob instead of four sliders and four panning knobs.

By first adjusting the track volume for each track you are insuring that each track does not exceed or come too close to the 0dB ceiling. By assigning the Stem controls to the Sub Shop you are enabling the submix track to control the volume and panning properties of all four Shop tracks at once. After you get your individual clips to the exact dB level that you want, you can then easily begin mixing all of the individual tracks with one volume slider and panning knob. The technical term for this is *stemming*.

11. Toggle on the Track Output Audio for your VO and Music tracks. Play back the sequence to get a sense of the volume adjustments that will be necessary in the next lesson.

By sending certain tracks to be processed and controlled by the submix track, you have the ability to position and place clips on top of each other while still allowing the clips to have the same effect processing. An additional advantage is that within the submix paradigm, you can still boost or tweak each sent track individually to further add depth to the mix. If you want to increase the volume of an individual element, you can adjust the gain of that individual track with its Volume slider. If you want to add an EQ effect to one of the tracks, you can apply that effect within the track. The resulting audio from the track-plus-effect will be processed by whatever track it is sent to with whatever effects are applied to the track.

A good way to think about Sends and submixing is to visualize an effects track that does not contain clips or media, just effects. Using a Send, you can send a physical track with content to use the effects of the submix track. Depending on how much volume from the physical track you send, the sound of the track will either be low and subtle or loud and obvious.

Automation and Live Mixing

Another option for mixing your sequence is using the four Automation modes—Read, Write, Touch, and Latch—which save your live track adjustments as keyframes into the track being adjusted.

Every volume adjustment, left or right pan, or effect change, such as expanding the pre-delay of a Reverb, can be seen visually in the form of assigned keyframes in the adjusted track. Instead of using the Pen tool and manipulating keyframe handles, you can use Automation to adjust the knobs, sliders, and interface controls live, while translating those adjustments into track-based keyframes.

In this lesson, you will create a track volume adjustment using Read Automation mode, then investigate the other modes. You will also make a panning adjustment using the Pen tool, then create another using automation.

1. Open the Automation_Start.prproj file from the APPST Lesson Files/Chapter 18 folder.

   All of the files for this project are in the primary Chapter 18 folder and its SFX sub-folder.

2. Expand the VO track and turn on the track display for Show Track Volume. In the full Audio Mixer, solo the VO track by pressing the Solo Horn above its Volume fader. Click Play to play back the timeline while you monitor the sound level registering in the master VU meter. Using the Volume slider in the VO track, raise and lower the volume to get the master VU meter registering a peak halfway between 0dB and –6dB. The level that I found to be about right is –1.7dB for the VO track volume, set the volume fader to –1.7dB. Notice that the VO track is in Read Automation mode.

   Get a feel for making live adjustments and knowing where to look to see how much effect your adjustment is making to the overall sound level. Because your VO track is in *Read mode*, the live adjustments you are making will not be keyframed and assigned, instead the final resting point of the Volume fader position will update the display of the Track Volume in the sequence's VO track. It's a good idea to monitor the sound work in this section with headphones or good speakers.

3. Collapse the VO track, and press the Lock icon in the track header to lock it. Expand the Music track. Set the Track Display to Show Track Volume. With the

Timeline window active and no clips selected, press the Home key to get the Edit Line back to the head of the sequence. Click the Solo Horn for the Music track so that you can hear both the Music and VO only. Set the Automation mode of the Music track to Touch. Position the Volume Fader at –oodB, then click Play. While the timeline plays back, click and drag the Volume fader for the music up and down between –oodB and 0dB. Play with the volume so that you can hear it fading in and out. Once you get near the end of the disclaimer, stop pressing the mouse and let playback come to a stop. (See Figure 18.7.)

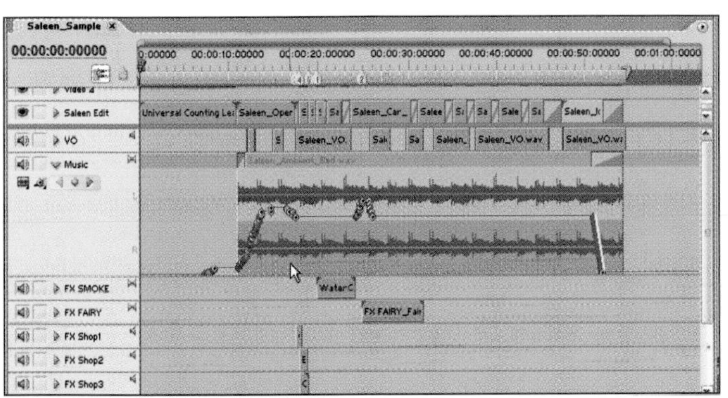

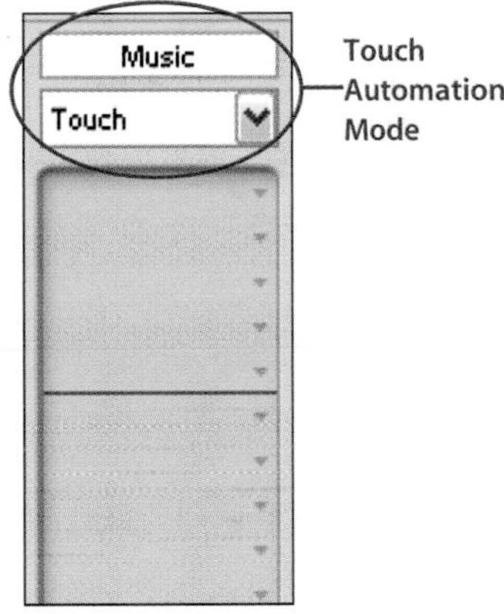

Figure 18.7 After you play back your timeline and adjust a track in either Write, Touch, or Latch Automation mode, you will have keyframes written into the automated track that reflect the live adjustments you made. Here, the volume keyframes reflect the fading up, leveling off for awhile, and fading out at the end. Although these keyframes could be assigned manually with the Pen tool, automation assigns them automatically.

Touch Automation writes keyframes on the parameters that you are adjusting while you playback. Unique to *Touch mode* is that whenever you click off your mouse and release the parameter you were adjusting, the parameter automatically goes back to its start position. In this case, you started the volume at –oodB, so when you released the mouse during the disclaimer it dropped from the current volume position down to –oodB. This is called *Automatch.* When you release a knob or fader in Touch mode it automatically shifts back to its start position. You can dictate the amount of time it takes to

Automatch in the Edit>Preferences>Audio>Automatch Time field.

4. Press the Home key, and then click Play to play back the timeline with your new fade adjustment. Watch the Music Volume fader in the Audio Mixer. Once the timeline finishes playing back, press Ctrl+Z to undo the volume adjustments.

   If you watch the Music track's Volume fader in the Audio Mixer, you will see its position automatically update and move in accordance with the adjustments you defined in the previous step. Notice how your Volume fader now *automatically* adjusts over the course of playing back, and you can see the moving fader live during play back. In Automation mode, you essentially can create a mixing road map for the mixer to follow automatically.

5. Switch the Automation mode to Latch in the Audio Mixer for the Music track. Set the Volume fader to –oodB. Press the Home key to get to the head of your sequence, and click Play in the Audio Mixer. While the timeline plays, adjust the Volume fader so that you fade your music up as the music comes in. After you have faded it up, you can release the mouse. When the Disclaimer comes on, slowly click and drag the Volume fader back down to –oodB.

   Latch mode is different from Touch mode in that when you click off the fader, it will latch onto its current position until you click and drag to modify it again. If you don't have a steady hand, but want to fade up your volume, keep it level, then fade it back down, Latch mode is your best bet.

6. Using either Latch or Touch mode with the Music track, automate the volume level so that the music has a good presence beneath the voiceover. Once you are finished, lock the Music track and then click the Solo Horn for the FX Smoke track, so you can hear all three tracks together.

7. Position your Edit Line at approximately 17;00000 in the timeline, and press the I key. Move the Edit Line to 24;37000, and press the O key. Leave the FX Smoke track in Read mode. Click Loop in the Audio Mixer, and then click Play. While the In/Out instance plays, adjust the volume level for the FX Smoke track so that the sound effect is present, but not overwhelming (see Figure 18.8). The volume I found to be perfect was –3.0dB.

TIP

As you remember from Chapter 16, "Editing Your Voiceover," you can use the Pen tool to group/marquee select and move groups or sections of keyframes. If you have automated a fade that starts too late, you can use the Pen tool to grab the group of keyframes that make up the fade and drag them left so that they start earlier.

Figure 18.8 This instance is looping while the audio level is being adjusted. Read mode allows for the setting of a static track level, whereas Latch and Touch mode write keyframes for any adjustment made. If you were in Write mode, every time you looped, Premiere would update the keyframes with the adjusted values. In Latch and Touch, once you release the mouse button and looping re-engages, you will not overwrite the previous assigned automation.

This is a perfect example of how well looping supports the tweaking and finding of adjustment levels. Because Read mode just updates the volume on a static level, you can keep sliding the fader up and down to find the sweet spot.

8. Collapse and lock the FX Smoke track. Click the Solo button for the FX Fairy track. Expand the FX Fairy track in the timeline. Create a new In point at 24;00000

and an Out point at 32;46000. Using the same technique of adjusting the volume in Read mode, find the right volume level for the Fairy effect. I used –5.1 dB. Instead of automating a fade for the end of the clip, add the Audio Transition Constant Power at the tail of the clip to fade it out. I gave the transition a duration of 1 second.

After setting the proper volume for this track, you quickly slapped on a transition to accommodate a quick one second fade out. Now the Fairy FX audio plays and then fades out seamlessly.

9. In the track header for the FX Fairy track, change the Keyframe Display to Show Track Keyframes. From the Track drop-down menu, select to show the keyframes for Panning>Balance (see Figure 18.9). In the Audio Mixer, twist the Panning knob for the FX Fairy track all the way to the right. Using Latch or Touch mode, click Play and slowly pan the knob from its full right position to a full left position while the Fairy Dust effect plays.

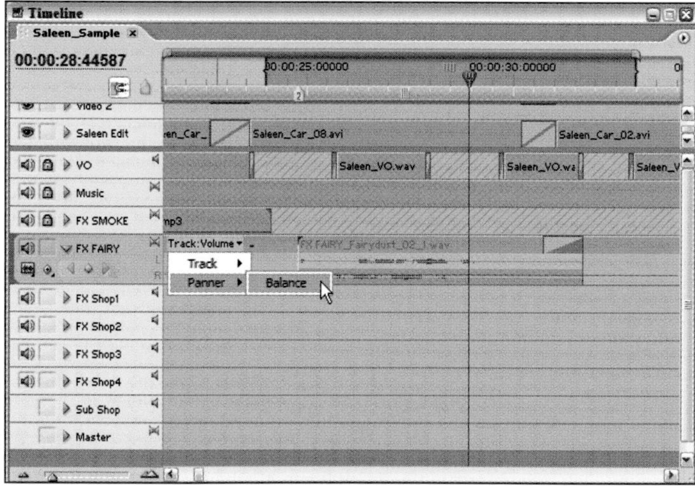

Figure 18.9 Depending on the display mode, if there are multiple keyframe parameters to view, you will be able to pick them from the selected track's drop-down menu.

If your mixer is still in Loop mode, you can let the loop re-engage to hear your adjustment. If you don't like it, then wait for the loop to re-engage again and click and adjust the pan for another pass.

What you have done here is adjusted the panning of the sound so that it "moves" with the image of the car on the screen.

10. Collapse and lock the FX Fairy track. Solo each of the FX Shop tracks. Using this lesson's technique, set timeline In and Out points around the Shop Sound effects and adjust their overall volume by sliding the Volume fader in the Sub Shop submix track. If you want their volume level to have a static adjustment, use Read mode. To keyframe or have an automated volume fade, use either Latch or Touch mode.

    Because you are stemming the output of each track to the fade and pan controls of the submix Sub Shop track, you don't have to adjust each track's Volume fader individually. In the last lesson, you preset each level within the group, and you now can bring the entire group up or down accordingly for your final mix. I used –11.4dB for the Sub Shop track's Volume fader level.

After you make all of these adjustments, clear your timeline In and Out points, turn up your speakers, and listen to what you have mixed. If you want to see my finished result, open the Automation_Finish.prproj file from the APPST Lesson Files/Chapter 18 folder. If you encounter any stuttering playback, be sure to press Enter to render any necessary preview files.

Write Mode Automation and Converting to Surround Sound

Write mode is a bit different from Read, Latch, and Touch. In *Write mode*, every parameter is written during automation, even parameters you are not adjusting. Because it can be very destructive to your mix, I don't recommend using Write mode, unless you are familiar with its behavior. A visual illustration and explanation can much more effectively explain Write mode's behavior than words on a page. I, therefore, encourage you to consult Set 3 of my "Total Training for Adobe Premiere Pro 1.5" series for a more visual reference to what is covered here. The lessons are dedicated to audio mixing, automation, and converting a stereo mix into a 5.1 surround sound mix.

Things to Remember

Although exact sound effects serve an exact purpose, there may be instances where one sound can substitute for another. In the case of the wave crashing file, a few adjustments in the EQ reshaped that file into something that worked perfectly for the car appearing through the mist.

Another important technique is the choice of creating and naming individual tracks to be used for specific clips. To have better control over your final sound mix, use individual unique tracks for specific sound effects and sound elements. In a narrative film scene, every character would have a dedicated dialog track and foley track. The ambient noise would be on its own track, as would natural noises and specific sound effects. By isolating specific noises on their own tracks, you are creating a much easier final mix process. As revealed through the last two chapters, track-based mixing and effects are much easier to use and manipulate than clip effects. This becomes especially true with 5.1 surround sound mixing and having all your unique sounds on their own tracks, enabling a quick and painless conversion from mono or stereo into 5.1 surround.

In terms of mixing, get in the habit of using the VU meters to gauge the safe range of the audio levels you are playing back. You don't want to see anything registering red either in the individual track meters or the Master VU meters. While automation is very cool to use, sometimes the Pen tool easily does the trick to apply a simple fade or pan adjustment. You can also ensure that no damage comes to any mixed track, by locking it after you have finished work on it.

Advanced Editing Techniques

CHAPTER

19

Advanced Timeline Editing Techniques

To explore how Premiere Pro's timeline editing tools behave in a real-world environment, you will edit a typically photographed film scene in this chapter. Specifically, you will piece together an initial edit, inserting and overlaying footage from my short film, *Bleach.* As I did for the original scene, you will then clean up and fine-tune the rough cut using the Ripple Edit, Rolling Edit, Slip, Slide, and Trim tools.

Your editing should always be motivated by the story and ideas being articulated in the scene you are cutting. The story and its various scenes are captured with numerous shots from multiple angles, each with a different emphasis or focus. The available shots for this example scene are a straightforward mix of actor shots (medium shots) and point-of-view shots (of the objects or people at which the actor is looking, commonly referred to as POVs). You will have the flexibility, for instance, to cut from a shot of the character looking at something to a shot of what the character sees. Whether you show the character or the character's point of view (POV) will be dictated by the scene's rhythm and tempo. Finding that rhythm is the essence of editing.

Assembling Your Edit

When initially editing a scene, first identify the shots and takes that you like most. When I am working with an editor on a film, for example, I make sure I know all of my footage and material inside and out. I identify which shots convey the right emotion and have the actors' best performances. My initial rough cut of a scene is a loose edit based on the original script that was photographed. I cut from one shot to the next feeling out the story

For more information on Bleach, go to **www.bleachyoursoul.com** or **www.formikafilms.com**.

being told and the performances given. In many cases, the rough cut of Scene B, for example, may need to be overhauled once I see it in juxtaposition to Scenes A, C, and D.

To successfully reflect a scene's mood and tempo, you need to understand not only what's happening in the scene, but also how it fits into the film's greater story. In the example scene from *Bleach*, the main character, Fulton (played by Adam Scott), has already gone into his friend Zach's house to deliver some stereo equipment and get some money. While his girlfriend Laura (played by Katrina Holden Bronson) impatiently waits for him to emerge, Fulton's recent sobriety is challenged by an uncanny offer from his crazed friend. With a promise to clean the stains from his life, Fulton returns to Laura with the money and a surprising new perspective.

The scene that you are editing is supposed to reveal through the eyes of Fulton that the world he sees is not the same as the world others see him in. Cutting from his "cleaned up" point of view to the dirty environment that he occupies, you will establish a distinct difference between the real world and the bleached world of Fulton's mind.

The Rough Cut

The steps in this section will guide you through an initial rough edit, explaining a specific order for placing all of the scene's clips. You will use the Ctrl modifier key to toggle between inserting and overlaying the clips. In the next lesson, you will trim and fine-tune the edits to make the scene flow better. As you become more comfortable in Premiere Pro, you will probably combine these three processes into a single workflow. For now, however, concentrate on the rough cut only.

1. Open Edit_Start.prproj in the APPST Lesson Files/ Chapter 19 folder. Watch all the source material in the Video Files folder to familiarize yourself with the entire content of each clip.

   I can't emphasize enough that you need a good understanding of the scene's flow. After linking all of the material to the project (all associated clips are in the

Chapter 19 folder), open and look at 13E_TK01. This clip is a master shot that shows the entire scene from beginning to end. Watching it, you can see the basic structure of the scene and perhaps start sensing when you want to cut and to which shot. Looking at the rest of the shots, you can see the options and choices you have; these are your shot selections.

2. Open clip 13E_TK02. Mark an In point at 12;00 and an Out point at 22;00. Add the clip to the head of the timeline using an Overlay edit (drag and drop it into position). Open clip 13G_TK02, mark the In point at 10;00, and the Out point at 18;00. With Snapping turned on, drop the second clip so it snaps to the end of the first. Open clip 18E_TK01, and mark In and Out points at 1;18 and 3;20, respectively. Overlay this clip after the second shot. Open clip 13G_TK01, mark an In at 11;07 and an Out at 27;13, then drag the clip into position at the end of 18E_TK01. Your edit should look like Figure 19.1.

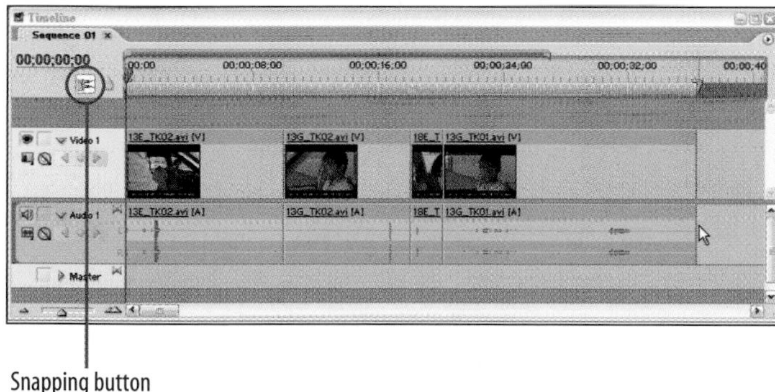

Figure 19.1 A first edit is not meant to flow perfectly from shot to shot. Once assembled, the shots and moments can be refined in a second pass. Here, the first four shots are placed back to back so that none of the material is edited out. Notice the Snap icon indicates Snapping is active (at top).

Clip 13E_TK02 is the master shot that establishes the scene's setting: Fulton sits down in the car and looks to his left at Laura, who appears as she is in reality.

Continuity is important in editing; you do not want to surprise or jar the audience when cutting from one shot to another. Cutting on the movement in one shot to the movement in another shot is a way of making the editing feel more fluid. This technique is referred to as *continuity editing*.
Note that this lesson's edit is purposefully loose without exact continuity, so that I can demonstrate techniques to fix and clean an edit in the next lesson.

The key to this scene is Fulton's altered point-of-view, so you cut from the master, establishing shot to a medium shot of Fulton turning his head to look at Laura. This edit works because the medium shot (13G_TK02) is of the character who is the focus of the scene and it continues the action of the scene. With the cut to the medium shot, you now see Fulton looking directly at Laura. He is clearly perplexed and responding to what he sees. His reaction in this medium shot motivates the next cut, which reveals his exact POV of Laura (18E_TK01).

To continue on with the scene and show him looking in the back seat, you edited in an alternate shot, 13G_TK01, in which he looks at Laura and then into the back seat.

3. Continue adding the necessary shots into the edit: Open clip PU_01 in the Source Monitor window, mark an In point at 1;03 and an Out point at 8;03, and drop the clip at the end of 13G_TK01 (the fourth clip). Open a second instance of clip 13G_TK02 in the Source Monitor window. (Do not double-click and open the instance already in the timeline.) Mark In and Out points at 29;13 and 42;26, respectively. Drop this down as the sixth clip. Finally, open a new instance of clip 13E_TK01, in the source side and mark an In at 47;17 and an Out at 51;13, and add it to the timeline as the seventh clip.

   From the fourth clip (13G_TK01) set in step 2, you cut to a POV shot of Fulton looking at himself in the side mirror (PU_01). You then cut back to the medium shot (13G_TK02), this time using a different take that has better eye contact and action that matches the previous shot. You finish the scene back on the master shot of the two characters seated in the car (13E_TK01).

4. So far, you have created a rough, shot-to-shot template and you still have to insert a few more shots (clips) into and between shots already in the edit. The same way you cut to the POV on Laura (18E_TK01) after the second shot, you now need to edit in the other POV

shots in their proper places. Table 19.1 lists markers for placing the remaining shots, as well as their In and Out points. To switch from the default Overlay mode, use the Ctrl key modifier while dragging and dropping for Insert edits. Your complete sequence should look like Figure 19.2.

To follow the table, consider the example of inserting the second POV shot: Give 18A_TK02 an In point at 9;03 and an Out point at 10;21 in the Source window. Overlay it in the timeline at marker 1 by holding the Ctrl key while dragging it to the timeline. Holding the Ctrl key modifier switches from the default Insert edit to an Overlay edit.

Table 19.1: Shots and Edit Points

Shot	In Point	Out Point	Timeline Marker	Edit Type
18C_TK01	2;22	4;15	0	Overlay
18A_TK02	9;03	10;21	1	Insert
18E_TK01	4;15	10;25	2	Insert

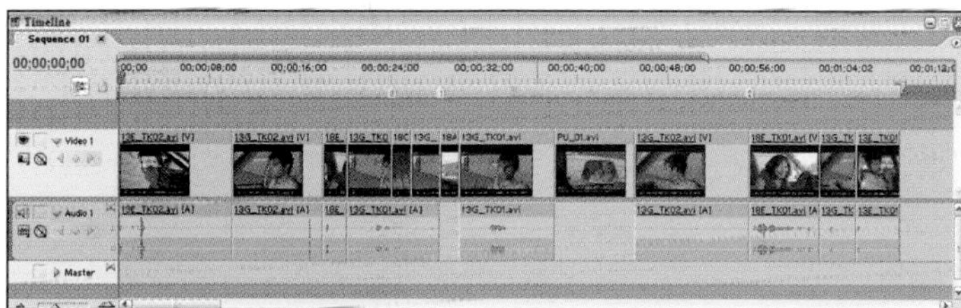

Figure 19.2 With all the shots in place, your rough cut is an exact copy of my initial cut of the scene for *Bleach*.

You overlay the first shot on top of existing material because you do not want to shift the placement or ripple any of the surrounding media. By overlaying this shot you are still relying on the pacing of the shot you covered up; however, you alter the pacing with the next two Insert edits. For the other two shots, you use Insert edits to add the material to the timeline and ripple the existing material right from the cut point, so that nothing is overwritten. Because the response time by the actor looking at each of the things in the car is not that long, you are extending the moment by inserting the shot.

With all the pieces in place, pause for a moment and consider the scene you've made. Keep in mind the toggling of the edit modes (Insert/Overlay) that you used to piece the scene together, the snapping of clips and the rhythm or flow of the scene.

Reflect and Reorganize

Play back the entire sequence to get a feel for the flow of the scene and the pacing of the cuts. I sat with this exact order of shots for this scene for a couple of months while we worked on the sound mix. Eventually, I decided it needed reworking, and re-edited the scene with a few very minor, but very effective changes. The next few steps reflect this re-editing and re-placement process. Using the Ctrl key to Extract and Insert edit, you will make a few simple changes to adjust and get the proper placement for the shots.

1. Right-click on clip 18A_TK02 at timeline marker 1, and select Ripple Delete.

   Because this clip was inserted into at timeline marker 1, ripple deleting the clip instance brings the separated shots back together by rippling the timeline media left to fill the gap that 18A occupied. If you scrub over the cut and observe the burned in timecode in the frame, you will see it flow continuously. (See Figure 19.3.)

   I removed this shot primarily because it seemed a bit overkill and unnecessary. I had already established that what he sees in the car is different from what is really in the car, so the shot of the dashboard was not as important as the shot of him looking around. In this case, more attention is given to Fulton and his realization that the car is different than at the beginning of the film.

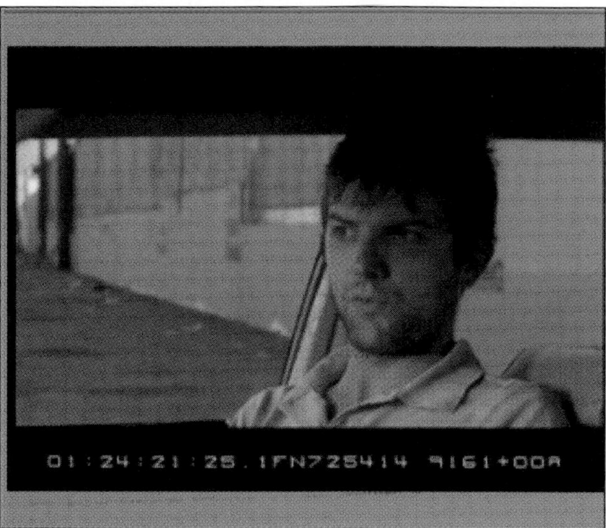

Figure 19.3 The numbers at the bottom of the video frame reflect timecode (left) and keycode (right). The timecode value is a window burn from the master Digibeta tapes onto which *Bleach* was transferred from film. The keycode numbers reflect the literal frame counting format from the original film negative. Using timecode and keycode you can find out where the shot originates on your video master and where the shot originates on your film negative.

2. Holding down the Ctrl key, grab (extract) the third clip in the sequence (18E_TK01), which is the first shot of Laura. Continuing to hold down the Ctrl key, insert the shot right before the second shot of Laura (18E_TK01) near timeline marker 2 (see Figure 19.4). Holding down the Ctrl key before selecting a clip puts the pointer tool in Extract mode.

3. Using the same technique, select the second, longer clip of Laura (18E_TK01, right next to the newly inserted shot), extract it, and then insert it at the cut that the previously moved clip occupied. (See Figure 19.5.)

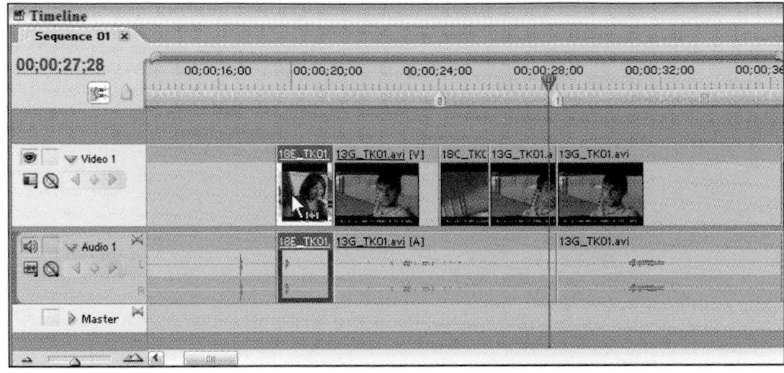

Figures 19.4 Holding down the Ctrl key before you grab the first shot puts the Selection tool into Extract mode (top). Extract ripple deletes the selected clip from its current position when you drag it. Continuing to hold down Ctrl enables you to drop the shot at a new timeline position as an Insert edit (bottom).

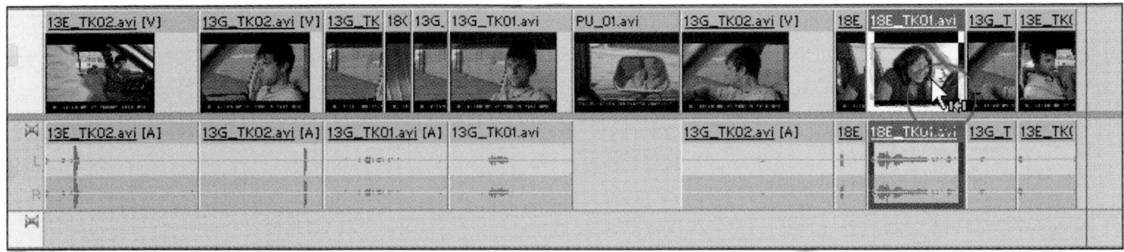

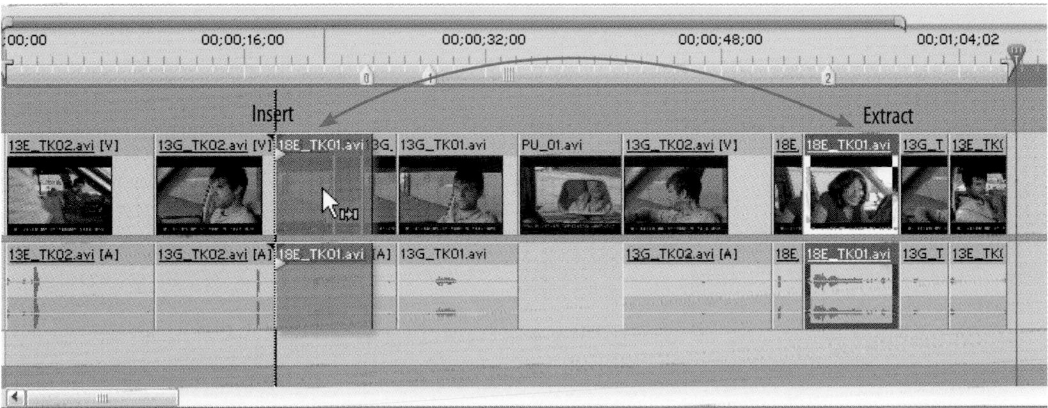

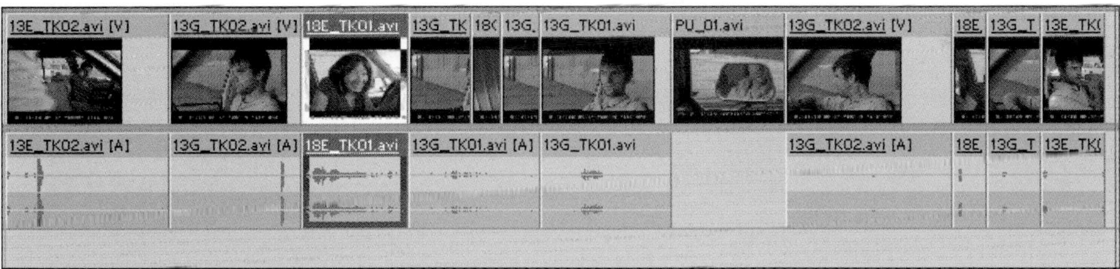

Figure 19.5 The Extract tool icon appears next to the curser as you Ctrl-grab the clip to move it (top). Continuing to hold the Ctrl key down, you are then in an Insert edit mode (middle). Dropping the clip into the same position that the former clip (from Figure 19.4) occupied produces the revised cut (bottom).

In two moves, you swapped both shots and quickly changed the order of the edit. Swapping the two shots of Laura distinctly changed the rhythm and tone of the edit. In the former version, Fulton sat down and slowly took in the altered environment culminating in the dialog from Laura. In the adjusted version, Fulton is immediately engaged by Laura and her dialog. This image contradicts her portrayal throughout the film and the rest of the scene serves as a reassurance that the world Fulton perceives is truly different. In the last POV shot of Laura, she smiles at him in a manner affirming the fantasy. Two shots later, the audience sees a stark contrast to the POV images from Fulton's eyes and ends on a master shot of the two in the car.

With the adjustments made here, the sequence now reflects the final version of the film. Although the looseness of the edit still needs trimming, the basic scene structure is intact. The lesson establishes a workflow of finding the In and Out points in your source material, and then one by one editing the clips together. Using the Ctrl key, you can use the Insert, Overlay, Lift, and Extract edit functions to quickly add, replace, and shuffle the material of your edit. Now it's time to play with the tool box!

Trimming and Modifying Your Edit

Now that you have the pieces and structure in place, you need to clean up the edit and adjust the timing to fit the flow of the scene. In this lesson, you will establish continuity of action between shots to create a better rhythm.

1. Open the project Trim_Start.prproj from the APPST Lesson Files/Chapter 19 folder. Notice that I renamed the timeline instances of each clip so it is easier to identify the clips and cut points that you need to adjust. You will start at the beginning of the timeline and work your way right.
2. With Video 1 and Audio 1 targeted in the Timeline window, press Ctrl+T to open the Trim window. Press Page Down to advance the Edit Line to the cut between shots 1 and 2 (see Figure 19.6). Place the cursor within the frame boundary for the outgoing shot on the left, click and drag to the left, trimming off –3;19 of material; the new Out point for the clip should be 18;12. (See Figure 19.7.) Using the Jog wheel below the incoming shot, jog to the right to move the In point to 11;19, which is a shift of +1;19. (See Figure 19.8.) Press Play Edit to preview the trim that you just made.

Figure 19.6 The Trim window enables you to perform Ripple and Rolling edits on the cut points between material in your sequence. The left frame shows the outgoing shot, and the right frame, the incoming. Like the Ripple Edit tool in the timeline, the Trim window enables you to grab the edge of a clip and drag it, but with greater clarity because of the frame size and detailed window feedback.

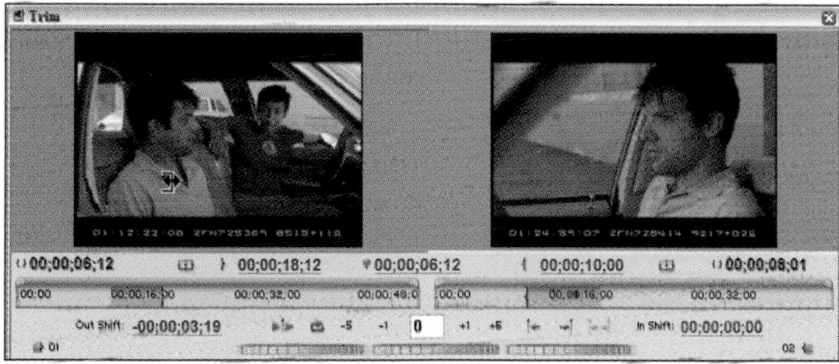

Figure 19.7 Holding the cursor inside the frame boundary puts the Trim window into Ripple Edit mode. Clicking and dragging left inside the outgoing frame reduces the duration of the clip being trimmed. All the material to the right of the cut will be shifted left so that no gaps are created between the shots. Notice the out shift is –3;19, meaning 3 seconds and 19 frames have been trimmed off and the new Out point of the subclip in the timeline is 18;12.

Figure 19.8 The same way clicking and dragging within the frame enables you to perform a Ripple edit, jogging the wheel below either the outgoing or incoming shot achieves the same effect. Dragging to the right on the incoming shot trims off material from the head of the subclip in the timeline. Jogging the wheel to the left adds material to the head of the incoming shot. In both cases, a Ripple edit occurs either replacing the space created or pushing material right to make room for added content.

The Trim window is essentially a glorified Ripple and Rolling Edit tool that enables you to clearly see the frame you are trimming. Additionally, you have corresponding visual data about the entire range of the clip you are trimming, the number of frames you are trimming off or adding, and so forth. Although using the Ripple Edit tool in the timeline reveals a two-up display in the Program Monitor, the Trim window can be as large asyou like with a lot more detailed information.
A few rules about the Trim window: To trim linked audio and video tracks together, both audio and video tracks need to be targeted in the track header area. To trim just video, target only the video track you want to trim. To trim just audio, target only the audio track you want to trim. If you happen to move the Edit Line off of a cut point in your sequence, the Trim window automatically closes.

To cut from shot 1 to shot 2 without the edit feeling too abrupt, you want to cut in the middle of action or movement that hopefully exists in both shots. You trimmed off the tail of the first shot and the head of the second shot so that as the character's head turns left you cut from one shot to the other. When you have a rough cut sketched out, it's very simple and easy to open the Trim window, trim the Out and In points at each cut, preview the adjustments, then move on to the next cut.

3. With the Trim window still open on the cut between shots 1 and 2, enter 9 in the text box above the center jog wheel. Press Enter, then press Play Edit to preview the adjustment. (See Figure 19.9.) Close the Trim window.

Figure 19.9 Holding the cursor in the gray space between the two frames reveals the Rolling Edit tool. If dragged to the right, the Rolling Edit tool synchronously extends the Out point of the outgoing shot and retracts the In point of the incoming shot. Dragging left extends the In point of the incoming shot and retracts the Out point of the outgoing shot. In both cases, there is no shifting or rippling of the timeline, only the edit rolls to reveal a new cut point between the shots. The center jog wheel is the one for rolling the edit. The empty text box above the center jog is for entering a rolling edit value (frames or samples).

Entering a value of 9 rolls the edit forward nine frames, so that the Out point from the outgoing shot is extended by nine frames and the In point from the incoming shot is reduced by the same number. Positive values roll the edit right, and negative values roll the edit left. In this trim adjustment, you rolled the cut point between shots 1 and 2 to a spot a bit more in the middle of the action for a more subtle cut.

4. Back in the timeline, make sure Snapping is turned on and move the Edit Line to 11;00. Hold down the Ctrl key to toggle the Selection tool to the Ripple Edit tool. Click and drag from the tail of clip 2 to the left, snapping the edit to the Edit Line. (See Figure 19.10.) Move the Edit Line to 13;19, and holding down the CTRL key, ripple the In point of clip 3 so that it snaps to the Edit Line.

Figure 19.10 Holding down the Ctrl key turns the Selection tool into the Ripple Edit tool. Using the Edit Line as a guide to the new cut point's location, you can drag and snap the Out point of shot 2 to the Edit Line. When using the Ripple Edit tool, notice how the Program Monitor reveals the small two-up displays of the frame being trimmed (left) and the first frame of the next shot (right).

Using the Ctrl key, rippling an edit point in the timeline is quite quick and simple. First, scrub through the clip in the timeline to find the moment at which you want the cut to occur, then use the Ripple Edit tool to trim off the tail or head of the clip that needs trimming. Because of timeline snapping, you can have exact precision as to where the cut occurs.

For this cut, Fulton looks at Laura and you will notice that his eyes size her up. After his eyes go from down to up is a perfect moment to cut. Although this cuts in the middle of Laura's dialog, you will use the Rolling Edit tool to roll the audio cut separate from the video cut.

The Alt key can be very useful when you want to trim and adjust the audio or video separately from each other. This can happen when you have an abrupt sound just before the end of a shot that is being used in your edit. Instead of trimming both the audio and video, you can try rolling the audio back a bit from the next shot in the sequence to cover the unwanted sound. In this case, you would want to be sure you had the extra material from the incoming shot to extend.

5. Press the N key to switch the cursor to the Rolling Edit tool. Hold down the Alt key, and click in Audio Track 01 at the cut point of clips 2 and 3. Click and roll the cut left –3;02 (see Figure 19.11). Press the V key to switch back to the Selection tool, move the edit before the clip 2, and play back the adjustment you made.

Figure 19.11 Holding down the Alt key allows you to temporarily break the link between the audio and video to select and adjust only one or the other. In this case, you are rolling only the audio edit between the two shots. When using the Rolling Edit tool, notice how the Program Monitor gives you feedback as to the exact value of the edit. Rolling to the left would reveal a negative value, and rolling right, positive. For this example, you needed to roll back –3 seconds and 2 frames.

This edit is called a *J cut*, because the audio portion of shot 3 occurs before the video portion. An *L cut* is when the video cuts out before the audio cuts out. (These names are based on the shape of the letters, of course.)

The audio of Laura's voice further helps to motivate the cut to the POV of Fulton. Even though Adam's performance was not in response to Katrina speaking dialog, it looks as if he is quite taken by what he is seeing and hearing. I think it works very well.

6. Move the Edit Line to 14;04, and ripple the Out point of clip 3 to the Edit Line. Move the Edit Line to 15;07, and ripple the In point of clip 4 to the Edit Line. Move the Edit Line to 16;13, and press the U key to switch from the Selection tool to the Slide tool. Click and drag clip 5 left so that the left edge of the clip snaps to the Edit Line. (See Figure 19.12.)

Figure 19.12 The Slide tool is essentially a double-sided tool for rolling edits. With it, you can select a clip and slide it left or right while retaining the clip's In and Out points. As you slide it left, you trim off frames from the adjacent clip to the left and reveal frames of the adjacent clip on the right. Notice how the four-up display in the Monitor window shows the In and Out frames from the selected clip smaller at the top. On the bottom, the large frames reveal the new Out point from the clip to its left and the new In point from the clip to its right.

After adjusting the edit point for better timing between clips 3 and 4, you used the Slide tool to slide the entire clip 5 to the left. Now when Fulton looks to the back seat, the scene cuts directly to his POV shot. The Slide tool moves the entire selected clip, not just one edge. The Slide tool works very well when you have a clip that exists in the timeline for an exact duration and you want to adjust its position. The Slip tool, preserves the position of the selected clip, but modifies the content of the clip.

7. Press Y on your keyboard to select the Slip tool. Click and drag just slightly to the left for –10 frames. (See Figure 19.13.) Release the mouse button, and play the section you just adjusted.

The easiest way to visualize what the Slip tool does is to mark an In and Out point in a clip in the Source Monitor. The In and Out points have a specific duration, say one second. If you click in the center of the In/Out point markers in the Source Monitor, you can drag that In/Out duration to cover a different portion of the source clip. The Slip tool essentially does the same thing. As you drag left, you are slipping the content of the subclip left, revealing a later portion of the clip. If you drag right, you slip the clip material to the right, revealing an earlier portion of the clip.

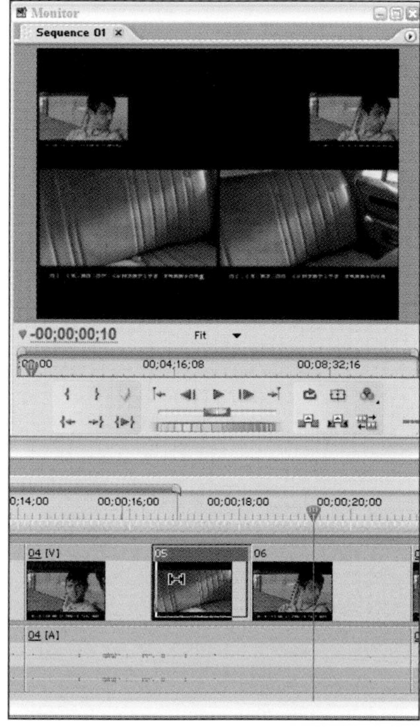

Figure 19.13 The Slip tool takes the defined edges of your edited clip in the timeline and slips the material left or right to reveal new content using the same duration and clip position. The four-up display shows the adjacent Out frame and In frame from left to right on the top with the updated slipped to In point on the bottom left and the slipped to Out point on the bottom right. The counter value in the bottom right corner displays the frame adjustment. Negative values equal slips left, and positive values slips right.

For this step, you slipped the clip material to reveal a different portion of the shot. The adjustment you made of –10 frames slipped the material up so that the beginning and end of clip 5 was ten frames later than before. This fit the head movements of the characters you were cutting from and to, much better. The Slip tool is very effective for updating the contents of a subclip without disturbing the overall duration of the shot or affecting the surrounding media.

The Slide tool modifies the physical position of the clips being adjusted, but the Slip tool modifies just the material inside of the clip at its current timeline position.

8. Using the tools and techniques illustrated in this lesson, continue editing the sequence so that you have continuity of action and better timing for the rest of the cuts between the rest of the shots.

   To see what I came up with, open the Trim_Finished.prproj file from the APPST Lesson Files/Chapter 19 folder.

Despite the number of steps in this lesson, there are a great number of details and techniques to be extracted. Using the Ctrl key to quickly toggle from your Selection tool to the Ripple Edit tool is very intuitive. Using the Alt key to adjust only the audio or only the video of linked clips is another gem not to be forgotten. If at the end of the day, you find yourself struggling with the editing tools behavior, then you can use the Trim window to help with a solid visual reference for Ripple and Rolling edits.

Once you are comfortable with the editing tools and the ideas introduced in this chapter, I encourage you to stray from the lesson and explore a different version of the scene, trying to edit it in a slightly different manner with different timing or shot selection.

Things to Remember

At the end of the day, your content rules, so the more preplanning and preparation you do before you shoot, the more secure the editing process can be. If you are unsure how to handle a scene, then take some risks and try some new ideas and shoot more than you need. Editing should serve the story, but should also reveal new ideas and new structure that may not have been anticipated before shooting. I see editing as possibly the single most important part of the filmmaking or videography process. In editing many problems can be solved and new options can be explored.

Once you understand which tool serves which purpose, editing efficiency simply becomes a matter of necessity. First you preview your material, then begin assembling it in a linear fashion. Using the Insert, Overlay, Extract, and Lift functions you can add or change the order. Moving a step further, use the timeline tools to make any small or large adjustment in relation to the accuracy and details of your edit. If you want a bit more control and details from your editing modifications, target specific tracks and use the Trim window to adjust the cut point further.

When working with multiple scenes or different sections of a large project, I always find that the first and most important step is to roughly put together one scene in its own sequence. Instead of adding other scenes to the same sequence, make each new scene its own sequence with another sequence that is used to tie all the scenes together. The nesting of individual scenes reduces clutter and enables you to control and better manage the individual pieces of the project. For this workflow, I also make individual bins for each scene, with each holding the scene sequence and sub-bins containing all the footage for the scene.

In the next chapter, you will get your hands on some bona fide multi-cam material and edit a live three-camera shoot into a seamless sequence of shots.

CHAPTER

20

Multi-Cam Editing: Live Shoot

So far, you've learned how to cut together your scenes with all the timeline editing tools. Now it's time to up the ante: In this chapter and the next, you will get your hands on some bona-fide multiple-camera shoot material. Here, you will focus on editing a live three-camera shoot, and in Chapter 21, "Multi-Cam Editing: Music Videos," you will use similar techniques to edit two music videos.

A successful multi-cam project requires attention to all phases of the production. How you set up your shoot, for example, affects your ability to synchronize the material from multiple cameras in post-production. This chapter will provide guidelines to ensure success. During editing in Premiere Pro, you will re-assign the timecode for the individual shots to create a sychronized timecode value to which all your shots will adhere. You also will learn how to create individual sequences for each shot so that you can apply different effects to the various shots with greater ease.

Establishing Sync

The goal of a multiple-camera shoot is to record the same action from a variety of angles, getting different shots of the same moment. In a professional environment, such as a newsroom, multi-cam shoots are live and edited as they are shot. The command center of a multi-cam shoot is the *control room*, which houses a small screen for every camera and a *switcher*. The *live director* sits in the control room and calls out which cameras to cut to. The *live editors* then execute the edits on the switcher. Because the shoot is live, the cameras are automatically synchronized.

Slates have long been used on film sets. Because film cameras do not record audio, a device was needed to create an audible and visual sync point for a film shoot. Enter the clapping slate. At the beginning of each shot, the camera and audio crews visually film and audibly record the slate closing. To synchronize the audio and visual after the fact, the film editor marries the film frame in which the slate closes to the audio frame in which the slate makes its clapping sound. Once these two are properly combined, the material after the slate is in sync.

Without the luxury of multiple monitors and a live switcher, syncing your cameras requires a little more ingenuity: You need to first establish a clear *sync point* at which all of the cameras record the same thing before they record their individual shots. That sync point will be identified as the same moment in physical time, even though it exists at different tape positions in each camera that is recording.

An excellent way to establish a sync point for multiple camera shoots in which all cameras can record the same image is to clap a *slate*, like they do in the movies. This is the technique I used for recording the multi-cam footage for this chapter. First, you point every camera at the slate and start each camera recording. Clap the slate closed, and then continue recording with each camera until you have recorded *all* of the necessary material. After you establish the sync point, do *not* stop any of the cameras in mid-shoot. If a camera does happen to stop, you must establish an intermediate sync point for that camera to be synchronized with the other cameras. Recording a new slate mark with the stopped camera and one of the already synchronized cameras, which continue recording, is usually enough.

If you are setting up a multi-cam shoot where some cameras are recording separate angles and cannot all identify the same image, you can use a camera flash bulb instead of a slate to create a sync point. Recording a slate relies on seeing the hinged clapper come together or hearing the clap; however a flash bulb creates a short instantaneous burst of light that covers a very broad area. Because the moment of the actual flash can be isolated as a single frame of video, the frame of the flash occurring can be your sync point. After you recorded the sync point, keep all cameras recording until the shots are complete.

Editing a Multi-Cam Shoot

Editing multiple-camera material comes down to one simple adjustment: timecode. Because each camera has a different tape with different timecode, the resulting footage does not have a shared timecode value. (See Figure 20.1.) Regardless of the timecode values of the individual clips, however, all the cameras do share one instance: the sync point. You will use this to create the shared timecode value and synchronize the shots.

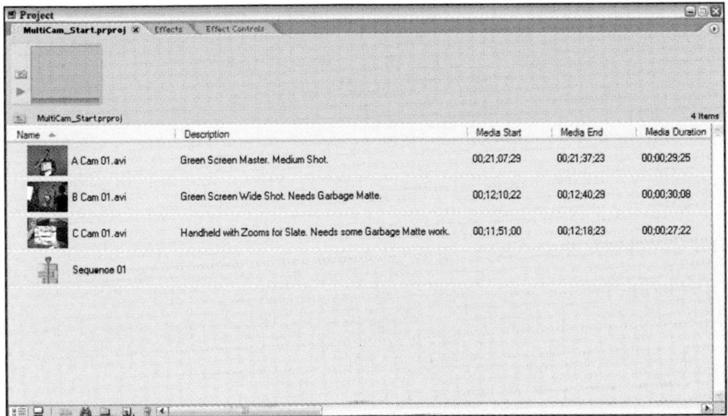

Figure 20.1 Each shot name is preceded by a letter—A, B, or C—which allows you to immediately distinguish between the shots. Notice how the Media Start timecode value for each shot is different. Using Premiere Pro's Timecode feature, you will alter the timecode of each clip so that it is based on the same value.

1. Open MultiCam_Start.prproj from the APPST Lesson Files/Chapter 20 folder. Open A Cam 01.avi in the Source Monitor, and scrub to the frame where the slate completely claps together: 21;10;25. Add an unnumbered marker to this frame (press * on the keyboard's numeric pad or the Unnumbered Marker button in the Source Monitor). With the clip still active in the Source Monitor, choose File>Timecode. In the Timecode dialog, enter the value 1;00;00;00 for Timecode, click Set at Current Frame, and click OK. (See Figure 20.2.)

   This step isolates the sync point at which the slate claps together and then reassigns the timecode of the clip so that you have not only a marker for the sync frame, but also a unique timecode value. You will next reassign the timecode at the same slate-clapping moment in the other shots to establish timecode synchronization between the separate shots.

If you accidentally assign the incorrect timecode, you can immediately open the Timecode dialog and click Revert to switch the timecode back to its previous state. Revert is good for only one step: If you change the timecode of a clip twice, you can never get back to its original timecode value.

If you end up going too far and cannot get your original timecode back, you can always recapture the clip instance from your tape.

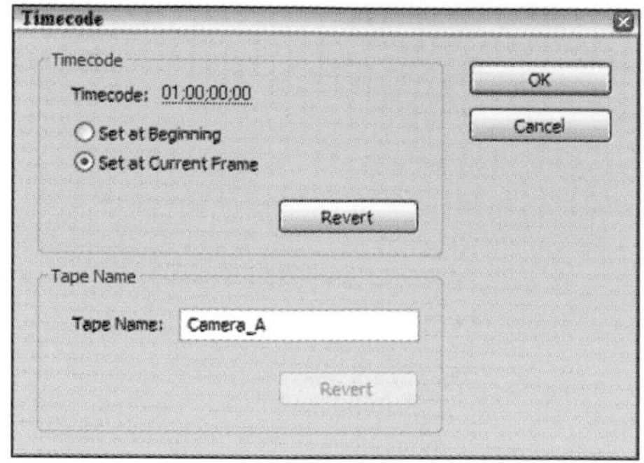

Figure 20.2 The Timecode dialog allows you to re-assign the timecode value for the selected clip at either the beginning of the clip or at the current frame. To establish a unique timecode value for the exact frame at which the slate claps, assign the timecode at the current frame to be the unique value of 1;00;00;00.

2. Open B Cam 01.avi in the Source Monitor, and scrub to the slate-clapping frame (12;13;10). Add an unnumbered marker to this frame, and then reassign the timecode to be 1;00;00;00 at the current frame.

   After identifying the exact same sync point, you gave it the same timecode value as the first clip. Now two clips share the same timecode value for the exact same moment in time: when the slate first comes together.

3. Open C Cam 01.avi in the Source Monitor, scrub to frame 11;52;09, add an unnumbered marker to the frame, and then reassign the timecode value of the current frame to be 1;00;00;00.

   Having added markers to all three clips and assigned a shared timecode value at the sync point, you are just about ready to begin editing.

   In theory, the hard work is done and the shots are synchronized. Because you reassigned the timecode values to be equal for the same moment in time, 1;00;05;00 will be the exact same moment in time for each of the different shots.

4. Select Sequence Zero Point from the wing menu of the open sequence, set Sequence Zero Point to 59;50;00 in the resulting dialog (see Figure 20.3).

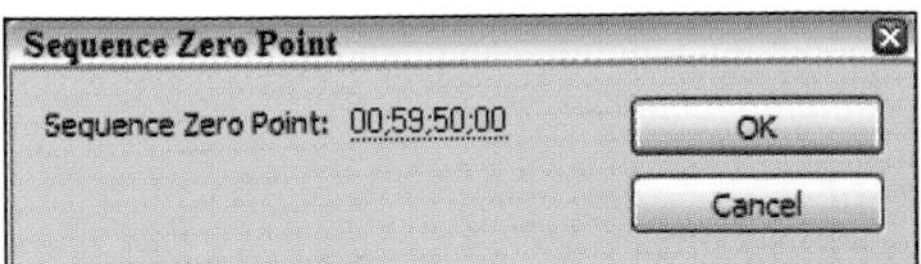

Figure 20.3 As you can reassign the timecode of a source clip, you also can reassign the timecode value used as your counter. Choose Sequence Zero Point from the open sequence's wing menu to reassign your sequence's timecode to match your synchronized timecode. The value 59;50;00 provides for 10 seconds of extra space before the timecode 1;00;00;00 occurs.

In this step, you reassign the sequence timecode to include 1;00;00;00. This timebase matches the value to which the source clips are synchronized. Once your sequence contains the same timecode value as your source material, you can easily drop in and edit each shot, placing the shot at the exact same timecode value that you want the edit to occur.

Remember, all of your shots are synchronized because they have the same timecode value for the same moment in time. 1;00;05;10 in A Cam 01 reflects a different angle of the same moment in time from B Cam 01, which also has the timecode 1;00;05;10. As long as you edit your source clips into the timeline so that their timecode matches that of the sequence timecode, everything will remain in sync.

5. Drop the A Cam 01 clip into the Video 1 track. Move the Edit Line to the timeline position 1;00;00;00. Click and drag A Cam 01 to the right so that the clip marker snaps to the Edit Line. (See Figure 20.4.)

   Placing a clip marker at the same frame as the sync mark (1;00;00;00) creates both a snapping point and a visual timeline reference to the established sync point. Positioning the timeline Edit Line at 1;00;00;00 and snapping the clip marker to the newly positioned Edit Line shifts the clip so that the sync point of the source clip now rests in the timeline at the same timecode value as the source material.

   If you were to navigate through the sequence with the repositioned source clip, the timecode value displayed for the sequence would match that of the timecode for the source clip.

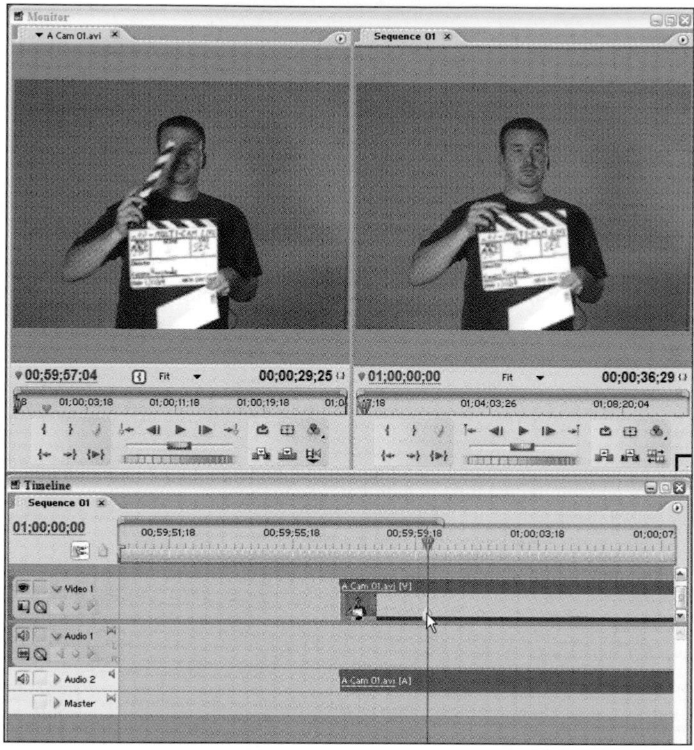

Figure 20.4 After you create a visual marker for the sync point of the source material, you can drag the source clip to a new position so that the sequence timecode matches the source clip timecode. Using this technique, you can drop in shots based on their start timecode position.

TIP

If you want to play your multi-cam shots side by side or at reduced sizes all at once, you can easily stack the clips on top of each other in different video tracks, lining up and snapping the markers' positions to the same frame. Once the shots are lined up, it's up to you to pick the frame sizes and frame positions in which you want the clips to play. (See Figure 20.5.)

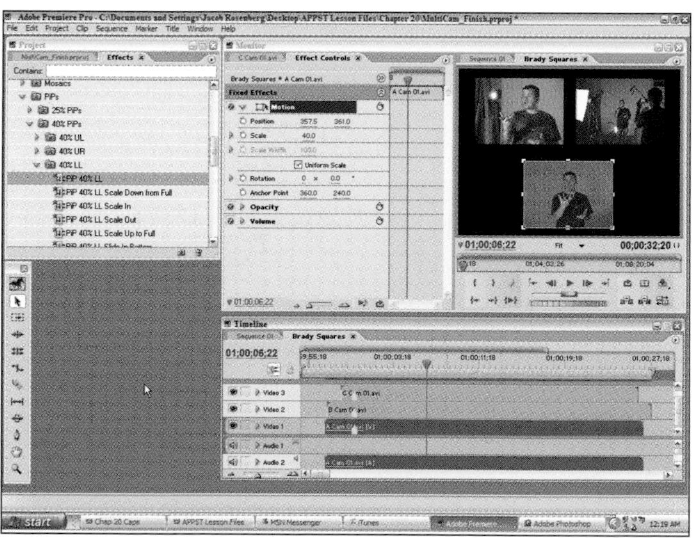

Figure 20.5 In the timeline, you can see the clips stacked one on top of the other with each of their clip markers aligned. With the scale of each clip reduced and its position modified, you can easily position each frame in a different region so that you can see all shots at the same time.

6. Reposition the timeline Edit Line to 1;00;11;05. Here the script references to the second camera, so cut to that shot. Open B Cam 01 in the Source Monitor, and navigate to 1;00;11;05. Mark an In point for the source clip at the current timecode position and an Out point at 1;00;13;09. Click the Toggle Take Audio and Video button so that you are taking video only from the source clip. Drag and drop B Cam 01 into Video 1 so that the head of the clip snaps to the Edit Line. (See Figure 20.6.) Play the sequence to see how it looks.

Figure 20.6 The lynch pin for this technique is that the timecode for the source clip's In point matches the timecode value of the timeline position where the clip is being placed. To ensure you maintain the sync you created, all edits should occur at the same timeline timecode value as they occur in the clip. Here, the source clip has an In point of 1;00;11;05 and the Edit Line rests at the same value in the sequence.

The key to this multi-cam editing technique is that once you establish sync between the separate shots, the timecode for the In point of the clip being added to the timeline must match the timecode of the timeline position to which it is being added.

7. Position the timeline Edit Line at 1;00;12;12, where the third camera is mentioned. Open C Cam 01 in the Source Monitor, and mark an In point in the source clip at 1;00;12;12. Mark an Out point at 1;00;15;14, and toggle to Take Video Only. Drag and drop the source clip into the timeline so that the In point snaps to the Edit Line position. Play the sequence.

Because you established a unified sync point (1;00;00;00), as long as you position the edits at the same timecode in the timeline as they occur in the source material you remain in sync. Of course, dragging or shifting a clip's timeline position once the clip is edited moves the clip out of sync. If you want to update or adjust an edited clip's In or Out point, you must use the Rolling Edit tool.

8. Press the + key to zoom into your sequence to get more details out of the next adjustment. Select the Rolling Edit tool, and roll the edit point between A Cam 01 and B Cam 01 a few seconds to the left (see Figure 20.7). Using the same tool, roll the edit point between C Cam 01 and A Cam 01 a few seconds to the right. Play the timeline to view your results. Roll the edits.

Figure 20.7 With the Rolling Edit tool, the timeline positioning of the clips being rolled stays the same, only the exact cut point from clip A to B is updated. The new cut point is previewed in the Program Monitor's two-up display.

As reiterated in the last chapter, the Rolling Edit tool preserves the timeline positions of both adjoining clips and updates only the cut point between them. The Rolling Edit tool is the tool of choice for adjusting and modifying the editing positions of multi-cam material. Additionally, as you roll the edits you can very clearly see the synchronization between the shots in the Program Monitor's two-up display.

Now that you have the fundamentals of the multi-cam editing technique, practice the technique by adding different clip instances at different points in time and rolling the edit points between the shots. To see what I came up with, open the MultiCam_Finish.prproj from the APPST Lesson Files/Chapter 20 folder.

Nesting and Multi-Cam Editing

Now that you have the groundwork for the principal technique of multi-cam editing, I want to incorporate *nesting* as a means of simplifying the process of adding effects to individual shots. Imagine you have 20 cuts between these three shots and you want one of the source clips to be black and white. You would have to drop or copy the Black & White effect to each of the individual clip instances to which you wanted the effect applied. Considering that in later chapters you will white balance each shot and key out the green screen background, it's in your best interest to find an easier structure for accommodating the adding of effects to multi-cam edits. Here is a solution.

1. Open MultiCam_Nest_Start.prproj from the APPST Lesson Files/Chapter 20 folder. Create three new sequences, and name each sequence for each of the separate camera shots, as in A Sequence, B Sequence, and C Sequence. In each of the new sequences, adjust the Sequence Zero Point so that it starts at 59;55;00.

   Because you identified the sync point in the previous lesson, all you have to do is create an individual sequence for each of the shots that make up your multi-cam edit and then reassign the timecode of the sequences to match the synchronized value of the source clips.

2. Open A Sequence, and add the entire A Cam 01 source clip to the timeline. Zoom in to the timeline, and position the Edit Line at 1;00;00;00. Drag A Cam 01 so that the clip marker snaps to the Edit Line position.

   Having assigned the synchronized timecode value of 1;00;00;00 to A Sequence, you moved the A Cam 01 clip to put the sync marker for the source clip at the 1;00;00;00 frame in the timeline. Now the timecode of the source clip matches the timecode of the timeline.

3. Repeat step 2 for B Sequence with B Cam 01 and for C Sequence with C Cam 01.

   By repositioning all the source clips to a timeline position that matches your synchronized timecode value, each sequence accurately simulates the timecode of its source material. Because a sequence can be opened in the Source Monitor and edited the same way as a clip, you will re-edit the multi-cam material with the A, B, and C Sequences as opposed to their individual source clips.

4. Create a fourth sequence, and name it MultiCam Nest. Reassign the Sequence Start timecode to 59;55;00.

   Step 4 of this lesson matches Step 4 of the previous lesson. With a synchronized timecode value for the multi-cam material established, that timecode value becomes the timebase for the sequence into which you are editing the multi-cam material.

5. Hold down the Ctrl key and double-click on the A Sequence icon in the Project window. Mark an In point at 1;00;00;00. Position the MultiCam Nest sequence Edit Line to the same timecode value (1;00;00;00). Drag and drop the A Sequence from the Source Monitor down into the timeline so that its In point snaps to the Edit Line position. (See Figure 20.8.)

Figure 20.8 Notice how A Sequence is loaded into the Source Monitor and appears exactly as a normal clip would. Assigning an In point at 1;00;00;00 in the source sequence and moving the Edit Line to the same timecode position in the timeline allows you to add the source sequence to the timeline, preserving synchronization to the timecode value. Notice how both the Source Monitor and the Program Monitor display the same frame for the same timecode value.

Once again, step 5 uses a sequence to mirror step 5 from the previous lesson.

6. Hold the Ctrl key down, and double-click the B Sequence icon from the Project window. Toggle to Take Video Only. Mark an In point at 1;00;03;02 and an Out point at 1;00;06;19. Add this In/Out instance to the MultiCam Nest sequence at the timecode position 1;00;03;02. Make a second In/Out instance from 1;00;10;27 to 1;00;11;24, and add the instance to the sequence timecode position 1;00;10;27. Make a third and final In/Out instance from 1;00;19;22 to 1;00;21;13, adding it to the sequence at timecode position 1;00;19;22.

Because you are using the audio from A Sequence as your master audio track, you turned off the audio of B Sequence so you were only editing with its video. By isolating specific In/Out instances and using the default Overlay method of adding the source material to the timeline, you are overlaying the existing sequence content with different, but still synchronized material.

7. Hold the Ctrl key down, double-click the C Sequence icon from the Project window, and toggle to Take Video Only. As shown in Table 20.1, mark the In/Out instances in the source sequence and add them to the corresponding sequence timecode position.

Table 20.1: Timecode for In/Out Instances

Source In	Source Out	Sequence In
1;00;02;20	1;00;03;18	1;00;02;20
1;00;11;25	1;00;14;01	1;00;11;25
1;00;22;15	1;00;24;11	1;00;22;15

Positioning these three instances, you quickly cut together a short edit of the three-camera shoot using nested sequences. Now take a look at how easy it is to apply an effect to an entire camera shot, despite the fact that each shot is cut into a number of pieces.

8. Click on the Sequence tab for B Sequence to bring it to the front of the Timeline window. Click on your Effects tab, and locate the Black & White effect from the Video Effects>Image Control folder. Drag and drop the Black & White effect onto the B Cam 01 clip in the B Sequence timeline. Click on the MultiCam Nest sequence tab in the Timeline window, and play the sequence to view your results. (See Figure 20.9.)

Figure 20.9 Applying the Black & White effect to the source clip in B Sequence, notice that any instance of the nested B Sequence yields the result of the applied effect. Here you can see that the B Sequence in the Source Monitor displays properly with the Black & White effect, as does its edited instances in the Multi-Cam Nest sequence.

Using this workflow and sequence structure, it is very easy to add effects and titles to each of the separate shots that make up your edit, without having to apply the effects multiple times to short clip instances.

From this point, you can springboard to either Chapter 23, "Using the Color Corrector," to see how to properly white balance and correct the individual shots that make up the multi-cam edit or to Chapter 26, "Green/ Blue Screen Keying and After Effects," to see how to use the green screen effects to key out the background of each shot.

For this lesson, you essentially performed the same steps as you did in the previous one, except you nested each individual shot into its own sequence. The advantage of this workflow is that any applied effect to the nested shots updates all the instances to which the nested sequence is edited. Instead of applying the Color Corrector effect to three different instances of the same source clip, you can now apply the Color Corrector effect to the original nested clip in its host sequence and see that result in every instance where that sequence was edited.

Things to Remember

The biggest thing to remember about multi-cam work is to not stop any of your cameras until the shoot is complete. If a camera is stopped, you will lose your referenced sync point and have to create a new one for that camera. If you do stop one of your cameras, you must break the resulting clip up and create a second sync point for the new clip that starts after the initial sync point.

The workflow for shooting is:

1. Start all cameras recording.
2. Use a slate or flash bulb to establish a sync point.
3. Continue recording material.
4. When all the material is complete, stop each camera.

The workflow for editing is:

1. Identify the sync point in each shot.
2. Add an unnumbered marker to the sync point to create a visual timeline reference for the sync point that can be snapped to and from.
3. Reassign the timecode value of the sync point to be a unique number that is shared by all of the clips from your shoot for that same frame of time.
4. Establish the same timecode value for the host editing sequence as the synchronized source material.

5. Edit all source clips to the timeline using the default Overlay method with the In point of the source clip matching the In point in the sequence where the source clip is added.
6. Adjust and modify edit points between shots in sequence using the Rolling Edit tool.

A few multi-cam plug-ins and third-party applications can enable you to view all of your multi-cam shots simultaneously and pick between the ones you want to cut to and when. You can find the plug-in listing in Appendix E, "Third-Party Plug-Ins and 24P Support."

This technique differs from the others by building a foundation and workflow that is applicable not only to live multi-cam shoots, but also to the editing of music videos. You will get to explore the multi-cam technique for editing music videos in the next chapter.

CHAPTER

21

Multi-Cam Editing: Music Videos

Synchronizing and editing music videos can be quite simple, especially when you think of them as multiple camera shoots. The only difference is that in a music video, you shoot the same song 30 times from 30 different angles, instead of shooting with 30 cameras at once.

Building on the previous chapter's timecode technique, this chapter will show you how to create a unique timecode value to synchronize both the audio soundtrack and each of the unique video clips of your music video project. Marrying the audio and video in the timeline, you will use Premiere Pro's Match Frame function to identify and assign the exact sync point.

In the chapter's first lesson, you will use the "eye match" method of synchronization, which involves matching a moment in the video clip when you can clearly make out the word the singer is singing with the same word being sung in the soundtrack. The second lesson matches moments with the assistance of a Smart Slate for a sound reference. A Smart Slate is basically a slate with a digital readout that displays the timecode value of the tape being used for playback during the music video.

Whichever method you choose for your own projects, by the end of the chapter you will be able to easily and efficiently create sync between your audio and video.

The clips for this lesson are four shots from a music video I made way back in 1998. It was a "guerilla" shoot, and I ended up editing, directing, and photographing the video for the rap group Hieroglyphics. The song is called "You Never Knew," and the concept was to make a very down home, organic, and intimate video of the band having fun in Hawaii.
My producer, Alex Tse, wore a DAT player in a backpack with speakers attached to the shoulder straps. Because we were filming in the midst of normal city life, in a number of different locations, we didn't have the luxury to set up elaborate shots and record 20 times. We got to the location, figured out the shots, then played back the DAT while I filmed the band lip-synching to the music. As soon as we got the shot, we quickly moved to the next spot before we disturbed anyone. . . or got arrested.

The Eye Match Technique

On a music video set, the band performing needs music to lip sync to while the film/video is recording, so that when you edit it together the band appears to be really singing the song. The most basic method of synchronizing video and audio is the eye match technique: Through sharp-eyed observation, you clearly identify a word being sung on the video clip and match that moment with the instant the same word is sung in the soundtrack. This technique is well-suited for low budget music videos shot on film and for synchronizing a videotaped performance with the original song. For the technique to work, you need to make sure that the sound being played back while you were filming the video is the same sound being used to synchronize the video in the editing room.

For the sake of this lesson, assume that you have captured the audio for your song off of a DAT (digital audio tape) or copied it from a CD. You also captured four clips that reflect four different shots. You, of course, know the lyrics to the song inside and out. This last point is very important for the eye match technique, because you need to be able to follow the song without having to consult the music and be able to clearly identify moments where specific words that are easy to spot are being sung. Believe me, after spending a day shooting one song, you will never forget the words!

1. Open the file YNK_Start from the APPST Lesson Files/Chapter 21 folder.

   You will find the source material for this project in the APPST Lesson Files/Chapter 21/YNK Media folder.

2. Open the Audio folder in the Project window, and open the YNK_Audio.wav file in the Source Monitor. Navigate to 25;25, and set an unnumbered marker at that frame. Drag the clip down to the beginning of the timeline on Audio 1 track. From the timeline wing menu, select Sequence Zero Point and enter the value 1;00;00;00. Lock the Audio track.

With the audio file open, the first step in the eye match technique is to identify a moment where the word being spoken has an obvious *plosive*. In this case, you identified the "ttt" sound as the artist sings the word "towel," assigned a marker to that exact frame, and dropped the marked clip into the timeline. Out of habit, I always re-assign the sequence to begin its timecode counter at 01;00;00;00, which makes the timecode value for the sequence more appropriate and more unique than the default 00;00;00;00. Because the audio is the master sync device, you locked the track so it will not shift or move.

In essence, the new timecode value for the sequence now becomes the master timecode value for the audio in sequence, now you must synchronize each of the clips with the audio and timecode of the sequence.

3. Navigate back to the root folder, open the Video folder, and then open the YNK_Beach01.avi file in the Source window. Scrub the CTI to 16;06, and set an unnumbered marker. Drag and drop the video clip down into the Video 1 track. With Snapping turned on, slowly drag the clip over the region of the audio clip so that the two markers snap together (see Figure 21.1). Play the timeline to see how the clips synchronize together.

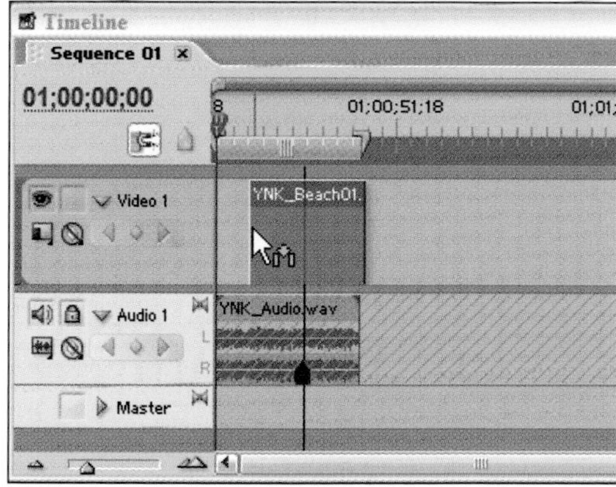

Figure 21.1 When Snapping is on, Premiere considers markers acceptable snapping points. When you drag the source clip over the audio clip, move it slowly until you get a snapping line that indicates that the two markers are lined up and snapped together.

A little secret for my choosing the T in towel as the sync point is that Del, the artist performing, does a gesture in all four shots where he over dramatically rubs his face before he says the word "towel." When searching through each individual take to find the T sync point, I just looked for the obvious gesture that preceded it.

In step 2, you identified and marked the sound to act as your sync anchor. In step 3, you identified and marked the frame of video that shows the artist forming that same sound. Finally, you aligned the marker for the video with the marker for the same sound in the audio. This is the eye match technique in a nut shell. Playing back the timeline you can see that the two line up quite well. In the next step, you will adjust the timecode of this shot so that it is completely synchronized with the audio in the sequence. This enforces the eye match multi-cam technique used for the next series of shots.

4. With the audio and video synchronized, position the timeline Edit Line over the clip boundary of the YNK_Beach01 file at 1;00;27;14. With the Video 1 track targeted (the track header should be dark gray), press the T key. Select File>Timecode, and enter the value 01;00;27;14 in the resulting Timecode dialog. Select the option Set at Current Frame (see Figure 21.2), and click OK. Clear the YNK_Beach01 instance from the timeline.

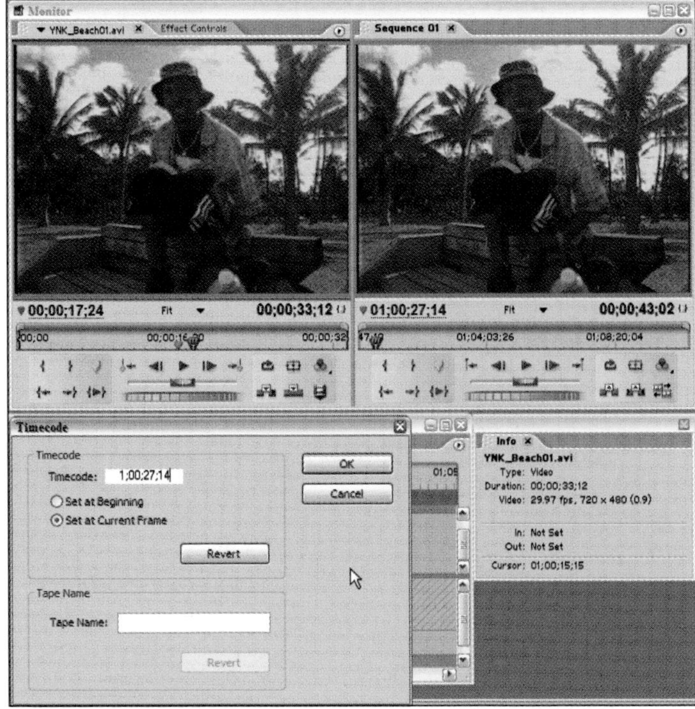

Figure 21.2 The Match Frame function opens the YNK_Beach01 source clip in the Source Monitor at the exact frame at which the Edit Line is resting in the timeline. The timecode for the timeline reflects the synchronized timecode for the music video. If you reassign the timecode of the source clip at the current frame to match the exact timecode in the timeline for that same frame, you are essentially creating a perfect link to preserve the synchronization between the source material and the audio.

Because you assigned a unique timecode value to your sequence and the audio in the sequence has been locked in place, the timecode is just as important for synchronizing as the audio. After you aligned the video file to perfectly match the audio, you reassigned the timecode value of the video to match the timecode of the sequence, creating a virtual lock of synchronization between the video clip and the sequence. The Match Frame T key automatically opened the subclip underneath the Edit Line from the target track in the Source Monitor with the CTI positioned on the exact same frame that the Edit Line is on in the timeline. You then reassigned the timecode of the source clip to match the timecode of the sequence at the exact frame open in the Source Monitor.

5. Open YNK_Mall01, and add a marker at 15;20. Drop the clip to the timeline aligning the video clip marker with the audio marker. Play the timeline to watch the synchronization of the audio and video.

   Based on the marker placement in the source clip, the lip sync is a bit off. The words of the song occur just a little bit earlier than the lip movement in the video clip. The next step adjusts that.

6. With the YNK_Mall01 subclip selected in the timeline, hold down the Alt key and press the < key six times. Play the timeline to check the synchronization again.

   Moving the video clip six frames to the left allows you to easily get it into sync with the audio. This frame-by-frame moving with the keyboard shortcut is called *nudging*. To nudge a selection one frame left, you press Alt then <. To nudge a clip one frame to the right, press Alt then >. To nudge either direction five frames at a time, hold down Shift and Alt then press either < or >.

7. Place the Edit Line on top of any portion of the YNK_MALL01 clip in the timeline, and press the T key to perform a match frame. Reassign the timecode of the current frame displayed in the Source Monitor to match the timecode value that corresponds to the frame in the Program Monitor.

Although the two markers didn't exactly line up, you manually nudged the video file into sync with the song. You were then able to use the technique illustrated in step 4 to match frame and then assign the synchronized timecode value to the source clip.

8. Using what you've learned, sync up and reassign the timecode for the remaining two clips: YNK_Market02 and YNK_Store01. Ironically, you can add a marker on frame 17;10 in both clips to synchronize them with the audio. Use the nudge keyboard shortcut to help perfect the synchronization before you match frame and reassign the timecode. After you reassign all the source clips' timecode, clear all the markers in source clips.

   Clearing the markers helps ease the editing process because it will reduce the number of potential snapping points with the source material.

   After you assign the adjusted timecode values, the primary leg work is complete and your creative editing juices can take over. There are two different methods for editing in sync with the reassigned timecode. The last two steps illustrate your options, you must of course first synchronize these shots to the timecode value that matches the sequence.

9. Open the source clip YNK_Market02.avi in the Source Monitor. Mark an In point in the source clip at 1;00;25;21 and an Out point at 1;00;31;02. Press Q to snap the CTI to the In point. In the Program Monitor, position the Edit Line to 1;00;25;21. Drag and drop the source clip into the timeline so that it snaps to the position of the Edit Line. (See Figure 21.3.)

   By positioning the timeline Edit Line at the same timecode position as your source clip's timecode In point, you are creating a snapping point for the head of the source clip to be placed at and preserving synchronization between the audio and video.

   This step illustrates how you can search within the source material to find the exact segment you want to edit into the sequence. Once you identify the In point of the source clip you want to add, you simply need to make sure that there is either an In point or Edit Line in the timeline at that corresponding timecode value.

Figure 21.3 The Edit Line is positioned at 1;00;25;21 and the In point of the source material reflects the same timecode value. When dragging the source clip down into the timeline, be sure that you are snapping the head of the clip to the Edit Line. Notice how the black snapping line replaces the red Edit Line and the black snapping arrows point toward the Edit Line as the snapping point.

10. With the Timeline window active, press the Page Down key to advance the Edit Line to the cut at the end of the newly placed subclip. Note the timecode value. Open the YNK_Store01 clip, and position the CTI at the same timecode value from the sequence. Mark an In point in the source clip on that frame. Without worrying about a pre-determined Out point, drag the source clip down into the timeline so that it snaps to the tail edge of the YNK_market02 subclip and the Edit Line. Play the sequence to see the edit between the two clips.

In this step, you identified a position in the timeline where you wanted an edit to occur. You then moved the Edit Line to that position to see the timecode value of that cut point. Finding a source clip with material that could be edited at that cut point, you assigned the In point timecode value of the source clip to be the same as the timeline Edit Line's position.

This step is sort of the opposite of step 9. Instead of fishing through the source clip to find what portion of the clip to use, you identified a position in the timeline that needed material. By moving the Edit Line to the position where the timeline edit should occur, you knew the exact timecode value that the In point of the source clip needed to be. Snapping the source clip's In point to the position of the Edit Line preserved the synchronization of the sequence.

11. Press the N key to select the Rolling Edit tool. With the Rolling Edit tool, roll the edit between the YNK_Market02 shot and the YNK_Store01 shot left or right to find a new cut point.

Ripple editing would shift the synchronized position of the subclips, but using the Rolling Edit tool enables you to roll the edit point between two clips while leaving the clips at their originally synchronized position.

From here you can explore this technique and repeat steps 8, 9, 10, and 11 with different clips in the project to create your own order of edits. Feel free to open the file YNK_Finish01.prproj to see how I edited the clips together and matched certain cut points by gestures that were repeated in different shots (see Figure 21.4).

Figure 21.4 Having started my version of the cut on the beach and then cut to the mall, I can use the Rolling Edit tool to roll the edit point to a moment in the song where Del makes a similar gesture in both shots. As discussed in Chapter 19, "Advanced Timeline Editing Techniques," cutting on action helps with the fluidity of the edit.

Many multi-cam editing techniques will force you to leave material in the timeline or stack the different shots on different tracks, one clip above the other. This technique teaches you to create a synchronized timecode value for both your edited sequence and your source material. The value of this technique is that in using the unique timecode value, you can search for moments to use in your source material or moments to fill in your sequence, without having to worry about their synchronization. Clearly the only time consuming part of this process is synchronizing the individual shots and assigning the timecode. The better you know the song and performance of the song, however, the easier that process becomes.

Working with Smart Slates

Instead of recording your band's performance in its entirety and matching mouth movements to the music in post, what if you could simply queue up the DAT to the point of the song you want to film, play it back while the band performs that scene, and sync them up easily? With the addition of one piece of equipment—a Smart Slate—you can.

Here's how it works: During a video shoot, the band's song comes from a DAT with pre-striped timecode. You cue up the DAT to the portion of the song you wish to film. Via a wireless adapter, the DAT transmits its timecode to a Smart Slate (see Figure 21.5). You film the timecode value displayed back on the Smart Slate before or after the band performs that particular section. Because the timecode on the Smart Slate corresponds with the timecode of the DAT, you can easily marry the captured video and audio by reassigning the timecode of the video file to match the timecode displayed in the smart slate. This lesson will show you how.

Figure 21.5 Timecode from the DAT that provides the music for lip syncing is sent via a transmitter to the Smart Slate. Film a few frames of the Smart Slate as the music plays from the DAT to show exactly which frame of the audio is playing at the exact moment being filmed. With this information, you can easily sync the video with the audio.

The primary difference from the last lesson is that the audio for this lesson comes with timecode assigned already. Because the audio comes off a captured DAT tape, you will use the tape's pre-written timecode as the basis for synchronizing the sequence.

Another small difference between the lessons is that the timecode format for the eye match method was drop-frame (with semi-colons) and the timecode for the Smart Slate method is non-drop-frame (with colons). Drop-frame timecode skips the ;00 and ;01 for all minutes except those that are even multiples of 10. Non-drop-frame, the typical timecode for music DATs, does not.

For this lesson, assume you captured your DAT audio and its associated timecode into Premiere Pro. You then captured all of your source clips off of the master BetaCam tapes onto which the film from the video shoot was transferred. Your ultimate goal is to assemble an edit in Premiere Pro that can be exported onto an uncompressed system that will take your edit list and master the video onto 1-inch and DigiBeta tape or another format. You will use footage from the music video I directed titled, "If You Must" by Del tha Funky Homosapien. You have five full camera takes to work with. Practice the technique first, then experiment with different versions of the edit using the various shots.

1. Open the file IYM_Start.prproj from the APPST Lesson Files/Chapter 21 folder.

   The media for this project can be found in the APPST Lesson Files/Chapter 21/IYM Media folder.

2. Open the IYM_Audio Clip in the Source Monitor. Notice the timecode value displaying for the audio, its In point is 01:01:56:09. From the timeline wing menu, select Sequence Zero Point. Assign the value 01:01:56:09, and click OK. Drag and drop the entire audio clip into the timeline starting at the head of the timeline. Scrub the timeline Edit Line to 01:02:30:08, and press the T key. (See Figure 21.6.) Lock the Audio Track.

   The important step is to assign the timecode value of the timeline to be exactly the same as the existing timecode value for the source audio. Using the Match Frame function, you can check that the audio is properly placed. Now that the timeline reflects the timecode of the audio, putting your shots in sync and editing is very simple. Locking the audio track ensures that no edits disrupt the audio placement.

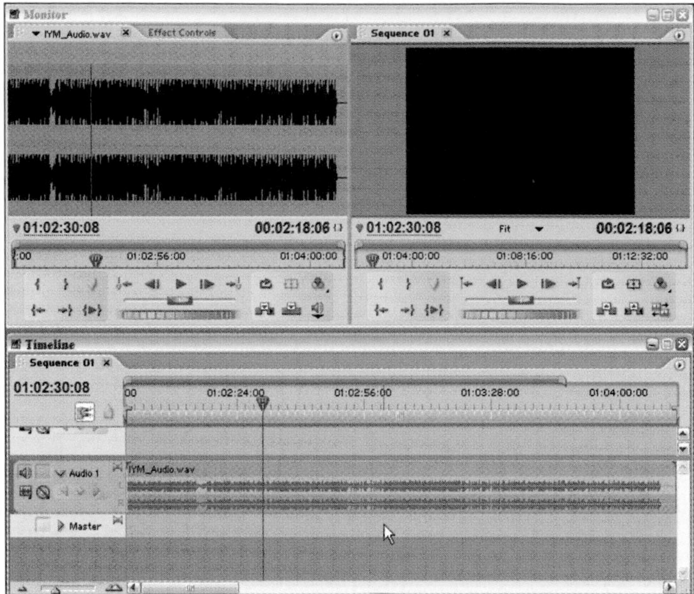

Figure 21.6 Use the Match Frame T key to verify that the audio added to the timeline displays the correct timecode. Because there is no video in the video track, the T key opens the source clip for the clip in the targeted audio track. In this case, the opened source clip properly displays the exact same timecode value as the Edit Line position in the timeline.

3. Open the IYM_BBoys clip in the Source Monitor. The first frame reveals a very clear timecode value in the Smart Slate, 01:02:44:02. From the File menu select the Timecode option. Enter the timecode value 01:02:44:02, and then click OK. At 01:02:58:21, mark an In point in the source clip. Move the Edit Line to the same position in the timeline. With Snapping turned on and the Video 1 track targeted, press the . (period) key.

   After you create sync between the source video clips and the timeline audio, you can begin editing—but make sure that the source clip's In point timecode value matches that of the timeline at the frame at which you are adding the clip.

4. Reassign the timecode value for the four other clips in the Project window. Because a few of the clips don't have easy values to discern, here are the timecode values from the Smart Slate at the first frame of every clip:

IYM_ChorusMaster	**01:02:41:14**
IYM_Crew	**01:02:49:08**
IYM_DelDoll	**01:01:57:05**
IYM_DelVerse	**01:01:56:09**

IYM_Crew, IYM_DelDoll, and IYM_DelVerse may have difficult timecodes to discern. Stepping through the DelVerse shot frame by frame, you can make out 01: 01:56:0 at the first frame, but not the last digit. If you step forward one more frame, the answer becomes very clear. Because a 1 appears before the last digit on the second frame it is easy to conclude that the first frame ends with 09.

For the DelDoll shot, the first frame is 01:01:57:05. When you step through frame by frame, however, you will see that some frames repeat themselves. The first two frames display 05 and 06 as the end value. The third frame is 07, the fourth 09, the fifth 10, and the sixth 11. Once you have a clear frame-by-frame value, such as the 9, 10, and 11, you can step back and count the frames backward to check your work. Starting at the frame displaying 11 (the sixth frame), you click back 10, then 9, then 8 (even though it displays 07), then 7 (it displays 06), and then 6, which display the 05 that you counted down to. Because the frame-by-frame digital read out of the Smart Slate can be changing numbers or not updating its display at the exact film frame exposed (then transferred to video), you may have to step through the individual frames counting them off to double-check your value before assigning it.

5. With all of your timecode values assigned for your source clip material, feel free to explore the edit using the techniques illustrated in this chapter.

The original timecode values of the source clip are important, because they match the timecode from the clip's original video tapes. Over the course of this lesson, however, you have reassigned your timecode. Next, you will revert the timecode back to its original values so that you can export an EDL of your sequence.

6. Having adjusted all of the clips in the current project, open the file IYM_Finish01.prproj, which contains an edited sequence of the example clips. Select each clip from the video folder in the Project window. Open the File>Timecode dialog, and click the Revert button. (See Figure 21.7.)

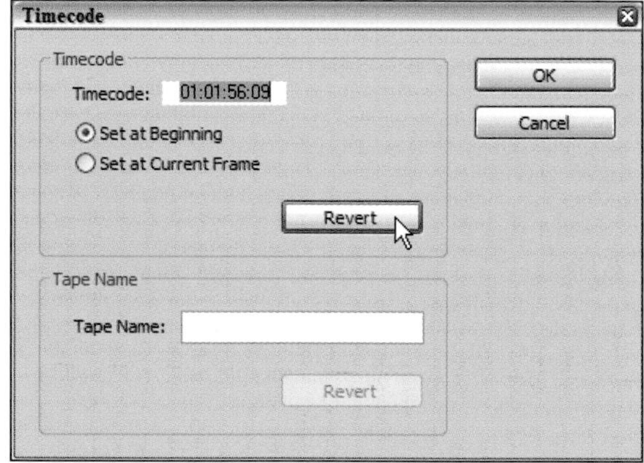

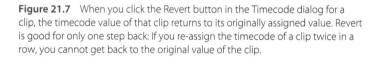

Figure 21.7 When you click the Revert button in the Timecode dialog for a clip, the timecode value of that clip returns to its originally assigned value. Revert is good for only one step back: If you re-assign the timecode of a clip twice in a row, you cannot get back to the original value of the clip.

After you complete your offline edit, you revert your source material back to its original timecode. Now you can export an edit list that can recreate the same edit on another editing system, provided you have the same source material (tapes and audio).

The Timecode dialog's Revert feature gives the Smart Slate technique even more power. Not only can you create sync between multiple clips with the technique, but with Revert, you can also preserve the original timecode values of the source clips. For most of my offline editing work, for example, I arrange my preliminary cut in Premiere Pro then rent time on an expensive online system to master the DigiBeta version of the video. Using the Smart Slate and Revert technique, I can quickly put together an offline edit on a laptop or desktop computer and then export an EDL to piece together the final edit on an online editing system.

To learn about exporting EDLs, you need only advance to the next chapter.

Things to Remember

Don't worry about having the Smart Slate or all the audio bells and whistles, just put as much money into making the video look good as you can. There are easy ways to solve your audio problems in post production.

By simply sharing a unique timecode value between multiple clips, you can easily synchronize your elements. Make sure the timeline edit point matches the In point of the source clip, and you can search for your edit by looking for holes in your sequences or identifying the pieces of the source material that you want to use. Because this technique does not involve stacking of clips, your timeline remains quite manageable. It's certainly not a typical multiple camera editing technique, but it is very easy and efficient to work using the same timecode numbers between multiple clips and sequences.

If you are interested in viewing each of these videos in its entirety you can see them on my website at **www.formikafilms.com**, just click on the Music Videos link.

Showcasing one of the new features in Premiere Pro 1.5, the next chapter will help you learn to use the Project Manager. Say your original raw captured footage has a total duration of nearly eight minutes, but your final edit is just under one minute. The Project Manager is streamlined to remove some of the excess unused material, giving you the option to reduce a version of your project to only the elements essential for your edit.

CHAPTER

22

Exporting EDLs and the Project Manager

With version 1.5, Premiere Pro provides a new degree of portability and flexibility. One of the most important reasons is the Project Manager, with which you can consolidate, back up, and trim your project to its essential elements. (See Figure 22.1.) Another is Premiere Pro 1.5's support of exporting and importing EDLs (edit decision lists) and AAF (advanced authoring format) files. If you anticipate your project may be edited on multiple nonlinear editing systems, then the EDL and AAF options can help secure your experience passing from one application to another. On all systems, disk space is very valuable, and using the Project Manager is an excellent way to cut unused material from your project and save a compact version with only the necessary files.

This chapter will show you how to get the most out of these new features. It will start with how to properly use the Project Manager and what results to expect. Then, the chapter will focus on practical examples and explanations of when and how to export EDL and AAF files.

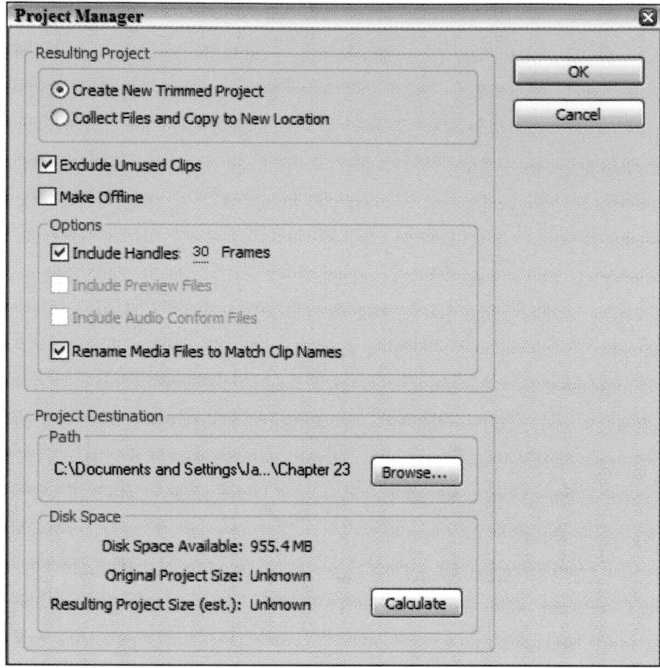

Figure 22.1 From the Project menu, you can access the Project Manager, which enables you to trim or consolidate your active project.

Using the Project Manager

When using the Project Manager, you can either trim your project or collect the files associated with it. *Trimming* reduces the project's overall file size and narrows it down to only the media being used in the edit, creating a new project with new media trimmed to the essentials. *Collecting* backs up the files associated with your project to a separate folder with copies of all the media in the project. You may wish to run Project Manager once to trim, and a second time to collect files.

Trimming a Project

If you want to keep a back-up copy of your completed project, saving only the clips used in your edit so that you can tweak some effects or use it again later, trimming your project is the best option. Trimming offers you the choice of trimming into a new project retaining the media online or trimming a project with all the media offline. In addition, you can use trimming to simplify your project by removing unused media, which frees up disk space. Give it a try.

1. Open the file PM_Trim.prproj in the APPST Lesson Files/Chapter 22 folder.

   For this example, you are using the car scene that you edited in Chapter 19, "Advanced Timeline Editing Techniques." All of the associated media with this project is in the APPST Lesson Files/Chapter 19 folder.

2. With the Project Window active, select Project>Project Manager. Click the following check boxes:

   Create New Trimmed Project
   Exclude Unused Clips
   Make Offline
   Include Handles
   Rename Media Files to Match Clip Names

Remember that when you trim or collect a project you are not destroying or altering your original project file and media. Instead, you are creating an exact copy based on your original with the parameters that you define in the Project Manager dialog box.

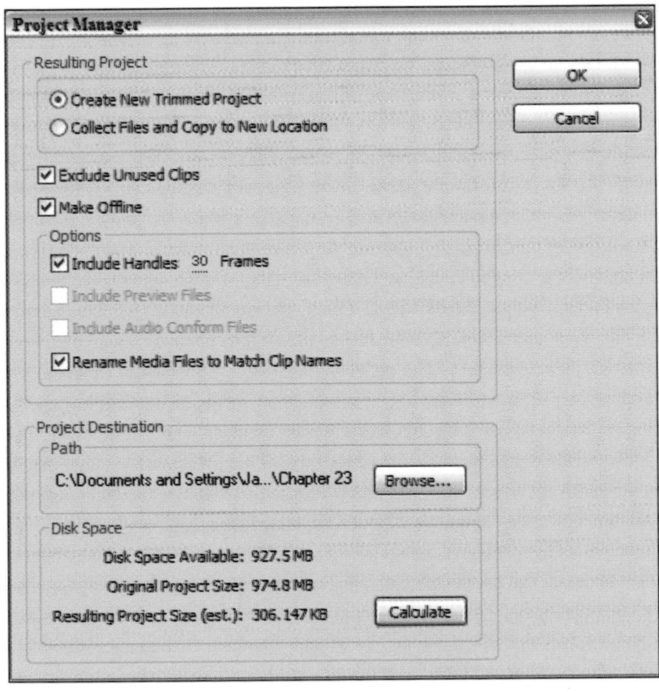

Figure 22.2 The top group of check boxes refers directly to the resulting project that trimming or collecting creates. The bottom group of check boxes refers to the destination of the project being managed.

When capturing from a DV camera (or tape deck with proper timecode) into Premiere Pro, timecode values and reel names are associated with every clip that is captured from your original tapes. Assuming that your master tapes remain intact, you can delete the captured media from your drive. Your project will retain all of the references to each of the captured clips, but detect the media for the clips as being offline. Because the clip information in the project preserves the timecode In and Out points as well as the reel name, bringing the media back online is only a matter of putting the tape back into your camera and batch capturing the offline files. When trimming a project into an offline state, make sure you have access to all the original source tapes with timecode values that match those of the clips used in your project. Because trimming to offline doesn't copy the media, you need to batch capture and re-link all the clips used in the project to get it back into its original online state.

Create New Trimmed Project enables you to reduce the existing project to a new project that includes only the media being used in your edited sequences.

Exclude Unused Clips excludes any reference to clips or media that is not included or edited into any of your sequences.

Make Offline creates the trimmed project without copying any of the media. Unless you have a lot of graphic, audio, and video media that cannot be re-digitized or easily retrieved, this is the most space-efficient way to back up your project. Simply load the offline project, and, assuming all the video content was logged with tape names and timecode values, batch capture all the offline files from their original source tapes to bring them back online.

Include Frame Handles is a way of allowing you to trim your project media while still preserving some extra frame information beyond the assigned In and Out points of the media in your sequences. For example, a clip was 100 frames long, and you used only frames 40 to 60 in your final piece. A standard trim with no handles would create a new clip of the same name with only frames 40 to 60. Including handles of 30 frames would result in the same trimmed clip starting at frame 10 and ending at frame 90, while still being used from 40 to 60 in your edited sequence. It is a good practice to always leave at least 30 frames of handles to allow for minor adjustments later.

Notice that the clip names in the Project window do not exactly match the clip names in the sequence. To help ease the editing flow for Chapter 19, I renamed each timeline subclip to a two digit number. If you have renamed clips in your Project window, any used instances of these clips will trim with their renamed value when you turn on the Rename Media Files to Match Clip Names check box. Because these clips are renamed in the sequence window (subclips are renamed), the trimmed master clips will still retain the original named value.

3. Browse and locate your desktop as the Path Destination for the trimmed project. Click Calculate.

   Choosing your path directly affects the calculation results in the following Disk Space area. Once a path is specified, the Available Disk Space value reflects that of the drive chosen.

   For Calculate, you can see that the Resulting Project Size is relatively very small. To see the size of the trimmed project if the media was copied, turn off the Make Offline check box. (See Figure 22.3.)

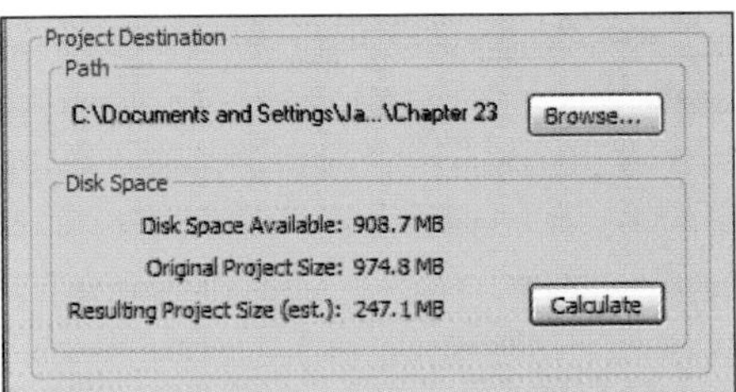

Figure 22.3 If the project was trimmed with all the files online, its overall file size is less than one-third that of the original. Keep in mind that all sequence effects and settings remain perfectly intact when trimming or collecting; therefore, you are creating a much more compact duplicate of your original project in a few simple clicks.

You can re-check Make Offline and click OK to trim the current project, then feel free to launch the project and analyze the results. If this were a real-world trim and you were satisfied that everything was intact with the trimmed version, you could throw away all the media associated with the original and store or use the trimmed version instead. This is an excellent way to prepare to archive a project when it has been completed.

The most valuable feature of the Trim option is that you can trim your project and create an offline version of your project that includes only the media used in your edit. With this feature you could send a tiny project file and the tapes that the media came from to another Premiere Pro system and the exact same edit could be created. When bringing your project back online and re-digitizing everything, you will need to digitize only the media that is being

You will appreciate the Rename function when you capture an entire tape using scene detection and Premiere Pro assigns less than descriptive names to the resulting files: Clip_01, Clip_02, and so on. When going through these clips, manually give them more descriptive, content-related names in the Project window. Then, when you trim the project, Premiere Pro will use your new clip names as the names for the trimmed files.

used and nothing extra. This is especially useful when the offline edit is being done on a DV workstation or laptop and the project needs to be moved to an SD or HD Premiere Pro finishing station.

Collecting Files

Trimming cuts down and removes unused media, while collecting gathers all your files for a separate self-sufficient complete backup. To see how the operations differ, try collecting for the same PM_Trim.prproj file.

1. With PM_Trim.prproj open, click on the Project window to give it focus, then choose Project>Project Manager. Click on the Collect Files and Copy to New Location check box. (See Figure 22.4.)

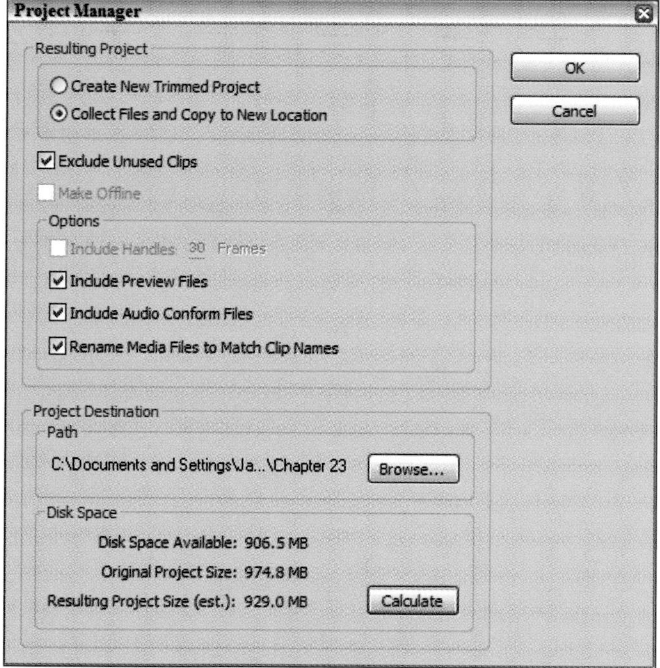

Figure 22.4 The Project Manager looks slightly different for collecting. Because collecting includes the entire duration of each file in your project, Make Offline and Include Handles are inactive. Include Preview Files and Include Audio Conform Files are now available options.

Because collecting literally collects and copies all your original source files from the beginning to end of the master clips in the Project window, Make Offline and Include Handles have been dimmed this time.

2. If you wish to reduce rendering and conforming time later, check Include Preview Files and Include Conformed Audio Files. The newly created project file will point to Preview Files and Conformed Files folders that are populated with files relevant to the collected project.

   In terms of overall disk space, collecting is not the most efficient way of reducing a project's size. It is, however, an excellent way to archive an entire project and gather all the media associated with the project into one folder.

In certain cases, you may have content spread across multiple drives and multiple folders. Collect Files copies every file from every location into a specified folder with all the other media used in your project. If you want to send an entire project with all its media elements to someone else, you can easily collect the project, then burn the media to a DVD, for example. Collecting is also perfect if you want to be able to load a project to other systems without having to always conform and render preview files. You could collect the project and include both previews and conformed files, thus having immediate access to the audio and preview areas in the project file whenever you copy it to a new system.

Either by trimming or collecting you can reduce the overall size of your project or enhance the portability and archival options for any project created in Premiere Pro 1.5.

Exporting to EDLs and AAF Files

For all work using EDLs and AAF files, capturing from source material with timecode is the only way to ensure that the exact media being used in the originating project can be reloaded and found with the exported EDL and AAF files being used.

Premiere Pro's AAF support is optimized for use with Avid Xpress and Avid Media Composer. Other AAF implementations may or may not be compatible with Premiere Pro's AAF files. This is a growing pain that should be resolved as AAF implementations mature.

Another angle for looking at this workflow is that Premiere Pro is being adopted as an HD finishing station. From several hardware vendors at a range of reasonable price points, there are numerous, affordable uncompressed HD systems that Premiere Pro supports. With this in mind, offline compressed HD edits from Avid and FCP systems could be exported as EDLs or AAF files and imported into Premiere Pro. Bringing the edits online in an uncompressed HD environment with Premiere Pro gives you more choices in your editing process and more financial choices in your online editing solution.

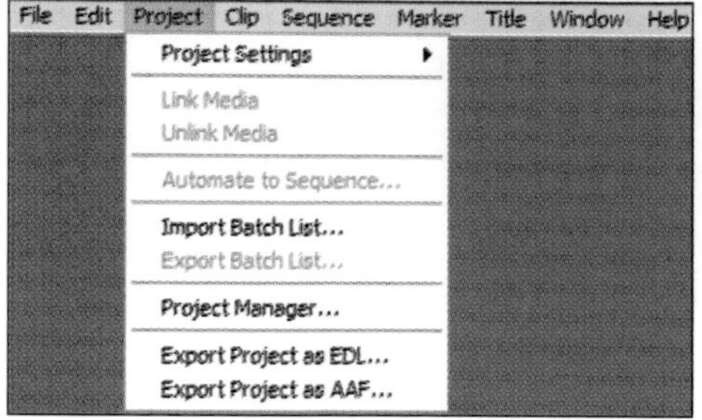

Figure 22.5 When your Project window is active, you can access the options to export to EDL or AAF.

Depending on the system you are going to and how much of your project you want to retain, you can export either an EDL or AAF file. EDLs are very versatile and supported by the broadest group of applications. However, EDLs export only one video track and four audio channels (two stereo tracks) with basic transitions. They do not support effect settings, audio levels, or effect listings. To export more project details, you can export an AAF file that contains multiple track information and such sequence-sensitive information as effect settings and speed adjustments. On the downside, AAF is a new format, and although many companies have announced support for AAF, very few implementations are available at this writing.

To better understand the advantages of each format, consider them in the light of a common scenario: Say you are editing a project coming from DigiBeta or BetaCam material (these are your masters). You want the flexibility of creating an initial offline edit on your laptop with Premiere Pro and standard DV. Your goal is to create a project or edit list that can be imported into an alternate online editing system that can digitize and play out at full quality from DigiBeta or BetaSP (a finishing station). Assume that your master tapes have proper timecode assigned and that you will digitize directly into your laptop for your initial Premiere Pro offline edit.

To accommodate this workflow you need to purchase:

- **A DV bridge.** Hardware that converts the analog video and audio signal coming from your Beta deck into a DV stream. Connects to your computer's FireWire port.

- **ProVTR.** A combination of a device-control plug-in for Premiere Pro and a cable that transfer the RS-422 device-control signal from your Beta deck directly to your editing system. Available from Pipeline Digital, ProVTR connects to either a COM or USB port.

With these two components you can digitize the audio/video signal from your master Beta tapes directly into Premiere Pro, preserving the timecode value of the material captured from the tapes. With all the material digitized in the DV format with all the proper source timecode, you can piece together an edit on virtually any PC system.

Transferring your Beta tapes and their accompanying timecode to DVCAM tape is another option that might reduce the overhead of having to rent an expensive deck. DVCAM supports proper timecode, so you would have a frame-accurate copy of your master tapes on a less expensive format. MiniDV does not support true timecode and you cannot dub from Beta down to MiniDV and have the exact timecode track on the MiniDV tape match that of the Beta.

Finding the Right DV Bridge

You have a number of options when purchasing a DV bridge that converts almost any signal to a DV stream. Some DV bridge solutions accept the RS-422 timecode signal, as well as digital or analog format inputs. Here are a few DV bridge solutions and the format conversions they support:

- **DV-Bridge+, DV-Bridge Pro.** *(Miranda, www.miranda.com)* A bi-directional bridge, the DV Bridge+ converts digital SDI video, AES/EBU audio, and timecode (RS-422) information into a single DV stream. The DV-Bridge Pro does standard analog audio and video conversion to DV, also integrating RS-422 support. Unless you have only digital SDI and AES signals to convert, the DV-Bridge Pro is the better choice, because it also offers the integration of audio faders to turn up or down the audio being transmitted.
- **DVMC-DA1.** *(Sony, www.sony.com)* The DVMC-DA1 is Sony's basic bridge that converts S-Video and Composite Audio/Video (RCA) to DV. It offers no RS-422 control, only bi-directional analog to DV conversion. Note that this bridge is a bit old, but it still works fine. You may not find it directly on Sony's website; however, it is out there.

- **ADVC-100, ADVC-300, ADVC-1000.** *(Canopus, www.canopus.com)* The basic bi-directional bridge from Canopus, the ADVC-100, offers standard analog RCA/ S-Video to DV conversion. The ADVC-300 offers the same conversion support but adds technology to perform digital noise reduction, as well as image stabilization for transferring VHS or Hi8 to DV. The company's top of the line bridge, the ADVC-1000, offers SDI to DV conversion with a host of other bells and whistles, such as a color bars generator, RS-422 support, plus digital audio and timecode reference track support.
- **Hollywood DV-Bridge.** *(Dazzle, www.dazzle.com)* Another option for bi-directional analog to DV conversion, the DV-Bridge supports analog RCA/S-Video conversion to DV.

For each of these options, price and flexibility are the primary variables. If you are simply coming off BetaSP, then consider a standard S-Video to DV bridge, which connects to the S-Video output monitor and audio monitor output and your system's FireWire port. To communicate with your deck, you connect your RS-422 and control the device using ProVTR. If you have a DigiBeta deck or other high-end decks with SDI routing, you can look to one of the bridges with that option.

ProVTR and Offline Editing

When using Premiere Pro in an offline capacity with video decks that support device control, you need a plug-in and device-control interface to accurately poll the decks and capture video with exact timecode information into the DV file format. If your DV bridge comes with RS-422 support, then you're all set. If your bridge only converts signals and lacks an RS-422 port, then you will need ProVTR to control the deck that provides the video stream.

The ProVTR package is comprised of one cable and one plug-in. The cable connects the RS-422 port on the back of the deck to a COM or USB port on your digitizing system. If you do not have a free COM port, you will have to purchase a USB adaptor cable to change the nine-pin RS-422 cable to USB interface.

You install the ProVTR plug-in into Premiere Pro's plug-in folder. When you launch Premiere Pro and open your project, choose ProVTR as your device-control method from the Device Control Preferences. After you assign the proper settings in the ProVTR setup dialog (see Figure 22.6), all the shuttle and playback controls in the Capture window will execute on the attached deck. In the bottom left corner of the Capture window, timecode from the playing tape will be visible. When you capture individual clips, the exact timecode value coming off the tape at that moment will be stamped on the clips.

If you plan to export to an EDL, try to keep the tape names to six characters and clip names to less than 12 when you initially capture your media. The EDL format has a character limit, and you don't want filenames to be too similar and truncated. I always use simple alpha numeric combinations, such as Blch01 for the tape name and Car01 or CarInt01 for clip names.

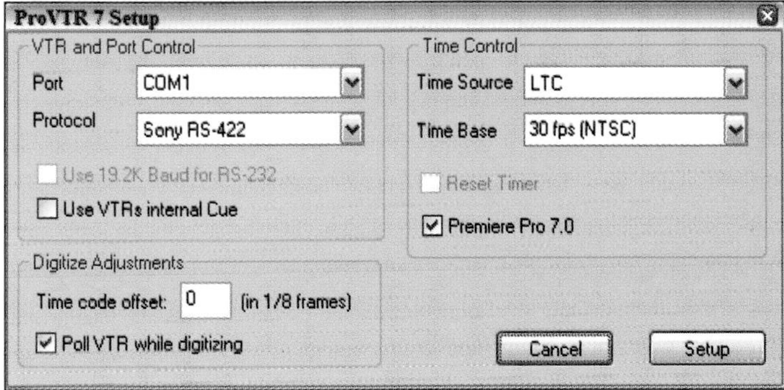

Figure 22.6 In the ProVTR dialog box, you can specify a number of parameters associated with your device-control protocol (RS-422/232) or the deck you are using.

Additionally, if you ever want to export out of Premiere Pro back onto your attached deck, you can use the Export to Tape function and insert or assemble your edits back to your deck.

Exporting an EDL

Having digitized and edited your project into its final form, you are ready to export an EDL so that you can emulate your edit on another system. Premiere Pro supports the CMX3600 EDL format, so make sure your target system does as well. Most all editing systems do.

Because the CMX3600 EDL format supports only one video track and four audio tracks, you need to build your project accordingly. Technically, the four audio tracks are four single-channel (mono) tracks. This means that two stereo tracks mix down into four mono tracks with one track for each of the channels of the stereo file.
Remember, too, that the EDL format does not retain any effects or filter information. It exports only edits and certain transitions, as well as the timecode and reel name associated with each of the clips in the sequence.

Here are the steps to exporting a CMX3600 EDL:

1. With your edit pieced together, click on the Project window to make it active. Choose Project>Export Project as EDL. Click OK to save your project.

   The Exporter first saves your current project, then asks you to provide a filename for the EDL that you want to export.

2. Name and target the destination of the EDL, click Save. Next, the EDL Export dialog appears. Select the sequence you wish to export from the Select a Sequence to Export drop-down list, and then assign the tracks that you want exported. Click OK. (See Figure 22.7.)

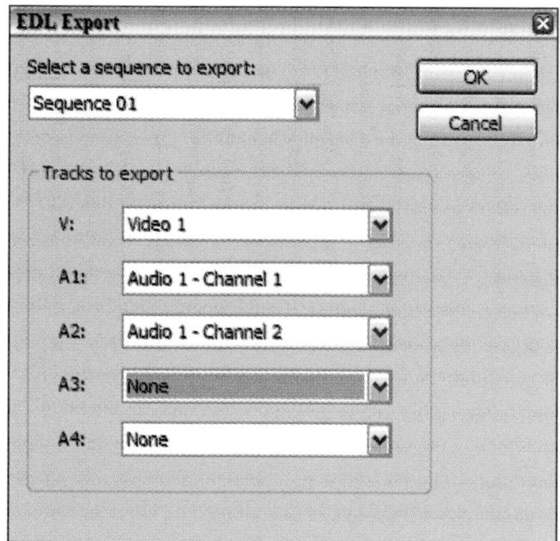

Figure 22.7 Because EDLs can accommodate only one sequence at a time, you have to individually export EDLs for each sequence in your project. First select which sequence to export, then select which tracks to include in the EDL.

Once you specify the single sequence that you wish to export, you must specify which tracks to include in the EDL. Remember only one video and four audio tracks can be exported. If you have more than two stereo tracks in your Premiere Pro edit, you must eliminate or reduce the tracks that you want to export. Choose wisely, because the EDL format supports four channels for audio and not technically four tracks.

You can pop your exported EDL file onto a disk or e-mail it to the online editing system. Then, load the EDL in the online system, and you can digitize the media again and re-create your exact cut.

Exporting to AAF

When you export to an AAF file, you can preserve a little more project metadata than you can in an EDL. The AAF exporter in Premiere Pro is tailored to import accurately into the Avid Xpress DV system. It exports multiple sequences, clip effects, speed adjustments, motion effects, and transition settings, as well as other details from your source project.

To export an AAF, follow the same steps as specified for the EDL; having your Project window active allows access to the Projects>Export Project to AAF menu item. After saving your project, you rename it and tell Premiere where to save the exported AAF file.

As with the EDL structure, you need to be aware of a few parameters when exporting to an AAF file:

- When naming clips, files and sequences, avoid characters, such as /, >, <, ®, and ü. These do not translate properly, because the AAF format uses them internally as special characters.
- If you are exporting to AAF and passing the file between applications on the same system, you must manually re-link the files associated with the project when it is imported into the alternate program. All files appear as offline, but can then be re-linked.

When exporting to AAF and opening the file in Avid Xpress DV, here are the features that you can expect to be supported and what the export results will be:

- All stereo audio, mono audio, and video cuts translate properly. Any specific audio panning, gain, or level adjustments do not convert. 5.1 surround sound files and track information do not convert, because these features do not exist in Avid Xpress DV.

Automatic Duck (**www.automaticduck.com**) develops a number of AAF and OMF importer and exporter modules. Just as this book was going to press, I received word that the company has created an OMF import tool, Pro Import PPRO, which enables Premiere Pro to import OMF files from either FCP or Avid DV Express. OMF files support even more project information than EDLs or AAF files, and they allow more features and effects to be translated when converting a project from those systems into Premiere Pro. According to company president Wes Plate, Automatic Duck plans on eventually adding direct XML import support from FCP to Premiere Pro to further enhance conversion among project formats.

- All footage that is greater than 720×480 automatically is scaled to 720×480 when imported into Xpress DV.
- Premiere titles, Bars and Tone, black video, color mattes, and Universal Counting Leaders are not supported by Xpress DV and appear as offline files. Be aware that all other still or graphic media also appear offline, unless the format is directly supported by Xpress DV.
- If you have a multiple bin structure in your Project window, all files are converted to a single bin in Xpress DV.
- Because nesting sequences are not supported, the source clips replace the nested sequence. In essence, nested sequences do not appear as individual nested clips, instead the source content of the nest is added.
- Markers are retained during export; however, the chapter, URL, and frame target metadata is not preserved.
- A majority of transitions are exported accurately, as long as the underlying clip's duration is not less than the transition's duration.

This list covers the main points only. The Premiere Pro 1.5 documentation provides more details on AAF export functionality, as well as details on how specific transitions translate between applications.

Things to Remember

When configuring Premiere Pro for offline editing, make sure you have the proper DV bridge to convert your deck video signal into a DV stream. If you do not have a DV bridge with RS-422 ports, you will need to purchase a device-control plug-in, such as ProVTR, to control your deck and have accurate timecode stamped on your captured files.

For single-track projects with cuts and transitions only, consider exporting to an EDL. The EDL format is widely supported by online systems, and I use it for interacting with most high-end editing systems. Just be warned that it does not come close to containing the same amount of project information as an AAF file.

When exporting to an Avid Xpress DV system, use the AAF export option. AAF exports an offline project with all your source clips' names, timecode, comments, and other metadata information, as well as reflecting the multiple sequences and effects used on the clips in each of the sequences. Although not all effects translate from one application to the other, the AAF file will contain a number of pointers and references to get the projects mirroring each other as much as possible.

Keep in mind that all tasks of the Project Manager do not touch, delete, or move the original media that makes up your project. The Project Manager simply creates a new project in a new location with new media files that match the names you defined in your project.

If you want to trim your project down to its basic elements so that you can pass it off to someone else or archive only what was used in the edit, use the Project Manager's Trim function.

If you have captured without timecode, have a ton of media spread across multiple drives, or may have difficulty going back to get some of the media used in your project, use the Collect Files option of the Project Manager.

Advanced Effect Techniques

CHAPTER

23

Using the Color Corrector

Color correction is the process of altering and modifying the color information that makes up your video image. Premiere Pro 1.5 offers two primary color correction effects: Color Corrector and Color Match. You use the Color Corrector effect to white balance your shots or make subtle adjustments to the coloring of your image. Color Match matches the color set of one image to the color set of another.

The Color Corrector effect (see Figure 23.1) makes adjustments within the red, green, and blue (RGB) color range, as well as adjusts the hue, saturation, and lightness (HSL) with the tonal ranges of your image. By altering the settings for these ranges, you can "correct" the look of your image to be more rich and vibrant or to have a customized color value.

You can view the physical implications of your adjustments in a number of different monitor views. For example, the waveform monitor analyzes and displays the light and darkness (luminance) values of your image (see Figure 23.2), and the vectorscope analyzes the color (chroma) value of your image (see Figure 23.3).

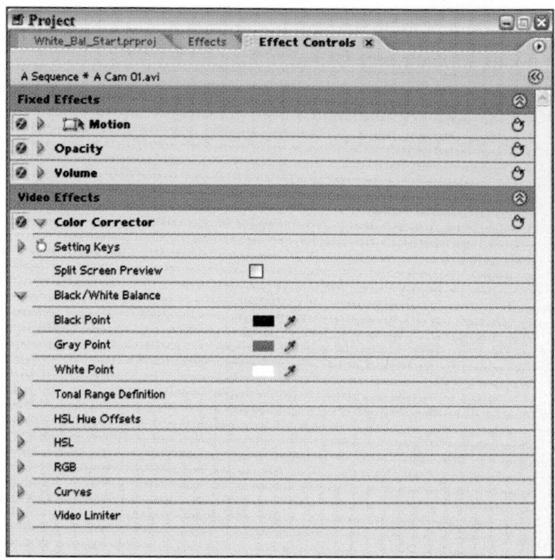

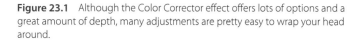

Figure 23.1 Although the Color Corrector effect offers lots of options and a great amount of depth, many adjustments are pretty easy to wrap your head around.

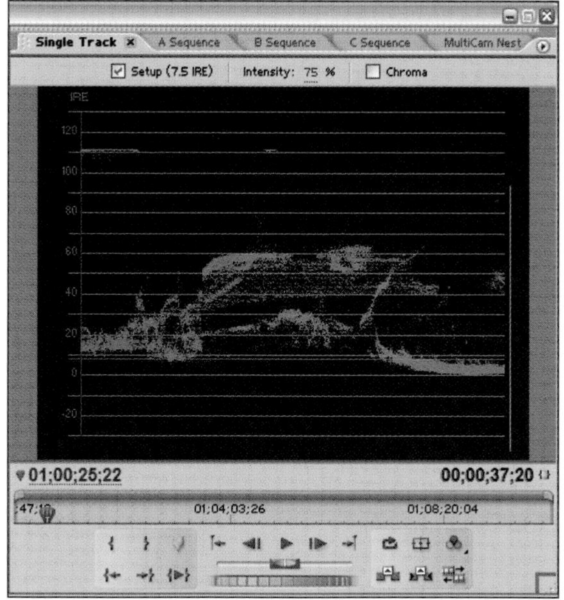

Figure 23.2 The YC waveform monitor introduced for Premiere Pro 1.5 has a few new options, including the ability to see chroma values in the waveform view as well as adjusting the intensity of the waveform image. The vertical lines of the waveform measure IRE levels. In order to stay within a safe considered broadcast range, keep your IRE levels contained between 7.5 and 100IRE.

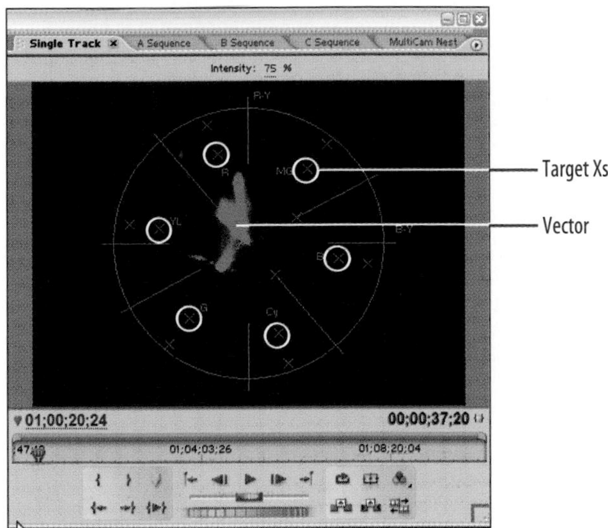

Figure 23.3 The vectorscope has specific color coordinates that map exact color values. The letters in the scope reflect the specific values for yellow, red, magenta, blue, cyan, and green. The absolute middle of your vectorscope is considered pure black, and each coordinate reflects the peak hue and saturation value for the color it represents. The farther a vector extends from the center, the greater the saturation of the color. As the vector changes its angle, it measures or reflects an adjustment in hue. Generally you don't want your saturation to exceed the target Xs or the outer ring of the scope, as the image would be considered over saturated and potentially unsafe for broadcast. Many custom looks, however, rely on increased saturation.

The Color Match effect (see Figure 23.4) enables you to sample color (RGB) or HSL values from one image and to match them with another. In the next chapter, you will use Color Match to match two film shots that don't naturally have the same color information.

This chapter will give you a good taste for some of the features that the Color Corrector offers. In the first lesson, you will learn how and where to apply white balance to your footage in order to make the colors look more accurate for the light in which they were shot. You also will try a subtle HSL adjustment that helps unify the look between the various shots in an edit. The second lesson goes a step further, introducing how to use the color corrector effectively for creating a custom look. Here you will set your Black, Gray, and White Points, as well as make some HSL Offset adjustments.

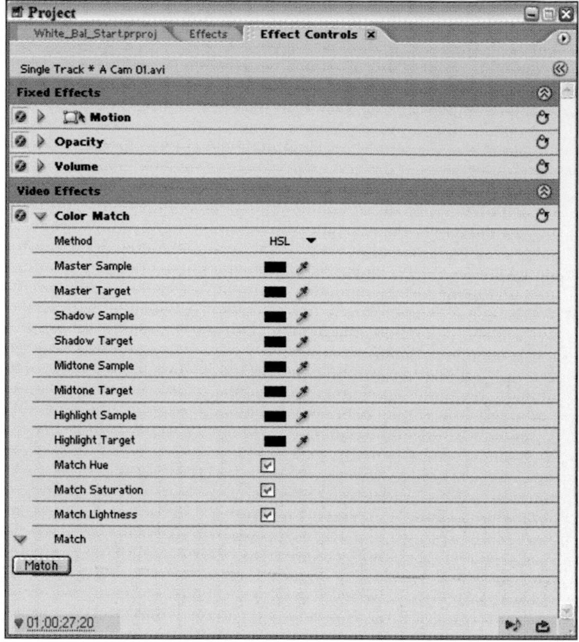

Figure 23.4 With the Color Match effect, you can make subtle adjustments to your clips so their color tones are consistent from cut to cut.

When you finish these lessons, check out the video tutorial "Color Corrector Limiter with Scopes" in the Advanced Techniques section of the accompanying DVD. The tutorial is a short demonstration of using the broadcast video limiter and waveform monitor.

Setting Your White Balance

Each type of light has a characteristic *color temperature* that affects the color of the objects it illuminates. Although the human eye cannot often discern the effect, film and video cameras can. Fluorescent lights, for example, cast a slightly green- or blue-tinged light. Although your eye might not see it, your camera will: Look through the viewfinder at a pure white sheet of paper held under the fluorescent lights, and you will notice the tinge or slight color differences on the paper.

So, how do you ensure the colors you are recording are true? You *white balance* your video. White balancing is the act of finding and assigning the color that you consider pure white—which brings us back to that white sheet of paper. By recording a sheet of white paper under the same light as you record your scenes, you have a reference to the exact color that may not appear white, but should be considered pure white. Then, when you get your footage into Premiere Pro, you can use the Color Corrector to white balance your shots by targeting the color of the recorded white paper to be pure white.

Setting your white balance is even more important when you're working with footage from multiple cameras. Sometimes lighting variations can cause subtle shading differences among the shots. For example, when I recorded the live multiple camera shoot used in Chapter 20, "Multi-Cam Editing: Live Shoot," I had three cameras recording the same event. Despite one slight exposure variation, the footage looks somewhat similar, but it could be more accurate. To establish proper color unity between the shots, in this lesson you will assign the white balance value for those three shots and fix the variant shot.

1. Open White_Bal_Start.prproj from the APPST Lesson Files/Chapter 23 folder.

   The source material for this project can be found in the APPST Lesson Files/Chapter 20 folder. Even though the final sequence of these shots has been nested within the MultiCam Nest sequence, applying the Color Corrector effect to the source clips in the separate sequences will reveal the effect in all places where those sequences are nested.

2. Start working on the first shot: Click on the A Sequence tab in the Timeline window to open the sequence. From the Effects window, type the word "Color" into the Contains field. Drag and drop the Color Corrector effect onto the A Cam 01.avi clip in the Video 1 track. Click the Effect Controls tab to open the Effect Controls window, then twirl down and expand the Color Corrector effect.

When making color correction adjustments, set your Program Monitor window to display at Highest quality. This ensures that you are seeing the image with as much detailed accuracy as possible.

If you are working with the current project and want to have more space for doing your color correction adjustments, select Window>Workspace>Color Correction.

You now have the Color Corrector effect applied to the clip in the initial sequence. Whenever you are looking for an effect in the Effects window, you can enter part or all of the effect's name in the Contains field. Premiere will reveal all matching results in expanded folders. To find other effects or to get the full listing back, clear the text in the Contains field.

3. You can now assign the white balance settings. From the Effect Controls window, twirl down the Color Corrector effect and expand the Black/White Balance parameter (see Figure 23.5). Position the Edit Line at 01;00;03;20 in the timeline. Click on the eye dropper for White Point, and continue holding the mouse down while you drag it out to the center of the white card in the middle of the image. Release the mouse while the eye dropper is on top of the card (see Figure 23.6).

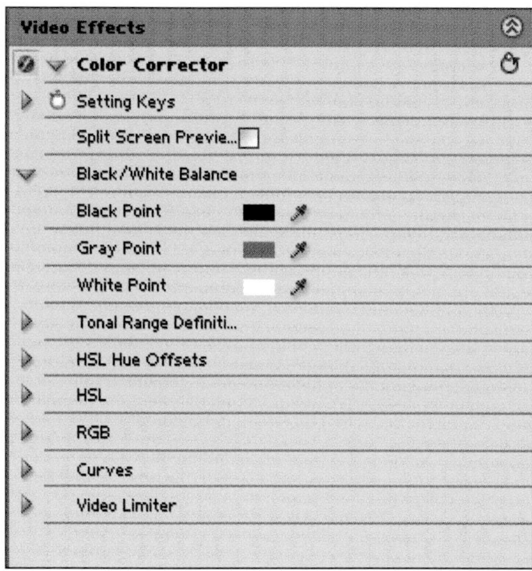

Figure 23.5 Using the Color Picker for the Black, Gray, and White Points is the same as picking colors in the Adobe Title Designer. Clicking in the Color Picker box enables you to target and assign an exact color from the color swatch. Clicking on the eye dropper allows you to pick from any color in the application window. Because the color changes preview automatically, holding down the Shift key picks the color but does not apply the adjustment until after you release the Shift key.

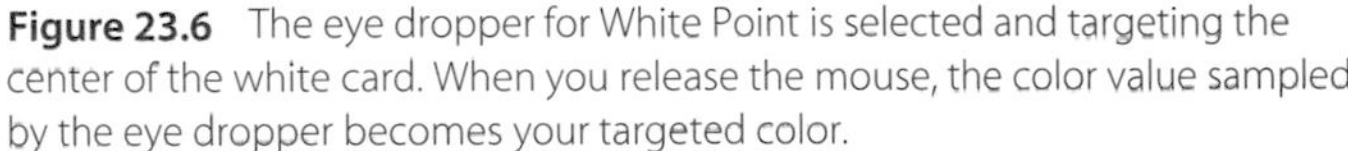

Figure 23.6 The eye dropper for White Point is selected and targeting the center of the white card. When you release the mouse, the color value sampled by the eye dropper becomes your targeted color.

NOTES

To ensure greater accuracy between different shots or better color accuracy in general, you can target and sample the Black Point and Gray Point, as well as the White Point. When targeting the Black and Gray Points, your color sample will assume the value of either pure black or pure gray. In the next lesson, you will identify and assign Black, Gray, and White Points.

This step is all you need to do to white balance your shot. First, you find the frame displaying your pure white card or paper, then you choose the White Point eye dropper and sample the color value displayed on the card. Having assigned the white balance for sequence A, you're ready to do the same for sequences B and C.

4. For B Sequence, apply the Color Corrector effect to the B Cam 01.avi clip and position the Edit Line at 01;00;03;04 to find the white card frame (see Figure 23.7). Do the same for C Sequence, applying the effect to C Cam 01.avi and targeting the white card at 01;00;03;05 (see Figure 23.8).

If you are having difficulty targeting or sampling a small region of the frame, you can zoom in the Program Monitor's view. Using the Hand tool, you can then move the image so that the exact area of the frame is visible in the Program Monitor window.

Figure 23.7 Target the White Point in B sequence and sample it.

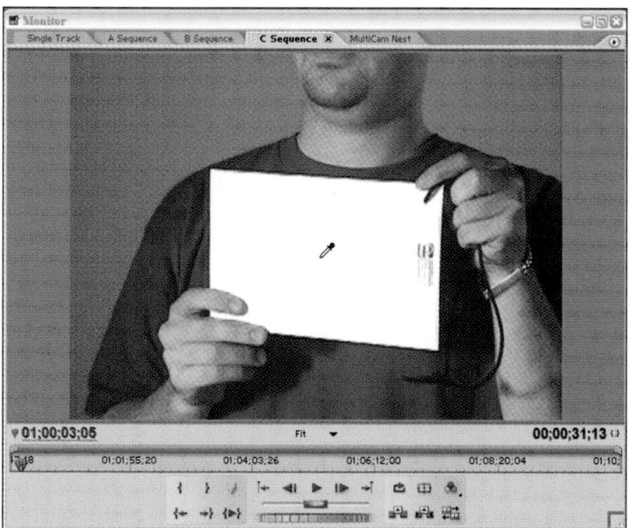

Figure 23.8 Target and sample the White Point of the shot in C Sequence.

By sampling a White Point from each shot you unified the white balance between the three. Because the shots were recorded by different cameras, however, you still can see some slight color differences between the images—most noticeably the over-exposed C Sequence shot. Looking at the results of the color correction in the MultiCam Nest sequence, C Sequence still sticks out as inconsistent with the other shots.

Because the clip in C Sequence is slightly over exposed, you need to adjust the image's brightness with the HSL parameters in the Color Corrector.

5. Change your window workspace layout to Editing. Grab the tab for the Effect Controls window, and drag it into the Project window. While pressing the Ctrl key, double-click on the A Sequence icon in the Project window to open the sequence in the Source Monitor. (See Figure 23.9.)

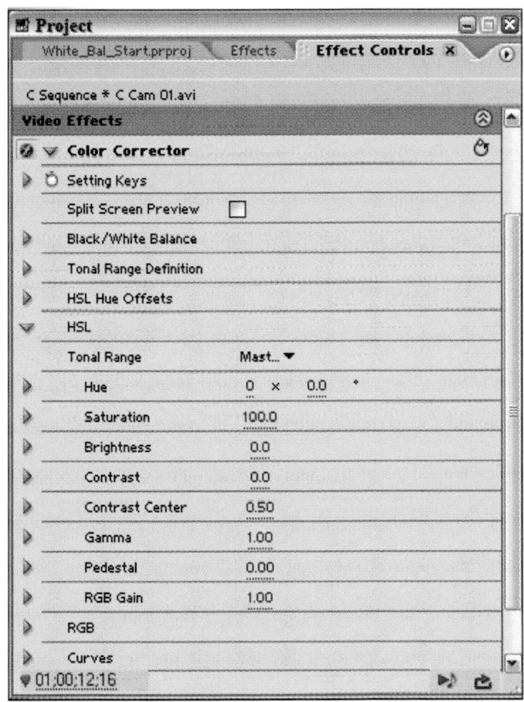

Figure 23.9 By docking the Effect Controls window in the Project window, you free up both Monitor windows to view the clip being adjusted (C Sequence in the Program Monitor) next to the clip you want it to reference (A sequence in the Source Monitor). A Sequence is in the Source Monitor because it contains the white balanced instance of the A Cam01 shot. Opening the A Cam01 shot on its own would not include any added effects, just the original clip.

Docking the Effect Controls window in the Project window frees more window space for your images, so you can adjust and see your results as clearly as possible. Opening one of the sequences in the Source Monitor gives you a visual reference side by side with the adjustments you are making.

6. Position the Edit Line in both monitors at 1;00;12;16. With the C Cam01.avi clip selected in C Sequence, go into the Effect Controls window and twirl down the HSL parameter for the Color Corrector effect. From the Tonal Range submenu, select Midtones (see Figure 23.10), and set:

   Brightness: **–12**
   Gamma: **0.9**
   Pedestal: **–0.05**

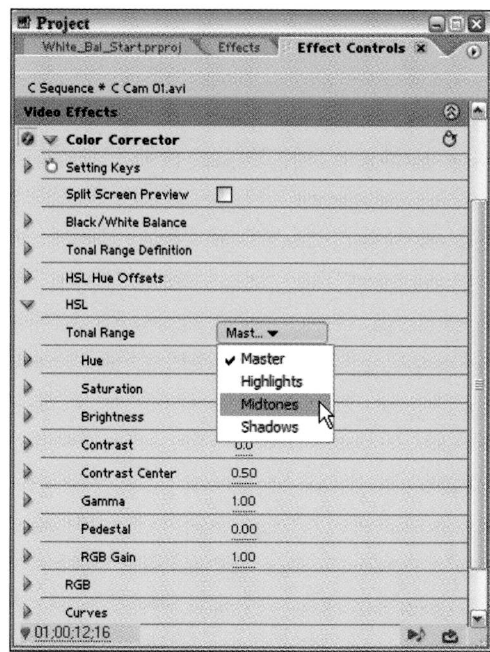

Figure 23.10 With the Color Corrector's HSL controls, you can adjust all three tonal ranges (Master), bright areas (Highlights), the middle area between bright and dark (Midtones), and the dark areas (Shadows). With the HSL Offset controls you can go one step further, changing the exact color emphasis within those four definable tonal areas.

By isolating and adjusting the Midtones ever so slightly, you preserved the integrity of the image and brought its appearance closer to that of the other shots. If you had selected HSL Master and set the same levels for Brightness, Gamma, and Pedestal, all three tonal ranges would have been darkened instead of one specific tonal range.

Figure 23.11 shows before and after versions of your color correction adjustments. To preview the differences yourself, toggle the Effect Toggle button next to the Color Corrector effect listing in the Effect Controls window. To see the results of all three adjusted sequences, render and play the Multicam Nest sequence. Because all the sequences are nested into the final edit, the results of the color correction adjustments in the original sequences appear in the final nested edit.

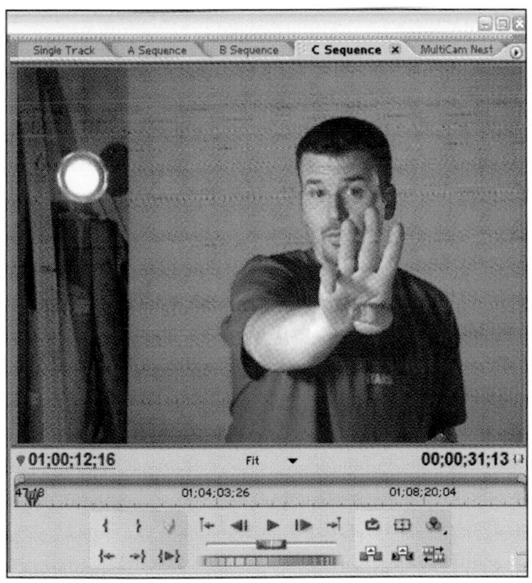

Figure 23.11 Contrast the clip with no color correction applied (left) with the clip after white balancing and HSL Midtones adjustment (right). The result is subtle, but enough to make a difference in your final edit. By bringing down both the Brightness and Pedestal, you reduced the brightness of the image and then increased the darkness of the blacks. The Gamma slightly altered the strength of the color.

Rather than trying to learn every facet of the Color Corrector, concentrate on specific adjustments and their results. For accurately depicting the light in your given shots, for example, using the Color Corrector to assign your white balance is an excellent choice. In this lesson, you reduced the overall brightness and gamma emphasis within a specific tonal range to produce more unity between the shots.

You can explore this technique in your own work by tinkering with slight adjustments in specific ranges, as opposed to the master level. Keep in mind that the HSL Hue Offset color wheel allows you to change the *emphasis of a color* within a tonal range, while the HSL parameters enable you to adjust the *Hue, Saturation, and Lightness values* within a tonal range. In plain terms, HSL Hue Offsets can change your entire shadow tone to a specific shade of blue, and the HSL adjustment can make that shadow tone brighter, darker, or more saturated in color.

The color correction adjustments you make may be minor or only slightly noticeable, but developing healthy habits with the Color Corrector goes a long way toward making your video look better overall.

Creating a Custom Look

Now that you have the fundamentals, this lesson opens up the full power and potential of the Color Corrector. Remember the scene from *Bleach* that you edited in Chapter 19, "Advanced Timeline Editing Techniques?" The colors in a few shots need to be distinctly richer and more vibrant than what was recorded. Why? In the film, as you may remember, the main character's point of view is altered so the reality that the audience sees through his eyes does not match the reality that they see him in. To nail this idea home, you need to color correct the POV shots that are taken through "his eyes." Using the Color Corrector, you will define the White, Gray, and Black Points then adjust the HSL Hue Offset values to make the overall images warmer with a unique look.

1. Open the file Color_Correct_Start.prproj from the APPST Lesson Files/Chapter 23 folder.

   The media for this project can be found in the APPST Lesson Files/Chapter 19 folder. For this lesson, you will concentrate on the POV shots: clips 03, 05, 08, and 10 in Sequence 01.

2. From the menu bar, choose Window>Workspace>Color Correction. From the Program Monitor's wing menu, select New Reference Monitor. Grab the Reference Monitor by its tab, and dock it into the source side of the Monitor window. Click the Gang to Program Monitor button, and set the Output display to All Scopes or your own choice of scope. (See Figure 23.12.)

Figure 23.12 The Reference Monitor is docked into the source side of the Monitor window. Because the two monitors are ganged together, their Edit Line positions are exactly the same. The Reference Monitor displays the All Scopes view for the frame that is being displayed on the right.

Using the Reference Monitor and Program Monitor together, you can see the physical results of your color correction adjustments. In this arrangement, the Reference Monitor mirrors the current sequence loaded in the Program Monitor. Because the monitors are ganged together, any update to the Edit Line in one updates the Edit Line in the other. I recommend this setup for most, if not all, color correction work.

When making color correction adjustments, set your Program Monitor window to display at Highest quality. This ensures that you are seeing the image with as much detailed accuracy as possible.

You may notice that the colors of clips 01 and 12 do not match those of the other shots in the sequence. For example, the shirt is blue in clip 01 and green in clip 02. Don't worry. You will use the Color Match effect to fix this in Chapter 24, "Color Match and Color Effects."

3. Apply the Color Corrector effect to clip 03 in the timeline. Position the Edit Line at 12;05. Twirl down the Color Corrector effect listing, and click the check box for Split Screen Preview. Expand the Black/White Balance listing. Based on Figures 23.13 through 23.15, sample and target the Black, Gray, and White Points. After you assign these values, turn off Split Screen Preview to view your results.

Split Screen Preview shows you half of your image corrected and half of your image uncorrected. Be sure to turn off the preview when you finish your adjustments, otherwise the effect is processed split screen.

By selecting the dark color in the dash as your Black Point, you targeted and anchored your pure black value. Targeting and anchoring your Gray Point in the window frame resulted in the most extreme and noticeable adjustment to the image. Because the window frame is a green/blue color, assigning it to be gray removes that green/blue tinge from your entire image and adjusts it to gray instead. Immediately the image warmed up with the washed out colors removed. Targeting and anchoring the bright light reflection in the side mirror as pure white removed a slight yellow tinge and replaced that as pure white. If you were simply correcting and balancing this image, these would be excellent results. You are, however, going to take this effect a bit further.

Figure 23.13 By holding the Shift key down while you target and sample your Black Point with the eye dropper, you temporarily disable the automatic color adjustment of the image. For the Black Point, the suggested target area is inside the dash on the right.

Figure 23.14 To set the Gray Point, target and sample the light green side of the door frame. Be sure to hold the Shift key down while making your selection from this region.

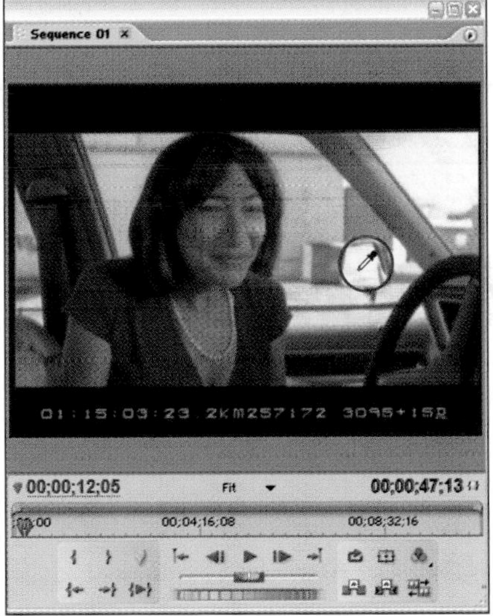

Figure 23.15 Holding the Shift key down once again, target and sample the bright light reflecting in the side mirror. This selection assigns the slightly yellowish light reflecting in the mirror to be pure white.

4. Collapse the Black/White Balance parameter, and twirl down Tonal Range Definition. Click the Preview check box, set Shadows to 0.60, and set Highlights to 0.80. (See Figure 23.16.) When finished with your adjustments, turn off the Preview check box.

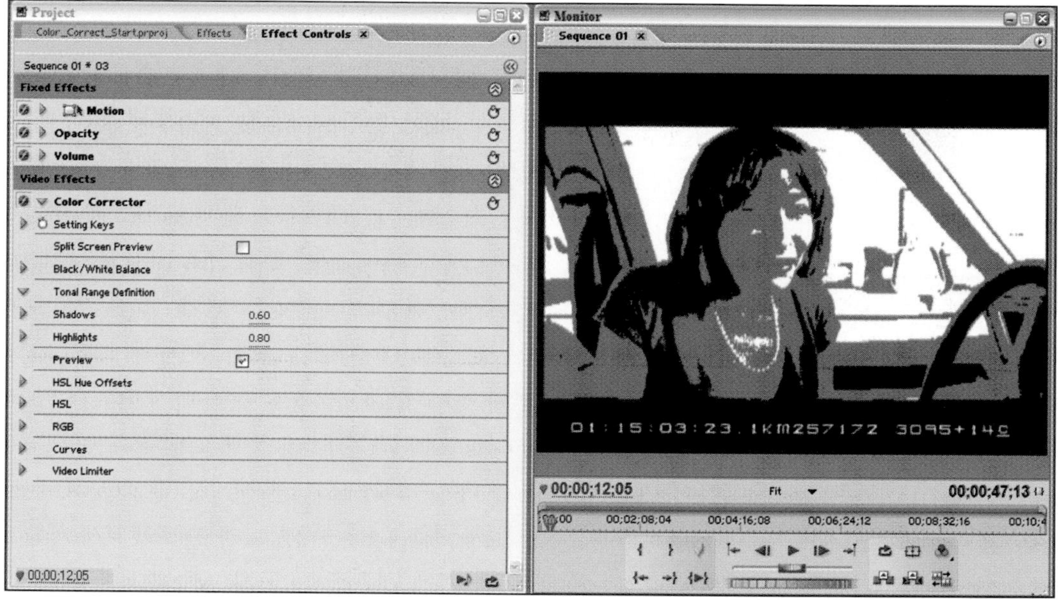

Figure 23.16 Turning on Tonal Range Definition displays a grayscale rendering of your color image. The rendering reflects the three tonal ranges of your image: white for the highlights area, gray for midtones, and black for shadows. When the Color Corrector makes adjustments to a tonal range, this image gives you an idea as to which parts of the image fall into which range.

Slightly increasing both the shadow and highlight range definition means you will get more noticeable results when you adjust the HSL Hue Offset for Shadow and Highlight. By that same token, you de-emphasized the midtone area, because some of the midtones are now associated with either the Shadows or Highlights range.

5. Collapse the Tonal Range Definition parameter, and expand the HSL Hue Offsets. Adjust the values for Shadows, Midtones, and Highlights by clicking in the same regions as shown in Figure 23.17.

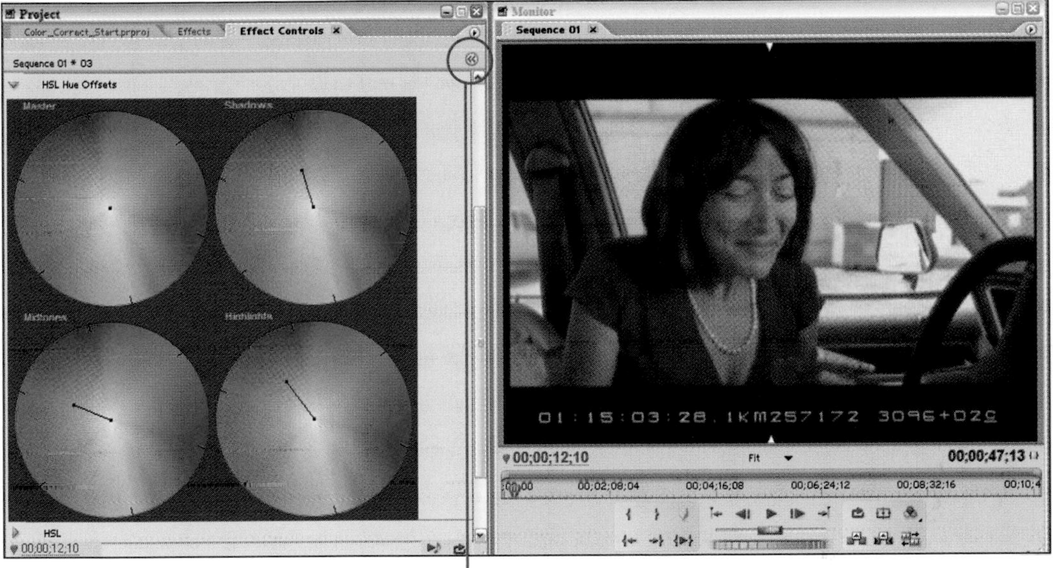

Figure 23.17 In each of the three tonal range color wheels, click in the color region that you want assigned to the specified range. To warm up this image, I chose a yellow/orange/red combination for all three tonal ranges. Notice the difference in the split screen of the adjusted image and the original.

The first thing you should notice in this step is the size of the HSL Offset color wheels. If you find that you need more horizontal space in your Effect Controls window to see the wheels you can close the timeline view of the Effect Controls window (See Figure 23.17.)

Instead of applying a general warm adjustment to all three ranges using the master, you adjusted the hue of each range separately. The result is an image that is much warmer. It's important that the flesh tone of the actress still looks like a flesh tone and that the red in her shirt sticks out. If you were to adjust the master hue, you risk altering those specific areas because a more dramatic color shift would be applied.

A unique feature of Premiere Pro's Color Corrector is its ability to define and adjust the tonal ranges of your image. Tonal Range Definition does not alter any color information, but adjusts the emphasis or strength of what is defined as either a shadow or highlight. This feature is incredibly powerful, because it enables you to increase or decrease the presence of an adjustment within a tonal range by increasing or decreasing the range definition.

For example, say you lower the Shadow range to 0.0 in Tonal Range Definition. Next, you give the shadow range a red tinge using HSL Hue Offset's Shadow color wheel. Because you reduced the overall presence of the shadow range, the red color adjustment is barely noticeable. By slowly increasing the range, you slowly introduce that red value. To put it simply, Tonal Range Definition can help control the dominance of any adjustment in any of the three tonal ranges.

As an experiment, try cooling off the warm image in step 5. Assign the highlight hue to a blue color. Immediately all the warmth in the highlight will take on a blue-ish tone, cooling off the image entirely. Additionally, try taking the midtones to a green hue offset. This will keep the image looking nice, but reduce some of the warmth.

6. Right-click on the Color Corrector effect listing, choose Save Preset, and enter:

   Name: **Bleach Color Correction**
   Description: **Bleach POV overall warmth**

   From your custom Presets Effects folder, drag and drop the Bleach Color Correction effect onto clips 05, 08, and 10 in the timeline.

   By saving the Color Corrector effect as its own preset, you can quickly apply it by dragging and dropping it onto any clip. The custom effect will also be available for use when other projects are loaded.

Congratulations. Using the Color Corrector, you warmed up a very washed out, overly blue/green image to look much more vibrant and colorful—all of this without taxing the image and distorting the color set in any noticeable way. The key to this lesson was removing the blue and green emphasis by picking the window frame's green/blue color and assigning it as the Gray Point. When adjusting your Black and White Points, keep in mind how much power the Gray Point offers. It might not always be appropriate to assign, but when necessary it can create some excellent results. Remember too that by defining the tonal range of your image you can add or subtract the emphasis of any adjustment within that range.

Using the Limiter and Scopes

The Color Corrector effect has its own broadcast limiter that allows you to quickly limit the overall Luma or Chroma values of your image. To see an overview of using the limiter and a walkthrough of using the waveform monitor, watch the "Color Corrector Limiter with Scopes" tutorial in the Advanced Techniques section of the video training on the accompanying DVD. You will see the previous lesson file go through the limiter and have its levels adjusted and viewed in the waveform monitor.

Things to Remember

The chapter introduced several fundamentals:

- Always record a pure white sheet of paper in the same lighting setup as the scene that you are recording. If you switch locations in the same shoot, record a white balance reference for each location.
- Using the Color Corrector, you can quickly target and assign your White, Black, and Gray Points.
- By nesting the source material for your edit, all color correction applied to a sequence appears in every instance where the sequence is nested. This technique reduces the redundancy of copying and pasting the Color Corrector effect to multiple shots.
- Adjusting your Tonal Range Definition can help you make slight or dramatic changes within specific tonal ranges.

In addition, remember to save your successful color correction efforts as presets in the Custom Presets folder. This enables you later to apply common adjustments in one drag and drop of the preset.

Color correction can be an art form unto itself. If you want to dig deeper into it, I recommend *Color Correction for Digital Video: Using Desktop Tools to Perfect Your Image,* by Steve Hullfish (CMP Books), which is an excellent resource on the subject.

In the next chapter, you will use the Color Match effect on the first and last shots of the same *Bleach* scene, matching their colors to those of the other shots in the scene. You will also learn about a few new plug-ins for Premiere Pro 1.5 that enable you to brighten and quickly adjust problematic video clips.

CHAPTER

24

Color Match and Color Effects

As you learned in the last chapter, color correction is a subtle art, composed of patient and practical adjustments designed to get your image looking exactly how you want. Part of that art is color matching, which involves matching the color set of one image with the color set of another. Premiere Pro takes some of the guesswork out of this complicated process by offering a color match tool to help you better blend your scenes.

In the first half of this chapter, you'll use the Color Match effect to match two shots of the *Bleach* car scene so that they edit seamlessly with the other shots in the sequence.

In the second half, you will explore the Auto Levels, Auto Colors, Auto Contrast, and Shadow/Highlight effects. These four effects have been taken from Photoshop CS and imported for use as brand new effects for Premiere Pro 1.5. These effects can dramatically improve and quickly clean up troublesome shots that may appear too dark or not vibrant enough.

Practical Color Matching

In Chapter 19, "Advanced Timeline Editing Techniques," you cut between multiple shots to achieve a good editing flow for your scene. Because each shot was photographed from different angles at a different time of day, however, each shot had slightly different lighting. Your final sequence had a good flow, but the shots themselves had minor color differences between them. Although subtle, these differences distract and detract from the scene's overall effect. (See Figure 24.1.)

Figure 24.1 These two shots from the same scene need to be color matched. As you can see easily in the man's shirt, the left shot has a blue color tinge and the right one has a green tinge.

With the Color Match effect, you can match the color set from one shot to the color set of another. Although the effect seems straightforward enough, you will need to pick wisely and carefully what you are matching to get the shots to look like each other.

As you learned with the Color Corrector effect, making slight adjustments in specific tonal ranges can yield excellent results. With color matching those same rules apply. Instead of trying to match the entire tonal range of an image, experiment with which tonal range matches provide the most accurate results. Give it a try.

1. Open the project Color_Match_Start.prproj from the APPST Lesson Files/Chapter 24 folder. Play the first two clips back and notice the difference in the color of Fulton's shirt.

   The media being referenced in this project is located in the APPST Lesson Files/Chapter 19 folder.

   Notice that the Effect Controls window is already docked into the Project window, so that you can use the Source Monitor to view and sample the colors of one clip while the Program Monitor displays another.

2. Double-click on clip 02 in the timeline to open it in the Source Monitor. Drag and drop the Color Match effect from the Effects window onto clip 01 in the timeline.

Position the Edit Line at 3;25 in the sequence. Activate the Effect Controls window tab in the Project window. (See Figure 24.2.)

Figure 24.2 The Effect Controls window is active for the selected clip (01) in the timeline. With the Source Monitor displaying the clip that you want to match your colors to (clip 02), you can easily navigate between the Color Match effect and the two Monitor windows.

Because you are going to target colors from clip 02 to match with clip 01, you need both clips open in a monitor. Placing the Effect Controls window in the Project window streamlines your workspace so you have the effect and the two frames next to each other.

3. Expand the Color Match effect for clip 01. From the Method drop-down menu, select RGB.

   The RGB match method tends to give the best results. For all color matching, start in RGB mode and see where you can get. If your results aren't satisfying, then try either Curves or HSL (see Note).

Color matching using HSL rotates or shifts all of the colors in your image so the result will be dramatic. If you want to match the Saturation or Lightness of two images, try using HSL with the Match Hue check box turned off. Turning that off should keep your color values intact, so you affect only the Saturation and Lightness levels.

The Curves method of matching is very good for slight adjustments, but if there is too much of a change you can get some color clipping.

To get exactly the same results as the example, you need to enter the RGB color value for each target/sample point in its associated color picker.

Notice that I did not use the Master and Highlights settings to match these images. Master controls the entire image, which makes subtle changes more difficult, and this image pair did not include an obvious highlight to match to. I found the best results using just Midtone and Shadows.

Matching Master, Shadow, Midtone, and Highlight can often be too much for your image to handle, and the results won't match. Because of this, work on one tonal range at a time and see how your cumulative results look.

4. Click the Shadow Target eye dropper. While holding the Shift key down, target the shadows on the headrest in clip 02 (Source Monitor), which reveal a slight difference in color. The RGB color value of the example's target point is R93, G96, B86. (See Figure 24.3.)

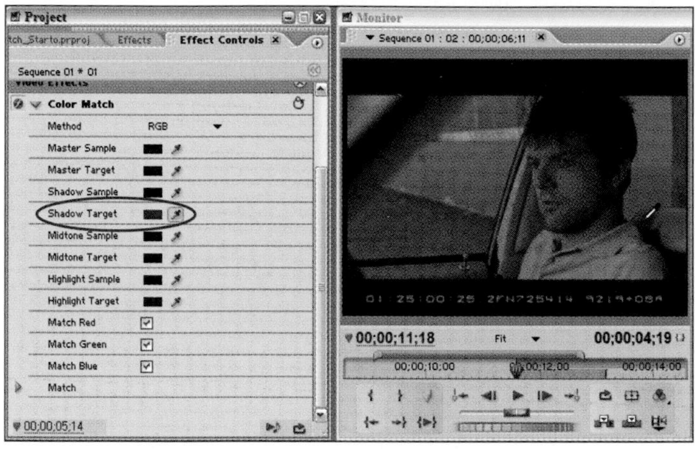

Figure 24.3 Shadow Target: Target the shadow area of the image that best reflects the color difference between the shots.

Color Matching operates on a target/sample basis. First, you *target* the color that you want the result to be like, then you *sample* the color you want to change to match the target. The target clip is usually placed in the Source Monitor. Because the results can vary dramatically one way or the other, you may need a few attempts to properly match your images and find the right target/sample combinations.

You start by matching the shadows or dark areas of the image—not the pure black spots, but the dark grays where there is a slight difference between the green/gray of the target and the blue/gray of the sample.

5. Select the eye dropper for Shadow Sample, and sample the small shadowed area on the headrest in clip 01, as shown in Figure 24.4. The color value for the example's sample point is R73, G91, B92.

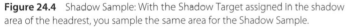

Figure 24.4 Shadow Sample: With the Shadow Target assigned in the shadow area of the headrest, you sample the same area for the Shadow Sample.

You need to find a dark color value that reflects the shadow area, but retains enough of the color needed to sample from the image. The shadow sample on the headrest incorporates a blue/gray color that needs to be removed from the image in order for it to be matched. The blue/gray sample and green/gray target shadow colors are not too radically different in their general tone; this will help with your match.

6. Click the eye dropper for Midtone Target, and, in the Source Monitor, target the area of Fulton's shirt shown in Figure 24.5 (R126, G166, B143). Click the Midtone Sample eye dropper, and sample the shirt area from the Program Monitor (R94, G147, B189), as shown in Figure 24.6.

   To get the best results, target and sample the bright colors of the shirt. Notice that the saturation of the color looks almost identical, except the target is green and the sample is blue.

Figure 24.5 Midtone Target: To best reflect the midtones, choose the most obvious even-balanced color that exemplifies the color differences.

Figure 24.6 Midtone Sample: To get the perfect match, sample a similarly bright area of the shirt in the Program Monitor. The blue color of clip 01 will now be matched against the green color of clip 02.

7. Expand the Match listing of the Color Match effect, and click the Match Button. (See Figure 24.7.)

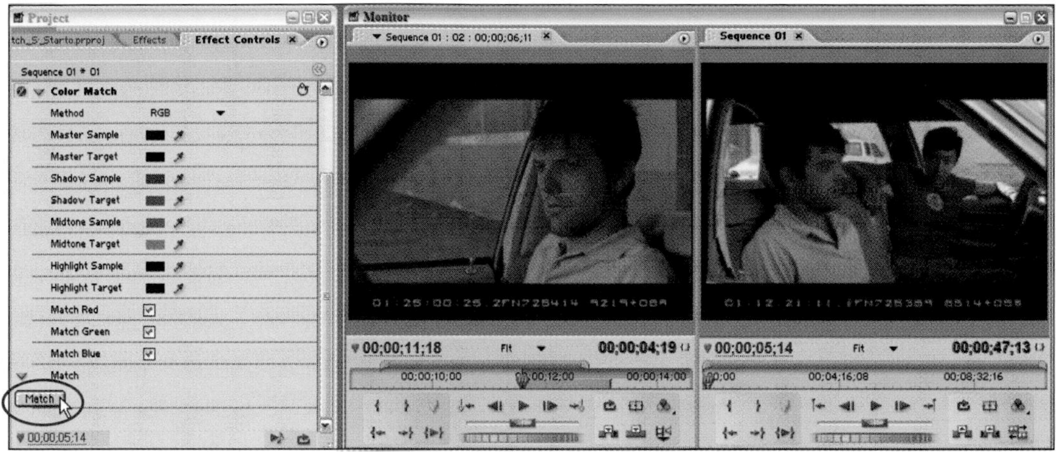

Figure 24.7 Click the Match button to match the images based on the current settings in the Color Match effect.

Clicking the Match button initializes the effect and assigns the values to the image being matched. If you go back into the Color Effect settings and sample/target other colors after you click the Match button, the effect updates automatically after you click the eye dropper or Color Picker. To avoid this and temporarily disable the Color Match effect, hold down the Shift key while you target your colors. Disabling the effect displays the original image in the Program Monitor as opposed to the matched image; that way you can sample the original values of the clip, rather than the adjusted ones.

For this pair of images, the results are quite good, and no further color matching is needed. In the next step, however, you will reduce the brightness and contrast of the first image slightly so that it is a tiny bit darker with a little less color range.

8. Drag and drop the Brightness & Contrast effect onto clip 01 in the sequence. Expand its effect parameters, and adjust the Brightness to –5 and the Contrast to –15. (See Figure 24.8.)

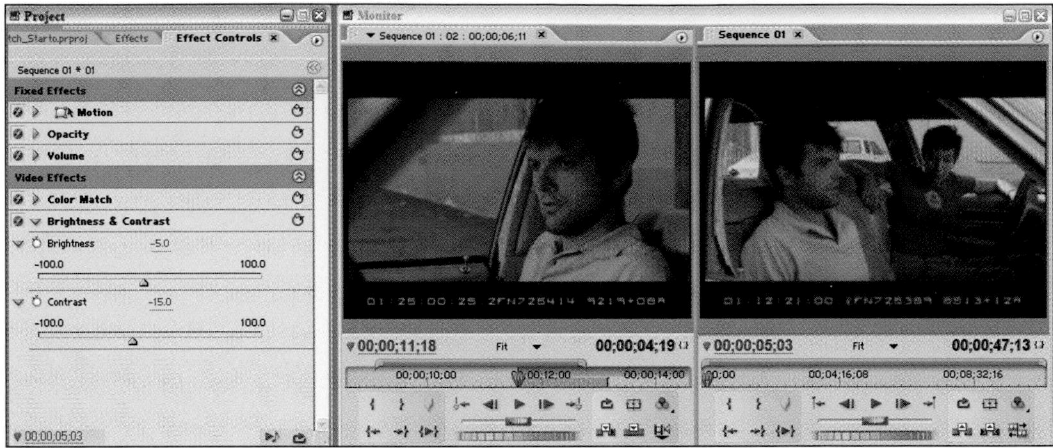

Figure 24.8 To reduce the overall brightness of the image you want to match and to give it a little more of a washed out look, you reduce the Brightness and Contrast settings for the matched clip. Comparing this image to Figure 24.7 you can see a nice slight difference.

Reducing Brightness brings down the overall levels of the image. Reducing Contrast contracts the overall color range. This works perfect for matching the rest of the clips in this sequence, because they are very low contrast shots.

9. Right-click on the Color Match effect listing in the Effect Controls window for clip 01, and choose Save Preset. Name the custom effect preset Color Match 01, and describe it with the phrase "Bleach Color Match settings to remove blue from clips 01 and 12." Ignore Type for now. From your Effects Presets folder, select the newly created preset and apply it to clip 12, the last clip in the sequence. Select clip 01 in the timeline. In the Effect Controls window, right-click on the Brightness & Contrast effect listing and choose Copy. Select clip 12 in the Timeline window. In the empty space of the Effect Controls window, right-click and choose Paste.

   Saving a Color Match preset as its own custom effect preset means you can apply it later to another clip. You can also copy individual effect parameters from one clip and paste it into the Effect Controls window for another clip. With the preset and clip 01's Brightness

& Contrast parameter applied to clip 12, there is now a final visual unity to the edited sequence.

The final results are a tremendous difference from the images that you started with and are enough to make the cut work. Using the Color Match effect, then going in and making further adjustments with the Color Corrector or other image adjusting effects, can help resolve image differences between shots that don't match.

In the APPST Lesson Files/Chapter 24/Presets folder, you'll find two Color Match presets. Color Match 01 holds the settings you used in this lesson to match clips 01 and 12 to the rest of the sequence. Color Match 02 will enable you to do the opposite: match the sequence to the blue-ish tint of clips 01 and 12. I encourage you to look at the results of matching clip 02 to clip 01 using the Color Match 02 preset, the results are excellent!

The New Auto Effects: Color, Contrast, and Levels

Among the new image adjusting effects in Premiere Pro 1.5's tool box are the Auto effects: Auto Color, Auto Contrast, and Auto Levels. You can find all three in the Video Effects/Adjust subfolder.

Auto Color adjusts the contrast and colors of your image by identifying the shadows, midtones, and highlights, then automatically neutralizing the midtones. Based on the new value of the midtone, Premiere shifts and sometimes clips the black and white colors of your image.

Auto Contrast adjusts an image's contrast by looking for its lightest and darkest colors and auto-assigning them to true white and true black, respectively. Unless you want to see an automatic white/black balance, you're better off determining true black and true white in the Color Corrector's White/Black Balance settings.

Giving you two effects for the price of one, Auto Levels adjusts your highlights (white) and shadows (black) automatically. Although similar to the Auto Color effect, Auto Levels is much more powerful, because it adjusts the black and white values in each of your three color channels. (See Figure 24.9.) The result can often be a change in contrast and a slight shift in color. Here's what each parameter adjusts:

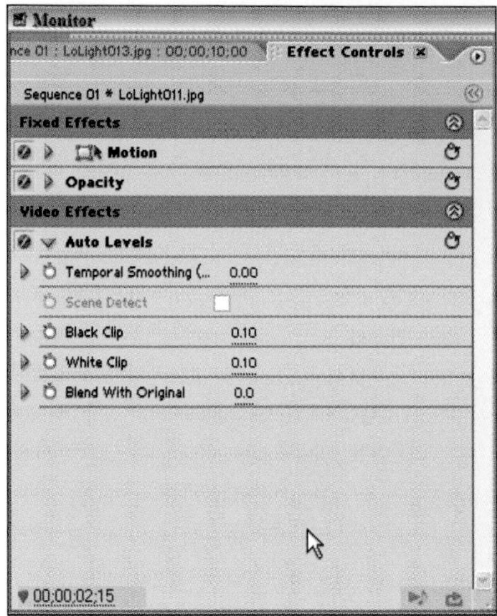

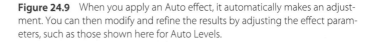

Figure 24.9 When you apply an Auto effect, it automatically makes an adjustment. You can then modify and refine the results by adjusting the effect parameters, such as those shown here for Auto Levels.

- **Temporal Smoothing.** Enables you to define how many surrounding frames you want the effect to sample when making its adjustment. A value of 0 means the effect adjusts each frame independently. A value of 3 means the effect analyzes the frame information 3 seconds before each adjusted frame to determine the proper level adjustment. To calculate how many frames are analyzed for a value of 3.3, you multiply the temporal smoothing value by the frame rate of the media: 3.3×30fps=3;09.
- **Scene Detect.** Adjusts the effect to look for the nearest frame of the same scene if there is a scene change between the frame being sampled and the frame being analyzed. Active if Temporal Smoothing is higher than 0, Scene Detect is based on a general light and image consistency.
- **Black Clip and White Clip.** Enable you to clip the black and white (shadows and highlights) levels of your image. Premiere Pro recommends you clip between 0.0% and 1.0%. The default clipping for all effects is 0.1%.

- **Blend With Original.** Blends the Auto effect adjustments with the original image underneath, similar to the Mixing feature for Audio effects. A 50% blend puts a 50% transparent version of the adjusted image on top of the original image. It is not a ghosting effect; it simply reduces the prominence of your color adjustments.

Images that do not really "snap" alive with color and seem somewhat flat in contrast can greatly benefit from the Auto effects. In each case, adjust the Black and White Clip levels to emphasize the lightness and darkness of the images, while experimenting with blending to get the right look. You may be able to make a radical adjustment and slightly blend it with the original for a very cool effect.

The Shadow/Highlight Effect

Although in many cases the automatic adjustments of Auto Color and Auto Levels may be too subtle to be noticed, the Shadow/Highlight effect is obvious and sometimes drastic. Because of this, it can actually be a great way to bring potentially lost footage (too dark, too muddy, no contrast, or too much contrast) back from the dead. (See Figure 24.10.) In essence, the Shadow/Highlight effect increases the lightening of shadow areas, increases the darkening of highlights, or both.

Figure 24.10 The Shadow/Highlight effect can distinctly brighten an image (right) from its original state (left).

The Premiere Pro manual has an excellent breakdown of all the Shadow/Highlight effect's parameters. Instead of repeating it here, I want to give you some hands on experience adjusting a few bad clips. (See Figure 24.11.)

Figure 24.11 Using the Shadow/Highlight effect, you can quickly correct shots like these. The clip on the left needs more contrast and detail where the skateboarder is doing his trick. The clip on the right has a great color set and harsh contrast, but there are no details to extract from the skater's face.

1. Open the Effects_Start.prproj file from the APPST Lesson Files/Chapter 24 folder.

   The media for this project is located in the APPST Lesson Files/Chapter 24/Skate Clips folder.

   The first clip in the sequence has a somewhat typical problem: The exposure is set for the bright area of the image, as opposed to the area of interest (the dark zone where the skateboarder does his trick).

2. Drag and drop the Shadow/Highlight effect from the Video Effects/Adjust folder, onto Skate01.avi in the sequence. (See Figure 24.12.)

   You can immediately see the difference in the image after the effect is applied. Although the blacks do start shifting to grays, the clip is in a better state than it was. And you're not done yet: You can make further improvements by adjusting individual effect parameters.

Figure 24.12 Before (left) and after (right) applying the Shadow/Highlight effect.

3. Select the Skate01 clip instance in the timeline, and expand the Shadow/Highlight effect listing in the Effect Controls window. Turn off the check box for Auto Amount. Change Shadow Amount to 30 to lighten the shadows up, and set Highlight Amount to 25 to take down the lightness of the highlights so that they are not too blown out.

   When Auto Amounts is on, the effect automatically samples the image and makes adjustments based on the shadow and highlight values it detects. Turning that option off enables you to manually set the Shadow and Highlight levels. Increasing Shadow Amount increases the lightening of the shadow tonal range in your image. The higher the Highlight Amount, the darker the emphasis on the Highlight tonal range. In both cases, a setting of 0 means no effect is applied.

4. Twirl down the More Options parameter, and set Shadow Radius and Color Correction both to 40.

   Increasing the Color Correction value gives the colors of this image a little more punch, increasing their saturation within each of the adjusted shadow and highlight tonal ranges. The greater the Color Correction value, the more saturated the colors become. If you have a lightly applied Shadow Amount, then the color adjustment in the shadow amount will not be too noticeable.

3. From the Effects window's Video Effects/Keying folder, drag and drop the Track Matte Key effect onto the first video clip in Video 1. Select the video clip, and activate the Effect Controls window so that you can view the effect properties. Twirl down the Track Matte Key effect listing, set Matte to Video 2, and set Composite Using to Matte Alpha (default value). Turn off the track output eyeball for Video 2 to see the result of the track matte. (See Figure 25.6.)

Figure 25.6 With the proper settings in the Track Matte Key effect listing (left), the video composites perfectly through the text of the title. Although the Track Matte effect is using the alpha information of the title to key through, because the title is still visible in the video track, you can see the final results only after you turn off the video overlay of the track (right).

To get the proper matte results, you have to specify which video track you want the Track Matte Key effect to composite through. Here you assigned Video 2, which contains the title. By compositing with the Matte Alpha option, the title's alpha channel becomes a transparent matte and the video punches through the text. When using the Track Matte Key effect with titles, you can safely assume that all drawn objects in a title are treated as alpha, while the background/empty area is completely transparent. This means that when you apply the Track Matte Key effect to key through the alpha of a title, it keys through object area, in this case the text.

Because the title contains objects and because the Track Matte Key effect is applied to a video clip and not the title, you need to turn off the video overlay for the track with the title in order to reveal the key through its alpha channel. This might seem a bit confusing, but because the effect is using the information for the media on Video 2, you can turn the video information off and still see the results of the effect.

When you use the Track Matte Key effect you can either composite using the alpha or luma information. Choosing Matte Alpha composites through the alpha information of the image, makes the alpha channel completely transparent and keyed through. Compositing using Matte Luma enables you to punch through the pure white areas of the image regardless of the alpha channel information, but the surrounding alpha area also punches through. The most effective way to use the luma composite method is as a reverse key, meaning you key through pure black and the alpha channel is transparent.

4. Copy and paste the Track Matte Key effect from the first instance of the LIL124.avi clip in Video 1 to the other two instances. Right-click on the Track Matte Key effect listing in the Effect Controls window for the first instance, and select Copy. Select the second clip, right-click in the Effect Controls window, and select Paste from the drop-down menu. Paste in the selected Effect Controls window for the third clip.

To copy and paste the effect settings from one clip to the next, you copied the adjusted effect from the first clip then pasted it directly into the Effect Controls window for the other two.

5. Drop the Title_Stroke file onto the Video 3 track directly above the content on the tracks below. Press Enter to render your sequence and view your results. (See Figure 25.7.)

Figure 25.7 Because the two titles are duplicates with alternate Fill settings, the video composited through Title_Fill appears perfectly inside Title_Stroke for a very clean effect.

Dropping Title_Stroke on top of the two video layers completes the look of the title. So that you can use this title as a single clip instance for later projects, however, you need to nest it.

6. Click on the Nest sequence tab in the timeline to open the sequence with the nature clip on Video 1. Drag and drop the icon for the Track Matte sequence in the Project window onto the Video 2 track. For a finishing touch, apply the Drop Shadow effect (Video Effects/ Perspective) onto the Track Matte clip on Video 2. In the Effect Controls window, twirl down Drop Shadow and set (see Figure 25.8):

   Shadow Color: **White**
   Opacity: **75**
   Direction: **0 x 115**
   Distance: **8**
   Softness: **30**
   Shadow Only: **Off**

For ideas on how to make this title a tad more dynamic, open Static_Matte_Finish.prproj to see the transitions and simple motion effect that I applied.

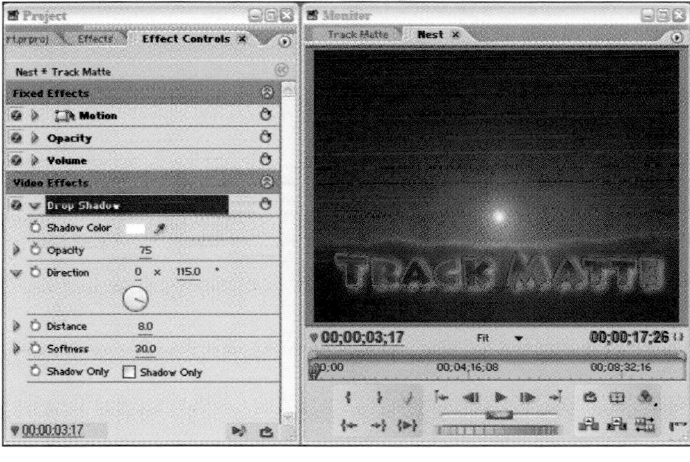

Figure 25.8 By nesting the entire track matte, you can now apply effects, such as this Drop Shadow, to the entire nested clip as opposed to every layer of the original.

The Drop Shadow effect would have affected the initial composite of the track matte if you applied it to either of the title elements. By nesting the Track Matte sequence as an individual clip, you were able to apply Drop Shadow as a clip effect to give the finished title some depth.

By applying the Track Matte Key effect to your basic title elements then adding more effects to the nested sequence, you can create a pretty compelling graphic image. Consider using this technique for creating lower-third backgrounds or objects for use in a DVD menu.

Adding Effects to Your Track Matte

This second lesson reveals a slightly different structure for arranging track matte elements, one that enables you to apply effects to the graphic used as the matte. You will create a quick track matte and add effects, such as a blur, to smooth its edges.

A common mistake is to apply the effect to the graphic in the same sequence that the Track Matte Key effect is being applied. Take a look at TM_Blur_Start.prproj in the APPST Lesson Files/Chapter 25 folder, and you'll see why this doesn't work. View the Bad Blur sequence shown in Figure 25.9. A Gaussian Blur was applied to the graphic file, assuming it would only soften the edges of the rectangle. Then, a Track Matte Key effect similar to the previous lesson's was applied to the video clip on the track below. Video 1 was properly composited through the rectangle on Video 2, but the Gaussian Blur affects the video information of the graphic and not the alpha channel information that the clip below is keying through.

Figure 25.9 Applying a blur to the graphic or title that serves as the track matte does blur the edges of the graphic element, but it does not blur the information in the alpha channel for the element. Notice how the white rectangle is blurred, but the video is still keying through the original rectangular shape.

To correctly apply effects to the matte graphic, you need an alternate workflow.

1. From Premiere Pro 1.5's File menu choose File>New>Photoshop File. (If you do not have Photoshop, import Circle.psd from the APPST Lesson Files/Chapter 25 folder.) Specify a path and name (such as Circle) for the file you are about to create. When Photoshop opens, use the Ellipse tool (M key) to create a large circle in the center of the frame. Press the G key to access the paint bucket, and fill the circle with white. (See Figure 25.10.) Save the file.

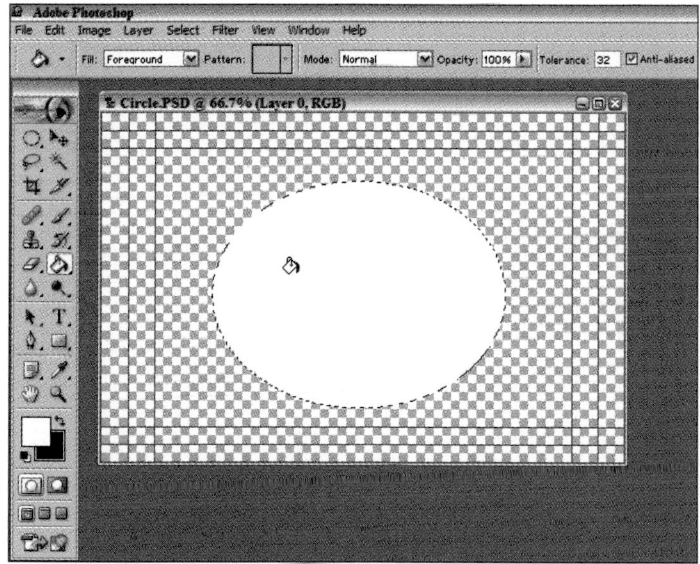

Figure 25.10 Choose Files>New>Photoshop File to quickly create a Photoshop file that has the same frame size as the project in which you are working. Here you created a large circle and filled it with white.

Create New Photoshop is a brand new feature for Premiere Pro 1.5. With it, you quickly named and created a Photoshop file that adhered to your exact Premiere project frame size (720¥480).

2. Go back to Premire Pro 1.5, and you will find that exact Circle.psd file inserted in your Project window automatically. Drag and drop it onto Video 1 of the Blur Matte Sequence. Extend the graphic to be about 25;00 in duration. Apply the Gaussian Blur to the file, and adjust its Blurriness to 25.0. (See Figure 25.11.)

Figure 25.11 Circle.psd will serve as the track matte, and the Gaussian Blur softens the graphic's edges. To ensure the blur applies properly and integrates into the final track matte, you must keep the graphic with blur effect in a separate sequence. This way the alpha information of the graphic is preserved and used when the graphic serves as your track matte.

Because you will use this graphic in another sequence later, you extended its duration here. The Gaussian Blur softens the edge of the graphic. For Premiere to recognize the blur as part of the matte graphic and its alpha channel, you next need to nest this sequence.

3. Open the Blur Matte Nest sequence, drag Blur Matte Sequence from the Project window, and drop it into the Video 2 track. Drag and drop the LIL124.avi file directly below the nested sequence in Video 1.

   In this step, you nested the blur sequence with the matte sequence. With the two elements in the same sequence, you can now apply the Track Matte Key effect to the clip on Video 2. From here, the steps follow the workflow of the previous lesson.

4. Apply the Track Matte Key effect to the clip on Video 2. Assign Video 1 for Matte, and set Composite Using to Matte Alpha. (See Figure 25.12.)

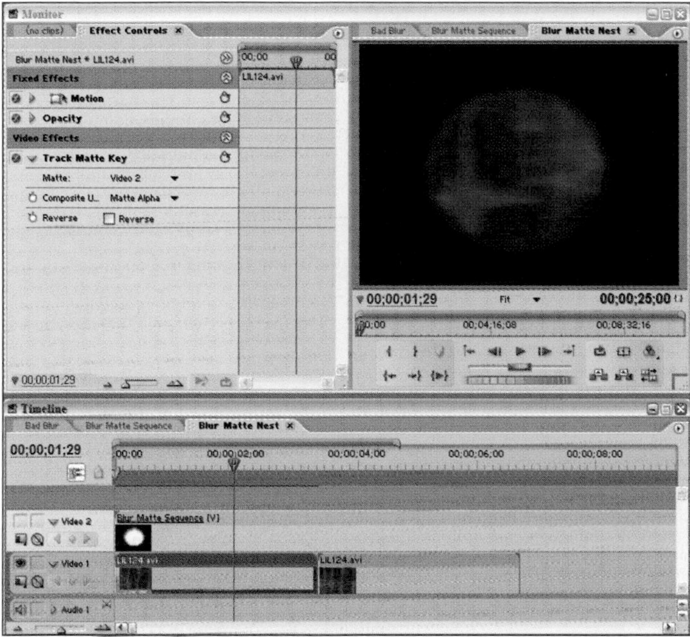

Figure 25.12 Use the nested sequence as the track matte for the clip on Video 1 to composite through. Remember to turn off the video output eyeball so that the graphic does not overlay the track matte video. Notice the soft edge of the blurred circle is preserved.

When you applied the Track Matte Key effect this time, the sequence composited correctly. You can add further effects, as well. If you want to apply motion to the matte, for example, just manipulate the nested sequence. For a drop shadow, nest Blur Matte Sequence and apply Drop Shadow as a clip effect to the new nested sequence.

To update the Gaussian Blur effect, open Blur Matte Sequence and modify the effect at the graphic's level. If you do adjust the graphic's Gaussian Blur, however, you will see only the adjustment of the graphic as black and white in the Program Monitor. You will not see the end result of the composite (the circle with the video composited). Fortunately, you can work around this.

5. Holding down the Ctrl key, double-click on the Blur Matte Nest in the Project window. Dock the Effect Controls window in your Project window. In the Timeline window, open Blur Matte Sequence. With your Effect Controls window open and the Circle.psd file selected in the timeline, adjust the Blurriness of the Gaussian Blur to 76. Watch it update in both windows. (See Figure 25.13.)

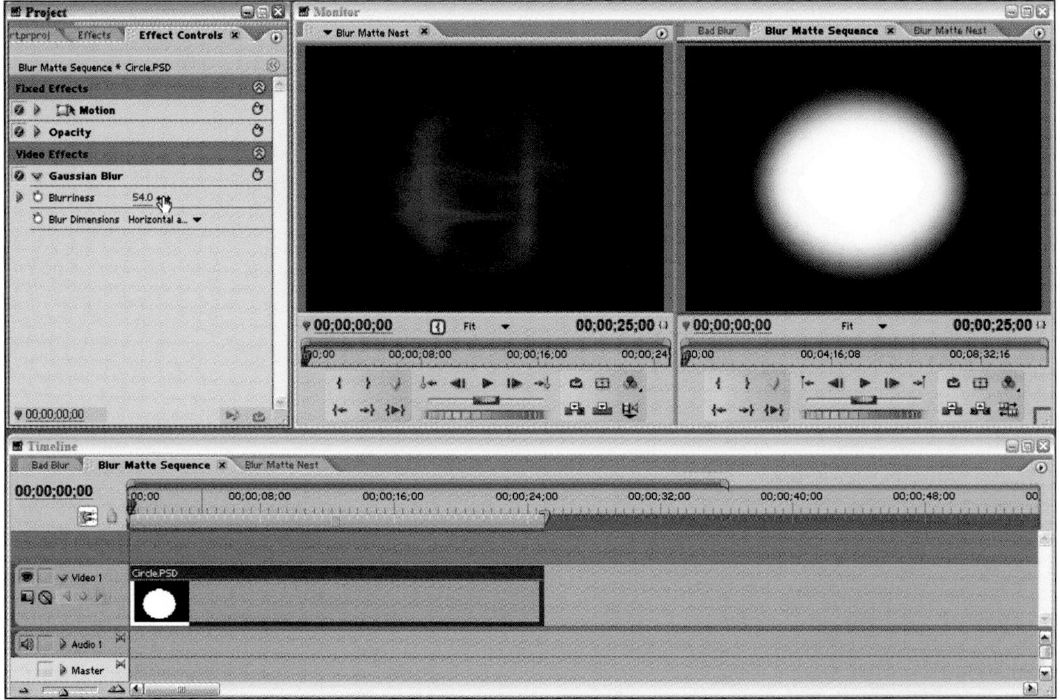

Figure 25.13 Having the Blur Matte Sequence active in the timeline, open the Blur Matte Nest sequence in your Source Monitor. By docking the Effect Controls window in your Project window, you can select the graphic element in the Blur Matte Sequence and adjust its effects settings. With this workspace you see the graphic update in the Program Monitor and the nested instance update in the Source Monitor.

Docking the Effect Controls window in the Project window gives you access to the Effect Controls window while you view the Source Monitor's contents. In other words, with the Blur Matte Nest sequence loaded into the Source Monitor you can look at the results of your adjustments. With the Effect Controls window available and the final sequence open in the Source Monitor, you opened Blur Matte Sequence, selected Circle.psd, and manipulated its blurriness directly in the Effect Controls window.

I encourage you to watch this chapter's video lesson, "Track Mattes, Source, & Program Monitor," which is featured in the Advanced Techniques section of the DVD training. It reveals an even more technical and specific workflow that involves adjusting the track matte and previewing the results at an exact frame of the nested sequence and an exact frame of the track matte sequence.

For such effects as blurring to be incorporated in the track matte composite, remember that the effects must be applied to the graphic *in its own sequence*, then the track matte graphics *must be nested.* By nesting the graphic, you are ensuring that the alpha channel of the nested sequence will reflect the effect adjustments to the graphic in the sequence.

Exploring Full Motion Video Track Mattes

Now that you understand the basic components of creating and setting a proper track matte, I want to leave you with some footage that will enable you to explore the track matte technique further. On the DVD, you'll find a number of video clips generously provided by Artbeats.

Two interesting files are RF108.avi and RF108M.avi. These files are exact copies of each other, except RF108M.avi is a grayscale rendering of the color file for you to use as a matte. Because the RF108M.avi file does not have any alpha information to key through, you can use the Matte Luma Composite setting to get a cool result. The project file TM_Video.prproj will give you an idea of the necessary stacking order and results of a Track Matte Key effect applied to these video clips. (See Figure 25.14.)

Artbeats provides grayscale matte files as well as full color versions of many different clips that can be used for Track Matte Key effects. The one-time purchase fee allows you to use and reuse the content royalty free. I use Artbeats clips often, and I encourage you to check out the company's online library at **www.artbeats.com**.

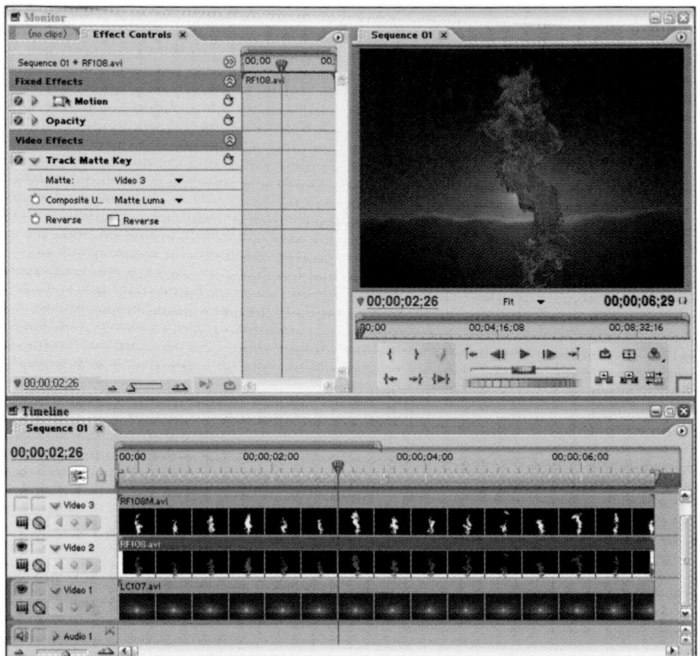

Figure 25.14 The background for the composite is on Video 1, the track matte video source is on Video 2, and the clip that you are using as the track matte is on Video 3. Because the clip on Video 3 has only grayscale information associated with it, you use the Track Matte Key effect for the clip on Video 2 keying through the content on Video 3. To key through only the white portion of the clip (in this case the flame), you set Composite Using to Matte Luma. If you want fire blowing from one side of the frame instead of the bottom, simply rotate the files on Video 2 and 3 exactly 90 degrees.

Things to Remember

The Track Matte Key effect is a powerful effect in Premiere Pro's arsenal. Because you can use alpha channel information to matte out elements, there is no resolution compromise when you output and render your final results.

When creating your track matte graphic elements, remember that the Matte Luma setting of Composite Using composites through pure white and should be used only if you don't have any alpha channel information to key through. If you want to key through the black information of a clip without an alpha, check the Reverse option to composite through the black using Luma. With Matte

Alpha, Premiere Pro composites through the nontransparent alpha channel information of your media. With titles and Photoshop files, their empty space is not considered the alpha channel, instead the graphic and object within the frame will be attributed to the alpha channel.

When adding any blurs or image adjustment effects to the clip, graphic, or title used as your matte, be sure to apply those effects to the *source clip* in a *separate* sequence. You can then nest that sequence and use it as the material for the track matte.

From the Track Matte Key effect, you'll move to another type of compositing. In the next chapter, you will use green/blue screen keying to finish the Live MultiCam lesson you started back in Chapter 20, "Multi-Cam Editing: Live Shoot."

CHAPTER

26

Green/Blue Screen Keying and After Effects

As you learned in the last chapter, keying involves replacing elements of one image with those of another. Green and blue screen keying keys out the green and blue information from one image, making it transparent so other images can show through. Using green and blue screen keying techniques, you can make a person appear in different locations or environments. In the *Lord of the Rings* films, for example, green screen tarps were hung up around actors to enable full flexibility for incorporating computer generated background elements in hundreds of shots.

In this chapter, you will learn how to set up and light a green/blue screen shoot, as well as how to key out the recorded green/blue elements in Premiere Pro. The first lesson provides an overview of setting up your shoot and of the tools you can use to make green/blue screen keying much easier and more accurate. The second lesson takes some imperfect green screen elements from Chapter 20's live multi-cam shoot and shows you how to key out the green screen to introduce different backgrounds for the material. You also will use garbage mattes to clip sections of your image, removing excess material in a single action.

To get things started, let me first give you some tips about the fundamentals for setting up a good looking green screen shoot.

Setting Up Your Green/Blue Screen Shoot

From the screen itself to properly placing your lights, here's what you should consider when setting up a green screen shoot.

A *cylcorama* is a stage with walls that smoothly curve into the floor, instead of meeting it perpendicularly. (See Figure 26.1.) Because of this slightly curved transition, no harsh shadows get caught in the angle of the wall hitting the floor. Cycloramas painted white give the appearance of an infinite background, as in George Lucas' film *THX-1138* where characters wandered aimlessly, lost in an empty, sterile pure white world.

Ultimatte, a company that is synonymous with green/blue screen compositing, offers several plug-ins that assist with green screen post-production work, as well. For a complete list of Ultimatte plug-ins and hardware acceleration products to lower rendering times, go to **www.ultimatte.com**.

Any place where you can rent lighting or grip equipment you can likely pick up a big roll of thick green screen paper. The rolls are typically six to ten feet wide, and you can hang them from the ceiling and unroll them to reveal a flat, pure green background. I used this type of green screen for the example material. If you want more space and more room to move around, you might consider renting a stage that has a cyclorama painted the proper green color, which is technically called Ultimatte Green.

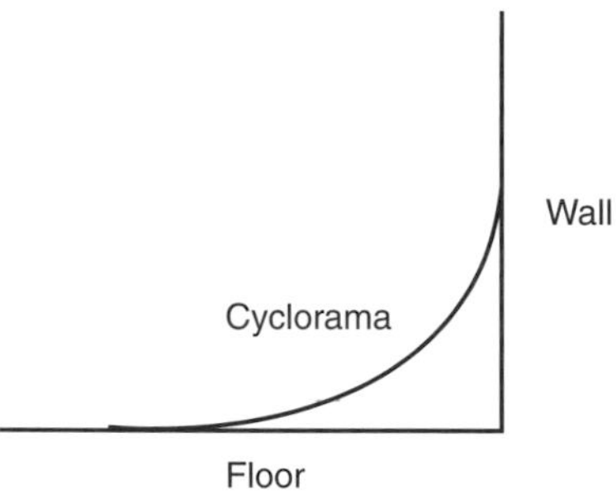

Figure 26.1 Where a regular wall meets the floor, a shadow hits the floor and also hits the wall in a slightly disjointed fashion. With a cyclorama, you cannot see where the floor ends and the wall begins, and the shadow appears as one continuous shadow.

Your screen is hung, now you need lights. Figure 26.2 illustrates proper lighting for the subject and green screen in medium to close-up shots. Do the best with the resources you have; even the lighting for the example footage wasn't perfect. Premiere Pro and other tools can help you later.

Position your subject far enough from the green screen that the shadows created from the lights on the subject do not cast on it. Keep an even light source on the green screen itself (L1 in Figure 26.2), producing an even tone rather than various shades of green. An evenly lit green screen background can be more effectively keyed out. If the light is severely angled and very close to the screen, you'll see color shades and a noticeable bright spot. If a green screen is lit too brightly or the subject is too close to the screen, you risk the green color reflecting off the screen and spilling onto the subject. The spill color, which could end up on clothes or the side of your subject's face, is the same color as the screen; when you key the screen, the spill area will be keyed out as well.

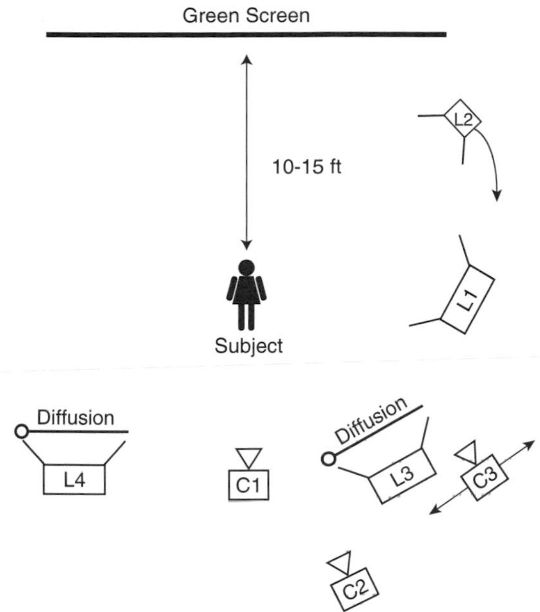

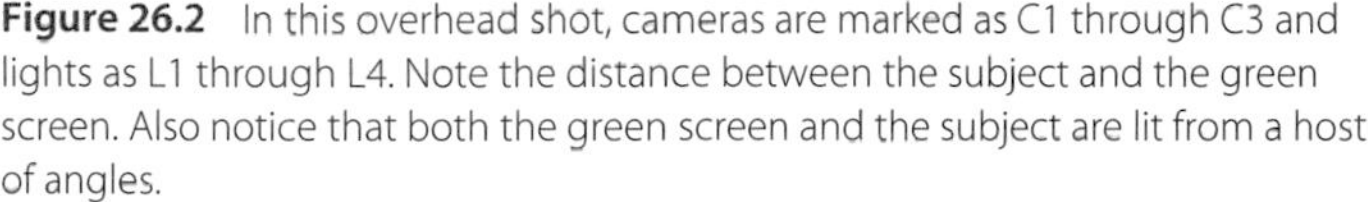

Figure 26.2 In this overhead shot, cameras are marked as C1 through C3 and lights as L1 through L4. Note the distance between the subject and the green screen. Also notice that both the green screen and the subject are lit from a host of angles.

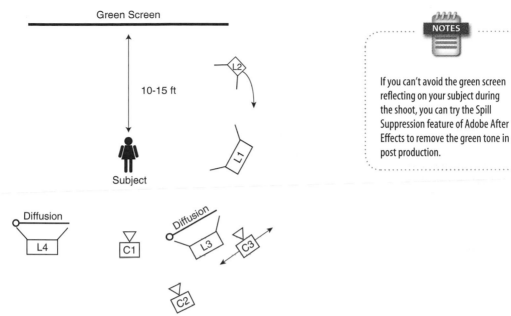

If you can't avoid the green screen reflecting on your subject during the shoot, you can try the Spill Suppression feature of Adobe After Effects to remove the green tone in post production.

Pointing one light directly at your subject produces a flat effect. Instead, place at least two lights at or slightly above head height, pointing downward on the subject (L3 and L4 in Figure 26.2). Of these two lights, one light should be half as bright as the other. With each light coming from a different angle, the lighting has some mild depth.

To create a clear distinction between the background green screen and the foreground subject, you need a back light. This third light (L2 in Figure 26.2) should be small, bright, and narrowly focused at an angle so that it hits the back of your subject's head and shoulders. (See Figure 26.3.) In terms of exposure, the background green should be equal to the exposure of the foreground subject. The back light should be brighter so that it is visible above the lighting of the other elements. With your subject well lit, both front and back, you can more easily get an exact edge to your subject, meaning it will integrate better with whatever is keyed into the green screen. With your lighting set up, you're ready to find the right camera angle and start recording.

If you have the budget, you might consider some new alternatives to hanging a literal green screen. In the last couple of years, there have been some great breakthroughs that aid the green/blue screen process.

For example, Reflecmedia's LiteRing enables you to create a sharp blue or green screen by using a small ring of light and a reflective gray screen. The LiteRing fits around the lens of your camera and emits a blue or green light. A custom fabric screen reflects this light directly back into the lens of the camera. Although the screen appears gray to the naked eye, the blue or green color can be seen perfectly and evenly through the camera's lens. One advantage to using this technology is that you need to light only your subject, and you don't have to worry about lighting the screen. With the LiteRing around the lens, the technology of the fabric takes care of a perfect looking blue or green screen. The other advantage is that you will never have any reflective blue or green spillage onto your subject. For more information on LiteRing, see Reflecmedia's website at **www.reflecmedia.com**.

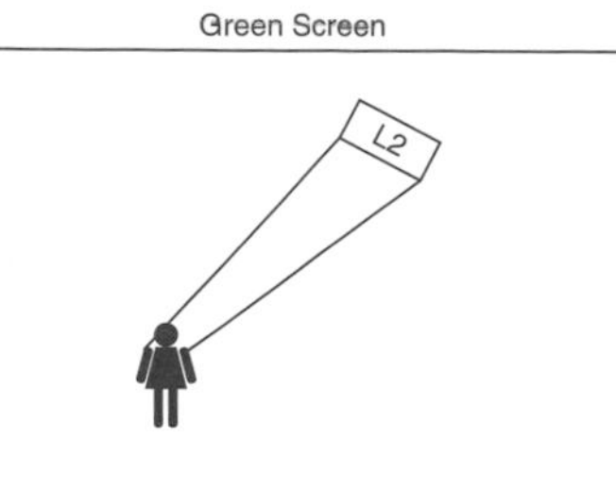

Figure 26.3 In the aerial view, you can see that the back light (L2) is pointed at an angle at which it can spread light over the entire back of the subject without pointing directly into any of the shooting cameras. In the head-on camera view, the outline to the subject shows the result of the light.

Green/Blue Screen Keying and Premiere Pro

Premiere Pro has adequate green/blue screen keying tools, but does not have a wide range of controls for fine-tuning the key, which is a hot topic. I recommend using Premiere for a rough cut that you then import into After Effects for final editing.

In this lesson, you will separately key out each of the backgrounds from Chapter 20's multi-cam shoot. Once you have the proper key set, you will then use the Garbage Matte effect to remove some excess material from the frame of the cluttered B and C cameras. As you work, you quickly will understand why you must have a bright and strong green screen background to get good results in Premiere Pro.

1. Open Key_Start.prproj from the APPST Lesson Files/Chapter 26 folder on the accompanying DVD. This project picks up after you white/black/gray balanced the shots that make up the multi-cam shoot.

   The multi-cam media in the project can be found in the APPST Lesson Files/Chapter 20 folder. The remaining files can be found in the APPST Lesson Files/Artbeats folder.

2. Open A Sequence in the Timeline window, and set up the proper hierarchy for keying a green screen. Drag the clip in Video 1 up to Video 2. (See Figure 26.4.) From the Project window, drag and drop the Artbeats file named LC107.avi onto Video 1, snapping its head to the Edit Line. Press the X key to activate the Rate Stretch tool, and extend the tail of the added clip to snap to the end of the clip on Video 2. (See Figure 26.5.)

Effects applied in the Effect Controls window are processed hierarchically; Premiere applies the top effect listed first, then applies the remaining effects on top of each other. In step 3, you adjusted the order of the Green Screen Key effect so that it applies after the Color Corrector effect. The new order ensures that the key will take advantage of the image adjustments made with the Color Corrector.

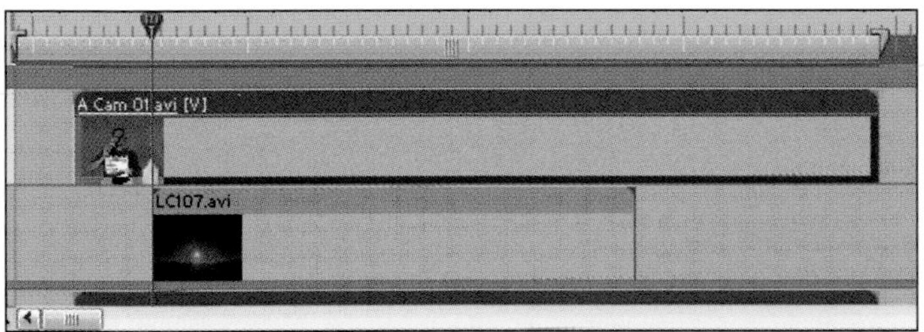

Figure 26.4 For the key effect, you must move the green screen clip above the content that you want to appear through the key. Here the green screen is on Video 2 and the background is underneath on Video 1.

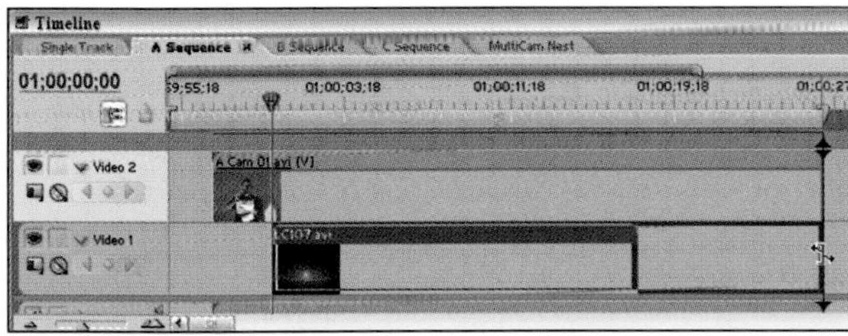

Figure 26.5 Rate Stretch is the perfect tool for adjusting a clip's speed to accommodate a set duration. Here, you use the Rate Stretch tool to extend the end of the background clip to the end of the clip on Video 2.

For successful green screen keying, the green screen material needs to be on a track above the background. If, like here, your background's duration is somewhat less than the green screen clip's, the Rate Stretch tool can extend the duration of the background clip by slowing its speed while preserving the clip's assigned In and Out points in the timeline. Rate Stretch will also speed up a clip if you need to shorten it.

3. Drag and drop the Green Screen Key effect from the Effects/Video Effects/Keying folder onto the clip in Video 2. In the Effect Controls, window, drag and drop the Green Screen Key effect so that it is applied after

the Color Corrector. Twirl down the Green Screen Key effect listing, adjust the Threshold to 70, and set Smoothing to High. (See Figure 26.6.)

Figure 26.6 By default, the Green Screen Key effect applies itself to the clip keying through the green. Because the green screen background of this image was not incredibly bright, the composited background appears through a slight haze. Note that you will want the Program Monitor's Preview mode set to Highest Quality for the most accurate results.

With the effect applied, the results are not perfect. Because the green screen is not strongly lit, the very vibrant green area is not completely keyed out. Adjusting the Threshold reduces the strength of the composited image, allowing the key to be stronger. In addition, when you play this clip, you can see that the background seeps through the subject, even though he is not green. To correct this as much as possible, you will use the brand new Auto Contrast effect to adjust the contrast of your corrected image. Setting Smoothing to High ensures a higher level of sensitivity and smoothness when differentiating between the edge of what is keyed out and what is not.

4. Position the Edit Line at 1;00;08;04 in the sequence. Drag and drop the Auto Contrast effect into the Effect Controls window for the selected clip below the Color Corrector effect listing and above the Green Screen Key effect listing. Twirl down the Auto Contrast effect listing, and assign White Clip to be 0.01. (See Figure 26.7.)

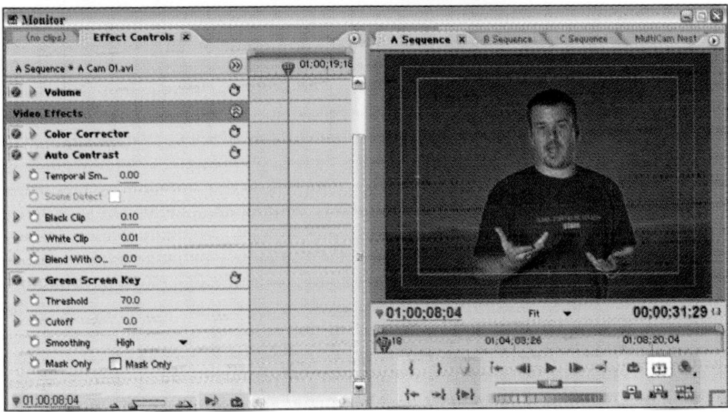

Figure 26.7 The current frame before contrast adjustments (top) and the results of the Auto Contrast adjustment (bottom). Although this slightly changes the color structure of the image, it clearly does a more accurate job of removing the key and reducing the transparency of the subject. The Auto Contrast also reduced the flat, washed out coloring of the original image.

By applying the Auto Contrast to the results of the Color Corrector effect, you reduced the gray, washed out coloring of the clip. Once the contrast of the clip became more defined, the Green Screen Key did a more accurate job of keying out the background and green area. Although the default Auto Contrast effect yielded a result with a bit too much bright white in the image, you lowered the White Clip value to make sure that the bright white was not as prominent in the image. This step certainly emphasizes the power and ease of using the new Auto effects in Premiere Pro 1.5.

5. Right-click on the Green Screen Key effect from the active Effect Controls window, and choose Copy. Open B Sequence in the Timeline window, and select B Cam 01.avi. Right-click in the Effect Controls window with this clip selected, and choose Paste. Select C Sequence and the clip in the timeline, and paste again into the Effect Controls window.

   This cutting and pasting technique is very useful when you want to share effects between clips whether they're in the same sequence or different sequences.

6. In the Color Corrector for the clip in B Sequence, adjust the HSL>Master>Contrast value to 40. This better differentiates the green screen from the subject.

   For this step, you are essentially problem solving in a different manner than for the last. If you apply the Auto Contrast effect to this clip, you will find the results are not that dramatic or very noticeable. (See Figure 26.8.) This is because the original clip already has a decent contrast range.

   To manually create a more noticeable contrast difference for the clip, go into the HSL controls of the Color Corrector effect, selecting and adjusting Master Tonal Range Contrast. The result will be noticeable. (See Figure 26.8.)

Figure 26.8 The original image (top left), the result of applying Auto Contrast to the clip (bottom left), and the result of adjusting the Master Tonal Range Contrast to 40 in the Color Corrector's HSL controls.

7. Open C Sequence, select C Cam 01.avi, and open the Effect Controls window. Twirl down the effect listing for Green Screen Key. Reassign the Threshold to 50, and adjust the Color Corrector HSL>Master>Contrast value to 20 as shown in Figure 26.9.

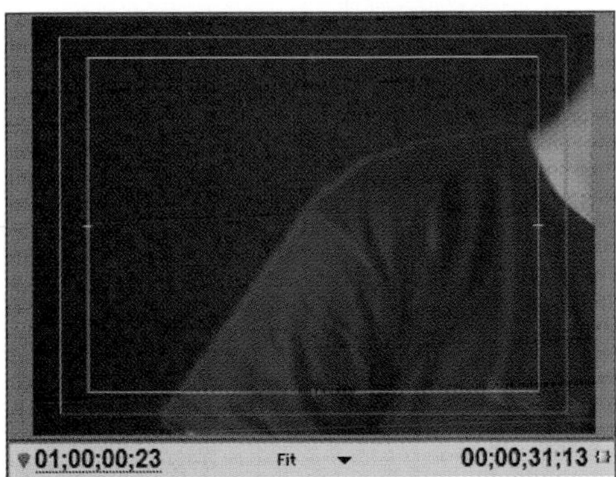

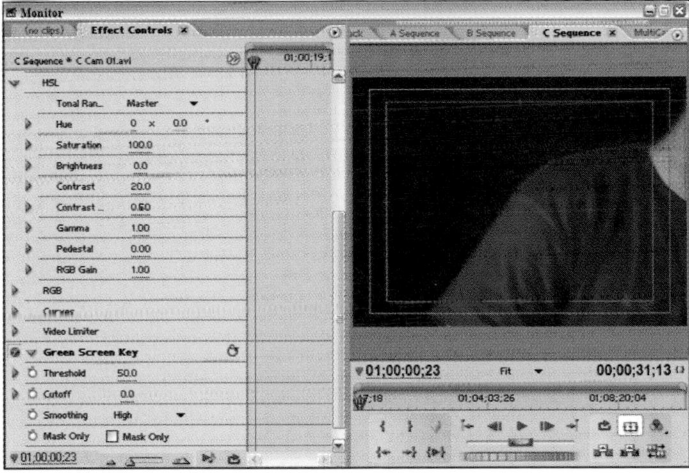

Figure 26.9 Despite the Green Screen Key effect, there are still some areas of the top image that aren't completely keyed out. After adjusting Threshold and HSL Contrast, the key improves (bottom).

This step pushes the integrity of the files even further to achieve a decent green screen effect. Even so, some of the moments in a few of these shots will not be usable because the green screen is slicing too thick into the image; fortunately, you have three cameras to cut among.

Reducing Threshold makes the image even more transparent by reducing the strength of the overlaying image. Increasing the contrast makes the green key color that much more definable and adds to the quality of the key. The shot should match fine with others, and the key will be more effective.

8. For B Sequence, move the video clip on Video 1 up to Video 2, and place the RT113.avi background file end to end a number of times so that it appears beneath the green screen shot for its entire duration. For C Sequence, move the video clip to Video 2, and place eight instances of the WA114.avi background end to end beneath it on Video 1. Open the MultiCam Nest sequence, and press Enter to render the sequence and see your results.

   The C Sequence content is a bit troublesome still and doesn't match as well with the other shots. Part of the reason is that adjusting contrast and other fundamental image settings can have dramatic results. If you have a problem sequence like C Sequence, consider moving to After Effects, which offers more controls to draw out the green screen without devaluing the integrity of your image that is being keyed.

9. Save your work so you can clean up the project a bit more with Premiere's Garbage Matte effects in the next lesson.

Keying out the green screen and adding the different backgrounds makes you better appreciate the value of the nesting structure you set up when editing this multi-cam material. Having each clip in its own sequence, you can update all the clip instances in the final sequence with just one keying adjustment. With your Green Screen Key effect assigned, you're ready to use the Garbage Matte effects to remove the extra elements from B Sequences and C Sequence.

Garbage Mattes

Eight- and Sixteen-Point Garbage Matte effects have been added to Premiere Pro 1.5. With them, you can clean up and remove unnecessary elements that appear in a clip.

Garbage Mattes are a way of cropping your image so that certain frame areas are cut entirely. Take a look.

1. Open Garbage_Start.prproj from APPST Lesson Files/Chapter 26 folder. In your desktop workspace, be sure you have the Effect Controls window and Effects window open.

2. In B Sequence, click and select the video clip on Video 2. Open the Effect Controls window, and click the Effect Toggle button for Green Screen Key to temporarily turn the effect off. Position the Edit Line at 1;00;00;00. From the Effects/Video Effects/Keying folder, drag and drop the Sixteen-Point Garbage Matte effect on top of the selected clip. Reposition the Garbage Matte effect so that it is at the top of the Video Effects list. Click on the Sixteen-Point Garbage Matte effect listing in the Effect Controls window. (See Figure 26.10.)

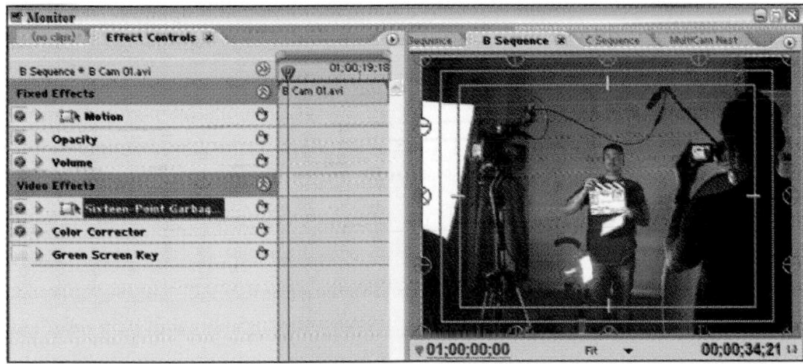

Figure 26.10 With the Green Screen Key effect toggled off, you can see which elements need to be cropped out: the hanging microphone cord and the camera objects. Clicking on the Garbage Matte effect listing enables direct manipulation; you then can manually drag any of the visible handle points to a new position to crop the image.

A bunch of elements need to be removed from the B camera shot. Because this shot is from a tripod and the camera remains stationary, you can safely crop out certain areas of the frame to remove the objects surrounding the subject. Turning off the Green Screen Key effect enables you to see clearly the definition of the objects surrounding the subject and to identify which need to be matted out.

Because direct manipulation is available for the Garbage Matte effects, clicking on the effect listing displays each of the 16 points that you can move and reposition to crop out extra elements.

3. Clicking on the various points for the Garbage Matte effect, drag each inward so that the wires, lights, cameras, and cameraman are cropped out. (See Figure 26.11.)

Figure 26.11 With 16 points to manipulate, you can easily crop a cluttered frame. As the image is cropped, you can see the background clip beneath it appear in the cropped area.

A Garbage Matte enables you to crop an image so that you can easily erase and entirely remove whatever portions of the image reside outside the matte's boundary.

4. Increase your Program Monitor zoom to 150%. Select the Hand tool (H), and reposition the frame in the Program Monitor so that you can see the top of the subject's head. Press V to get back to the Selection tool, and be sure that the matte is cropping out the wire and not the top of the head. (See Figure 26.12.)

Although the Program Monitor zoom is not used that often, this is a perfect example of when and where it is practical to zoom in and study your image to make sensitive adjustments.

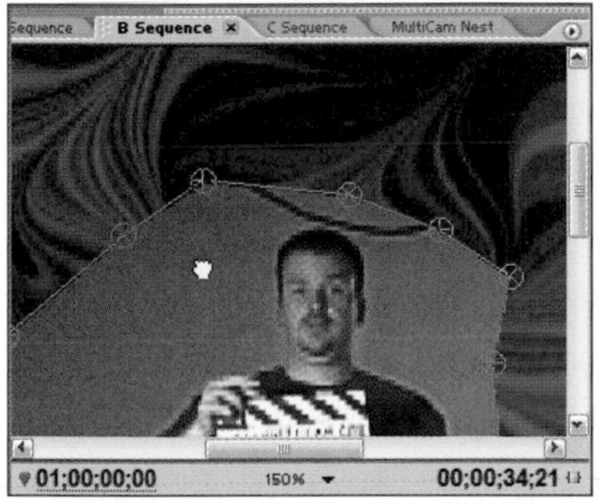

Figure 26.12 In version 1.5, the Hand tool not only helps you reposition the timeline, but it also allows you to reposition the image in the zoomed Program Monitor (left). In the image on the right, because you are zoomed in, you can define the garbage matte so that it properly crops out the microphone cable.

5. Click off the Garbage Matte effect in the Effect Controls window, and toggle on the Green Screen Key effect. Scrub through the sequence, and check out the results.

   The image is obviously much cleaner, but you still can see a slight haze surrounding the subject in a few spots because the green screen was not perfectly and entirely keyed through the footage. Once again, After Effects can help you.

6. Switch to C Sequence, and try what you've learned by applying the Eight- or Sixteen-Point Garbage Matte.

   C Sequence is a bit more difficult to matte, because the camera moves. Like all effects, however, the Garbage Mattes are keyframeable, and you will need to use keyframes to remove the light that keeps appearing on the left side of the frame. Once you start cropping out C Sequence, you may have to continue to reduce the Green Screen Key effect threshold to make the edge less noticeable. To see how this is done, consult Garbage_Finish.prproj in the APPST Lesson Files/Chapter 26 folder.

Using the Garbage Matte effects, you can quickly crop out areas of your image. Because there is a video clip beneath your clip with the Garbage Matte, as soon as you start making matte adjustments the clip elements are removed and the background shows through. By clipping out the extra pieces of the image you can clearly see that the Green Screen Key effect has not totally keyed out the screen.

If you have a perfect green screen key, then Premiere Pro can do the job just fine, however if you have a troublesome or less than desirable green screen key, try taking the project into Adobe After Effects. Adobe After Effects and its Keylight plug-in (available with the Production Bundle) can complement Premiere Pro by adjusting keys further without compromising the integrity of the original image.

Green/Blue Screen Keying and After Effects

Included with the After Effects Production Bundle and developed by The Foundry, the Keylight plug-in is absolutely amazing at keying out green and blue screen material. For example, all those values you struggled to find and adjust in Premiere Pro can be found and assigned in the click of a few buttons with Keylight.

You can launch After Effects and easily import the Premiere Pro multi-cam project directly into a new composition. Next, you apply the Keylight effect to each of the green screen source clips in their source sequences to key the video through them. Because After Effects recognizes the project and nesting structure of the sequences, your final edit remains intact with all the elements properly keyed. Figures 26.13 through 26.15 should give you an idea of the quality of a simple default Keylight adjustment; consider the following image comparisons for each of the source files.

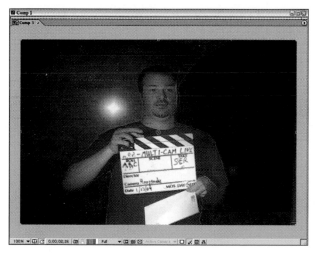

Figure 26.13 The frame keyed in Premiere Pro (top) and After Effect's adjustments to the same frame (bottom). You can remove the green screen in just a few clicks with Keylight and not have to manipulate or adjust the integrity of the original image.

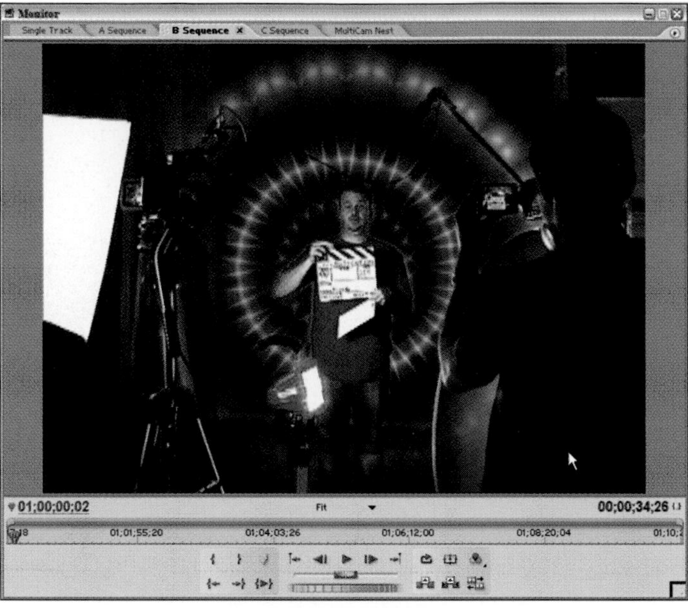

Figure 26.14 The Premiere Pro 1.5 frame (top) and the frame from the After Effects Production Bundle 6.5 with Keylight (bottom). The minor After Effects adjustments did not alter the inherent properties in the source material to accommodate the green screen key.

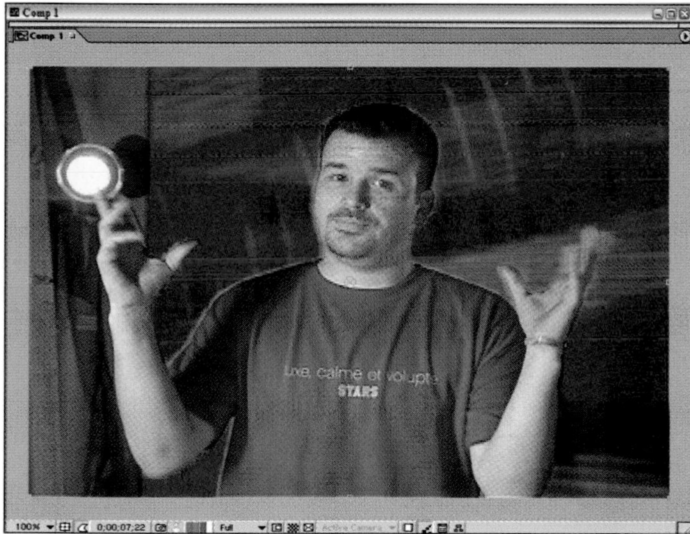

Figure 26.15 Compared to the Premiere Pro 1.5 frame (top), notice the definition and boundary of the key adhering to the edge of the screen in the After Effects Production Bundle frame (bottom). You can continue to tweak and adjust to get that slight green edge off the subject's shoulders, then you can keyframe a Garbage Matte to cut out areas.

For more on how to work with the Keylight plug-in and After Effects 6.5, see the video tutorial "Keying in Adobe After Effects 6.5," in the Advanced Techniques section of the accompanying DVD.

Things to Remember

If you are in a studio and can't paint or hang your matte, you may want to explore Reflecmedia's LiteRing option, which I have found to be very reliable and effective. Using LiteRing also ensures that the power and brightness of your screen is consistent and easier to key out.

This chapter presented a common production scenario: The footage wasn't perfect and needed tweaking. As the comparative results demonstrate, Premiere Pro does leave room to be desired in terms of crisp edges, spill suppression, and enhancing a poor key. For the example, a brighter image in the source footage and better exposure on both the subject and the green screen would have produced better results from Premiere Pro—but you still would be limited to the tools of the Green Screen Key effect. If you are serious about your green/blue screen work then I won't pull any punches: You're better off using the After Effects Production Bundle and Keylight.

Beyond green/blue screen keying, Premiere Pro's Garbage Matte effects enable you to crop your image. Simply drag the handles to remove entire sections or areas of your image.

Whether you enhance your image from the get go by having a cleaner brighter key (LiteRing) or you use another tool for compositing (After Effects or Ultimatte), this chapter has outlined and exposed a number of issues involved in the shooting and post-production process working with green/blue screen material.

In the next chapter, you will learn a great technique for creating a picture-in-picture (PiP) template using the Adobe Title Designer, as well as how to maximize the custom PiP presets that come with Adobe Premiere Pro 1.5.

CHAPTER

27

Creating a Good Picture-in-Picture

A picture-in-picture effect (PiP) is quite easy to achieve in Premiere Pro: Drop a clip in the timeline on one video track, then drop a second clip above it on another track. Resize the top clip to make it smaller, add a drop shadow, and quickly you've created a simple PiP. The result is a small video clip on top of another full-size clip. This effect is useful when you are trying to put more information on the screen or when you want to reference a video clip that someone on screen is talking about. The best and most common PiP examples play every night on the news.

To help your PiP image stand out from the image it's covering, however, you need more than a basic drop shadow. You need a frame. In this chapter, you will learn the Adobe Title Designer settings that make up a great looking frame, then you will marry the title and the video to build a simple, clean picture-in-picture effect. You will then learn how to transform your settings into custom presets that can be used for multiple PiP effects.

Building a Custom Frame

The most common question I hear about Premiere picture-in-picture effects is how to create a strong border or edge for the image that is overlaid on the other clips.

Using effects only on a clip, you might add a Bevel Edge and a soft Edge Feather, but this typical look doesn't frame the PiP image well or make it stand out.

Using the Adobe Title Designer, I discovered a picture perfect way of creating a custom frame that you can resize and adjust to look different every time you use it. Here's how:

1. Open PiP_Start.prproj from the APPST Lesson Files/ Chapter 27 folder. Press F9 to open the Adobe Title Designer, and create a rectangle in the center of the Designer's drawing area by selecting the Rectangle tool. Drag from the upper-left corner down to the lower right, trying to stay in the safe-area boxes. To ensure the resolution and position of the rectangle are correct for this lesson, assign it the following values in the Transform panel (see Figure 27.1):

   Opacity: **100%**
   X Position: **324**
   Y Position: **240**
   Width: **648**
   Height: **480**
   Rotation: **0.0**

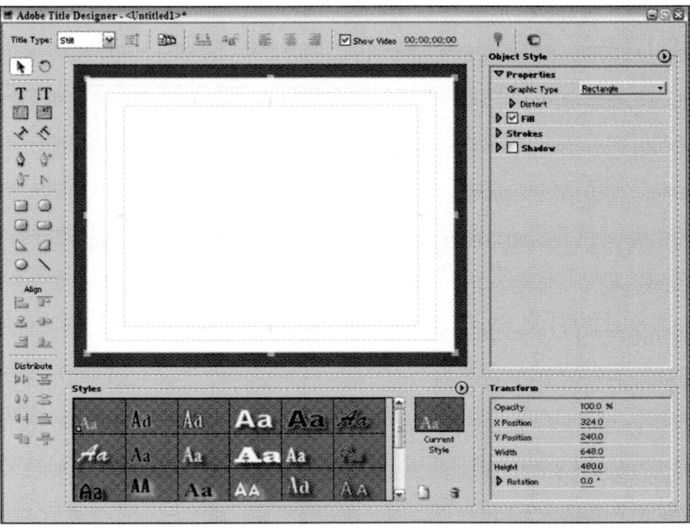

Figure 27.1 The rectangle fits exactly to the edge of the title frame, because the Title Designer window size is not 720×480, but 648×480. For this lesson that actual size is important to remember.

You now have a title that fits to the exact edge of the frame. Using what you learned about inner strokes in Chapter 12, "Advanced Titling: Styles," you next can create an inner stroke that grows inward from the outer edge to help build a border or frame for your PiP effect.

2. In the Title Designer's Object Style panel, click off the check box for Fill. Twirl down Stroke, and add one inner stroke.

   By making the fill of the rectangle empty, you can see directly through the center of the title. The inner stroke provides an "outline" that is bound to the edge of the frame and will expand inward, always locking to the edge of the frame when you increase its size. Next, you'll give that inner stroke a personality to transform it into a beautiful frame, or at least a good looking frame.

3. Assign the following settings to the inner stroke:

   Type: **Edge**
   Size: **40**
   Fill Type: **Bevel**
   Highlight Color: **47,35,100 (HSB, Golden)**
   Highlight Opacity: **100**
   Shadow Color: **46,35,69 (HSB, Brown)**

   Using a Bevel fill for the inner stroke gives the appearance of a more three-dimensional stroke, one that stands out a bit more. Although I used a skin tone type of color, you can use your own color choices to customize the frame. The highlight color should be a bright color, and the shadow should be a darker setting of the same color.

4. Click the Lit check box (see Figure 27.2), then click on the Tube check box (see Figure 27.3). Click off the Lit check box (see Figure 27.4).

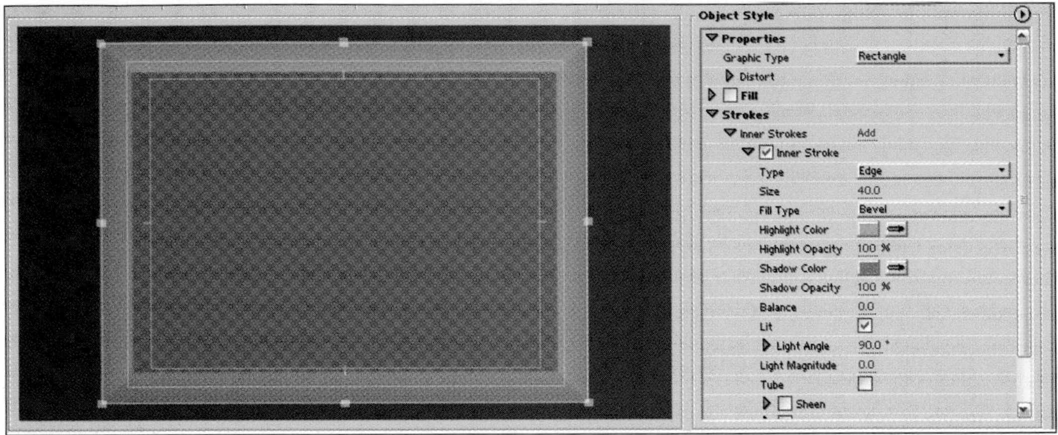

Figure 27.2 With only Lit checked, the result is a typically angled looking flat frame. Changing the Light Angle adjusts the direction the light comes from, while altering Light Magnitude affects the strength and presence of the light.

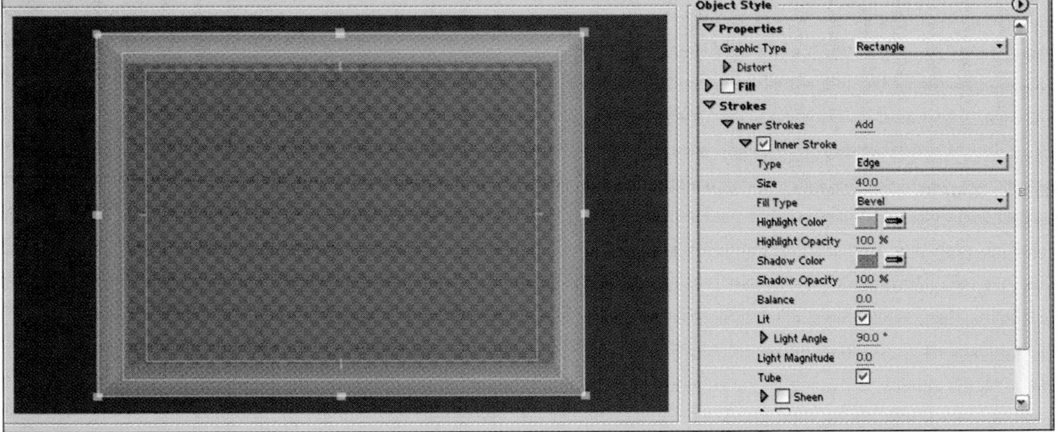

Figure 27.3 With both Lit and Tube checked, the result is a rounded bevel edge with a gentle lighting effect. Increasing Light Magnitude adds even more emphasis to this effect.

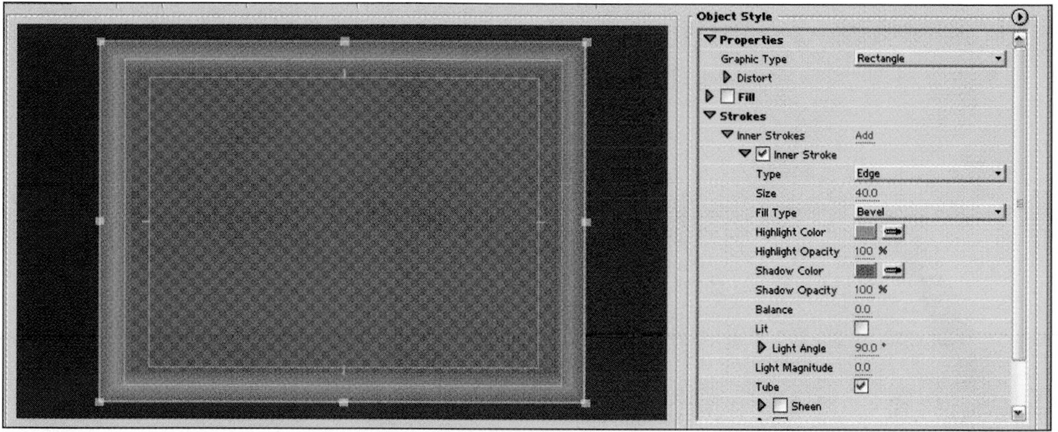

Figure 27.4 Turning off Lit and checking Tube creates a simple rounded frame rim with the light shadowing bleeding off to the sides of the edges.

The Lit check box engages an effect that assumes a light source is shining down on the edge and provides a more three-dimensional look. The light source comes from whatever angle you like; you can increase or decrease the magnitude to heighten or lesson the effect. When checked, Tube makes the bevel edge rounded; turn it off for a flat edge. Lit and Tube offer a good selection of options for creating an attractive PiP frame.

5. Save the newly created title as PIP_Frame. Click the Templates button to open the Templates dialog. From the wing menu of the Templates dialog, select Save <PIP_Frame> as Template. Name the template the same as the title, PIP FRAME, then click OK.

   By saving your new title as a custom template, you can use it time and again with any project. Because of what you learned about modifying templates in Chapter 13, "Advanced Titling: Templates," you can quickly load this PIP Frame template and change its color and lighting properties to make it unique and appropriate for subsequent projects.

This PiP frame technique is quite simple and straightforward, offering excellent results that you can customize and vary as you like. Additionally, you can increase or reduce the size of the stroke depending on how much emphasis you want to give the frame and its image.

Nesting Your PiP

To make your PiP files easier to manage you can add your custom title frame to the video file and nest the two elements in their own sequence. You will then be able to use the frame and video file synonymously as one file. With the two files nested, you can more easily explore additional effect settings to help complete the look and position of your PiP.

1. Open PiP_Nest_Start.prproj from the APPST Lesson Files/Chapter 27 folder.

   The video file for this project is in the APPST Lesson Files/Chapter 20 folder. The titles are in the APPST Lesson Files/Chapter 27 folder. And the LIL124.avi file is located in the APPST Lesson Files/Artbeats folder.

2. Drag and drop the file A Cam 01.avi to the Video 1 track in Sequence 01. Drag and drop PiP_Frame.prtl to the Video 2 track, covering the clip. Extend the duration of the title to cover the entire clip beneath it. (See Figure 27.5.) Preview the results in your Program Monitor.

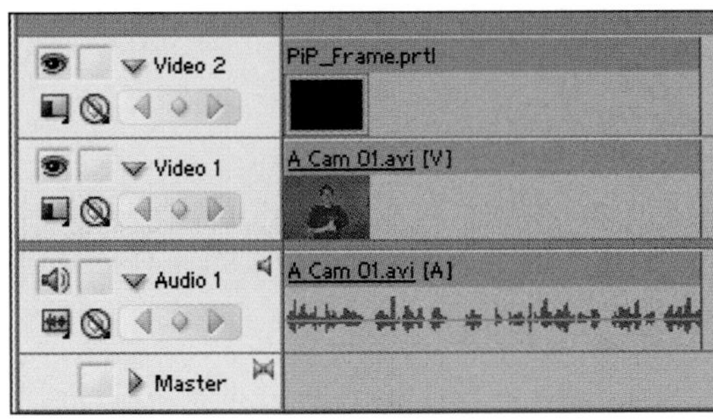

Figure 27.5 When you are nesting your title and video clip, keep the duration of the title equal to the duration of the video clip it is covering, unless you want the border to disappear.

Because the title frame is bound to the exact edge of the video frame, placing the title above the PiP video file is all you need to do to merge the picture frame with the video clip. Now that these two elements are merged into one sequence, you can develop the final look of the PiP.

Because the title picture frame is using an inner stroke, it is technically cropping inward onto the video clip that it surrounds. You can adjust the size of the stroke to reduce the size of the frame, or you can reduce the size of the video clip on Video 1 so that it fits inside the inner edge of the inner stroke. To reduce the size of the video clip on Video 1, select it and from the Effect Controls window's Motion listing, reduce Scale to the appropriate size.

3. Rename the Sequence 01 file in the Project window to A Cam PiP. Create a new sequence with two video tracks and one stereo audio track, naming it Final Comp. In the Final Comp sequence, drag and drop the LIL124.avi clip to Video 1 four times in a row. Drag and drop the A Cam PiP sequence to Video 2. Press the \ key to snap the zoom of your sequence to completely contain the added clips. (See Figure 27.6.)

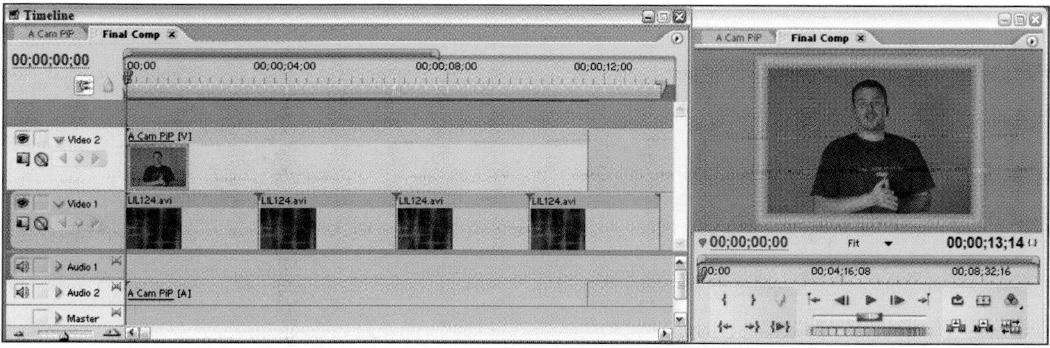

Figure 27.6 By nesting the title and video element into one sequence (A Cam PiP), you can now drag and drop the sequence file as if it were an individual clip. The Artbeats graphic on Video 1 will serve as the background under the PiP image.

Because you have married the title border with the video clip, you can now treat them as a single clip by dragging and dropping the host sequence. For the PiP to appear on top of the background video element, the PiP sequence must be placed on Video 2 above the background on Video 1. With the two files stacked in the proper hierarchy, you can reduce the scale, change the position, and then add a nice drop shadow effect to give the appearance that the PiP is on top of the other video.

4. Turn on the Safe Margins in the Program Monitor. Select the A Cam PiP clip on Video 2, and open the Effect Controls window. Open the Motion effect, and reduce the Scale to 40%. Click on the PiP clip, and in the Program Monitor physically reposition the clip in the upper-right area of the frame. (See Figure 27.7.) My final position was 530×127.

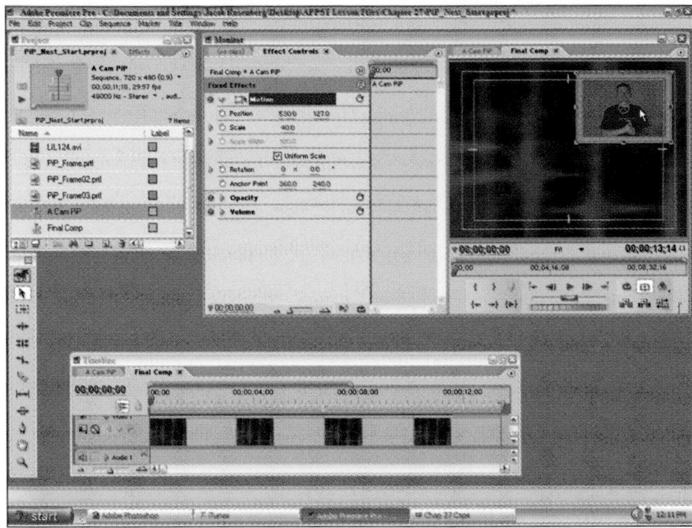

Figure 27.7 A new feature for 1.5 is the ability to click on a clip in the Program Monitor and have direct manipulation automatically activated. For any effect displaying the Direct Manipulation square next to its name, you can click and make adjustments directly inside the Program Monitor window. For the PiP effect, you dragged the selected clip to the upper-right frame region.

Turning on Safe Margins enables you to see the title- and action-safe areas of your frame. By positioning the PiP on the line of the title-safe margin, you are ensuring that the entire clip will be visible on a standard television. Placement and scale of your PiP is entirely up to you. I recommend 40% as the half size and 25% as a small size.

5. From the Effects window, drag and drop the Drop Shadow effect from the Video Effects>Perspective folder onto the clip A Cam PiP in the Video 2 track of your Final Comp sequence. In the Effect Controls window, assign these Drop Shadow effect settings:

   Color: **Default Black**
   Opacity: **45**
   Direction: **0×135**
   Distance: **40**
   Softness: **40**

A drop shadow gives a sense of depth to the composition. The direction and settings of the shadow are entirely up to you. I chose a simple and subtle lower-right falling shadow. The shadow is not too dramatic, yet it still gives off the appearance that the PiP is floating on top of the video that it covers.

6. For the final step, target Video 2 by clicking its track header or holding Ctrl while pressing the + key. Target the Audio 1 track by clicking its track header or pressing Ctrl+Shift++. With both Video 2 and Audio 1 targeted, press the Home key, then Ctrl+D, then Ctrl+Shift+D. Press Page Down so that the Edit Line snaps the end of the A Cam PiP, Ctrl+D, and Ctrl+Shift+D again. (See Figure 27.8.) Press Enter to render your sequence and see the final results.

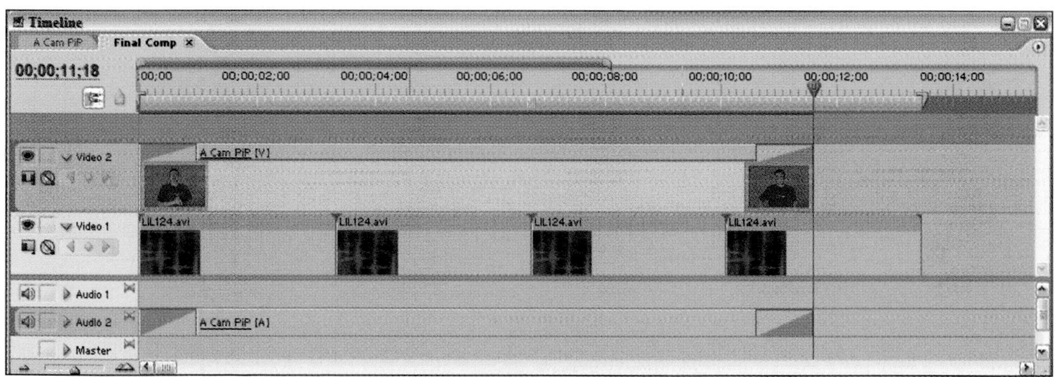

Figure 27.8 On Video 2, you can see the purple effect line signifying that effects have been added to the clip. Also, the one-sided dissolve transitions appear at the head and tail of the clip. Having applied all the effects and transitions to this clip, you can move it up to another track or down the timeline to a different position without reassigning effects or reapplying transitions. The integrity of the clip with effects will remain unchanged until you manually adjust it.

By targeting Video 2 and Audio 1, you activated each track to receive keyboard editing commands. After you pressed Home to snap the Edit Line to the head of the timeline, you added video and audio default transitions to the clips on those tracks. Page Down advanced you to the next edit point, which happened to be the end of the same clips. Here you added two more default transi-

When using the PiP custom presets, take note of the abbreviations UR (upper right), UL (upper left), LR (lower right), and LL (lower left). The effects are organized by the start or end position, so all UR effects either start or end in the same upper-right position.

tions. The end result is an attractive PiP effect that fades in and out to the upper right with a nice drop shadow for added depth.

With the files nested, making refinements is easy. If you want to add any effects or color correction to the video in the PiP, simply adjust the original file in the nested sequence. If you want the title border to be thicker, open the title and adjust the size of the inner stroke. Once you save the adjustment to the title, all instances where the title is used will update to reflect its saved state.

While you're in the mood to make adjustments, take a look at some of the custom PiP presets that came with Adobe Premiere Pro 1.5. You can easily customize them for your projects.

Using Custom Effect Presets

Part of my contribution to version 1.5 of Premiere Pro was to create a bunch of custom effect presets that you can quickly apply to clips in the timeline for immediate results.

This lesson will show you how to use the custom effect presets to quickly create and enhance a PiP effect—a moving PiP. For this effect, the PiP will slide in from the left side of the frame to hold in the upper-right corner. As the clip finishes, the PiP will spin out and off to the right. Three custom presets make this easy: Drop Shadow LR, PiP 25% UR Slide In Left, and PiP 25% UR Spin Out Right.

Because of how Premiere Pro handles effect settings, however, you can't just add the three effects to the same clip at once. To accommodate two separate motion adjustments, you must razor the clip into two pieces.

1. Open PiP_Presets_Start.prproj from the APPST Lesson Files/Chapter 27 folder.

   This project starts midway through the last lesson, just before you assigned the PiP effects.

2. From the Custom Presets/PiPs/25% PiPs/25% UR folder drag and drop the PiP 25% UR preset onto the A Cam PiP clip on Video 2 in the sequence.

Here you dragged and dropped a custom effect preset onto a clip in your sequence. The clip automatically updated with the settings of the preset, in this case Scale resized to 25% and Position updated to the upper-right picture-in-picture location.

3. Press the C key to access the Razor tool. Make incisions at 2;00 and at 6;00 in the A Cam PiP clip.

   With the clip split into three pieces, you can apply two different keyframed presets to begin and then end your PiP effect.

4. Drag and drop the PiP 25% UR Spin In custom effect preset from the Presets/PiP>25% PiP/25% UR preset folder onto the first instance of the A Cam Pip clip. Drag and drop PiP 25% UR Scale Out from the same folder onto the third instance of the same clip. (See Figures 27.9 and 27.10.) Press Enter to preview your results.

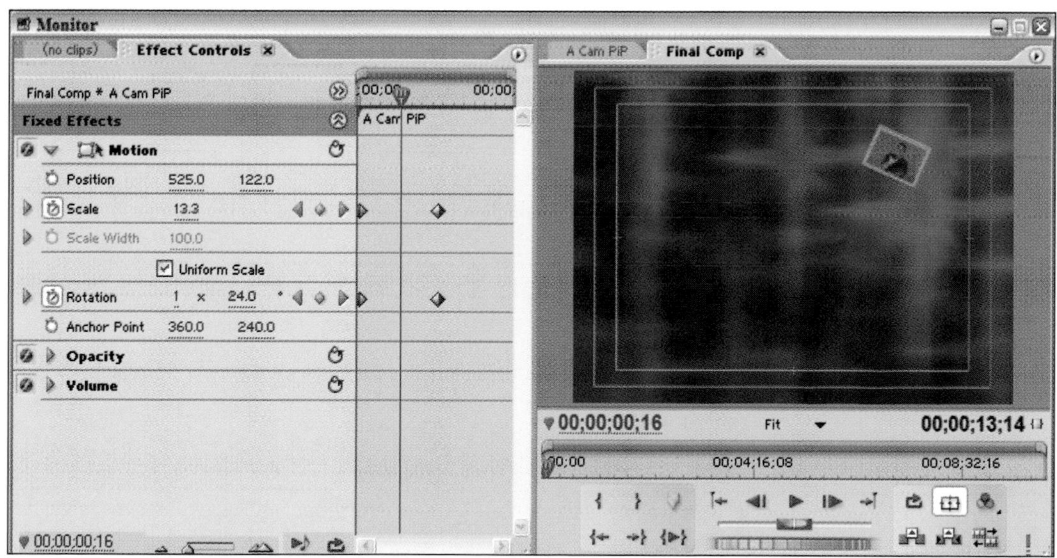

Figure 27.9 In the Effect Controls window, two scale keyframes represent the scale in so that the PiP zooms into position. At the same time, two rotation keyframes represent two full rotations from the first keyframe to the second. If you want to slow the scaling, just slide the second keyframe to the right. If you want to increase the number of rotations, position the Edit Line on top of the second rotation keyframe and increase the number of rotations from 2 to 4.

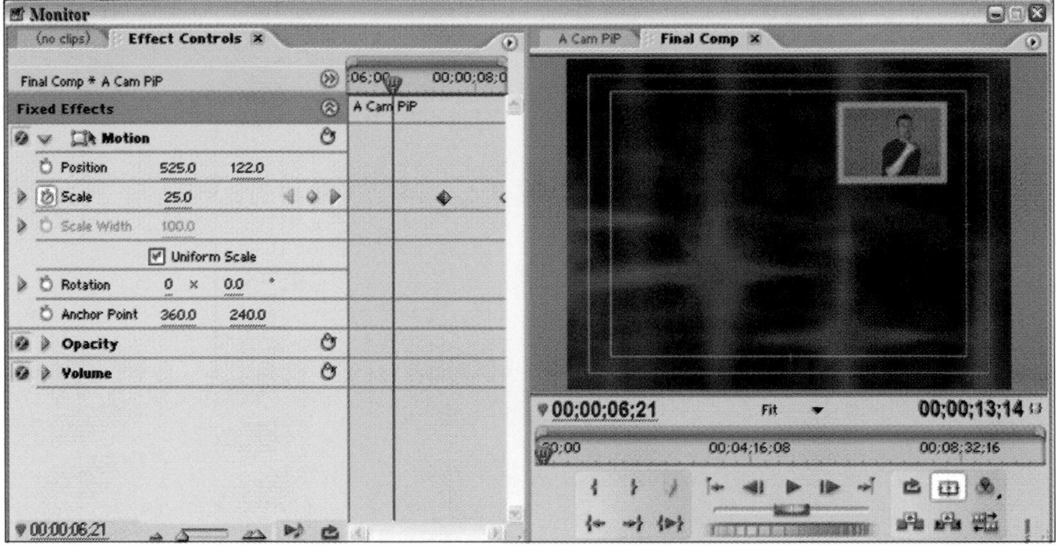

Figure 27.10 The last clip has two scale keyframes that represent the clip scaling from its current 25% down to 0%. If you want to slow the scale, just move the first Scale keyframe to the left.

All Custom presets have a default duration of one second. Any preset displaying the word "In" anchors its first keyframe to the first frame of the clip it applies to. Any preset displaying the word "Out" anchors its last keyframe to the last frame of the clip it applies to.

Having properly split the clip into three pieces, you can't see the seam when you play back the shots, although the division is clear in the timeline. Each clip accommodates a different move, and the result is a more dynamic PiP effect. The next step will show you how to adjust the keyframes created from the preset, in case you decide to adjust timing of the effect.

5. Select the first instance of the A Cam PiP clip in the timeline, and open the Effect Controls window displaying the timeline view. Marquee select the second two keyframes for scale and rotation. (See Figure 27.11.) With both keyframes selected, move them to the right to move their position closer to the end of the clip. (See Figure 27.11.)

By either Marquee selecting or holding down the Shift key and clicking multiple keyframes, you can select and move multiple keyframes in unison. To deselect the keyframes, click off of them.

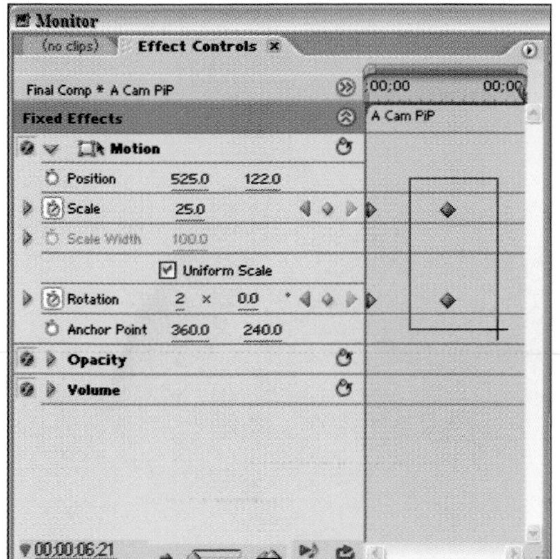

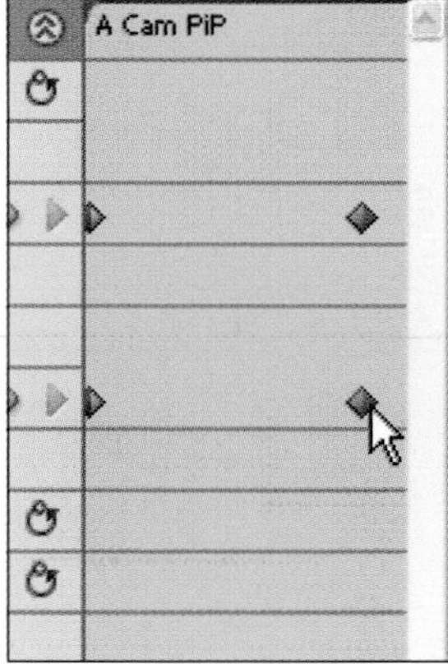

Figure 27.11 Marquee select the separate keyframes in the timeline view of the Effect Controls window (left). Once the two keyframes are selected, you can quickly drag them to a new position to adjust their timing (right). Now the scale and rotation are a little slower.

You cannot see literal time positioning when moving keyframes, but you can reposition the Edit Line to give you an Idea as to the time value of the adjustment you are making.

6. Holding down the Shift key, select all three pieces of the split clip. Right-click on the selection, and choose Group from the context menu. If you like, you can add audio and video transitions to the head and tail of the shot.

   To ensure that these three clips remain together, joined as a seamless trio, you grouped them. Grouping the clips creates a hard link that binds them together, enabling you to physically drag them to another track or timeline position while they are locked together. If you want to update or modify individual effect or keyframe settings, you must right-click and select Ungroup to get the individual clip effect parameters back.

   Adding the transitions puts the finishing touches on the PiP effect. You can now move the group of clips anywhere in the timeline; the PiP will appear as you intended with a custom slide in and custom spin out.

Presets are great for streamlining effect building. The lessons from this chapter should help you not only to use the custom PiP presets to their highest potential, but also to create an attractive PiP easily. Keep in mind that all your clips with anchored In or Out custom presets should have a duration of a least one second to ensure all the keyframes can be displayed. If you want to add multiple keyframed presets to one clip, remember to split the clip before you apply the In and Out presets.

Things to Remember

With a few simple steps you can use the Title Designer to create an adjustable border that adds a great look to your PiP effects. To change the emphasis of the frame size around your PiP, adjust the size of the inner stroke in your title frame. To change the shape and look of the frame itself, play with the Lit and Tube options to toggle between a flat frame and a rounded one. As for the colors, you can specify them on a project-by-project basis.

Adding a slight drop shadow helps give the PiP a greater feeling of depth on top of the image that it covers. You can even add a slight edge feather if you want to soften up the edges a bit.

Finally, using the custom PiP presets can save you a lot of time if you apply them properly. If you intend on using two keyframed effect presets, remember to split the clip in half before adding any of the keyframed presets.

Having one custom title frame and all the custom presets should make your life much easier when it comes to creating a good looking PiP effect.

Further Reading

Congratulations, you've reached the end of the book's lessons section.

If you haven't already explored the additional appendices that are included on the DVD, check them out. They offer more information on troubleshooting, third-party plug-ins, 24P support, and the Adobe Media Encoder. To open the appendices, click on the Appendices button in the DVD's menu to copy the PDF Appendices files onto your system. After they copy, just double-click to open the appendices you want to view.

Index

B

D

F

G

H

I

J

K

L

M

N

O

P

Q

R

T

W

X-Y

Z